THE LIFE OF

BENJAMIN DISRAELI

EARL OF BEACONSFIELD

THE MACMILLAN COMPANY
NEW YORK · BOSTON · CHICAGO · DALLAS
ATLANTA · SAN FRANCISCO

MACMILLAN & CO., LIMITED
LONDON · BOMBAY · CALCUTTA
MELBOURNE

THE MACMILLAN CO. OF CANADA, LTD.
TORONTO

The Right Honble. B. Disraeli. M.P.
1852.
from the picture by Sir Francis Grant. P.R.A.
at Hughenden.

Printed in England.

THE LIFE OF
BENJAMIN DISRAELI
EARL OF BEACONSFIELD

BY WILLIAM FLAVELLE MONYPENNY
AND
GEORGE EARLE BUCKLE

VOLUME III

1846—1855

WITH PORTRAITS AND ILLUSTRATIONS

Reaa no history, nothing but biography, for that is life without theory. — CONTARINI FLEMING.

New York
THE MACMILLAN COMPANY
1914

Set up and electrotyped. Published December, 1914.

Norwood Press
J. S. Cushing Co. — Berwick & Smith Co.
Norwood, Mass., U.S.A.

CONTENTS OF VOL. III.

LIST OF ILLUSTRATIONS TO VOL. III.

FROM A MURAL TABLET IN FARNHAM ROYAL CHURCH.

TO THE GLORY OF GOD

AND IN AFFECTIONATE MEMORY OF

WILLIAM FLAVELLE MONYPENNY,

OF THE STAFF OF 'THE TIMES,' BIOGRAPHER OF DISRAELI,

BORN 7 AUGUST 1866, DIED 23 NOVEMBER, 1912,
AND BURIED IN THE ADJOINING CHURCHYARD,

THIS BRONZE IS PLACED HERE BY SOME OF HIS MANY FRIENDS, TO COMMEMORATE A LIFE CUT SHORT IN MID CAREER, RICH IN PERFORMANCE, RICHER YET IN PROMISE, SPENT IN SERVING HIS COUNTRY AND THE BRITISH EMPIRE, WITH PEN AND SWORD IN S. AFRICA, AND WITH THE PEN IN ENGLAND AND IRELAND.

'A man of understanding shall attain unto wise counsels.' —*Proverbs* i. 5.

PREFACE.

When Mr. Monypenny was completing for the press the second volume of this biography his health was rapidly failing, and he died within ten days after its publication. Consequently, though he had arranged and classified most of the papers in the keeping of the Beaconsfield Trustees, and had collected a large mass of other material bearing on the remainder of Disraeli's life, he left no consecutive manuscript written for the printer, with the exception of an analysis of *Tancred*, which forms the basis of the second chapter of the present volume. For the rest, save for a very few detached paragraphs and sentences here and there, I am solely responsible. My aim has been, to the best of my ability, to continue the work on Mr. Monypenny's lines and in his spirit. I was a warm admirer of my friend's two volumes, and I realise to the full the extreme difficulty of reaching the standard which he set. I venture, in view of the delicate nature of my task, to plead for indulgence to my shortcomings.

I am very grateful to Lord Rothschild and the other Trustees of the Beaconsfield estate for extending to me the confidence which they reposed in Mr. Monypenny, and for lightening my labours by their constant encouragement and support. My other obligations for assistance in the preparation of this volume are too numerous for individual acknowledgment; but my thanks to those I do not specifically name are not on that account less sincere. To His Majesty the King I am particularly indebted for his gracious permission, not only to make use at my discretion of the invaluable series of historical documents contained in *The Letters of Queen Victoria*, but also to print some unpublished Royal letters which have a special bearing on Disraeli's career. By far the most important correspondence reproduced or quoted in this volume is that between Disraeli and his chief, the fourteenth Earl of Derby; and I have to thank the present Earl very sincerely for the privilege which he accorded to Mr. Monypenny of searching the archives of Knowsley, and for the kindness with which he has allowed me to enter into my predecessor's labours and to lay before the public the material documents. I also owe special acknowledgment to Lord Londonderry, the Duke of Rutland, the Duke of Richmond and Gordon, Sir Philip Rose, and Mr. Gladstone's family and Trustees; to Mr. Arthur Willyams, Mrs. Brydges-Willyams's nephew; and to Mr. Coningsby Disraeli, from whose collection at Hughenden most of the illustrations are again derived. I have greatly benefited by the criticisms of Mr. Murray, my publisher, who has carefully read the proof-sheets; and I should be ungrateful indeed if I did not record my obligations to my wife, who has not only prepared the index but co-operated with me throughout.

I have not been able in this volume to carry the story down so far as I had originally hoped. But the same number of years is covered as in Volume II., and there is a larger proportion of original material available than there was for the earlier part of Disraeli's life.

G. E. B.

October, 1914.

THE LIFE OF

BENJAMIN DISRAELI

EARL OF BEACONSFIELD

CHAPTER I

Bentinck and Disraeli

1846–1847

On the day of Peel's resignation, Disraeli wrote from the Carlton Club to his wife: 'The Ministry have resigned. All *Coningsby* and "Young England" the general exclamation here.' All *Coningsby* and 'Young England'! In *Tancred*, which was being written during this year 1846, Disraeli seems to give the same reason for Peel's overthrow, when he makes Coningsby say, speaking of the earlier Sir Robert, Sir Robert Walpole, but obviously glancing at the Sir Robert of the hour: 'The "boys" beat him at last.' The suggestion is, of course, a whimsical exaggeration. *Coningsby* and 'Young England' had indeed begun the uprising against Peel's system, but could never have dislodged him had it not been for the revolt of the agricultural interest due to his abandonment of Protection. If, however, the words be taken as a claim on behalf of the author of *Coningsby* and leader of 'Young England' to the chief share in the movement which defeated the great Minister, they are, as has been shown in the last volume, fully justified; and the Country party, reluctant as many of them were to admit Disraeli's superiority, found themselves driven before long to accept, and even to acknowledge, his leadership in the House of Commons.

Meanwhile a purely Whig Cabinet was formed[1] under Lord John Russell, with Lord Palmerston as Foreign Secretary. A coalition with the Peelites, which had

[1] July 5, 1846.

been Lord John's 'original scheme,' was, Disraeli notes in a memorandum, 'frustrated by Peel himself.' At any rate, the offers of office which were made to Lord Dalhousie, Lord Lincoln, and Sidney Herbert, were declined, though subsequently Dalhousie accepted the Governor-Generalship of India. The new Ministry was in a minority, as Whigs, Radicals, and Irish together fell decidedly short of half the House of Commons; its strength consisted in the absence of opposition. Peel was determined to keep the Protectionists out of office, and was, as he said to the Queen, 'anxious not to undertake the Government again.'[1] The Protectionists, Disraeli tells us, so far from contemplating opposition, 'retained their seats beneath the gangway on the Ministerial side. . . . As it was their intention to support the general policy of the new Government, it was unnecessary for them to cross the House with the late Cabinet, which they had themselves driven from power.'[2] Such being the state of mind of Peel and the Protectionists, it is no wonder that some well-meant but premature efforts of Lyndhurst, the retiring Lord Chancellor, to reunite the Conservative party, were fruitless. Lord George Bentinck was emphatic in his repudiation of the whole idea. 'My mind revolts and my heart sickens at the thought of any such easy reconciliation,' he wrote to Lord Stanley. Far from seeking reunion, the Protectionists, as Greville notes on July 18, were 'very busy in rallying and remodelling' their party. They celebrated their success in overthrowing Peel by a dinner at Greenwich, given by members of both Houses, including Disraeli, to their leaders Stanley and Bentinck. The proceedings were harmonious and enthusiastic. Stanley pointed to the strong controlling power which the Protectionist party manifestly possessed, placed as it was by the force of circumstances, as well as

[1] *Queen Victoria's Letters*, July 6, 1846.

[2] *Lord George Bentinck*, ch. 20. This book is the principal first-hand authority for the political history of the years 1846–1848, as viewed by Disraeli; and it is from its pages, where not otherwise specified, that the bulk of the quotations in the early chapters of this volume are taken.

by the talent and energy of its members, in a commanding position in the Legislature. Bentinck announced his consent to continue his temporary leadership in the Commons, but at the same time made it clear that he regarded Stanley as leader of the whole party.

Policy as well as principle urged the new Ministry to introduce measures to confirm and develop the Free Trade system. This would tend to widen the breach in the Conservative party, and insure a steady Government majority through the support of Cobden and Bright on the one side, and the Peelites on the other. The sugar duties were the first to be attacked. 'Within a month of his accession to power, at the end of an exhausting session, the new Minister announced a sweeping measure which was at once to admit sugar, the produce of slave labour, to the British market.'

> Sugar was an article of colonial produce which had been embarrassing, if not fatal, to many Governments. Strange that a manufacture which charms infancy and soothes old age should so frequently occasion political disaster. The Minister therefore was resolved to rid himself of this perpetual difficulty by precipitating a settlement while the elements of opposition on this question, though powerful, were distracted.

Lord John Russell had no difficulty in showing 'the inconsistency of our receiving slave-grown cotton, and slave-grown coffee, and slave-grown tobacco, and rejecting slave-grown sugar'; but it was felt, and not merely by the Protectionists, that the new policy was a condemnation of all that England, under the guidance of the Whigs, had done for the abolition of slavery. 'Having deprived our colonies of those successful means of general competition, it would seem that the metropolis was at least bound to secure them a home market.' Bentinck accordingly moved an amendment condemning the proposed reduction as tending to check the advance of production by British free labour, and to give a great additional stimulus to the slave trade. It was the identical language of the famous Protectionist amendment which was moved, and carried, under Peel's auspices, to the Whig project of sugar duty reduction in 1841, and which contributed so greatly to placing in power the Minister who had now fallen because he had abandoned Protection. 'With Sir Robert Peel sitting opposite Lord George Bentinck . . . this was rather a dainty device of the Protectionist leader.' We may well believe that the device originated with Disraeli, who chronicles it with so much complacency. The motion was rejected by a large majority; but the Government were only saved by 'violent sacrifices of Parliamentary consistency, and even of personal conviction, on the part of those who had no political connection with them.' Among these was Peel, who avowed that he supported Ministers solely in order to keep the Protectionists out of office. Disraeli, as 'a follower of Lord George Bentinck,' spoke in the debate, and,

lamenting the destruction of our colonial system and expressing the belief that we should ere long have to reconstruct it, observed that it was a characteristic of our history that this country generally retraced its steps. . . . We did not commit less blunders than other countries, but we were a people more sensible of our errors. The history of England, he said, is a history of reaction. We destroyed, for example, our church establishment and we replaced it. We destroyed our ancient monarchy and we restored it. We destroyed the House of Lords, and yet we were now obliged to take up our Bills to them for their sanction. We even abolished the House of Commons, and yet here we were at the end of the session debating a great question.

Russell ridiculed this view of English history; but, though paradoxically heightened after Disraeli's fashion, it would be admitted to have much truth in it to-day, when, though nobody proposes exactly to restore our old colonial system, some of the best minds are devoting themselves to the problem of how to 'reconstruct' it, and consolidate it into a coherent imperial edifice.

The Protectionists did not confine their exertions to Parliament, but, even before the session was over, Bentinck and Disraeli, with several of their friends, started on a political tour which involved meetings at King's Lynn, Bentinck's constituency, and Waltham, in the neighbourhood of Belvoir Castle, where Lord Granby[1] and Lord John Manners, the sons of the house, were pillars of the cause. It was one of the very few excursions of the kind in the life of Disraeli, who was emphatically a Parliament man.

To Mrs. Disraeli.

KING'S LYNN, *Aug.* 4, 1846.—We carried the railroad, but lost the general train; the special train, however, was all ready for us (only G[eorge] B[entinck] and myself), and though we started an hour after them, we caught them up halfway at Cambridge. . . . At Cambridge we joined Lord Orford,[2] the Duke of Richmond[3] and Granby, Miles[4] not having appeared. . . .

This morning, as soon as I woke, I found a note from Neilson[5] of *The Times* requesting an interview. He is sent down with two other *Times* reporters, and all for my speech. . . . In the meantime, I have not a thought ready, and if we are to be reported in *The Times* it must be something for the nation, and not merely for the farmers of Lynn.

KING'S LYNN, *Aug.* 5, 1846.—Our dinner was very successful indeed, as far as speaking and enthusiasm remarkable. G. B. did very well, Granby particularly so, and your humble servant quite to his satisfaction. I hope the reporters managed also. Lord Orford a capital chairman. The only fault in my mind was the expense of the tickets, £1 a head; 5s. should have been the outside. This prevented that overflow which should always be at these meetings: however, we sat down more than 500 substantial squires and yeomen. G. B. on the right of Lord Orford, and Duke of Richmond on the left:

[1] Afterwards 6th Duke of Rutland.

[2] The 3rd Earl, High Steward of King's Lynn, father of Disraeli's friend, Lady Dorothy Nevill.

[3] The 5th Duke, whose sons, the 6th Duke and Lord Henry Lennox, were both subsequently colleagues of Disraeli.

[4] William Miles, of Leigh Court, Bristol, M.P. successively for Somerset, Chippenham, and Romney, created a Baronet in 1859.

[5] J. F. Neilson (1809–1881), a leading member of *The Times* staff of Parliamentary reporters. He took a prominent part in reporting most of the great speeches of the mid-Victorian period, both in and out of Parliament, and Disraeli's in particular. Disraeli respected him greatly, and often rehearsed his speeches, or the important parts of them, to him in private. As Prime Minister, he wished to confer a Civil List pension upon Neilson, but the proprietors of *The Times* objected, and themselves augmented Neilson's salary by an equivalent sum.

certain difference of tendency between leading Protectionists. Already the wiser heads among them, and assuredly Disraeli, in spite of his outburst to a sympathetic audience at Lynn, realised that it was hopeless, for the present at any rate, to try to reinstate the sliding scale. But there were two possible alternatives — either to concentrate upon the fixed duty, which had been the old Whig policy and had been advocated to the last by Palmerston, or to turn to the alleviation of local burdens as a compensation to the agriculturists for what they had lost by the abandonment of protection for corn. Bentinck, as we have seen, suggested both policies in turn. The latter was that which Disraeli was ultimately to adopt, but it almost inevitably led to the abandonment of the fight for any Protection at all. The former, the fixed duty, was pressed upon Disraeli by John Manners a few days after the Waltham meeting.

From Lord John Manners.

LONGSHAW LODGE, *Aug.* 15, 1846. — . . . It seems to me that the Protection Leaders are foolishly determined to fight the identical battle they have just lost over again in the new Parliament. Can't something be done to prevent such a shipwreck? . . . Can't G. B. be prevailed upon to 'go for' his second alternative in the first place? Corn might be reinstated in a Tariff, and Cattle too, at moderate duties. To belong to a party with only one idea is unsatisfactory; and methinks 'tis far wiser and more statesmanlike to fight a second battle on a fresh field and with new dispositions, than on the old battleground strewed with the symbols of defeat. . . .

Stanley is here, full of fun and chaff; but he does not give me the idea of a statesman. . . .

Disraeli received this when he had returned to London for the closing weeks of an arduous session. He must have been much tried by the behaviour of his leader Bentinck, who discredited himself by a number of petty personal charges of jobs and blunders against members of Peel's late Government, particularly Lyndhurst, Ripon, and Gladstone. *Lord George Bentinck* observes a discreet silence on these episodes, and the charges were all satisfactorily repelled. Disraeli himself, while endeavouring to justify Bentinck's attack on Ripon, strongly defended the honour of his old patron, Lyndhurst.

To Lady Londonderry.[1]

GROSVENOR GATE, *Sept.* 1, 1846.

DEAR LADY LONDONDERRY, — . . . Kielmansegge[2] is at Wiesbaden, and you will therefore probably meet him.[3] He is just fresh from Drayton, where Sir Robert said that no man's health would permit him to be Prime Minister of this country for more than five years, from which we infer he counts on the feeble frame of Johnny sinking very shortly under the burthen, though I don't see that will help him, as the Peelites do not in any way rally, and the Tory rancour flourishes in all its primal virulence and vigor.

By the time you return, you will see the Duke's statue[4] on the Hyde Park arch. In future, he is to be called the Arch-Duke. The secret history of this rally is rather curious. The D. of Rutland,[5] the eve of our departure, a Sunday eve, his Grace entering desperate, confided after dinner his wrongs and disappointments to Lord Geo. Bentinck and myself. I observed that he had made no fight, and that there were at that moment four men in the room (Granby and John Manners being there) who were all able not only to vote but to speak. Fired by the idea, flushed with claret and sympathising with our injured host, we all agreed to go down to the House, on our arrival in town on the morrow, and make a struggle. Whereupon G. Bentinck, the instant he arrived, gave a notice, by way of amendment to the iconoclastic motion of Craven Berkeley,[6] which so alarmed Morpeth[7] with its dark insinuations of royal pledges broken, that the Government surrendered without firing a shot, notwithstanding the whole House of Commons, all the newspapers, and what they call public opinion, were in their favour. Trench[8] looks as if the

[1] See Vol. II., p. 261.

[2] Hanoverian Minister.

[3] Lady Londonderry was at Homburg.

[4] The statue of the Duke of Wellington is now at Aldershot.

[5] The Duke of Rutland was chairman of the Committee which decided to place the statue on the arch — a decision which found little favour either with public opinion or with the Government, but which was nevertheless carried out.

[6] M.P. for Cheltenham, son of 5th Earl of Berkeley.

[7] Afterwards 7th Earl of Carlisle, at that time Chief Commissioner of Woods and Forests.

[8] General Sir Frederick Trench, M.P. for Scarborough, and principal promoter of the project for placing the Duke's statue on the arch at the top of Constitution Hill.

perished;[1] but Bentinck's letters, which have been preserved, contain frequent proofs of his admiration for, and confidence in, his colleague. In June Bentinck had discarded the formal 'My dear Sir' in addressing Disraeli, and always afterwards subscribed himself, 'Ever yours most sincerely.' Bentinck had, as his letters and Disraeli's narrative of his life show, been working hard at politics the whole autumn. In order to devote himself more completely to his political duties, he had finally, at the Goodwood meeting, severed his connection with the turf, of which he was 'the lord paramount,' parting with the whole of his racing stud 'at a moment when its prospects were never so brilliant.' He thereby lost 'the blue ribbon of the turf,' the Derby, which was won in 1848 by Surplice, a horse he had sold with the rest.

Before coming to Bradenham, Bentinck had visited Knowsley, where he had been 'hatching secret plans for the next session,' in concert, no doubt, with Stanley. The Protectionist leaders in Lords and Commons were old friends and fellow-sportsmen; but Stanley's prejudice against Disraeli seems to have been still active, and these two apparently had as yet no personal relations. The events of the autumn necessarily directed the attention of the Protectionists to other issues than the Corn Laws. Famine in Ireland — the apprehension of which had determined Peel's momentous action in 1845—, though it was averted that year, came in grim earnest in the next. Three-fourths of the potato crop failed, and the normal poverty of the people made what would have been a severe visitation to any country a crushing calamity to Ireland. Legislation for helping the Irish by employing their labour on public works had produced disastrous results. 'The number of persons employed under the Labour Rate Act, principally in useless and entirely in unproductive works, which in the month of September had amounted to thirty thousand, reached, when Parliament met, the awful sum

[1] Lady Ossington, Bentinck's sister, wrote in 1884 that 'all Lord George Bentinck's political correspondence was probably destroyed by the Duke of Portland, his father' (*Croker Papers*, Vol. III., p. 116).

of half a million, representing, it was said, as far as the means of subsistence were concerned, two millions and a half of her Majesty's subjects. A nation breaking stones upon the road!' It was determined by the Protectionists, in these circumstances, to press on Parliament the policy of substituting productive for unproductive labour by promoting in Ireland that construction of railways which was proving so beneficial to England.

The opening of the session on January 19, 1847, formed an epoch in Disraeli's parliamentary career. He took then for the first time his seat on the front bench in the House of Commons, a position he was to occupy continuously, in opposition or in office, for thirty years. He has explained in *Lord George Bentinck*[1] how it happened that the Protectionists, who had at first made a point of separating themselves from the Peelites in the House, and remaining on the same side as the Whig Ministry whom they had placed in office, now crossed the floor. Considerable inconvenience resulted from the original arrangement.

> The Protectionists were so numerous that the greater portion of the habitual supporters of the Whigs were obliged to range themselves on the benches opposite the men whom they had always supported and with whom they were still voting. This led to some conversation between the Treasury Bench and Lord George Bentinck, and it was finally agreed that on the whole it would be more convenient that, on the meeting of the House in '47, he should take the seat usually occupied by the leader of the Opposition, and that his friends should fill the benches generally allotted to an adverse party.

Disraeli, it will be noted, says nothing of his own position; but he and Bankes, member for Dorset, who had previously held office, and possibly others, took their seats by their leader, on the same bench with Peel, Lincoln, Sidney Herbert, and Goulburn. Gladstone had retired from Newark, and was out of Parliament, and Graham preferred the obscurity and independence of a back bench. '*Three off* Sir Robert Peel' is the way in

[1] Ch. 20.

which *The Times* describes the position of Disraeli and Bentinck, whom it mentions in that order. 'There is, however, we presume,' it adds, 'to be no connection with the adjoining shop."[1] According to a descriptive writer in a provincial journal, Disraeli changed more than his seat. He modified the extravagance of his clothing. The 'motley-coloured garments' which he still wore at the close of the session of 1846 were exchanged for a suit of black, 'unapproachably perfect' in every stitch, 'and he appears to have doffed the vanity of the coxcomb with the plumage of the peacock.' He was also thought to have acquired a weightier manner of speaking, suited to his more responsible position, though in a day or two he crushed his old opponent, Roebuck, in quite a familiar vein. Indeed, we shall note from now onward, with the exception, perhaps, of the final fling of the publication of *Tancred*, an increase of gravity in his political actions and speeches, and a greater reluctance to let himself go as his natural genius would dictate. Nobody ever felt more strongly than Disraeli the responsibility of those who control a party. He had thoroughly grasped the principle, which neither Peel nor Gladstone ever fully apprehended, that a great party is an organ of government which cannot be broken and destroyed without confusion and danger. Now for the first time his action would affect a party. He was the first lieutenant, and largely the inspirer, of the party leader in the Commons, and he had before his eyes the wreck that Peel's disregard of party had produced. No wonder that his words were more measured, even at the risk of their sometimes becoming dull to us who read them when the issues are no longer living.

At the moment it was uncertain exactly what the size of the party was for which Bentinck and Disraeli were responsible. Could they count upon the 240 who had voted against the Corn Bill, or only upon the 76 stalwarts who had voted with the Whigs and Irish for ejecting Peel from office, or upon some indeterminate number in

[1] *The Times*, Jan. 20, 1847.

THE FRONT OPPOSITION BENCH, 1847.

From a sketch by John Doyle ('H. B.').

between? In the division on the sugar duties in the autumn they had been supported by 135 members in a House which was two-thirds full; but on that occasion they were able to appeal to anti-slavery sentiment. This uncertainty caused Bentinck to write to Stanley shortly before the session, expressing his unwillingness to thrust himself forward 'as though he were the acknowledged leader of the Protectionists in the House of Commons.' But he yielded to the necessities of the position, and was ready, when Parliament met, to give an attentive consideration to the Ministerial proposals for dealing with Irish distress, in the hope that they might be sufficiently comprehensive to obviate any interference on his part. The first proposal to suspend the temporary duties on corn established in 1846, met with his approval. Then there were to be loans for the improvement of private estates, extension of the drainage system, encouragement of fisheries, and a better Poor Law: 'Projects for ordinary times, hardly adequate to absorb the teeming millions of the public works, whose numbers increased with every telegraph, and alarmed the Cabinet like a fresh invasion of some barbaric host appalling the trembling senators of Rome.' The famine was getting worse; relief committees were formed, to be aided by public grants, half of the whole charge to fall upon the Treasury of the United Kingdom.

These proposals seemed to the Protectionist leaders to be peddling and inadequate. Early in February Bentinck brought forward the measure which he and Disraeli had prepared in the autumn 'to stimulate the prompt and profitable employment of the people by the encouragement of railways in Ireland': £16,000,000 was the amount which he proposed that the Government should lend, during four years, for this purpose. He disclaimed any motive of hostility to Ministers, and hoped all parties would consider his Bill on its merits. The Bill was received with general favour, especially in Ireland; but the state of the money market, and the dislike of Peelites and Radicals, dominated by the doctrines of *laisser-faire*, for any policy of the kind, led the Government to oppose it on the second reading, and to announce that, if it were carried, they would resign. 'There was not a section or an individual in the House of Commons who wished to disturb the Government, least of all Lord George Bentinck . . . but he was not a man who would ever shrink from the consequences of his acts.' He was 'not appalled,' he said, by the difficulties in Ireland; and he formally notified Stanley, and explicitly stated in the House of Commons, that he would not shrink from any responsibility which, unsought, might be forced upon him. 'It must be confessed, however,' says Disraeli, 'that he was the only member of his party who was undaunted. A sort of panic pervaded the Protectionist ranks.' The division was naturally very unfavourable, only 118 following Bentinck into the lobby. Even the Irish, who had loudly acclaimed his policy, deserted him; a change which led Disraeli, a few weeks later, to comment somewhat severely on their instability. 'I hope it will never be said of the Irish that they are a light and frivolous people; but the rapidity with which they pass votes of confidence, and then of illimitable condemnation, is certainly not an encouragement to public men, and is not the best evidence of popular consistency.'

Disraeli supported Bentinck in the debate in a long and elaborate speech in which he repeated his conviction —a conviction he declared to be held by the great body of his countrymen—'that no hallucination . . . had been greater than to suppose that a political panacea could cure the ills of Ireland.' He quoted facts and figures in defence of the railway policy, and pointed out finally 'that the commercial principle came into contact with circumstances in Ireland with which it was not fitted to cope.'

Bentinck and Disraeli had not long to wait for an admission by the Government of the justice of their arguments. It was in February that, under urgent Ministerial pressure, Bentinck's Bill was defeated; before the end of April the Chancellor of the Exchequer announced to an astonished House that he would recommend a vote to assist Irish railways of £620,000. Peelites and Radicals were indignant. Bentinck cordially welcomed the repentant sinners, and must have been especially gratified by Peel's remark that 'the measure of Lord George Bentinck was free from some of the objections that forcibly applied to the present measure.' When the Government Bill came on for second reading, Disraeli made the sarcastic comment that the overwhelming majority against Bentinck's Bill 'was, at least, one animated by a too precipitate spirit.' He maintained that Bentinck's policy, though hastened by the potato famine, was quite independent of it, and good for a backward country like Ireland in all circumstances. Ireland was the disgrace of England; her people were suffering, miserable, and unemployed. It was only by the creation of public works that the people could be employed; and Bentinck's scheme insured that employment without loss to England. The real question, Disraeli declared, was : Did the people of England care more for the good government of Ireland than for the principles of political economy? Was the House to be animated in its legislation by national sympathies, or 'to take refuge in mere dry pedantic political aphorisms'? The Protectionists had the satisfaction of helping the Government to carry their Bill by a large majority against the opposition of Peelites and Radicals. It is noteworthy that Bentinck and Disraeli were among the first to proclaim the principle, now generally accepted, that, as England and Ireland, though a united kingdom, were in very different stages of economic development, it was right to use English wealth to forward the material prosperity of Ireland. The policy of the Land Purchase Acts is honourably associated with the names of Bright, Ashbourne, Balfour, and Wyndham ; the underlying principle is to be traced to those politicians whom it has been the fashion to despise, the Protectionist leaders of the late forties.

The session was so much occupied with the Irish distress, and the measures necessary for coping with it, that all other subjects were dwarfed. Disraeli spoke several times on external questions, but it will be more convenient to consider his attitude towards Palmerston's foreign policy in a subsequent chapter.[1] The Poor Law and its administration came up, as usual, for consideration. On 'the great Mott case'[2] Disraeli had another small fling at Peel. He referred to the condemnation of Ferrand in 1844 for his attacks on Graham. It had been the case of a solitary member against the whole House; he had against him both 'the most powerful Minister that England has seen for a century,' with a 'Macedonian phalanx' of supporters, and also an Opposition dominated by the manufacturing interest. In another Poor Law debate Disraeli protested against central control of Poor Law administration in London. He was all for local control — county control. But he uttered one characteristic caution: 'I have always believed that the power of the Crown has diminished, is diminishing, and ought to be increased; and therefore any increase in the patronage of the Crown is a proposition I would never oppose.' In general, Disraeli contented himself during the session with a steady and efficient backing of his leader, Bentinck, whether it was in resisting inquiry into the Navigation Laws, in criticising the Bank Charter Act, in demanding justice for distillers, or in all the numerous phases of the Irish Railway question. One personal reference may be quoted. In a debate at the end of the session he described the transference of Stanley from the Commons to the Lords, in 1844, as a misfortune for the country.

Disraeli's friends noticed his steady advance. In a letter written about this time, Lady Londonderry passes on to him a charming compliment: 'I send you my best wishes and a pretty speech I heard about you. "Le talent regne en Angleterre et ne gouverne pas."' An admiring cousin goes to hear him speak in the House, and reports:

[1] See below, ch. 7. [2] See Vol. II., p. 236.

B. E. Lindo to Sarah Disraeli.

March 25, 1847.—I was very charmed with Dizzy's display last Tuesday,[1] and astonished at the command and control of the House which he possesses—the buzz everywhere in the lobbies and the galleries when he rose, and the rush into the House, which filled in no time after he had begun. In every way I was astonished and pleased.... Dizzy's figure suits the floor of the House admirably, while his voice is so various, modulated musically at one moment and pouring out its thunder the next, and you hear plainly every whisper. He extracted cheers from a full House of opponents. What would they have been if they had gone with him! He certainly is the wonder of the day, and begins to be universally acknowledged so.

The General Election was approaching, and an opportunity offered for the attainment of one of Disraeli's most cherished ambitions—to sit in Parliament for the county of Buckingham. Since the time when, as a member of his father's household, he came there twenty years before, first for summer visits, and afterwards to reside at Bradenham, his attachment to his 'beloved and beechy Bucks' had been steadily growing. He had resolved to make his permanent home in it, and had been for some time on the lookout for a suitable house. We have seen that his extravagant fancy had once, when he was a bachelor and heavily in debt, hovered round the thought of Chequers Court;[2] and at the present time, as a married man, and, though still in debt, in a comparatively stable position, he had just agreed to purchase the more modest estate of Hughenden, a few miles from Bradenham. It was in Bucks that his earliest political efforts had been made. He had stood three times unsuccessfully for High Wycombe; and once, in 1832, had even issued an address to the electors of the county—'a juvenile indiscretion,' as he now felt, but 'prophetic' if 'presumptuous'—though, on that occasion, he withdrew almost immediately, so as not to embarrass his friend Lord Chandos, now the Duke of Buckingham. He had

[1] The speech about Cracow. See below, p. 171. [2] Vol. I., p. 353.

been careful to accept opportunities to speak on political occasions in the county, recognising, he wrote in 1836, that 'in all probability I am addressing my future constituents.'[1]

He was not altogether happy in his relations with his present constituency, Shrewsbury. Though the general body of the electors seem to have appreciated their distinguished member, and to have recognised how completely he had carried out the pledges that he had given to them, there was trouble with the local wirepullers; and there did not appear any likelihood of that fixity of tenure which a leader of the country party might well hope to obtain from the squires and farmers of Bucks. One of the three members for the county announced his intention of retiring. There was some expectation that the Lord Chandos of the day, the son of Disraeli's friend, would come forward; but he absolutely refused, and the way was clear. On May 24 Disraeli issued his farewell address to the electors of Shrewsbury, dwelling on the seven eventful sessions during which he had been their member, and on his pride and satisfaction that, trying as the circumstances had been, he had never forfeited the confidence of his constituents. The next day appeared his address to the electors of the county of Buckingham, a characteristic and historic document, which excited much attention at the time, and has a permanent interest for all students of his ideas.

The paragraphs in it referring to the question of the hour were these:

It is now many years ago, since, in your County Hall, I upheld the cause of the Territorial Constitution of England, as the best and surest foundation for popular rights and public liberty, imperial power and social happiness. The maintenance of the agricultural industry of the Country is the necessary condition of the enjoyment of that Constitution; and I have, therefore, independently of all other considerations, opposed, during the ten years in which I have had the honor of sitting in Parliament, every attempt which had a tendency

[1] *Ibid.*, p. 352.

to diminish the numbers and influence of those classes which are directly dependent on the land.

Influenced by this principle, I offered, during the recent assault on our protective system, a faithful, though fruitless, opposition to that project. What has since occurred has not, in any degree, changed the conclusions at which I then arrived as to the scheme of the late administration. The temporary high price, that is stimulated by famine, is not the agricultural prosperity which I wish to witness; while, in the full play of unrestricted importation, I already recognise a disturbing cause, which may shake our monetary system to its centre, and which nothing but the happy accident of our domestic enterprise has prevented, I believe, from exercising a very injurious effect on the condition of the Working Classes of Great Britain.

Notwithstanding this opinion, I am not, however, one of those who would counsel, or who would abet, any attempt factiously and forcibly to repeal the measures of 1846. The legislative sanction which they have obtained, requires that they should receive an ample experiment; and I am persuaded that this test alone can satisfy the nation either of their expediency, or their want of fitness. If, however, as I hold, the result of this great change must be a reconstruction of our financial system, it will behove the various classes connected with the cultivation of the soil to be vigilant, that their interests may be adequately represented and fitly enforced at a crisis, when their more compactly organised rivals will not be oblivious of their claims, or over-scrupulous in urging them.

Disraeli proceeded to explain that he was in favour of placing the education of the people in the hands of the clergy, their legitimate guides and instructors, and that he would heartily maintain the alliance of Church and State. He continued:

In the great struggle between popular principles and liberal opinions, which is the characteristic of our age, I hope ever to be found on the side of the people, and of the Institutions, of England. It is our Institutions that have made us free, and can alone keep us so; by the bulwark which they offer to the insidious encroachments of a convenient, yet enervating, system of centralisation, which, if left unchecked, will prove fatal to the national character. Therefore, I have ever endeavoured to cherish our happy habit of self-government, as sustained by a prudent distribution of local authority. For these reasons, I am of opinion that the right of supreme control, necessary to the due administration of the Poor Law, should be exercised by the chief Depositary of power in every County, and that the supervision of our Parishes should not be entrusted to strangers.

It is unnecessary for me to state that I shall support all those measures, the object of which is to elevate the moral and social condition of the Working Classes, by lessening their hours of toil — by improving their means of health — and by cultivating their intelligence. These are objects which, it is not unpleasing for me to remember, I endeavoured, in common with some of my friends, to advance, before they engaged the attention of Governments, or were supported by triumphant Parliamentary majorities.

The leading journals of the day, though the great majority of them were supporters of the Free Trade policy, nevertheless treated the candidate and his address with a respect and consideration which show the position which Disraeli had now won in the opinion of his countrymen. The points on which they chiefly fastened were the admission that the measures of 1846 must not be factiously repealed, but should receive an ample experiment; and the contrast set up between 'popular principles' and 'liberal opinions.' These two phrases were naturally ridiculed, as meaning merely, on the one hand, the views with which Disraeli agreed, and, on the other, those from which he differed. Really they represent a distinction running through the whole of his political philosophy, which always contrasts principles which bring classes together in accordance with the spirit of the Constitution, with the Liberalism which sets class against class and exalts political economy at the expense of human nature and patriotism. The Tories, he held, must be the popular party as opposed to doctrinaire Liberalism. In his first speech at Newport Pagnell, he illustrated his meaning. It was a popular principle, he said, to interfere to protect the factory workers; but the advocates of Liberal opinions said that in no circumstances must labour be interfered with. It was a popular principle to make a difference between the industry of our fellow-subjects and that of foreigners; Liberal opinion treated them alike. It was a popular principle that the National Church should be independent of the State, exercising a beneficial effect on public feeling and morals, and vindicating the cause of liberty; but Liberal opinion treated the Church as a mere stipendiary of the State. That the administration of justice should be conducted by an independent proprietary was a popular principle; that it should be conducted by a man paid by the State a Liberal opinion. 'In one word, it is a popular principle that England should be governed by England, while the Liberal opinion is that England should be governed by London.'

At Aylesbury, Disraeli insisted — and Bentinck took a similar line in his election address — that Free Trade must have a fair trial.

I told you in my address that I would not attempt factiously and forcibly to repeal the measure which was passed in the course of last year. What is the use of discussion, what is the use of a Legislature, if it is not that a great public question is to be settled for a time, at least, by the decision of your representatives? I care not how that decision may have come; it is a resolution of Parliament, and we must see the experiment fairly tried. You are in the position of a man who has made an improvident marriage. You have become united to Free Trade, and nothing can divorce you except you can prove the charmer to be false. Wait, then, till that period has arrived; when you find that you have been betrayed, then will be the time to seek a divorce from that pernicious union. You have become united to the false duenna, and you must take the consequences; and the consequence, I venture to predict, will be that the House of Commons, after a fair, full, and ample trial of this great measure, will be driven to repeal it from absolute necessity, though at the termination of much national suffering; but that that suffering will be compensated for by the bitterness and the profundity of national penitence.

The trial has been fuller and more ample than Disraeli anticipated, but it is evident that the end is not yet. At Newport Pagnell he had made it clear that the Protection which he believed to be expedient for the country was of a moderate, but at the same time Imperial, character.

He did not advocate that they should go back to what was perhaps a too limited application of a principle, but that they should reconstruct a system on a broader basis and foundation. They had heard much of the Customs Union of Germany, but when they looked to the numerous colonies over which the Queen of this country ruled, they saw Great Britain possessing a greater area than any other European Power, except Russia, and they were tempted to ask why should not England have her Imperial Union, the produce of every clime coming in free which acknowledged her authority, and paying no tax to the public Exchequer?

These sentiments fell on deaf ears at the moment; but they contain the germ of the idea of Imperial consolidation which Disraeli elaborated in a more favourable atmosphere in 1872, in a famous speech at the Crystal Palace.

The candidates at this election were — on the Conservative side, Du Pré and Tower, who had both sat in the last Parliament, and Disraeli; on the Liberal side, a member of the Whig house of Cavendish, who was afterwards created Lord Chesham. During the contest Tower withdrew, and attempts were made to get Chandos, in spite of his unwillingness, to come forward, in the hope of securing for the county three members of the Country party. But these attempts were unavailing. It was thought by some that, if Chandos were nominated, Disraeli might very likely fail. However that might be, a contest was avoided, and Du Pré, Disraeli, and Cavendish were returned unopposed. Thus began a connection of which both Disraeli and his county of Bucks had reason to be proud; which lasted for nearly thirty years, until his elevation to the peerage; and of which he wrote in 1860, 'This is the event of my public life which has given me the greatest satisfaction.' In a speech at Amersham during the election he made his profession of faith, often repeated in similar terms, in the political greatness of the county.

The county of Buckingham has always taken a lead in the political fortunes of this country. The parliamentary constitution of England was born in the bosom of the Chiltern

Hills; as to this day our parliamentary career is terminated among its hundreds. The parliamentary constitution of England was established when Mr. Hampden rode up to Westminster surrounded by his neighbours. Buckinghamshire did that for England. It has done more. It gave us the British Constitution in the seventeenth century, and it created the British Empire in the eighteenth. All the great statesmen of that century were born, or bred, or lived in this county. Throw your eye over the list — it is a glorious one — from Shelburne to Grenville. Travel from Wycombe to Buckingham, from the first Lord Lansdowne, the most accomplished Minister this country ever produced, to the last of our classic statesmen. Even the sovereign genius of Chatham was nursed in the groves of Stowe, and amid the *templa quam dilecta* of Cobham; and it was beneath his oaks at Beaconsfield that Mr. Burke poured forth those divine effusions that vindicated the social system, and reconciled the authority of law with the liberty of man. And in our own time, faithful to its character and its mission, amid a great parliamentary revolution, Buckinghamshire called a new political class into existence, and enfranchised you and the farmers of England by the Chandos clause. Now let the men of the North, who thought that they were to govern England — let them bring a political pedigree equal to that of the county of Buckingham.

Throughout the contest Disraeli emphasised his independence, and spoke as a leader of men. In his address he had said: 'I am not the organ of any section, or the nominee of any individual.' He was justly indignant at being described as a nominee of the Duke of Buckingham, seeing that he came forward at the request of leading yeomen and proprietors in the county, and relied mainly upon the farmers for his support. He said at Buckingham:

Independence is the necessary, the essential element of my political position. . . . I cannot take a seat in the House of Commons if I am not the master of my political destiny. I have not gained the position which I am proud to remember I occupy there but by my own individual exertions. It has cost me days of thought and nights of toil — it has cost me unwearied industry, frequent discomfiture, and many unequal contests. I have gained that position by myself, and I must maintain it by myself.

For Lord Stanley he said he entertained great respect, and believed no difference could exist between them at present on great public questions, but 'he would not pin his faith and his political creed to the robe of any senator, however exalted.' In referring to the struggle against Peel, he spoke of himself as the protagonist, who appealed for their approval, but who would not pursue the quarrel on the hustings or 'desecrate the recollections of the combat by allowing it to degenerate into a squabble.' Bentinck appears little in these speeches, and as a colleague rather than a leader. After the election was over Disraeli expressed his strong conviction, that 'the great question of Protection is not dead, but is only sleeping. You may rely upon it that Protection to native industry is a fundamental principle.' In this opinion he never varied. Lord Rowton, after the Tariff Reform movement had begun, though a Free Trader himself, told a friend that Lord Beaconsfield had always said that England would return to Protection.

As the Protectionists — or, at any rate, the Protectionist leaders — did not advocate the immediate overthrow of the new commercial system, there was at the General Election of 1847 no clear-cut issue before the country; and consequently very little alteration was effected in the relative strength of parties. The Whigs gained slightly, mainly at the expense of the Radicals and the Peelites; there were roughly 325 Ministerialists of all shades, and 330 Conservatives, of whom not more than 100 were followers of Peel. Russell's Ministry were still in a minority without Peel's support, but could fairly claim that they had been encouraged by the constituencies to confirm and develop the Free Trade policy. Disraeli has put on record his explanation of the general result. 'The high prices of agricultural produce which then prevailed naturally rendered the agricultural interest apathetic, and although the rural constituencies from a feeling of esteem again returned those members who had been faithful to the protective principle, the farmers did not exert themselves to increase the number of their supporters.' Indeed, as we have seen, in Disraeli's own county of Bucks a seat was given up, and two Protectionists and a Whig sat where three Protectionists had sat before. Of the personal changes owing to the election, four had a special bearing on Disraeli's fortunes. His great opponent of the future, Gladstone, returned to Parliament, after an absence of a year and a half, as member for Oxford University; his Protectionist ally, the veteran Herries, who had failed to obtain a seat in 1841, was elected, along with Granby, for Stamford; his intimate friend, John Manners, who retired from Newark, attempted in vain to capture a seat at Liverpool, and was out of Parliament till 1850; and the election of another friend, Baron Lionel de Rothschild, the head of the great financial house, as a colleague of the Prime Minister, for the City of London, forced to the front the question of Jewish disabilities, on which Bentinck and Disraeli held views very repugnant to the main body of their supporters.

'Had the General Election been postponed until the autumn, the results might have been very different,' writes Disraeli. No sooner was it over than the condition of general content which prevailed during its progress was suddenly changed for one of widespread commercial disaster. Bentinck, supported by the great financial authority of Thomas Baring, had called attention in the spring more than once to the signs of an approaching monetary crisis, mainly due, no doubt — though it was not generally recognised at the time — to excessive railway speculation. They had recommended the suspension of Peel's Bank Charter Act, which separated the currency from the banking department of the Bank of England, and limited the issue of banknotes, not permitting it to go beyond £14,000,000 in excess of bullion. The Government, supported by Peel, refused to interfere. But in September 'that storm, which had been long gathering in the commercial atmosphere, burst like a typhoon.' In that month fifteen houses in the City of

London failed for between five and six millions, the Governor and three directors of the Bank of England being involved. Large firms went at Manchester, Liverpool, and Glasgow. When the Chancellor of the Exchequer, Sir Charles Wood, hurried to London on October 1, he found the interest on money was 60 per cent. But Government refused to act for three weeks more, during which extensive disasters occurred in London and the country.

> Perish the world, sooner than violate a principle, was the philosophical exclamation of Her Majesty's Ministers, sustained by the sympathy and the sanction of Sir Robert Peel. At last the Governor and the Deputy-Governor of the Bank of England waited on Downing Street and said it could go on no more. . . . In four-and-twenty hours the machinery of credit would be entirely stopped. The position was frightful, and the Government gave way. They did that on the 25th of October, after houses had fallen to the amount of fifteen millions sterling, which they had been counselled to do by Lord George Bentinck on the 25th of April. . . . No sooner had the Government freed the Bank of England from that stringency than the panic ceased. The very morning the letter of licence from the Government to the Bank of England appeared, thousands and tens of thousands of pounds sterling were taken from the hoards, some from boxes deposited with bankers, although the depositors would not leave the notes in their bankers' hands. Large parcels of notes were returned to the Bank of England cut in halves, as they had been sent down into the country; and so small was the real demand for an additional quantity of currency, that the whole amount taken from the bank, when the unlimited power of issue was given, was under £400,000, and the bank consequently never availed itself of the privilege which the Government had accorded it.

In consequence of the Government having authorised an infringement of the law, Parliament met on November 8, the Queen's speech being delivered on the 23rd. Manners, 'compelled, like one of the unwilling Homeric gods, to witness the strife, a passive spectator,' wrote from Belvoir to counsel vigorous action. He thought his friends might look for strong support on all leading questions from various and conflicting quarters. What he dreaded was 'this horrid question of

Lionel Rothschild's election. . . . If you can put that matter into a right train you will perform a greater feat than when in five minutes you induced three Dukes, one after the other, to say you had convinced them about Cracow. I see no daylight through that Cimmerian darkness.'

To Lord John Manners.

GROSVENOR GATE, *Nov.* 16, 1847.

MY DEAR JOHN,—Your letter was forwarded to me from Bradenham. I had come up to have a couple of days' counsel and conference with G. B., before he went to Welbeck, which he did on Thursday—and I have stayed here since, and shall, I suppose, for the next eight months, with very slight intervals.

What I thought of your letter will be best shown by my immediately sending it off to G. B., who returned it yesterday. He writes: 'I send you back John Manners' sensible and spirited letter. I am low-spirited for want of such comrades in arms as this very John Manners.' I need not say how completely I echo this sentiment. What would I not give to find you again at my right hand; with the talent ever ready, the courage that never faltered, the indefatigable industry, and, above all, the honor and fidelity in which one could place implicit trust.

It will always be the first object of my life, and I am sure also of G. B.'s, to restore you to that place, where you are destined to occupy the most conspicuous post, and where in your presence we shall find the comrade and colleague for whom both of us feel devoted friendship. As for G. B. himself, he is a little taken by surprise by the early meeting, but full of courage, and I think much more matured; very earnest, and conscious of a great office, 'to save if possible,' he says in his last letter, 'the greatest commercial empire of the world engaged in a life and death struggle for existence.' . . .

G. B. has been terribly annoyed by the Rothschild affair, which he looked upon as a sad *début*, whatever he did. I had the pleasure yesterday of informing him, as I do now yourself, that the peril is not so imminent. It is even on the cards that the Bill will be introduced in the Lords; and whatever the result there, it will be a great relief to us. But, if introduced into the Commons, Lord John will only give notice before Christmas, and the battle is not to be fought until next year. Lionel, as at present counselled, will not even take his seat to choose the Speaker. Are you aware that, if Rothschild were to go to the table and ask for the Roman Catholic oath, which they could not refuse him, he could take his seat? The words 'faith of a Christian' only being in the oath of abjuration, from which the Romans were relieved. . . .

As for our domestic affairs, I will to-day say nothing. It is out of my power to give you the faintest idea of the feeling of terror, panic, despair, which seems to pervade all classes and people in this town. Every moment brings a fresh rumor; Cabinet Councils every other day, and frequent differences therein, as I am assured. . . . — Yours ever, D.

Lady Dorothy Walpole went down to Wolterton to-day to be married, which makes me very glad: an excellent match — Reginald Nevill with a *good* £8,000 *per ann.* and a real good fellow.

The special business which had occasioned the early summoning of Parliament was taken in hand at once. The Chancellor of the Exchequer moved to appoint a Committee to inquire into the causes of the commercial distress, and in the course of the debate Disraeli extracted an admission of some consequence from Russell. That statesman was arguing that the Bank Charter Act could not of itself prevent panics. There was a tendency to give credit to Acts of Parliament for doing more than they could perform. That was so in the case of Catholic Emancipation and various other measures. 'Free Trade, for example,' suggested Disraeli; and Russell, though apparently somewhat taken aback, agreed. Other urgent business which the Government brought forward at once was a Crimes Bill for Ireland, famine in that country having produced an outbreak of crime. Disraeli supported the Bill, and had no difficulty in reconciling his support with his action against Peel's Coercion Bill of 1846. That measure, though declared to be urgent, was not really proceeded with for six months; and one of its most important clauses, the Curfew clause, was unnecessary and arbitrary. The Protectionists, he held, had a 'legitimate opportunity' in 1846 to overthrow a Ministry in which they had lost confidence.

Disraeli attended a council of the leading Protectionists at Stanley's house in London, and from there sent his wife a gloomy account of the health of his colleagues:

To Mrs. Disraeli.

Nov. 29, 1847,—Our Cabinet is just over, having lasted three hours. . . . Lord G. B. is so ill with the influenza, that he is obliged to go home to bed. Herries has only just got out of bed after three days, and is still very ill.

Lord Chandos has been in bed for four days, the Duke has just told me.

If the physical health of the Protectionist leaders was bad, the political prospect immediately before them was worse. Rothschild had 'found a difficulty in taking one of the oaths appointed by the House to be sworn preliminarily to any member exercising his right of voting. The difficulty arose from this member being not only of the Jewish race, but unfortunately believing only in the first part of the Jewish religion.' The oath contained the words 'on the true faith of a Christian.' Russell moved, on December 16, that the House should resolve itself into a Committee 'on the removal of the civil and political disabilities affecting Her Majesty's Jewish subjects'; and the peril, which Bentinck and Manners had foreseen and dreaded, and Disraeli had been sanguine enough to think he could conjure away, was immediately upon the Protectionist party. The bulk of the rank and file considered it to be a religious duty to exclude from the supreme council of the nation, which regulated the Church as well as legislating for the State, those who denied the Divinity of Christ. Both Bentinck and Disraeli, for different reasons, supported the Jewish claims. To obtain a proper comprehension of Disraeli's point of view on this and other religious questions, we must turn to *Tancred.*

CHAPTER II

Tancred

1847

When Disraeli began a 'Young England' novel, he had intended, as we saw,[1] to deal with three principal topics: the origin and character of political parties, the condition of the people, and the duties of the Church as a main remedial agency in our present state. The two former had been treated in *Coningsby* and *Sybil*, published in 1844 and 1845; and the third novel, *Tancred; or, The New Crusade*, treating of the Church, was intended to follow in 1846. It appears to have been begun at once after the publication of *Sybil*, and was no doubt the subject of Disraeli's labours during that quiet autumn holiday in 1845 at Cassel, in French Flanders; but, owing to the great political struggle of 1846, it was not finally completed till the end of that year, and was only published in March, 1847. Its purpose was to develop the views respecting 'the great House of Israel' which he had first intimated in *Coningsby*.

In considering the Tory scheme, the author recognised in the Church the most powerful agent in the previous development of England, and the most efficient means of that renovation of the national spirit at which he aimed. The Church is a sacred corporation for the promulgation and maintenance in Europe of certain Asian principles, which, although local in their birth, are of Divine origin, and of universal and eternal application.

In asserting the paramount character of the ecclesiastical polity and the majesty of the theocratic principle, it became

[1] Vol. II., p. 250.

necessary to ascend to the origin of the Christian Church, and to meet, in a spirit worthy of a critical and comparatively enlightened age, the position of the descendants of that race who were the founders of Christianity. The modern Jews had long laboured under the odium and stigma of mediæval malevolence. In the dark ages when history was unknown, the passions of societies, undisturbed by traditionary experience, were strong, and their convictions, unmitigated by criticism, were necessarily fanatical. The Jews were looked upon in the middle ages as an accursed race, — the enemies of God and man, — the especial foes of Christianity. No one in those days paused to reflect that Christianity was founded by the Jews; that its Divine Author, in his human capacity, was a descendant of King David; that his doctrines avowedly were the completion, not the change, of Judaism; that the Apostles and the Evangelists, whose names men daily invoked, and whose volumes they embraced with reverence, were all Jews; that the infallible throne of Rome itself was established by a Jew; and that a Jew was the founder of the Christian Churches of Asia.

The European nations, relatively speaking, were then only recently converted to a belief in Moses and in Christ, and, as it were, still ashamed of the wild deities whom they had deserted, they thought they atoned for their past idolatry by wreaking their vengeance on a race to whom, and to whom alone, they were indebted for the Gospel they adored.

In vindicating the sovereign right of the Church of Christ to be the perpetual regenerator of man, the writer thought the time had arrived when some attempt should be made to do justice to the race which had founded Christianity.[1]

Looking back in 1870, Disraeli further expounded his views and aims:

Some of the great truths of ethnology were necessarily involved in such discussions. Familiar as we all now are with such themes, the house of Israel being now freed from the barbarism of mediæval misconception, and judged, like all other races, by their contributions to the existing sum of human welfare, and the general influence of race on human action being universally recognised as the key of history, the difficulty and hazard of touching for the first time on such topics cannot now be easily appreciated. But public opinion recognised both the truth and the sincerity of these views.[2]

[1] Preface to the fifth edition of *Coningsby*, 1849.

[2] General Preface to the Novels, 1870.

By Disraeli himself and most of his critics, *Tancred* has been regarded as merely the third novel in a trilogy. In a certain external sense it is that, of course. The theme with which it deals had been touched on in *Coningsby*, and the principal characters of *Coningsby* reappear. But a good many things had happened before *Tancred* was issued; and the reader is soon conscious of a breach of continuity with the previous novels, of being in a different atmosphere and a different world of ideas. 'Young England' had disappeared, and the political purpose, in the narrower sense, underlying *Coningsby* had disappeared with it. In the sphere of actual politics Disraeli had shown great and striking genius, and had become one of the foremost men in the House of Commons; but he had, on the other hand, become sensible of the weight of prejudice against him, and of the difficulties to be overcome if he was to continue his ascent. And *Tancred* strikes the reader less as the accomplishment of a political purpose, than as a sudden revolt of the author against the routine and hollowness of politics, against its prejudice and narrowness; and as an assertion of his detachment and superiority to it all by the glorification of his race and by the proclamation of the mystic ideas, inherited from the Jews, which marked him out from the commonplace mediocrities around him.

Tancred falls at once into two main portions: in the first, which occupies about a third of the book, the scene is laid in England; in the second in Palestine and the adjacent regions. Tancred, Lord Montacute, is the only child of the Duke and Duchess of Bellamont; his father a man of gentle but serious nature; his mother a woman of fixed opinions and of firm and compact prejudices, Puritan in religion and precisian in morals; both living entirely aloof from the world of fashion. The child of such parents, Tancred's upbringing has been serious; and his mother is able to say that he has never given her a moment's pain. His grave and reserved but enthusiastic nature has been brooding over the eternal mysteries;

he is discontented with his age, mourns over the decay of faith, and has entered a world of ideas into which his father and mother cannot follow him. He is, in fact, a type of religious discontent, as Coningsby was of political. When pressed by his father to enter Parliament after his coming of age, he astonished his parents by announcing his desire to make a pilgrimage to the Holy Sepulchre.

'When I remember' [he says to the Duke] 'that the Creator, since light sprang out of darkness, has deigned to reveal Himself to His creature only in one land; that in that land He assumed a manly form, and met a human death; I feel persuaded that the country sanctified by such intercourse and such events must be endowed with marvellous and peculiar qualities. . . . Our castle has before this sent forth a De Montacute to Palestine. For three days and three nights he knelt at the tomb of his Redeemer. Six centuries and more have elapsed since that great enterprise. It is time to restore and renovate our communications with the Most High. I, too, would kneel at that tomb; I, too, surrounded by the holy hills and sacred groves of Jerusalem, would relieve my spirit from the bale that bows it down; would lift up my voice to heaven, and ask, What is DUTY, and what is FAITH? What ought I to DO, and what ought I to BELIEVE?'

His mother at once calls in her favourite Bishop, whose character is so drawn that it was immediately recognised as an unfriendly portrait of Blomfield, Bishop of London.

He combined a great talent for action with very limited powers of thought. Bustling, energetic, versatile, gifted with an indomitable perseverance, and stimulated by an ambition that knew no repose, with a capacity for mastering details and an inordinate passion for affairs, he could permit nothing to be done without his interference, and consequently was perpetually involved in transactions which were either failures or blunders. He was one of those leaders who are not guides. . . . Placed in a high post in an age of political analysis, the bustling intermeddler was unable to supply society with a single solution. Enunciating second-hand, with characteristic precipitation, some big principle in vogue, as if he were a discoverer, he invariably shrank from its subsequent application, the moment that he found it might be unpopular and inconvenient. All his quandaries terminated in the same catastrophe — a compromise.

In a long interview with Tancred he makes no impression. He was as little able as the Duke to solve Tancred's difficulties. As a proof of the vitality of the Church he solemnly announced that they would soon see a Bishop at Manchester. 'But I want to see an angel at Manchester,' replied Tancred.

The Bishop having failed, the Duke decides that the best man to deal with a visionary is a man of the world, and the man of the world is now called in, in the person of an old friend, Lord Eskdale.[1] He receives the announcement of Tancred's resolve to go to Jerusalem with the light-hearted remark that it is 'better than going to the Jews, which most men do at his time of life'; and he recommends a policy, not of opposition, but of delay, sets Tancred searching for a yacht, and meantime introduces him to the allurements of London society. There Tancred meets a certain Lady Constance Rawleigh, 'a distinguished beauty of two seasons; fresh but adroit.' 'It had got about that she admired intellect, and, though she claimed the highest social position, that a booby would not content her, even if his ears were covered with strawberry leaves.'

She fascinates Tancred, and becomes a serious rival in his thoughts to Jerusalem; but the spell is broken when she recommends him to read *The Revelations of Chaos*,[2] a new book which 'explains everything.'

'It explains everything!' said Tancred; 'it must, indeed, be a very remarkable book!'

'I think it will just suit you,' said Lady Constance. 'Do you know, I thought so several times while I was reading it.'

'To judge from the title, the subject is rather obscure,' said Tancred.

'No longer so,' said Lady Constance. 'It is treated

[1] See Vol. II., p. 203.

[2] Mrs. Disraeli writes to Sarah Disraeli, in January, 1845: 'We have just got *Vestiges of the Natural History of Creation*. Dizzy is enchanted with it. It does and will cause the greatest possible sensation and confusion.' The book, by Robert Chambers, the Edinburgh publisher, issued anonymously in 1844, set forth a theory of development, and was praised by Darwin as preparing the ground for his own 'analogous views.'

scientifically; everything is explained by geology and astronomy, and in that way. It shows you exactly how a star is formed; nothing can be so pretty! A cluster of vapour, the cream of the milky way, a sort of celestial cheese, churned into light. You must read it, 'tis charming.'

'Nobody ever saw a star formed,' said Tancred.

'Perhaps not. You must read *Revelations;* it is all explained. But what is most interesting, is the way in which man has been developed. You know, all is development. The principle is perpetually going on. First there was nothing, then there was something; then, I forget the next, I think there were shells, then fishes; then we came: let me see, did we come next? Never mind that; we came at last. And the next change there will be something very superior to us, something with wings. Ah! that's it: we were fishes, and I believe we shall be crows. But you must read it.'

'I do not believe I ever was a fish,' said Tancred.

'Oh! but it is all proved.' . . .

'I was a fish, and I shall be a crow,' said Tancred to himself, when the hall door closed on him. 'What a spiritual mistress!'

He resumes his preparations for departure, and at the instigation of Lord Eskdale calls on Sidonia[1] with a recommendation, as the great banker is of the Hebrew race, not to 'go on too much about the Holy Sepulchre.' Sidonia, whose place of business in the City, Sequin Court, is clearly drawn from New Court, St. Swithin's Lane, the famous Rothschild establishment, listens to his talk with sympathy. 'When Tancred had finished speaking, there was a pause of a few seconds, during which Sidonia seemed lost in thought; then, looking up, he said: "It appears to me, Lord Montacute, that what you want is to penetrate the great Asian mystery."' 'The great Asian mystery!' 'How often,' writes Disraeli, 'when all seems dark, and hopeless, and spiritless, and tame, when slight obstacles figure in the cloudy landscape as Alps, and the rushing cataracts of our invention have faded into drizzle, a single phrase of a great man instantaneously flings sunshine on the intellectual landscape!' Reanimated by Sidonia, Tancred resumes his purpose; but he has more adventures first. At a dinner at Sidonia's he meets some

[1] See Vol. II., ch. 7, especially pp. 206, 209–212, and 222.

more of our old friends of *Coningsby* and *Sybil.* The critics tell us that in *Julius Cæsar* Shakespeare has deliberately made the figure of the great dictator, for whom he shows elsewhere so warm an admiration, a little ridiculous in order to insure that the real hero, Brutus, should stand out more distinctly; and so it seems here as if Disraeli, possessed of his high religious theme, took an iconoclastic delight in shattering his lesser idols. Sybil and Egremont are spared; so is Henry Sydney, now spelt Sidney; but Coningsby has become a somewhat commonplace young man, at once pompous and saucy, engaged in a prosperous career; and Edith is represented so that she draws a protest from Sarah Disraeli: 'I am so sorry that the beautiful and pure Edith should have turned out what she is. . . . We were very much in love with her; but I cannot forgive her for saying her child has a "debauched look."' A new character, Vavasour, who is famous for his breakfasts, and to whom we shall return, is now added to the 'Young England' group. Tancred pours scorn on the Parliamentary career in which they are all striving. Parliament seems to him the very place which a man of action should avoid.

'In this age it is not Parliament that does the real work. It does not govern Ireland, for example. If the manufacturers want to change a tariff, they form a commercial league, and they effect their purpose. It is the same with the abolition of slavery, and all our great revolutions. Parliament has become as really insignificant as for two centuries it has kept the monarch. O'Connell has taken a good share of its power; Cobden has taken another; and I am inclined to believe,' said Tancred, 'though I care little about it, that, if our order had any spirit or prescience, they would put themselves at the head of the people, and take the rest.' . . .

'I go to a land,' said Tancred, 'that has never been blessed by that fatal drollery called a representative government, though Omniscience once deigned to trace out the polity which should rule it.'

In the same symposium Sidonia expounds some of Disraeli's favourite ideas:

'If development be progressive, how do you account for the state of Italy? . . . Has the development of Western Asia been progressive? It is a land of tombs and ruins. Is China progressive, the most ancient and numerous of existing societies? Is Europe itself progressive? Is Spain a tithe as great as she was? Is Germany as great as when she invented printing; as she was under the rule of Charles the Fifth? France herself laments her relative inferiority to the past. But England flourishes. Is it what you call civilisation that makes England flourish? Is it the universal development of the faculties of man that has rendered an island, almost unknown to the ancients, the arbiter of the world? Clearly not. It is her inhabitants that have done this; it is an affair of race. A Saxon race, protected by an insular position, has stamped its diligent and methodic character on the century. And when a superior race, with a superior idea to Work and Order, advances, its state will be progressive, and we shall, perhaps, follow the example of the desolate countries. *All is race;* there is no other truth.'

'Because it includes all others?' said Lord Henry.

'You have said it.'

'As for Vavasour's definition of civilisation,' said Coningsby, 'civilisation was more advanced in ancient than modern times; then what becomes of the progressive principle? Look at the great centuries of the Roman Empire! . . .'

'What an empire!' said Sidonia. 'All the superior races in all the superior climes.'

Tancred has yet another adventure before he sets forth for Palestine. A married beauty, Lady Bertie and Bellair, wins him by her sympathy with his high aspirations, till he learns by chance that she is the most inveterate female gambler in Europe.

This first part of *Tancred* is perhaps the best comedy that Disraeli ever wrote. Besides the principal characters and the main intrigue, there are some delightful vignettes. There is the low comedy of the cooks, with which the book opens; and the amusing scene in which Lord Eskdale soothes an unappreciated *chef* by the delicate compliment, 'Why I wished you to come down here, Leander, was not to receive the applause of my cousin and his guests, but to form their taste.' Then there is Lady Hampshire, a character always familiar in society. She 'was an invalid; but her ailment was one of those mysteries which still remained insoluble, although, in the most liberal manner, she delighted to afford her friends all the information in her power. The further social progress of the Guy Flounceys, and especially of Mrs. Guy Flouncey,[1] is admirably depicted. They had 'a good fortune, with good management, no country house, and no children'—it was 'Aladdin's lamp.' They had already attracted the best men; but Mrs. Guy meant also to conquer the great ladies. This is how she proceeded:

> A great nobleman met Mrs. Guy Flouncey at a country house, and was fairly captivated by her. Her pretty looks, her coquettish manner, her vivacity, her charming costume, above all, perhaps, her imperturbable good temper, pierced him to the heart. The great nobleman's wife had the weakness to be annoyed. Mrs. Guy Flouncey saw her opportunity. She threw over the earl, and became the friend of the countess, who could never sufficiently evince her gratitude to the woman who would not make love to her husband. This friendship was the incident for which Mrs. Guy Flouncey had been cruising for years.

She determined to test her position by giving a ball. Her great friend, the countess, asked the guests; a royal duchess was prevailed upon to come; so was the 'Dictator,' the Duke of Wellington. 'All the great ladies, all the ambassadors, all the beauties, a full chapter of the Garter, a chorus among the "best men" that it was without doubt the "best ball" of the year—happy Mrs. Guy Flouncey!'

The social satire in *Tancred*, it will be seen, is bitter; more bitter than in *Coningsby* or *Sybil.* In fact, it is to be noted that, if we regard the three novels as a trilogy, as the theme grows higher, passing from party in *Coningsby* to the people in *Sybil* and religion in *Tancred*, the detachment from the world and the readiness to flout and trample upon it grow more marked.

We now leave London society and pass to the Holy Land and Tancred's attempts to penetrate 'the great

[1] See Vol. II., p. 223.

Asian mystery';[1] and the tone at once changes to Disraeli's highest vein of seriousness. A rhapsody in Jerusalem sounds the note of all that is to follow in an allusion to 'the most illustrious of the human, as well as of the Hebrew, race, the descendant of King David, and the divine son of the most favoured of women.' Disraeli's great conception of Christianity as completed Judaism pervades the whole. After a visit to Gethsemane, Tancred falls asleep in a garden near Bethany, and on awaking beholds a beautiful young woman the description of whose dress illustrates a side of Disraeli's mind and taste. She wore an amber vest of gold-embroidered silk fastened with buttons of precious stones, and white Cashmere trousers fastened with clasps of rubies. Over the vest was a violet silk pelisse; and over this an outer pelisse of amber Cashmere lined with white fox fur. There were costly jewels on her arms; her cap was thickly incrusted with pearls; her hair was fastened up with bunches of precious stones.

In the long dialogue that follows, the lady displays an intellect as marvellous as her jewels:

'Pray, are you of those Franks who worship a Jewess; or of those other who revile her, break her images, and blaspheme her pictures?'

'I venerate, though I do not adore, the mother of God,' said Tancred, with emotion.

'Ah! the mother of Jesus!' said his companion. 'He is your God. He lived much in this village. He was a great man, but he was a Jew; and you worship him.'

'And you do not worship him?' said Tancred, looking up to her with an inquiring glance, and with a reddening cheek.

'It sometimes seems to me that I ought,' said the lady, 'for I am of his race, and you should sympathise with your race.'

[1] During Disraeli's last period of office as Prime Minister, a clergyman wrote to ask him the meaning of 'the great Asian mystery' mentioned in *Tancred*. Disraeli endorsed the letter for his private secretary: 'Write to this gentleman that, as I have written three volumes to answer the question he asks, and, so far as he is concerned, have failed, it would be presumption to suppose I could be more fortunate in a letter. Recommend repeated, and frequent, study of the work as the most efficient means for his purpose.—D.'

'You are, then, a Hebrew?'

'I am of the same blood as Mary whom you venerate, but do not adore.'

She is, as a matter of fact, Eva, known as the Rose of the banker Sharon, the daughter of Besso, to whom Tancred has a letter of credit, and she stands in the book for the genius of Judaism. The other principal character in the second part is Fakredeen, an Emir of the Lebanon, Eva's foster-brother, a scheming and ambitious Syrian, clever, subtle, volatile, and utterly unscrupulous. 'I am of that religion,' he says, 'which gives me a sceptre.' 'What is the use,' he asks Eva, 'of belonging to an old family, unless to have the authority of an ancestor ready for any prejudice, religious or political, which your combinations may require?' 'Ah! Fakredeen,' replies the lady, 'you have no self-respect.' He has 'the two greatest stimulants in the world to action, youth and debt.' He wants Europe to talk of him. His ambition hovers between being Prince of the Lebanon, on the one hand, and, on the other, conquering the East in order to establish the independence of the Oriental races. For him all life and conduct was a matter of force or fraud, and he preferred the latter, on æsthetic grounds.

Though it was his profession and his pride to simulate and to dissemble, he had a native ingenuousness which was extremely awkward and very surprising, for, the moment he was intimate with you, he told you everything. Though he intended to make a person his tool, and often succeeded, such was his susceptibility, and so strong were his sympathetic qualities, that he was perpetually, without being aware of it, showing his cards.

After a week's solitude and fasting, Tancred has kneeled at the 'empty sepulchre of the divine Prince of the house of David,' but no voice from heaven has yet sounded for him. However, as Sinai led to Calvary, he resolves to go from Calvary to Sinai. On his way across the desert, through the machinations of Fakredeen he is captured and held to ransom by a tribe of Rechabites, children of

Jethro, whose chief is Eva's grandfather. But Fakredeen, meeting Tancred, comes under the spell of his heroic and enthusiastic nature; and the simple-minded Tancred pours out his ideas to the fickle Syrian. Nothing great, he tells him, was ever effected by management. Fakredeen's system of intrigue might suit the wretched eighteenth century, when there was no faith in God or man. In the nineteenth century you must appeal to popular sympathies.

'If you wish to free your country, and make the Syrians a nation, it is not to be done by sending secret envoys to Paris or London, cities themselves which are perhaps both doomed to fall; you must act like Moses and Mahomet. . . . The world was never conquered by intrigue, it was conquered by faith. Now, I do not see that you have faith in anything.'

'Faith,' said Fakredeen, musingly, as if his ear had caught the word for the first time, 'faith! that is a grand idea. If one could only have faith in something and conquer the world!'

'See now,' said Tancred, with unusual animation, 'I find no charm in conquering the world to establish a dynasty: a dynasty, like everything else, wears out; indeed, it does not last as long as most things; it has a precipitate tendency to decay. . . . One should conquer the world not to enthrone a man, but an idea, for ideas exist for ever. But what idea? There is the touchstone of all philosophy! Amid the wreck of creeds, the crash of empires, French revolutions, English reforms, Catholicism in agony, and Protestantism in convulsions, discordant Europe demands the keynote, which none can sound. If Asia be in decay, Europe is in confusion. Your repose may be death, but our life is anarchy.'

Fakredeen, revolving the strange idea of faith in his mind, thinks something might be done by heading the Desert, and making the tribes pour out like an irresistible simoom. 'The Arabs are always young; it is the only race that never withers.' He was an Arab by race himself, whereas Tancred could only claim to be an Arab by religion.

At the end of the conversation the Emir, suddenly inspired, bursts out: 'The game is in our hands, if we have energy. There is a combination which would entirely change the whole face of the world, and bring back empire to the East.' One thing was clear: 'it is finished with England.' But all might be saved by a *coup d'état*.

'You must . . . quit a petty and exhausted position for a vast and prolific empire. Let the Queen of the English collect a great fleet, let her stow away all her treasure, bullion, gold plate, and precious arms; be accompanied by all her court and chief people, and transfer the seat of her empire from London to Delhi. There she will find an immense empire ready made, a firstrate army, and a large revenue. In the meantime I will arrange with Mehemet Ali. He shall have Bagdad and Mesopotamia, and pour the Bedoueen cavalry into Persia. I will take care of Syria and Asia Minor. The only way to manage the Affghans is by Persia and by the Arabs. We will acknowledge the Empress of India as our suzerain, and secure for her the Levantine coast. If she like, she shall have Alexandria as she now has Malta: it could be arranged. Your Queen is young: she has an *avenir*. Aberdeen and Sir Peel will never give her this advice; their habits are formed. They are too old, too *rusés*. But, you see! the greatest empire that ever existed; besides which she gets rid of the embarrassment of her Chambers! And quite practicable; for the only difficult part, the conquest of India, which baffled Alexander, is all done!'

Fakredeen's confident assertion that 'it is finished with England' is not yet true; but the British Crown does hold Alexandria, though not in quite the same way as it holds Malta; and the seat of Eastern empire is now at Delhi, where a British King has held his court as Emperor of India. Moreover, these developments are due, directly or indirectly, to Disraeli's policy.

Tancred at length finds himself on Sinai, and there, during a night spent in prayer on the sacred soil, a vision is vouchsafed to him; a form appears which announces itself as the Angel of Arabia. In this ambitious scene Disraeli, it must be said, completely overreached himself. What is meant to be solemn and impressive is grotesque. The Angel talks a couple of pages of fluent journalese, and gives him this message:

'The equality of man can only be accomplished by the sovereignty of God. The longing for fraternity can never be satisfied but under the sway of a common father. The relations between Jehovah and his creatures can be neither too numerous nor too near. In the increased distance between God and man have grown up all those developments that have made life mournful. Cease, then, to seek in a vain philosophy the solution of the social problem that perplexes you. Announce the sublime and solacing doctrine of theocratic equality.'

Tancred, on his return to the Rechabite encampment, nearly dies of a brain fever, but is nursed back to life by Eva, who has come from Jerusalem to her grandfather. He is now 'all for action,' ready to place himself at the head of the Asian movement. 'A man might climb Mount Carmel,' he says, 'and utter three words which would bring the Arabs again to Grenada, and perhaps further.' He proceeds :

'The most favoured part of the globe at this moment is entirely defenceless; there is not a soldier worth firing at in Asia except the Sepoys. The Persian, Assyrian, and Babylonian monarchies might be gained in a morning with faith and the flourish of a sabre.'

'You would have the Great Powers interfering,' said Baroni.

'What should I care for the Great Powers, if the Lord of Hosts were on my side!'

'Why, to be sure they could not do much at Bagdad or Ispahan.'

'Work out a great religious truth on the Persian and Mesopotamian plains, the most exuberant soils in the world with the scantiest population, it would revivify Asia. It must spread. The peninsula of Arabia, when in action, must always command the peninsula of the Lesser Asia. Asia revivified would act upon Europe. The European comfort, which they call civilisation, is, after all, confined to a very small space: the island of Great Britain, France, and the course of a single river, the Rhine. The greater part of Europe is as dead as Asia, without the consolation of climate and the influence of immortal traditions.'

And again:

'Unhappy Asia! Do you call it unhappy Asia? This land of Divine deeds and Divine thoughts! Its slumber is more vital than the waking life of the rest of the globe, as the dream of genius is more precious than the vigils of ordinary men. Unhappy Asia, do you call it? It is the unhappiness of Europe over which I mourn.'

'Europe that has conquered Hindostan, protects Persia and Asia Minor, affects to have saved Syria,' said Eva, with some bitterness. 'Oh! what can we do against Europe?'

'Save it,' said Tancred.

'We cannot save ourselves; what means have we to save others?'

'The same you have ever exercised, Divine Truth. Send forth a great thought, as you have done before, from Mount Sinai, from the villages of Galilee, from the deserts of Arabia, and you may again remodel all their institutions, change their principles of action, and breathe a new spirit into the whole scope of their existence.'

Disraeli by this time was clearly beginning to find the impossibility of bringing his hero to any satisfactory bourne, and his story to any satisfactory conclusion. As in *Vivian Grey* and *Contarini Fleming*, he had let his thoughts run; and the true completion of *Tancred*, as of them, is to be found in his own career. In the deepest sense, it stands with those two as the most autobiographical of his novels. From the point of view of art, the true scheme would have been to bring Tancred to the threshold of his vision on Sinai, and then let all end in tragedy. Sarah Disraeli foresaw the difficulty. When she had only read the first volume, she wrote to her brother: 'We are as eager as Tancred to reach the Holy Sepulchre, but, as Sidonia says, when we arrive there, what is to happen? How are these great questions to be answered? When are these mighty truths to be discovered?' Disraeli, however, persevered, but, though much of the detail in the remainder of the book is good—especially the comedy scenes—it is really incoherent. As he wrote to Lady Londonderry, Tancred had turned out a much more troublesome and unmanageable personage than he had anticipated.

Fakredeen carries Tancred off to Canobia, his mountain castle in the Lebanon. There he collects round him and reconciles the Druses and the Maronites; but the allies feel that their purposes require further support. They accordingly endeavour to enlist in their cause a mysterious and isolated tribe, the Ansarey, settled in the north of Syria, and ruled over by a Queen Astarte. With difficulty they manage to pay these Ansarey a visit, and find them to be Hellenes still worshipping the old Greek gods. This gives Disraeli an opportunity of bringing out in another aspect his theory of race.

The Queen of the Ansarey has a pompous and absurd Prime Minister, Keferinis, who affords some comic relief in the latter part of the book. But the best comedy scenes in Syria are those in which the gossips of Jerusalem discuss the high politics of the world.

'Palmerston' [said Barizy of the Tower] 'will never rest till he gets Jerusalem.'

'The English must have markets,' said the Consul Pasqualigo.

'Very just,' said Barizy of the Tower. 'There will be a great opening here. I think of doing a little myself in cottons; but the house of Besso will monopolise everything.'

'I don't think the English can do much here,' said the Consul, shaking his head. 'What have we to give them in exchange? The people here had better look to Austria, if they wish to thrive. The Austrians also have cottons, and they are Christians. They will give you their cottons, and take your crucifixes.'

'I don't think I can deal in crucifixes,' said Barizy of the Tower.

'I tell you what, if you won't, your cousin Barizy of the Gate will. I know he has given a great order to Bethlehem.'

'The traitor!' exclaimed Barizy of the Tower. 'Well, if people will purchase crucifixes and nothing else, they must be supplied. Commerce civilizes man.'

At the end of many adventures and many complicated intrigues on the part of Fakredeen, who turns round and betrays Tancred, we are admitted to a dialogue between Eva and Tancred in that garden at Bethany where their acquaintance began. She is despondent, and says:

'Your feelings cannot be what they were before all this happened; when you thought only of a Divine cause, of stars, of angels, and of our peculiar and gifted land. No, no; now it is all mixed up with intrigue, and politics, and management, and baffled schemes, and cunning arts of men. You may be, you are, free from all this, but your faith is not the same. You no longer believe in Arabia.'

'Why, thou to me art Arabia,' said Tancred, advancing and kneeling at her side. 'The Angel of Arabia, and of my life and spirit! Talk not to me of faltering faith: mine is intense. Talk not to me of leaving a Divine cause: why, thou art my cause, and thou art most divine! O Eva! deign to accept the tribute of my long agitated heart! Yes, I too, like thee, am sometimes full of despair; but it is only when I remember that I love, and love, perhaps, in vain.'

But even this solution of the problem has its difficulties. The lovers are interrupted by the approach of a crowd, shouting Tancred's name. 'The Duke and Duchess of Bellamont had arrived at Jerusalem.' And with these words the novel ends.

Thirty years later Disraeli told Jowett that he still liked *Tancred* the best of his novels. That is easy to understand. It embodied those deeper dreams which had not yet faded, and which he was still trying to realise. In 1877 he was far closer to the spirit of *Tancred* than to that of *Lothair*, which had been published a few years before. He once told someone else that, when he wanted to refresh his knowledge of the East, he read *Tancred*. As a picture of the East it is a wonderful *tour de force*. Lady Blessington, on reading it, wrote to Disraeli: 'You have made me comprehend the East better than all the books I have ever read on it.'

The book was an astonishing publication for a man who had just forced himself into the front rank of a great political party. Nothing in Disraeli's whole career is more illustrative of his range than the production — at a critical moment of his life, when it appeared to be his business to conciliate the prejudices of the respectable, the decorous, and the commonplace — of this remarkable work, with all its daring and its dreams, its firm handling of sacred subjects and its visionary spirit, its fierce protest against Western material civilisation and Philistinism. The reviewers, with some reproofs for the audacity that at times seemed to border on irreverence, were friendly on the whole in their reception of the novel; but *Tancred* had not the success of *Coningsby* with the public at large. It was above their heads. Isaac D'Israeli, whose own admiration was expressed in superlatives — 'a work for its originality and execution without a rival; faultless in composition, profound in philosophy, and magical in the loveliness of its descriptions' — anticipated a dubious reception. 'I am waiting with more curiosity than anxiety to learn its effect on the unenlightened public. We may have to listen to the squeak or the bray of the obscure animals in their forests whenever a new light breaks into their dark recesses.' Colburn, who published *Tancred*, as well as its two predecessors, wrote to Mrs. Disraeli shortly after its appearance. 'The sale of *Tancred* is progressing, tho' not quite so quickly as I could wish. . . . I have, however, got through the first edition of 1,500 copies (including the *gratis* books), and have disposed of about 50 of the second edition.' Disraeli's share of the profit, on 2,250 copies, was £775.

The bewilderment of the public over *Tancred* has been shared by eminent critics. Sir Leslie Stephen can only explain the book 'by accepting the theory of a double consciousness, and resolving to pray with the mystic, and sneer with the politician, as the fit takes us.' He writes of 'the strange phantasmagoria of *Tancred*,' and the 'strange antics' of its character; but suggests that the judgment of the harsh realist must be that, 'after all, it is a mere mystification.' 'A mere mystification' was what the ordinary man and the rank and file politician considered it; and hence the legend sprang up which treated Disraeli as a mystery-man, a conjurer, who performed by verbal dexterity the same kind of tricks that the juggler effects by sleight of hand. This was the view that *Punch* adopted for years; and few things did more in Victorian days to fix the character of public men in the public mind than Leech's and Tenniel's cartoons. Even Carlyle, whose teaching was in many respects so similar to Disraeli's, treated him as a 'superlative Hebrew conjurer.' The book therefore, on the whole, did its author a disservice. It increased the distrust already existing in many minds; it hindered and delayed public recognition of the real seriousness of his political ideas and of the lofty nature of his patriotism. And yet those who penetrated deep into the spirit of the novel found there more of Disraeli's message to his age than in any other of his writings.

Before we consider this message in detail, it may be as well to recur to one of the *dramatis personæ* in *Tancred*, where we have the advantage of being able to compare Disraeli's recorded estimate of an eminent man with his portrait as depicted in the novel. In the first part, perhaps the most elaborately sketched character is that of Vavasour.

Mr. Vavasour was a social favourite; a poet and a real poet, and a troubadour, as well as a member of Parliament; travelled, sweet-tempered, and good-hearted; amusing and clever. With catholic sympathies and an eclectic turn of mind, Mr. Vavasour saw something good in everybody and everything. . . . Mr. Vavasour's breakfasts were renowned. Whatever your creed, class, or country, one might almost add your character, you were a welcome guest at his matutinal meal, provided you were celebrated. That qualification, however, was rigidly enforced.

It not rarely happened that never were men more incongruously grouped. Individuals met at his hospitable house who had never met before, but who for years had been cherishing in solitude mutual detestation, with all the irritable exaggeration of the literary character. Vavasour liked to be the Amphitryon of a cluster of personal enemies. . . .

A real philosopher, alike from his genial disposition and from the influence of his rich and various information, Vavasour moved amid the strife, sympathising with everyone; and perhaps, after all, the philanthropy which was his boast was not untinged by a dash of humour, of which rare and charming quality he possessed no inconsiderable portion. Vavasour liked to know everybody who was known, and to see everything which ought to be seen. He also was of opinion that everybody who was known ought to know him; and that the spectacle, however splendid or exciting, was not quite perfect without his presence.

His life was a gyration of energetic curiosity; an insatiable whirl of social celebrity. . . . He was everywhere, and at everything; he had gone down in a diving-bell and gone up in a balloon. As for his acquaintances, he was welcomed in every land; his universal sympathies seemed omnipotent. Emperor and king, jacobin and carbonaro, alike cherished him. He was the steward of Polish balls and the vindicator of Russian humanity; he dined with Louis Philippe, and gave dinners to Louis Blanc.

There was no difficulty in recognising in this careful portrait one of the best-known men of the day — Richard Monckton Milnes, afterwards Lord Houghton. How he came to figure in *Tancred* is explained in a memorandum written by Disraeli in the sixties:

Monckton Milnes was a good-natured fellow, and not naturally bad-hearted; he was highly instructed and very clever. But he was always ridiculous, — from an insane vanity. This excess of a sentiment, which, when limited, is only amusing, was accompanied by a degree of envy which made him unamiable.

When I published *Coningsby*, he complained to me that I had not introduced his character among the Young England group, to which he was attached in feeling, and with whom he wished to act — and had sometimes. He spoke to me on this matter with great earnestness — tears in his eyes — I had never appreciated him, and all that sort of thing. As his father was a friend of mine, and I always wished to be on good terms with Milnes, . . . I at length promised that, if the opportunity offered, I would remember his wish. Accordingly, when I wrote *Tancred*, in which the Young England Group reappeared, I sketched the character of Vavasour, and I made it as attractive as I could consistent with that verisimilitude necessary. I don't know whether he was over-satisfied: but between 1844 and 1847 when *Tancred* was published (*Sybil* in 1845, and *Tancred* was intended for 1846, but the publication postponed in consequence of the great Corn Law Repeal) much had happened in my position: the Young England myth had evaporated, and I had become, if not the recognised leader, at least the most influential organ, of a powerful parliamentary party. Milnes was full of envy.

'It is impossible that I and Sidney Herbert,' he went about saying, 'can be led by Disraeli.'

No one expected that Sidney Herbert would be led by me. He was a member of Sir Robert Peel's Cabinet, which had been mainly, if not entirely, destroyed by my efforts. Milnes was one of the most insignificant members of the House of Commons: but he gratified his vanity by classing in his own talk himself with S. Herbert.

In Easter, 1846, when the success of Peel was doubtful, Milnes, who had not a rural taste or accomplishment, came up from Yorkshire after the recess in a squire's cutaway green coat, with basket buttons. As he entered the House, G. Smythe exclaimed: 'See Dicky,—Protection looking up.'

When he found that Peel was flung in a ditch, he changed his politics, and took to Palmerston, whom, as well as Lady Palmerston, he toadied with a flagrant perseverance that made everyone smile. His passion was office. He wanted to sit on the Treasury Bench, with folded arms, and to be a man of business. Palmerston was ready to do anything for him except give him office, and refused him everything on every occasion. He always went to relieve his feelings and plead his cause to Lady Palmerston, who smoothed him down, asked him to perpetual dinners, and said he was a 'social favourite.' . . .

It is well known that Palmerston offered a peerage to Milnes's father, Pemberton Milnes, who greatly annoyed his son by declining it. Disraeli's memorandum proceeds:

In this quandary, Dicky, who was himself not incapable of generous feelings and conduct, gave me credit for a similar constitution, and determined to appeal to me. His father, in order probably to vex him, always declared that he was a follower of mine, and could not as a man of honor accept a dignity from my opponents. Dicky threw himself upon my good feelings, and I saw his father and said and urged everything which should induce him to reconsider his course: but in vain. I even ventured to represent to him, that, even if the Tories returned to power, and Lord Derby were to consult me as to the commoners who should be promoted, the number must necessarily be limited, and would be confined to those members of the House of Commons who had served the party long, made great sacrifices, and left behind them great influences; that private friendship merely could not be a ground of promotion. I thought that this representation of affairs at one moment a little shook him: but he was ultimately firm, and he died a commoner.

Eventually, in 1863, after Pemberton Milnes's death, Monckton Milnes became, on Palmerston's recommendation, Lord Houghton.

Milnes, the father, was a tall, handsome man, with a distinguished presence. Lord Houghton was unfortunately short, with a face like a Herculaneum masque, or a countenance cut out of an orange. . . . He never caught the House of Commons tone. Too easy and familiar in Society, the moment he was on his legs in St. Stephen's he was nervous, took refuge in pomposity, and had no flow; a most elaborate style and always recalling his words. His irresistibly comic face, becoming every moment more serious, produced the effect of some celebrated droll, Liston or Keeley, and before he had proceeded five minutes, though he might be descanting on the wrongs of Poland or the rights of Italy, there was sure to be a laugh.

Disraeli's judgment of Milnes seems to be unduly harsh, and betrays, perhaps, the contempt of a literary man who has gone into politics and there succeeded, for a literary man who has gone into politics and there failed.

'Mr. Vavasour's breakfasts were renowned.' Disraeli has left on record a description of an actual breakfast-party given by Monckton Milnes in the forties:

Mem. of breakfast at Monckton Milnes', the only one I ever attended—and why? Because he came to me and said Ibrahim Pacha, who was then in England, was going to breakfast with him, and he had requested his Highness to make a list of those he wished to meet him; and he had put down my name among those who had visited Egypt, etc., etc. I believe a fudge; but having refused M. M. a 1000 times, hating breakfasting out, and he very urgent, I agreed Went late (half-past 11 perhaps), as his breakfasts were 10 o'clock-ers, but kept up at the house. All the breakfast eaten: that nothing, as I never eat in public at that time. Some coffee on a disordered table; M. M. murmured something about a cutlet, not visible, which I did not notice.

Strange scene. Ibrahim not there, but Suleiman Pacha, the renegade Frenchman (Col. ——, I think), and some Egyptian Grandees. They were fighting the battle of Konieh (I think) like Corporal Trim. 'Voilà la cavalerie,' said Suleiman, and he placed a spoon. L'infanterie est là,' and he moved a coffee-cup, etc., etc.; D'Orsay standing behind him and affecting immense interest in order to make the breakfast go off well. A round table: at the fireplace, Milnes' father; a Shandean squire, full of humor and affectation, and astonished at the scene, not accustomed to in Yorkshire. Cobden there: a white-faced man whom I did not know, who turned out to be Kinglake, then the author of *Eothen*, which I had not read and never have; and other celebrities.

I declined to sit down, but watched the battle, and was regretting I had come, when someone touched me on the back. I looked round: it was Prince Louis Napoleon. 'Are you very much interested in this?' he said. 'Not at all; for I am neither the Conqueror nor the conquered.'

'Come here then,' and he invited me to the recess of a window.

'Have you any news from Paris?' he asked me with earnest inquiry—excited.

'None, sir.'

'Then I tell you the most important. Two thousand Sous-Lieutenants have signed a document that they will not rest until the family of Buonaparte are restored to the throne.'

'That indeed, sir, is most important,' and I thought I was talking to a madman. I believe it now to have been quite true. (This was after Ham.)

CHAPTER III

Religion and the Jews

1847–1858

The ruling sentiment of *Tancred*, as the reader will have seen, is intense pride of race; its underlying philosophy is Disraeli's philosophy of race. Race even lies at the root of all his conceptions of religion. 'All is race — there is no other truth,' he makes Sidonia say. A few years later, in *Lord George Bentinck*,[1] he suddenly proclaims, in the midst of a prosaic description of the fortunes of a Sugar Bill, 'Progress and reaction are but words to mystify the millions. They mean nothing, they are nothing, they are phrases and not facts. All is race. In the structure, the decay, and the development of the various families of man, the vicissitudes of history find their main solution.' This doctrine of race is akin to the belief in aristocracy. It is 'entirely opposed,' he tells us, 'to the equality of man and similar abstract dogmas, which have destroyed ancient society without creating a satisfactory substitute.'[2] This doctrine he enforced to the end of his life. The principle of race is 'the key of history,' he repeats in the novel of his old age, *Endymion*. Baron Sergius, the Ambassador, descants to Endymion on the distinctive qualities of Teutons, Slavs, Celts, and Semites, and proceeds:

> The Semites now exercise a vast influence over affairs by their smallest though most peculiar family, the Jews. There is no race gifted with so much tenacity, and such skill in organisation. These qualities have given them an unprece-

[1] Ch. 18.

[2] General Preface to the Novels, 1870.

dented hold over property and illimitable credit. As you advance in life, and get experience in affairs, the Jews will cross you everywhere. They have long been stealing into our secret diplomacy, which they have almost appropriated; in another quarter of a century they will claim their share of open government. Well, these are races. . . . But what do they mean by the Latin race? Language and religion do not make a race — there is only one thing which makes a race, and that is blood.[1]

While Tancred meditates, by the pools of Solomon, over the 'superb relics' of the 'inimitable magnificence' of the great Hebrew Kings, his creator bursts out:

And yet some flat-nosed Frank, full of bustle and puffed up with self-conceit (a race spawned, perhaps, in the morasses of some Northern forest hardly yet cleared), talks of Progress! Progress to what, and from whence? Amid empires shrivelled into deserts, amid the wrecks of great cities, a single column or obelisk of which nations import for the prime ornament of their mud-built capitals, amid arts forgotten, and populations destroyed, the European talks of progress, because, by an ingenious application of some scientific acquirements, he has established a society which has mistaken comfort for civilisation.

One cannot but admire this pride of race, in presence of which all the triumphs and interests of the West are mere vanity. The note may be too much forced; there may be something rhetorical, declamatory, violent, and self-assertive about it, that makes it fall short of the truest art and the truest wisdom. Still, it is certainly refreshing to turn from the self-satisfied laudations of material progress and the confident prophecies of corresponding moral enlightenment, which were the commonplaces of the politicians and publicists of the day, to a criticism of life from so different and so much more spiritual a standpoint. The material progress of the mid-Victorian age was largely bound up with the progress of science. Here, again, Disraeli refused to swim with the tide. The note of hostility, not to science, but to its extravagant claims, is sounded clearly in that passage

[1] *Endymion*, ch. 56.

of *Tancred* where Lady Constance Rawleigh disgusts the hero by her cheap evolutionary theories. The note was struck again, still more insistently, in the famous Ape or Angel speech at Oxford in 1864. This attitude of hostility was inevitable in a man of Disraeli's temperament and race in the days when science was far more arrogant than it is to-day, and attempted to dethrone the spiritual, the religious, and the imaginative from the proud position which he assigned to them. It was hardly possible then to accept what were confidently claimed to be the results of science, and yet relegate her to her proper place; to find the spiritual shining through and rising above the scientific. But in the main he and those who sympathised with him were nearer the truth than the enthusiasts who, in the first eagerness of enlightenment, mistook a part for the whole.

The feeling of race is so strong in *Tancred* that it almost swallows up that which it was designed to illustrate. The topic that was to be treated in the novel was 'the duties of the Church as a main remedial agency in our present state.' The Church was, we were told, a powerful agent of development in the past, and a most efficient means of renovation of the national spirit in the future. No society could be durable 'unless it was built upon the principles of loyalty and religious reverence. The writer and those who acted with him looked, then, upon the Anglican Church as a main machinery by which these results might be realised. There were few great things left in England, and the Church was one.'[1] Yet the Church plays but a small part in the novel. It fails entirely to satisfy the religious longings of Tancred, as the Constitution had failed to satisfy the political aspirations of Coningsby. And no wonder, for it is represented far from sympathetically. We find, indeed, no longer that sentiment of regret for pre-Reformation Christianity which is visible in some of Disraeli's earlier works, and is especially conspicuous in *Sybil*. Yet even in *Sybil* there

[1] General Preface to the Novels, 1870.

is a worthy parish priest; in *Tancred* the only clergy introduced are a time-serving Bishop, a mild 'high and dry' tutor, and an 'honourable and reverend,' who is an epicure and nothing else. The sole recorded action of the Church is the promotion of a great fund for converting Roman Catholic Ireland to Protestantism; and its condition and the nature of its rulers are caustically described:

> The Church of England, mainly from its deficiency of oriental knowledge, and from a misconception of the priestly character which has been the consequence of that want, has fallen of late years into great straits; nor has there ever been a season when it has more needed for its guides men possessing the higher qualities both of intellect and disposition. About five-and-twenty years ago, it began to be discerned that the time had gone by, at least in England, for bishoprics to serve as appanages for the younger sons of great families. The Arch-Mediocrity who then governed this country . . . was impressed with the necessity of reconstructing the episcopal bench on principles of personal distinction and ability. But his notion of clerical capacity did not soar higher than a private tutor who had suckled a young noble into university honours; and his test of priestly celebrity was the decent editorship of a Greek play. He sought for the successors of the apostles, for the stewards of the mysteries of Sinai and of Calvary, among third-rate hunters after syllables. These men, notwithstanding their elevation, with one exception,[1] subsided into their native insignificance; and during our agitated age, when the principles of all institutions, sacred and secular, have been called in question . . . not a voice has been raised by these mitred nullities, either to warn or to vindicate; not a phrase has escaped their lips or their pens that ever influenced public opinion, touched the heart of nations, or guided the conscience of a perplexed people.

The first indication is here given — 'misconception of the priestly character' — of opposition to the later phases of the Oxford Movement. Disraeli obviously blamed the Church for seeking its inspiration at that time rather in mediæval traditions than in its Jewish origin; and for joining, in consequence, in the oppression of the Jews instead of upholding their cause. Hence his readiness

[1] Bishop Blomfield. See above, p. 35.

to make his hero find Anglicanism profoundly unsatisfying, and determine to seek faith and inspiration in the country which was the cradle of the Christian religion. Though the great Asian mystery is never thoroughly revealed, certain large ideas about God and man and the world pervade the book — that the world was made and is governed by God, and not by blind natural forces; that before, and in relation to, God their Father men are equal, but that all other equality of man is absurd; and that faith is essential, and the spiritual order, not the material, the thing that counts, Disraeli's teaching is, in fact, a protest against materialism; he preaches that the soul and the mind are more than the body; faith and ideas above material progress. 'Power is neither the sword nor the shield, for these pass away, but ideas, which are divine.' Like other great truths, these are elementary, but none the less needing proclamation and emphasis in an age of gold and iron and cotton. What he adds to these high religious themes is the corollary that the Jews, as the original depositaries of these and all other revelations of true religion, are a highly privileged, and should be a highly regarded, race.

This is the lesson that he is especially anxious to drive home. In *Tancred* he expresses it in the guise of fiction; four or five years later he interpolates a famous chapter on the same subject in a political and historical treatise.[1] Religion and race, he tells us in both, are intimately bound up together. God has only spoken to one race, the Jewish; his full revelation was made by a Divine Jew, Jesus; the Apostles, the preachers of the true religion to the world, were all Jews. 'The greatest of legislators [Moses], the greatest of administrators [Solomon], and the greatest of reformers [Christ]: what race, extinct or living, can produce three such men as these?' The religion of the great Western races, Saxon, Slav, and Celt, is derivative, and comes entirely from the Jew. In proportion to their adherence to, or rejection of, the Semitic principle

[1] *Lord George Bentinck*, ch. 24.

are those races prosperous or decadent. Disraeli exults over the failure of the attempt, during the French Revolution, to substitute the worship of the Goddess of Reason for the worship of Christ:

> Half a century ago, Europe made a violent and apparently successful effort to disembarrass itself of its Asian faith. The most powerful and the most civilised of its kingdoms, about to conquer the rest, shut up its churches, desecrated its altars, massacred and persecuted their sacred servants, and announced that the Hebrew creeds which Simon Peter brought from Palestine, and which his successors revealed to Clovis, were a mockery and a fiction. What has been the result? In every city, town, village, and hamlet of that great kingdom, the divine image of the most illustrious of Hebrews has been again raised amid the homage of kneeling millions; while, in the heart of its bright and witty capital, the nation has erected the most gorgeous of modern temples, and consecrated its marble and golden walls to the name, and memory, and celestial efficacy of a Hebrew woman.

In another passage he writes: 'Since the great revolt of the Celts against the first and second testament . . . France has been alternately in a state of collapse or convulsion.' England, however, 'despite her deficient and meagre theology, has always remembered Sion.' America is prosperous, and Russia has been consolidated, by this sacred principle. Even at Rome, 'an old man on a Semitic throne baffles the modern Attilas and the recent invasion of the barbarians, under the form of red republicans, socialists, communists, all different phases which describe the relapse of the once converted races into their primitive condition of savagery.' Austria is held together by the Semitic principle; Germany's failure to achieve an imperial position is due to the imperfect conversion of the north of her country. The decline of Spain, in spite of her adherence to the principle, is due to her expulsion of the Semitic population. It all appears very fantastic; but if we interpret the Semitic principle as a phrase summing up all those spiritual and moral ideas which we derive from the sacred books of the Hebrew race, this view of modern history becomes comprehensible.

'Righteousness exalteth a nation,' and faith has always gone far to win victory. Modern civilisation derives from various sources. Disraeli's teaching is that those elements of it which have their origin in a wider spread and a better comprehension of the great truths of the Old and New Testament are more vital to the greatness of a nation than those which spring from the literature of Greece, the Empire of Rome, the advance of science, and the development of invention. This, after all, is very much the teaching of Matthew Arnold, that the Hebrew sense of conduct is far the most important thing for man, as conduct embraces three parts of life.

In order to heighten the obligation of the Western races to the Jews, Disraeli reduces to a minimum the differences between the Old and New Testament. He insists that the morality of the Gospel is 'not a thing apart and of novel revelation.'

There cannot be two moralities; and to hold that the Second Person of the Holy Trinity could teach a different morality from that which had already been revealed by the First Person of the Holy Trinity is a dogma so full of terror that it may perhaps be looked upon as the ineffable sin against the Holy Spirit. When the lawyer tempted our Lord, and inquired how he was to inherit eternal life, the great master of Galilee referred him to the writings of Moses. There he would find recorded 'the whole duty of man'; to love God with all his heart, and soul, and strength, and mind, and his neighbour as himself. These two principles are embalmed in the writings of Moses, and are the essence of Christian morals.

So Tancred, Christian from the Saxon north-west though he was, felt that he was no stranger in the wilderness of Sinai.

Had he not from his infancy repeated, in the congregation of his people, the laws which, from the awful summit of these surrounding mountains the Father of all had himself delivered for the government of mankind? These Arabian laws regulated his life. . . . The life and property of England are protected by the laws of Sinai. The hard-working people of England are secured in every seven days a day of rest by the laws of Sinai. . . .

Who is the most popular poet in this country? Is he to

be found among the Mr. Wordsworths and the Lord Byrons, amid sauntering reveries or monologues of sublime satiety? Shall we seek him among the wits of Queen Anne? Even to the myriad-minded Shakespeare can we award the palm? No; the most popular poet in England is the sweet singer of Israel. Since the days of the heritage, when every man dwelt safely under his vine and under his fig-tree, there never was a race who sang so often the odes of David as the people of Great Britain.

Vast as the obligations of the whole human family are to the Hebrew race, there is no portion of the modern populations so much indebted to them as the British people. It was 'the sword of the Lord and of Gideon' that won the boasted liberties of England; chanting the same canticles that cheered the heart of Judah amid their glens, the Scotch, upon their hillsides, achieved their religious freedom.

That being so, why persecute the Jews? It is because they are supposed to be expiating by dispersion among the nations the crime of betraying and crucifying Christ. Disraeli maintains that this is neither historically true nor dogmatically sound. It is not historically true, because the dispersion of the Jews began, in the wanderings of the ten tribes, long before Christ; moreover, if some rejected and betrayed him, many preached, wrote, and shed their blood as witnesses for him. Nor is it dogmatically sound.

The imprecation of the mob at the crucifixion is sometimes strangely quoted as a divine decree. It is not a principle of jurisprudence, human or inspired, to permit the criminals to ordain their own punishment. Why, too, should they transfer any portion of the infliction to their posterity? What evidence have we that the wild suggestion was sanctioned by Omnipotence? On the contrary, amid the expiating agony, a divine voice at the same time solicited and secured forgiveness. And if unforgiven, could the cry of a rabble at such a scene bind a nation?

In arguing the point of dogma, Disraeli shocked many of his contemporaries by his free handling of the doctrine of the Atonement. He makes Eva, who stands for the spirit of Judaism, say:

'A sacrificial Mediator with Jehovah, that expiatory intercessor born from the chosen house of the chosen people, yet blending in his inexplicable nature the divine essence with the human elements, appointed before all time, and purifying, by his atoning blood, the myriads that preceded and the myriads that will follow us, without distinction of creed or clime, this is what you believe. . . . The human race is saved; and, without the apparent agency of a Hebrew prince, it could not have been saved. Now tell me: suppose the Jews had not prevailed upon the Romans to crucify Jesus, what would have become of the Atonement?'

'I cannot permit myself to contemplate such contingencies,' said Tancred. '. . . I must not even consider an event that had been pre-ordained by the Creator of the world for countless ages.'

'Ah!' said the lady; 'pre-ordained by the Creator of the world for countless ages! Where then was the inexpiable crime of those who fulfilled the beneficent intention? The holy race supplied the victim and the immolators. What other race could have been entrusted with such a consummation? . . . Persecute us! Why, if you believed what you profess, you should kneel to us! You raise statues to the hero who saves a country. We have saved the human race, and you persecute us for doing it.'

'Could that be a crime,' exclaims Disraeli in *Lord George Bentinck*, 'which secured for all mankind eternal joy?' A reviewer in *The Times* has suggested the obvious Scriptural answer to this pleading: that it must needs be that offences come, but woe unto that man by whom they come. On the whole, perhaps Disraeli would have been well advised to confine himself to his historical argument, and avoid the dangerous ground of dogma.

Persecution had, no doubt, degraded the Jews. It was the law of all persecuted races: 'The infamous is the business of the dishonoured. . . . This peculiarity, however, attends the Jews under the most unfavourable circumstances; the other degraded races wear out and disappear; the Jew remains, as determined, as expert, as persevering, as full of resource and resolution as ever.' The Jew is 'sustained by a sublime religion.' However degraded he may be, 'the patriarchal feeling still lingers about his hearth.' 'The trumpet of Sinai still sounds in the Hebrew ear, and a Jew is never seen upon the scaffold, unless it be at an *auto-da-fé*.' Moreover, though there is a partial degradation of the race, still as actors, dancers, singers, musicians, and composers,[1] they deserve honour and favour from Europe, so much have they done to 'charm the public taste and elevate the public feeling.'

Statesmen should consider how injurious were the consequences to society of persecuting the Jews.

The Jews represent the Semitic principle; all that is spiritual in our nature. They are the trustees of tradition, and the conservators of the religious element. They are a living and the most striking evidence of the falsity of that pernicious doctrine of modern times, the natural equality of man. The political equality of a particular race is a matter of municipal arrangement, and depends entirely on political considerations and circumstances; but the natural equality of man now in vogue, and taking the form of cosmopolitan fraternity, is a principle which, were it possible to act on it, would deteriorate the great races and destroy all the genius of the world. What would be the consequence on the great Anglo-Saxon republic, for example, were its citizens to secede from their sound principle of reserve, and mingle with their negro and coloured populations? . . . The native tendency of the Jewish race, who are justly proud of their blood, is against the doctrine of the equality of man. They have also another characteristic, the faculty of acquisition. . . . Thus it will be seen that all the tendencies of the Jewish race are conservative. Their bias is to religion, property, and natural aristocracy; and it should be the interest of statesmen that this bias of a great race should be encouraged, and their energies and creative powers enlisted in the cause of existing society.

Persecution, however, had driven this conservative element into the ranks of the secret societies, who were at war with the Semitic principle — 'the people of God co-operate with atheists!'—and the provisional governments of 1848 were largely officered by Jews. Take the case of Manini at Venice — 'Manini, who by-the-bye is a Jew who professes the whole of the Jewish religion, and believes in Calvary as well as Sinai, "a converted Jew!" as the Lombards styled him, quite forgetting, in the confusion of their ideas, that it is the Lombards who are the converts, not Manini.'

[1] See Vol. II., p. 212.

'It is no doubt to be deplored that several millions of the Jewish race should persist in believing in only a part of their religion;[1] but it must be remembered that Christianity cannot have been presented to the Jews who sprang from the pre-Christian dispersion till centuries after Christ, when 'it came from a very suspicious quarter and was offered in a very questionable shape. . . . It appeared to be a Gentile religion, accompanied by idolatrous practices, from which severe monotheists, like the Arabians, always recoil, and holding the Jewish race up to public scorn and hatred. This is not the way to make converts.'

In *Tancred* Disraeli had contented himself with a passionate appeal to Christians to recognise their indebtedness to the Jews, and to honour instead of persecuting them. At the end of the famous twenty-fourth chapter of *Lord George Bentinck*, he turns to the Jews, and endeavours to persuade them of the reasonableness of believing in 'the most important portion of the Jewish religion.' It should not, he maintains, be very repugnant to the feelings of a Jew to learn 'that the redemption of the human race has been effected by the mediatorial agency of a child of Israel'; or 'that a Jewess is the queen of heaven, or that the flower of the Jewish race are even now sitting on the right hand of the Lord God of Sabaoth.' Might not 'the pupil of Moses' ask himself 'whether all the princes of the house of David have done so much for the Jews as that prince who was crucified on Calvary?'

Has not He made their history the most famous in the world? Has not He hung up their laws in every temple? Has not He vindicated all their wrongs? Has not He avenged the victory of Titus and conquered the Cæsars? What successes did they anticipate from their Messiah? The wildest dreams of their rabbis have been far exceeded. Has not Jesus conquered Europe and changed its name into Christendom? All countries that refuse the cross wither, while the whole of the new world is devoted to the Semitic principle and its most glorious offspring, the Jewish faith. . . . Christians may continue to persecute Jews, and Jews may persist in disbelieving Christians, but who can deny that Jesus of Nazareth, the Incarnate Son of the Most High God, is the eternal glory of the Jewish race?

Fantastic as Disraeli's view of the true relations of Judaism and Christianity appeared when it was published, and, indeed, to some extent appears still, much of it is perfectly sound. That Christianity is the completion of Judaism, and that Judaism — at any rate the Judaism of the Old Testament — is undeveloped Christianity, is the teaching of the Bible throughout. But Disraeli is very unconvincing when he attempts to show that there is no distinction between the morality of the Old Testament and that of the New. The development brought about by Christ was marked in the sphere of morals. Against the story of the lawyer which Disraeli quotes, instances at once rise to the recollection in which the teaching of Christ was after this fashion: 'Moses, because of the hardness of your hearts, gave you this commandment; but I say unto you,' or, 'Ye have heard it said by them of old time; but I say unto you.' And, of course, Disraeli's theory has the great weakness of minimising the importance of the fundamental distinction involved in accepting or repudiating the Divinity of Christ. His language sometimes almost suggests that his religion was pure Judaic monotheism, only prolonged and perhaps softened by the teaching of a great Jewish reformer; and the fact that Christ was the son of Israel seems, now and again, more important than the fact that he is the Son of God. But, when all deductions are made, Disraeli rendered a great service to his somewhat intolerant generation by insisting on the intimate relationship between the two religions.

It was under the influence of the views which we have set forth at length, and with a strong sense of the claims of the race from which he sprang to the most honourable treatment from the professors of the faith which he had embraced, that Disraeli took part in the debate on Russell's motion, in December, 1847, for the removal of the remaining civil and political disabilities of the Jews. The debate was a remarkable one, and the most remarkable speech in it was Disraeli's. Russell proposed his motion on the general ground 'that every Englishman born in the country is entitled to all the honours and advantages of the British Constitution,' and that religious opinions should be no disqualification. Most of the Jewish disabilities, he pointed out, had been already removed. Popular prejudice against them had clearly weakened, otherwise Rothschild would never have been returned by nearly seven thousand votes for the City of London. The opposition was led by Sir Robert Inglis, senior member for the University of Oxford, on the ground of the vital importance of preserving the Christian character of every person holding any share in the government of the country. But the speaker who carried most weight in opposing the motion was Lord Ashley, the evangelical philanthropist, who based himself largely on Dr. Arnold's view that there could be no plea of justice for the Jews; 'they are voluntary strangers here, and have no claim to become citizens but by conforming to our moral law, which is the Gospel.' Though he regarded the Jewish people with 'reverence,' Ashley could not consent to abolish the oath 'on the true faith of a Christian,' because he thought that in so doing he should be making a public declaration of the utter uselessness of Christianity for the government and superintendence of public affairs. Gladstone, who had just been elected for Oxford University, spoke and voted against what he knew to be the wishes of his constituents, and what had till recently been his own views. But he very reasonably held that 'we may consistently affirm that Christianity is in the highest degree needful for our legislation, and yet decline to follow out that proposition to a conclusion so rigid as this, that every individual who is not a Christian should be excluded from the possibility of becoming a legislator.' Other leading speakers were: against the motion Goulburn, Bankes, Sir Thomas Acland, and Newdegate; and for it Fox the Quaker, Lord Morpeth,

Sir Harry Verney, Bentinck (whose standpoint was much the same as Russell's), and Disraeli.

Parliament was well accustomed to hearing this and similar questions discussed, as on the present occasion, upon religious grounds; and it was as a religious question that Disraeli proposed to treat it. But while most speakers were wont to dwell upon the one great distinction between the Jewish and the Christian faith, Disraeli insisted on the intimate relation between the two as constituting the special claim of the Jew to favourable treatment. 'Who are these persons professing the Jewish religion? They are persons who acknowledge the same God as the Christian people of this realm. They acknowledge the same divine revelation as yourselves. They are, humanly speaking, the authors of your religion.' It was on the ground of religious truth rather than on that of religious liberty that he should vote for the motion.

> If religion is a security for righteous conduct, you have that security in the instance of the Jews, who profess a true religion. It may not be in your more comprehensive form. I do not say it is *the* true religion; but although they do not profess all that we profess, all that they do profess is true. You must admit, then, that in men who are subject to the Divine revelations that you acknowledge, whose morals are founded on the sacred oracles to which we all bow, that, as far as religion can be a security for their conduct — for their public morality and justice — you have in the religion of the Jews the best sanction in the world except that of our own Christianity. . . . The very reason for admitting the Jews is because they can show so near an affinity to you. Where is your Christianity if you do not believe in their Judaism? Do not mix up, then, the consideration of a question which is so intimately allied to your own faith, with the different considerations that would apply to the Pagan and the Mahommedan. I am prepared to lay down the broadest principles as to the importance of maintaining a Christian character in this House and in this country; and yet it is on this very ground you will found and find the best argument for the admission of the Jews.

The Jew was necessarily a religious being, but not a proselytising one, and so would support and not undermine the Christian Church.

In Europe — that Europe which you have baptised Christendom — how stands the Jew in relation to the Church of Christ? What possible object can the Jew have to oppose the Christian Church? Is it not the first business of the Christian Church to make the population whose mind she attempts to form, and whose morals she seeks to guide, acquainted with the history of the Jews? Has not the Church of Christ — the Christian Church, whether Roman Catholic or Protestant — made the history of the Jews the most celebrated history in the world? On every sacred day you read to the people the exploits of Jewish heroes, the proofs of Jewish devotion, the brilliant annals of past Jewish magnificence. The Christian Church has covered every kingdom with sacred buildings, and over every altar . . . we find the tables of the Jewish law. Every Sunday — every Lord's day — if you wish to express feelings of praise and thanksgiving to the Most High, or if you wish to find expression of solace in grief, you find both in the words of the Jewish poets. . . . All the early Christians were Jews. The Christian religion was first preached by men who had been Jews until they were converted; every man in the early ages of the Church by whose power, or zeal, or genius, the Christian faith was propagated, was a Jew.

Disraeli's argument was very distasteful to the House. There were cries of 'Oh! oh!' at intervals, and many other signs of general impatience. He was stung by these interruptions into some heat:

In exact proportion to your faith ought to be your wish to do this great act of national justice. If you had not forgotten what you owe to this people, if you were grateful for that literature which for thousands of years has brought so much instruction and so much consolation to the sons of men, you as Christians would be only too ready to seize the first opportunity of meeting the claims of those who profess this religion. But you are influenced by the darkest superstitions of the darkest ages that ever existed in this country. It is this feeling that has been kept out of this debate; indeed, that has been kept secret in yourselves — enlightened as you are — and that is unknowingly influencing you as it is influencing others abroad. . . .

I cannot sit in this House with any misconception of my opinion on the subject. Whatever may be the consequences on the seat I hold — and I should not have referred to such a consideration unless other gentlemen had done so — I cannot, for one, give a vote which is not in deference to what I believe to be the true principles of religion. Yes, it is as a Christian that I will not take upon me the awful responsibility of excluding from the legislature those who are of the religion in the bosom of which my Lord and Saviour was born.

Disraeli sat down without a cheer, and amid cries of 'Divide.' Though he spoke on the first of the two nights of debate, no subsequent speaker showed any appreciation of his point of view; indeed, very few referred to it at all. It was too strange, and to most of his political friends it was repulsive. The only appreciation came from his own family. His sister wrote: 'Papa thinks Dis' speech the most important ever delivered in the House of Commons: stamped with all the characteristic novelty and boldness of the orator.' The motion was carried by sixty-seven votes, and Bentinck and Disraeli went into the lobby in its favour, while their followers in a body voted against it.

Substantial as this majority in the Commons was, the struggle was only beginning, as there was in the Lords a constant and convinced majority on the other side. During the ten years and more that the controversy lasted, Baron Lionel de Rothschild was again and again elected for the City of London, without being permitted to sit; and he favourably impressed the House of Commons by the quiet dignity with which he bore himself in this ambiguous situation. Throughout Disraeli maintained unchanged the attitude which he took up on Russell's motion. He voted for the second and third readings of the Jewish Disabilities Bill of 1848 which Russell founded upon his motion, and he voted steadily for similar Bills which were brought forward, mostly by the same indefatigable champion of civil and religious liberty, in the years 1849, 1851, 1853, 1856, 1857, and 1858. All the Bills were carried safely through the House of Commons, only to perish in the House of Lords. In 1850 the procedure was varied. Rothschild came to the table, and endeavoured unsuccessfully to get the Clerk and the House to allow him to take the oath in his own form, omitting the words 'on the true faith of a Christian' as not binding on his conscience. Changes of Government and other disturbing causes accounted for no Bill being pushed forward in either 1852 or 1855; and in 1854 a general Oaths Bill, which would indeed have relieved the Jews, but proposed at the same time to make a number of other changes, deemed to be of a Romanising character, was opposed by Disraeli by speech and vote, and defeated on second reading by four votes. To this occasion we will return later. Finally, in 1858, when Derby and Disraeli were in office — after the Lords had wrecked the Commons' Oaths Bill of that year by striking out the really operative clause, and the Commons had retorted by placing Rothschild, though still unsworn, on the Committee for drawing up reasons for restoring it — the wiser heads among the Peers began to realise that a compromise was desirable. There was some dispute as to the form which the compromise should take, but eventually the Peers, under the guidance of one who was a soldier rather than a politician — Lord Lucan, initiated a measure, which was quickly passed into law, giving each House power to alter, by resolution, its own form of oath. A strong Committee of the Commons had only failed by a bare majority to lay it down that that House inherently possessed such a right; and this view had been supported by Disraeli. Now it was not necessary to assert it. As Chancellor of the Exchequer and leader of the House, Disraeli had the satisfaction of finding the necessary time for Lucan's Bill, and of helping to carry it by his vote; and also of voting with the majority for Russell's consequential resolutions, which enabled Rothschild and all subsequent Jewish members to omit the declaration 'on the true faith of a Christian,' and nevertheless to take their seats in the House.

The compromise was not arranged without some friction inside the Government, where the Jews had few friends except Disraeli and the Prime Minister's son, Stanley. Disraeli's efforts to settle the question exposed him to a temporary misunderstanding both with Derby and with others of his colleagues.

From Lord Derby.

Confidential.

St. James's Square, *Sunday*, [? *Spring of* 1858]. — I am sorry to find that you have given any hint to John Russell of the suggestion which I made to you confidentially as to a *possible* solution of the difficulty respecting the Jew Bill. If ever it can be brought to bear, of which I am not confident, time is absolutely necessary; and to urge it on now would, I am convinced, ensure its failure. I must beg of you, if you have in any way introduced my name in speaking to Lord John, to let him know that I cannot be a party to any such arrangement; and should the suggestion be now made, which I hope it will not, I must hold myself quite free to act as I may think advisable respecting it.

To Lord Stanley.

Sunday, June 20, 1858. — Pursuant to your father's instructions to ascertain whether the Ho. of C. would respond to the arrangement which he contemplated for the settlement of the Jewish question, — I placed myself in confidential communication with Bethell,[1] who entirely acceded to the plan, and offered, himself, to prepare the proposed amendment, previously submitting it to me for the approval of my friends. I thought, therefore, all was right: but, yesterday, I met Sir Jas. Graham at dinner, who gave it as his opinion that the Ho. of C. would not, and could not, take the course intimated in the Ho. of Lords a few nights since, — and that Ld. John Russell disapproved of it. . . .

I have heard nothing from Bethell since Friday night, and he is so strange a man that his whereabouts is not definable, and I don't know how to get at him. To-morrow night, I shall be unable to leave the Bench; for, independently of the general conduct of affairs, the whole business of the night is in my department. Would you, therefore, see Bethell,[2] and take steps that all goes right? If he sees his way, and there is no foundation for what we heard respecting John Russell, Bethell ought to place himself in instant communication with Ld. Lyndhurst, for his (L.'s) bill comes on next Friday.

[1] Sir Richard Bethell, afterwards Lord Chancellor Westbury.

[2] Bethell, Stanley reported, said to him: 'If Lucan does it, there will be a blunder; if Lord Lyndhurst does it, there will be a blunder; but, if it is done in the Commons, I shall do it, and then there will be no blunder.'

The matter generally requires great energy and vigilance, for I hear the Lord Chancellor and Redesdale are manœuvring deeply; and the unfortunate illness of the Premier, no doubt, facilitates their intrigues. . . .

Steadily as Disraeli had voted for all Bills directly brought forward to remove Jewish disabilities, he spoke on them but seldom; and Russell lamented his silence during the second reading of the Bill of 1849. It was possibly in response to this that he said, in Committee on that Bill, that he was very anxious to see no obstruction offered to its passing, as he supported it warmly for reasons which were not merely political. In the following year, in the discussions that arose out of Rothschild's attempt to take the oath in his own form, Disraeli defended his silent vote in language that showed how entirely he adhered to the principles he had expounded in December, 1847:

Sir, if I thought that anything which I could say would have tended to accomplish an object dear to my heart as to my convictions, my vote would not have been a silent one. But, inasmuch as I believe that my opinions upon the subject are not shared by one single member on either side of the House, I thought that it was consistent, both with good sense and good taste, that, after having once unequivocally expressed the grounds on which my vote was given, I should have taken refuge in a silence which at least could not offend the prejudices of any hon. member on either side. . . . Although I have no wish at any time to dilate upon feelings or views which may not be prevalent or popular in this House, I never will relinquish them; and even now, shrinking as I do from offending the feelings of anyone, I will still express my hopes that full and complete justice will speedily be done to the descendants of a race which you acknowledge to be sacred, and the professors of a religion which you admit to be divine.

Disraeli's plea for his silence carries conviction. It was not as if the Bills required special assistance in the Commons. There they were regularly carried. It was in the Lords, where his leader procured their rejection, that the Jewish cause needed all the help it could get. Disraeli renewed his profession of faith in 1854 and in 1856. In 1854 he said: 'When I remember for how much we are indebted to that people, of what ineffable blessings they have been the human agents — when I remember that by their history, their poetry, their laws, our lives are instructed, solaced, and regulated — when I recall other considerations and memories more solemn and reverential, I confess that I cannot as a Christian oppose the claims of those to whom Christianity is under so great obligations.' In 1856: 'With all becoming respect, I may be allowed to say that this would not be a Christian State or a Christian community, had it not been, under Divine inspiration, for the efforts and exertions of a Jew.' It may not be possible to accept in its entirety Disraeli's point of view, but it is difficult to read these repeated and fervent declarations to the House of Commons without being impressed with the depth and sincerity of the religious conviction underlying them.

Nevertheless, in spite of these persistent votes and unhesitating speeches, Disraeli's consistency and sincerity in his support of the Jewish cause have been called in question. To substantiate the calumny, reliance has been placed on his conduct in 1850, when Rothschild's attempt to take the oath in his own way led to some complicated proceedings, and on his speech and vote on the Bill of 1854. Rothschild's action in 1850 was taken quite near the end of the session, on July 26, and the House and the Whig Government had very little time in which to decide upon their course. After some hesitation the Attorney-General moved two resolutions — the first declaring that Rothschild was not entitled to sit and vote till he should take the oath in form prescribed by law; the second, that the House would take the subject into serious consideration at the earliest opportunity next session. Disraeli voted against both resolutions, and his reasons are perfectly straightforward and satisfactory. A resolution declaratory of the law, such as the first, was not a very constitutional proceeding, and a resolution pledging the future policy of the House, such as the second, was not a very politic one; recourse should not be had to either, he thought, save in extreme necessity. Where was such necessity in this case? What excuse, he asked, had the Government for not having introduced a Bill at the beginning of the session, as in 1848 and 1849, instead of resorting to resolutions of this kind at its close? In short, the whole question was one of procedure; and only malice could strain and twist a vote given against pledging the House to take up the subject the first thing in the next session into a vote against the Jewish cause.

The question on the Bill of 1854 was really one of procedure also. Here was a Bill doing one thing which Disraeli desired, and other things to which he was opposed: relieving the Jews on the one hand, but also altering the oaths in other ways to please, in his view, Romanising Protestants and Roman Catholics. There were three courses, any one of which with perfect honour and consistency he might take. He might either oppose the second reading, notwithstanding his approval of part of the Bill, in order to prevent the changes he disliked; or he might accept the second reading, in the hope of making in Committee the modifications he desired; or he might, in so uncertain a situation, leave the House without voting. In 1854 he adopted the first course; in 1856, when on the Bill of that year a somewhat similar question arose, he adopted the second; it was foreign to his intrepid nature to adopt the third. The debate in 1854 turned much more on the alterations calculated to arouse Protestant feeling than on the relief proposed for the Jews. Disraeli, in a speech from which we have already quoted[1] his eloquent reaffirmation of his support of the Jewish claims, clearly explained the reason of his hostile vote.

Here is a bill in which the word 'Jew' never appears, in which a person not versed in our political tactics could not for a moment divine that the object of the noble lord [Russell] lay concealed in it. From the debate that has arisen to-night, we find that the noble lord has made propositions which have excited great controversy and very acrimonious

[1] P. 73.

feeling. Why has the noble lord prejudiced the Jewish claims, which, though objected to, were only objected to by a minority, and which were objected to on single and simple grounds which we might meet by argument and master by time—why has the noble lord, I say, prejudiced those claims by mixing them up with subjects that to the people of this country must appear of infinitely greater importance?

No doubt Disraeli was not sorry to be able honourably to oppose this Bill of 1854. For it was a Government measure, brought in by Russell as a member of that Coalition which drifted into the Crimean War; and the loss of it by four votes, in a session which had already proved unfortunate for Ministers, was a mortifying rebuff. This may explain some petulant words in which Russell, smarting under the defeat, taunted Disraeli with inconsistency and insincerity: 'Notwithstanding his great anxiety to see the Jews in possession of those privileges, the right hon. gentleman sometimes stays away, and sometimes votes against them: the political convenience of the hour always seems to overcome his attachment to the cause.' Disraeli's reply was clear and simple:

I give the noble lord's statement an unequivocal and unqualified denial. . . . Suppose I had got up, and said that the noble lord made Parliamentary reform a mere political convenience—that when it suited him, he made it convenient to quit the House, and did not vote at all on the subject: and then again, when it suited him, he also knew how to give his vote against that principle. I might, and without much ingenuity, make a very admirable case against him on that head; but I should scorn to do it. I am convinced that the noble lord is sincere in the views which he professes on the subject of Parliamentary reform, and that whenever he has voted against any measure of Parliamentary reform, he has done so from a sense of duty, convinced that by so doing he was benefiting the cause to which he wished success. But the noble lord can make no colourable case against me. I never on any occasion have quitted the House—I never absented myself from any division in which the claims of the Jews were concerned;[1] and, if I voted against his bill the other

[1] Microscopic scrutiny of Hansard enabled an opponent to discover one division of the kind in which Disraeli's name did not appear; but it was at a time when he was absent for some weeks from Parliament owing to illness.

night, I tell the noble lord that I do not consider that I voted against a bill which could have benefited the Jews, but, on the contrary, that I voted against a bill which I believe would have been of greater injury to the Jews than any measure ever brought forward.

The last sentence was a rhetorical exaggeration, but it was surely no service to the Jews to associate their cause with other changes certain to rouse the Protestant feeling of the country, at that time very suspicious, owing to the re-establishment of the Roman hierarchy in England on the one hand, and the spread of Ritualism and the wholesale conversions to Romanism on the other. Disraeli's colleague, Walpole, although a stanch opponent of the Jews, vindicated him at once: 'If there is one thing more than another for which my right hon. friend is entitled to the respect of both sides of the House, it is for the manly and honourable way in which he has come forward in support of the Jewish race.' Russell himself must have felt that he had been unjust to Disraeli, for, in a rejoinder on the same night, he apologised if he had done him an unintentional wrong, and added: 'I am quite persuaded that the right honourable gentleman has intended to serve the cause of the Jews in the course which he has taken;' and he was careful, two years later, on the third reading of the next Bill of the kind, to describe Disraeli explicitly as 'one who, on the peculiar ground of the merit of the Jews, always advocates their cause, and always votes in their favour.' That testimony of the statesman to whose perseverance the final success was mainly due may be taken as conclusive.

The verdict of history must surely be that Disraeli's course throughout this Jewish controversy was highly honourable to him. When it first assumed an acute form owing to the election of a Jew to Parliament, he had forced his way, over great obstacles and not without rousing strong animosities, to the front of the Parliamentary stage, had become the Chief of the Staff to a party leader, had gathered round him a band of stanch political friends, and was in a fair way to overcome the ingrained prejudices of the country gentlemen. It was a critical time; a false move might imperil all he had won. He had everything to gain by leaving the question alone, speaking not at all, and absenting himself on one pretext or another from the vote. There was pretty certainly a majority in the Commons for the measure without his aid; the House had passed Jew Bills before, and would pass them again, whatever his action. He knew well that there was no subject on which the men whom he aspired to lead felt more strongly than the proposal to admit to a share in the Government of a Christian State anyone who denied the Divinity of Christ. The fact that the position has now been entirely abandoned must not blind us to the religious fervour with which it was then upheld by some of the best men in the country. Yet, in spite of his ambitions and his critical position, Disraeli did not hesitate to put in action the principles which he had outlined in *Coningsby* and developed in *Tancred*, and, on the first possible occasion, to deliver a speech in which his esoteric philosophy of religion was set forth. And it should not be forgotten that he stood practically alone in his party. After Bentinck's death, there was for many years no leading Conservative of the main body, except Thomas Baring, who gave Disraeli any countenance in his action;[1] there were certainly some leading Peelites, such as Peel himself and Gladstone, but their concurrence would rather do him harm with his own followers. On the other hand, those who were foremost in the fight against the Jews were prominent personages among his colleagues, whose good-will so ambitious a man would be anxious to conciliate. They were, the principal lawyer of the party, Sir Frederic Thesiger, who was Attorney-General in 1845 and 1852, and Lord Chancellor in 1858 and 1866; Sir Robert Inglis, the stout old Tory who sat for Oxford University; Bankes, the unofficial chairman of the party;

[1] Towards the close of the struggle Pakington changed his view and supported Disraeli, who also received the reinforcement of the younger Stanley.

Walpole, whose name and abilities both commanded respect; Newdegate, one of the Whips; and, last but by no means least, Stanley, soon to become Lord Derby, the party Chief, and the Prime Minister under whom Disraeli served. During the ten years of controversy he was dependent on these men for securing and consolidating his leadership in the Commons; and yet he was courageous enough to remind them year by year, regularly by his vote, and sometimes by his speech, that he was himself of the Jewish extraction which they despised, and that his religious convictions were very different from theirs, but quite as strongly held. There is a story that, on one of the occasions when Disraeli was elaborating his favourite thesis that Christianity is completed Judaism, and that therefore the Jews should be respected rather than subjected to disability, Russell could not resist turning to a colleague[1] and expressing his admiration for a Parliamentary leader who could so intrepidly stand forward and enunciate doctrines which he knew the men behind him abhorred. There was, it should be remembered, in spite of that inbred conservatism which Disraeli claimed as characteristic of the Hebrew race, no party interest to serve. Success could only add another vote to the opposite side; for Rothschild, though a personal friend of Disraeli's, was, like most of the Jews of the day, a Liberal in politics and a follower of Russell. When all the circumstances are considered, it cannot be gainsaid that in his unfaltering support of the Jewish claims Disraeli manifested in a very high degree adherence to principle, disregard of self-seeking, and courage. He proved in the most convincing manner that he was ready to act, even when strongly against his own interest, on the doctrine proclaimed throughout his writings, that 'All is race.'

[1] The colleague was Gladstone; and I am indebted to Lord Morley for the story.

CHAPTER IV

The Question of Leadership — I

1847–1848

Lord George Bentinck's speech and vote in favour of the removal of Jewish disabilities brought to an end his leadership of the Country Party in the House of Commons. From that time onwards there was no acknowledged leader till Disraeli's undisputed pre-eminence compelled his recognition. The Parliamentary history of the next few years, on its personal side, is largely the story of the steps by which he became indispensable and inevitable, in spite of much active, and more secret, disparagement and ill-will.

Great efforts were made to persuade Bentinck to stay away from the Jewish debate and division, so as not to separate himself from his followers. His opinions in the matter were not based, like Disraeli's — it would have been strange if they had been — on the intimate relationship of the Christian and the Jewish religions. They were the honourable remnant of his old Whiggism, and sprang from 'his devoted attachment' to what Disraeli, in *Lord George Bentinck*,[1] characteristically calls 'the equivocal principle of religious liberty, the unqualified application of which principle seems hardly consistent with that recognition of religious truth by the state to which we adhere, and without which it is highly probable that the northern and western races, after a disturbing and rapidly degrading period of atheistic anarchy, may fatally recur to their old national idolatries, modified and mythically dressed up according to

[1] Ch. 25.

the spirit of the age.' As it was a matter of principle, Bentinck could not be moved. 'After long and deep and painful pondering, when the hour arrived he rose from his bed of sickness, walked into the House of Commons, and not merely voted, but spoke, in favour of his convictions.' On an intimation from the Chief Whip of the dissatisfaction felt with his conduct by many sections of the party, he retired from the leadership at once, rejoicing, as he told Stanley when he gave him notice of his intention, 'like a caged wild bird escaped from his wired prison.' He had accepted the post of leader with the utmost reluctance, after repeated refusals; he had often tried to relinquish it and find some colleague, now Thomas Baring, now Sir Robert Inglis, now Lord Ashley (who was not even a Protectionist), to take his place; he was frequently dissatisfied, and occasionally indignant, with his old friend and Chief, Stanley, whom he suspected of lukewarmness in the cause, because he was incapable of such exclusive devotion to politics as himself; and, in addition, he felt that his health was failing.

To Lord John Manners.

BRADENHAM, *Dec.* 26, 1847. — . . . By this time, you have heard of the Hebrew explosion. The truth is, but I say this in the greatest confidence, I doubt whether this would have taken place, but for the previous irritating causes, which could no longer be endured by G. B. Every day something occurred, which disgusted him. And at no time were censure and criticism less justifiably exercised on his career, for he was speaking rarely, and always with great improvement, and had given up his own opinion every time in council, which, in my belief, was the cause of the very ineffective way in which our affairs progressed; as he really is the only head of decision and real native sagacity, that we possess: but he was depressed by the influenza, and desirous of conciliating, for which he has received his reward. . . .

As for finding a new leader, these *frondeurs* little know the qualities that are required for such an office. It is something more than asking a question at 4 o'clock or making a speech at 11. Independent of the knowledge and management of mankind, the great spirit and social position, the even profuse generosity, which are required, and were so eminently practised and possessed by G. B.; the mere conduct of correspondence, and reading of blue books and making calculations, demand physical powers of herculean range. He said to me: 'It is not merely what I have done or spent for them: but during these two years, I have shaken my constitution and shortened my days.' . . .

[BRADENHAM, *Jan.* 1848.] — . . . Your letter is capital. You have sketched, with the hand of a master, the two characters:[1] especially the first. As for the second, I have always shrunk from him: he appeared to me coarse and commonplace, not a man of much *moyens:* more rapacious than ambitious, and rather cunning than shrewd: but he has vigor, tho' deficient in tact.

I hope you have seen G. B. if he were in London at the same time as yourself. I believe in his career as I do in yours: but, at all events, I would sooner be his companion in adversity than share the sunnier hours of those who do not possess my confidence and heart. At present, I would write to you as Lord Bolingbroke did to the immortal Dean, when Queen Anne died, 'Love me, for tho' all is over, I am in the very best spirits in the world.' At least I should be so, were you well, and in Parliament: but Nature will cure you, and your friends must contrive the second remedy. Then all would go right, and our friend would be at the head of a party, that would ultimately carry all before it. I hope Granby will stand by him, in spite of the Jews, as your brother, not only from his position, but his grand *character,* and strength of purpose, is a tower. . . .

Your sort of kinsman, Carington,[2] or rather his wife, has christened their new daughter Eva![3] So the Jews go down here better than was expected.

Bentinck had no intention of sulking, and immediately endeavoured to obtain for the Protectionists a competent successor. He was ready to support anyone on whom the party would unite; but 'his efforts, though indefatigable, were not successful,' says his biographer, 'for those who were competent to the office cared not to serve under anyone except himself.' Was there anyone, after Bentinck's withdrawal, competent to the office, except Disraeli? 'Nobody can think of a successor to Bentinck,'

[1] Of the Whips, Newdegate and Beresford, to whose mismanagement Manners attributed the dissensions in the Protectionist party.

[2] The 2nd Baron, father of the present Marquis of Lincolnshire.

[3] The name of the Jewish heroine of *Tancred.*

writes Greville on January 7, 1848; 'and, bad as he is, he seems the best man they have. It seems they detest Disraeli, the only man of talent, and in fact they have nobody.'

Let us pass in review the more prominent personalities of the party, and see how poor was the field, how limited the choice. The whole of the leading Conservatives in the House of Commons—that able administrator Graham, the experienced Goulburn, the accomplished Sidney Herbert, the high-minded Lincoln, and the once 'rising,' now risen, hope of the party, Gladstone—had followed Peel. The only men available with any official experience were Herries and Bankes. John Charles Herries had great knowledge of finance, and had proved an excellent and hard-working administrator. He had been Financial Secretary to the Treasury in 1823, when he first entered the House of Commons, Chancellor of the Exchequer under Goderich, Master of the Mint after that Minister had fallen, President of the Board of Trade in 1830, and Secretary at War in Peel's first Ministry. Disraeli, who admired his tact—tact which was 'so supreme that it amounts to genius'—wrote of him as an 'invaluable coadjutor' of Bentinck, and 'a gentleman whose official as well as Parliamentary experience, fine judgment and fertile resource have been of inestimable benefit to the Protectionist party.' But he was sixty-seven years old, had been out of Parliament during the eventful five years of Peel's Great Administration, and had thus no sufficient touch with the party which had come together in opposition to Peel's policy; and was, moreover, of a retiring disposition and a poor speaker. George Bankes was a substantial Dorset squire, who had sat for the family borough of Corfe Castle till it was disfranchised by the Reform Bill, and had re-entered Parliament as member for the county in 1841. He was the last Cursitor Baron of the Exchequer, and had been Chief Secretary to the Board of Control in 1829, and a Lord of the Treasury in 1830. He was 'popular and much esteemed,' Disraeli tells us, and carried weight in the inner councils of the party, of which he acted as a kind of unofficial chairman, but he took no leading part in Parliament.

A man of much higher calibre was Thomas Baring, a Conservative member of a Whig family, younger brother of Melbourne's Chancellor of the Exchequer. At this time he carried on his shoulders the chief burden of the operations of the Baring firm, and was one of the leading financial authorities both in the City of London and in the House of Commons. *Lord George Bentinck* bears repeated testimony to the considerable impression he produced in Parliament. We are told of his 'animated manner, which, while it never passed that line of restraint which good taste requires, was remarkable for a freshness of handling which is rare, and a sort of winning naturalness that often broke spontaneously into very telling points.' He had in the spring endeavoured vainly, though 'the first merchant of Great Britain,' to make the Government realise the seriousness of the impending monetary crisis; and on another occasion he delivered what Disraeli describes as one of the best speeches ever made in the House of Commons.

> Few more combine mastery of the case with parliamentary point than this gentleman. . . . A man who at the same time understands a question and can handle it before a popular assembly in a popular style, who teaches without being pedantic, can convey an argument in an epigram, and instruct as the Mexicans did by picture, possesses a talent for the exercise of which he is responsible to his sovereign and his country.

But Baring preferred business to high politics, and, in spite of this eulogium — published in the winter of 1851–52, when a Conservative Ministry was clearly imminent, and written doubtless to stir his ambition — declined, it is believed, more than once to be Lord Derby's Chancellor of the Exchequer.

Besides these three there were Sir Robert Inglis, a genial and popular man of high character but mediocre ability, who had ousted Peel from the representation of Oxford University over the Roman Catholic question; Joseph Warner Henley, the shrewd and businesslike, if somewhat narrow, Chairman of Quarter Sessions who sat for Oxfordshire; and the three brothers Manners, 'a family phalanx,' as Bentinck called them. Of these brothers, the most distinguished, Lord John Manners, Disraeli's close political and personal friend throughout, had failed in his attempt to represent Liverpool, and, having no seat in Parliament, was impossible as a leader. Lord George Manners, the member for Cambridgeshire, was considered by Bentinck the ablest man of the three, but he never took a prominent position. There remained Lord Granby, the eldest brother, who had been member for Stamford since 1837, who was a convinced and ardent Protectionist, and had, indeed, resigned a high post in the Prince Consort's household because of his opposition to Peel's Corn Law, who was popular in the country and in the House, and whose position as heir to the dukedom of Rutland commanded respect among a party of country gentlemen. 'The earnestness of his disposition and the firmness of his character' won him the confidence of Bentinck and the praise of Disraeli. Beyond those we have mentioned there was no one else possible. Spencer Horatio Walpole, great-grandson of Sir Robert's brother and nephew of Spencer Perceval, had only just entered Parliament; and Sir John Pakington was still reckoned a Peelite.

It was a beggarly array, when all is said that can be said in their favour. Who among these mediocrities, except, perhaps, Baring, who had no ambition of the kind, could stand up night after night and cross swords without discredit with Peel and Palmerston and Russell and Cobden? But the party had a man who had challenged all these giants, and at least held his own with them, and who was now acknowledged to be, as a Parliamentarian, in the very first flight. Yet for the moment he was tacitly ruled out. No wonder that Malmesbury should write under date February 10, 1848:

It seems strange that in these proceedings Disraeli's name was not put forward, but whoever may in future take the lead in the House of Commons by election he must virtually and practically hold that office. There can be no doubt that there is a very strong feeling among Conservatives in the House of Commons against him. They are puzzled and alarmed by his mysterious manner, which has much of the foreigner about it, and are incapable of understanding and appreciating the great abilities which certainly underlie, and, as it were, are concealed by this mask.

It must be admitted, however, that, apart from the strong feeling in the House of Commons against Disraeli, he was ineligible at this moment for a vacancy caused by the resentment of the party against Bentinck's support of the Jewish claims. His course had been the same; and his reasons for taking it even more distasteful.

Bentinck was fully conscious of the enormous superiority of Disraeli to all the rest of his colleagues in the House of Commons, and he was the less likely to restrain the expression of his feelings as both of them were under the ban of the extreme Protestant wing of the party, represented in the House by Beresford the Whip, and in the press by the *Morning Herald*, of which the editor, or principal writer, was then Samuel Phillips. On the eve of the party meeting to choose a new leader, he wrote to Stanley an indignant protest on his friend's behalf.

Lord George Bentinck to Lord Stanley.

HARCOURT HOUSE, *Feb.* 9, 1848.—Disraeli is very much disgusted, as well he may; but, judging from what I hear from the best men of the Party, there will be an indignation, which you don't seem to feel, expressed at the meeting to-morrow at the conduct of Mr. Phillips, the *Morning Herald*, and their copartners and accomplices, which I doubt not will go a long way to heal his wounded feelings.

Disraeli, who was earning by his writings £6,000 or £7,000 every two years or so, was dragged out from his retirement and literary occupation by special invitation from the Protectionist Party in the hour of their greatest need, before I was even thought of as their Leader; and the reward he has met with (were it not that as I believe a manly, a generous, and an honest English indignation promises to be expressed to-morrow) would leave a blot upon the fair name of the Country Gentlemen of England.

I tell you none of all this could have happened, had you played a generous part: you have suffered and parleyed too long with Mr. Phillips, and if you care to be free from the stain which cannot but attach to those who touch such filth, we must have something more than a half-and-half, mincing, milkwarm disavowal of Mr. Phillips, the *Morning Herald*, and their 'Conservative' Alliance.

And a month later Bentinck told Croker, who probably made a wry face on reading the prophecy, that Disraeli's leadership was certain and not distant.

Lord George Bentinck to J. W. Croker.

HARCOURT HOUSE, *March* 2, 1848.— . . . You ask me of Disraeli's manner of speaking and effectiveness in debate . . . His speeches this session have been first-rate. His last speech[1] . . . was admirable. He cuts Cobden to ribbons; and Cobden writhes and quails under him just as Peel did in 1846. And mark my words, spite of Lord Stanley, Major Beresford, and Mr. Phillips and the *Herald*, it will end before two sessions are out in Disraeli being the chosen leader of the party; but I think it will not be under Lord Stanley's banner, whether he turns his coat on the Jew bill or not.[2] . . .

Such being Bentinck's views, in looking for an immediate successor he was careful to select a man with whom Disraeli could cordially co-operate. So his choice fell upon Granby, 'as the only man of the party,' he wrote to Disraeli, 'whom you might be disposed to unite with me in upholding.' 'His high station, noble bearing, mild and conciliatory manners would combine and rally the whole party under his banner, and then you and I, sitting one on each side of him, would easily — when he required help, which I do not think would be often — carry him through.' Disraeli had at first joined others in recommending Bentinck to take his own course, lead his own friends, and wait for the party to return to him. This Bentinck would not do, so anxious was he to keep the party together. If this arrangement was impossible, Disraeli, who probably

1 On the revised Budget on Feb. 28. See p. 95.

2 *The Croker Papers*, Vol. III., p. 165.

believed that Bentinck, if he remained in Parliament, would be compelled by circumstances to resume the leadership, was quite ready to second the nomination of Granby, who was one of his own intimate political circle, and whom he might hope to guide as he wished. Accordingly he joined Stanley and Bentinck in pressing the reluctant Granby to come forward.

Nothing, however, was settled when Parliament reassembled on February 3, and many members of the party still hoped that Bentinck would reconsider his resignation. But he made his position quite clear; he would not even continue to sit on the front Opposition bench, but 'walked up to the head of the second bench below the gangway on the Opposition side, and thus significantly announced that he was no longer the responsible leader of the Protectionist party.' Disraeli has been blamed for not following him, and very gratuitous doubt has been thrown on the truth of his explanation. 'It was the wish of the writer of these pages, who had resolved to stand or fall by him [Bentinck], to have followed his example, and to have abdicated the prominent seat in which the writer had been unwillingly and fortuitously placed; but by the advice, or rather at the earnest request of Lord George Bentinck, this course was relinquished as indicative of schism, which he wished to discourage.' The correspondence of the day confirms this statement. It is quite clear that Bentinck felt that, though at the moment Disraeli could not be the leader, it was essential that the greatest Parliamentarian in the Protectionist ranks should be at the right hand of whomsoever the party might choose. No cloud ever came between these close allies since they joined forces in the spring of 1846; and all the evidence shows that they were acting in concert now.

In a party meeting in the following week Granby was chosen leader without opposition. But his modesty, stimulated, perhaps, by the distracted and factious spirit in the ranks, proved to be insuperable; and in a few days it was announced that he had refused, expressing his willingness to co-operate but not to assume the foremost place. 'He recommended his friends to consult Ld. G. B. and Mr. D.,' wrote Disraeli to Sir Philip Rose. 'The whole Protectionist party is in confusion,' was Malmesbury's entry in his journal. Hence the session began 'without a leader, without any recognized organ of communication between parties, or any responsible representation of opinion in debate. All again was chaos.'[1] As the session began, so it ended. Some attempt seems to have been made in May to procure a leader in Herries, but nothing came of it. Such a condition of affairs was eminently favourable to Disraeli's ambition. He puts it rather quaintly, that in this session he 'was subject in the House to a greater pressure of debate than his experience warranted.' His experience may not have warranted it, but his genius was fully equal to the demands. He himself writes as if the session was peculiarly a triumph for Bentinck:

> Notwithstanding the formal renunciation of the leadership of the Protectionist party by Lord George Bentinck, it was soon evident to the House and the country that that renunciation was merely formal. In these days of labour the leader of a party must be the man who does the work, and that work cannot now be accomplished without the devotion of a life. Whenever a great question arose, the people out of doors went to Lord George Bentinck, and when the discussion commenced he was always found to be the man armed with the authority of knowledge. There was, however, no organised debate and no party discipline. No one was requested to take a part, and no attendance was ever summoned. The vast majority sitting on the Protectionist benches always followed Bentinck, who, whatever might be his numbers in the lobby, always made a redoubtable stand in the House. The situation, however, it cannot be denied, was a dangerous one for a great party to persevere in, but no permanent damage accrued, because almost everyone hoped that, before the session was over, the difficulty would find a natural solution in the virtual chief resuming his formal and responsible post.[2]

Undoubtedly Bentinck showed to great advantage, especially over the West India Committee, of which he was

[1] *Lord George Bentinck*, ch. 25. [2] *Ibid.*, ch. 27.

the indefatigable and successful chairman; but the most striking interventions in debate were those of Disraeli, who made it clear, in a number of masterly speeches on all sorts of subjects, that, if Bentinck could not be persuaded to resume the position, there was a leader to the party's hand who would be equal to any emergency that might arise.

In a letter written to Manners before the party meeting Disraeli describes the opening debate, which resulted in the unopposed appointment of the Committee on the West India sugar question for which Bentinck moved.

To Lord John Manners.

GROSVENOR GATE, *Feb.* 5, 1848.—The W. India debate terminated last night at two o'clock in the morning, and was without exception the best supported debate by our friends that has occurred since we were a party. Indeed it was one of unbroken interest, and scarcely flagged on either side for a moment, except of course when old Bernal[1] discoursed, upon whom both parties dined.

G. B. made his exposition in a speech of three hours and ½, which never for an instant flagged. His voice capital, strong and clear without effort, which he ascribes to quinine which has entirely cured him: no pumping, and action in consequence greatly modified and subdued. By far his most successful effort. After him the Chancellor of the Exchequer. Then next night Wilson,[2] who is a great accession to the House, and delivered one of his best essays. He was followed by Tom Baring from our red box, sitting between G. B. and myself, with a vigor, an earnestness, and a freshness, which were quite captivating, and which wonderfully took. Later in the evening your humble servant spoke not to the dissatisfaction of the House; and after Lab[ouchere] and Goulburn, G. B., at ½ past one, made an effective reply.

I have not seen Granby, if he be in town, but I had a conversation with Miles on the *coup d'apoplexie* of the party, and spoke without reserve of my own views and feelings thereon. It is a curious thing that the three men who supported this sugar debate for the Country party, G. B., Tom Baring and myself all vote for the Jews!

There is a new note by Beresford; a lithograph circular, in

[1] Bernal Osborne.

[2] James Wilson, the political economist, M.P. for Westbury, afterwards financial member of Council in India.

which the name of Protectionist party disappears and is succeeded, not by the 'Country' but by the 'Conservative' party. Miles is indignant, having declared at our first meeting in 1846 that the epithet 'Conservative' had become a byword of reproach.

G. B. has written to Stanley acknowledging the receipt of this invitation to his house, but informing Lord S. that he, G. B., does not belong to the 'Conservative' party, adding that he wonders anyone has the audacity to do so, after it had been 'justly denounced by Disraeli as an "organised hypocrisy."' . . .

Disraeli might have pointed out that his famous phrase was that a Conservative *Government* — not party — was an organised hypocrisy; but, of course, he had written and spoken very severely about that party as manipulated by Peel. It will be noticed that, while reporting the views of Miles and Bentinck to Manners, Disraeli expresses no judgment of his own. It may well be that, while retaining his opinion as to the abuse of the term in the past, he was becoming alive to its profitable use in the future. In *Lord George Bentinck* we see signs of change. In reference to the past he writes of 'the great Conservative party that destroyed everything';[1] but in reference to the present and future he declares, in a more friendly and hopeful tone, that there is 'something so vital in the Conservative party that it seems always to rally under every disadvantage.'[2]

There is no doubt that in the matter of the name the Whips, of whom Disraeli and Manners had so low an opinion, were right, and Bentinck and his friends wrong. In spite of the ridicule which Disraeli had poured on the name Conservative, it had been accepted by the country as the recognised designation of the party of order, and the name Tory had dropped out of general use. Of the Conservatives of both wings returned at the General Election, decidedly more than two-thirds followed Stanley rather than Peel; and, as Malmesbury shrewdly remarked, Peel's declaration that he did not mean to take office again would be likely to send some of the rank and file of

[1] Ch. 16. [2] Ch. 25.

his followers into the Protectionist camp. That movement would be greatly aided by the assumption, on the part of the majority, of the party title, to which they had every right, not only by their numbers, but by the consistency of their opinions. After all, the backbone of the Tory or Conservative party were the country gentlemen, and they, speaking broadly, were with Stanley and against Peel. They might not produce at the moment competent Parliamentary leaders; leaders are not improvised in a session, and the whole of their General Staff had deserted them; but they had themselves much practical capacity, and were the men to whom their fellows looked up in their various counties. Peel, with his business origin and financial leanings, had superinduced on the old, aristocratic country party a surface of *bourgeoisie*, and his overthrow marked the reassertion of essential tendencies. The men who overthrew him rightly claimed to be the traditional representatives of the party, and the claim was tacitly conceded after a while by public opinion, and by their old comrades, who were content to be called Peelites after their great chief, or Liberal-Conservatives, to mark their hybrid position.

Though the Opposition were disorganised and without a leader, they made a very good fight for their principles during the session of 1848. The Monetary Crisis, the Famine in Ireland, the distress in the West Indies, and the general depression of trade, showed that Free Trade was, at least, no panacea. Bentinck's committee brought into relief the serious facts about the sugar industry and the West Indian colonies, to which the Free Traders wished to close their eyes. Though his own resolutions were negatived by the Committee, Bentinck had the satisfaction of carrying, by his casting vote as chairman, a report recommending a differential duty of ten shillings in favour of colonial sugar for six years, so as to secure time for bringing measures of relief into operation. He had the further satisfaction of compelling the Government to introduce and pass a measure adopting this principle, by establishing a gradually diminishing difference in favour of the Colonies till 1854. Disraeli delivered a series of powerful speeches criticising the new commercial system, and showing the falsity of the hopes held out by its supporters. In the first sugar debate[1] he declared that this system had been applied to only one branch of our imperial industry, and had been found wanting. Their legislation had brought ruin in India, Mauritius, and the West Indies.

Tell a Government of the present day that a million of H.M.'s subjects, previously enjoying great prosperity, are suddenly involved in almost inextricable difficulty; tell them that the sugar colonies of the Empire are in a perilous position, and all classes connected with them — proprietors, merchants, shipowners, labourers — agree in attributing their danger and suffering to our inconsistent and vacillating legislation; and the Government have always one peculiar class of remedies at hand. These remedies appear to consist of a certain number of abstract qualities and cardinal virtues. Competition is always at the head of the list; then follow, you may be sure, energy and enterprise. These remedies are not facts — they are only phrases. What is this competition, of whose divine influence we hear so much? Define it, tell us its sex and character. Is it a demigod or a nymph? It inspires all their solutions of economical difficulties. Is the shipping interest in decay? Competition will renovate it. Are the Colonies in despair? Energy will save them. Is the agricultural interest in danger? Enterprise is the panacea.

It was hopeless, he thought, to attempt to influence the House with any consideration which had not its growth in the prosperity of their ledgers. 'The commercial principle now rules this country. We had an Imperial principle in the time of those who preceded us; but you may rest assured that, if you convert the senate into a counting-house, it will not be long before the nation degenerates into a factory.' There was 'something in the catastrophe of nations *sævior armis*. These are the *longæ pacis mala*.'

On the Budget, which renewed and — as at first proposed — doubled the income tax, Disraeli observed[2] that

[1] Feb. 4. [2] Feb. 18.

the new principle of commercial legislation had not brought to the Treasury 'all those advantages which, like the picture of some Arabian tale, we were brought to believe was to be the happy appanage of the people of England'; and now the income tax, which was originally proposed as a temporary sacrifice for great national purposes, was to be permanent. Cobden's policy, it was claimed, was to give us the blessings of perpetual peace. That was no new idea. At Utrecht the Abbé St. Pierre proposed that the nations should agree to perpetual peace; but he was prepared to use force to compel them. In fact, his system 'assumed war as a necessary element of itself.' It was easy to entertain the dogma of perpetual peace, looking only at the material interests of such nations as America, France, and England. But war was produced, 'not by the Powers which are contented and satisfied,' but 'by the race or the prince who agitates for a position.'

> Take a remarkable case. At this moment Liberal gentlemen refer to it with great delight; and certainly, omitting our own country, of whose position we are hardly impartial judges, there is probably no nation in Europe, whether we look to general civilisation, diffused knowledge, public intelligence, or fame in arms and science, that can be placed superior to Prussia. But only a few years before St. Pierre laid down his principles Prussia did not exist. But Margraves of Brandenburg, conscious of great talents and power, determined, instead of being Margraves, to become Kings of Prussia, and that produced many struggles, and among them a Seven Years' War. If you reason in favour of universal peace from existing circumstances, you reason from circumstances that are essentially superficial.

Trade between England and France, Disraeli pointed out, had not prevented war in the end of the eighteenth century. The commercial tendency was not stronger than the religious tendency; all Europe was Christian, but that had not brought fighting and armaments to an end. The principles of the Radicals were totally opposed to the permanent maintenance of the Empire.[1]

[1] With regard to this speech, Baroness Lionel de Rothschild wrote to Mrs. Disraeli, of 'Friday night's glorious success. Lord Palmerston told me he had never heard a more magnificent speech.'

Cobden, in reply, urged Disraeli to give up the idea of forming a party on Protection. 'You have no principle, it is a sham and a fudge'; 'the thing is dead and gone and disposed of'; Disraeli and his friends had better join the Radicals in diminishing expenditure. Between this debate of February 18 and its resumption ten days later, Louis Philippe had fallen and France had set up a revolutionary government. So Disraeli, on February 28, rejoined with some force that the country would have to test Cobden's opinions, not merely as to the policy which would fill the Treasury, but also as to the policy that would secure the happiness and independence of the country. 'The hon. gentleman stands before us with all his talents as the supporter of a bankrupt exchequer, and as having, only within these last few days, appealed to a revolutionary nation as the model of political perfection.'

To Lord John Manners.

March 8, 1848.—. . . Where is the pilot to weather the storm? The Whigs are dished, dead, in spite of all our forbearance, and I mean, D.V., to give the last blow to 'Progress' on Friday, if the Muse inspire and aid me. What then?

As for G. B., he rises to the occasion. If you had seen him at ¼ past 11 on Monday, when Peel sate down, spring from a back bench, and making his most effective speech without a paper, or notes, you would have been astonished.

We were all, like so many gibbed cats, going to vote the Income Tax by an overwhelming majority when he declared his intention of supporting Hume's proposition,[1] and at least 100 men changed in a moment.

Had it not been for Peel's speech, G. B. would have said nothing. It was a great effort, and has affected a revolution in our parliamentary position here.

The Paris crash has no parallel; since Aladdin's palace vanished when his fool of a wife sold his old lamp!

As for general affairs, Madeira chaplains, Rio Plata jobs, Irish do, are all swamped and merged in the mighty theme of how the devil Europe, or perhaps England, is to be governed. 6 men shot at Glasgow: here, cockney riots of little boys, egged on by Charles Cochrane, and breaking the windows of club houses: then to wit Dicky Milnes asking questions at five o'clock of Secretaries of State about the collision between

[1] For limiting the Income Tax to one year.

'the people' and the police in Trafalgar Square amid groans and ironic cheers. Dicky dying of envy of Lamartine, and ready to put himself at the head of the 'gamins' and break the windows of Buckingham Palace. . . .

Granby, of whom I perpetually inquire of you, delighted me by telling me that you were really better. I am in force, tho' not equal to G. B. Nothing but a revolution will satisfy him: or at least the repeal of the Regency Act. Smythe has gone off to Paris to see his friend Louis Blanc, and some other successful blackguards. I remain at my post, and should enjoy it all amazingly, if you were at my right hand.

Disraeli's 'last blow to Progress' was delivered on March 10. He began by drawing a distinction between the commercial principles of 1842, which he supported, and those of 1845 and 1846, which he opposed. When the income tax was introduced in 1842, Peel's policy was 'to terminate prohibitions, to reduce protective duties to a moderate and practical amount, to raise a revenue by moderate duties on raw materials, and to admit the manufactures of other countries at duties varying from 12 to 20 per cent.' Reciprocal treaties were also to be concluded with other nations, following the traditional policy of Bolingbroke, Shelburne, and Pitt. This policy Disraeli supported: he was a 'Free Trader' in this sense, not a 'freebooter,' like the Anti-Corn Law Leaguers. The Leaguers never pretended that they accepted the 'principles of regulated competition and reciprocal intercourse'; their principle was buying in the cheapest, and selling in the dearest, market — a principle really only applicable to retail trade. When the commerical treaties failed, Peel adopted League principles, renewed the income tax, and cut off a revenue of £4,500,000, following this up by the repeal of the corn duties. The correct test of commercial legislation was commercial prosperity; but we had as a result of the new policy commercial distress and financial disorder. There were no signs whatever that the other great trading nations, Prussia, the United States, and France, were abandoning Protection. Where was the £100,000,000 extra revenue this policy was to give us? Cobden and Bright claimed to be the representatives of two great principles, Peace and Plenty. 'Yes. Peace and Plenty amid a starving people and with a world in arms!'

'The session of 1848, one of the longest on record,' wrote Disraeli, 'may be said to have commenced with sugar and to have concluded with sugar'; and at the end of June the Government narrowly escaped defeat on their Sugar Bill.

> Singular article of produce! What is the reason of this influence? It is that all considerations mingle in it; not merely commercial, but imperial, philanthropic, religious; confounding and crossing each other, and confusing the legislature and the nation lost in a maze of conflicting interests and contending emotions.[1]

Accordingly, Russell's measure, which Disraeli in retrospect described as a 'temperate and statesmanlike one,' pleased no one when it was produced, but was denounced by Free Traders and Protectionists alike—by the former as violating the principles laid down in 1846, and by the latter as affording the West Indian Colonies very inadequate relief. It led to protracted debates, which were envenomed by the personal charges brought, after his too frequent fashion, by Bentinck against Ministers, of withholding important information from the cognisance of his Committee. The charges had some foundation in this case, but Bentinck showed more vigour than discretion in his way of pressing them, and had to be rescued more than once by his friend's adroitness and skill. One famous scene in these debates, when Bentinck had reiterated his accusation against the Colonial Office, is depicted in the biography:

> Nettled at these observations, and partly perhaps executing a design contemplated, the first Minister took advantage of the motion for the adjournment of the debate to make a severe personal attack on Lord George Bentinck. The Minister said that these mean frauds, these extremely dishonourable tricks, which Lord George Bentinck imputed, were not the faults and characteristics of men who are high in public office in this country; they were characteristics of men who were engaged in pursuits which Lord George Bentinck long followed. Upon

[1] *Lord George Bentinck*, ch. 26.

this there was a burst of disapprobation from all sides, in the midst of which the Minister, feeling perhaps that the drift of his retort had been somewhat misapprehended, went on to say that Lord George Bentinck some years ago had greatly distinguished himself in detecting a fraud of that nature with respect to the name or the age of a horse, in which he showed very great quickness of apprehension. But the House would not be diverted from its first impression, and the Minister, though he pursued his observations for some minutes, was continually interrupted. It was clear that the taste and feeling of the House were both offended. This unusual indiscretion from so eminent a personage, and one who both by temper and discipline is acknowledged to be superior to passion, called forth a rejoinder from a friend of Lord George Bentinck [Disraeli], who reminded the Minister that his brother, the Duke of Bedford, had taken the lead in honouring Lord George Bentinck for his great services to public morality in this instance. A scene of great and prolonged excitement occurred.[1]

To the Government scheme Sir John Pakington moved a hostile amendment, which the majority of the Peelites were disposed to support. But, after many days of anxiety, Peel was able to collect sufficient of his followers in the Government lobby to save Ministers from defeat by fifteen votes. The fact that Goulburn, Gladstone, Cardwell, and other eminent Peelites, voted with the Protectionists stimulated the exertions of those who desired a reconciliation between the two wings of the Conservative party; and Lord Londonderry, the soldier and diplomatist, Castlereagh's half-brother, made, in a letter to his friend Disraeli, the first of several overtures to this effect. He suggested Goulburn as a man round whom all might rally — neither a happy nor a successful idea, though it was one which Disraeli suspected Stanley himself of entertaining two years later.[2]

Disraeli made several important speeches this session on foreign affairs; also one defending the 'ancient and national system' of the navigation laws; and one warmly supporting the Government in their measure for suspending the Habeas Corpus Act in Ireland, in view of the impending insurrection there, which he regarded as a Jacobin

[1] Ch. 26. [2] See below, p. 260.

movement. One speech deserves particular attention. It was delivered on June 20, on Hume's motion for Parliamentary reform. It is the first of Disraeli's considered utterances on a subject with which his fame is intimately bound up, and contains besides much of his political philosophy. People talked, he said, about the right to a vote. The suffrage was not a right[1]; it was not even a trust — 'that very vague and somewhat canting phrase'; it was a privilege. The Commons were a privileged order, and the Reform Act of 1832 was a reconstruction of that order. That settlement was most unsatisfactory to him and his friends, but it was fully supported and sanctioned by the people, and should not be disturbed now unless they could be sure of arriving at a new reconstruction, which would give satisfaction to the people and security to the State. Not that he was an advocate of finality. 'I conceive there may be circumstances, there may be a period, when we shall do that which we have done for five hundred years in this country — reconstruct the estate of the Commons.' The most striking mistake in the settlement of 1832 was that it took property as the only qualification for the exercise of political rights. Hume's project was open to the same objection; there was no educational suffrage, no industrial suffrage, no attempt to increase or vary the elements of suffrage, but property alone was its basis.

Besides household suffrage, Hume's motion also advocated the ballot, triennial Parliaments, and more equal electoral districts. As for the ballot, Disraeli preferred rather to trust to the influence of opinion organised by a free Press, as the best safeguard against corruption and

[1] Here Disraeli interposed an interesting passage about female suffrage: 'In a country governed by a woman, where you allow women to form part of the other estate of the realm — peeresses in their own right, for example — where you allow a woman not only to hold land, but to be a lady of the manor and hold legal courts, where a woman by law may be a churchwarden — I do not see, when she has so much to do with State and Church, on what reasons, if you come to right, she has not a right to vote. All this proves that right has nothing to do with the matter.'

intimidation. As for triennial Parliaments, they were part of the old Tory creed advocated by Sir William Wyndham[1] against a corrupt Minister, and the only objection to them was that they were an unnecessary change, and as such to be deprecated. Of equal electoral districts he spoke with great scorn in language that sounds strange to-day. Such a system presented itself to him as a proposal to take members from his historic county of Bucks and give them to Manchester, Liverpool, Glasgow, and London. Was it to be tolerated that the county of Hampden and the Grenvilles, the elder Pitt and Burke, should be deprived of its hereditary weight in a free Parliament because its population might not be equal to the number of some great town 'born in a day, and destined, perhaps, to vanish in a day'? 'The realised experience of a nation' was one of the most important elements in reconstructing the franchise.

This was a middle-class movement, to aggrandise the power of that class at the expense, not merely of the aristocracy, but of the working classes. What was the history of its legislative enterprises? The middle classes emancipated the negroes, but never proposed a Ten Hours Bill for English workmen. In their reform Bill they destroyed, under the pretence of its corrupt exercise, the old industrial franchise, and they never constructed a new one. Again, in their commercial legislation, while the interests of capital were unblushingly advocated, the displaced labour of the country was offered neither consolation nor compensation, but was told that it must submit to be absorbed in the mass. There was no evidence in any of these reforms of any sympathy with the working classes. Disraeli then discussed the origin of the movement, and in a vivacious passage depicted the working of professional agitation, at that time comparatively in its infancy, now grown to herculean proportions, but in its methods always the same.

[1] See Vol. I., pp. 218, 219.

It is a profession which requires many votaries — chairmen, deputy-chairmen, secretaries, committeemen, missionaries, pamphleteers, lecturers, hired orators —

> 'Rhetor, grammaticus, geometres, pictor, aliptes,
> Augur, schenobates, medicus, magus.'

The business of this profession is to discover or invent great questions. When a great question is settled, it is the ruin of the profession. There is no need of a chairman, for there is no chair to fill; no want of a deputy-chairman to represent his hon. friend; there are no committees to be attended; no pamphlets to be written; the lecturer is idle and the orator is dumb. The rule, however, is, when a great question has been settled, immediately to look out for a new one.

After Free Trade was settled, the Anti-Corn-Law Leaguers first tried perpetual peace as the next great question, but the unhappy affair at Paris stopped that movement. So they had turned to electoral districts, which was a new cry, and would serve to flavour the somewhat stale pretexts of triennial Parliaments and vote by ballot.

Disraeli proceeded to draw a favourite moral of his from 'this playing and paltering with popular passions for the aggrandisement of one too ambitious class:'

Why are the people of England forced to find leaders among these persons? The proper leaders of the people are the gentlemen of England. If they are not the leaders of the people, I do not see why there should be gentlemen. Yes, it is because the gentlemen of England have been negligent of their duties and unmindful of their station that the system of professional agitation, so ruinous to the best interests of the country, has arisen in England. It was not always so. My honourable friends around me call themselves the country party. Why, that was the name once in England of a party who were the foremost to vindicate popular rights — who were the natural leaders of the people and the champions of everything national and popular; and you must blame yourselves alone if you have allowed the power that has been entrusted to you by the Constitution to slip from your hands, to be exercised for other interests than the general good of your country. When Sir William Wyndham was the leader of the country party, do you think he would have allowed any chairman or deputy-chairman, any lecturer or pamphleteer, to deprive him of his hold on the heart of the people of this country? No, never! Do you think that, when the question of suffrage was brought before the House, he would have allowed any class who had boldly avowed their determination to obtain predominance to take up and settle that question? Read what Sir J. Hynde Cotton,[1] in the days of Walpole, said on the question of the suffrage. He was one of the greatest gentlemen in the country; he did not run away every night from the House and pair till half-past eleven, and let the country go to the dogs. If it be true that we are on the eve of troublous times, if it indeed be necessary that changes should take place in this country, let them be effected by those who ought to be the leaders in all political and social changes. Then we shall not find changes carried into effect for the unblushing purpose of securing a middle-class Government, but an English and a national Government, the pride of the people, and in which confidence can be placed.

There is much that is interesting and informing as to Disraeli's views in this speech. He disclaims finality in reform, and he claims for the Country party the right and, at the proper time, the duty itself to take up and settle the question — a task which he attempted in 1859, and carried through successfully in 1867. He desires also to base the franchise, not merely upon property, but upon educational and other qualifications; here we have the germ of the fancy franchises of 1859 and 1867. On the other hand, household suffrage, which was the basis of the Act of 1867, and was then recognised to be the transference of power from the middle class to the working men, was opposed by Disraeli in 1848, rather oddly, as a measure to secure a middle-class Government. He was perfectly justified in his suspicion of its origin. The Manchester School, as we have seen, were in their Free Trade movement at least as much concerned with the profits of the manufacturers as with the improvement of the industrial class; and it was not unreasonable that their opponents should suspect that, in desiring to extend the suffrage to the artisans, they were really aiming at increasing the political power of the class most likely to influence the new voters. Disraeli's aim throughout was to curb the excessive power which, in his view, the middle-class had

[1] See Vol. I., p. 221.

obtained under the Reform Act of 1832, and to counterbalance it by strengthening the landed interest on the one hand, and on the other by admitting, in such proportions as political cross-currents would permit, a real representation of the industrial class.

The session did not close without a further long stride being made by Disraeli towards the leadership. Parliament had been sitting ten months, from November to September, with but slight intermission; and yet Ministers had accomplished little of their programme, and had met with repeated rebuffs and humiliations.[1] They had naturally laid the blame on the forms of the House and on the loquacity of their opponents; but Disraeli, in a long and detailed speech on August 30, put the story of the session in a juster perspective. 'The speech that made me leader,' he said to Lord Rowton, on being shown a reprint more than thirty years later. How he came to speak at all, he has told us in *Lord George Bentinck:*

Lord George Bentinck was very anxious that there should be a parliamentary summary of this enormous and eventful session of '48, that the conduct of business by the Ministry should be traced and criticised and the character of the House of Commons vindicated, and he appealed to the writer of these observations to undertake the task. But the writer was unwilling to accede to this suggestion, not only because at the end of August he shrank from a laborious effort, but principally because he did not hold that his position in the House of Commons warranted on his part such an interference, since, after all, he was only the comrade in arms of one who chose to be only an independent member of the House. He therefore unaffectedly stated that he thought the office was somewhat above his measure. But Lord George Bentinck would not listen to these representations. 'I don't pretend to know much,' he said, 'but I can judge of men and horses.' It is difficult to refuse those who are themselves setting a

[1] Meeting Hobhouse at one of Lady Palmerston's parties in July, Disraeli told him the Government 'might last as long as it liked. It was a weak Government, and therefore durable. Strong Governments always fell to pieces—*e.g.*, Lord Grey's and Peel's' (*Broughton's Recollections*, under date July 22). The prediction was verified, as the Government lasted three years and a half more.

constant example of self-sacrifice, and therefore, as far as the labour was concerned, the writer would not have shrunk from the exertion even on the last day of the month of August; and when the particular wish of Lord George was found to be more general than the writer presumed to suppose, he accordingly endeavoured to accomplish the intention.[1]

It appears from Disraeli's private correspondence that this is not a complete account of the origin of the speech. Not only Bentinck, who was always anxious to further his comrade's ambitions, but Stanley himself, urged him to deliver it. During this summer there seems to have been the first approximation to friendly personal relations between these two eminent men, Stanley and Disraeli, destined to be allied so long and intimately in public duty. It is possible that the differences and misunderstandings which frequently occurred in these years, 1846–1848, between the somewhat *nonchalant* Stanley and the strenuous and irascible Bentinck, may have inclined Stanley to view Disraeli with less disfavour. In the spring[2] Manners could still write to Disraeli: 'Do you see more of Stanley than you gave me to understand you were seeing of him when I was last in London? I hope so, though I agree with you there is something queer in his whole behaviour.' But in July we find Stanley cordially accepting an invitation to dine at Grosvenor Gate, in the first of his letters to Disraeli which has been preserved; and on August 7 Disraeli writes to Lady Londonderry: 'I was with Lord Stanley this morning, who wants me (this quite between ourselves) to sum up the session in the House of Commons; but I am wearied, and occupied with that arrear of private business which always awaits me in August, which distracts without exciting.' A day or two later he tells the same correspondent that, late as it is, he must remain in town two or three weeks more, 'as I have promised Lord Stanley to sum up the session for the edification of Her Majesty's lieges, and must not precipitate the performance, which should be a final ceremony, the dropping of the curtain — the last flavour, which is to give a tone to

[1] Ch. 27.

[2] March 12.

public opinion and an impulse to public discontent for some months.'

The speech takes the form of a vindication of the House of Commons from the charges of vacillation and incompetence, and fastens the responsibility for the unsatisfactory state of affairs on the misgovernment of Ministers. Parliament, Disraeli reminded his hearers, was called together unusually early owing to the monetary crisis and the licence given to the directors of the Bank of England to infringe the Bank Charter Act, and he commented on the delay and inconsistency of Ministerial proceedings:

> I scarcely know to what to compare their conduct, except something that occurs in a delightful city of the South, with which hon. gentlemen are familiar, and which is now, I believe, blockaded or bullied by the English fleet. There an annual ceremony takes place, when the whole population are found in a state of the greatest alarm and sorrow. A procession moves through the streets, in which the blood of a saint is carried in a consecrated vase. The people throng around the vase, and there is a great pressure — as there was in London at the time to which I am alluding. This pressure in time becomes a panic — just as it did in London. It is curious that in both cases the cause is the same: it is a cause of congealed circulation. Just at the moment when unutterable gloom overspreads the population, when nothing but despair and consternation prevail, the Chancellor of the Exchequer — I beg pardon, the Archbishop of Tarento — announces the liquefaction of St. Januarius's blood, as the Chancellor of the Exchequer announced the issue of a Government letter; in both instances, a wholesome state of currency returns; the people resume their gaiety and cheerfulness, the panic and the pressure disappear, everybody returns to music and macaroni — as in London everybody returned to business; and in both cases the remedy is equally efficient and equally a hoax.

Much time had been wasted by the financial mismanagement of the unlucky Sir Charles Wood, the Chancellor of the Exchequer. Disraeli poured scorn and ridicule on the four Budgets which had been presented to the House: one in February, when the Prime Minister emphasised the importance of the occasion by taking on himself the task of the Chancellor of the Exchequer, and on the score of the imperative necessities of defence announced that the income tax would be doubled; the second, ten days later, when — owing to the 'unearthly yell' as of 'a menagerie before feeding-time' which went up at the prospect from those friends of free trade, the middle classes — the Chancellor of the Exchequer announced that 'by filching on the one hand and screwing on the other' Ministers, in spite of the needs of defence, could do without the £3,500,000 which a doubled income tax would bring in; the third Budget in June, interposed by the Chancellor of the Exchequer in the midst of a debate on Colonial sugar; and the fourth in August, the introduction of which Disraeli thus describes:

I shall never forget the scene. It irresistibly reminded me of a celebrated character who, like the Chancellor of the Exchequer, had four trials in his time, and whose last was the most unsuccessful — I mean the great hero of Cervantes when he returned from his fourth and final expedition. The great spirit of Quixote had subsided; all that sally of financial chivalry which cut us down at the beginning of the session, and which trampled and cantered over us in the middle, was gone. Hon. gentlemen will remember the chapter to which I refer, which describes the period when the knight's illusions on the subject of chivalry were fast dispelling, and, losing his faith in chivalry — or finance — he returned home crestfallen and weary. The villagers, like the Opposition, were drawn out to receive him; and Cervantes tells us that, although they were aware of his weakness, they treated him with respect. His immediate friends — the barber, the curate, the bachelor Samson Carrasco — whose places might be supplied in this House by the First Lord of the Treasury, the Secretary of State for Foreign Affairs, and, perhaps, the President of the Board of Trade [Labouchere], were assembled, and with demure reverence and feigned sympathy they greeted him, broken in spirit, and about for ever to renounce those delightful illusions under which he had sallied forth so triumphantly; but just at the moment when everything, though melancholy, was becoming — though sad, was in the best taste — Sancho's wife rushes forward and exclaims, 'Never mind your kicks and cuffs, so you've brought home some money.' But this is just what the Chancellor of the Exchequer has not brought. Such was the end of the fourth and final expedition, and such is the result of the fourth and final budget. The Chancellor of the Exchequer during the whole session has been bringing home barbers' basins instead of knightly helms; and at the last moment, true to his nature, to his vocation, and to his career, he finds instead of a surplus a deficiency, and, instead of reducing taxation, he commemorates his second year of finance by a second loan.

Time had been muddled away over the Public Health Bill, the Jewish Disabilities Bill, the various Sugar Bills, and the Bills dealing with delinquent boroughs. No wonder that time had not been found to pass the repeal of the Navigation Laws, and that there were forty-seven other Bills, two-thirds of them Government measures, abandoned, withdrawn, or postponed. During this long session there had been 'sedition in England, insurrection in Ireland, and revolution in Europe,' but the Opposition had taken no advantage of these opportunities. Palmerston had admitted the consideration shown in foreign affairs; there had been no discussion of the condition-of-England question, and, when stringent measures were proposed for Ireland, the Government were neither attacked nor even hampered, in spite of the fact that the Opposition were without a leader, split into sections, with everything left to the discretion of individual members. No, it was not the Opposition, it was not the House of Commons, that was in fault: it was the Treasury Bench, to which Disraeli pointed amidst the cheers of his party. Though the Whigs were justified by the exigency of the case in assuming office without a Parliamentary majority, they ought not to have retained it in such circumstances. What was the result?

In the first place, we have a Cabinet who, in preparing their measures, have no conviction those measures will be carried. The success of their measures in this House depends on a variety of small parties, who, in their aggregate, exceed in number and influence the party of the Ministers. The temper of one leader has to be watched — the indication of the opinion of another has to be observed — the disposition of a third has to be suited; so that a measure is so altered, remoulded, remodelled, patched, cobbled, painted, veneered, and varnished, that, at last, no trace is left of the original scope and scheme; or it is withdrawn in disgust by its originators, after having been subjected to prolonged and elaborate discussions in this House. . . .

There is another inconvenience resulting from the present position of the Government — in my opinion more serious, if not so flagrant — and that is, it is impossible to expect from Ministers thus situated those matured, finished, and complete measures which, under other circumstances, we should have a right to demand from them. Men in their situation will naturally say: 'What is the use of taking all these pains, of bestowing all this care, study, and foresight, on the preparation of a measure, when the moment it is out of our hands it ceases to be the measure of the Cabinet, and becomes essentially the measure of the House of Commons?' . . . The House of Commons, as now conducted, is a Great Committee sitting on public affairs, in which every man speaks with the same right and most of us with the same weight. No more the disciplined array of traditionary influences and hereditary opinions — the realised experience of an ancient society and of a race that for generations has lived and flourished in the high practice of a noble system of self-government. That is all past. For these the future is to provide us with a compensatory alternative in the conceits of the illiterate, the crotchets of the whimsical, the violent courses of a vulgar ambition that acknowledges no gratitude to antiquity — to posterity no duty. . . .

Sir, I trace all this evil to the disorganisation of party. I know that there are gentlemen in this house who affect to deprecate party government. . . . I say, you can have no parliamentary government if you have no party government; and, therefore, when gentlemen denounce party government, they strike at that scheme of government which, in my opinion, has made this country great, and which I hope will keep it great. I can foresee, though I dare not contemplate, the consequences of the system that now prevails. They are weak words that would describe them as prejudicial to the realm, perilous to Parliament, fatal to that high tone of public life that is the best security for national grandeur and public liberty. It is more than this: it is the *finis fatorum* of the great Dardanian house. . . . I know no institution in the country that can long withstand its sapping and deleterious influence. As for the class of public men that have hitherto so gloriously administered the affairs of this country, I believe they will be swept off the face of our political world. For my part, I protest against the system: I denounce it. Even at the eleventh hour, I call upon the country to brand it with its indignant reprobation.

It was a brilliant peroration, and the concluding portion, which emphasised the crucial importance, for Parliamentary government, of maintaining party association, embodied one of Disraeli's profoundest convictions. It was for the break-up of his party that he reproached Peel; it was to the reorganisation of that party that he himself devoted successfully the best years of his life. His remarks on the evils of government through a Parliamentary minority are equally true; but it is a strange irony that he should have been destined to illustrate three times in his own person the disadvantages that he depicted so clearly.

The speech produced a marked effect, and Russell, in replying, though he professed not to understand why it should have been delivered, complimented the orator on his abilities and eloquence. Disraeli, in his account to his wife, is even more infectiously enthusiastic than usual, and is also naturally anxious that *The Times* report of his great effort should be correct:

To Mrs. Disraeli.

Aug. 30, 1848.—The success has exceeded our most sanguine expectations and hopes!

I spoke exactly three hours, and omitted scarcely one point of great importance, and very few of secondary.

The attendance on our side was admirable. G. B. had scoured the country—Hudson[1] and all sorts of fellows by express trains. The cheering capital and genuine: not factitious. We had, in fact, a considerable majority over the Government, and could have turned them out, had there been a division.

The Peers' gallery crowded, and all the Foreign Ministers; among them, De Beaumont, the new French one.

All my friends delighted: universally admitted my greatest speech. Smythe beyond expression. He tells me that in the Peers' galleries—*especially his father—all the* 18*th century*, say there never was anything like it.

I am now going to Delane—God knows how long and how often I shall be there, as the speech must be eight columns at least.

[1] The Railway King.

On the previous day Disraeli had written to Lady Londonderry: 'To-morrow is my Waterloo, but whether for triumph or discomfiture, I dare not now foresee. . . . This is the first day of the campaign that I have felt utterly exhausted and dispirited — a sad mood on the eve of a general engagement'; he now reports exultingly that he has 'won the battle completely.' But we have other evidence than his own. Newspapers of all parties recognised the brilliance and general accuracy of his exposure of Ministerial inefficiency. Brougham wrote to him: 'You have closed the session most magnificently'; and Greville, though he calls the speech 'nothing but a theatrical display,' admits that it was 'very sparkling and clever.' Moreover, letters of both the Whips of the Protectionist party — Beresford and Newdegate — neither of whom was specially well affected to Disraeli, have come down to us. Newdegate sent an 'impartial' but flattering account to Mrs. Disraeli. Beresford reported to Stanley that the speech was 'very able and powerful,' and shrewdly added: 'One feature of Disraeli's speech that demands some attention is the character, which he attempts to assume in more than one instance, of being the organ of the Opposition, and thereby bidding for the station of their Parliamentary leader. No doubt but his ability is sufficient for that station, but he must not claim it merely on that score until it is conceded to him by the party.'

In the prostration which, as usual, fell upon Disraeli when the labours of the session were over, he was cheered and consoled by the delicate appreciation of his oratory shown in a letter from Prince Metternich,[1] whom the troubles of this year of Continental revolution had driven to take refuge in England.

From Prince Metternich.

EATON SQUARE, *le* 9 *Sept.* 1848. — . . . Vous avez une constitution, qui doit vous engager à ménager la partie matérielle de votre être, qui tend à user l'élément moral, dont le créateur vous a si richement dôté. Ce qui se

[1] See below, ch. 7.

présente en vous comme de la prostration, n'est que la suite d'une lésion de l'équilibre entre l'esprit et la matière. Le travail parlementaire est un travail très lourd; il équivaut parfois à celui d'Hercule et je suis convaincu que, malgré sa demie divinité, ce héros a un besoin de se reposer après ses exploits! Vous êtes doué d'un fort rare talent oratoire, et on n'est orateur que quand on sait remuer les questions fortes et qui par celà même sont pesantes. La différence entre un orateur et un causeur *de rien* est immense; cette différence se présente dans toutes les directions et il ne suffira de m'arrêter à une seule; *l'orateur* use ses propres forces et éveille celles de son auditoire; le *parleur* use les facultés des écouteurs et ne court pas le risque de compromettre les forces qu'il ne possède pas en lui-même. L'un marche dans le plein, et l'autre établit autour de lui le vide. Le premier fait, ou du bien, ou du mal; l'autre ne fait rien; et le mouvement qui ne produit pas, détruit! Usez des dons dont vous êtes favorisé et ménagez-vous pour faire vie qui dure. Après vous-même, je vous en saurai le plus grande gré. . . .

Donnez-moi de vos nouvelles pour que je sache ce que vous faites. Vous n'avez pas besoin de m'apprendre ce que vous pensez; je ne le mets pas en doute.

CHAPTER V

THE QUESTION OF LEADERSHIP — II

1848–1849

Before the echoes of Disraeli's triumphant speech had subsided, the political outlook was changed, in a moment, by Bentinck's sudden death. On the afternoon of September 21 he started to walk, from his father's house at Welbeck, some five or six miles across the woodland to Thoresby. As he walked he had a heart attack, and his body was found, some hours afterwards, lying by the path. It seems strange that the event should have taken the world entirely by surprise. He had been prostrated by influenza in December, and the condition of his health had weighed heavily in his resignation of the leadership. Nevertheless, in the protracted session of 1847–48 he worked, largely in consequence of his chairmanship of the West India Committee, harder than ever. The news caused everywhere an immense sensation; 'all men seemed to mourn over this untimely end, and there was that pang in the public heart which accompanies the disappearance of a strong character.' Like the rest of the world, Disraeli seems to have assumed that his friend had regained all his vigour, and he was accordingly quite unprepared and overwhelmed. He and Mrs. Disraeli were staying at Wynyard with the Londonderrys at the time, and after a melancholy parting he went to London for the funeral.

To Lord Henry Bentinck.

GROSVENOR GATE, *Sept.* 25, 1848.

DEAR LORD HENRY, — The desolating news reached us at Wynyard yesterday morning. I do not write this to intrude on your affliction. My own is too vast. It is the greatest

Lord George Bentinck.
from a pencil drawing by John Doyle. (H.B.)
at Hughenden.

nted in England.

sorrow I have ever experienced. A peculiar and unparalleled spirit has departed: at all times a loss; in an age of degeneracy, an irreparable one. It seems to me, that the pulse of the nation beats lower after this.

I can neither offer, nor receive, consolation. All is unutterable woe! And I only write this because, when the occasion is fitting, there are reasons which make it necessary I should see you.—Ever, dear Lord Henry, yours, B. DISRAELI.

Writing to Manners, Disraeli used much the same phrases of profound grief, and added: 'Arriving in town I found on my table a letter[1] of six sheets, written an hour before the fatal walk, and full of his accustomed vigor and keen interest in existence.' To another friend he wrote that he was 'shaken to the core'; and to a third, that he was 'overwhelmed by a great calamity' in 'the death of one to whom I was bound by personal ties, far stronger even than those political connections which knit us together.' Of the loss to the party he spoke in Parliament at the beginning of the next session:

At a time when everything that is occurring vindicates his prescience and demands his energy, we have no longer his sagacity to guide or his courage to sustain us. In the midst of the Parliamentary strife his plume can soar no more for us to rally round. But he has left us the legacy of heroes: the memory of his great name, and the inspiration of his great example.

Disraeli did not rest content with this Parliamentary tribute. With the assistance of the Bentinck family he erected a lasting monument to his friend's memory in *Lord George Bentinck, a Political Biography*, published in December, 1851. Here is the full-length portrait which he draws:

His eager and energetic disposition; his quick perception, clear judgment, and prompt decision; the tenacity with which he clung to his opinions; his frankness and love of truth; his daring and speculative spirit; his lofty bearing, blended as it was with a simplicity of manner very remarkable; the ardour of his friendships, even the fierceness of his hates and prejudices: all combined to form one of those strong characters who, whatever may be their pursuit, must always direct and lead.

[1] The text of this letter is given in Appendix A.

Nature had clothed this vehement spirit with a material form which was in perfect harmony with its noble and commanding character. He was tall, and remarkable for his presence; his countenance almost a model of manly beauty; the face oval, the complexion clear and mantling; the forehead lofty and white; the nose aquiline and delicately moulded; the upper lip short. But it was in the dark brown eyes that flashed with piercing scrutiny that all the character of the man came forth; a brilliant glance, not soft, but ardent, acute, imperious, incapable of deception or of being deceived. . . .

In politics he was a Whig of 1688, which became him, modified, however, by all the experience of the present age. He wished to see our society founded on a broad basis of civil and religious liberty. He retained much of the old jealousy of the Court, but had none of popular franchises. He was for the Established Church, but for nothing more, and very repugnant to priestly domination. As for the industrial question, he was sincerely opposed to the Manchester scheme, because he thought that its full development would impair and might subvert our territorial constitution, which he held to be the real security of our freedom, and because he believed that it would greatly inspire Ireland, and certainly dissolve our colonial empire.

He had a great respect for merchants, though he looked with some degree of jealousy on the development of our merely foreign trade. His knowledge of character qualified him in a great degree to govern men, and if some drawbacks from this influence might be experienced in his too rigid tenacity of opinion, and in some quickness of temper, which, however, always sprang from a too sensitive heart, great compensation might be found in the fact that there probably never was a human being so entirely devoid of conceit and so completely exempt from selfishness. Nothing delighted him more than to assist and advance others. All the fruits of his laborious investigations were always at the service of his friends without reserve or self-consideration. He encouraged them by making occasions for their exertions, and would relinquish his own opportunity without a moment's hesitation, if he thought the abandonment might aid a better man.[1]

In describing his last talk with Bentinck in Harcourt House, about a fortnight before the end, Disraeli added some further reflections over this 'singular and sudden career':

[1] Ch. 2.

Never was a reputation so substantial built up in so brief a space. All the questions with which he had dealt were colossal questions: the laws that should regulate competition between native and foreign labour; the interference of the state in the development of the resources of Ireland; the social and commercial condition of our tropical colonies; the principles upon which our revenue should be raised; the laws that should regulate and protect our navigation. But it was not that he merely expressed opinions upon these subjects; he came forward with details in support of his principles and policy which it had been before believed none but a minister could command. Instead of experiencing the usual and almost inevitable doom of private members of parliament, and having his statements shattered by official information, Lord George Bentinck, on the contrary, was the assailant, and the successful assailant, of an administration on these very heads. . . .

Though his manner, which was daily improving, was not felicitous in the House, the authority of his intellect, his knowledge, and his character made him one of the great personages of debate.[1]

It is a fine tribute by a friend to the character and work of his colleague and leader, and much fairer than the estimates current in histories mostly written from the Free Trade standpoint. Bentinck has suffered, like Disraeli, from his sturdy opposition to a policy which was for many decades treated by the ordinary Englishman almost as a religion; and he has frequently been denied both ability and character. That his Parliamentary capacity was greatly improved through his association with Disraeli is unquestionable; but without his co-operation Disraeli would hardly have overthrown Peel. It may be that Bentinck, when he died, had done his best work. In Disraeli's opinion, given to Greville, he would have failed as Minister and Leader of the House, owing to the deficiencies of his education and the want of flexibility in his character. 'In his speaking there were physical defects he never could have got over, and as it had been proved that he could not lead an Opposition, still less would he have been able to lead a Government.'[2] Stanley

[1] Ch. 27. [2] Greville, under date Nov. 24, 1851.

shared this view. He told the Queen in November, 1852, that Bentinck, if alive, 'would have made confusion worse confounded' from his excessive violence.[1] Such speculations, however, as to what might have been are always unsatisfactory. It is impossible to fix a limit to the development which responsibility may produce in a strong and resolute character. What is certain is that by Bentinck's death one of the two forceful personalities in the Protectionist ranks in the Commons was removed; and the path was cleared for Disraeli's advance.

'No one but Disraeli can fill his place. Although of perfectly different natures, they pulled together without any difficulty. It will leave Disraeli without a rival, and enable him to show the great genius he undoubtedly possesses without any comparisons.' So wrote Malmesbury in his diary on hearing of Bentinck's death. There is no doubt he was right. No new man had arisen in the ranks of the country party. Bentinck's successor in the representation of Lynn, Edward Henry Stanley, Lord Stanley's eldest son, afterwards 15th Earl of Derby, was indeed a notable accession; but he was only twenty-two, and did not make his maiden speech till May, 1850. The only choice, outside Disraeli, lay among the mediocrities whom we have already passed in review. His claims were greater than ever, owing to his successes during the past session. He was, moreover, as the Duke of Newcastle wrote to him on October 22, Bentinck's 'Prime Minister, fellow-labourer, and most confidential friend.' Almost immediately a movement was begun in his favour. The Bentinck family, who knew the wishes of Lord George, and were grateful to Disraeli for his constant attachment and unfailing support, very naturally took the lead, Lord Henry, who sat for Nottinghamshire, being specially active. The Duke of Newcastle, to whom Lord George was the beau-ideal of a true patriot, and who resented his son Lord Lincoln's following Peel, went with the Bentincks. Christopher and Trollope,

[1] *Queen Victoria's Letters*, under date Nov. 28, 1852.

members for Lincolnshire, and Miles, member for Somerset, were also forward in promoting the movement. Disraeli seems himself to have done a little discreet wire-pulling at an early stage. He was in London, off and on, a good deal in the weeks after Bentinck's death.

To Mrs. Disraeli.

Half-past six [Oct. 12, 1848].

MY DEAREST WIFE, — I am going to dine with Lord Hardwicke[1] alone, before he goes off by the train. . . .

Pollington[2] is in town — alone.

I met Mrs. Dawson,[3] who was painfully condoling; Jemmy McDonald,[4] who turned and would walk with me, full of G. B.; Exmouth,[5] who cried, so I suppose it is the fashion to weep. All the newspapers go on praising him up to the seventh heaven, and discovering all the great qualities which they never before would acknowledge. . . .

[*Nov.* 4, 1848.]

MY DARLING, — I am going to dine with Herries — alone. Lord Hardwicke is in the room; I think I shall tell him that his letter is in the box.

The Duke of Bucks just returned from Scotland; very well, quite renovated by the grouse shooting. Thinks of going abroad; 'anything better than kicking one's heels in London,' where, however, I have no doubt he will remain. . . .

Disraeli took care, when he was in town, to propitiate the Protectionist party organ, the *Morning Herald*, whose guiding spirit, Phillips, had shown himself so hostile in the previous winter. He gained also an influential adherent in Lord Mandeville,[6] who wrote on October 16 that Phillips had told him 'the line you proposed to take in politics, and I did not hesitate to state to him, as I now repeat to you, the readiness with which I should tender any support or assistance I can afford to one who

[1] The 4th Earl, Postmaster-General 1852, Privy Seal 1858. See Vol. II., p. 20.

[2] Viscount Pollington, M.P. for Pontefract 1835–1837 and 1841–1847, afterwards 4th Earl of Mexborough.

[3] Sir Robert Peel's sister. See Vol. II., pp. 28, 125, and 230.

[4] See Vol. II., p. 195.

[5] See Vol. II., p. 25.

[6] M.P. for Bewdley. Afterwards 7th Duke of Manchester. His Duchess, after his death, married the 8th Duke of Devonshire, the Liberal Unionist statesman (1833–1908).

has been of such eminent service to the party as you have.' What attracted Mandeville especially were Disraeli's economic principles and his resistance to the advance of Popery. In his reply, which does not seem to have been kept, Disraeli showed apparently considerable reserve, expressing doubts of his own competence and of the character of the party to be led. Other clear-sighted observers had a poor opinion of that party in its then condition. Both the rank and file, and the mediocrities at the head, were trenchantly castigated in a letter from Henry Drummond, the banker, member for Surrey, who urged Disraeli to assert himself and disregard them. 'I think,' he wrote, 'that there is great danger to your future prospects if you link yourself to a lazaretto of incurables. . . . The men around you are at your mercy; they have not an idea touching any course of policy; all their ideas of parties are like those of rival attorneys, rival public-houses, pastrycooks, etc., in a county town. . . . I have no doubt that your party will try to get some titled nonentity to be its nominal head in the House of Commons, although every individual knows he cannot stir without you; but if you stand your ground and civilly say to all (*i.e.*, covertly, though not openly) that you will be *nulli secundus*, they will be as meek as mice.'

Disraeli spent most of the autumn in Bucks. He flattered himself that he had been able to secure an important ecclesiastical ally in his own diocesan, Samuel Wilberforce, who had become Bishop of Oxford in the last few years. But the Bishop proved in the long run to have greater affinities with Disraeli's future rival; and, as the years went by, it became more and more difficult for a man to retain the close friendship of both Gladstone and Disraeli.

To Lord John Manners.

BRADENHAM, *Nov.* 19, 1848.—It was most vexatious our missing each other. I had gone down to Cuddesdon to assist Samuel Oxon in the foundation of a diocesan training school for masters, in which we have succeeded. I made his acquaintance at Wimpole, and we have made, not only a cordial understanding, but a compact alliance between Church and State; and are henceforth to work together. He is young and vigorous, and repents of his backslidings: for the future, I expect to find him a pillar of the Church in our sense. . . . I am in the agonies of transition from Bradenham to Hughenden, and never was more annoyed. . . .

Disraeli's host at Wynyard, which he had quitted hurriedly after Bentinck's death, was anxious for news of him. 'Of politics,' Lord Londonderry wrote from Mount Stewart on November 18, 'I hear and know nothing. Some say it's a toss up for a leader for the Pro's between you and Bankes — not very flattering, I think, to superiority.' Disraeli represents himself as adopting a passive attitude.

To Lord Londonderry.

Hughenden Manor, High Wycombe, *Nov.* 22, 1848. — It is very kind of you to remember me, and I feel sensibly flattered by it. I should, long ere this, have reminded you of my existence, if I could have told you anything interesting or important. But after leaving Wynyard, I remained a whole month, in this place, in that apathy, which often arises after excitement and startling events, and found myself incapable of touching a pen, even to write to you; tho' I should have been happy to have expressed some sense of an agreeable visit to your splendid halls, and of the kindness which will always make us remember your roof with regard. But I felt I ought also to write about other things, and I was nervously incapable of it. This is my frank reason for my brutal silence, which I admit to have been a gross outrage, but which, I trust, you have pardoned. . . .

I have seen very few people, and those only by chance. I have avoided, as much as I could, all sort of political communication. Letters I have received by shoals. There have been all kinds of rumors — most of them unfounded, all untrue: and many little efforts, as there naturally would be, resulting, as was to have been foreseen, in nullity. From my knowledge of the things and persons in question, I feel as aware of all that is said, done, or thought, as if I were present at all their confabulations, and were the dæmon of their innermost mind. It is not little commonplace intrigues that can reconstruct parties in this country. The quandary is too complex. What is wanted, and what alone will do it, are great events, and men equal to them. The former are sure to arrive. . . .

As the year drew to a close, the movement in favour of Disraeli increased. The newspapers began to discuss the situation; and on December 16, in an article which attracted much notice, the *Morning Chronicle*, the organ of the Peelites, treated his leadership as a practical certainty. It compared him to the first Napoleon at the time when he assumed the Imperial crown. 'We cannot help regarding the election of Mr. Disraeli to the Leadership of the Protectionists in the House of Commons as an analogical example of what conscious merit and inborn superiority, backed by strong volition and utter insensibility to the ordinary weaknesses of a sensitive or shrinking nature, may effect.' Disraeli was as indispensable, it held, to the Protectionists as Napoleon to the French. He was their only man of genius. But though public opinion pointed to Disraeli as inevitable, and there was a growing feeling in his favour in the party, Stanley was still unconvinced. He recognised Disraeli's genius, but did not believe that he would be able to unite the Protectionists, and was probably still disinclined to enter into those close personal relations with him which are eminently desirable, if not always attained, between the leaders of the same party in the two Houses. His first idea was to recur to Granby; but Granby was as reluctant now to put himself forward as he had been in the winter before. He agreed with Stanley about Disraeli, but added: 'Remembering how great his talents are, the intimate friendship that existed between him and George Bentinck, the immense service he has rendered to our party and cause, do you not think it would be a proper and deserving compliment to pay him if you were to write to him explaining the difficulties of our position, placing confidence in the rectitude of his judgment, good sense, and patriotism, and asking him to unite with you in inducing and inviting Herries to accept the office?' Newdegate confirmed Stanley's view that Disraeli was not trusted by the party. 'I have been warned repeatedly not to trust Disraeli, while I see nothing in his public conduct to justify the want of confidence so many seem to feel. This I conclude is attributable to some circumstances of his earlier life, with which I am not familiar, but have little doubt you are. I can scarcely help believing there must be some foundation for so general an opinion as I have alluded to, and it makes me very uneasy.' Supported by this opinion from the Whip, Stanley took Granby's advice, and immediately opened his long political correspondence with Disraeli by the following letter:

From Lord Stanley.

Confidential. KNOWSLEY NEAR PRESCOT, *Dec.* 21, 1848.

MY DEAR SIR, — I am sure that no apology will be necessary either for troubling you with a letter, within little more than a month of the reassembling of Parliament, on the state and prospects of the party with which we are both connected, or for the entire frankness with which I intend to write.

For I conceive that our position as a party is a critical one, and that upon our continued cohesion much of the future welfare of the country depends. Now all the reflection I have given to the subject, and the experience of the last Session, convince me that that cohesion is not to be hoped for, unless there be in the House of Commons a recognised Leader, whose decision as to the course to be taken on any sudden emergency will be taken as final by the body of the party, who should enjoy their confidence, and through whom, by means of continual private intercourse, I may have the opportunity of letting my opinions be known. Such a Leader, and in many respects admirably qualified, we had for a considerable time in poor George Bentinck. With talents of the highest order, dauntless resolution, and indefatigable perseverance, he commanded the entire confidence of a large portion, and the respect of the whole of our friends; and though I did not agree with him in all his views, his frank and generous spirit, and our long personal friendship, enabled me in general to carry on business with him to our mutual satisfaction.

I need not now advert to the circumstances under which he felt it to be his duty to withdraw from the Leadership in the House of Commons. Even after that unfortunate division among us, his co-operation was as readily given on all questions connected with the great principle of our union, as if he had still retained his ostensible post; and his loss, as an ally, I consider as quite irreparable. You are aware that on his retirement it was wished by many that Lord Granby should allow himself to be put forward; but that his invincible diffidence in his own powers prevented him from accepting a post which it was the general desire that he should occupy. I cannot doubt but that the same feeling still actuates him; and indeed his difficulties would now be much greater than they would have been last year, because he could then have always relied on George Bentinck's aid, which would have been given to *him* with peculiar cordiality. The result of his refusal was to leave the Leadership in abeyance; but the inconvenience of that state of things was felt to be so great that I am bound to make an effort to put an end to it if possible. In making this effort, I must write to you with an absence of reserve which nothing short of the critical state of our affairs would justify: and must appeal to your public feeling to afford me assistance which is all but indispensable to success.

I am doing you bare justice when I say that as a debater there is no one of our party who can pretend to compete with you; and the powers of your mind, your large general information, and the ability you possess to make yourself both heard and felt, must at all times give you a commanding position in the House of Commons, and a preponderating influence in the party to which you are attached. But, believing also, as I do, that, from whatever cause, your formal establishment in the post of Leader would not meet with a general and cheerful approval on the part of those with whom you are acting, I pay you the much higher compliment of thinking that you have both the clearness of perception to be aware of the truth of what I have just said, and the manliness of character so far to acquiesce in the feeling of the party, as to be willing to waive a claim which your talents might authorise you to put forward, and, satisfied with the real eminence of your position, to give a generous support to a Leader of abilities inferior to your own, who might command a more general feeling in his favour.

The difficulty of finding such a Leader is hardly less obvious than the necessity of doing so, if possible; and after the most anxious consideration on my part, I can think of no one open to so little objection, provided he agrees with the bulk of the party on one question to which I will advert by-and-bye, as Herries. His age, his long experience, especially in financial and commercial matters, his knowledge of the House of Commons, and his habits of business, though without any great powers of debate, give him, on the whole, a claim which may be admitted without jealousy by some who would not willingly consent to act under a younger and less experienced man. I propose therefore to communicate confidentially with Herries without loss of time; but I have thought it due to you to lay open to you both what I am doing, and my motives, even before I name the subject to himself; and should you receive my communication (which I need hardly say is made in the strictest confidence) in the spirit in which alone I make it, of anxiety for the promotion of great public interests, I think you have an opportunity of greatly serving the party, and also of establishing a strong personal claim on them for the future, if, consistently with what you feel due to yourself, you can set to others the example of promising him, should he become the Leader, a support of which he will stand greatly in need, and the assurance of which may materially affect his decision. Should you write to him on the subject, the secrecy which I would beg you to observe to all others on the subject of this letter need not apply to him, unless you prefer writing as from yourself, without reference to anything you may have heard from me. And now let me once more ask your indulgence for the freedom with which I have written; a freedom which I would not have used had I not given you credit for being able to appreciate my motives; and to postpone all personal feelings to the consideration of the public advantage.

I have been suffering much lately, and am hardly recovered from a very severe and lengthened attack of gout; but I hope to be fit for my work at the opening of the Session, and to be in Town a few days previous. I apprehend that the main subject of contest on principle will be the Navigation Laws, on which I know we are cordially agreed, and on which I hope that you will take an active part in a vigorous resistance to the proposed change.

Ireland will also, of course, occupy a large portion of time and talk; but after the indication of feeling in the country, I doubt much whether Government will venture to propose a measure for the endowment of the R.C. clergy. On this, the subject to which I before alluded, I think it right to say, that I do not share in the objections of principle entertained by a large body of our friends, who see *moral guilt* in the endowment; but as a measure of policy I am prepared to oppose it, as revolting the feelings of a great majority of the English and Scotch people, and the best friends of English connection in Ireland, and as incurring a very heavy expense, with a very faint prospect of effecting the *real* object, that of diminishing the community of feeling between the R.C. Priest and his flock, and of bribing him to allegiance, and to exercise in favour of the constituted authorities the influence which may remain to him. I hope, though I do not feel quite assured, that your opinions coincide with mine on this point; but I have thought it my duty, in such a communication as this, to be quite explicit on a subject which *may* be brought forward, and which, if it is, will supersede every other in the public mind.

I will not add to the unreasonable length of this letter by saying anything on foreign politics; on which, however, I shall be glad to have some conversation with you when we meet, and where I think the policy of the Government, and their management, are open to very serious animadversion, especially on the Italian and Sicilian questions. — Believe me, my dear Sir, sincerely yours, STANLEY.

Greville calls this, not unfairly, a 'flummery' letter.[1] All that Stanley wrote about the disorganisation of the party in the Commons, and the necessity of having a recognised leader, was indisputable; but he could hardly expect his correspondent to see why in those circumstances one whom he described as an incomparable debater, with a commanding position in the House and a preponderating influence in the party, should be ruled out. The doubt expressed as to the 'general and cheerful approval' of such an appointment must have appeared but a poor reason to one who knew that he had at any rate a strong body of friends at his back. The 'Prime Minister' of Bentinck was not disposed to be the 'Prime Minister' of Herries, or of any other mediocrity on whom Stanley might wish to bestow a strictly limited and constitutional sovereignty over the Country party. If the party for whom he had done so much was not disposed to give him the post to which he alone in the ranks was equal, he would prefer to take up an independent position.

To Lord Stanley.

ERLESTOKE,[2] WESTBURY, *Dec.* 26, 1848.

MY DEAR LORD, — Your letter of the 21st reached me only this morning — having been sent into Bucks, and, then, forwarded here, where we are passing Christmas.

[1] The text of the letter has never before been published, but Disraeli may have shown it to Greville, or to Greville's friend, Delane, the editor of *The Times*.

[2] The Disraelis were spending Christmas with the Hobhouses; and Disraeli there told Hobhouse that 'the summit of Heaven's bliss was to be possessed of £300 a year, and live a retired life amongst books.'

I am gratified by the frank manner in which you have communicated with me, and I will reply to you with as little reserve.

The office of leader of the Conservative party in the H. of C., at the present day, is to uphold the aristocratic settlement of this country. That is the only question at stake, however manifold may be the forms which it assumes in public discussion, and however various the knowledge and the labor which it requires. It is an office which, in my opinion, would require the devotion, perhaps the sacrifice, of a life; and, however his great qualities for its fulfilment, would not be wisely undertaken by any man, who did not possess, not only the confidence, but even the warm personal regard of those with whom he acted in political connection. If you had been in the House of Commons you could have fulfilled this office, and dark and difficult as I deem our future, I would have acted cordially under your banner, because I am sure it would have led always to honor, if not to triumph. But unhappily you have quitted us. Honor, and personal feelings, stronger than any public consideration, attached me to George Bentinck in his able, tho' hopeless, career, and as long as his course had continued, I would never have quitted him. But I am now free from all personal ties; and I am no longer disposed to sacrifice interesting pursuits, health, and a happy hearth, for a political career, which can bring one little fame, and, even if successful in a vulgar sense, would bear me a reward which I now little appreciate.

These are personal considerations. There are, as you well remind me, others, and far superior ones, which should influence all men in a responsible position. I am not insensible, especially in this age, to the principle of duty — but in the present distracted state of parties, it is my opinion, however erroneous, that I could do more to uphold the cause to which I am attached, that I should have better opportunities of reviving the spirit, and raising the general tone of feeling among our friends throughout the country, by acting alone and unshackled, than if I fell into the party discipline, which you intimate.

I heard, with great regret, from Lord Hardwicke, of your sufferings, and trust that, when I have the pleasure of seeing you in town, I shall find you quite yourself. I feel persuaded that yours is an instance in which the water cure would prove completely effective. I have just seen a case, in the person of the Rector of my own parish, a man about your Lordship's time of life, and a still greater sufferer, which prevents me having any further scepticism on this subject. In advanced years I believe the remedy is perilous, as it proved to poor Sir Francis Burdett.

It gave me great pleasure to observe your son's return,[1] as I have great confidence in his abilities. — Pray believe me, dear Lord Stanley, yours sincerely, B. DISRAELI.

In the mood of temporary disgust and despondency produced by Stanley's letter, Disraeli wrote to a correspondent in Glasgow, on December 29, that he 'would not take the trouble of riding up to Town to be installed leader of any party whatever' and that 'the time for such factitious supremacies has gone past.'

Stanley does not seem in the least to have been able to realise Disraeli's feelings and legitimate aspirations, or to have recognised the impossibility of a Granby, a Herries, or a Bankes, pretending to lead the party, with Disraeli as a candid friend on the leader's flank. Before he had received an answer from either Disraeli or Herries, he wrote to his Whip, Newdegate, with some confidence about Herries's leadership: 'I hope to arrange this before Parliament meets, and that Disraeli will have the good sense to acquiesce in, and aid, the arrangement. I have never seen, of late years, any reason to distrust him, and I think he will run straight; but he would not be acceptable as Leader.' This letter was written on Christmas Day. The next morning Stanley must have received Herries's reply, dated December 24, declining the leadership primarily on the ground of insufficient health — he was now sixty-eight; and a day or two later came that 'cold but civil answer,' in Greville's words, of Disraeli's which we have already given. Herries suggested the appointment of a confidential Committee as a possible way out of the difficulty. Stanley's next letter to Disraeli shows a considerable advance from his original position:

From Lord Stanley.

Confidential. KNOWSLEY, *Jan.* 6, 1849.

MY DEAR SIR,—I need hardly tell you that I received your letter of the 26th ult. with deep regret, though with gratitude

[1] To Parliament for King's Lynn.

for the feelings which you express towards me personally. I cannot be surprised at any man, in these days, being desirous of escaping from the thankless labours of political life; and least of all can I wonder at it in one who, like yourself, possesses in literary pursuits ample means of enjoyment for himself and of usefulness for others. Without so good an excuse to myself, I should desire nothing more than to be able to withdraw altogether from a mode of life which requires a constant sacrifice of comfort, independence, and health, and holds out no personal inducements to compensate for the sacrifices it entails.

But I feel that I — and excuse me if I add that you — cannot so withdraw. He who has once put his hand to the Parliamentary plough cannot draw back. I do not speak, of course, of the great majority of members of both Houses, who act as Parliamentary units, giving numerical strength, and nothing else, to the party to which they attach themselves, but of those whom talent, or station, or accident has placed in the foreground and enabled them to exercise, whether they will or no, an influence over numbers of their brother members. For them there is no retreat—none at least so long as they retain their seats; and in times like the present, their abandonment of them would be justly regarded as a dereliction of public duty.

This, supposing him to be sincere in his professions, is the difficulty, or rather the impossibility, of Peel's position at the present moment. He *must* be *a* Leader in spite of himself; and the course which he took in 1845 alone prevents him from being *the* Leader. Hence the disruption, which we have all seen and regretted, of the great Conservative party; and what I now anticipate with anxiety, and am desirous, if possible, to avoid, is a similar disruption, into minute sections, of that portion of the party who, as Protectionists, adhered to their original principles. The adoption, by you, of the line which you lay down, would, in my judgment, go far to produce this disastrous result. You cannot divest yourself of the influence which your abilities and your debating powers give you: and you cannot place yourself in a position of complete independence, or rather isolation. Some will follow you, others will attach themselves more particularly to other Leaders: and thus the Opposition will be broken into a number of small guerrilla parties, without the means of organising or conducting any combined operations.

Nothing, as it seems to me, can prevent this state of things, but the selection, by the party at large, of some one Leader, and a cordial support given to him by the other 'notables' of the party. I have, on this subject, no personal objects, and no personal predilections to gratify. I have nothing at heart but the support of the views which I entertain on public affairs and, as a means to that end, the maintenance of union and *Party*. What I should most anxiously urge would be the selection of *a* Leader of the House of Commons; and whether that Leader be Lord Granby, Mr. Herries, or yourself, I should be ready to act with him with the same cordiality in concerting the means of furthering our common objects: but what I most of all deprecate is that which I fear that I foresee, the 'restoration of the Heptarchy' which is sure to follow any repeal of our union.

Pray reconsider the decision you seem inclined to take, or rather to have taken; and at all events let me have the pleasure of seeing you before Parliament meets on this all-important subject. I shall be in Town on Monday the 29th.—Believe me, my dear Sir, yours sincerely, STANLEY.

Meanwhile Disraeli's friends within the party redoubled their activity, with the object of creating so strong a current of feeling in his favour as to overbear Stanley's hesitation. Henry Bentinck was the prime mover in what the party Whips denounced as an intrigue.

From Lord Henry Bentinck.

LINCOLN, *Tuesday* [Jan. 2, 1849].—Trollope needed no instigating; he was keen enough. But Christopher is the man. Heart and soul in the cause—without a crotchet or a wrong feeling, and will work like a navvy. Two warm letters from Bankes and Billy Miles. The way it is proposed to play the game is this: to collect in Town a small conclave of 14 or 15 of the most influential *fighting* men—no mutes—on Saturday next. That a paper should be drawn up, signed by them all, and sent to Lord Stanley, pointing out the course they think well should be followed, and urging him to be himself the means of bringing over to their views all those of the party that might be likely to throw difficulties in the way.

We fancy Stanley will be the most effective tool to make use of for the awkward crotchety fellows, and when he sees a strong body in earnest our way, he will feel the necessity of coming over and exerting himself heartily. Christopher will be in Town on Friday, and he is anxious that you should be within call on Saturday next. Turn the following matter over in your mind: we think it would be a good move that in answer to a letter which C. should write to you that he should have one from you in some such form as this—That you would not accept the post unless you were assured of the cordial support, etc., and a clear understanding come to on the following points: first, that on the questions concerning the Endowment of the Catholic Clergy and the Education Questions you should have the assistance of Mr. Henley and Mr. [name illegible] to guide you in the course that would best accord with the feelings of the entire party; and on the Jew Question, that while you would not conceive it to be proper in any way to make use of the power the party would put into your hands, to further a measure obnoxious to them, you must claim for yourself the right of individually following the same course you had followed before, and to have an unfettered discretion to take the line that you would deem fair to your own Church[1] and just to the party.

We fancy that something of the sort that could be shown about would bring over great numbers — also old Henley, whom we can't do without, and we fear might be crotchety. . . .

Disraeli himself, however much he might affect a detached and indifferent attitude on occasion, was as resolved as any of his friends that he should be established in a post which there was none other competent to fill. Once again, as in the spring of 1845, when he had begun the open attack on Peel,[2] the opportunity had come; and he determined to spare no effort to turn it to account. 'Never lose an occasion,' he had just written in *Tancred*. 'Opportunity is more powerful even than conquerors and prophets.' His wife remained at Hughenden during that critical month of January, 1849, but he was in town most of the time, and wrote to her constantly about the progress of the movement. His letters reveal the extraordinary union there was in his character of emotion and resolution. Along with the firm determination to carry his point there is an almost boyish eagerness and delight in the details of the political game.

To Mrs. Disraeli.

Jan. 5, 1849.—I long to read to you Lord H. B.'s letter, of which I have made out almost every word. It is a most remarkable one. The Duke of Portland has been dangerously

[1] Lord Henry Bentinck writes as if he thought that Disraeli was a Jew in religion.

[2] See Vol. II., pp. 304, 305.

ill, and though out of immediate danger, it is evident that his son thinks he is dying. Lord H. will not hear of Stanley's project. He is going to get the Duke of Newcastle to write to Stanley, and Trollope is to ride over to Granby for the same object. He impresses on me the importance of getting Mandeville to do the same. M. will be in town on Sunday, and therefore I wish you could send me by post Stanley's letter and copy of my answer, that I may show them, and the others, to Mandeville before he writes.

Saturday [*Jan.* 6, 1849]. — Granby came up to town last night from Belvoir about the leadership — Stanley in confidence having sent him our two letters, and entreating him to interfere, etc., etc.

He came into the Coventry about ½ of an hour after me, and saw the very man he wanted. We dined together. Fortunately I had Henry Bentinck's letter, etc., etc., in my pocket. All was read and digested. Details when we meet. Nothing could be more happy than this meeting. Providence sent me up to London and prevented my going to B[righton] yesterday.

The Leader question excites much interest. Except the Gold Mines nothing else is talked of, and every day, every hour, it of course becomes more interesting: like the election of the President.[1]

Disraeli ran down to Brighton for a few hours to pay a visit to Metternich.

To Mrs. Disraeli.

Sunday night [*Jan.* 7, 1849]. — I got to Brighton at ½ past two and caught M[etternich] before he went out. He said directly he hoped I had come to stay a few days, but when I replied only a few hours, that business demanded my presence in London, and that it was only to see him that I had come down, he replied: 'Well, then, I know by your letter[2] what you want. I am no longer a Minister; I am Professor Metternich'; and he broke into a gallop immediately. I never heard such divine talk: he gave me the most masterly exposition of the present state of European affairs, and said a greater number of wise and witty things than I ever recollected hearing from him on the same day. He was indeed quite brilliant, and his eyes sometimes laughed with sunny sympathy with his shining thoughts. He was looking very well indeed. I saw the Princess, who, whether from my

[1] Louis Napoleon was elected President of the French Republic on Dec. 10, 1848.

[2] See below, ch. 7.

not congratulating them before on the important events that had occurred in their favor, or at my knocking up her morning excursion, or mere caprice, was rather short, I thought: but that did not signify, as I was most anxious to get away and shrunk from hospitalities.

After the state of Europe, strange to say, the subject which most interests M. at this moment is the 'Leadership.' He mentioned to me the famous article in the *Morning Chronicle*[1] on it, and then asked many questions, and gave his view of what should be my course, if I undertook it. I endeavoured to make him understand the complicated question. But he requested me to state the case precisely in a confidential despatch, with copies of all the correspondence, and he would draw up his views on the whole case. It was impossible to refuse such a man such a request; to say nothing of the interest and importance of having such a document as his decision in our archives: but the consequence is, that I have almost the whole of this morning been employed in copying the letters of Lord S[tanley] and Lord H. B.: a tolerably arduous task: besides an interview with Granby of two hours. Mandeville has not arrived, though hourly expected from Scotland. It is of the utmost importance that a certain letter to Lord S. should be written by him. However he may be here to-night.

I have not drawn up the statement for M[etternich], which I hope to do to-morrow morning, but I really have not had a moment of relaxation since we parted. . . .

Monday [*Jan.* 8, 1849]. — . . . Phillips has just gone, having set immense machinery to work. . . . Affairs get more complicated and exciting every moment. This morning brings *another letter from Stanley!*[2] He seems at my feet, but the difficulties are immense. Yet they may be surmounted. An idea has just crossed me on which I shall act. It is to make Delane my confidant and ask his advice. I think some articles in *The Times*, done with discreet thunder, might do the business.

Tuesday [*Jan.* 9, 1849]. — I am harassed to death. Herries has just come up! Just arrived. There is to be a Congress at Burleigh next week, where Granby is going, and where I suppose they must settle something. I have been with Delane all this morning.[3] Nothing can be more difficult than my position, and it requires the greatest tact and discretion to manage it. I hope to get back to-morrow, though it will be late, as I have promised to see Herries at ½ past two. I shall decide on nothing: merely main-

[1] See above, p. 120. [2] See above, pp. 126–8.

[3] Delane must have discountenanced the idea of articles in *The Times*, as none appeared in this month.

taining the position which I took in my reply to Sir John Trollope, and which I have *impressed* on Granby, and which I trust he now fully understands. *Deciding* on nothing, I shall have the benefit of your advice, which I have several times wanted; but which will be much more important during the next three weeks than at this moment. . . . I am too tired, too hurried, and too anxious to be able to write anything worth reading, or to anyone but you. I have not been able to compose my despatch to Prince M.

Half-past six. — Lord Henry Bentinck is going to give up hunting, and give himself up to politics in order to support me!

[*Jan.* 10, 1849.] . . . Nothing, as it has turned out, could be more opportune than my visit, and, I hope, more discreet than my departure. For having set every wheel at work, it is just as well that I should be off the scene when everyone is on it.

Disraeli could not keep off the scene for long. He had time to draw up and send off his promised memorandum for Metternich, but after little more than a week's absence we find him back in town.

To Mrs. Disraeli.

Saturday [*Jan.* 20, 1849]. — A hurried line. Christopher has been here these two hours. I think there is no doubt about the result, though there are delicacies and difficulties. I must keep in the background, but always ready to counsel and aid Christopher, who is one of the most generous and hearty of men. Lord Henry is in town, but I have not yet seen him.

Sir John Yarde Buller has come up about it, and is for me. This is a great adhesion.

I can give you no idea of Bankes' letter. I have been very much mistaken about him. It is the highest praise and the most unqualified adhesion you can imagine.

I am a little too excited at this moment, from travel and talk, to write more.

They say that Peel will never get over my appointment.

GROSVENOR GATE, *Jan.* 22, 1849.

DEAR LADY OF HUGHENDEN, — What would I not give to be with you in these almost spring mornings, surrounded by birds, flowers, and running waters! 1000 thanks for your letter, the violets, and the enclosures. It was, however, lucky that I came, as I don't think H. B. would have ever pardoned my want of interest and energy, had I been quiet.

What do you think he did? Yesterday he went to Goodwood and returned the same day, and made the Duke write a strong letter to S[tanley]!

I must write in initials, and even that is dangerous. H[erries] has entirely declined. Lord Exeter wants Lord G[ranby] — who of course has declined. Christopher goes down to-night to Burleigh. The personage[1] respecting whom the letter was *about* calls at G[rosvenor] G[ate] to-morrow at two o'clock. This is most important.

Jan. 23, 1849. — The interview with the gentleman[1] to-day was *most cordial and satisfactory.* In short, as he himself exclaimed, where are the opponents? He thinks, however, that the false position of Lord S., in consequence of his first letter, is so great and unmanageable, that he counselled my setting up for myself, *without Lord S.* Time will settle all this.

Jan. 24, 1849. — I think there cannot be a shadow of doubt of all happening as we desire; and with greater éclat from Lord S.'s letter, and my continuing to hold back.

Jan. 25, 1849. — You remember the Prince of Lucca? He is now Prince of Parma. He called at Gros. Gate a few days back, and yesterday came a royal invitation from an aide-de-camp to *prier* me to dine with him and her Royal Highness, sister of the Duke of Bordeaux, but I have refused, as I can't work and stand the excitement of Society too, and certainly shall not be tempted anywhere without you.

Baroness Brunnow is at home on the 30th, and has sent us an invitation. I don't particularly want to go, but very much wish you should, and maintain your position in Society, and feel the public sentiment on many affairs.

A most interesting and *affectionate* despatch from Prince M. this morning, returning the documents.

Metternich's despatch was wordy and involved, and he declined to give Disraeli any definite advice on the personal question. He was anxious not to mix himself up too much in English party politics; Princess Mélanie, his wife, in her Journal, complains that he had to defend himself against 'les obsessions du parti conservateur' in England.[2] But he very shrewdly pointed out the desirability of merging the name Protectionist in the wider title Conservative — a change of nomenclature which was indeed, as we have seen, already in progress. The views of the greatest Conservative statesman in Europe on this

[1] It is not clear who this was — possibly Lyndhurst.

[2] *Metternich Memoirs*, Part III.

crisis in the Conservative party in England have a permanent interest for the student of politics, and the letter will be found in full in Appendix B. There is a peculiar irony in contemplating the mind of the most determined enemy of Parliamentary government applying itself to solving a difficulty in the working of Parliamentary institutions.

To Lord John Manners.

GROSVENOR GATE, *Jan.* 29, 1849.

MY DEAREST J. M.,—1000 thanks for your welcome letter![1] I have been silent, lest, at this moment, you might misconceive my purpose in writing. I have therefore studiously avoided to communicate with everyone, save in reply to their letters. I had the good fortune of seeing Granby in town casually, as I was passing thro' to Brighton, to pay a little visit to Metternich. I make no doubt that Granby made you acquainted with all that passed between us, as in our most confidential communications there is always a reservation in your favor—on both sides.

With respect to the great question, nothing will induce me to attempt the task unless it is with the general wish and consent of the whole party: for nothing but that unanimous feeling could sustain me in the terrible struggle which, as you well know, I have long seen looming in the distance between the aristocratic and democratic principles. Sincerely I say, I wish the duty had fallen to the lot of another: but if it falls to me, I will attempt to fulfil it to the death.

I have heard nothing from Stanley since the 6th inst., when he expressed an anxious wish to see me the moment he arrived in town. I replied—in order to throw the fixing the appointment on him. I believe he has arrived. I have kept in the country as quiet as possible, and since I have been in town, have avoided the Carlton: but I have received a great many letters and communications. I have received the adhesion, unqualified and complete, of every shade of Church Party. Inglis did me the honor of paying me a visit a few days back: nothing could be more cordial and satisfactory. Yesterday I was informed that on Saturday there was a meeting at the National Club, Colquhoun, whom I have never seen, at the head, and that it was unanimously resolved, in that mysterious conclave, that I was the man, and that if I accepted the office, I had a right to expect an unreserved confidence, which after due explanations, respecting which

[1] Expressing earnest hope for Disraeli's unanimous election as leader.

they anticipated no difficulty, they were prepared to give me! I am told Inglis was present and Walpole. Will you believe it, that Plumptre[1] is going to support me?

In the meantime, I have literally not entered into the intrigue, which was not only justifiable, but which was almost my duty to myself and the party generally; so convinced am I, that the result you wish will be disappointing, unless it be almost unanimous. I have not written to Stafford, for the same reason I have written to no one. I am not a candidate for the Leadership, tho' I am prepared to undertake the task at the unequivocal desire of the party. . . .

Ah! my dear John, if that happens which you wish, how I shall miss you—my best and earliest political friend. You would be invaluable to me.—Ever yours, D.

The Whips were much perturbed by the activity of Disraeli's friends.

William Beresford to Lord Stanley.

2, Eaton Square, *Friday night* [*? Jan.* 5 *or* 12, 1849].—. . . Yesterday and to-day for the first time for above a month I have seen a few persons, and I have discovered that there has been a deep intrigue carrying on in the Party to force Disraeli on us as our Leader. . . . I have never flinched from admitting since last summer that Disraeli has shown an amount of talent that places him above *all* in the House, and if the Party choose to be led by him and agree to that generally, I do not say unanimously, I shall not be found as one creating disunion. But I must say that I am not prepared to yield to an intrigue and to assist in an arrangement which I verily believe will bring great obloquy upon a Party, which I have joined from principle, and which has its weight from character. . . .

Jan. 22.—. . . I have discovered that the plan that they at present intend to adopt is not to propose D. as Leader in a general meeting of the Party, but being themselves organised to go down to the House, and for him thus backed to virtually undertake to be Leader, not by election but *de facto*. . . .

The other Whip, Newdegate—according to some notes written by Corry in 1876, after conversation with Disraeli—told Stanley during this winter that, if Disraeli became leader, he should whip to empty

[1] M.P. for East Kent.

benches, 'and, as things turned out, resigned his post and, as we now see, his prospects, the victim of jealousy and self-conceit, though rich, capable, and a gentleman. Beresford, not very friendly before, bowed to the rising star.'

There is no reason to impute any discreditable motives to the Whips, any more than to their Chief, Stanley, for their hesitation about Disraeli and their reluctance to see him appointed leader. Whips, though frequently very bad judges of policy owing to the shortness of their views, are usually good judges of men. In this case they spoke undoubtedly for a considerable body of feeling in their party, rather perhaps in the country, where Disraeli was less known, than in the House, where his powers extorted admiration. It was admitted that his public conduct gave him great claims to confidence, that he had been a most zealous and faithful lieutenant to Bentinck, and that without him Peel's betrayal of his party could not have been adequately punished. But the bad character, derived from earlier exploits, and especially from malignant distortions and misrepresentations of them, still clung to him in many minds. Stanley wrote significantly that he had 'never seen, *of late years*, any reason to distrust him'; but he was evidently of opinion that confidence is a plant of slow growth. Greville could write of him so recently as February 6, 1847, as having 'a character so disreputable that he cannot be trusted.' Disraeli was a Jew by birth, had been much of a dandy and something of a Bohemian, had been flighty and incomprehensible in his early political efforts, was a literary man, and had hardly yet been converted into a country gentleman by the very recent purchase of Hughenden; his look and manner were mysterious and foreign. These facts gave some colour, it was felt, to the constant calumnies of certain newspapers, which represented him as an unprincipled adventurer, animated by a merely selfish ambition; especially as there was no adequate journalistic reply. Even the *Morning Herald*, the Protectionist organ, had until recently joined in depreciating him; and the *Standard*, another Conservative newspaper, did not find its prejudices against him removed until his speech on the Address in 1849. *The Times*, indeed, though a supporter of Free Trade, was wont to treat Disraeli and his opinions with respect; but what was at that date the most authoritative political and literary oracle of Conservatism, the *Quarterly Review*, absolutely ignored his existence. Neither Murray nor Croker had forgotten; but the respectabilities of the party could hardly be expected to understand that this ominous silence was due largely to personal reasons, or to place themselves readily under the command of one whom their famous *Review* could not bring itself even to mention.

Then the less progressive and more prejudiced of the party, who formed a very considerable contingent, were well aware that Disraeli did not share their prejudices, and had in every respect an open mind. *Coningsby* and *Sybil* had shown them that, while he maintained that the government of the country should rest with the gentlemen of England, he had no sympathy with an Eldonian policy of exclusion and restriction. His attitude about Protection had always been that it was a matter of expediency and not of principle, though he held strongly to the view that moderate Protection was expedient for England and the Empire. He was a steady supporter, but also a candid critic, of the Church; and his religious views, as set forth in *Tancred*, his persistent support of the removal of Jewish disabilities, and his readiness to accord generous treatment to the Roman Catholics, were not calculated to recommend him to the high-fliers. They felt dimly about his elevation to the leadership what the exiled Guizot said to him: 'I think your being the leader of the Tory party is the greatest triumph that Liberalism has ever achieved.' Disraeli made no secret of his conviction — a conviction shared by Peel, at least after 1832, and in a lesser degree by Stanley, who had served his political apprenticeship among the Whigs — that a mere policy of negation was impossible for a Conservative party in the nineteenth century; that, to secure that predominance of aristocracy which he desired in the government, an alliance in some form with democracy was indispensable. It would be too much to affirm that he had thought out a definite programme of Tory Democracy; but the phrase accurately describes the spirit in which he conceived that the administration of the country should be carried on.

We must therefore recognise that those who hesitated to assist in Disraeli's elevation had plausible grounds for their distrust. Their difficulty was that there was no alternative; and two-thirds of the party, it was claimed by Disraeli, gave in their formal adhesion to him. All that could be done to propitiate the reluctant was to gloze over what was really taking place; to provide an arrangement which should give Disraeli's genius full play and the party the benefit of his initiative, while apparently still keeping the actual leadership an open question. Accordingly, in a personal interview on the day before the session began, Stanley laid before Disraeli the proposal which Herries had suggested, that a confidential Committee, of which Disraeli would be the leading spirit, should be appointed to manage the party affairs in the Commons.

To Mrs Disraeli.

Most confidential. Jan. 31, 1849. — A proposition that the party should be led by myself, Granby, and Herries *with equal power;* that I should, or rather must, be the real leader; that this would remove all jealousies for the moment; and that when Granby was called to the Upper House, soon to be anticipated, I should, of course, become the only leader, and every jealousy and distrust would, by that time, have been removed.

Very friendly and cordial.

Says it is all over with the party if I retire.

Refused: but at his request left it open, as he has not yet even consulted Granby.

Very hurried. All details when we meet.

From Lord Stanley.

St. James's Square, *Feb.* 1, 1849.

My dear Sir,—I very much wish you could do me the favour of calling here, as you cannot attend the meeting, about one o'clock, or ½ past. Lord Brougham is to be with me at 2, and I do not know how long he may stay. There was a strong feeling among the Peers who dined with me yesterday that an amendment should be moved on the Speech, which is most *audacious;* but if anything of the kind is to be done in the Commons, we should come to an understanding about it before you speak.—I am, dear Sir, yours faithfully, Stanley.

P.S.—If it would suit you better, I would call on you, if I have a moment to spare after Lord B. leaves me—but I have to consider what course I am to take in moving an amendment, if moved, and shall be much hurried for time.

The meeting at Stanley's house approved the suggested Committee of Herries, Granby, and Disraeli; but Disraeli, who was not present, seems never to have definitely withdrawn his refusal. Phillips, writing to him on the following day, says: 'I am pleased to find that you resist the arrangement'; and the same correspondent, more than three years later, recalls the proposal 'to place the leader of the Conservative party like a sandwich between two pieces of bread (very *stale* bread—Herries and Granby), in order that he might be made fit for squeamish throats to swallow. Sympathising with genius,' Phillips proceeds, 'I honestly recommended you to reject the proposed connection, and to vindicate your own true position. You acted upon the suggestion.' But, though Disraeli may not have formally accepted, he apparently tolerated the Committee, only setting himself to make his own pre-eminence clear. George Smythe took the news of the appointment of this Committee of Three to his old chief, Aberdeen, 'who said with one of his grim smiles, "Sieyès, Roger Ducos, and Napoleon Bonaparte."' There might be a doubt who was cast for the part of Sieyès, and who for that of Ducos; but it was certain that Disraeli would reduce the other members of the Committee to practical insignificance, just as Napoleon treated his two consular colleagues after the 18th Brumaire.

From Lord John Manners.

Belvoir Castle, *Feb.* 2, 1849.—. . . On you presses the intellectual and even physical burden of this 'terrible struggle,' as you most justly characterise it. I can compare your position to nothing save that of the Duke's in Spain, with a few good, hardy English troops to rely upon, an energetic and powerful enemy to oppose, and a confused mass of friendly partisans who, from pride, jealousy, superstition, or stupidity, were eternally thwarting his combinations or deserting him in the hour of need. Well—I wished and worked that the leadership might have been a Monarchy, but, as a Triumvirate has been established, I must salute the new power, and wish it well; possibly your power will be greater, for being nominally less; let us hope so. . . .

The inevitable happened. Disraeli, at Stanley's request, became the mouthpiece of the Opposition on the Address, moving the official amendment; and Malmesbury noted at once that the 'triumvirate' was an evident failure, Granby and Herries being in their colleague's way. It was feared that a deficiency in general civility to mediocrities and bores might keep him back; and a strong well-wisher, the Duke of Richmond, urged, through a friend, on February 11, the adoption of more conciliatory manners. He thought that Disraeli, with his commanding talents, must be declared leader shortly if he removed the personal prejudice entertained by some against him. But this drawback—after all so common in political leaders—proved no obstacle, and on February 22 Disraeli wrote triumphantly to his sister: 'After much struggling, I am fairly the leader.' Three weeks later the Prime Minister, in his official letter to the Queen, treated this leadership as an accomplished fact: 'Mr. Disraeli shows himself a much abler and less passionate leader than Lord George Bentinck.'[1] In March or April, Beresford, who had hitherto taken his orders directly from Stanley, recognised Disraeli as the responsible Chief in the Commons; and before the end of the session definite acknowledgment of the position was made by the Government and their supporters in the debate,[2] in July, on the vote of

[1] *Queen Victoria's Letters*, March 16, 1849. [2] See below, pp. 208–212.

want of confidence. The Chancellor of the Exchequer then spoke of him as 'the avowed leader of a powerful party'; Russell referred to the Protectionists as Disraeli's 'supporters'; Peel protested his anxiety to show 'no disrespect to the hon. member's ability or station'; and Roebuck offered him congratulations 'upon this his first appearance as the acknowledged Chief of the party.' Thus, without any regular nomination or election, but by a natural evolutionary process, the lead of the Opposition passed to the fittest.[1]

[1] This account of Disraeli's accession to the leadership, based mainly on contemporary correspondence, is borne out by a statement made by him to his secretary in 1876, that the session of 1849 was opened with the leadership, as it were, in commission; but that, as Granby and Herries were unequal to the task, a few weeks placed it in his own hands. Two somewhat different stories, however, in which the Committee of Three was entirely ignored, were told by him, with characteristic carelessness about detail in 1860, when the events referred to were more recent. Writing to Miles in that year, he said: 'When . . . we lost Lord George, Lord Derby, with whom I had very slight relations, wrote to me, and asked me to undertake, under certain conditions, the management of our party. I declined to do so, though duly honoring the offer. I saw personal difficulties ahead, and the engagement on my part would have involved the sacrifice of several thousands a year, which I would willingly, having no children, have relinquished, if I possessed the confidence of the gentlemen of England, but which, without that great reward, I was not willing to give up. After long and earnest representations, principally urged by Lord Derby, the present Duke of Rutland, yourself, and Lord Henry Bentinck, I undertook the office.' The other version was given in the same year to a biographer who asked Disraeli for the principal details of his career. To him he wrote: 'After the death of Lord George Bentinck, I was chosen leader of the Tory party in the House of Commons, at the commencement of the Session 1849. Sir John Buller and Mr. Miles were deputed formally to announce to me the choice; and I had the satisfaction, in due season, of recognizing their undeviating fidelity to myself, by making one a baronet, and elevating the other to the peerage.' Undoubtedly Sir John Buller was created Lord Churston in 1858, and Mr. Miles Sir William in 1859, on the recommendation of the Derby-Disraeli Government. But we happen to have a letter of January, 1852 (see below, p. 315), from Buller to Miles, definitely stating that Disraeli was *not* appointed in 1849 the one acknowledged leader of the party in the Commons. No doubt the Committee was practically superseded by Disraeli within a few weeks; but it maintained a shadowy existence till the winter of 1851–52, when Granby resigned his membership of it. See below, pp. 311–13.

CHAPTER VI

Family Affairs and Hughenden

1847–1863

In Disraeli's private life, no less than in his public career, the years during which he overthrew Peel and established his own leadership were critical and decisive. In those years his mother and his father, having happily lived long enough to witness his success, both died, within a few months of each other; and he acquired, and took possession of, the country home where it was his pride and delight to dwell for the rest of his days.

Mrs. D'Israeli's death took place rather suddenly at Bradenham on April 12, 1847, in her seventy-second year. She had been ill, but not sufficiently to call for her eldest son's presence, and he was in London attending to his Parliamentary duties when the end came. She had, as we have seen,[1] counted for little in his life. Indeed, one of her few recorded marks of interest in his career is chronicled by Sarah Disraeli in a letter to her sister-in-law in March of this same year: 'This wonderful speech,[2] too, that everyone praises. Mama at last confesses that she never before thought Dis was equal to Mr. Pitt. So you see it pleases all varieties of hearers or readers.'

'Sa bears up under all this sudden calamity,' wrote James Disraeli on the day of their mother's death, 'but we must break it to our father.' Isaac D'Israeli was now eighty-one, and for more than seven years had been blind.[3] When the blow fell, in 1839, he was, in spite of his

[1] See Vol. I., pp. 11, 12. [2] The speech on Cracow. See below, p. 171.
[3] See Vol. II., p. 73.

seventy-three years, confidently prosecuting his ambitious design of a comprehensive History of English Literature.[1]

Considering the bitterness of such a calamity to one whose powers were otherwise not in the least impaired (writes the son in his Memoir of his father), he bore on the whole his fate with magnanimity, even with cheerfulness. Unhappily, his previous habits of study and composition rendered the habit of dictation intolerable, even impossible, to him. But with the assistance of his daughter, whose intelligent solicitude he has commemorated in more than one grateful passage, he selected from his manuscripts three volumes, which he wished to have published under the becoming title of 'A Fragment of a History of English Literature,' but which were eventually given to the public under that of 'Amenities of Literature.'

He was also enabled during these last years of physical, though not of moral, gloom, to prepare a new edition of his work on the Life and Times of Charles the First, which had been for some time out of print. He contrived, though slowly, and with great labour, very carefully to revise, and improve, and enrich these volumes.

Such were the literary labours of Isaac D'Israeli's last years; outside of them, his principal delight was in watching the growing renown of his favourite son in literature and Parliament. In his very last year of all he busied himself to secure for him that permanent home in the country on which both father and son had set their hearts. Before, however, the purchase of Hughenden was completed and possession taken, Isaac D'Israeli had passed away. His illness was short, and ended on January 19, 1848, nine months after the death of his wife. 'For an author,' wrote his son, 'his end was an euthanasia, for on the day before he was seized by that fatal epidemic, of the danger of which to the last moment he was unconscious, he was apprised by his publishers that all his works were out of print, and that their republication could no longer be delayed.'

To Lord John Manners.

Carlton Library, *Jan.* 29, 1848.—I can't let a line, which I have written to Lord Granby, reach Belvoir, without also a word to you. Your letter poured balm into the bruised

[1] See Vol. I., p. 13.

spirits of our circle. My only consolation for the death of my father is his life. . . .

Lord G.[1] is at Wimpole. That kind Lord Hardwicke sent me the life of his great ancestor, and my father was in the second vol. revelling in the extraordinary interview or Cabinet scene, between Lord Hardwicke and George II., when the King would not speak — when my father was seized with his attack. It was his last book!

'He leaves you proud memories to cherish,' wrote Manners to Disraeli, 'and a great name to guard and augment in praise. Rarely does such an heir succeed to such an heritage: and I feel confident the future will add other crowns to those already bestowed on your house.' The son did cherish to the end of his life[2] the memory and reputation of a father for whom he entertained the highest respect and the warmest affection, whose literary work he keenly appreciated, and of whose influence upon his own character and intellect he was profoundly conscious.[3] Isaac D'Israeli was wont to say that 'the best monument to an author was a good edition of his works.' His son, in spite of the political anxieties and labours of 1848, and the worries necessarily involved in winding up his father's estate and in his own installation at Hughenden, set about providing this memorial with such promptitude that he was able to publish a new edition of the *Curiosities of Literature* in the last days of the year, with the Memoir, dated Christmas, 1848, from which we have quoted; and to follow it up in subsequent years with the *Charles I.* and the collected works. He could not have done this without the devoted aid of his sister, as he acknowledged in conversation a quarter of a century later.

Note by Montagu Corry.

I read to-day,[4] by Mr. D.'s advice, his father's chapter on Shakespeare in the *Amenities of Literature*, which he told me

[1] Bentinck.

[2] In May, 1866 (Lord Rowton records), Disraeli and the younger Stanley, who were at that time intimate friends, dined together at Bellamy's on the hundredth anniversary of Isaac D'Israeli's birthday, and drank to his memory in a bottle of champagne.

[3] See Vol. I., ch. 2.

[4] Easter Sunday, 1873.

he had read last week, for the first time (he was ashamed to confess), and considered to be the finest piece of literary criticism in the language. To my remark that he had himself edited the *Amenities*, he replied that in reality the work was done by Miss Disraeli, in whose talent and discretion he was able thoroughly to trust.

Of all his possessions, what Isaac D'Israeli naturally valued the most were his books. He often said to his son, 'The Octavos are my Infantry, my Cavalry are the Quartos, and the Folios are my Artillery.' There were 25,000 volumes in all, of which Disraeli transferred the best to Hughenden, but the larger part were sold. A note by his secretary in 1873 is interesting, when we remember the friendship of the father and the admiration of the son for Byron:—

D. much laments the loss of a much prized copy of the first edition of his father's first work, *Curiosities*, which had belonged to Byron. It was much marked and noted. On the title-page was written 'Byron Athenis relegit.' It had been sent to Mr. I. D. by Murray who secured it, it having been seized in the Albany under a writ of execution. Mr. I. D. valued it beyond measure. It was abstracted from the Library, after 1850, and Mr. D. has told me who he conceives appropriated the volume.

Disraeli was his father's executor and heir. The will directed that the personal property should be realised and divided into twelve parts, four to go to Sarah, two to Ralph, and two to James, the rest to be sunk in the residue, which was, with the real estate, to pass to Benjamin, the eldest son. To his 'beloved daughter-in-law, Mary Anne D'Israeli,' Isaac Disraeli left his collection of prints; to Sarah his portrait by Denning, 'as a mark of my sense of her devotion and my entire affection.' The value of property converted into money was returned as £7,553, and of property not so converted as £3,500. The net residue was declared by Disraeli as £10,803. The home at Bradenham was broken up. His sister went to live first at Hastings, and then at Twickenham. His brother Ralph he had already been able to start in life, having procured for him in 1841, through Lyndhurst, then Lord Chancellor, a clerkship in Chancery of £400 a year, which was eventually to lead to the post of Deputy Clerk of the Parliaments. His brother James, for whom his applications had so far been unsuccessful, settled down to farm at the Manor Farm, Bradenham, until Lord Derby gave him a small post in the Treasury in 1852, promoting him to a Commissionership of Inland Revenue in 1858.

Benjamin Disraeli and his wife moved in the autumn to Hughenden Manor. It was a place he had long known and admired—'the prettiest place in the county,' Lord Mahon, the historian, who took him there in 1829, called it. It lay only a few miles over a spur of the Chilterns from Bradenham, and was even nearer to High Wycombe. The Norrises, its recent owners, were friends, as well as neighbours, of the Disraelis; and the Disraeli boys, in their early Bradenham days, used frequently to go over there, to visit and flirt with the Norris girls. So Disraeli was very familiar with his future home. Hughenden, or Hitchenden, has had its modest relation to English history. The manor formed part of the possessions of Edith, Queen of Edward the Confessor, was granted by William the Conqueror to Odo, Bishop of Bayeux, and duly appears in Domesday Book. In the thirteenth century Richard de Montfort, youngest son of the creator of Parliament, settled in Hughenden parish, but not at the manor; and there is a Montfort Chapel in the church, with family monuments. More than a century earlier the manor had become part of the endowment of the Black Canons of Kenilworth Priory. At the Reformation it was granted by Henry VIII. to one of the Dormers of West Wycombe, from whom it passed to the famous Philip Dormer Stanhope, fourth Earl of Chesterfield, statesman and letter-writer. The Norris family acquired it later in the eighteenth century; and on the death of John Norris in October, 1845, it was offered for sale. Negotiations on Disraeli's behalf were carried on for some months, and on March 3,

1847, he agreed to purchase the estate for £27,700, excluding timber but including the advowson. The timber was ultimately valued at £7,250, and so the total purchase-money amounted to £34,950. How was Disraeli to find this sum?

We have already seen[1] that marriage, though it had provided him with a house in London and an income, had by no means extricated him from debt. At the time of his election for Shrewsbury in 1841 his liabilities were more than £20,000, and he was still in the clutch of usurers. A year later, in a document which testifies at once to his love for his wife, his confidence in his father, and his serious financial embarrassments, he stated that his wife had already satisfied claims upon him for £13,000, and that there was as much more which she was prepared to liquidate. This paper is endorsed in his handwriting: 'To be given to my father after my decease. Δ. August 13, 1842.'

To Isaac D'Israeli.

GROSVENOR GATE, *Aug.* 13, 1842.—The uncertainty of life impels me to draw up this note, which in the event of my death before that of my father, I request should be immediately given to him. At this date, after a life of constant struggle, I find myself commencing an era of worldly prosperity and mental satisfaction. I am entirely indebted for this position and this state of mind, doubly appreciated by one whose lot has hitherto been so much the reverse, to the unexampled devotion of my beloved wife, to whom I am indebted not only for all these worldly accidents which make life desirable, but for that peace of mind and consequent physical health which render it even delicious. Since our marriage, it should be distinctly known, which indeed in conversation I have already mentioned to my father, that she has defrayed either for those parliamentary contests so indispensable to my career, or for debts incurred before our union, no less a sum than thirteen thousand pounds sterling, and is prepared to grapple with claims and incumbrances to an amount not inferior. I place these facts on record, that in the event before referred to, her moral claim to my patrimony,

[1] Vol. II., p. 115.

as described in my father's will recently executed, may be clearly comprehended. But I have such confidence in the justice of my father, and in the affection and gratitude which every member of my family must feel towards her to whose ceaseless vigilance and unbroken devotion I am indebted for even existence, that I feel that, in expressing these wishes, I am only sanctioning their own affectionate anticipations.

I solemnly commend her to their unbroken love.—B. DISRAELI.

It is clear from this touching document that no further pecuniary aid could be looked for from Mrs. Disraeli's property. All that could be spared was already mortgaged, so to speak, to meet old debts, which there is too much reason to fear were still mounting up owing to Disraeli's extraordinary financial methods. One sensible step he had taken. In 1846, when the struggle against Peel was entirely engrossing his energies and attention, he placed his affairs in the hands of an old acquaintance and Buckinghamshire neighbour, a business man of the highest reputation for ability and integrity, the late Mr. (afterwards Sir) Philip Rose, of the firm of Baxter, Rose, and Norton, solicitors. For the rest of Disraeli's life Rose was by his side as his confidential agent in regard to his complicated private affairs, and also for many years as the political agent of the Conservative party; and was constituted by his will his executor and trustee along with Lord Rothschild. We may perhaps doubt, in view of the subsequent story, whether, at any rate in the first instance, Disraeli revealed to Rose the full extent of his indebtedness, any more than he had revealed it to his father or his wife. He probably had great difficulty in ascertaining it himself.

To Philip Rose.

GROSVENOR GATE, *April* 28, 1846.

MY DEAR SIR,—I want a confidential man of business in whose talents, zeal, and fidelity, I can repose a complete trust. The pressure of public life has become so extreme of late on me, that I can no longer attend to my private affairs, which require great consideration. I have, more than once, from my early knowledge of you, and my occasional observation of your career, thought, that I might find in you the adviser and agent I contemplated; but I fear, that the engrossment of your parliamentary business may perhaps render it difficult, or even impossible, for you, to undertake the transaction of my affairs. If, however, I be mistaken on this head, oblige me by sending me a line directed to me at the *Carlton Club;* and believe me, very faithfully yours, B. Disraeli.

Bradenham, Wycombe, *Oct.* 25, 1846.

My dear Rose,—I learnt with great pleasure, from your brother on Friday, that you had returned to England, much benefited by your travels.

Your services to me, performed with a zeal, that I never can forget, and the circumstance that, many years ago, I suffered much, and for a long time, from a disorder which I believe to be similar to your own, makes me much interested in your welfare.

My present condition of health and career may convince you, that there is more of distress, than danger, in these exhaustions of the nervous system. But if not duly checked, the trial they inflict is severe. Repose is the best medicine, and we should guard against the belief, that there is any cure for them but a gradual one. Repose, however, is a rare medicine, and impatient suffering is too apt to take refuge in quacks.—Yours very sincerely, B. Disraeli.

Carlton, *Dec.* 8, 1846.—. . . It would give me the greatest pleasure to find my title deeds[1] under your roof, but I should not like to take a decisive step without a line from you, that you saw your way.

Could you command £25,000 to complete the purchase, I supplying the balance, say £10,000; the Estate your security?

Carlton Club, *March* 24, 1847.—A thousand thanks for your indefatigable kindness! It is quite true that I have purchased Hughenden, or rather that my father has purchased it, but for me; and the conveyance is to be made to me.

Isaac D'Israeli thus stepped into the breach for the moment, but it was many months before his son found the money to complete the agreement. The period originally fixed for completion was June, 1847; it was put off till the following Christmas for a revaluation of the timber; and, after a somewhat heated correspondence regarding the delay, the purchase was actually

[1] Of Hughenden.

completed in September, 1848. In the end it was to the Bentinck family that Disraeli was mainly indebted for his country house, as it was with them that the movement originated to make him leader of the Conservative party. They were loyal friends to him, as he had ever been to Lord George. Lord Henry Bentinck told a friend in later years that his brother George used to complain that he had found for the Tory party a marvellous man as leader, whom they would not accept just because he was not a country gentleman. So the three brothers, Lord Titchfield, Lord George, and Lord Henry, determined to make him one; and the Bentinck family found the money to buy Hughenden. The correspondence suggests that Lord George, as might be expected, was the original mover in the scheme; his brothers carried out his wishes after his death.

From Lord George Bentinck.

Private. HARCOURT HOUSE, *Feb.* 6, 1847.—I have just got a note from C. Lloyd to tell me he has placed £5,000 to my account at Drummonds', so when you want it it is all ready; if you require the other £2,000, it will only be necessary for me to know a day or two at most in advance, and it will be forthcoming; Drummonds will let me have a couple of thousand for six months without a bond, and by that time I shall have my other £5,000. . . .

To Philip Rose.

BRADENHAM, *Oct.* 27, 1847.— . . . I am very sensible of your most friendly offer about Hughenden. Ld. George Bentinck wrote to me, a few days back, offering to be my security for £10,000, if that would help me to tide over. At any other time, he would have lent me the money, and indeed offered it to me last year, but I waived it until affairs were more mature with respect to the purchase.

He is a man now of ample independence, and will on the death of his father, nearly as old as mine, accede to some 20 or 30 thousand *per ann.*, to say nothing of his chance of being Duke of Portland, his brother, Titchfield, not being married, and very ailing.

If, by any chance, you knew any person, who might not be disinclined to serve Ld. George and myself in this matter, it might be prudent to avail oneself of the opening: the rest I could arrange without any ruinous sales of stock or any expensive arrangements.

HOUSE OF COMMONS, *Wednesday evening*, [? 30 *Aug.*, 1848].—I can't help thinking, on reflection, that the inconvenience of obtaining the temporary loan from your banker is so much less, than that of connecting Lord George's name with mine in a public office with respect to a pecuniary transaction, that it would be better at once to decide on your bankers, and get the business done on your return.

The public or the private nature of the act on the part of Ld. G. B. makes all the difference, and tho' I am sure that he would not hesitate in doing anything, even of a very serious and important nature, for my advantage, I think he is a man who would wish anything of that kind to be confined to your roof and personal clients. . . .

The actual payment in September, 1848, seems to have been temporarily met by borrowing £5,000 from the solicitors, obtaining an overdraft from the bankers of £14,000, and utilising, it may be presumed, the inheritance from Isaac D'Israeli. The final arrangements with the Bentincks were made subsequently, after Lord George's death, which followed hard upon the completion of the purchase. Lord Henry was the intermediary. 'What an admirable man,' wrote Disraeli to Manners, 'worthy of being our dear friend's brother!' 'With some eccentricities, one of the ablest men and finest characters I have ever met,' was his verdict in later life.

To Mrs. Disraeli.

[GROSVENOR GATE] *Oct.* 18, 1848.—Lord Henry has only just left me after four hours. Neither he, nor his brother, have yet spoken to the Duke, of whom they appear in great awe; and I think the object of his interview was to beg me, on the part of himself and T[itchfield], not to demur to any arrangement the Duke might propose. They would be content, that the Duke should pay off the £25,000, and take to the whole estate, receiving the rents — in short, realising, without raising money, the original scheme of Lord George. Then, on his death, they could act as they liked.

I would not be drawn into any suggestion, saying, that, if the Duke asked me for a proposition, I could only propose to pay my debt to the family by the sale of the estate, which their funds had purchased, and then, of course, resign the County. This he declared to be utterly impossible, and that the Duke would not listen to it. Then I went on [to] the state of my affairs, observing that it would be no object to them and no pleasure to me, unless I played the high game in public life; and that I could not do that without being on a rock. And then I went into certain details, showing that I could not undertake to play the great game, unless your income was clear. That was all I required, and ample.

Finally, he entreated me not to mention this to the Duke, or to anyone but himself: that the moment affairs were settled, he would himself see what he could do about my private affairs; that he was resolved I should play the great game; and that I must trust to him. He remained with me four hours, and appears more devoted than even Lord G.

I write this, as you may suppose, very wearied.

What were the exact arrangements made we do not know, but the two brothers took over the complete responsibility, and Disraeli was enabled to play the great game at the cost of owing them £25,000. The whole business must be pronounced, from a financial point of view, to have been very imprudent. Disraeli was still seriously in debt when he entered into the negotiations for Hughenden. But if he incurred no fresh liabilities, his prospects were good. On his father's death, which could not be long deferred, he would come into property sufficient, by careful management, to put his affairs straight, and his marriage secured him a permanent income. Economy, however, was repugnant to his large ideas. To play the great game he needed a position beyond what his marriage had given him. So he light-heartedly assumed the expense of a country house in addition to a town house, and probably increased his indebtedness to a total of £40,000. Worse was to come. Titchfield, who was a Peelite, and therefore always in imperfect sympathy with Disraeli's politics, succeeded to the dukedom in 1854, and three years later, either from political reasons or owing to that eccentricity which became so strong a feature of his character in his later life, suddenly called in his money, and Disraeli had once more to resort to the usurers whom he had already found so expensive. Thus the load of debt, which at the time of his father's death might with a very little care have been lifted entirely from his back, went on accumulating. Still, however imprudent the acquisition of Hughenden may have been financially, undoubtedly it both consolidated his political position in the county and in the party, and, by immensely increasing the amenities of his life, conduced to his happiness, his health, and his powers of work. Fortunately his temperament was such that, save at occasional periods of depression, he was able, so long as he was not absolutely liable to arrest, to ignore his debts altogether, and to pursue his literary and political career entirely undisturbed by their shadow.

It must have been a proud moment for Disraeli when the purchase was completed, and he was the lord of Hughenden. Hebrew as he was by origin, and with a deep feeling of race, he was also in a very real sense a patriotic Englishman. Indeed, it is one of the most pleasing characteristics of the Jews that, without in any way losing their distinctive nationality, the best of them are able to associate themselves intimately with the peoples who treat them well. This is so even in the case of some international Jewish families, where the strong Jewish family feeling might be expected to override national obligations. Take the conspicuous instance of the Rothschilds, where the family tie has been very close from the first. Few are more markedly Austrian, French, or English respectively in sympathy and political bias than the Rothschilds of Austria, France, and England. If that is a feature of those who remain Jews in religion, national attachment comes still more readily to those who are Jews only in race. Disraeli had never had a specially Jewish bringing up, and was baptised before he was thirteen. In 1853 he wrote: 'I was not bred among my race, and was nurtured in great prejudice against them.' His father's circle and surroundings were far more Christian than Jewish; and the society which he himself had frequented had been English society, fashionable, artistic, literary, and political. From his father he had derived a strong interest in English history and tradition; both his father and himself were ornaments of English literature. From his years of adolescence he had been familiar with, and had become attached to, the typically English county of Bucks, and gloried in this association. To be an English country gentleman was as natural an object of ambition to him as it has ever been to true-born Englishmen who have distinguished themselves in the service of their country abroad or made a fortune in commerce at home. There was, besides, in his case a very special political satisfaction in the position. He had long regarded the country gentlemen as the backbone of the State, the natural leaders of the people. The great Whig nobles were, in his opinion, an official oligarchy, who had grown wealthy on robbery of the Church, had reduced their King's power to a shadow, and had arranged the policy of the State to suit in the first place their own interests, and afterwards the convenience of manufacturers and Dissenters. The country gentlemen were a natural aristocracy, firmly rooted in the soil of England, the proper counsellors of the King, the supporters of the Church, and the friends of the poor, who yielded them a voluntary respect and confidence. From their intimate acquaintance with all sorts and conditions of men in their various localities, they were familiar with the wants and necessities of working people, of whom they were much more really representative than the middle classes could possibly be. By the purchase of Hughenden, he who was already a political leader of the squirearchy became a squire himself.

Surprise has often been felt at Disraeli's ready identification in sympathy with the country gentlemen, and it has been suggested that the sympathy was spurious and interested. What could there be in common between a Jew adventurer and the English territorial aristocracy? It is apparently forgotten that, in Disraeli's eyes, to be a Jew was not to be a despised outcast, but to belong to an aristocracy among peoples, a race as old as history, and the only one to whom God had vouchsafed to reveal Himself. Not only was he of an aristocratic race, but he believed, though it may be without certain warrant, that he was descended from some of the most illustrious families of that race. Moreover, he had that genius to which aristocracies, to their credit, have seldom been entirely blind. No wonder that he felt that in English aristocratic society he could mix as an equal, and that the country gentlemen, though they might be, and were, slow to recognise the fact, had in him a leader who, however apparently exotic, was yet essentially sympathetic and congenial.

Hughenden Manor stands on a projecting tongue of the Chilterns which falls south towards High Wycombe. The history of the house does not seem to be exactly known, but it has obviously been built at very various dates. Though Disraeli chose to think that some alterations which Mrs. Disraeli made in 1862–63 'restored the house to what it was before the Civil War,'[1] there is no remaining work in the present building which appears to be earlier than the eighteenth century. When Disraeli bought it, it was an oblong house of three storeys, built of brick but white-washed, with very little external ornament. While the entrance is on the north side, the house faces due south; and the south front is broken by two bays, running the whole height of the building, with a garden door between them. A pergola extends over the ground-floor windows across the whole length, and immediately below is a terrace which enjoys the sun the greater part of the day. The interior is irregular, the ceilings of the rooms being at very different levels. The oldest part, the centre of the house and the east wing, is of a Gothic character, with groined ceilings, though the ornamentation may only date from Mrs. Disraeli's reconstruction. This part comprises the entrance-hall and passages and the library, which are low, and the dining-room and saloon,

[1] See below, pp. 471, 472.

which are lofty. The library, where Disraeli kept the larger part of his books, is a picturesque room occupying the east end of the south front, including the east bay. The other two reception-rooms are behind. The principal bedrooms are on the floor above, looking south; and there, too, is the small study in which Disraeli worked. The halls and staircase, as well as the principal rooms, were mainly decorated by portraits of his family, friends, and colleagues. Queen Victoria, by Von Angeli, held an honoured place, and most of the portraits in these volumes are copied from originals at Hughenden. Dignified without pretension, comfortable but not luxurious, the house was a thoroughly suitable home for a statesman and man of letters of moderate fortune.

In front of the terrace the garden extends towards the south, flanked by fine trees on either hand, with an opening at the end, affording a pleasant view over part of Wycombe, including the church tower, and the woods of Wycombe Abbey on the hill beyond the town. On the west side the ground falls very steeply from the house and garden, and is thickly covered with a beech wood, which is prolonged southwards beyond the garden, and shelters a green walk with a gentle gradient, known as the Beech Walk—a favourite resort of the statesman. There is a charming irregularity about this south front and garden and lawns; nothing is quite at right angles or in the centre, owing to the haphazard way in which the house was built.

Behind the house, up the hill-slope to the north, come the stables and kitchen-garden. Beyond and to the west of these stretch the woods up to and over the crest of the chalk down. They are mainly of beech; but after a short walk you pass into what Disraeli called the German Forest, where Mrs. Disraeli planted pines and yew-trees and laurels in the more open parts among the beeches, and cut numerous paths like those in the pine-woods surrounding German watering-places. These paths sweep round to the west, and catch the southern sun.

The park is on the east and south of the house, and

HUGHENDEN MANOR, VICARAGE, AND CHURCH, 1840.

From a drawing by R. Green at Hughenden.

stretches to the Wycombe and Missenden road. It slopes gently past the church and churchyard, which stand in an enclosure almost hidden by trees, down to a trout stream which flows along the valley from the north-east and spreads out at one place into a small lake. The church, much of which dates from the thirteenth or fourteenth century, was in its unrestored state when Disraeli came to Hughenden, and the square block of its tower was a feature in the landscape. The park is well timbered, and the private grounds are shut off on practically every side by dense masses of foliage, so that you can seldom catch a glimpse of the house, 'bosom'd high in tufted trees.'[1] The estate, which lies close round the grounds and park, comprised about 750 acres when it was bought, but by enclosures on Hughenden Common and subsequent purchases was increased in Disraeli's time to 1,400 acres.

Hughenden was exactly the country retreat for which, after the strife of politics, Disraeli's nature craved. When the session was over, he hurried down, autumn after autumn, entirely exhausted with the constant strain, and there found the peace and the books and the woods in which he rejoiced. Every year, in August and September, as his letters show, there was the same nervous depression, the same need for a period of absolute retirement, to be alone with his wife in that corner of his beloved county which he had chosen for his home. He might well have appropriated to himself the lines of Catullus:—

> O! quid solutis est beatius curis?
> Cum mens onus reponit, ac peregrino
> Labore fessi venimus larem ad nostrum . . .
> Hoc est, quod unum est pro laboribus tantis.

Disraeli has left a note showing the kind of *dolce far niente* life which he preferred to lead when he came away from town:—

I have a passion for books and trees. I like to look at them. When I come down to Hughenden I pass the first week

[1] Quoted by Bulwer Lytton in writing of Hughenden to Disraeli.

in sauntering about my park and examining all the trees, and then I saunter in the library and survey the books. My collection is limited to Theology, the Classics, and History. Anything miscellaneous in it is the remains of the Bradenham Collection, but the great bulk of the Belles Lettres I parted with after my father's death.

As he came down August after August, and September after September, he would see the picture he so lovingly described in *Endymion*:—

The woods were beginning to assume the first fair livery of autumn, when it is beautiful without decay. The lime and the larch had not yet dropped a golden leaf, and the burnished beeches flamed in the sun. Every now and then an occasional oak or elm rose, still as full of deep green foliage as if it were midsummer; while the dark verdure of the pines sprang up with effective contrast amid the gleaming and resplendent chestnuts.

From the terrace in front of the house, where—as formerly on the terrace at Bradenham[1]—he was wont to pace up and down and muse over politics or letters, Disraeli looked out on trees to right and left, with the woods of Wycombe Abbey in the distance. There he would watch his peacocks—'My dear lady, you cannot have terraces without peacocks,' he told a guest—and then stroll down the beech walk at the end of the garden. Or he would walk up the hill behind to the German Forest, along the paths his wife had cut, basking occasionally in the sun on one of the numerous rustic seats at view-points where the trees had been opened out. She would often accompany him, generally in a pony carriage.

Everything to do with the woodland country appealed to him, those who worked there as well as the trees themselves, the woodman as well as the wood. Here is a memorandum of 1860:—

I find great amusement in talking to the people at work in the woods and grounds at Hughenden. Their conversation is racy, and the repose of their natural manners agreeable. An old, but very hale, man told me to-day, that he was going to be married, and that his bride would not be much younger than himself, but he had lodged in her cottage now for more than a year, and he thought she would do for him. He said he

[1] See Vol. I., p. 144, note.

was a widower, and he added, speaking of his first wife, 'And I can truly say, from the bottom of my heart, that for fifty years I never knew what it was to have a happy hour.' I told my wife of this, and they are to have a wedding dinner.

I like very much the society of woodmen. Their conversation is most interesting. Quick and constant observation and perfect knowledge. I don't know any men, who are so completely masters of their business, and of the secluded, but delicious, world in which they live. They are healthy, their language is picturesque; they live in the air, and Nature whispers to them many of her secrets. A Forest is like the Ocean, monotonous only to the ignorant. It is a life of ceaseless variety.

To see Lovett, my head-woodman, fell a tree is a work of art. No bustle, no exertion, apparently not the slightest exercise of strength. He tickles it with his axe, and then it falls exactly where he desires it. He can climb a tree like a squirrel, an animal which, both in form and color and expression, he seems to me to resemble.

If Disraeli did not find his enjoyment, like his great rival, in felling trees himself, he at least took an artistic pleasure in seeing them fall under an expert woodman's axe. But he was sparing of that pleasure. It was much more congenial to him to plant than to cut down. He planted innumerable trees, especially ornamental ones—cedars and firs of various kinds—in the private grounds; and he seldom allowed an eminent friend or colleague who paid him a visit to depart without adding one more. The result was that the lawns, both before and behind the house, became choked with foliage; and Disraeli's nephew and heir had regretfully to clear away most of these memorial trees to let into the rooms sufficient light and air. The pine, however, which Queen Victoria planted when she visited Hughenden was carefully preserved, and still decorates the south lawn.

It was Disraeli's regular habit when in the country to attend Quarter Sessions. He had been a justice of the peace since 1836, and a Deputy-Lieutenant since 1845. With his county neighbours he became on excellent terms. The Carrington family at Wycombe had long been his friends; and he was warmly welcomed as a resident landowner by Sir Harry Verney, the leading Whig in the county. 'Few things,' Sir Harry wrote, 'have occurred in Bucks lately so gratifying to me as your purchase of Hughenden.' With his tenants Disraeli always kept in good relations. They were largely new men, whom he had accepted himself. He found the estate greatly under-rented, and as, being a poor man, he was unable to allow the easy terms which contented his wealthy predecessor, the old tenants mostly went. He made the well-being of everyone on the estate his care; and delighted in a friendly chat with farmer or cottager. The annual flower-shows and harvest-homes in the park were great occasions of local festivity; and the lord of the manor always attended when he could, and spoke on agricultural topics suitable to his audience — sometimes, it was thought, going into more detail than his technical knowledge warranted, though at other times showing a surprising amount of practical rural wisdom. For instance, in 1864 he pressed upon the farmers the expediency of crossing Cotswold rams with Southdown ewes — then a new system; and subsequently he had the satisfaction of receiving from Sir George Jenkinson, a well-known agriculturist and breeder, an emphatic endorsement of his advice: 'My own actual experience entirely accorded with your recommendations.' The duties of a country gentleman, in fact, Disraeli performed punctiliously; of the ordinary sports of a country gentleman he was innocent. Though, with his feeling for dress, he wore in the country the clothes of a sportsman, at first in a somewhat accentuated form, he did not shoot, and he did not preserve game; nor did he ride to hounds, though he had certainly once made the experiment, in Essex in 1834, and, according to his own story, with 'great *kudos*.'[1] Consequently he would gladly have spent the closing months of the year in London, and returned to the country for May

[1] See Vol. I., p. 246. The hero in the *Young Duke* says: 'I have hunted; it was not very disagreeable. I sometimes shoot; it is not very stupid.' These may very well have been Disraeli's own sentiments when he was a young man.

and June. 'If we could only so contrive our lives,' he writes in *Lothair*,[1] 'as to go into the country for the first note of the nightingale, and return to town for the first note of the muffin-bell, existence, it is humbly presumed, might be more enjoyable.'

It was on September 6, 1848, that Disraeli was able to report to his wife: 'It is all done, and you are the Lady of Hughenden.' The autumn and winter were occupied with moving from Bradenham and settling in. Most of the arrangements had to be made by Mrs. Disraeli, as the question of the leadership took her husband often to London.

To Mrs. Disraeli.

[GROSVENOR GATE] *Jan.* 25, 1849.— . . . My darling, you have, I am sure, done at Hughenden what no other woman, or man either, could do. You have gained a year in our enjoyment of that place, where I trust every year we shall be happier and happier. It was for this great result of which I was sensible, and also for the importance of getting well acquainted with your new staff, to whom we must leave so much for the next months, that I did not like to press you to come on to me on Tuesday, tho' I have much wanted you. . . . Pussy now comes into my room every morning at breakfast, and jumps on my head, and rubs my nose. He seems colossal after our little favourite—and very dirty—I don't think he will ever be clean again. . . .

'You have done wonders,' he writes in another letter; and his brothers and sister, when they saw what improvements had been made in a house and grounds which they knew well, were enthusiastic over Mrs. Disraeli's 'magical touches' and clever arrangements. But considerable as were the changes made by her directly she came to Hughenden, in the interior of the house, in laying out the garden, and in cutting walks through the forest, her greatest period of activity was some fourteen years later. In the winter of 1862–1863 she both entirely rearranged her garden, and also gave what Disraeli called, in a letter to Lady Dorothy Nevill, 'a new form and character' to the house. This she did by remodelling it inside, and outside by adding an ornamental parapet and varying

[1] Ch. 9.

the hitherto smooth surface of the walls with florid Gothic decoration.[1] Earlier in 1862 she showed her grateful affection for her father-in-law, 'the most lovable, perfect old gentleman I ever met with,'[2] by erecting, on a conspicuous hill within the estate, to the south-west, a monument to Isaac D'Israeli. The work was carried out without the knowledge of her husband, who was busy at the time in London, and upon whom it burst as a welcome surprise on his return. Hughenden bears many signs of its mistress's careful management. Disraeli might be reckless in money matters; his wife was a most excellent housewife. All her account-books for household expenses, with the entries in her own hand throughout, are preserved at Hughenden, and testify to her proficiency in domestic economy.

To Sarah Disraeli.

HUGHENDEN, *Aug.* 25, 1849.—. . . The alterations here seem very successful. It is quite another place, and of far more pretension and effect. It is really a park now. The library also is arranged; it took me several days, and I think you will like it. It has quite lost the circulating-library look which you noticed. Did I tell you Sir W. Molesworth had presented me with a copy of his *Hobbes*, eighteen vols.? This is an accession, and I got it through that impudent friend of mine, Bernal Osborne, which makes it more amusing.[3] . . .

The parish church at Hughenden is, as we have seen, within the park, and the vicarage lies between the church and the manor-house, quite close to the private grounds. Good relations with his Vicar were, therefore, even more than usually desirable for the lord of the manor. When Disraeli acquired Hughenden the Vicar was the Rev. John R. Pigott, who welcomed him cordially, but with whom he had a curious little misunderstanding in the first few months. Disraeli was a regular churchgoer and communicant. He has described in *Lothair* his satisfaction in passing Sunday in the country,

[1] The work was carried out under the superintendence of E. B. Lamb, a distinguished Gothic architect of the day.

[2] See Vol. I., p. 379.

[3] *Letters*, p. 223.

and has given us, without a doubt, a picture of his practice at Hughenden. 'There is something in the essential stillness of country life which blends harmoniously with the most divine of our divine laws. It is pleasant, too, when the congregation breaks up, to greet one's neighbours; to say kind words to kind faces; to hear some rural news profitable to learn, which sometimes enables you to do some good, and sometimes prevents others from doing some harm. A quiet domestic walk, too, in the afternoon has its pleasures.' But it so happened that on one of the early Sundays of his residence at Hughenden Disraeli travelled to London after morning service. The Vicar, more earnest than wise, without making any inquiry, dealt very faithfully with the truant. Disraeli's action, he wrote on the Sunday evening, was 'a breach of that commandment which, though not so rigidly enforced as on that people from whom with a natural pride you record your descent, is still not less binding on a Christian.' He was bound to act towards Disraeli as towards his 'poorer and less intellectual neighbours,' and to admonish him to set a better example.

To the Rev. John R. Pigott.

GROSVENOR GATE, *April* 16 [*or* 17], 1849.

DEAR SIR,—It is quite true that, in consequence of public circumstances of urgency and importance, I was obliged suddenly to leave Hughenden on Sunday to my great personal annoyance and inconvenience. I departed without even a servant.

Had you made any temperate inquiry, you might perhaps have ascertained that it is not my habit to travel on Sunday, and I would venture also to observe that my object in attending Divine service is not merely or principally to set an example to others. The duties of a spiritual pasture[1] should be fulfilled without regard of persons, but these duties are often of a delicate nature, and it is therefore desirable that they should fall to the lot of those who act with reflection, and not in a hasty and precipitate spirit.—My dear Sir, yours faithfully, B. DISRAELI.

[1] The word perhaps should be 'pastor.' The letter is printed from a copy made by Mrs. Disraeli; but her spelling is not impeccable, and the copy was probably written down from dictation.

The Vicar took the snub on the whole well. 'I freely receive your somewhat severe rebuke. It is the *first* of the kind bestowed on me during the twenty-six years in which I have been in holy orders — it may not, however, be the less deserved.' He trusted that Squire and Vicar might learn to know each other better; but they did not long remain in parochial relations. Pigott left in 1851; and with the new Vicar, of his own appointment, the Rev. Charles Whishaw Clubbe, Disraeli got on admirably.

'Unusually drained this year,' Disraeli wrote to his solicitors in 1849. It is not to be wondered at that during the preceding winter he was very glad of any sums that his pen could produce. His negotiations with Colburn in regard to the popular edition of his own novels, and with Moxon in regard to the republication of his father's *Curiosities*, crop up in the letters to his wife from London.

To Mrs. Disraeli.

[*Dec.* 12, 1848.]

My dearest Wife, — I have just come from Colburn — a most satisfactory interview. He is eager for the *Commentaries*, and wants to get on with the printing immediately, but I don't think it prudent to make an engagement until the *Curiosities* are published, as I think, from all I observe, the book is likely to make some stir. I have succeeded in securing the publication of the *Curiosities* before Xmas. This is an immense *coup*.

The arrangement for the publication of the popular edition of the novels is all on hand: estimates, engravings, prospectuses, etc., etc. The usual excuses made by the little man; but he is really at work. He also particularly asked about the Library, as his contribution is getting ready, and he hopes to send them to Hughenden as a Xmas present.

I got the £300 from Moxon; very *apropos* for our Xmas balance, and expect another £300 from the same quarter, before the year is out. . . .

Though I have been successful with my business, I have not at all enjoyed myself; very dispirited and lonely last night, so that had it not been for Ld. George's solicitor at Lincoln's Inn I should have attempted to have got back to-day. A very bad night — the weather very close and muggy, and wifie much missed. . . .

When the new edition of the *Curiosities*, including the Memoir of Isaac D'Israeli, was published, Disraeli bethought him of a friend of his early manhood, and sent the volumes to Lady Blessington, with a letter in which he referred to her kindness to his father, and his father's sincere regard for her. Her reply opened with a flattering blend of affection and deference. 'My dear Dis,' she wrote, 'I am tempted to smile at my own presumption in addressing so unceremoniously the most remarkable man of our time. But I believe that you are so unspoilt by fame that you will prefer the familiarity of a friendship so old as ours to the coldness of the more deferential "Mr. Disraeli," which I can never use to one I so truly like.'

Disraeli was about to lose his old friends, Lady Blessington and Count D'Orsay. In April, 1849, there came the financial crash which had long been impending over the pair; and D'Orsay first, and Lady Blessington a fortnight later, retreated to Paris, where they had a powerful friend in Louis Napoleon, just elected President. Disraeli was not in the secret of their intentions, and called at Gore house to find Lady Blessington gone. 'It was a pang,' he wrote to her; 'for though absorbing duties of my life have prevented me of late from passing as much time under that roof as it was once my happiness and good fortune through your kindness to do, you are well assured that my heart never changed for an instant to its inmates, and that I invariably entertained for them the same interest and affection.' He would now, he told her, have an object in coming to Paris.[1] He never saw her again. A few weeks later, on June 5, he sent the news of her sudden death to his wife: 'Alas! poor Lady Blessington! Died of apoplexy! The day before she was to enter her new house!'

To Count D'Orsay.

HUGHENDEN, HIGH WYCOMBE, *Jan.* 1, 1850.—We are very anxious to hear from you, and we ardently wish that this year may bring you happiness, and solace for the sorrows of the last.

I need not tell you how entirely we have sympathised with your affliction, who knew so well, and valued so completely,

[1] Madden's *Lady Blessington*, Vol. III., ch. 4.

the faithful friend that has departed. For myself my knowledge of her is a considerable volume in my life. It spread over many years, during which I received at her hands nothing but acts of sympathy, grace, and affection.

I have exposed myself to [so] many griefs, and am worn by so many cares, that the present always demands my energies, and I seldom venture to indulge in memory, for the past has too many pangs. But I find sometimes a melancholy pleasure in recalling her cordial and accomplished existence, and the past is linked with the present, when I recollect that you are left, between whom and myself the relations will never expire.

What are you going to do, and can anything be done in your unfortunate country? England is only sinking. France is finished. What a mournful fate to be born in the decline and fall of great countries! Europe, at least the Europe of our fathers and our youth, approaches its end. We ought to have found our careers across the great waters.

D'Orsay survived Lady Blessington three years. He resumed the practice of the arts of painting and sculpture in Paris, though he never carried out that project of making a large portrait of the Disraeli of this period to which Sarah Disraeli alludes in a letter of October 10, 1848: 'It rejoices my heart to hear that Count D'Orsay will endeavour to make a large picture of Dis; there is every chance of it being a great success.' Disraeli's own tribute to his friend's powers at this time may be added to his sister's: —

To Count D'Orsay.

Oct. 7, 1848. — I came in a spirit of severe and even savage criticism, despairing of seeing that countenance of blended energy and beauty reproduced to my eye and heart by the pencil of even so felicitous an artist as yourself.

I beheld again my beloved friend, and after gazing on the bust with an eye which would glance at nothing else in your studio, I left your room with the consolation that the magic finger of art had afforded the only solace which his bereaved and devoted friend can now welcome — the living resemblance of George Bentinck.[1]

D'Orsay died in Paris in August, 1852, having lived long enough to see his friend of twenty years arrive, if not at power, at any rate at office, and to forward congratulations in his last letter: —

[1] Brit. Mus. Addit. MSS.

Count D'Orsay, 1841.
from the picture by J. Wood, R.A.
at Hughenden.

nted in England.

From Count D'Orsay.

49, Rue Ville l'Evêque, Paris, 7 *Avril*, 1852.

My dearest D'Is,—I wanted to write to you all this time, but I have been ill, I may say for the first time of my life. Fancy me on a sofa with an atrocious lumbago for the last six weeks, and obliged to write with a pencil! I cannot resist longer to congratulate you, and myself, on your present position. I say myself because for many many years I said that there was no power which could prevent you to arrive at the Ministry, and at the head of the House of Commons. Therefore I let you judge how pleased I was when I saw you in your right place. My sister was also delighted, as she knows that I always liked you as a brother. Your dear kind wife must be very happy, and I am sure that she has been thinking of me on this occasion, as she always sympathised with me about all your triumphs. She felt that I was of the Trio *sacré*.

When you have time write to me one line; it will give me pleasure on my sofa to see again your handwriting. Most affectionate regards to your good wife.—Your best friend, D'Orsay.

CHAPTER VII

Foreign Policy and Metternich

1846-1849

The years that followed the fall of Peel were fertile in Continental troubles and complications. The old European system, which had been in a fashion restored by the Treaty of Vienna, showed unmistakable signs of breaking down, and in 1848 there came an upheaval which seemed for the moment to threaten as serious a disturbance of the existing order as the Revolution of 1789. Disraeli did not allow the absorbing interest of the political struggle at home to prevent him from following keenly the course of events in Europe and the trend of British foreign policy. The Foreign Office was once more under the direction of the masterful personality of Lord Palmerston, whom Disraeli had satirised in the *Runnymede Letters* as the 'Lord Fanny of diplomacy,' but whom he subsequently depicted in *Endymion,* under the name of Lord Roehampton, in a decidedly favourable light.

The Earl of Roehampton was the strongest member of the Government, except of course the Premier himself. He was the man from whose combined force and flexibility of character the country had confidence that in all their councils there would be no lack of courage, yet tempered with adroit discretion.[1]

That distinguished man . . . had been Minister for a long time, and had left a great name. Foreigners rarely know more than one English Minister at a time, but they compensate for their ignorance of the aggregate body by even exaggerating the qualities of the individual with whom they are acquainted. Lord Roehampton had conducted the affairs of his country

[1] *Endymion*, ch. 42.

always in a courteous, but still in a somewhat haughty spirit. He was easy and obliging, and conciliatory in little matters; but when the credit, or honour, or large interests of England were concerned, he acted with conscious authority. On the Continent of Europe, though he sometimes incurred the depreciation of the smaller minds, whose self-love he may not have sufficiently spared, by the higher spirits he was feared and admired, and they knew, when he gave his whole soul to an affair, that they were dealing with a master.[1]

Lord Roehampton, like Palmerston, was 'absorbed, and naturally absorbed, in his department, the most important in the State, and of which he is master.' 'His despatches to Ministers . . . were unrivalled.' 'The composition of these despatches was a source to Lord Roehampton of much gratification and excitement. They were of European fame, and their terse argument, their clear determination, and often their happy irony, were acknowledged in all the Cabinets, and duly apprehended.'[2] He 'was a man who really cared for nothing but office and affairs'; but he was 'always playful, and even taking refuge in a bantering spirit.' Lady Montfort says of him: 'Look to Lord Roehampton; he is the man. He does not care a rush whether the revenue increases or declines. He is thinking of real politics; foreign affairs; maintaining our power in Europe.'

All this is true of Palmerston, and is generously said. But there was another side to his foreign policy, which made it the constant subject of criticism in these years from Stanley and Disraeli, and, indeed, from Aberdeen and Gladstone and Cobden too, and which was largely responsible for the Continental distrust of England that has so often in subsequent times hampered the action of our statesmen. For fifty years after the Battle of Waterloo, Great Britain was recognised as the first Power in Europe. Palmerston conceived that the position which she had acquired justified her in meddling in all the affairs of other European countries, their internal

[1] *Endymion*, ch. 72.

[2] But see below, p. 193, for a disparaging estimate of some of Palmerston's despatches.

difficulties as well as their external relations. He was popular at home for his constant upholding of British interests; he by no means confined himself, however, to this his proper sphere, but was forward with his advice on all occasions and to all countries, whether British interests were concerned or not. In particular, he was wont to lecture despotic Governments on the advantages they would derive from adopting constitutions after the British pattern, and to make no secret of the support and countenance he was prepared to afford to revolutionary movements. While he thus acquired for his country valuable sympathies in some quarters, notably in Italy and Hungary, he roused strong suspicion in most of the Governments of Europe, and courted unnecessary rebuffs in matters over which he was not prepared to resort to arms.

Disraeli, in a thoroughly patriotic spirit, had endeavoured, when in Paris in the winter of 1845–46,[1] to smooth the way for Palmerston's return to the Foreign Office, by endeavouring to remove the prejudices against him of Louis Philippe and Guizot; and Palmerston himself visited Paris at the following Easter, and confirmed in person Disraeli's assurances that he would make a good understanding between France and England the foundation of his policy. But his accession to office unfortunately coincided with a critical period in the discussion of the proposed marriages of the Spanish Queen and her sister — an arrangement by which Louis Philippe and Guizot hoped that a grandson of the French King might eventually sit on the throne of Spain. To Queen Victoria and Aberdeen Louis Philippe had expressly disavowed this policy; but an unfortunately-worded despatch to the British Minister at Madrid roused all the old French distrust of Palmerston, and was the reason, or the excuse, for a breach of his word by Louis Philippe. The marriages were hurried on. Strong resentment was felt in England, and Palmerston fanned the flame. It argued

[1] See Vol. II., pp. 338–343.

a want of sense of proportion to see in Louis Philippe, that worthy bourgeois monarch, with his clumsy intrigues, a Louis XIV. or Napoleon Bonaparte, plotting to combine the nations of Europe under the hegemony of France. The solemn parade of British remonstrances in the Queen's Speech of 1847 afforded some justification for the flippant comment of Disraeli, who lamented the relaxation of the *entente cordiale* between France and England, and said that he should have thought that the correspondence on the occasion of the marriages would have been of a congratulatory character. The breach between England and France encouraged Austria, with the consent of Russia and Prussia, to annex the little republic of Cracow, the last remnant of Polish independence, where a revolutionary movement in the spring had had to be suppressed by the three partitioning Powers. Cracow enjoyed its freedom under the Treaty of Vienna, but the Western Powers could no longer act together in defence of the treaty, and England registered a forcible but futile protest. On this policy of the Government Disraeli made a very elaborate attack, which, however, though Bentinck[1] admired his knowledge, and his family[2] and friends his eloquence, rather missed fire. His main point was that there was no violation of the Treaty of Vienna, as Cracow was the subject of a separate arrangement between Austria, Russia, and Prussia, which was indeed recognised by the Treaty, but was not, strictly speaking, incorporated in it. Palmerston convinced the House that there was no substance in the objection. But, though the Minister was successful on this technicality, it could not be denied that his foreign policy, largely owing to the mistrust which his name inspired, had placed the country, as Disraeli pointed out, in bad relations with all the Great Powers within six months after his return to office.

[1] Bentinck wrote to Stanley, in reference to the question of Cracow, on Dec. 6, 1846: 'D., as you probably know, has the foreign policy of Europe quite at his fingers' ends.'

[2] Sarah Disraeli wrote: 'That admirable speech; how commanding is the tone, and how true and wise the politics!'

Throughout 1847 Europe was in a very restless condition, but the year closed without serious disturbance in the larger States. The Revolution came in 1848, and, strangely enough, it began in no despotically-governed country, but in France,[1] which enjoyed constitutional Monarchy and Parliamentary institutions. A memorandum by Disraeli illustrates public feeling just before the storm burst:

[At the] Meeting of Parliament, 1848, George Smythe brought the last news from Paris. He had been under-Secretary of State with Lord Aberdeen, and had had a conversation with Guizot at his reception. G. S. considered affairs at Paris critical: but described Guizot as 'transcendentally bumptious.'

Comte de Jarnac at the Coventry Club on the critical day—a little nervous but most sanguine.

'What do you think?' he said to me.

'I cannot doubt but with such notice and such men all must be prepared.'

He nodded entire assent, and said, 'It must be right.'

I did not know then, that he had at that time, though I should think not more than thirty years of age, his appointment as Ambassador of France to our Court, I may say, in his pocket. But he bore his bitter disappointment well. Seldom a greater fall. He had to retire to Ireland, having married, and live on a meagre paternal allowance, and occupied himself with writing a novel, instead of living in a palace, with a large revenue, and writing despatches on the fate of the world.

This was at the Coventry Club, where only a season before the same Comte [de] Jarnac exerted all his influence to secure the black-balling of Louis Napoleon.

It was on February 24, about a fortnight after the meeting of Parliament, that the Monarchy of July suddenly collapsed. Louis Philippe and his Queen fled to England, followed by Guizot, his unpopular Minister. France was declared a Republic, and a provisional Government was set up, of which Lamartine, the poet, was the leading spirit and Minister of Foreign Affairs.

[1] There was, indeed, an outbreak in Sicily two or three weeks before the Revolution in France, but it was the latter that set Europe ablaze.

National workshops were established under the inspiration of Louis Blanc. Louis Philippe's fall was the signal for a 'general convulsion, with four pitched battles fought in Europe in eight weeks, and the Adriatic and Baltic both blockaded.' The Revolution spread to Austria and Hungary, where the Emperor had to abdicate and Metternich to go into exile; to Prussia and Germany, where representative institutions were vehemently demanded; and to Italy, where there were premature revolts against Austrian dominion in the north and against Bomba's tyranny in the Two Sicilies.

Disraeli had a theory of his own about the subversion of the Orleans dynasty and the subsequent revolutionary movements all over the Continent. They were, he was convinced, the work of secret societies:

> The two characteristics of these confederations, which now cover Europe like net-work, are war against property and hatred of the Semitic revelation. . . . Alone, the secret societies can disturb, but they cannot control, Europe. Acting in unison with a great popular movement, they may destroy society, as they did at the end of the last century. The French disturbance of '48 was not a great popular movement. It was a discontent which required nothing more for its solution than a change of ministry; but the sovereign and his subjects were in sudden confusion; the secret associations are always vigilant and always prepared; they took society by surprise, but having nothing really to rely upon except their own resources, the movement, however disastrous, has been an abortion.
>
> It is the manœuvres of these men, who are striking at property and Christ, which the good people of this country, who are so accumulative and so religious, recognise and applaud as the progress of the Liberal cause.[1]

Inadequate as this theory may be to cover the whole ground, it cannot be neglected in judging European history in the nineteenth century. In particular, the history of the unification of Italy cannot be written or understood without giving full weight to the action of secret societies, to one of which, the Carbonari, Napoleon III. had himself belonged.

[1] *Lord George Bentinck*, ch. 27.

To Sarah Disraeli.

March 8, 1848.—What will happen in these times of unprecedented horrors! I know not whether I am standing on my head or my heels. . . .

March 20.—The mob are in possession of Vienna, and Metternich, they say, almost as badly off as Louis Philippe.

Guizot called on me on Saturday, and I was fortunately at home. He is unchanged, and has taken a house in Pelham Terrace, Brompton, at £20 per annum. The last time I saw him he was starred, ribboned, and golden-fleeced, and surrounded by Ambassadors and grand personages.[1]

Affairs are very bad, but in my opinion will be much worse. All one can hope for now is to put one's house in order during the temporary lull—if there be one. . . .[2]

Disraeli had a great regard for Louis Philippe, who had shown him many marks of friendship in his days of power in Paris; and he manifested his sympathy and respect for him, both in public and private, now that he was fallen and in exile. Four days after the abdication he said in the House of Commons:

I have no hesitation in saying that I lament that the late Ruler of France has fallen. Whatever his errors to his people may have been, he was a great prince, a great gentleman (a laugh), a great man. There may be those who are ready to laugh over fallen royalty. I, for one, would shrink from such a course; and least of all does it become us to do so; for, whatever were his errors, to us in England and to Englishmen at least he always extended an appreciating sympathy; and I cannot forget that for eighteen years he did secure, he did maintain for Europe, the blessings of peace.

And towards the end of the session Disraeli eulogised Louis Philippe as a Sovereign who succeeded 'in bridling, for a period of seventeen years, the Jacobin tiger'; as a man, without question, of great sagacity, and of unrivalled experience. He has left a memorandum of his first visit to the exile:

I shall never forget my first visit to Claremont after the catastrophe of 1848. I shrank from it, but it was impossible

[1] Guizot resumed his decorations in exile next year. The Disraelis met him at dinner '*très decoré*. His wearing the Golden Fleece I think more than insensibility, I call it impudence,' Disraeli wrote to Lady Londonderry.

[2] *Letters*, pp. 210, 211.

to be avoided. If there were an occasion, in which one should show respectful sympathy, this was one. . . . I was ushered into a drawing-room, where there were groups of gentlemen. The King, who was standing, and speaking to General Fox, who was taking his leave, then advanced, bowed to me with some dignity, and asked some ordinary questions in a friendly tone. A strange question he asked was, whether I was thinking of paying a visit to Paris,—quite in an ordinary tone. Then H.M. approached me quite closely, and said in a clear but hushed voice, 'If you will follow me, Mr. Disraeli, we shall be able to converse together undisturbed.'

So we quitted the room, and then the King led the way down a passage, which at the end was rather gloomy, and there was a door open, and all I saw was a common mahogany glass on a painted table; and it was a bedroom, a very ordinary one, looking on the walls of back premises, very gloomy: but apparently the King's bedroom, and then he sate down in a small painted rush-bottomed bedroom chair, and at the same time placed one for me exactly opposite and close to him, and without any further preface said in French, which he spoke the whole time, 'I am desirous of telling you how all this happened.' And then he began a narrative, which commenced with the beginning, and never ceased until he had quitted the Tuileries, an abdicated monarch. I am sure I am understating when I say, that the narrative considerably exceeded an hour. During this time, the King never paused, never hesitated. He spoke with volubility: not apparently with much feeling. He rarely looked at me as he spoke. He seemed to me to be making a clean breast of it, and speaking as it were to the reporters.

I concluded from his narrative, that the whole thing was a surprise; an accident. And that Lagrange and the secret societies, finding everything in disorder, and no master, rose suddenly at the eleventh hour when they found the ball was at their feet.

At last it ended; the impetus was arrested; the excitement which had carried on the King was over, and he went into hysterics. I have seldom felt more distressed. It was a position in which one could not even speak. Feeling deeply for this kind-hearted and clever man, who in his great prosperity, and when I was young and little known, had showered many kindnesses upon me, I with respectful tenderness took His Majesty's hand and pressed it to my lips: he took my hand and held it in both of his own. Then he rose, and in his usual voice said, 'Now I will take you to the Queen.'

So he led me into a drawing-room, where I found the Queen working at embroidery with some ladies. General Dumas and some other attendants were standing in the background. The King presented me as if it were the Tuileries, — quite cheerful. Her Majesty received me without the slightest embarrassment, with cordiality and sweet serenity, and asked me after my wife. After a short conversation, I preparing to go, the King came up and made some inquiry after Lord George Bentinck, who had spoken with sympathy and respect of the King in the House of Commons recently, and began talking of his uncle, Lord William, whom he had known in Sicily. Then he went on in a rather rambling way about some papers which he had which he thought might be interesting to Lord George. Of course, I assented. Whereupon the King, just as if he were at the Tuileries, called for General Dumas, and gave orders, that copies should be prepared of certain documents, and sent to Lord George Bentinck, without loss of time. I was told afterwards that the papers, like all other public papers, were not at Claremont, and that the King was in the habit of giving his orders on all subjects to his aide-de-camps just as if he were at Paris or St. Cloud.

This account of the visit was written, apparently, several years afterwards, in the sixties, and does not tally in all its details with a letter which he wrote to a friend at the time: —

To Lady Londonderry.

Grosvenor Gate, *May Day*, 1848. — . . . Have you yet recovered the great catastrophe? Its cause is inexplicable, its consequences an alarming mystery. No judgment and no imagination can fathom its probable results. The King of France in a Surrey Villa, Metternich in a Hanover Square Hotel, and the Prince of Prussia[1] at Lady Palmerston's! The toil of public life and private affairs have so absorbed me, that I did not pay my respects at Claremont until a fortnight ago. The King received me in his bedroom, in order that we might not be disturbed. I found him little changed. I sat with him two hours; the first occupied with an almost uninterrupted narrative of the three fatal days, but varying little from the received accounts, except his warm vindication of the Duc de Nemours, whom he greatly praised: his approbation of Montpensier's too eager counsel of abdication much more reserved. This last seems to have been in a great fright. The whole affair a series of blunders, and it was only at the last moment that Lagrange and the secret societies, seeing

[1] Afterwards the Emperor William I. of Germany.

everything in confusion and that everybody had lost their head, resolved to make an impromptu dash, and clutch the prize.

The King's description of the abdication, his room crowded with councillors of all parties, and all talking at the same time, most distressing! Poor old man—75 years of age, scarcely recovered from a severe influenza, and with Mme. Adelaide[1] hardly buried! No wonder his nerves gave way! His narrative was affecting, and he was much softened, but not feeble. Afterwards, when he had relieved his mind, and talked of political affairs in general, I found him quite himself, perfectly alive to all the questions of the hour, even keenly interested about them, and prompt and vivacious.

The state of Belgium[2] seemed his great consolation. He more than once recurred to it. I fancy his hope, perhaps conviction, is, that if a general war be prevented, all may yet end well, so far as his grandson's destiny, but he did not directly touch on this. The interview ended by his saying he would take me to the Queen, with whom he left me alone. The moment he had shut the door, she exclaimed, 'Ah! Monsieur Disraeli, quelle catastrophe!' She, however, here ceased to weep, and harped much upon Belgium.

The King did not mention to me, that he had seen M. Guizot, but he spoke of him several times without any bitterness. They say that Guizot has less reserve, but during the only interview which I have had with him, when he called at Grosvenor Gate, he imputed no blame to His Majesty, but said that if the King had gone to St. Cloud on the second day, and summoned the chambers there, all would have been saved. Guizot I found quite unchanged. You heard, perhaps, that he called on Lord Palmerston in Carlton Gardens, and asked for Lady Palmerston, when he was told his lordship was not at home. Ushered up, he said when he met her, 'I used to think that in England nothing ever changed, but I find I was in error, for I called at your old home, and found that I had knocked at the wrong door!' Cool!

Guizot said to me that Palmerston had done it all, by his patronage of Thiers, and the encouragement that Normanby, etc., gave to the Reform Banquets.

F. Mills, who returned from a railroad (I mean about some railroad company) visit to Paris, on Sunday week dined with Lamartine, who used, in old days, quite to affect splendor and *luxe*. There were several present, all in boots and black cravats, and smoking after dinner — only two dishes, a scanty one of broiled soles, and, unmentionable horror! an immense

[1] Louis Philippe's sister.

[2] King Leopold I. of Belgium had married, as his second wife, Louis Philippe's daughter.

portion of *foie de veau!* How puerile this affectation of republican simplicity! and what confidence can we have in anything durable being effected by such men! The King, by the bye, said to me several times, 'One thing alone has been proved by what has taken place — that in France nothing can endure.'

Affairs, however, *on dit,* are worse in Germany than in France. Kings and Princes are turned off as we turn away servants, and worse, without a character, and nobody resists. Fifty mad professors at Frankfort, calling themselves a Diet, self-appointed, have absolutely invaded Denmark, and will not conclude their labours till they have established a federal republic like the U.S.

Did you hear of Lord Hardinge's interview with Metternich on the 9th March? Lord Ponsonby and P. Esterhazy both present and listening, as if to an oracle, while Metternich announced that Austria never was so sound, while he moralised over the miserable fate of the French. Esterhazy kissing his (P. M.'s) hand, like the Emperor's, when he quitted the room! Lord Hardinge told me this. . . .

HOUSE OF COMMONS, *Tuesday* [? *Aug.* 15, 1848]. — . . . The accounts from Paris are very émeutish: the question being whether Louis Blanc is to be arrested or not. What a noise for so little a man, not so tall as Tommy Moore at his best, and twelve months agone calling in vain at a café for a waiter. But such is the magnetic power of brains. Who could ever have supposed that Louis Blanc would have beaten Louis Philippe?

General Dumas came to me from Claremont on Friday last to thank me in the name of the King for my mention of His Majesty in my speech.[1] I was glad to receive his grateful congratulations, for I was by no means certain that the King would have altogether approved of what I said. But the fact is one must manage an audience like the House of Commons, with a strong party hating all Kings. . . .

[*Aug.* 17, 1848.] — I send you a line in the midst of a brawling debate about the Pope of Rome. Sir Robert Inglis horrified at the idea of red stockings being seen in England. I have less fear of them, than of blue.

What I wanted to tell you at the end of my last letter, was the feeling at Claremont about Palmerston, but I have not time to do it justice. He persecutes them, according to their story, prevents people calling, notices every little attention of the Court. The Queen and Prince Albert are obliged to show their sympathy under the rose, and they do it frequently. Claremont speaks most gratefully of their disposi-

[1] See above, p. 175.

tions, but of Palmerston as of an ogre. One trait, L. Philippe paying them a visit, and the talk being of Jenny Lind, he said, 'Alas! I shall never see her, for I don't think it will do for the Comte de Neuilly[1] to go to the Opera.' The Queen did not dare to ask the C. and Comtesse de Neuilly to the Palace, but a few days after, at Her Majesty's instigation, the Q. Dowager asked the illustrous exiles to a little concert. They came, and they heard Jenny! . . .

Sept. 2.— . . . To-morrow we go to Claremont, having received a notification to that effect. In such weather the drive alone will be charming. . . .

Dick,[2] who has just come in, tells me that Louis Blanc is positively staying over the way (Pall Mall) with Monckton Milnes! I really think that the frequent guest of Louis Philippe might have grudged his hospitality in this respect.

Sept. 5.— . . . I spoke to the Queen,[3] very naturally, on the subject you hinted at.[4] I found Her Majesty had already written to you, what she also stated to me. I ventured to observe, that there was a great difference between being the guests of a country house and mixing in the miscellaneous crowds of London saloons, and that there were occasions when the Princes might create sympathies and make friends, whose good feeling and influence might hereafter be useful. This view of the case was not without effect, but the answer had been written and sent. The Queen more than once desired that I would personally express to you her sense of your kindness and consideration, which she said much touched her.

The poor Princes do nothing but fish, and have not much sport. They have no horses, of which they complain. The King and Queen have now a carriage and a pair of horses. There is also one riding-horse for one of the generals, who is too fat to walk, and a pony. All this she said herself.

Coming home in the park, we met a most graceful child, about three years, with a singularly sweet face, and the bluest eyes I ever saw. His nurse called him Monseigneur, and the unhappy little exile was the Prince de Condé. There are six grandchildren at Claremont! On Sundays all six dine with their grandparents, on other days three only. . . .

There was, as we have seen,[5] an even more notable exile in England in this year than the French King or

[1] The King and Queen of the French passed, in exile, as the Comte and Comtesse de Neuilly.

[2] Quintin Dick, M.P. (C.), for Maldon 1832–47, and for Aylesbury, 1848–52.

[3] The Queen of the French.

[4] An invitation to the Joinvilles and D'Aumales to go to Wynyard.

[5] P. 110.

his Minister. On May 17, Londonderry, who had formerly been Ambassador in Vienna, took Disraeli to Eaton Square to introduce him to Prince Metternich. That eminent man had been mainly responsible for the policy of Austria for nearly forty years. Throughout that period he had been the leading representative of Conservatism in Europe, the man to whose influence was principally due the preservation of the *status quo* both in the relations of the European Powers to one another and in their internal affairs. He was the chief bugbear of Continental Liberalism, and in foreign politics was at the opposite pole to Canning first, and to Palmerston afterwards. But, if he was insensitive to abuses and sceptical about popular rights and parliamentary institutions, he could fairly claim that he had resuscitated the power of Austria after her defeat by Napoleon, and had succeeded in keeping her motley States together, including the large territories in Italy which were wrenched from her a few years after his fall. This was no small achievement. He was now seventy-five years old, and could entertain little hope of restoration to high office; but his mental powers were quite unimpaired. Disraeli had long admired 'the serene intelligence of the profound Metternich.' It was indeed natural that one who aspired to lead the Conservative party in England should be attracted to the living embodiment of the cause on the Continent of Europe. The attraction seems to have been mutual. Metternich was living as a hermit, in Londonderry's phrase; but, though he saw few others, he saw and corresponded with Disraeli frequently. 'I have seen Metternich twice at great length,' Disraeli writes to his sister on May 30. 'He talks very much, and is very kind.' Metternich's wife, Princess Mélanie, notes in her diary for May, 1848, that a complete understanding was at once established between the two men. Both were prone to philosophise about politics; Metternich prided himself upon being 'un diplomate philosophe,' as Disraeli was eminently a statesman of ideas. They agreed in

Prince Metternich.
from the Mezzotint by S. Cousins
after the portrait by Sir Thomas Lawrence. P.R.A.
at Hughenden.

inted in England.

deploring the socialistic doctrines which were promulgated from Paris, in wishing to stem the revolutionary tide throughout Europe, and in reprobating Palmerston's policy of constant interference, in the interests of Liberalism, between Continental Governments and their peoples. The following passage in *Lord George Bentinck*[1] would have been adopted by Metternich, even if it did not owe something to his inspiration :

> It is very desirable that the people of England should arrive at some conclusions as to the conditions on which the government of Europe can be carried on. They will, perhaps, after due reflection discover that ancient communities like the European must be governed either by traditionary influences or by military force. Those who in their ardour of renovation imagine that there is a third mode, and that our societies can be reconstructed on the great Transatlantic model, will find that when they have destroyed traditionary influences there will be peculiar features in their body politic which do not obtain in the social standard which they imitate, and these may be described as elements of disturbance. A dynasty may be subverted, but it leaves as its successor a family of princely pretenders; a confiscated aristocracy takes the shape of factions; a plundered Church acts on the tender consciences of toiling millions; corporate bodies displaced from their ancient authority no longer contribute their necessary and customary quota to the means of government; outraged tradition in multiplied forms enfeebles or excruciates the reformed commonwealth. In this state of affairs, after a due course of paroxysms, for the sake of maintaining order and securing the rights of industry, the state quits the senate and takes refuge in the camp.
>
> Let us not be deluded by forms of government. The word may be republic in France, constitutional monarchy in Prussia, absolute monarchy in Austria, but the thing is the same. Wherever there is a vast standing army, the government is the government of the sword. . . . [An] irresistible law . . . dooms Europe to the alternate sway of disciplined armies or secret societies; the camp or the convention.

Two speeches of Disraeli on foreign affairs, in June and August of 1848, were clearly made under Metternich's influence; and Princess Mélanie's diary shows the importance which Metternich attached to both of them.

[1] Ch. 27.

The first, on June 5, arose out of an awkward complication with Spain. Palmerston had carried a policy of meddling with the internal affairs of that country so far as to instruct the British Minister, Sir Henry Bulwer, to recommend earnestly to the Queen of Spain the adoption of a legal and constitutional course of government. In view of Louis Philippe's downfall, she would do wisely to call to her councils 'some of those men who possess the confidence of the Liberal party.' The advice may have been good, but it was certainly impertinent, and it led to the immediate expulsion of Sir Henry Bulwer, who had previously rendered himself obnoxious to the Spanish Government by his political intrigues. In the debate, Disraeli, while defending Bulwer, who was his friend, took the opportunity to criticise the whole system of Liberal foreign policy. He said his objection to Liberalism was that it endeavoured to carry on the very practical business of the foreign affairs of the country by means of philosophical ideas and abstract theories.

You could not find a country governed by an absolute form without telling it that the only way to be happy and prosperous was to have a House of Lords and a House of Commons, and an English treaty of commerce. All this ended in confusion. All that was practical you never obtained. You never obtained the treaty of commerce, but you fostered confusion and convulsion. By lending all the aid of a great country like England to some miserable faction, you created parties in domestic policy in every country, from Athens to Madrid, deteriorated the prosperity and condition of the people, and laid the seeds of infinite confusion. The noble lord opposite proceeded in this course — the great prophet of Liberalism in foreign affairs.

The Liberals had introduced a sentimental instead of a political principle into the conduct of foreign affairs:

You looked on the English Constitution as a model farm. You forced this Constitution in every country. You laid it down as a great principle that you were not to consider the interests of England, or the interests of the country you were in connection with, but that you were to consider the great system of Liberalism, which had nothing to do with the interests of England, and was generally antagonistic with the interests of the country with which you were in connection.

The second speech was delivered on the Foreign Office vote in supply on August 16, and dealt mainly with British relations with Rome, Naples, Sardinia, and Austria. 'Last August,' said Disraeli, 'the Lord Privy Seal [Minto] went on a very peculiar and roving mission . . . to teach politics in the country in which Machiavelli was born.' Disraeli had an easy task in demonstrating the failure of the mission by pointing to the chaotic state of Italy. Palmerston had sympathised with the abortive revolutions in the peninsula founded on nationalist ideas; but Disraeli was scornful of 'this modern, new-fangled, sentimental principle of nationality.' Yet this was the basis on which Palmerston proposed to mediate. Palmerston was suspected of encouraging France to invade Italy and drive out the Austrians, who, under Radetzky, had just put down the insurrections in Lombardy. Of good relations with France Disraeli was a strong supporter. 'If you mean, by an alliance with France, by a cordial understanding with France, or whatever other phrase you may use, that those important affairs and those great events which periodically and surely occur in the world should be regulated and managed in concert by these two leading nations, after previous council, animated by a wise spirit of concession and compromise, and leading to a cordial co-operation, that is a system of which I shall ever be a feeble but a warm supporter.' Queen Elizabeth worked thus with Henri IV., and Cromwell with Mazarin; Bolingbroke and Walpole, who differed so widely in many things, agreed in supporting an Anglo-French *entente* of this kind. 'But an understanding which is only founded on forced occasions and forced opportunities—the incidents invented to justify and occasion the co-operation, instead of the co-operation arising from the natural order of the events—that is an understanding and that is an alliance which, before this time, has occasioned the greatest evil, and which, in the present case, might lead to the greatest possible disasters.' France had no right to invade Italy. He protested against the attempt to regulate the world by a contrived concert with the Jacobin party, then in power in Paris. 'It is the system that commences with "fraternity" and ends with assassination; it is the system that begins by preaching universal charity, and concludes by practising general spoliation.' Happily, no such invasion as Disraeli deprecated took place.

In this speech, which Disraeli himself thought would make a noise, and which Greville calls 'very brilliant' and Hobhouse 'amusing and striking,' there were, according to Princess Metternich, certain expressions which Palmerston maintained could only have been furnished to Disraeli by her husband; and Metternich certainly called the particular attention of the Austrian Foreign Office to it, and pointed out that 'ce grand orateur' had borrowed from him the idea of the difference between political and sentimental mediation, the first based on treaties, the second on nationality.[1]

Even before making Metternich's acquaintance, Disraeli had scoffed in the House of Commons[2] at the principle of nationality as a ground for international action. This was on the dispute between Germany and Denmark over Schleswig-Holstein. Here Palmerston and he were in general agreement. Indeed, few public men in England, with the conspicuous and creditable exception of the Prince Consort, appreciated or sympathised with the movement for German unity. Disraeli treated the 'dreamy and dangerous nonsense' of German nationality as merely a thin pretext for Prussian invasion; but, on the other hand, long before his countrymen in general awoke to the meaning of what was passing before them, he realised the vitally important fact that Germany had embarked on a policy which would make her eventually a great maritime Power, the rival of England in the North Sea. It was actually laid down as a principle, he

[1] Metternich, *Mémoires*, Vol. VIII.

[2] April 19, 1848.

said, by men occupying seats in the Cabinets of Europe, that wheresoever the German language is spoken, there the German flag ought to wave. But if so, why did not the Prussians invade Alsace, and meet at once the high spirit of France? Or why did they not occupy Livonia, and thus encounter the colossal power of Russia? That would be consistent and national; but the principle only held good towards the north.

And why? Because it is in the north, when surrendered, that the pretext vanishes and the cause appears. Germany is the centre of Europe, and has no reason, one would think, to complain of the territorial advantages which have been allotted to it. Its broad and rich lands are watered by the three most considerable rivers of Europe—the Rhine, the Elbe, and the Danube. But Germany, which possesses almost every other advantage, is not a great naval Power, and Germany wants a coast. This is the real reason why Denmark, supposed to be weak, is to be invaded in this age of liberty on the plea of nationality. It is to gain the harbours of the Baltic, and to secure the mouths of the Elbe, that the plea of German nationality is put forth. Hitherto in the Baltic Russia and the Scandinavian Peninsula have prevented this project of Germany; while Holland and Great Britain have intercepted in the North Sea its maritime development. But now, under shelter of the plea of nationality, taking advantage of the fact that the King of Denmark possesses in Schleswig perhaps 150,000 subjects of German race, his dominions are to be invaded, and may be conquered, notwithstanding the valour of his few but determined subjects, in order that Prussia may suddenly appear as a great maritime Power.

I do not wish to argue this case with respect to the interests of England. I do not wish to say anything about whether it is or is not for the interest of England that a new naval Power should spring up among the nations of the Baltic or the Northern Seas. But this I wish to lay down as a principle that it is for the interest of England, and not of England alone, but of all Europe, that peace should be maintained. And peace cannot be maintained if the policy of Prussia be permitted to pass unnoticed and uncensured.

'I never can believe,' Disraeli added in memorable words, 'that the peace of Europe is to be maintained by hiding our heads in the sand, and comforting ourselves with the conviction that nobody will find us out.' We had guaranteed Schleswig to Denmark, and must not shirk our obligations. The speech was naturally welcomed warmly in Denmark, which for the time was saved from dismemberment, and Disraeli's portrait was in all the library windows as Denmark's spokesman. The speech, moreover, initiated or confirmed a friendship, which Disraeli greatly valued, with Count Reventlow, the Danish Minister; who formally conveyed to the orator the thanks of his Sovereign and of the whole Danish nation. The relations between Reventlow and Disraeli became so close that, when Reventlow died, Disraeli wrote (October 4, 1851) to his sister: 'I am much shocked at the death of Reventlow. He was one of the best-hearted and most genial beings I ever knew, and clever, too; and, independent of all this, was my secret agent in the Diplomatic Corps, and I always found him faithful and accurate. It is a great loss to me in every way.'

It is not difficult to collect, from *Lord George Bentinck* and from the speeches which we have quoted, Disraeli's views on foreign policy at this time. They avoid the extremes of Palmerstonian meddlesomeness on the one hand, and of Cobdenite pacificism on the other. Owing to his opposition to Whig adventures, the Disraeli of these years has sometimes been claimed as a supporter of non-intervention. Non-intervention, it may be observed, is an ambiguous word. It is most frequently used nowadays to describe a policy of complete detachment from European politics of all kinds; but in the debates of the middle of the last century it generally meant only the policy of abstention from intervening in the domestic affairs of other nations. In this latter sense, no doubt, Disraeli then and afterwards was a non-interventionist, as most subsequent British statesmen have been, but Palmerston emphatically was not. To claim, however, that Disraeli advocated at any time a policy of isolation argues a very superficial reading of his speeches; and, as it happens, he took care, in the debate on the Address in 1849, to define his position. After blaming the Government for their 'mock mediations,' he continued: —

> In making these remarks, I am far from wishing to enforce a pedantic adherence to that passive policy which, in the barbarous dialect of the day, is called 'non-intervention.' On the contrary, I am persuaded that, in the settlement of the great affairs of Europe, the presence of England is the best guarantee of peace. But it should be the presence of England in accordance with the law of nations, and with the stipulations of treaties.[1]

Disraeli's foreign policy may, indeed, be summarised thus: The preservation of peace, guaranteed mainly by a steady understanding with France; the strict observance of treaty obligations; the avoidance of intermeddling in the domestic affairs of other nations, and especially of stirring up disorder in other countries under the specious pretext of promoting liberal institutions; the discouragement of sentimental politics, based either on the idea of nationality, which tends to alter the existing boundaries of States, or on Jacobin notions, which are subversive of all established and traditional order — in a word, the maintenance unimpaired of British interests and British prestige with a due respect for the rights and interests of others. It may appear strange that Disraeli, who had so strong a belief in race, should have had so little faith in nationality. The ideas are surely akin; but it must be remembered that race, as Disraeli has told us, depends on blood, and nationality is often more a matter of locality. To a Jew, therefore, nationality could never make so powerful an appeal as race. Race, moreover, was not being used as a lever to upset territorial arrangements and overthrow Governments, whereas nationality was proving to be an eminently explosive force. It is, however, a serious blot on Disraeli's reputation for prescience that he entirely failed to foresee what the principle of nationality was to effect for Germany and Italy. His general principles of foreign policy were, in the main,

[1] The intervention of Great Britain to-day (1914) on behalf of Belgium exactly fulfils Disraeli's conditions.

right; but his sympathies were often, especially at this period, on the wrong side.

The revolutionary movements of 1848, which threatened to carry all before them in the spring, did not maintain their ground as the year wore on. Great Britain was unscathed by the upheaval; the Chartist demonstration was a fiasco, the Young Ireland insurrection almost a farce. The rioting in Paris in the summer was put down by Cavaignac; and subsequently Louis Napoleon was elected President by an enormous majority of votes, and France had once more a fairly stable government. This did not happen till December; but by the autumn all over the Continent the reaction had begun, and Metternich could philosophise with comparative cheerfulness over the events and tendencies of the time: —

From Prince Metternich.

BRIGHTON, *ce 2 Octobre*, 1848. — . . . J'ignore si je vous ai jamais fait part de mes pronostiques pour l'automne dans lequel nous sommes entré avec le mois de Septembre. Si je l'ai fait, alors vous trouverez que mon pressentiment ne reçoit point un démenti par la marche des évènements. Si je ne vous ai rien dit, alors sachez que ma prévision a reposée sur la valeur que j'attache à l'action qui dans le monde politique, comme dans celui matériel, est propre aux deux saisons qui, parmi les quatre qui composent l'année astronomique, sont actives, en opposition avec l'été et l'hiver, qui sont latentes. Jetez vos regards sur l'histoire, et vous verrez que j'ai raison. Si vous voulez une deduction sur ce sujet, je pourrais vous la livrer; comme je ne suis pas enclin à la pedantérie, il me suffira de vous dire que l'expérience m'a appris à fixer dans tous les temps mes regards avec une attention particulière sur ce qui, en règle commun, se fait jour au printemps et tire son premier bilan en automne.

Ceci dit, voyons où en est le monde à l'époque du bilan de 1848.

Si son résultat n'est point favorable aux principes sur lesquels peut seul reposer l'ordre qui forme la base de celui social, il n'est pas d'avantage satisfaisant pour les défenseurs des doctrines subversives. . . .

Où se trouve aujourd'hui le premier élément du désordre — l'enthousiasme? Quelle valeur ont encore les mots — de *fraternité*, de *nationalité*, de *progrès?*

highly to me of the young Emperor,[1] as a man of character and resource; firm, of great integrity, and warlike. He seemed to think he would develop greatly in these troubles. . . .

Disraeli endeavoured to get Metternich to visit him at Hughenden, but apparently without success: —

To Prince Metternich.

[*Undated, August or September*, 1849.] — It made me very happy indeed to see you before I left Town.

Great events have since occurred, and they will not, I am sure, retard your recovery.

I am now reading critically the papers on the affairs of Italy presented to the House of Commons at the end of the Session. Their perusal will very much redound to your honor. They have, I confess, somewhat lowered my opinion of Palmerston. He has been fortunate, but he has not deserved to be *felix*. These papers afford indubitable evidence of his want of temper in the conduct of affairs, and of a reliance on the views and information of very second-rate persons, such as our Minister, Mr. Abercromby, at Turin, whom I should be very sorry to employ. Lord Napier at Naples seems a flippant schoolboy turning theme sentences *à la* Tacitus. Palmerston's own despatches are very badly written, though they aim at composition. They very unfavorably contrast with your own, which are, as I ever find them, models of diplomatic communication: precise, singularly clear, founded on thorough knowledge of circumstances and principles, and, though always distinguished by that sunny temper which is your characteristic, not without a species of archness, which often exposes with happy humor the weak points of your less-disciplined antagonists. I have particularly in my mind at this moment your management of the Ferrara question.

I wish I could induce your Highness to find a total change of air and scene amid our Chiltern Hills. I can easily understand why you should decline invitations to grand châteaux, and shrink from the weariness of pompous circles. We have no golden saloons to welcome you with, but only affectionate hearts: but you would be master entirely of yourself and of your time, and the Princess should drive a pony-chair in our woods, which would suit her exactly. Little more than half an hour's course on the Great Western would carry you to Maidenhead, and there our carriages should meet you and yours, and carry you ten miles through a sylvan country to this roof. I would arrange that your despatches should come

[1] The Emperor Francis Joseph.

to you twice a day. Think of this, my dear master, seriously. I am so persuaded that it would do you good that I have almost the audacity to write to the Princess herself, and entreat her to support my proposition.

'Sur le point de quitter ce beau et bon pays-ci,' Metternich wrote on October 7, 1849, to Disraeli, to tell him how anxious he was that his departure should cause no break in personal relations which he highly valued. Their spheres of labour had been different, he said, but their principles were similar. They agreed in the aim of their policy, 'la conservation,' the only object worth spending a life in defending and cultivating. It was 'a beautiful and affecting letter,' Disraeli told his sister. 'I received it in time to embrace him, exactly half an hour before he left England.' The two men did not meet again, though occasional letters passed between them. Metternich never returned to office, but he was able to go back to Vienna in 1851, and there exercised great influence over the counsels of the Austrian Court till his death in 1859. Disraeli always retained an affectionate recollection of his intercourse with him in 1848–49.

To Lord Stanhope.[1]

GROSVENOR GATE, *Feb.* 12, 1864. — You have much gratified me by your kindness in sending me a copy of the letters of Prince Metternich to yourself, which are most interesting. Events have given them a fresh relish, but his letters are too full of thought ever to become obsolete.

What a different man he really was to what those fancied him, who formed their judgment in the glitter of Vienna! A profound head and an affectionate heart! Had he not been a Prince and a Prime Minister, he would have been a great Professor. He said to me once, 'J'étais né penseur.'

To Lady Londonderry.

HUGHENDEN MANOR, *Dec.* 30, 1849. — . . . I find the pressure of public life so great in this age of struggle that I have been forced to give up every country house except my own, and have been too much engrossed to ask anyone there. I am surrounded by piles of blue-books, and two posts a day

[1] The 5th Earl, the historian.

bear me reams of despatches; so that my recess of relaxation has combined the plodding of a notary with the anxiety of a house steward. Pleasant! and what is called gratified ambition.

What an imbroglio of affairs! Your friends, the free-traders, say, that if we retrace our steps, there will be a revolution; and most certainly, if we do not do something, there will be one, for before four-and-twenty months are passed, every farmer will be a Republican. Indeed, it requires unceasing vigilance, and constant resource, to keep them, now, steady. Can you solve the knot? . . .

I think I told you of my farewell with Metternich. Tho' nobody talks of foreign affairs, I hear, among the initiated, that there are odd whispers, and the general state of things is anything but satisfactory. The fact is the elements of government do not exist in the greater part of Europe, and we are destroying them pretty quickly in England. Russia alone develops herself, and will develop herself still more in the great struggle which is perhaps nearer than we imagine. Once destroy the English aristocracy, and enthrone the commercial principle as omnipotent in this island, and there will be no repelling force, which will prevent the Slavonians conquering the whole of the South of Europe. I look upon France as quite exhausted: insolvent in purse and soul: no Republic can restore it, for there is no plunder left to support a Republic: and plunder was the inspiration of the great movement of the last century.

Amid all this confusion, Ireland may rise from its ashes: it will repudiate the commercial principle, and you will become a feudal Princess in the Tower of Garron.

CHAPTER VIII

'The Hopeless Question of Protection'

1849–1850

'I found the Tory party in the House of Commons, when I acceded to its chief management, in a state of great depression and disorganisation. Lord George Bentinck had only mustered 120 in his motion on the Irish Railways, which was to try our strength in the new Parliament. By a series of motions to relieve the Agricultural Interest by revising and partially removing the local taxation of the country, I withdrew the Tory party gradually from the hopeless question of Protection, rallied all those members who were connected either personally or by their constituencies with the land, and finally brought the state of parties in the House of Commons nearly to a tie.' Such was Disraeli's succinct account, given in 1860, of his labours and successes during his early years of leadership.

The party was indeed depressed and disorganised when he became responsible for its management in the House of Commons. Its disorganisation had been shown in the difficulties which attended the choice of a leader; its depression was the natural result of the waning fortunes of its principal policy. In spite of all Disraeli's and Bentinck's efforts, the Whig Ministry, steadily supported by Peel and his friends, had broadened and deepened the Free Trade system. The fact that many of the hopes held out by the Free Traders had not been realised, that the change in the commercial system had been followed, not by plenty at home and peace abroad, but by domestic distress and European convulsions, had not caused the commercial and manufacturing classes or their Parliamentary leaders to lose confidence. A cause that could survive so unpromising a start would count an increasing body of adherents when better times came, and both in numbers and in wealth that part of the nation which believed in Free Trade must become more and more predominant. As Dr. Cunningham writes: 'In England the industrial classes hold the key of the position.' On Disraeli, as he surveyed the inheritance into which he had entered, reflections of this kind were inevitably forced. If he did not realise at the outset that, whatever justification there might be for Protection in theory, it was practically, in the England of that day, 'a hopeless question,' the experience of the session and the facts that came before him drove his mind surely, and not slowly, in that direction.

The duty to his hand was to build up a strong Opposition party which might be ready to carry on the Government whenever disaster should overtake the feeble Whig Ministry. In the first place it was necessary to hearten and solidify the strictly Protectionist ranks, and in the next place to attract support from the outside. An accession of strength could most readily be obtained from the rank and file of the Peelites, who were in general harmony with the Protectionists on all subjects except commercial policy. There was clearly no possibility of obtaining in the 1847 Parliament any repeal of the Corn Law of 1846. It was therefore wise policy not to push Protection into the foreground, but to endeavour to secure for the Agricultural Interest in other ways compensation for the loss which they had suffered. At the same time, though the conditions were not quite so bad in 1849 as in 1848, there was still famine in Ireland, and commercial suffering and agricultural distress in Great Britain, to show that the prophecies of the Free Traders had not been fulfilled. In his speech in moving an amendment to the Address, Disraeli said the new commercial system had had a fair trial and had failed. He pointed to reciprocity as the proper policy. On the principle of reciprocity, which was at once cosmopolitan and national, the commercial system could be reconstructed in a manner beneficial to the Mother-Country and advantageous to the Colonies. But questions of commercial policy occupied a comparatively small portion of a speech which an unfriendly journal[1] was compelled to describe as a 'masterpiece of comprehensiveness. . . . The world was all before him where to chose, and he chose the whole of it.' The state of Europe, and the interferences of the British Foreign Office, were his principal theme. 'There wanted but one ingredient in the mess to make the incantation perfectly infernal. A republic without republicans, an empire without an emperor, required only mediations without on object to mediate about; and the saturnalia of diplomacy could mix with the orgies of politics.' Retrenchment had been promised in the Queen's Speech, to meet the wishes of Cobden and Bright. Disraeli said that the Conservative party had always been in favour of retrenchment, but how could retrenchment be possible in 1849, when the world was everywhere disturbed, seeing that in the beginning of 1848, before the convulsions had occurred, increased expenditure was thought necessary? The Government had yielded to the clamour of the Manchester School, who, in Disraeli's paraphrase, 'counselled the people of England to lower their tone.' Disraeli, however, denounced the politics and defied the predictions of that school, because he had faith in the people of England, their genius, and their destiny. It was a spirited opening of the campaign; but Palmerston made a clever defence of his policy, and, as a motion for adjournment was defeated by a considerable majority, Disraeli withdrew his amendment.

The first of his motions to relieve the Agricultural Interest was introduced a month later, on March 8. In

[1] *Morning Chronicle.*

the interval the anxieties of the past weeks had brought on illness.

To Sarah Disraeli.

March 7, 1849.—I ought to have acknowledged your affectionate letter, but in addition to all my troubles, perhaps in consequence of them, I have had for the last fortnight one of my worst attacks of low fever, so that till to-day I have never had an hour to prepare for the speech of to-morrow, from which so much is expected. The country is up in arms about my motion. I have received between forty and fifty letters every day, from every county indeed, except Bucks. The meeting of the farmers in Willis's Rooms was remarkable, and my name received, Lord Malmesbury told me, with the greatest cheering he ever heard.[1]

The meeting to which allusion is here made was held on the previous day, and attended by a thousand tenant farmers from all parts of the country. They demanded revision of imperial and local taxation, and the repeal of the malt tax, in order to mitigate the evils produced by the abandonment of Protection; and the report in *The Times* bears out Malmesbury's statement that Disraeli's name was enthusiastically received, and his Parliamentary conduct spoken of in terms of warm approbation.

Disraeli's motion was that the House should go into Committee to take into consideration the burdens on land, and especially the unequal pressure of local taxation. He said he was not going to enter into controversy about recent changes, but he still believed that the only means to be pursued against hostile tariffs were countervailing duties. It was estimated that the income of the whole country was £249,000,000, while the rental of the land amounted to £67,000,000. Why should the £10,000,000 raised in rates be charged only on the £67,000,000, instead of also on the other £180,000,000? The maintenance of the poor was not specially a local duty. It was a social duty; and the same reasoning applied to the administration of justice and the repair of roads. The question was a simple one: Was it just or unjust that real property,

[1] *Letters*, p. 217.

forming one-fourth of the income of the country, should alone bear burdens imposed on account of matters in which all property was equally interested? His plan was to put half the local rates on the Consolidated Fund.

Disraeli ended with an impressive warning to the Government. The landed interest considered that it had been treated unfairly. It was proverbially loyal, but Ministers would do well not to abuse that loyalty. The descendants of those who refused to pay ship-money were not to be trifled with. Their motto was 'Live and let live'; while the Manchester School said that England could prosper without any agriculture at all, provided it became the workshop of the world.

> Your system and theirs (said Disraeli to the Free Traders) are exactly contrary. They invite union. They believe that national prosperity can only be produced by the prosperity of all classes. You prefer to remain in isolated splendour and solitary magnificence. But, believe me, I speak not as your enemy when I say that it will be an exception to the principles which seem hitherto to have ruled society, if you can succeed in maintaining the success at which you aim without the possession of that permanence and stability which the territorial principle alone can afford. Although you may for a moment flourish after their destruction, although your ports may be filled with shipping, your factories smoke on every plain, and your forges flame in every city, I see no reason why you should form an exception to that which the page of history has mournfully recorded; that you, too, should not fade like the Tyrian dye, and moulder like the Venetian palaces. But, united with the land, you will obtain the best and surest foundation upon which to build your enduring welfare: you will find in that interest a counsellor in all your troubles, in danger your undaunted champion, and in adversity your steady customer. . . . I wish to see the agriculture, the commerce, and the manufactures of England, not adversaries, but co-mates and partners — and rivals only in the ardour of their patriotism and in the activity of their public spirit.

The motion was opposed by Ministers, Radicals, and Peelites alike. Sir Charles Wood, for Ministers, in what Disraeli called 'a very plausible, well-managed speech,' maintained that, as rates were a deduction from rent, the proposal would benefit only the owner, and not the occupier; and assumed throughout that, in order to find the money to carry out Disraeli's views, there must be a great increase in the income tax. Cobden also held that the interests of landlord sand tenants were antagonistic, and that Disraeli's proposal would not benefit the farmer, who could only be benefited by a reduction of the material expenditure. The opposition of the Peelites was a disappointment to the Country party. Malmesbury held that the motion, as it had nothing to do with Free Trade, gave the Peelites a fair opportunity for reconciliation with their old friends; but Sidney Herbert and Goulburn both spoke against it, and their party as a whole voted with the Government. Disraeli, in reply to Wood and Cobden, pointed out that the present generation of farmers would enjoy the remission in full before it became absorbed in rent, and concluded with an assertion that the question could not be regarded as disposed of by this solitary discussion. The real property of the country would no longer consent to contribute two public revenues. They demanded justice; if they were rebuffed, they would come again and again with the cry of a 'protected and regenerated England.'

The motion was defeated on March 15 by 280 votes to 189—a majority of 91. Disraeli professed himself on the whole satisfied, and his friends and political rivals congratulated him. 'Egad, you are a stupendous fellow!' wrote Ferrand. At Lady Palmerston's evening party the congratulations on his opening speech, wrote Disraeli to his sister, 'far exceeded old days, even when I turned out Peel.' He heard indirectly what Russell had written to the Queen about it: 'Great praise as to its power of argument, thought, and rhetoric. Palmerston was still warmer; and Lord Malmesbury told me that Stanley, "who never pays compliments, you know, that's not his way," said it was one of the best things that was ever done.' Manners's compliment was in the grand style. He quoted in his letter the lines,

Cum tot sustineas, et tanta negotia *solus*,
. . . in publica commoda peccem,
Si longo sermone morer tua tempora, Cæsar.

To Lord John Manners.

GROSVENOR GATE, *March* 18, 1849.

MY DEAREST JOHN,— . . . I am much gratified by your opinion of the opening of the late movement: I trust the result has not disappointed you. I look upon the division as of great importance. It far exceeded my expectations, not only in the numbers we ourselves polled — but in the very diminished amount of our opponents. Trials of strength where the government majorities form only *two* figures commence to be interesting. At any rate, our friends ought not, I think, to be dissatisfied with the new management — when in the same week[2] — on vital questions — such a body of troops, and troops full of life and, almost, enthusiasm, have been brought into action with so much discipline and effect.

As a party move, I hold the last to have been most wise and discreet: but as a movement of advantage to the landed interest, I think it, tho' of course not successful in its form, very beneficial in its spirit. . . . We carried the war into the enemy's camp, and acted on the aggressive at the right moment. Our tactics will prevent any fresh addition to our burthens, and will give us a claim to relief if ever there be a surplus. Independently of all which considerations, it gives us a better position for future movements of a more determined character, if the occasion ever be ripe for them.

Granby spoke very well on my motion: I think the best speech he has yet made: with more fire, and not too many documents, which are dangerous materials to handle.

But, alas! my dear John — generally speaking — what is the result of the debate as far as abilities are concerned? Was there ever such an opportunity to develop men! I kept down Bankes, Miles for a long time, Newdegate, and all the old rubbish, and gave a list to the Speaker of men to bring forward — Seymer[3] (who, by the bye, disappointed me), now quite with us — Brooke[4]—Trollope, of whom I have some hopes — Jolliffe[5] — George Manners, etc., etc. I could scarcely get one of them out: the Speaker was absolutely sending Beresford with messages to our men to tell them to get up. They

[1] *Letters*, p. 216.

[2] The division on the second reading of the Navigation Bill was taken in the same week as that on Disraeli's motion.

[3] M.P. for Dorset.

[4] M.P. for South Warwickshire, afterwards 4th Earl of Warwick.

[5] M.P. for Petersfield, afterwards Conservative Whip, and raised to the peerage as Baron Hylton, on Derby's recommendation, in 1866.

funked, and the Speaker was obliged to call Miles and Newdegate, who were always on their legs, and who were the very men I wished to be silent — Miles speaking of nothing but butcher's meat, and Newdegate anathematising imports under any circumstances. Alas! alas! an army without officers! How Stanley, if the Whigs at the end of the season play him a trick, is to form a Government — find at least seven Cabinet Ministers in the Commons, and about five-and-thirty other officials there — surpasses imagination.

As for the Peelites, they are more mysterious and hostile than ever. No one knows what they are after. . . .

I should think on the whole, as far as I am concerned, matters are improving. It is quite clear, that March,[1] and that clique, have entirely waived their prejudices, and generally speaking the machinery works better. But, after all, it will be impossible to go on without some assistance. It is a fact, that I must have forced a division on Monday in order to reply to Wood. This will never do. All my hopes and my heart are turned, in this dilemma and these difficulties, to yourself. With you at my right hand, much might be done: and I cannot believe that any lengthened period can elapse without your returning to a post for which you are in so many respects so greatly qualified. — Ever your faithful friend, D.

The other great party fight of the early weeks of the session was over the Bill to repeal the Navigation Laws — a Bill which had failed in 1848, but was passed in 1849. It was the complement of previous Free Trade legislation; but many Free Traders, remembering Adam Smith's dictum, that 'defence is of much more importance than opulence,' hesitated to carry their principles to a logical conclusion which might impair the efficiency of the Royal Navy. Disraeli did not take the leading part in the fight over this Bill; the protagonist of the Opposition was Herries. The second reading was only carried by a majority of fifty-six, Gladstone, in spite of his Free Trade views, making a speech in favour of reciprocity. In Committee Disraeli made a lively sally against Labouchere, who was conducting the Bill for the Government, for throwing over certain clauses, and against Gladstone for abandoning his amendments in order not to imperil the Bill.

[1] M.P. for West Sussex, afterwards 6th Duke of Richmond, and Disraeli's colleague in 1859, 1866, and 1874.

To Sarah Disraeli.

HOUSE OF COMMONS, *March* 26.—Last Friday was most important, but quite burked in *The Times*, probably from being in Committee, where nothing is expected and little reported, yet there is a capital report in the *Morning Post*, which I have sent you; the men returning to the House when it was breaking up; Gladstone and Labouchere both standing, while the cheers after I had sat down resounded, etc., all very animated. Palmerston said he never remembered a more amusing scene; the way I brought the men back, as if I said, 'Hullo! you fellows, come back there!'

The Whigs will go out if the Lords throw out the Navigation Bill, and I think from present appearances the Lords will. I have had several conferences with Stanley as to our future and consequent movements, and the Cabinet is in embryo! He says I must be Chief Minister in the Commons. I confess myself that I think this a little too strong, and would willingly find a substitute. . . .[1]

In the middle of the fight over the Bill came the Easter holidays. From Hughenden, on April 12, Disraeli wrote to tell Lady Londonderry: 'There will be a hot and perhaps eventful campaign between this and Whitsun. Under ordinary circumstances the Whigs ought to go out and, perhaps even under the present, wish it. But what then? The agricultural distress is so great and the general prosperity is so doubtful that, even if we were inclined, fusion under the standard of Peel, or with his adherents even, seems impossible.' The Bill came up for third reading on April 23. Graham in the debate made a great point of quoting Stanley's declaration, on the first day of the session, in favour of Protection. Protection being the only alternative policy, Graham supported the Bill as 'the capital necessary to crown the work we have already accomplished.' Without it that work was imperfect. But if, said Disraeli in reply, the column they had raised had not realised the expectations of their creative fancy, they might hesitate before incurring the additional expense of crowning it with a costly capital. Graham had ended his speech by declaring that he was opposed to reaction, and favourable to pro-

[1] *Letters*, pp. 216, 217.

gress tempered by prudence and discretion. 'Progress where?' said Disraeli. 'Progress to Paradise, or progress to the Devil? People don't want to hear any longer of these undefined, windy phrases of "progress"; they want to know where you are progressing to. What are you at? What do you mean to do?' The Manchester School were intelligible. They wanted disestablishment, destruction of landed tenure, a change of the whole constitution. But what did the Peelites want? These 'dilettante disciples of progress' were very dangerous opponents. Disraeli asked the House by their vote to beat down 'that great statistical conspiracy which has so long tampered with the resources and trifled with the fortunes of a great country.'[1] The arguments of the Opposition had their effect, and the Bill was only carried by a majority of 61 — 275 to 214.

To Lord Stanley.

CARLTON, 2 *o'clock* [*April* 24, 1849]. — I send you, by Lord March, a little line, tho' it is long past midnight, to tell you of the result. I think we made a very good division indeed — but Newmarket and Dublin were rather defaulters — the first I think the most inexcusable.

The debate on our side was very well sustained — the best thing we have done. Herries, Walpole, and Tom Baring — the latter very good — and myself to my satisfaction, and, I believe, not to the dissatisfaction of our friends.

The most remarkable circumstance of the night was the elaborate and undisguised declaration of war against us by Graham. He assailed you with venom even, nearly at the conclusion of a very long, lumbering, stupid speech — the latter or, as he called it, the 'political' part, of course, more spicy, and cheered by the Radicals and, a little, by some of the Whigs. I thought it unwise any longer to refrain, as it would only have cheapened you and us, and therefore I tickled him a little.[2]

[1] Disraeli's defence of the Navigation Laws brought him a pretty compliment in the following spring, when there was launched at Milford Haven the good ship *Disraeli*, of 400 tons, described as the finest yet built in the harbour, and bearing as its figure-head an exact likeness of its sponsor, 'holding the Navigation Laws in his left hand and defending the same with his right.'

[2] 'I settled the disciple of Progress,' is Disraeli's phrase in writing to his sister.

To Lady Londonderry.

HOUSE OF COMMONS, *April* 30, 1849. — . . . There are all sorts of rumours, varying every hour. I think the truth is, that the Lords, at this moment, are about equally divided, but, for my part, I have, as Metternich said to me yesterday, an *instinct*, that the Bill will pass; a week, however, has yet to elapse, and that is time for many intrigues.

Most Confidential. A friend of mine had yesterday an interview of an hour with the Duke of Wellington. He is much agitated about the affair, though, I doubt not, will support the Government. Abused the Bill very much, although not so much as he abused Peel, on whom he lavished all sorts of execration. He said that Free Trade had ruined this country, that he had supported all their measures against his will in order to keep out Cobden and Co., and that he feared change now for the same reason. What he feared most, he repeated often, was Change, lest it might lead to that. But all had been a mistake from the beginning. . . .

Disraeli's instinct was right. The Lords, by the aid of proxies, passed the second reading by a majority of ten, in spite of the eloquence of Stanley, Brougham, and Lyndhurst. Perhaps Bright's opinion, which Disraeli reported to his sister, may have been not far from the truth. Bright said the Lords would swallow the Bill; 'for, though they are convinced it will both destroy the commerce and navy of England, they deem such results comparative blessings compared with Stanley being Minister.' That a Stanley Ministry was felt to be quite a possibility during this session is shown not merely by several references in the Disraeli correspondence and in Greville's *Diary*, but by a list in Disraeli's handwriting, preserved among the Beaconsfield papers, headed 'Cabinet for 1849.' It is interesting as including all the principal Peelites except Peel — namely, Aberdeen, Graham, Gladstone, Sidney Herbert, Lincoln, Goulburn, and Cardwell — as Stanley's subordinate colleagues. Disraeli has allotted the India Office to himself.[1] There is no indication who was to lead the House of Commons. But in a

[1] In another Cabinet list of the same character, also in Disraeli's handwriting, and relating to one of the years 1849–1851, he makes himself Home Secretary.

letter from his sister, written probably in July of this year the question is put: 'Is Gladstone to be your lieutenant?'

To Sarah Disraeli.

HUGHENDEN, *May* 28. — I came down here [1] very indifferent, having dined out the three preceding days running. . . . It is settled that there is to be no coalition between the Peelites and the Whigs, and therefore I conclude that after a decent interval the old Conservative party will be reconstructed under Stanley, and of course without Peel. If the distress continues after the next harvest, Graham and Co. must give up progress, and swallow a little moderate reaction; if it abate, we cannot pretend to disturb *un fait accompli.* I think, therefore, that this time next year all may be well, if one can stand the storm till then. . . .[2]

June 22, 1849. — I am so pressed with affairs, and have been, though much better, so poorly, that I have been unable to write you a line, and must now do it hastily. . . .

To-morrow we go *in state* to dine with the Lord Mayor, who gives a banquet to our party. Lord Stanley is to return thanks for the House of Lords, and I for the House of Commons. H. Bentinck refused, never going to Court and those sort of things, and not understanding the nature of the meeting; but when Trollope told him that he was to see me make a speech in the Egyptian Hall, in a red coat, as leader of the party in the House of Commons, he begged leave to recall his refusal, and is going to appear in a Court dress which I believe belonged to the old Duke of Bulstrode.[3]

The Mansion House banquet to the Protectionist party was a further recognition both of the status which the party had acquired and of Disraeli's leadership in the Commons. The Lord Mayor, Sir James Duke, who was a member of Parliament, was a Liberal, and therefore could not be actuated by party feelings in his hospitality. Londonderry, indeed, who, faithful to his rôle of peacemaker, was endeavouring at this time to bring Aberdeen and Stanley together, regarded the Lord Mayor as a marplot. 'Either my Lord Mayor is a great fool,' he wrote to Disraeli, 'or a very cunning man; if the latter, he has admirably managed to reinforce his own party, the Whigs, and to make it more evident than ever that

[1] For the Whitsuntide recess. [2] *Letters*, pp. 218, 219.
[3] Bulstrode Park formerly belonged to the Duke of Portland.

Pro[tectionist]s and Pee[lite]s can never join. 'Party politics were naturally eschewed, and Disraeli said nothing of importance; but Stanley took occasion to insist on the unflinching steadfastness with which he and his followers maintained their opinions — especially the great principle that legislative encouragement ought to be granted to every branch of domestic industry.

Fortified by this public tribute to the solidarity and efficiency of the party, and spurred on by the agricultural agitation out of doors, Disraeli in the last month of the session led a general action against the whole front of the Government. He moved for a Committee into the State of the Nation, and brought forward the motion as one of want of confidence. His speech in introducing it was a sustained effort. He had spent much thought on it, and had been assisted by Edward Stanley, who was entering politics rather under Disraeli's wing than under his own father's. There was nothing of the sportsman about the younger Stanley, but he felt an absorbing interest in politics, especially social politics, and he was attracted by Disraeli's keenness and by his democratic Toryism.

Disraeli, in opening his speech, pointed out that for three years the Government had held office uncontrolled and uncriticised. And yet, if the condition of England abroad and at home in 1846 were contrasted with its condition in 1849, it would be seen that in 1846 there was tranquillity abroad and prosperity at home, whereas in 1849 there were convulsions abroad and depression at home. This was the justification for an inquiry. He severely condemned the treatment of Ireland. Three years ago she was 'like a poor man struggling against entering the workhouse'; now she was 'a contented pauper.' The new commercial system, if it were not altered, bade fair to change the country 'from a first-rate monarchy into a second-rate republic.' He passed a sweeping condemnation on the administration of Colonial affairs — 'the darkest page in the history of the Government.' In foreign affairs, 'when the influence of England might have been exercised to appease the discontents and settle the difficulties which existed in Europe, England was left without the power of so doing, because she was recognised only as the handmaid and colleague of the discontented in every country.' The great Ministers of Europe, the Metternichs and Guizots, were treated as personal enemies, and passed over as unworthy of consideration.

In his concluding passages Disraeli summed up the transformation which, in his opinion, the new commercial system had effected and was effecting in the character of Englishmen:

> Some three years or more ago, as it appears to me, we thought fit to change the principle upon which the economic system of this country had been previously based. Hitherto this country had been, as it were, divided into a hierarchy of industrial classes, each one of which was open to all, but in each of which every Englishman was taught to believe that he occupied a position better than the analogous position of individuals of his order in any other country in the world. For example, the British merchant was looked on as the most creditable, the wealthiest, and the most trustworthy merchant in the world; the English farmer ranked as the most skilful agriculturist . . .; while the English manufacturer was acknowledged as the most skilful and successful, without a rival in ingenuity and enterprise. So with the British sailor —the name was a proverb; and chivalry was confessed to have found a last resort in the breast of a British officer. It was the same in our learned professions. Our physicians and lawyers held higher positions than those in other countries. I have heard it stated that the superiority of these classes was obtained at the cost of the last class of the hierarchy— at the cost of the labouring population of the country. But . . . I know of no great community existing since, I will say, the fall of the Roman Empire, where the working population have been, upon the whole, placed in so advantageous a position as the working classes of England. . . . In this manner, in England society was based upon the aristocratic principle in its complete and most magnificent development.
>
> You set to work to change the basis upon which this society was established; you disdain to attempt the accomplishment of the best; and what you want to achieve is the cheapest. But I have shown you that, considered only as an economical principle, the principle is fallacious; that its infallible conse-

quence is to cause the impoverishment and embarrassment of the people. . . . But the wealth of England is not merely material wealth; it does not merely consist in the number of acres we have tilled and cultivated, nor in our havens filled with shipping, nor in our unrivalled factories, nor in the intrepid industry of our mines. Not these merely form the principal wealth of our country; we have a more precious treasure, and that is the character of the people. That is what you have injured. In destroying what you call class legislation, you have destroyed that noble and indefatigable ambition which has been the best source of all our greatness, of all our prosperity, and all our power. I know of nothing more remarkable in the present day than the general discontent which prevails, accompanied as it is on all sides by an avowed inability to suggest any remedy. The feature of the present day is depression and perplexity. That English spirit which was called out and supported by your old system seems to have departed from us. . . . As far as I can judge, men in every place — in the golden saloon, and in the busy mart of industry; in the port and in the exchange; by the loom or by the plough — every man says, 'I suffer, and I see no hope.'

Disraeli said that he was prepared to offer a remedy for this state of things, but he omitted to specify it. The omission was naturally the subject of comment throughout the debate, which occupied two nights, July 2 and 6. The Chancellor of the Exchequer wanted to know whether the unnamed remedy was Protection; and Peel, who made an elaborate defence of his own opinions and conduct, and especially of the policy of fighting hostile tariffs by free imports, said the issue was, 'Shall we displace the Government for the purpose of subverting the commercial policy on which it has acted?' Both Wood and Peel disputed with considerable success the extent of the distress which Disraeli alleged; and Russell considered that their speeches covered the ground.

Disraeli, at the close of the debate, records Hobhouse in his *Reminiscences*, 'made a most lively and spirited reply, attacking Peel for his conduct and for his speech, ridiculing Charles Wood, whom he compared to a conjurer pulling yards of red tape out of his mouth, and not sparing Russell.' The reply to Peel is one of the very few instances in which, after 1846, Disraeli reproduced in any degree the famous criticisms of the Corn Law fight; but Peel's pontifical and professorial discourse afforded a legitimate opportunity.

> I must say, with all respect to the right hon. Baronet, that there is something in his manner when he addresses on these subjects his former companions, which I will not say is annoying, but rather I would style somewhat astonishing. One would almost imagine, from the tone of the right hon. gentleman, that he had never, for a moment, held other opinions on this subject; that he had never entertained a doubt upon it; that he had been born an infant Hercules, cradled in political economy, and only created to strangle the twin serpents of Protection and monopoly. He speaks with a sneer of those who think that the principle of buying in the cheapest and selling in the dearest market is a new principle invented by the Manchester School. I say the Manchester School. I have a right to use that phrase, for I gave them that name. I gave it them with all respect; I thought it a homage due to their deleterious, but well-disciplined, doctrines. . . . We admit fully the comparative antiquity of the dogma; what surprises us is not the comparative antiquity of the dogma, but the recent conversion of the dogmatist. The right hon. gentleman should view one's errors at least with charity. He is not exactly the individual who, *ex cathedrâ*, should lecture us on the principles of political economy. He might, at least, when he denounces our opinions, suppose that in their profession we may perhaps be supported by that strength of conviction which, for nearly forty years, sustained him in those economical errors of which he was the learned and powerful professor.

Disraeli declined, however, altogether to rest his case solely on the commercial question. He had already told the House that this was no flash-in-the-pan motion, but a serious one. 'Its object is to turn out the Government. We may not succeed; but we shall succeed some day.' He reiterated this view in his peroration, with some effective hits at those Peelites who abused Ministers in private, 'whispering about in corners,' and supported them in public. 'Vote your confidence,' he said, 'in the Government in which you do not confide; but if you give them your votes, at least in future have the decency to cease your accusations and silence your complaints.'

There was a storm of applause when Disraeli sat down, but the division was a disappointment. The Opposition only numbered 156, and were beaten by a majority of 140. There were many plausible excuses for this failure in the division lobbies. But the plain fact was that, weak and discredited as the Whig Government might be, the House of Commons was not prepared to turn them out by any vote that could be represented as a condemnation of the new commercial system, and a demand for the re-establishment of Protection.

To Sarah Disraeli.

July 8 [? 7], 1849.—My speech last night at ½-past 2 o'clock, and of which there is consequently not a semblance of a report in the journals, was I think the most successful I ever made: and my friends, in the lobby, during the division were really *enthusiastic.* Our division was not as good as it would have been had it not been for the number of false starts which we have experienced: but my friends say the speech made up for the numbers, and are in high spirits. We had thirty good men away without pairs: men who would not pair, but would vote. The division came on at four-and-twenty hours' notice, after a public declaration of the Chancellor of the Exchequer on Wednesday (in the absence of Lord John) that it was positively impossible for the Government to give another day; so, as Hume was obstinate, our friends went out of town. On the Tuesday preceding we had 196 men in the House, besides 20 pairs. Yesterday we had 25 pairs. It might have been better: but I have been worried the last week with anticipations of something much worse. The debate last night was very interesting and well sustained.

Peel elaborate in his courtesies to me, and talked of the 'respect due to my abilities and station,' at which my fellows cheered immensely. I am very wearied, having been up till nearly five, and this morning rose at ½-past 9. We dine at the Combermeres. I think I shall fall asleep.

Though Stanley would not hear of any change of policy, Disraeli was more and more being driven to contemplate it as a necessity. He had already, during the session, to use the language of one of his correspondents, been gradually leading the party 'to abandon the narrow defile of Protection and to give battle on the open plain of reciprocity'; but even so he had not yet conciliated public opinion. He received in August caustic comments from Henry Drummond, which did not even spare Stanley, 'a rash man, the Lord Gough of politics, who as long as he can make a Donnybrook Fair of the House of Lords cares little for anything else.' Drummond recommended the raising, by an equalisation of the land tax, of a sum which should be employed as a sinking fund; preferential treatment of the Colonies; an *ad valorem* duty on articles of foreign produce; and an extension of the franchise. Others pressed strongly for equalisation of taxation as a substitute for Protection, which was 'a lost game.' Ideas of this kind were readily assimilated by Disraeli. A shrewd and friendly journalist, Samuel Phillips, wrote from Folkestone, July 25: 'I would suggest that the time has arrived for a reconsideration of the political creed of the Conservative party. . . . There are two things very much wanted to give life to politics just now; first, a combined and strong opposition, and, secondly, opposition on grounds which command men's sympathies, and which have a reasonable chance of being finally driven home.'

Strangely enough, while Disraeli's thoughts were all directed to find some other mode of promoting agricultural interests than a return to the Protection of corn, there was for the first time a serious agitation in progress throughout the country districts for such a return. Though there had been several indignation meetings in the autumn of 1846 to denounce Peel's apostasy, yet in the General Election of 1847 the farmers had been apathetic. Now that three years had passed and the Free Trade policy had been solidified by the legislation of the Whig Ministry, while trade and even agriculture had largely accommodated themselves to the new system, a serious attempt was made to upset it out of hand. The movement was taken up with special vigour in Ireland, always, as one of Disraeli's correspondents wrote, belated in its politics. Disraeli did not believe that this movement, in England at any rate, had any support outside the agricultural classes; and he was convinced that the more thoughtful even among them shared his incredulity as to the practicability of a reversion to the old system. Accordingly he strongly discouraged the agitation, while Stanley viewed it with favour. On this subject Disraeli has left a memorandum, written in the sixties, explaining his action, and the nature of his relations with Stanley in this their first year of joint leadership:

In the autumn of the year 1849, when, taking advantage of distress, a Mr. G. F. Young and what was called the Protection Society to British Industry were agitating the country, I had made a strong effort to counteract their pernicious course, and to direct the public attention to more practical measures of relief in the remission of taxation, than the frantic reaction they advocated, and which I was convinced no great class in the country itself either desired, or deemed practicable.

This had brought strong remonstrances from Lord Derby [then Lord Stanley], with whom my relations during the whole of the year 1849 were uneasy. He was in the hands of the Protection Society worked by this George Frederick Young, who was not an agriculturist, but a commercial and mainly colonial interest man, ignorant of the temper and situation of the farmers; a man of great energy and of equal vanity, but of ordinary abilities and no cultivation, and who was piqued by the success of Cobden and Bright, men of his own class, in agitating England, and thought he would show himself as good and powerful as they. G. F. Young had got hold of Beresford, who had originally intruded himself into the office of First Whip of the Protectionist party, and was in daily communication with Lord Derby, who really saw nobody else but him and a few companions in the House of Lords, all greatly his inferiors in intellect and acquirement. Beresford was a tall, coarse man, who could blend with his natural want of refinement, if necessary, extreme servility: very persevering, capable of labor, prejudiced, and bigoted. Protection and Protestantism were his specifics for all the evils of the State, and the only foundation for strong and lasting Governments: and these were the results that he was always dinning into Lord Derby's ears. He persuaded Lord Derby, that they were the real sentiments of the Tory party in the House of Commons, and especially of the middle class of the country;

of which Beresford affected, as a man of business in his way, a director of banks and insurance offices, with which he eked out a precarious income, to have peculiar knowledge.

The correspondence between the two leaders entirely bears out Disraeli's phrase of 'uneasy' relations. Stanley was unwilling to allow his lieutenant in the other House the latitude which he claimed; and Disraeli probably did not feel that he and Stanley were sufficiently in sympathy for him to unbosom himself frankly as to his political projects. Moreover, his projects were at present rather undefined. He felt that a substitute for the crude policy of a reversion to the old system must be found, but he was during this autumn splashing about a little wildly, and taking up attractive ideas rather at haphazard. A speech delivered by him at Aylesbury at a private meeting in September, and imperfectly reported, the nature of which appears sufficiently from the letters which were exchanged, formed the occasion of the first of Stanley's remonstrances.

From Lord Stanley.

BALLYHISTEEN, *Sept.* 22, 1849.

MY DEAR SIR, — Within the last few days I have received from various quarters letters of inquiry, and, I am sorry to add, of remonstrance, in reference to the proposition supposed to be made in your late speech at Aylesbury; and it is a little embarrassing to me to have to answer the direct inquiry whether the proposition so made had been the result of previous and deliberate consultation with me, and to be obliged to say that I know nothing of the matter beyond what I have read in the newspapers. Such an answer is of itself a disadvantage to us, because it indicated either a want of concert and agreement between us, or a somewhat hasty promulgation of crude and lightly-considered schemes upon a most important part of our domestic policy. I am well aware of what is said of the necessity of having some 'watchword' or 'party cry,' but while I admit the convenience to a party of having such, that convenience is more than counterbalanced if the watchword be not one which will command universal sympathy, or the scheme such as will stand the severest test of criticism. I always differed on this subject with poor George Bentinck, and deprecated the practice, to which he was too much inclined, of starting detailed projects in opposition.

I know not whether I correctly understand your views and intentions; but as I read your speech in the papers, you appear to advocate a general equalisation, involving a very great increase in amount, of the existing land tax; and the application of the increased taxation so obtained to the formation of a sinking fund of nearly £5,000,000 annually, which you think would have the effect of increasing public confidence, and thus, by operating on the funds, render the acquisition of money comparatively easy, and in that shape afford efficient relief to the agriculturist. Now it appears to me that, even admitting that the establishment of a *bona fide* sinking fund would have the effect which you anticipate, the formation of the sinking fund involves the necessity of a large annual surplus (in itself a most desirable object)—that surplus to be obtained, however, by an immediate increase, to a considerable extent, of the direct taxation of the country; a principle which I cannot but look upon as fraught with great future and not very remote danger.

But even as a party cry, if it were legitimate to set one up without the fullest conviction of the practicability of satisfying it, I should much doubt the popularity of your suggested scheme. My friends in Lancashire will not thank you for raising their land tax in the first instance from 2d. to 1s. 6d. in the pound; and though that is an extreme case, I understand from you that there would be a large increase in the great majority of the counties. Bucks, to be sure, is not injured; but neither is it benefited, except indirectly; and I suspect your constituents would prefer the immediate boon of being brought down to the Lancashire level, to the contingent advantage of having Lancashire brought up to theirs. You do not, I think, explain how you would deal with *redeemed* land tax: that, of course, you could not touch; and the first promulgation of your scheme would probably lead to a very general redemption, depriving you of the benefit of your expected surplus.

Perhaps, however, I have altogether misunderstood your plan; even if so, I shall not repent having given you the trouble of furnishing me with an explanation of your views, by which I may be able to allay the jealousies and apprehensions which I have already found to have arisen. For my own part, I am not inclined to abandon the principle of raising revenue by returning to some of the duties on importation, which we have unnecessarily and, as I think, unwisely relinquished, and thereby obtaining the power of reduction, rather than increase, of our direct taxation. I much fear that the adoption of any other line of action, and especially its promulgation by so distinguished a member of our party as yourself, may have the effect of yet further dividing our forces, and weakening our efforts; and I cannot but have my fears that so much of your scheme as sanctions increased burthens on land may be eagerly adopted by our opponents, and the object for which you are willing to submit to it be wholly thrown over by them. . . . — Believe me, my dear Sir, yours sincerely, STANLEY.

To Lord Stanley.

HUGHENDEN MANOR, HIGH WYCOMBE, *Sept.* 24, 1849.

MY DEAR LORD, — . . . I am vexed that a coarse report of some casual observations,[1] though made on a very important and well-considered subject, should have led to so much misrepresentation. That they did not give to the persons to whom they were addressed the impression which has been conveyed by the Press will be obvious to you by the enclosed address of Mr. Lowndes of Chesham, which expresses the general conclusions arrived at on the occasion, and in which not the slightest reference to the land tax is made.

All I wished to impress upon my auditors was the policy of petitioning for equal taxation according to the principles which we had advocated in Parliament last year, and that, having secured equality of taxation, they should next aim at achieving mitigation of taxation by the only legitimate means — viz., a sinking fund.

My main grounds for the latter recommendation are very briefly these: Firstly, that in the event of a surplus there is really no tax on the landed interest to repeal; the consequence is that all the indirect taxation of the country will gradually slip away unless some breakwater like a sinking fund prevents it. Secondly, that a *bona fide* sinking fund, by lowering the rate of interest, would relieve the mortgagor and bring capital to improve cultivation.

It seemed to me that these were two good and even great principles for the landed interest to associate itself with. The first is just, the second not only just but honest, and I can't help thinking they might make their way. In an age when so many are prepared by vast reductions to create a huge surplus, and then apply it in such various ways, I thought it might not be altogether indiscreet to remind the country that

[1] Writing to Manners on October 15, Disraeli explained that 'the first start was not very fortunate, for it was not intended as a manifesto, there being no reporters apparently present; and the thing that did appear, though it appeared in several papers, was furnished by one individual and a county hand.'

it might be just as well to pay their debts before they take off the duties on timber and tea.

I am sure that on this as on every occasion I should hesitate before I opened my mouth without the advantage of your opinion. I venture to hope that my fault is certainly not to shrink from advice; but to communicate at this moment was difficult, and it appeared to me that I was only about to express opinions of which in the main the party generally approved, while the remainder were of so general a character that no one could possibly be trammelled by their utterance.

Their effect here was far greater than I contemplated, because the people in these southern counties must have something to rally round. The association was not formed at my instigation, and the chairman is not a political partisan, but quite the reverse. This is the first time that he has interfered in public life, though a gentleman of old family, large estate, and high character, the lineal descendant, indeed, of that Secretary Lowndes whose famous apothegm about pounds and pence you remember.

I have not answered any of the articles in the journals, thinking it better to do so at some public meeting, where the opportunity will soon offer to remove any misconceptions.

From Lord Stanley.

BALLYHISTEEN, *Sept.* 28, 1849.—I hasten to thank you for your letter received this morning. In the objects which you have in view, equalisation of taxation, and the establishment of a *bona fide* sinking fund, I cordially concur, though I think them both difficult of attainment: the one from the necessity of reconciling general taxation with local management; the other from the general prevalence of what Lord Castlereagh, with more truth than policy, called the ignorant impatience of taxation. But I hope that you will find an early opportunity of explaining away, publicly, that part of your supposed speech in which you are made to suggest, as the means of establishing a sinking fund, the increase of the land tax to the amount of five millions a year: this is what has alarmed the agriculturists of other counties, and makes them not very unreasonably apprehensive of a scheme which would seem to provide for the gradual reduction of the National Debt by means of a tax, which falls mainly, if not exclusively, on them. You will have achieved a great work, if you can succeed in turning the mind of the agriculturists to a permanent reduction of the national burthens, rather than to an immediate relief from some particular tax, which may happen to be clamoured for by the masses.

William Beresford to Lord Stanley.

Hughenden, *Sept.* 30 [1849].—I am writing to you from Disraeli's. . . . He is living here very quietly, and working very hard. He is reading up all the Blue Books of the past Session, having divided them into classes, and separated them so that each group should comprehend different subjects. He attributes Peel's great power and effect in the House to having always had Blue Books by heart, and having thereby the appearance of a fund of general knowledge greater than he really possessed. . . .

He strikes me as very zealous in the cause, and as feeling himself completely embarked now with us, and I do trust that he is fully compromised and will remain true. He certainly has great powers, and not the least among them is the great command he has evidently over himself and his own feelings and passions. He acts and speaks with the greatest cordiality, and shows the most complete confidence in me. Certainly times are rather altered within one year in that respect. I am sure that you will be gratified to hear that he speaks most highly to me of your son's great knowledge, application, and talent. . . .

To Mrs. Disraeli.

Boreham House, Chelmsford, *Oct.* 4 [1849].—I arrived here just in time, and Tyrell[1] greatly relieved by my presence. There was a large dinner-party yesterday: turtle without asparagus. . . .

When a man is in a scrape, as I am, one must not complain of annoyances and sacrifices; but I have paid dear for the misconceptions of the Aylesbury meeting. At two o'clock I go with Sir John, twenty miles across country, to a Mr. White's, where we dine and sleep, and on Friday is the festival: in honour of me, to be held in an ancient baronial castle, the hall of which remains. The affair will not be over till late at night, and so uncouth is the land that, next day, I must travel twenty miles overland again to find a train at Chelmsford, which will bring me to town late at night. Hard work! when one is not in particularly good spirits. However, if the meeting goes off well, the cause may be rallied. . . .

It was at Castle Hedingham, in Essex, on October 5, that Disraeli delivered the speech that was to get him out of the 'scrape.' In it he followed Stanley's advice, and made it plain that what he was advocating was

[1] Sir John Tyrell, M.P. for North Essex, a leading Protectionist.

equalisation of burdens as between land and other property; but he also elaborated his plan for a sinking fund, to be supplied by import duties on foreign produce. He wrote to his sister when he had returned to Hughenden: 'I think the Essex move is successful; it must, however, be followed up without loss of time by a great move in Bucks, and all this is very harassing.' [1]

The 'Essex move' was not successful enough to divert the Protection Society from their policy.

To Lord Stanley.

HUGHENDEN, *Oct.* 20, 1849.—I send you, by this post, a reply to a letter which I have received from Mr. G. F. Young, a shipbuilder, who, with Mr. Freshfield, a retired attorney, and a mad Surrey farmer, one Mr. Foskett,[2] are going to organise, throughout the country, hole and corner meetings to address Her Majesty to dissolve her Parliament, in order, to use their own language, 'that a Protectionist Ministry may immediately be formed' and Protection restored. These gentlemen deprecate any movement for specific measures lest this coming Government be embarrassed, as if they, and such as they, were not an embarrassment, which must upset any Government, future or paulo-post-future.

I had my reply privately printed, because I have no secretary here, and I wished that yourself, and some other leading members of the party, should know my feelings on the subject.

I wish you would gravely consider the question of a sinking fund. It is not merely as a plausible mode of obtaining import duties that I press it. I had a very long and confidential conversation with Mr. McCulloch, as I passed thro' town, and he told me that, in his opinion, the effect of a sinking fund of five or six millions would be to reduce the interest on the debt to 2½ and even 2 per cent. This was also Mr. Ricardo's opinion. But then, they say, the difficulty is to maintain the fund. Let us suppose a *strong* Government that can. Conceive the effect on our shattered and embarrassed aristocracy, of the interest on the debt reduced to 2½ or 2 per cent. They would be saved. With this,

[1] Sarah Disraeli reports to her brother the personal impressions of his Essex hostess: 'She [Mrs. Majendie] thinks you not at all altered — that is, not grown apparently older; though to your youthful air is superadded a look of melancholy: but that is as befits a statesman in these days of danger and distress.'

[2] This was rather ungrateful of Disraeli. Mr. Foskett spoke, at the farmers' meeting at Willis's Rooms, of their 'deep debt of gratitude' to Disraeli, and asked them to support him 'to the utmost of their power.'

but remember that all the merit of a sinking fund depends upon its being a *bona fide* surplus, and that the vice of the old sinking fund was that we borrowed with one hand to pay off debt with the other. No Act of Parliament, therefore, can give security to the maintenance of a fund the existence of which depends upon annual votes of the House of Commons. The House of Commons in these days is powerfully operated upon by the popular voice; and no Government can be strong which is not popular. Can we hope for much popularity, especially with those who are our natural supporters, in favour of a scheme which sets out with the maintenance, perhaps the increase, of the income tax, the addition of ten or twelve millions of taxes, and no immediate reduction of burthens, except what is to be derived (a great one, I admit) from the redistribution of Poor Rates and other local charges? accompanied also, I must add, by a tacit but virtual repudiation of the Protective principle which has hitherto been the basis of our policy, and the bond of our union. I am very far from undervaluing the attainment of a large sinking fund, if it can be effected; and I have no doubt but that it would to a great extent raise the credit of the country, and reduce the interest of money; both objects of great value: but I foresee immense difficulties in the way of its attainment; and I see no prospect of its announcement producing such a popular feeling in its favour, as should induce the country to submit to the sacrifices necessary to secure it. While, therefore, you say that you do not advocate a sinking fund merely as a covert means of obtaining import duties, I say that I advocate import duties *in the first instance*, with two avowed objects: first, the increase of the revenue necessary to enable it to defray a portion of the local burthens; and next, as a means of protecting domestic industry against an undue and injurious competition of foreign produce; and if, after providing for these objects, a surplus can be obtained, I am in favour of maintaining it for the gradual reduction of debt rather than sacrificing it by continued remission of particular taxes.

If it be true, as you think, that in Bucks 'no five men can be got together by a vague talk of recurrence to abrogated laws,' I believe it to be at least as true that you will neither reconstruct nor hold together a party, certainly not our present party, without holding out adherence, and, if possible, practical recurrence, to the principle of those laws; and it is on this account that I must regret that you have given publicity to some of the opinions contained in your letter, and, you must forgive me for adding, the tone of some of the observations, which I fear are calculated to give needless offence. In the concluding paragraph of your letter I entirely concur; I agree that 'the Country party, in honor and policy, are bound to adhere to the advocacy of the principles' of 'the juster distribution of local burthens, and the imposition of import duties'; but I hold also that we are bound to advocate the latter not only for the purposes of revenue, but also in accordance with the spirit of those laws, which, if abrogated, I am not prepared to abandon as irrevocably lost. . . .

In order, no doubt, to meet Stanley's views, Disraeli, in his speech at Aylesbury on October 31, at the first meeting of the Bucks Association for the Relief of Real Property, took care to make it clear that he adhered in principle to the general policy of Protection to agriculture, before he proceeded to recommend once more, as the proper course for agriculturists to adopt in the existing circumstances, the advocacy of a sinking fund provided by import duties. Though his sister thought the speech 'full of wisdom and philosophy,' he himself was dissatisfied with the effect produced.

To Sarah Disraeli.

HUGHENDEN, *Nov.* 4, 1849.—. . . I was not at all pleased myself with the Aylesbury meeting, though on the whole the world has not taken so ill a view of it. I thought it was a shabby concern. It has, I think, however, been productive of some little good, though for my part I give up the attempt of rousing the agricultural interest to any decided demonstration. They are puzzled and sluggish, perhaps; when they are a little more pinched they may bestir themselves. . . .[1]

Disraeli got some, but no very large, measure of support for this particular proposal from his party. Manners sent 'a few lines of hearty admiration of, and congratulation upon, the Essex manifesto. I go heartily along with it.' Henry Drummond thought the letter to Young excellent. Tyrell wrote: 'I am only a wheeler, and not a leader. . . . The old dry crust of Protection may be, and I believe is, quite right, but your plan is a much larger, and under the circumstances a more prudent and

[1] *Letters*, p. 224.

practicable, affair.' And even Beresford, though doubtful about the plan, took up the cudgels at a farmers' meeting in defence of Disraeli against Lord Braybrooke's criticisms. But others wrote in a different strain. The Duke of Newcastle said: 'We are against Free Trade, we are in favour of Protection. If we are, why dissemble in the slightest degree?' McCulloch, the economist, was convinced that nothing would come out of the cry of agricultural distress; the Rev. John Cox, an Essex parson of much influence in the Country party, preached patience; and even Manners, without retracting his approbation of the plan, hinted that it was unwise to produce detailed measures.

Early in November the Whip sent Disraeli from town depressing report of the general feeling, which was hostile to the sinking fund scheme. Accordingly, in his next letter to Stanley, Disraeli dwells mainly on the impossibility of Protection as an electoral cry, and seems to admit that his own substitute has not met with general favour:

To Lord Stanley.

HUGHENDEN, *Nov.* 9, 1849.—. . . If the party is to be managed by the Protection Society, against which I have no wish to demur, I think that Society ought to have apprised the members of the House of Commons of their plan of campaign, which I now hear has been long matured, as they must, or ought to know, that at no time, and especially the present, is it possible to return to our counties and be quite silent about public affairs.

Instead of this, the Protection Society—suddenly—pass resolutions, in October, condemnatory of my views, and order them to be 'published' throughout the country, without the slightest communication with me—the private letter of Mr. Young to me, enclosing these published resolutions, being nothing more than his Reigate speech. Under these circumstances I should hope that, on reflection, you would not continue of opinion that the tone of my printed reply was calculated to give needless offence, but that, perhaps, on the contrary, I have rather refrained from retaliating against an unprovoked public insult.

I had no wish to take any lead in this matter. The main reason why I attended the meeting in Essex was our wish that I should not unnecessarily lose a moment in removing a misapprehension then afloat. If, after the Essex meeting, the Protection Society had confidentially communicated with me, I would cheerfully have sacrificed any views of my own to a general purpose more approved; but a public reproof, and from such people, rendered it necessary that I should publicly vindicate my course.

It would be too great an intrusion on your time for me now to enter into the important consideration on which you have touched: and even if I were to trespass to such a degree, my remarks must, necessarily, be so imperfect, that they might lead to misapprehension. I would only make an observation on the state of opinion in this and the neighboring counties, of which I have taken the utmost pains to inform myself. The cry of Protection will rally no one to our standard here. The farmers think that they have been used as political tools. They require some immediate remedy, or, at any rate, some immediate hope. This is why they are all inclined to run to Cobdenism, and reduce the taxation of the country ten millions at one swoop. This is what I meant by running amuck against our financial system. I have endeavoured to combat this feeling by showing them that the Manchester scheme would bring them no relief, by instilling into them some hope from the present House of Commons, and at the same time by suggestions which, as I was instructed, would afford a golden bridge to many who are prepared to join us, if we do not unnecessarily wound their self-love. Mr. Evelyn writes to me from Surrey that he found no feeling for Protection in his canvass, but a strong democratic feeling generally, and a bad humor to the Church.

I would not speak so gloomily of these counties at present, but there is a recklessness afloat which, if they are not tended, will prepare them for anything. Generally speaking, the County of Buckingham, when led by any person of station or Parliamentary mark, from its geographical position and old custom, has always given the tone to Berks and Oxon, and very much influences Herts and Beds, including, of course, their boroughs. At present the impulse which I was earnestly solicited to give has been checked, but I hope I have covered the retreat. Affairs in this part of the world, however, are serious. There has been a general and a considerable reduction of wages, and a dismissal from labor. Yesterday a body of two hundred able-bodied laborers walked in procession in this neighbourhood. At the same time, I am bound to say, that so general is the impulse given to trade, that all the defunct manufactures of these counties have suddenly revived. A great trade in plait is now carried on — all for foreign demand: the lace trade is very brisk: the chairmakers are all working for the North of England.

On the whole, I cannot resist the conviction that these counties will run to Radicalism, tho' I think, with energy, the catastrophe might have been averted. However, this may be too gloomy a view. With temper and tact we may dissipate the disagreeable results of our late misapprehension, and we should never forget that the world in general is not, perhaps, so sensible of the unnecessary misunderstanding as ourselves.

Disraeli went up to town, and had long conversations with the Whip, to their mutual satisfaction.

To Mrs. Disraeli.

Nov. 12, 1849.—. . . I send this to say that I have seen Lord Granby, Newdegate, and that Beresford has just come in. Lord G. had been to Grosvenor Gate. I think things will turn out pleasantly, but it is very lucky I came up.

Nov. 13, 1849.—My interview with Beresford last night was so prolonged, that it was too late to write again: it did not end till past seven. I think on the whole it was promising. They are evidently much more afraid of losing me, than I them: but the difficulties are not inconsiderable, and there are many jealousies, as well as genuine misconceptions, which must not only be put an end to, but rooted out for ever. I think if I am firm, and keep high ground, though conciliating and temperate, things may end with being better than they were. . . .

Granby wants Stanley, myself, and some others, to meet. Granby returns from Paris on Saturday night. I have no particular wish to meet at present; I would rather things would more develop, and the meeting of Parliament were nearer, but, of course, must be decided by circumstances. . . .

The Protectionists are evidently excited, and think they are going to win. I do not. If they gain Cork, which comes off to-day, there will be no holding them in. . . .

Nov. 14, 1849.—It is impossible for me to go into details respecting political matters. I will therefore only say, that everything goes to my satisfaction, and that by keeping my temper I think I shall turn all this to good account, and be in a stronger position than before. I dined yesterday with Stuart,[1] who is excellent and of great use. He is also a good adviser, being of a judicial mind. He says that he has heard, that the D. of Richmond is quite with me, and

[1] M.P. for Newark, afterwards Vice-Chancellor.

praised much my letter to Young. By the bye, in my closet, there are some copies of that letter left. Send me one by post. They have never got about — no one having broken faith — which is satisfactory.

Beresford affects devotion. Asks me to dinner every day; yesterday went into the city after Young, who was at his house at Walthamstow, and has written to him to come up to town immediately, etc., etc. I take it all; but as Tyrell says in his letter to-day, 'If you did trip, I don't think B. is the first man who would pick you up.' However, he is a thermometer.

Nov. 15, 1849. — I have dined out every day: yesterday with B. who had seen Young. He says that nobody can be more anxious to get out of the scrape than Young, who could say nothing to the point, on which all hinges — viz., that he never communicated the plans of the Protection Society to the party. He confessed it was a great mistake, and murmured something that he thought the D. of Richmond would have apprised us. B. seems to have kept his temper, but threw on Young the responsibility of putting all right. But the position of Young is most difficult after the violent course he has taken. Thursday being a dead day, Young returned to Walthamstow, and on Friday (to-morrow) he is to attend a meeting in Kent with Lord Stanhope in the chair! where, no doubt, a great attack was to have been made on me, and where he must now take quite a different line. This, with Lord Stanhope in the chair, is no easy matter.

I think Stanley's letter highly satisfactory and conciliatory. Chatterton, after all, has won the Cork election by an immense majority![1] There will be no keeping our friends in. They have won four important elections since the Prorogation. The general impression in London is, that Stanley is safe to be Prime Minister next Session: but I confess I should like to lead the Opposition another Session, before the break-up takes place.

Stanley's letter deserved the epithets 'highly satisfactory' and 'conciliatory' which Disraeli bestowed on it; but it was also characteristically outspoken.

From Lord Stanley.

KNOWSLEY, *Nov.* 13, 1849. — I am much obliged by your letter of the 9th inst. When I wrote to you, I was not aware that the Protection Society had passed resolutions condemnatory of your views, nor have I indeed yet seen these. Indeed,

[1] The figures were — Chatterton, Protectionist, 793; McCarthy, Liberal, 584.

Geoffrey, 14th Earl of Derby.
after the portrait by Sir Francis Grant, P.R.A.
at Hughenden.

inted in England.

I think that when I wrote to you I named that I had not seen the letter to which yours was an answer. I cannot for a moment hesitate, from what you say, and what I hear from others, in condemning the course pursued by Mr. Young in his comments upon you as ill-advised and improper, nor have I the slightest wish that our course as a party should be guided by the Protection Society: but I think that body may be useful in keeping alive the spirit of the party, and counteracting the impression actively sought to be produced by our opponents, that a return to the protective principle is hopeless. That hope gone, our principal support is lost to us; and therefore it was that I saw with regret that in a published letter you had taken up a controversial, or I may say a hostile, tone against the Society. I must repeat I was not aware of the provocation you had received; but had I been so, I should equally have regretted that it had drawn forth a retort, and an apparent abandonment of Protection, on your part.

What Mr. Young may say, or what imprudence he may commit, is of comparatively little consequence. His declarations commit nobody, and if he pitches the key extravagantly high, there is no great harm done; but what falls from you is of far more consequence, and if *you* go into the other extreme, and pitch it discouragingly low, serious injury may be done to our friends, and certainly great encouragement will be given to our opponents to persist in their present policy. I hope you will excuse my plain speaking, and with the same plainness allow me to say that I thought the tone of your last speech at Aylesbury far more conciliatory of the feelings of our friends, and very well suited in its tone to meet their views. I entirely approve of inculcating the doctrine that the present Parliament is not to be despaired of; and you know that I have always supported the policy of showing a *pont d'or* to those who may be inclined to think they have gone too far in the Free Trade line.

I hope your gloomy views of the present state of feeling on the part of the farmers are somewhat exaggerated: but you must remember first that the circumstances of the County of Bucks have been rather peculiar; and next, that if there has arisen a democratic feeling among them, it is caused by distress and by the feeling that they have been *thrown over;* and our best hope of counteracting this tendency is in our convincing them that *we* are not of the number of those who have so treated them. When we meet, I do not think there will be much difficulty in so forming the plan of our Parliamentary campaign, as to remove any appearance of dissension, and show a front at least as united as we did during the last Session.

Beresford's report to Stanley of his conversations with Disraeli is interesting. Disraeli, he writes, 'was very free and confidential in his intercourse with me throughout. He appeared at first decidedly piqued and low about the turn which matters had taken. I strove hard to eradicate all feelings of disappointment or resentment, as beneath his position in the party, and I hope that he is more the thing than he was in that respect.'

The process of peacemaking continued. Young sent Tyrell a letter for publication, explanatory and apologetic. Disraeli was willing to be placated. He wrote to Malmesbury on November 21: 'The scandal of our provincial movement is great and flagrant, but I hope the evil is more superficial than it seems, and that, with tact and temper, the ship may be righted. I have spared no effort, nor has Beresford, but we have had to deal with a wrong-headed man.'[1] He also wrote a letter to Christopher, explaining his views in a conciliatory manner. Malmesbury, who had a few weeks before written to Stanley of the 'great consternation' caused by 'the muck' Disraeli had run, expressed himself satisfied, promised to try and keep Young 'quiet, I mean *silent*,' and added a friendly caution: 'As to yourself, my dear Disraeli, I have only to ask you on all occasions to remember that you have obtained a position which makes every word you say an arm in the hands of our friends or our foes. Every speech you make will be read, marked, learnt, and inwardly digested by all men for their own purposes, and you should never speak on politics without securing a good and friendly reporter.' Admirable advice to all leading politicians on all occasions, but not always possible to follow!

To Philip Rose.

HUGHENDEN, *Dec.* 2, 1849.—. . . I think stout Sir John Tyrell has bowled Young out. They eat their leek very quietly. I am glad I have myself not advanced a jot to

[1] A note in Malmesbury's *Memoirs* suggests that the wrong-headed man was Lord George Bentinck; but, of course, it was G. F. Young.

conciliate them. The next move is mine, and, if played with tact and temper, I have not the slightest doubt I shall get the whole country with me by the time I want it.

Disraeli may not have advanced, but he certainly took pains to conciliate. In his next speech, at Newport Pagnell, on December 5, at a meeting of the new Bucks Association, he said he was quite willing to see a dissolution. Let the farmers petition for it if they liked; but if they did not get it, let them take his practical remedies. So he bound both policies together. 'The meeting at Newport Pagnell was more than good,' he told his sister, 'both in quantity and quality. It surprised everyone by its numbers; nearly 300, and a great acreage. I spoke to my satisfaction, and I think, from all I hear and read, have quite managed the malcontents.' The speech effected its object. Within a few days Young and his friends formally accepted the direction of the Parliamentary leaders.

The breach was healed; but as to the sinking fund, 'we must not deceive ourselves,' wrote Cox; 'it does not take.' Accordingly, when Disraeli resumed correspondence with Stanley as to their programme for the next year, that plan was quietly given the go-by. Adderley, afterwards Sir Charles, and finally Lord Norton, was very anxious to get Disraeli's support for a newly-formed Colonial Government Society, and for its motions in Parliament. The society, which was supported by men of different parties, was primarily to secure local independence and Parliamentary institutions for the Colonies, with the view, it rightly maintained, of substituting for growing disaffection a loyal and devoted attachment to the Mother-Country. But absolute local independence seemed to conflict with preferential trade arrangements, and the society was therefore held at arm's length by Stanley and Disraeli.

To Lord Stanley.

Confidential. HUGHENDEN MANOR, *Dec.* 17, 1849.—I enclose you a letter I received a day or two ago from Adderley.

I declined, of course, being a member of the Council in question, on the double plea that I was not sufficiently acquainted with their purpose, and, were I so, was too much occupied to give the due attention. I offered also the usual and obvious reasons against the expediency of amendments on the Address, which particular circumstances can alone render advisable, and counselled a substantive and well-concerted motion, to which he might bring all the force of the Protectionist party, in addition to that of the new Colonial movement. I apprehend myself that all these Colonial motions and manœuvres, in whatever form and by whomsoever proposed, are, in fact, the stir of Wakefield,[1] in whom I have little confidence. One Godley,[2] in whom I have less, is, I think, the instrument that acts upon Stafford and Adderley in the first instance. However, there is no doubt that these Colonial Reformers have organised their force, and are determined to be troublesome to the Government. It is, therefore, of importance that we should decide upon the course to be taken by the party. I am now pretty well qualified to listen to your ideas and instructions on this head, which I was scarcely last Session, as I have given a good deal of time during the recess to the Colonial question in all its branches. To obtain our support, Molesworth and Co. would modify their motions and movements a good deal, and it is not impossible that a deadly blow might be struck in this district of the Administration. Your son, too, I hope, will have returned by that time, and may be of vast use to our not too powerful ranks.

And on this head I may venture to express my deep regret that the D. of Richmond could not have contrived to lend a helping hand to John Manners at Shoreham. He would be of great use to us, because he is really a working man, has mastered the great questions by reading blue-books (the only way), and is a fair and improving speaker. On the rumor, but only a provincial one, of Quintin Dick's impending demise, I tried to run Lord John for Aylesbury.

A general amendment to the Address depends, of course, on the complexion of the times when Parliament meets, but assuming that we may not think it advisable to embark on one, and that it is of importance to lose no time in making a considerable diversion, I take the liberty, in the roughest manner, as you will recognise, to sketch the scheme by which I think the question of local taxation should be worked at present.

I would introduce the question to the House totally in a

[1] Edward Gibbon Wakefield, the Colonial Reformer.

[2] John Robert Godley, friend and supporter of Wakefield; largely concerned in founding and guiding Canterbury, New Zealand; afterwards Assistant Under-Secretary at the War Office; father of Lord Kilbracken.

new aspect. I would accept the declarations of our opponents, that there is no difference in land from other property; that land, in fact, to use their often repeated phrases of last Session, is nothing more than a *raw material*, and to be dealt with as other raw materials. I would then ask how they can justify the extension to this raw material, and the most important of all raw materials, of a different economical and fiscal system from that which they extend to all other raw materials. I would pursue this in detail, and your lordship will easily see the gross and flagrant consequences to which it would lead. I would argue the question on its sheer merits, as a question of justice to the proprietors and of policy to the community, and would not introduce the inferential benefit to be derived by the farmers, because that would lead to controversy; and as the farmers have generally made up their minds that they would reap the benefits of the proposed change, it is unnecessary to discuss the point any further in Parliament.

Another and more important point. I would openly and formally include Ireland in the proposition. It would be a motion for a Committee of the whole House to consider the local taxation of Great Britain and Ireland. Two great points to consider: the form of the motion, or rather measure; and the means of supply of consequent deficiency. Is it necessary for us even to intimate the latter? Is it not the duty of the Chancellor of the Exchequer to satisfy all just claims, and to keep the Queen's Exchequer sufficiently replenished?

With regard to the nature of the measure, in order to retain local administration, etc., etc., I can't for the life of me devise any suggestion very different from that we produced last year. But all this I submit to your lordship's better judgment. . . .

Stanley, in reply, strongly advised having nothing to say to the Colonial Government Society. It was difficult to imagine a more heterogeneous combination of names than those of its supporters, who would be sure to differ in opinion on the most ordinary matters of Colonial government. With regard to relief for agriculturists, he thought the party must take the field in earnest next session, though there were difficulties attending all plans.

To Lord Stanley.

Private. HUGHENDEN, *Dec.* 28, 1849.—The Colonial Dilettante Society have given up their amendment to the Address, which I think is well. There is to be a substantive motion, to be made by Molesworth and seconded by Walpole (who seems to have strangely mixed himself up with these affairs), and which motion is to be submitted to us previously, and modified in any way we desire consistent, or rather not inconsistent, with their general aim. Adderley, who seems very excited, and sadly deficient in judgment, has sent me the programme of their society, which contains only one idea — what they call self-government — and is written without any dignity or depth.

Henry Baillie writes to me that he has been in correspondence with Lord John and Lord Grey, *re* Ceylon. They have refused to send over for the witnesses, by a promise to do which they avoided, at the end of the Session, the virtual vote of censure of the Ceylon Committee.[1] Joseph Hume is furious, and I believe will shortly appear in print anent. He writes to Baillie that he is prepared to join in any motion to upset the Government, and especially Lord Grey, and mentions with self-complacency that he did not vote confidence in them on my motion on the state of the nation. All this foretells and foreshadows, as far as the House of Commons is concerned, a serious Colonial crisis. What are we to do?

You have sketched with the hand of a master, and with the inspiration of experience, those difficult considerations which I had only arrived at by many painful months of plodding. Clearly, instead of more Wakefieldism, we want less: and it appears to me that the real key of Lord Grey's position is that he talked much too much Wakefieldism out of office, and found, when at length Secretary of State for the Colonies, that his theoretical Colonial Reform was a delusion. But being a clever, proud, strong, and rather wrong-headed man, he has endeavoured to reconcile his visionary projects with a sane practice — hence this imbroglio! Now it appears to me — I say it with unaffected deference — that it would be possible to arrange a motion on the part of the Colonial Reformers that our party, as a party, might support, provided they held their tongues as much as possible, while myself, or someone else, might make a speech which, while it justified our voting for the motion, should, at the same time, completely develop our own Colonial system, and express our own tenets on all the great points of local government, emigration, waste lands, penal settlements, etc.

Lord Grey is open to all attack, not only on account of the results, but of the system he has pursued with respect to the Colonial Committee of the Privy Council. I hold that no man

[1] The House of Commons had appointed in the previous session, at Baillie's instance, a Committee, of which Disraeli was a member, to inquire into the grievances of Ceylon.

has a right to aspire to be Secretary of State for the Colonies who has not arrived at personal conclusions on the subjects which he has referred, and proposes to refer, to that Committee: in many other respects also a most objectionable arrangement. But to the point. In this Colonial discussion we must deal with frankness with the commercial question. Can we again establish a commercial tie with the Colonies without the odium of inflicting high prices on the metropolitan consumer? Could this be done by terminating all import duties whatever on Colonial produce? By really making them integral portions of the United Kingdom? No sugar duties on either Indies, and a duty on foreign corn, might set the more important Colonies on their legs (a duty on foreign timber still existing), and would comprise some elements of popularity.

I conclude it is too late to introduce thirty Colonial M.P.'s into St. Stephen's. Were it possible, it would be a great element of future strength to the Conservative party of this country. . . .

I thought John Manners was whitewashed by leading the forlorn hope against Rothschild, and that thereafter he was to be considered not only a Christian, but a Protestant.

Sir Robert's letter is not, I think, very happy: at the same time pompous and trite. He has succeeded in conveying an impression that his estate is in very bad condition. He seems to think that drainage is an universal specific, tho' in truth a very partial one. Tho' he really says nothing which might not have been said if the Corn Laws had not been repealed, he nevertheless writes with an awkward consciousness of having led his friends into a hopeless scrape.

Peel's letter was one to his tenants, in which he told them that what had been done was irrevocable, and that Parliament would never again sanction the taxation of food. They must make up their minds to low prices. He recognised that there might be distress among them, and, though he would not make a general reduction of rent, he would consider any special case. He was prepared to co-operate with his tenants in beneficial improvements to farms — for instance, by drainage — and would remit 20 per cent. of the rents for that purpose for two half-years. The admission that there was distress, and a substantial ground for assistance to farmers, was welcomed by the Protectionists.

To Lord John Manners.

HUGHENDEN MANOR, *Jan.* 1, 1850.

MY DEAR J. M.,— . . . I have just come from Quarter Sessions, and hear even in the rural districts that pauperism is diminished. How is this? I hear also that the shipowners are building more ships than ever. How again?

Tell Dr. Trench that it will not do to agitate the sinking fund now, as the suggestion has not been generally taken up, and will distract. It must sleep till the right time.

The National Debt was incurred for the foreigners: levy from the foreigner 5 millions per annum to pay off the National Debt. By which means you have virtual Protection on a popular principle; gradually every year diminish general taxation; and in a short time pay off the £400,000,000 of mortgages, or rather reduce their interest to 2 per cent. This is the affair in brief, but 'tis the gist. *Multos et felices annos!*—D.

There should be more variety in the movement. Something to break the low, tho' welling, chorus of the agrestic multitude.

Stanley, in reply to Disraeli, postponed a detailed discussion of the Colonial question till the party leaders met at Burghley, but intimated that he was in favour of preferential duties, and against the admission of Colonial representatives to Parliament.

To Lord Stanley.

HUGHENDEN, *Jan.* 11, 1850.—I had written the day before I received your letter to Lord Exeter, begging leave to withdraw my refusal of his kind invitation to Burghley, as I thought the aspect of affairs had become critical, and that we had better, all of us, meet as speedily, and confer as amply, as practicable. It is possible that the Government suffrage scheme may be of a conservative tendency, and projected to arrest the progress of the 40s. freehold movement. At the same time, it is not likely that they will propose any measure of this kind without considering the interests of their party at our cost, and at all events the measure will occasion discussion, in which it will be difficult for us to avoid taking a distinct position on a question which will probably be the key to future power. I look forward with great interest to your views on this subject.

Cobden's evening invasion of Bucks was very sorry. He make a mistake. Had he met the farmers boldly, the result might have been very different.

The agitation of the 'National Association' has operated

much as I anticipated. It was evidently projected by men who were ignorant of the real state of the country. To address the Throne for a dissolution of Parliament, with commerce and manufacture thriving, the revenue increasing, money abundant, and pauperism reduced even in the rural districts, which is certainly the case, was the *delirium tremens* of politics. One could hardly present one of these addresses to the Queen without a smile or a blush. The injurious effects of this movement are otherwise, also, not inconsiderable. It has forced us into an extreme position when circumstances counselled a very moderate one. It has terribly cut away golden bridges. It has unnecessarily exposed the agricultural interest in the nakedness of its isolation. Not a single meeting has taken place among the shipping population, among the Colonial or commercial interests, among any class of the labouring multitude. I don't say that our friend Mr. Young has been ineffective. He has done a good deal, but what he has done he had better not have done. He has gained the trick by trumping his partner's best card.

'Cobden's evening invasion of Bucks' was a meeting which he held at Aylesbury on January 9, where, at an hour suitable to the labourers and the artisans of the numerous small industries of the county, he addressed a mixed audience, which included only a few farmers, on the advantages of Free Trade. He had invited Disraeli to meet him; but Disraeli preferred to dine with the farmers at Great Marlow on the previous day, explaining that he had the pleasure of meeting Cobden in the evenings in Parliament during seven months of the year. In his speech Disraeli made great fun of Cobden's flying visit, fixed for an hour very inconvenient to the farmers whom he desired to convert. One phrase which Disraeli used, in accordance with the proposals in his letter of December 17 to Stanley, that the land was 'a raw material,' and should be treated as such, was taken up and apparently accepted by Cobden, and frequently appeared in the debates of the following session.

To Mrs. Disraeli.

BURGHLEY, STAMFORD, *Jan.* 22, 1850.

MY DEAREST WIFE,—A hasty line to say all goes right. The exterior of Burghley magnificent and unique—in an immense park crowded with ancient timber.

Here I found Duke of Richmond, Stanley, Lord and Lady Sandwich, Lord and Lady Southampton (the only women), Sir Robert Inglis, Granby, Herries, Christopher, H. Bentinck, Trollope, Maunsell, and Stafford — M.P.'s for the county — Beresford, etc.

Lady Exeter is what we heard, but I have scarcely seen enough of her to say more:[1] of the other women nothing as yet. This house, which is immense, can only accommodate altogether *twenty!*

We had a Cabinet last night, and are to have another to-day at five, Stanley being now shooting. Granby would not bring his guns, in order that he might lose not a moment in conferring.

I did not go to the fine ladies yesterday, but they sent Wilton, or rather he brought himself after me, being most eager to talk politics 'with his leader.' . . .

Frank Grant[2] has asked, through Granby, to paint my portrait. He will charge nothing. He does it for the sake of the engraving. I made sufficient difficulties, but at last promised. His charge is 300 guineas. Adieu, my dearest. I count on hearing from you to-morrow. — Your affec. husband, D.

Henry Bentinck and Trollope went this morning.

The Duke of Rutland arrived: very cordial.

Jan. 23, 1850. Yesterday we had four Knights of the Garter at dinner. The D. of Richmond is very cordial and hearty. Stanley shoots too much, but draws well with me, and the result is altogether satisfactory.

Disraeli impressed upon the friends and colleagues whom he met at Burghley the fact, which was very unpalatable to the ultra-Protectionists, that every interest in the country, except the landed, was improving. The visit was successful in establishing better relations between the leading personages of the party, and giving Disraeli a more assured position among them. At Burghley, too, he completed an arrangement to restore Manners to Parliament, an object which he had much at heart. The Conservative member for Colchester resigned, and after a contest Manners was returned in February. 'May this step, my dearest John,' wrote Disraeli, 'lead to your prosperity and happiness; and may you secure both by serving that great country which we both love!'

[1] Writing to his sister, on Jan. 24, Disraeli says: 'Lady Exeter tall, still handsome, engaging, and very pious.'

[2] Sir Francis Grant, P.R.A. For the portrait, see frontispiece of this volume.

With friends and political acquaintances not belonging to his own party Disraeli seems to have made no concealment, about this time, of the direction which his thoughts were taking. His old friend and fellow-traveller, James Clay, now a Liberal member of Parliament, gave him a pamphlet in favour of Protection, and told him that the author thought Protection was in the plight of Lazarus — not dead, but sleeping, and might be awakened. 'Protection is not only dead, but damned,' said Disraeli. Early in 1850 he dined with John Bright at Bellamy's and admitted to him that Protection was gone, and that he had been doing all he could to prevent squires and farmers making fools of themselves in the recess. Mr. George Trevelyan has revealed to the world that about this time a considerable friendliness sprang up between Disraeli and Bright, each of whom undoubtedly had a fascination for the other. Mr. Trevelyan expresses surprise at this, and maintains that they were the two men in the House of Commons most unlike. But surely, if there were obvious points of difference between them, there was also much in common. Each sprang from a small and despised religious community, the one being a Jew, the other a Quaker; each had won his way to a front rank in the House by force of character and power of oratory; each looked at the political facts before him from his individual standpoint, and not by the aid of party spectacles; and each was strongly opposed to the domination of the Whigs. The present writer has more than once heard Bright, in his last decade of life, refer with severe condemnation to the days when 'those old men, Lord John Russell and Lord Palmerston, were misgoverning the country.' There was, moreover, a democratic fibre in Disraeli as well as in Bright; though, of course, there was also in Disraeli an aristocratic fibre, which was wholly wanting in Bright, and in Bright a prevailing middle-class feeling which Disraeli certainly did not share.

To Londonderry Disraeli talked in February in the same sense about Protection as he had to Bright. 'He had long seen Protection was out of the question, and was looking to practical measures.' As a corollary he was anxious to conciliate the leading Peelites, and especially Graham, their principal debater, after Peel, in the House of Commons. Graham and he had had many sharp encounters, but Disraeli never bore rancour. Accordingly he told Londonderry, who was on very friendly terms with Graham, that the time for action was approaching, and that he was ready, as Londonderry wrote to Graham, 'to call his friends together, and tell them they must look to the best practicable mode of governing the country; that Sir James Graham was the only man then to be at the head of the House of Commons; that *he* should cheerfully act under him; that whatever coolness now existed between Graham and Stanley he was himself not conversant with, but that he had always found Stanley so manageable and agreeable to act and deal with that he felt sure he would see these views as they would be placed before him; and that, with Stanley in the Lords and Graham in the House of Commons, the country would have a very strong Government.' Graham refused to entertain the suggestion, but expressed his satisfaction that Disraeli was convinced that Protection was out of the question, adding caustically: 'The public good will be promoted if the leaders of the Opposition act steadily and boldly in conformity with these convictions. As yet they are entertained in secret, and the measures taken in public seem to be at variance with them.'[1] There was some justice in the criticism; but, after all, it hardly became Graham to make it, as Peel and many of his fellow-Ministers were thorough Free Traders some years before the fact was revealed in 1845 to the world; and, as we shall see, Disraeli laboured hard to convert his colleagues and his party, with ultimate, but tardy, success.

[1] Parker's *Sir James Graham*, Vol. II., ch. 5.

CHAPTER IX

A Successful Opposition

1850–1851

The agricultural distress was so undoubted, and the agitation among the farmers so violent, that, when Parliament met on January 31, 1850, all parties felt that they must define their position on the question of the hour. Accordingly, the Government put up the great Whig Free Trader, Villiers, instead of some inexperienced member, to move the Address in the House of Commons, and he made a detailed defence of the new system. There had been a perfunctory mention of the distress in the Queen's Speech, and Villiers admitted its existence; but he frankly told the agriculturists that he saw no way of helping them. This attitude invited opposition. Trollope moved an amendment, attributing the distress to recent legislation and heavy local taxation; and Disraeli supported him. The agricultural party were not asking, he said, for a return to 'abrogated laws'; what they did ask was that the Free Traders should be true to their own principles. Those principles would not tolerate the taxation of raw materials. Land was the most important raw material of a nation's industry. Why tax it?

Russell professed not to understand what Disraeli meant, but asked the House not to sanction any change in the commercial system; and Cobden challenged a discussion on the whole question of Free Trade and Protection. The issue being thus judiciously shifted, the Government, after a couple of nights' debate, obtained a majority of 119. But this was only a preliminary skirmish. The principal fight was two or three weeks later, when Disraeli made the presentation of petitions from Buckinghamshire owners and occupiers the basis of a motion for a Committee of the whole House to mitigate agricultural distress by revising the Poor Law. He and his friends, he said, still believed in Protection; but they could not shut their eyes to the practical conclusion that it was the opinion of a large majority in both Houses[1] not to disturb at present the settlement arrived at. In that case they ought to adapt the position of agriculturists to the altered conditions. He had received no answer to his argument about the proper treatment of the land as raw material. The Poor Law charges of which he proposed to relieve the agricultural interest amounted to some two millions.

The debate, which lasted two nights,[2] was a full-dress one, in which all the leading politicians spoke. Grey, the Home Secretary, in opposing the motion, did Disraeli the justice of saying that he had not encouraged the delusions of the extreme Protectionists; 'that *ignis-fatuus*, the restoration of Protection, has been declared by him utterly hopeless and impracticable during the present Parliament at least.' Bright asked, if the old Corn Law was unjust, how could its abrogation give the agriculturists any just claim to compensation? Graham took the familiar line that the adoption of the motion would involve a reversal of the policy of the last few years. Then fortune, in Disraeli's language, sent him an unexpected champion who 'fairly unhorsed' Graham. This was Gladstone, who, acting with Sidney Herbert and other Peelites, was of opinion that the agriculturists had a grievance which ought to be redressed, and that this proposal was a legitimate method of redressing it. They should look, he said, to the merits of the actual proposal, and not, as Graham insisted, to possible ulterior proposals. The adoption of the motion would tend to weaken the agitation for Protection, as showing that just demands would be conceded by Parliament. As a matter of essential justice, all property should be made liable for support

[1] A Protectionist amendment to the Address in the Lords was defeated by 49.

[2] Feb. 19 and 21.

of the poor. Peel, answering Gladstone, reinforced Graham's argument, pointing out that Disraeli had never said that the removal of taxation to the extent of £2,000,000 would close the account. He then proceeded to another elaborate, but somewhat ineffective, vindication of his policy and character, while conceding to Disraeli that 'the land is the stable basis of the State.' Russell also trotted out the Protection bogey once more; and finally Disraeli, in Gladstone's words, 'showed the marvellous talent that he has, for summing up with brilliancy, buoyancy, and comprehensiveness, at the close of a debate.' The division amply justified Disraeli's tactics. The Government only had a majority of twenty-one — 273 against 252. More than twenty Whigs and nearly twenty Peelites, including Gladstone, voted with Disraeli; Herbert was away ill. Hobhouse tells us that, when the numbers were declared, 'the Protectionists set up a shout, as well they might, but they seemed overpowered by their success, and did not cheer as much as usual. Our friends looked foolish enough.'

It was a great thing to have reduced the majority against the claims of the agricultural party from ninety-one to twenty-one in one year; but it had not been accomplished without seriously taxing Disraeli's strength. At the end of February he had rather a severe attack of illness — apparently influenza — and was confined to his London house during most of March. His absence from the field of battle demonstrated how necessary he was to his party; foes as well as friends recognised the fact. Graham wrote to Londonderry: 'There can be no doubt that Disraeli has been seriously ill: the Protectionists cannot do without him; and his presence after Easter will be much wanted by them.' Beresford lamented to Disraeli on April 3: 'Never was there so unfavourable a state for a party to find itself in as ours for the last ten days before the Recess. No Leader whatever: I was left quite alone and unsupported.' One beneficial change in party arrangements was effected during this period of illness:

Newdegate, to Disraeli's relief, resigned his position as one of the Whips,[1] and was succeeded by Forbes Mackenzie, a capable man, with whom the new leader could work heartily.

To Lady Londonderry.

GROSVENOR GATE, *March* 21, 1850.

DEAR LADY, — I send you my first letter. I have not yet left my room. My illness turned out more serious than I imagined, and if we had not called in Dr. Ferguson about ten days ago, I might have been in a scrape. However, I have now quite recovered, or am rather fast recovering, and only mention all this to account for the stupidity of this letter, for I have not been out, even for a drive. . . .

I have seen my friends the last two or three days; Lord Stanley was here on Monday, and talked over everything. Tell Ld. L. under the rose that the fusion between Ld. Aberdeen, Gladstone and Co., with Stanley and Co., ripens rapidly, and assumes in every phasis an encouraging aspect, but our mysterious friend Graham continues to baffle all conjecture.

Private. I am told that Peel said to Aberdeen, that even he could not make out what Graham was after. Some say that, if the Whigs can get their Irish Reform Bill well thro' this year, they mean to try their hand next season at an English measure, that Graham has an understanding with them on this subject, and is to lead the new revolution. A pleasant prospect!

The Government are very shaky, and, if we could only agree among ourselves, could be extinguished in eight-and-forty hours. . . .

HUGHENDEN MANOR, *March* 27, 1850. — Being told that the morning was more genial, I slipped my anchor on Tuesday, like a ship escaping from one of Palmerston's blockades, and about twenty miles from town encountered a snow-storm. When I arrived, the landscape was Siberian, and almost the climate; nevertheless I bore my journey well, and am better daily. . . .

To Sarah Disraeli.

HUGHENDEN, *March* 31, 1850. — . . . The weather has been very ungenial ever since [our arrival], and constant east winds, which I cannot face; my progress has therefore been rather slow.

Never was the political position more complicated, difficult, and urgent. I hope, but dare not determine, to be in my place on the 8th. If I cannot lead the party after the holidays, I had better retire altogether. There will be a fierce and

[1] See above, pp. 135, 136.

eventful Session. The Whigs could be turned out in a week if we were ready. I don't think my absence as yet has been productive of any serious harm, the great before-Easter result having been obtained. . . .

HUGHENDEN, *April* 5, 1850.—I go to town to-morrow to catch a Council with Stanley, flitting between Whittlebury and Goodwood. The political position is interesting, and I should not be surprised if our troops are brought into line immediately. They will be so if my plans are adopted; but there are so many people to consult and to persuade that it is like commanding an army in Italy under the Aulic Council at Vienna. However, I have not much cause to complain, as they are sufficiently docile; but there are moments which require rapidity of decision and execution. I am sorry I could not stay here a few days more; this north-west breeze renovates me wonderfully, and I am quite myself again.[1]

Disraeli's grumble about the number of persons whom he had to consult and persuade was no doubt provoked by a phrase in a letter which reached him that morning from Stanley: 'Consult your friends, *including Herries.*' Disraeli, as we have seen, never seems to have done more than tolerate the Committee of management, consisting of Herries and Granby besides himself; he neglected to call his colleagues together and ask their advice; and Stanley, now that the Committee was practically superseded, was specially anxious that proper deference should be paid to the veteran of the party. A month before, in reference to the selection of a new Whip, he had pressed upon Disraeli, also with all the urgency of italics, '*Don't forget Herries.*' In truth, Stanley and Disraeli, both strong men, were alike in a disposition to take their own course on important occasions, and consult their colleagues afterwards.

To Lady Londonderry.

[LONDON] *Sunday, April* 20, 1850.—. . . Here we have only two subjects, and both gloomy ones—Religion and Rents. Schisms in the Church and the ruin of landed proprietors are our only themes. The Church question has scarcely commenced, and may, before a very short time, effect some startling consequences. It pervades all classes—literally from

[1] *Letters*, pp. 228, 229.

the palace to the cottage. Gracious Majesty much excited, and clapped her hands with joy, when the critical decision[1] of the Privy Council against the Bishop of Exeter was announced to her. On this you may rely. . . .

A member of Brooks' told me yesterday, that he now never went to that club, the controversies among its members about Protection having become so acrimonious. The Duke of Bedford, who has held up very well to this spring, now wails and gnashes his teeth, and says that Peel was mistaken in all his calculations. Assheton Smith,[2] throughout a Free Trader, asked, in a letter from a friend, what sport he had had this year, replied: 'Don't talk to me of sport; I can think of nothing but these infernal low prices.' Granby showed me the letter, which was, I think, to Sloane Stanley. Lord Poltimore's steward, after his audit a few days back, sent him £1,200, and told him to take care of it, as it was probably the last he would ever receive — this, Devonshire, where things are very bad indeed. But you hear these sort of stories everywhere; what I tell you all come from the Whigs. It is, however, too late for those who voted for the Repeal of the Corn Laws to repent or to complain. As long as the great body of the people are well employed at a good rate of wages, all the proprietors, and all the farmers, too, may be ruined without redress. If the evil goes deeper, then we shall have a change.

As for Parliamentary politics, it is impossible for an Opposition to do more than we have done without turning out a Government. We have had a pitched battle nearly every night since we reassembled, and in some of them the Government have received ignominious defeats. Even their Budget has been destroyed.

It was a cheering situation in the House of Commons to which Disraeli returned after his illness. Ministers were constantly being put in a minority over one question and another. The Budget, which was produced during his absence, was responsible for several checks. Sir Charles Wood, with an estimated surplus of a million and a half, proposed to repeal the excise on bricks, and to lower the value of the stamps on the sale and mortgage of land. The Stamp Bill had a troubled career. Disraeli's letters to his sister at this time are written in high spirits,

[1] The Gorham case. Judgment was given on March 8 against Bishop Phillpotts, who had refused to institute Mr. Gorham to a living on account of his supposed heretical opinions about Baptismal Regeneration.

[2] Well-known sportsman, master of hounds, and M.P.

owing to the frequent defeats of the Government, and his own increasing consideration in the social and political world.

To Sarah Disraeli.

House of Commons, *April* 18, 1850.—The great victory on Monday[1] quite redeemed the Friday check.[2] I hardly know what the Government will do—anything but go out. The Radicals so frightened at what they have almost unwittingly done, that Tuesday night, the moment I announced my intention to support the repeal of the excise on paper, they fled the House in confusion or voted with the Government. By these means the division was not good;[3] but their tactics have had this among other effects: destroyed the Radicals' monopoly of Liberal propositions, which they will take care no longer to make now there is a chance of their being carried. . . .

The Royal Academy have asked me to their annual banquet in May. One gets into a great many good things (at least what people think good things) by being leader of the Opposition; which, according to Sir Charles Wood, if you are not a Minister, is 'the next best thing.' . . .

House of Commons, *April* 26, 1850.—I have little to say, my life being passed in this House of which you are furnished daily in the journals. The Government have saved themselves from a crushing defeat to-night, on the Stamp Act, by an ignominious surrender at discretion yesterday: but they have troubles enough before them. . . .[4]

House of Commons, *May* 3, 1850.—The visit to the Jolliffes was very agreeable, notwithstanding a north-east wind, that really cut me in two. . . . Notwithstanding a blazing sun, I was obliged to keep in the conservatory, or could only venture out in a bearskin coat. It was the coldest day this year.

I hardly know what has happened since, I have been so busy; I think all politics. Tuesday was not a bad division[5] and, according to my friends, my best speech this year, though meagrely and coldly reported in *The Times.*

Yesterday the Government received another apoplectic stroke;[6] they are drifting—but I suppose, and perhaps hope, they may escape the breakers this year. . . .

I sat an hour with Lord Lyndhurst to-day; in good

[1] Defeat of Ministers on the Stamp Bill.

[2] Committee of inquiry into diplomatic salaries, etc.

[3] Majority of 101 for Government.

[4] *Letters*, pp. 229, 230.

[5] Majority of 96 for Government on Henley's motion to reduce salaries in the public service. See below, p. 251.

[6] Defeat of Government on a minor bill by 155 to 136.

spirits after a year of darkness. When the weather is warmer they will operate. . . .

CEYLON COMMITTEE ROOMS, *May* 13, 1850. — I am so much occupied that I must endeavour to send you a line in the midst of the hubbub of this never-ending committee. The dinner at the Academy was very agreeable, though they took me out of the wits, among whom I sat last year, and which were represented this by Rogers, Hallam, Milman, Thackeray, Lockhart, and placed me among the statesmen: I sat within two of Peel, and between Gladstone and Sidney Herbert. A leader of Opposition who has no rank is so rare, if not unprecedented, an animal, that the R.A.'s were puzzled how to place me; and, though they seem to have made somewhat of a blunder, it went off very well, Gladstone being particularly agreeable.

Afterwards we went to the first assembly of Mrs. Abbott Lawrence, the wife of the American Minister, which was very numerous. Mr. L. is a very opulent man, and has given for Ld. Cadogan's fine house on Piccadilly Terrace a rent equal to his salary, £2,000 *per annum*. All the world was there. Lawrence is a very fine specimen of the New World — good-looking and cordial and well-bred — a high Protectionist. I had heard much of him from John Manners, as he stayed a week at Belvoir, and they were all much pleased with him. There were a good many Americans, among them the Peabody family — great people. As Mrs. Lawrence says, 'the Peabodies are the Howards of America.' The chief Peabody was presented to me. He said of the D. of W[ellingto]n, who was there as well as at the Academy dinner, where he made a speech, 'The two hemispheres can't show a man like that, sir.'

On Sunday I dined with the Molesworths — a most agreeable party. The Lovelaces, the Rossis, Lady Morley, C. Villiers, Stafford, Milnes, Henry Hope, the Turkish Ambassador. I never saw a house better *monté* or a dinner better served.

The postponement of the Sugar battle on Tuesday was very unfortunate. The division on the Irish Franchise Bill was much better than I expected.

I dined yesterday (Saturday) with the Londonderrys *en petit comité*, and afterwards went with M. A. to Lady Palmerston's and Lady Stanley's. It was a hard day, as in the morning I was obliged to receive Professor Aytoun to breakfast. He had called on me several times and written often, and as I could not ask him to dinner, it was the only thing left. I was very jaded, but after breakfast got some sleep by taking bang, and woke quite fresh.

Lord Eglinton had asked me to a great banquet on Thursday which he gave to Aytoun, whom it is the fashion to *fêter* among the grand folks, in gratitude for the Protection articles in *Blackwood*, of which he is the author; but I declined, as I thought it a bore, which large male dinners are. I got J. Manners and young Stanley, Boo Lennox, Lord Mandeville, and Lord Naas[1] to meet him.

Lady Blandford, next to whom I sate yesterday at dinner (Brunnow on my other side), told me that she had heard that *Sin and Sorrow* was the joint production of George Smythe and Lady Sligo. I think if I saw it I should find him out. I suppose he supplied the sin, and his sister the rest.[2]

The February motion and division — 'the great before-Easter result' — was Disraeli's main effort this session on behalf of the agricultural party. But he constantly kept rural distress before Parliament and the Government. He began[3] by making sarcastic inquiries as to what it was really meant to do with the Budget which had been introduced in his absence. He understood that the Chancellor of the Exchequer, having got a surplus, voluntarily offered to relieve the agricultural interest. He could not believe that the repeal of one excise duty — welcome as that was — represented the whole Budget of the Government. He was answered tartly by Russell that all Wood had promised was to devote half the surplus to relieve public burdens. A day or two later[4] he supported a motion of Henley's to reduce salaries in the public service, in order to lighten the burden on those who paid most of the taxes. He maintained that economy was necessary, and that the Conservatives were the party of economy. Peel and Cobden opposed, and the Government were sustained by a majority of ninety-six. At the end of the session he supported ineffectually a motion to relieve tenant farmers of income tax. On two occasions independent Whigs, alarmed at the serious effect on agriculture of measures which their party had supported on the faith of representations that the land would not suffer, brought forward motions for its relief. One of these motions advocated the reimposition of an

[1] Afterwards sixth Earl of Mayo; thrice Chief Secretary for Ireland; and Governor-General of India.

[2] Brit. Mus., Addit. MSS. Part of this letter appeared in *Letters*, pp. 231, 232.

[3] April 26.

[4] April 30.

import duty on corn; the other the immediate repeal of the malt tax, involving a loss of nearly five millions to the exchequer. Neither would have been introduced by Disraeli, and he anticipated the large majorities (114 and 124) by which they were rejected. But he welcomed them as the acts of repentant Free Traders, and supported them because he thought it was the duty of the Government to do something to relieve agricultural distress, and they had procured the rejection of his own February motion without making any proposal in its place.

On the proposal for placing an import duty on corn, he explained[1] that he would not have approved its introduction because it was of a partial character, and took into consideration the interests of only one class. He would prefer to have compensation, not in this manner, but by a fair adjustment of taxation. However he might differ from the policy of 1846, he did not suppose that the country would, 'like a capricious woman,' turn round at once and rescind all it had done. On the proposal[2] to repeal the malt tax, the Ministerial speakers declared themselves to be horrified at this light-hearted suggestion to sweep away a revenue of over £4,500,000; and Russell quoted Stanley as having said that he would not vote for a motion which would create such a deficiency till he saw how to make it good. But these arguments, though they produced a good majority for the Government, did not deter Disraeli from supporting the motion. Ministers had rejected all other proposals for remedying the distress, and would propose nothing themselves: they must be brought to their senses. The present mode of raising revenue, which pressed so unfairly on the land, could not go on. The proper course was to reduce excise rather than customs, as, whatever dispute there might be in the case of customs, the foreigner certainly paid no part of the excise. In this connection Disraeli made an important profession of his faith as regards Colonial policy.

[1] May 14. [2] July 5.

If there be any object which, more than another, ought to engage the attention of the statesmen of this country, it is the necessity of consolidating our Colonial Empire. If we wish to maintain our political power or our commercial wealth, we can only secure those great results by the consolidation of our Colonial Empire. I will not advert to the political means by which such a consolidation might be maintained. I will not enter into the difficult but important consideration, whether the Colonies ought or ought not to be represented in this House — although these are questions which we ought not to discard from our minds — but looking only to the commercial and fiscal part of the subject, I cannot understand by what means in the present day, following the current of our recent legislation, that consolidation can take place unless we can reduce into a fact a phrase which political economists are so fond of using — namely, that our Colonies should be placed on the same footing as the counties of England. Now let me ask the House, when this claim has been made on behalf of the Colonies, what has been the objection? It has always been met by the plea that it is impossible the Colonies can have the same footing as our English counties, because they do not bear their share of the Excise duties. But in attempting the great commercial and fiscal reforms which have gone on for the last six or seven years, if you had directed your attention to the Excise, instead of the Customs, you would have increased the means of the people to provide themselves with articles of consumption, and diminished in a great degree the burdens of the people, while at the same time we should have destroyed the great barrier to that consolidation of our Colonial Empire; and, while we relieved and employed our people, we should have increased the imperial strength of this still, I hope, great Empire.

Though agricultural distress was Disraeli's main preoccupation, he discharged effectively the ordinary duties of Opposition leader. The Ministerial programme mainly consisted of two Irish Bills, one lowering the Irish suffrage, and the other abolishing the Lord-Lieutenancy. The first passed in a modified form. The second was abandoned. The lowering of the Irish suffrage was defended on the ground that, owing to famine and impoverishment, the electorate had seriously decreased. Disraeli replied that the Government should rather have attempted to settle in a statesmanlike and moderate manner the long-controverted relation between landlord and tenant. The abolition of the Lord-Lieutenancy involved a risk which Disraeli was not prepared to run; and, in any case, he strongly opposed the creation in its place of another Secretaryship of State. Such a procedure was very uneconomical. Every new office of the kind involved an 'equipage of clerks.' Why not, if you must change, put Ireland under the Home Secretary?

The most really important measure of the session was a Factories Bill, introduced by Lord Ashley and taken over by the Government, to settle the law about hours in factories. An Act of 1847 was supposed to have definitely limited to ten the number of hours during which women and young persons could be employed. But the Courts had construed it in such a way as made it possible for manufacturers to evade the spirit of the law. Unwillingly Ashley accepted a compromise offered by the Government, which implied a ten and a half hours' day. Manners protested against this as a breach of faith with poor working people, and Disraeli, who explained that, though he had voted for limitation, he had never spoken before on the question, supported him. An overworked population, he said, had started a movement for ten hours thirty years before, but only attained it in 1847. The Act had been successful; manufacturers were prosperous in spite of it; why abrogate it now? The honour of Parliament was concerned in not taking advantage of a legal flaw. 'The voice of outraged faith is no respecter of persons. Its cry cannot be stifled; it will penetrate the Senate and reach the Throne. . . . The most important elements of government are its moral influences.' The speech was instinct with the spirit of *Sybil*, and its objects have long since been more than attained. But for the moment the Government carried the day by announcing that they would take no further charge of the Bill if the compromise was disturbed.

In regard to another measure of social legislation, Disraeli seems to have rather listened to the voice of friendship than followed his natural political course. Inspection of coal-mines was proposed, and the coal-owners, among whom Londonderry, the lord of Seaham, was conspicuous, uttered strong protests, which Disraeli echoed in the House of Commons. He made use of familiar phrases; it was hasty and ill-considered legislation — an unreasonable interference with the rights of property. He was unable to do more than delay the measure for a short while, and was probably not inconsolable for his want of success. To Londonderry, disgusted at the passing of the 'infernal' Bill, Disraeli explained that he was helpless. 'My friends, who are philanthropists, could not with consistency, after the ten hours affair, oppose it, and to my surprise the political economists were also in its favour.'

The most memorable debate of the session was that on the Greek question and Palmerston's foreign policy. The system of intervening in other nations' affairs, and giving unasked advice, which we have already discussed,[1] had been continued; but Ministers could, and did, boast that, throughout all the convulsions of the last two years in Europe, England, under their auspices, had been orderly at home and at peace abroad. The Greek question arose out of several petty claims of British subjects, largely Ionians, against the Greek Government. The most important were those of Finlay the historian, some of whose land had been expropriated for a royal palace; and of Don Pacifico, a Portuguese Jew born in Malta, whose house had been sacked by an Athenian mob, headed by persons of position. Neither Finlay nor Pacifico endeavoured to put the Greek law in motion to secure damages, but applied for redress to Palmerston, who disquieted Europe by sending the British fleet to the Piræus. The mediation of France was offered and accepted; but, without waiting for its operation, the British Admiral proceeded to seize Greek vessels in order to enforce his demands, with the result that the French

[1] Ch. 7.

Ambassador was withdrawn from London. Russia also protested against British action. Palmerston's clumsy and high-handed proceedings, which were thoroughly disapproved by most of his colleagues, called loudly for criticism; but the debate was not of Disraeli's contriving, nor, though he summed up the case of the Opposition at the close of four nights' contention,[1] was it one in which he showed to special advantage. Palmerston made the finest speech of his life, defending himself for five hours through a summer night, 'from the dusk of one day until the dawn of the next'; Peel spoke for the last time; and Gladstone, Graham, Roebuck, Molesworth, Cobden, and Sir Alexander Cockburn, all made notable efforts.

The movers in the matter were the Peelites; and it was in concert with Aberdeen, if not under his inspiration, that Stanley proposed and carried in the House of Lords a vote of censure on the Government limited to the Greek question. No similar attempt at censure was made in the Commons; and the Government, who refused to resign, found some difficulty in getting whitewashed. Finally, Russell, after taunting the Opposition with their inaction, accepted what Disraeli called 'the obvious and offered machinery' of a motion by Roebuck, expressing confidence in the principles of the Government's foreign policy, but not specifically mentioning Greece. The leaders alike of the Protectionists, the Peelites, and the Radicals, combined in resisting the motion, but in each case failed to command the allegiance of the whole of their followers. The bogey of a Protectionist Government was used effectively by Ministers and their friends, though Molesworth protested that he did not believe that 'the landed gentlemen of England under leaders with the abilities of Lord Stanley, and with the talents of my hon. friend the member for Buckinghamshire,' would pursue a policy leading to confusion and revolution.

It may be doubted whether Disraeli's heart was in the movement against ministers. He told Bright that he

[1] June 24, 25, 27, 28.

was annoyed at the crisis, and had wished the industrial question to be settled finally before anything of this kind came up. He probably realised that it would be difficult to get the rank and file to vote straight; he was reluctant to attack Palmerston, whom he desired to separate from the Whigs and attract, if possible, back into his old Tory camp; and it was obvious that a combined movement in force would tend to bring Russell to Palmerston's rescue, and close the breach that had been opening between these two statesmen. Stanley endeavoured to push his lieutenant forward; he urged him not to let the debate have too much of a Peelite character, and not to spare Palmerston and the Government. 'You will,' he wrote, 'and I think very judiciously, follow Palmerston; and forgive me if I impress upon you the great importance, on many accounts, of hitting hard and not sparing. Anything short of *guerre à outrance* would have the effect of reviving, in suspicious minds, old misconceptions, and expose you to misconstruction on the part of those who may look with envy at your present high position.'

In spite of Stanley's exhortations, it was Gladstone who answered Palmerston, and not Disraeli, and Gladstone and the other Peelite leaders who dominated the debate. The rare spectacle was seen of Gladstone defending Disraeli against Russell's reflections. Why, he said, should Disraeli be expected to move in the matter?

> The purpose was to question the vote of the House of Lords and to neutralise and destroy its effect. Was this [Disraeli's] affair? Sir, it is not for me to speak the sentiments of the hon. member; but if on this occasion I may attempt to divine them, I really apprehend that he was not so ill-satisfied with the vote of the House of Lords as to be desirous to disturb it.

So much did Gladstone take the lead that Cockburn said he supposed they were now to consider him Stanley's representative in the House—'Gladstone *vice* Disraeli, am I to say resigned or superseded?' and Russell lamented Disraeli's eclipse, as he had always found him 'a fair opponent, ready to take issue on great questions of public interest, not seeking by any evasion or subterfuge to obtain any undue advantage.' If Gladstone were in future to conduct the debates in the House on behalf of the Opposition, they could not expect, Russell said, the same fairness or justice. The taunts did not move Disraeli, who, in reply, while entirely associating himself with Stanley, repudiated any obligation to move a vote of censure, and reviewed the foreign policy of the Government, characterising it as both meddlesome and unsuccessful. England must beware lest she suffered at the hands of the Powers the fate of Venice under the Treaty of Cambray, 'the sole object of which was to cut the wings of this high-flying Republic of Venice, to terminate the intolerable career of the great commercial aristocracy which had offended them by its wealth and insulted them by its arrogance.' To a proud and self-satisfied House of Commons these sentiments were not nearly so congenial as Palmerston's famous peroration in which he challenged a verdict on the question, 'whether, as the Roman, in the days of old, held himself free from indignity, when he could say *Civis Romanus sum*, so also a British subject, in whatever land he may be, shall feel confident that the watchful eye and the strong arm of England will protect him against injustice and wrong.'

The Government obtained the satisfactory and hardly expected majority of 46 — 310 against 264. On the morrow[1] of the division, Sir Robert Peel, who had both spoken and voted against the Government, had a fall from his horse on Constitution Hill, and within four days was dead. 'Peace to his ashes!' wrote Disraeli in *Lord George Bentinck*. 'His name will be often appealed to in that scene which he loved so well, and never without homage even by his opponents.' Rightly or wrongly, Disraeli was convinced that in his last months Peel was desirous of effecting a reconciliation with him; and he has left an interesting memorandum, written apparently in the sixties, dealing with their relations and with the

[1] June 29.

facts of Peel's death, as well as with the circumstances of the Pacifico debate.

A day or two after Peel's death Gladstone was at the Carlton, and said: 'Peel died at peace with all mankind; even with Disraeli. The last thing he did was to cheer Disraeli. It was not a very loud cheer, but it *was* a cheer; it was distinct. I sate next to him.'

I had concluded the great debate on the Greek (Pacifico) business at four o'clock in the morning. It was the first, and the only time, in which, the Protectionist party acting again with Sir Robert Peel, or rather he acting again with them, I had to assume, and fulfil, the duties of leader in his presence. I wished to avoid it, as I thought it might be distressing to him, and I shrink from anything presumptuous. I had means of communicating with him, through Forbes Mackenzie, who was one of my Whips and who had been a Lord of the Treasury under Peel. Though Mackenzie had resigned his office on the Repeal of the Corn Laws, he still maintained his friendly relations with Sir R. Peel and his old colleagues. Sir Robert answered Mackenzie that he certainly meant to speak, but had no wish to close the debate. And he thought that Mr. Disraeli, from his position, ought to close it.

The majority in favour of Lord Palmerston was unexpectedly large: 46. Mackenzie went to tell Sir Robert the numbers before they were declared. Sir Robert looked disappointed, and said: 'I had thought it would not have exceeded 20.' I heard this myself, for, in that strange state of affairs, I was only removed on the front bench by two persons from Peel, during the latter years of his life. He was very conciliatory to me. Partly because his was not a nature that bore rancor; partly because, as he esteemed success in the House of Commons the greatest of human possessions, he respected a triumphant adversary; and partly, as I know, because he wished to bring back his followers into office under Lord Derby by an arrangement which would have, of course, omitted himself.

Lord Aberdeen had planned the attack on Palmerston, under the inspiration of Madame Lieven and Guizot. The Court, who attributed the fall of the Orleanist family to Lord Palmerston, were favorable to it. Lord Derby [then Lord Stanley] had readily fallen into the scheme, and had brought forward the motion of censure in the House of Lords himself, to cancel the ill effects of which Mr. Roebuck's counter-motion in the House of Commons had been brought forward. Lord Aberdeen, of course, would have been Secretary for Foreign Affairs. There was all reasonable room for the other Peelites, for Lord Derby had at that moment no men with pretensions to Cabinet Office, except old Herries and myself. Indeed, his difficulty would have been to have had sufficient friends of his own in his own Cabinet; and perhaps Peel, or at any rate the Peelites, saw all this, and looked upon him only as a stopgap.

The great difficulty would have been the Leadership of the House of Commons. I was the Leader of 250 men, and, so far as numbers were concerned, no one could compete with me; but I not only had no official experience of high office, but I had positively never held even the humblest office. There was no confidential intimacy at that time between Lord Derby and myself, and I don't think he would have much hesitated in suggesting a Peelite, one of his old and even recent colleagues, as Leader, if I consented, and the party generally. But who? Gladstone, though he had made a capital speech in the Pacifico debate, and had stamped himself on the House as a man with a future, had certainly not then, without a party, the sufficient position. Lord Lincoln (Duke of Newcastle) and Sidney Herbert had only just got out of the egg. I have always thought that old Goulburn was the man whom Sir Robert Peel and Lord Derby (then Stanley) would have brought forward, and furbished up like an old piece of dusty furniture, under whom we might have all served without any great outrage of personal feelings. But I never could penetrate this. The majority, however, dispelled these dreams. It was caused by a section of the Tories, who saw through the affair and looked upon it as a plot to bring the Peelites back, and put them at the head of the party, and they acted accordingly. Next morning Peel was dead, or as good! He seemed quite well in the House, and spoke well—with none of the bitterness of his followers against Palmerston. (By the bye, Lord P. met me shortly after the debate, and said: 'You and Peel treated me like gentlemen: which no one else did.')

Although he could not have been in bed before 5 o'clock, devoted to the Prince, he rose early to attend a Council about the projected 'Great Exhibition.' There was some financial question. He took it up, but not with his usual lucidity. Then he put pen to paper, but seemed confused, and finally said he would think over the matter, and send his results to the Prince. He went home, and afterwards went out to ride, and it happened. Was it a fit? If so, it was brought on by unnecessary want of rest and repose. I know, as well as most men, what it is to get home at 4 or 5 in the morning after an exciting division. Sleep is not commanded under such circumstances, even by the philosophical. Had Peel taken his fair rest, would he have been saved? Bulwer Lytton thought not when we talked over these matters.

'He had done his work,' he said. 'No man lives who has done his work. There was nothing left for him to do.'

I did not rise, that fatal day, so early as Sir Robert Peel. And in the afternoon my guardian angel persuaded me, instead of going to Clubs and Houses of Commons, to take a drive in our agreeable environs. We were returning through the Regent's Park, and two gentlemen on horseback, strangers, stopped our carriage. 'Mr. D.,' they said, 'you will be interested to hear that Sir Robert Peel has been thrown from his horse, and has been carried home in a dangerous state.'

'Dangerous?' I inquired. 'I hope not. His loss would be a great misfortune for this country.'

They seemed a little surprised, but I spoke what I felt.

Next day (it might be the day after), Peel still lying on his couch, there was a great morning fête at Rosebank; a thatched cottage on the banks of the Thames, surrounded by groves of the flowers which gave it a name, and where, to render the romantic simplicity complete, Lady Londonderry, in a colossal conservatory, condescended to make tea from a suite of golden pots and kettles.

Lord Londonderry was restless and absorbed: he foresaw the revolution which the death of Peel might occasion in parties. He pressed my hand with affectionate anxiety, asked many questions, and, full of intrigue, showed, as usual, his cards. I missed him during the fête. He reappeared towards the end. He came up, and whispered to me. It was hopeless. He had actually galloped up to London, called at Whitehall, and galloped back again, while his band was still playing, and his friends still sipping ices.

In another memorandum, also of the sixties, Disraeli dwells on the increasing civilities of his old opponent:

I observed this also in Peel. He sate almost next to me during the last years of his Parliamentary life. . . . I had recourse to many little arts to spare his feelings, and to get fellows to sit between us and all that: but he never assisted me in these endeavours; quite the reverse, and I have since more than once suspected, that he meant to make our respective positions in the House a means of gradually bringing about a reconciliation.

In one of my great 'Protectionist' motions, as they were called, though I carefully avoided advocating Protection in them, which he was obliged to oppose, he took elaborate pains to assure the House, looking at me the whole time, that he bore no enmity to any member on account of former struggles and differences of opinion. His language was so cordial and his manner so marked, that it was much cheered by his own friends, and all the men of sense of [our] own party: as indicating ultimate fusion on honorable terms.

There were other traits and circumstances I could mention, and, as Gladstone said, he died cheering me.

This pretty story of Peel cheering Disraeli, and Gladstone testifying to it, was also recorded by Smythe[1] in 1854, who wrote that he was present on both occasions, and who may indeed have been Disraeli's authority. But it receives no corroboration either from Peel's correspondence or from Lord Morley's *Life of Gladstone.* On the contrary, in the latter a tale is told of Peel's repugnance to any association with Disraeli, which entirely conflicts with Disraeli's consolatory belief in Peel's forgiving humour. Gladstone wrote in 1897, a year before his death:

A very curious incident on this occasion [the Pacifico debate] evinced the extreme reluctance of Sir R. Peel to appear in any ostensible relation with Disraeli. . . . Disraeli, not yet fully recognised as leader of the Protectionists, was working hard for that position, and assumed the manners of it, with Beresford, a kind of whipper-in, for his right-hand man. After the Palmerston speech, he asked me on the next night whether I would undertake to answer it. I said that I was incompetent to do it, from want of knowledge and otherwise. He answered that in that case he must do it. As the debate was not to close that evening, this left another night free for Peel when he might speak and *not* be in Disraeli's *neighbourhood.* I told Peel what Disraeli had arranged. He was very well satisfied. But, shortly afterwards, I received from Disraeli a message through Beresford, that he had changed his mind, and would not speak until the next and closing night, when Peel would have to speak also. I had to make known to Peel this alteration. He received the tidings with extreme annoyance: thinking, I suppose, that if the two spoke on the same side and in the late hour just before the division it would convey the idea of some concert or co-operation between them, which it was evident that he was most anxious to avoid.[2]

[1] In an article in the *Press*, Jan. 7, 1854, unsigned but known to have been written by Smythe. 'This is not rumour or hearsay,' it said, 'for the writer of this article sat next to Sir Robert Peel on that occasion. A few days after, when the horrible tragedy was over, amid a group of mourning disciples, we heard Mr. Gladstone urge as a consolation, "Peel died at peace with all mankind. He even lived to cheer Disraeli."' See Vol. II., pp. 121, 122, and below, ch. 14.

[2] Morley's *Gladstone*, Vol. I., p. 369.

It is impossible to reconcile the two versions of Peel's disposition towards Disraeli at the last. Gladstone's memorandum was written nearly forty years after the event, and when he himself was failing. But he had a tenacious memory for detail, and was likely to be acquainted with Peel's sentiments. Disraeli's account was written within fifteen years of Peel's death; but then he was a man of high imagination, with no gift of accuracy in detail. Gladstone's statement is disfigured by obvious *animus* against Disraeli, as shown by the carping reference to Disraeli's leadership of the Opposition; and it is possible that the devoted follower of Peel may have imputed to his more magnanimous leader a resentment which was at that date felt only by himself. Disraeli is certainly justified in claiming that in Peel's later speeches his former assailant was always mentioned with respect; but, of course, he would wish to believe that Peel cherished no more animosity against him than he did against Peel, and he would be likely to magnify any tentative approaches towards reconciliation. In dealing, however, with men of large nature and wide outlook, as were both Peel and Disraeli, the more generous and less cynical view is likely to be correct; and in Smythe we have a witness who claims himself both to have seen Peel cheer, and to have heard Gladstone's testimony. Therefore, we shall not greatly err if we accept the words put into Gladstone's mouth by Disraeli: 'Peel died at peace with all mankind; even with Disraeli.'

No one more strongly seconded Disraeli's movement to dissociate the Conservative party from any attempt to revive Protection in its old form than his chief's son, Edward Stanley.

From the Hon. Edward Stanley.

ALBANY, *Monday, July* 29 [? 1850].—I cannot forbear telling you, in confirmation of our common opinion on the 'industrial question,' that I had a long interview with a constituent on Saturday morning—one on whom I can thoroughly rely—and he said that, except a few old and obstinate men who never would give up their crotchets (these were his words), all the gentlemen farmers of his neighbourhood were agreed in thinking a return to high duties at any time, and to Protective duties, however low, at the present, impossible. This man calls himself a stanch Protectionist, and was one until very lately—indeed upon principle he is one still, and the head of that interest in Lynn. . . .

Again, from Paris, on October 19, Edward Stanley writes: 'It really will not do to make another Protectionist demonstration; the very turnips of Norfolk will cry out against us, as the turnip-headed inhabitants thereof have already begun to do.' On the other hand, one of Disraeli's oldest political and personal friends, Manners, implored him to abide by their old cause. 'I am for thorough,' he wrote on September 10. 'The only three republics known to England (for Switzerland has just established a Protectionist tariff) are Protectionist, and so are at least one-half of our Chartists. . . . On what question can one stand an appeal to the country with a better prospect of success than that of Protection?' But Manners's remonstrances only served to draw Disraeli into a still stronger statement of his resolve to find a substitute for the policy of Protection.

To Lord John Manners.

HUGHENDEN, *Oct.* 16, 1850.

MY DEAR COMRADE,— . . . I am also greatly engaged in endeavouring to prepare some great measure, or rather scheme of policy, which may set us on our legs, but the labor is great, for the task is most difficult.[1]

If 'general prosperity' and agricultural distress be concurrent when Parliament meets, which is not improbable, and we are equal to the occasion, we might do something. The great point is to devise a scheme, which will rally the landed party, and yet be suited to the spirit of the age. As for Protection in its old form, I look upon that as dead. In this county, able-bodied pauperism is extinguished. I imagine the same result in Oxon made Henley make the unnecessary confession in which he indulged. In case of a dissolution on the old protective cry, it is not merely the manufacturing masses that would be arrayed against us: the peasantry would be

[1] To Lady Londonderry, on Oct. 22, Disraeli wrote: 'It is a difficult business to evolve order out of chaos, which is the present state of the Tory party of these realms.'

equally hostile. This is my judgment from what passes under my eye in this eminently agricultural county. The same report reaches me from the contiguous counties.

Your 'three republics' are very ingenious: but the classes directly interested in 'Protection' in those countries are very considerable in amount. The awkward feature of rent does not arise, too, among the peasant proprietors of France—our great republican authority for agricultural Protection.

Moreover, it appears to me pretty clear, that the landed interest is the only one that seriously requires something to be done for it. I think the shipping case is not a good one; and protection to W.I[ndian] sugar is involved in almost inextricable difficulties. If the W.I. colonies are protected on account of their deficiency of labor, why should the E.I. territories enjoy that Protection with a redundancy of labor? And could you make a distinction? And so on.

Well, then, it is impossible, independently of other objections, to attempt to revive the old form of Protection merely for the land. That would never do. All which leads me to the conclusion, that unless, when Parliament meets (the circumstances being such as I previously assumed), we have some comprehensive proposition, which meets the exigency, we are done, and shall fall to pieces: but if we could hit the right nail on the head, we might put the Government in a minority in their own house, when Lord Carington thinks they would dissolve, but I doubt that, if the *coup d'apoplexie* were dealt them in February.

Write whenever you can. I hope you will be able to decipher these Sibylline leaves, but I have been writing all day, and my hand is quite exhausted.—Ever yours, D.

Manners was not convinced: 'In my poor opinion, "Away with the Income Tax, and hurrah for the Custom House!" ought to be our cry.' But there can be no doubt that Disraeli, with his wonted insight, had discerned the current of public opinion. Abraham Hayward, who was always malignant in his hostility to Disraeli, wrote to Lady Morgan on November 2: 'Protection is dead, and Disraeli very nearly, if not quite, forgotten. How soon one of these puffed-up reputations goes down! It is like a bladder after the pricking of a pin.' The cause of Protection might be lost, and, indeed, that was Disraeli's own belief; but it was very short-sighted to suppose that Disraeli, who was steadily riveting his hold on his party and the House of Commons, would disappear with it. A close observer of politics had, with more discernment, written to him earlier in the year: 'The Whig game of misrepresenting you, I think, has fairly run itself out.'

The perennial topic of Protection was temporarily overshadowed in the autumn of 1850 by what was known as the Papal Aggression. What happened is graphically described in *Endymion.*[1]

At the end of the autumn, his Holiness the Pope had made half a dozen new Cardinals, and to the surprise of the world, and the murmurs of the Italians, there appeared among them the name of an Englishman [Cardinal Wiseman], Archbishop *in partibus.* Shortly after this, a Papal Bull, 'given at St. Peter's, Rome, under the seal of the fisherman,' was issued, establishing a Romish hierarchy in England. This was soon followed by a pastoral letter by the new Cardinal 'given out of the Appian Gate,'[2] announcing that 'Catholic England had been restored to its orbit in the ecclesiastical firmament.'

The country at first was more stupefied than alarmed. It was conscious that something extraordinary had happened, and some great action taken by an ecclesiastical power, which from tradition it was ever inclined to view with suspicion and some fear. But it held its breath for a while. It so happened that the Prime Minister was a member of a great house which had become illustrious by its profession of Protestant principles, and even by its sufferings in a cause which England had once looked on as sacred. The Prime Minister, a man of distinguished ability, not devoid even of genius, was also a wily politician, and of almost unrivalled experience in the management of political parties. The Ministry was weak and nearly worn out, and its chief, influenced partly by noble and historical sentiment, partly by a conviction that he had a fine occasion to rally the confidence of the country round himself and his friends, and to restore the repute of his political connection, thought fit, without consulting his colleagues, to publish a manifesto, denouncing the aggression of the Pope upon our Protestantism as insolent and insidious, and as expressing a pretension of supremacy over the realm of England which made the Minister indignant.

A confused public wanted to be led, and now they were led. They sprang to their feet like an armed man. The Corporation of London, the Universities of Oxford and Cambridge, had audiences of the Queen; the counties met, the municipalities memorialised; before the first of January there had been held nearly seven thousand public meetings, asserting

[1] Ch. 99. [2] This should have been the Flaminian Gate.

the supremacy of the Queen, and calling on Her Majesty's Government to vindicate it by stringent measures.

The Prime Minister's manifesto was Lord John Russell's famous Durham letter, so called because it was addressed to the Bishop of Durham. Besides protesting vehemently against the Pope's action, it also denounced the excesses of Puseyism as 'a danger within the gates' which alarmed the writer even more. The letter was dated November 4, and published on Thursday, November 7. Disraeli, naturally anxious, as a good party leader, that the rising Protestant indignation of the country should not be appropriated for the political benefit of the Whigs, immediately wrote a letter to the Lord-Lieutenant of his county, which he contrived to get into *The Times* of November 9. In it he requested the Lord-Lieutenant to call a county meeting to express reprobation of the Aggression, but at the same time pointed out that the Government, who expressed so much indignation at the establishment of a Romish hierarchy in England, had recognised officially on several occasions the corresponding Romish hierarchy in Ireland. 'I had no idea,' he wrote to his sister, 'of Lord John's riding the high Protestant horse, and making the poor devils of Puseyites the scapegoats, when he, after all, is the greater culprit.' Greville, coming to the rescue of his friend Clarendon, the Viceroy of Ireland, replied in *The Times* that the Whig Government were only conforming to the practice established by Peel in 1845 in a royal warrant issued under the Charitable Bequests Act. Stanley wrote to ask what was to be done to avoid the country being placed, after all this bluster, in a ridiculous position.

To Lord Stanley.

HUGHENDEN, *Nov.* 16, 1850.—I received your letter this morning. I will first advert to the Popish question. I believe the position of the Government with respect to it to be one of extreme embarrassment. Naas writes to me that Corry Connellan[1] had just left him 'furious.' He said: 'Johnny must

[1] Private Secretary to the Lord-Lieutenant of Ireland.

have for the moment forgotten the existence of Ireland.' It was a stultification of the whole Whig policy towards this country for the last half-century and more. 'It will lead to such a complication as has never even in Ireland been witnessed.' Naas himself adds: 'The whole Papist population are bursting with fury at Johnny's letter. If they only act up to one-quarter what they say, they will never let an Irish Member vote for a Whig measure.'

It has confidentially reached me also from a very great quarter in Ireland, that Clarendon himself is extremely annoyed and perplexed with the affair.

I assume from the sudden silence of *The Times*, after lashing up the agitation, no leader referring to the question appearing for four days, and all the meetings shoved into the back of the paper, that Lord John already repents of indulging in his hereditary foible — to wit, having a shy at the Papists.

What will the Government do? If after the Downing Street Bull they do nothing, in deference to the Romans, then the Protestant cry, now legitimately raised, will gather to us, and we will not let it dissolve: if they act against the Pope in the manner you have intimated, the Roman Members will take the earliest opportunity, probably by a vote in favor of the land, to which they are always predisposed, to embarrass the Government. This is my general view.

Knowing that Lord John, a week before his manifesto, had written in reply to the remonstrance of the Bishop of London quite on a contrary tack, believing that both through Lord Minto and by other means the Government had long been cognisant of the Pope's intention, and were far from unfavorable to it, I thought not a moment should be lost in giving some check to what I conceived, on Lord John's part, to be a disingenuous and audacious ruse — 'insolent and insidious,' in my opinion. His manifesto in Thursday's *Times* did not reach me until Friday morning, and to obtain the insertion of my rejoinder on Saturday I had, of course, not a moment to lose. I might have made the statement more complete, but there are times when the opportune is preferable to the excellent.[1] I wished to give a warning hint to our too eager friends of the Spooner school, who have no doubt all fallen into the trap, but who, when Parliament meets, will recover from their hallucination, when they find the champion of Protestantism still the ally of McHale.

You are under a misconception in supposing that I ever referred to the Charitable Trusts Act or to Lord Grey's circular. I made no allusion to either. It was Greville who

[1] Disraeli used this same phrase in writing the day before to his sister.

vindicated Lord Clarendon on the ground of the precedent afforded by the C. T. Act. That statute itself does not mention any member of the Roman Hierarchy, nor even with the addition of the warrant would it pass muster as a precedent if well squeezed. I have not replied to C. G., as newspaper controversy is not satisfactory, and the proper opportunity will occur.

I have before me, among other analogous documents, a letter from Lord Clarendon addressed to 'His Grace Archbishop Murray of Dublin,' requesting him to submit the statutes of the New Colleges for the consideration of the Pope, for whom he entertained 'a profound veneration'—also the address delivered to the assembled Irish Roman Catholic Hierarchy by the Lord-Lieutenant in 1847, beginning 'My Lords,' and well larded with Lordships, and which ends by 'desiring their counsel and co-operation.' Also a list which is represented to me as the official list of the *entrée* during the Queen's visit, in which I observe Archbishop Murray takes precedence of the Lord C. Justice of the Queen's Bench, of Lord Abercorn, and of the ten Bishops of our Church. I wrote my letter from memory, which, however, seldom deceives me in political matters, and I apprehend that these and other documents fully justify my statement. That statement was studiously confined to Ireland. It did not touch the Colonies or other branches germane to the matter.

These remarks have already run to such a length that I can venture only cursorily to notice the second, and in truth more important, division of your letter.

Assuming, as I have done for a long time, that 'general prosperity' and agricultural distress would be concurrent when Parliament meets, I have been busied in preparing some propositions for your consideration which might lead to a settlement of the controversy between Town and Country, for which, under the circumstances referred to, the occasion would be favorable. They are necessarily of a somewhat comprehensive character, but essentially practical and popular; and if introduced and conducted in a moderate and conciliatory tone, and rather as an adjustment between contending claims, than an attempt to give a victory to a party, I think might be jockeyed thro'. They would have a very good chance indeed if the Papists are disaffected to the Ministry.

These propositions would involve some relaxation of the restrictions on Banking in accordance with that system of relaxation which is now extended to all branches of our system. Upon this head I am in *strictly* confidential correspondence with Herries, between whom and myself in this particular I apprehend there will be no difference. It is, however, almost impossible to hold counsel on such affairs by the pen, and we have mutually made some attempts to visit each other, but in vain. These propositions are hardly yet quite ripe enough in their details to be submitted to your Lordship, but when they are sufficiently advanced I apprehend they will require very deliberate discussion. I hope, therefore, that if we meet before Parliament assembles we may have the advantage of a little more, and less hurried, counsel than last year. I should advise, if the propositions are ultimately approved of by you, that notice of their introduction should be given the first night of the Session, and not a day unnecessarily lost in bringing them to a vote. Under these circumstances I will not now enter into other financial measures, as if these resolutions be carried, or even very strongly supported, very important consequences must ensue either to the position or the policy of the Cabinet.

In my opinion London and your library is always the best place for business, and I would always attend your summons for that purpose if not in town, tho' at the time best for council, the latter half of January, I should probably be fixed at Grosvenor Gate.

I shall be in town for a few days at the beginning of next month in case you are passing thro'. . . .

The Government were indeed embarrassed. As Disraeli put it in *Endymion:*

Unfortunately, it was soon discovered by the Minister that there had been nothing illegal in the conduct of the Pope or the Cardinal, and a considerable portion of the Liberal party began to express the inconvenient opinion, that the manifesto of their chief was opposed to those principles of civil and religious liberty of which he was the hereditary champion. Some influential members of his own Cabinet did not conceal their disapprobation of a step on which they had not been consulted.

Disraeli can hardly have shared the popular alarm and indignation. He wrote to Londonderry in a jesting spirit on November 3: 'What do you think of Cardinal Wiseman? The people are very much alarmed in this country. Even the peasants think they are going to be burned alive and taken up to Smithfield instead of their pigs.' But however much Disraeli may have regarded the agitation with amused comtempt, he was deeply impressed by it, as the vivid account in *Endymion*, written in his old age, shows. It convinced him of the essential Protestantism of the British character, and its effect may be traced in the complete abandonment of the Tractarian tendencies of his 'Young England' days, in the unfavourable picture of Roman methods drawn in *Lothair*, and in the famous Bill to 'put down Ritualism.' For the moment he was chiefly concerned to secure that the commotion should be utilised to help, and not to hinder, the advance of the Conservative cause.

To Lord Stanley.

CARLTON, *Dec.* 7, 1850.—. . . I have now been in town two or three days, and have reconnoitred the position, which seems to be about this:

There is great discontent and disquietude in the Liberal ranks. I think that Lord John will propose a Bill, as limited as possible in its operation, to prohibit the assumption of ecclesiastical and other titles, conferred by foreign Powers without the permission of the Sovereign. With the present commotion in this country, this will be rather a technical remedy than a political one. He will be legislating rather against an isolated grievance than taking those measures for the security of the Protestant realm which are required. There will be great disappointment in the public heart, if he takes this course. If, while his technical remedy be supported, we propose something more comprehensive and satisfactory, Lord John will fall back upon the Romanist party, and say: 'See what you must meet if you upset my Government: a Parliament elected under a "No Popery" cry, a purely Protestant Ministry, and the repeal of the Emancipation Act.'

They will, under these circumstances, find it most expedient to swallow the technical remedy, and continue to support the Government on the old understanding.

I have seen Inglis,[1] and conferred with him at great length. He is well disposed to us, but his ignorance of human nature will render it quite impossible for him to steer the course without our counsel and co-operation. Even he, however, has given up talking of keeping Lord John to his manly and straightforward declaration, having discovered that, if Lord John be pledged to anything by his letter, it is only to make a scapegoat of a section of the Church.

Inglis would be prepared, if only the technical remedy I

[1] Sir Robert Inglis, who represented Oxford University, took the lead among the Tory party of the movement to repel the Papal Aggression.

have intimated be proposed by the Government, himself to propose the more decisive course under our advice and sanction. If beat on this, which probably we should be, we should, at least, have outmanœuvred Lord John from his 'insidious position' as Protestant leader, and then we shall have the legitimate Protestant feeling on our side.

I have seen Lord Londsale,[1] Lord Ponsonby, and Herries, who came up from St. Julian's to meet me. Lord Ponsonby tells me that the Cabinet would have been broken up if its successors were ready. But where are they? The general idea among the Whigs is that what are called the Peelites are pro-Catholic and all that, but this I think to be without any solid foundation. After all, of the Peelites, there are only two men of first-rate calibre, and who would give the tone and color to the section — Graham and Gladstone. The first remains in the North, alert even after dinner, and Gladstone is at Naples — *not at Rome.* The idea that the Peelites are very Catholic arises from the tone of the *Chronicle*, but that is Sidney Herbert, to whom, I believe, the journal belongs. He is in town, very fervent, acting under the influence of Archdeacon Manning, who, I believe, has gone over. . . .

I have discussed affairs very much with Herries, and on the whole very satisfactorily. I am still of opinion, stronger even every day, that, whatever may be the excitement as to religious questions, when Parliament meets our policy should be to launch, as early as possible in February, some agricultural motion, which may lay the basis of a settlement of the industrial controversy, and may attract support.

If there be any discontent among the Irish, it would, I think, be carried; and if the Government are placed in a minority by these means, and at such a moment, with the Protestant question unsettled, and the Income Tax looming in the distance, I think their position would be distressing. But the form of this motion requires the most deep deliberation.

Lord Lonsdale thinks that we have lost a great opportunity by the precipitation with which our friends gulped down Lord John's letter. But there is a great revulsion on this head, and a letter published by Mr. Bennett[2] is making an extraordinary sensation here, and, when read, must affect the country. You have probably seen it, and there has been a new edition every day. It rather touches Lord John's private honor. When one finds that for the last seven years he kept the fasts and festivals of S. Paul, subscribed to S. Barnabas, that Bennett was his father confessor, people are

[1] The 2nd Earl, Postmaster-General 1841–5, President of the Council 1852.

[2] The well-known Ritualist clergyman, of St. Paul's, Knightsbridge, and afterwards Vicar of Frome.

startled that, with the Eucharist from Bennett's hands almost sticking in his throat, he should denounce his spiritual pastor as a mime and an impostor. . . .

The difficulties of the Government indicated that a Ministerial crisis might be at hand, but the Conservative Opposition, though their discipline and their spirits were better, were still lacking in *personnel.* These political conditions, and the death of Peel, which had left his followers somewhat forlorn, naturally suggested to the leaders of the regular parties the desirability of making fresh overtures to the Peelites, who, though weak in cohesion and numbers, were strong in administrative capacity and experience. It is not surprising, therefore, to find, in the winter of 1850–51, Disraeli resuming, in a more formal manner, the overtures which he had made through Londonderry in the previous spring to Graham. But for that affair, it would seem rather strange that Graham should have been the Peelite approached. We have seen that there had been, during the past session, sufficient community of action between the leaders of the two wings of the Conservative party to suggest the possibility of association in government; but the Peelites who had shown conspicuous friendliness were Aberdeen and Gladstone. Graham, on the other hand, had ever since 1846 approximated more closely than any of his colleagues, save Peel himself, to the Whig Government; and this attitude had been so marked as to bring him in January, 1849, an offer of the Admiralty under Russell. Moreover, he had had several sharp passages in debate with Disraeli, who enjoyed tilting at the 'disciple of Progress.' The choice of Graham was no doubt due mainly to his outstanding position, after Peel's death, in the House of Commons, but partly to the accident of his friendship with that persevering peacemaker, Londonderry.

To Lord Londonderry.

Confidential. HUGHENDEN, *Dec.* 29, 1850.—I am still in time to wish you and Lady L. a merrie Christmas, unless, indeed, you think it too Popish. . . .

The political phenomena of an autumn, to be decided in February, are data much too distant for speculation. I can't even now decide with any confidence to what degree the fervor may subside, but of this I feel persuaded, that Ld. J. R. has shaken himself very much in the confidence of all those whose good opinion a statesman should wish to possess. . . . The whole affair seems to me hasty, vulgar, and cunning.

I make no doubt, that it would not be very difficult to subvert his Government on the meeting of Parliament, but I am not prepared myself to engage in such an enterprise, without the probability of forming a strong and enduring administration. Such an administration must represent great interests and great parties in the country. Any attempt to achieve or to retain power in England by a mere reputation for administrative ability will never do. Peel tried it, and even he, with great adventitious advantage, signally failed.

In the meantime, trust me, that unless such a Government be formed power will slip from the hands of the aristocracy for ever, and results be precipitated which might, perhaps, have been for ever prevented.

With respect to Graham, you know my opinion of him. Both from personal regard and my high sense of his abilities. I should be unaffectedly glad to see him assume that position in the House of Commons and the State for which he is so eminently qualified; but I really don't think that Mr. Pitt himself could stand four-and-twenty hours, unless he were prepared with some wise and comprehensive settlement of the industrial question. Unless I greatly mistake, public opinion in almost every class is in favor of some temperate adjustment of this long controversy. It would permanently array on our side a large body of the population, again loyal.

My chief was not 'mum,' as you say, because of a bad fit of the gout, from which he has not yet recovered, but because he is too proud to bid for power, either by writing letters or making speeches, and I think he is right.

To Lord Stanley.

CARLTON, *Jan.* 21, 1851.—I arrived in town last night. This morning I received a letter from Lord Londonderry, which had been forwarded to Hughenden, of interest and importance.

You know that he always maintains a political correspondence with me, under the guise of social, and had more than once pressed me to go to Wynyard on the 17th to meet Graham. I declined with courteous expressions as to G.

Pressed again, and many compliments to myself in an extract from a confidential letter from G., I thought the matter was now ripe, and near eno' to bring these long-cherished negotiations to a crisis; and therefore, while I again declined going to Wynyard, on the fair excuse of having friends with me, I took the occasion, in a letter strictly confidential, but which I knew would be shown, to speak definitely on the political position.

My main points were these: that I could contemplate no Government of which you were not the head; that I should be sorry to see you attempt to form any Cabinet which had not a fair prospect of governing the country for a considerable period, and that I knew you shared these feelings; that a strong Government required not merely ability in the Houses of Parliament, but sympathies of numerous and powerful classes out of doors; that with respect to G., while there was no one who would more gladly see him than myself in the position in the House of Commons and the State which his great talents and experience fit him for, still I was confident he was indulging in an illusion in supposing that any man or body of men could rise to power in this country by a mere reputation for administrative talent; that even Peel had tried it and failed; that a Cabinet must be supported by powerful classes; and that the settlement of the industrial question, as far as agriculture was concerned, was the only basis of a strong Conservative Ministry; that, in my opinion, a great change had taken place during the last year in the public sentiment on this head; that even among the trading classes it was felt that the land had not been fairly dealt with; and that I believed the great majority of the country would be glad to see an equitable and temperate adjustment of the landed question, and a remission of taxation which might be supplied by a moderate duty on foreign agricultural imports, etc.

Lord Ly. writes to-day, urgently, that Graham has expressed his assent to most of my views; that he appears to be perfectly reconciled to serving under you; that he is *d'accord* with you on foreign affairs, and on the Irish question, considering a partial measure to be fatal to the existence of the Irish Church. The industrial question remains, and is doubtless the key of everything. But as, without doubt also, he has read and digested my letter, I conclude, tho' he does not choose to commit himself on that head at this moment, he will ultimately swallow this draught as well as the subordinate office points. . . .

Stanley expressed his interest, and congratulated Disraeli on his diplomacy, but shrewdly doubted whether Graham would even be 'brought to a *pourparler*.' However, the two leaders held a conference, and Disraeli wrote on January 29 to Londonderry a letter[1] which might form the basis of negotiation. There was no obstacle, he said, on the part of Stanley, who had no other feelings towards Graham than those 'which the recollection of long years of confidence and cordial co-operation would naturally inspire.' He himself, too, would allow no personal feeling to stand in the way. 'I would, however, observe that such arrangements, generally speaking, do not entirely depend upon the readiness of an individual to concur in them. It is scarcely possible for any man to lead, under any circumstances, a powerful party in Parliament, without developing such a degree of sympathy in his behalf, that his followers may not be very content that one, who has sedulously represented their opinions in debate, should subside to a secondary post.' He was persuaded, however, that at present he could overcome these difficulties. But it was an essential element of reconstruction to adopt conciliatory measures to the agricultural interest. 'There is a very prevalent and growing feeling, that the land has been hardly used, and that a temperate and well-matured conclusion of the controversy between town and country would meet with very general acceptation, because it has, for some time, been very generally expected.' If Graham shared Stanley's and Disraeli's general views on the subject, and was equally desirous to obtain the meditated result, Stanley would listen with the utmost willingness and deference to suggestions. 'We have a painful but irresistible persuasion, that the continued neglect of the agricultural classes may considerably, and, in all probability, permanently, impair the future elements of Conservative government in this country, in the same degree as an unequivocal, though temperate, disposition to do them justice would confirm their predilection for the present constitutional forms.'

Londonderry had apparently omitted to let Graham know what he was doing ; so, in passing on this letter to

[1] Published in Parker's *Graham*.

him, he deprecated his annoyance, assuring him that his only object in the negotiation was to see the Conservative party consolidated under the best statesmen left to depend on. Graham did not conceal his displeasure and his feeling that he had been placed in an awkward and unsatisfactory position. It was incorrect to say that he wished for an opportunity of resuming his political connection with Stanley. 'My intimacy with Lord Stanley has been unfortunately interrupted. But the terms on which we lived together for nearly twenty years, and on which we even parted, were such that I could not allow any other person to interpret to him my feelings and opinions. When I wish to communicate them to Lord Stanley, I shall ask his permission to state them for myself. At the present moment I have no such desire.' It was the policy of Protection on which Stanley insisted that formed the barrier. Disraeli's letter could lead to no consequences. 'I hope, however, that Mr. Disraeli will be assured that I have never wished to supplant him in the lead of the Protectionist party in the House of Commons, which he has won by his superior abilities.' Only two parties could exist, and were he a candidate for office he should sink differences and make his choice; but the effects of the disruption of 1846 had not yet subsided, and he meant to hold himself free from engagements.[1] In short, Graham's refusal was absolute. Perhaps Londonderry, in his eagerness to promote reconciliation, had not been entirely discreet. But Graham could hardly have been won by any manner of approach. He was much in request this year, as Russell again offered him Cabinet office, both at the beginning of the session and in the autumn. But the offer was on each occasion declined.

Graham was not the only Free Trade statesman with whom Disraeli endeavoured to establish this winter friendly relations which might lead up to political cooperation. The following mysterious letter can hardly

[1] Parker's *Graham*, Vol. II., ch. 6.

refer to anyone but Palmerston, to whom Disraeli felt constantly attracted.

From Count Reventlow.

Feb. 19, 1851.—I met our friend last evening near the famous cul de sac of Downing Street, and as his lordship proposed me to accompany him to the House of Commons, I availed myself of this excellent opportunity pour m'acquitter de votre commission, et je pense avec un plein succès, car notre ami a exprimé qu'il serait charmé de s'entretenir avec vous, et je l'ai prié de vous en donner une occasion, ce qu'il a promis; il va sans dire que je n'ai pas fait la moindre allusion à l'objet sur lequel vous désiriez lui parler, ce qui aurait été d'un très mauvais goût.

About this time Beresford warned Stanley that Disraeli had been 'coquetting and trying to deal with Lord Palmerston; that the latter expressed the impracticability of their different creeds and opinions, one being a Free Trader, the other a Protectionist. D. challenged Lord P. to produce one sentence in any of his speeches in which he had ever advocated Protection *per se*.' It will be remembered that on the Pacifico motion Stanley urged Disraeli to give no colour to misconceptions which might arise from sparing Palmerston in the debate.

It was a busy winter with Disraeli; his mind occupied with three great questions—the relief of agriculture otherwise than by Protection, the Papal Aggression, and the negotiations with Graham—all involving much correspondence; besides the biography of Bentinck, to the writing of which all his spare time was now given. If we are to believe Beresford's gossip, he made experiments during this recess with his personal appearance:

William Beresford to Lord Stanley.

THE DEEPDENE, *Friday* [*Dec.*, 1850].—... Disraeli, I hear, is figuring about with a fierce pair of moustaches. Now this is very sad, for he is not the person who ought to attract attention by *outré* dress and appearance, but by his talents.

I do trust that this style is only assumed while he is rusticating in the beech-woods of Buckinghamshire, and that he will appear in the world in a more humanised form in January....

To Sarah Disraeli.

Wednesday, Jan. 1, 1851. — I went on Monday to the Q[uarter] S[essions]. A great meeting. All the magnates there. The Lord-Lieutenant, the three county M.P.'s, Chandos, Verney, Calvert. The dinner very crowded — even the Carringtons remained to do the honor to Sir Thomas Aubrey, who resigns the chair. A note from Jem, which I found on my table yesterday, informs me of your merry Christmas dinner, and of his incipient influenza; but I hope he overstates his case, as I am the same, but impute it to the strange weather, the walls of H[ughenden] House in and out reeking with damp. At first I thought I had a cold. . . .

I found on my table letters from Lord Lyndhurst, Hardwicke, Granby, Buller, J. Manners, and Lord March, and all, even L.'s, at length, some almost pamphlets, so you see I have enough to do, but cannot reply to-day. Lyndhurst apologises for his handwriting, as he was always a poor scribe . . .; but it was dark. The truth is, I thought his handwriting very much improved. I think I told you Edward Stanley had returned — 'to my great joy,' his mother adds.

I wish you a very happy new year. Our plans remain all unsettled, in consequence of Stanley's state. Belvoir, Burghley, and Wimpole are contending for the honor of being the seat of the congress.

Hughenden, *Jan.* 13, 1851. — I find myself very incapable of exertion in this weather, and particularly so of writing letters, which I daily and weekly postpone, till the arrear frightens me. My public correspondence becomes a great tax, as the paper in the country is always damp, ink thick, and pens consequently incompetent. I expect young Stanley to-morrow, and on the 24th we go to Burghley. Lord Stanley wrote me his first letter, proposing to come up to town the 17th to consult; but, as the Burghley arrangement had been made, I thought it too great an effort for him to come 500 miles, so I suggested waiving it. I have not the slightest idea what will happen.

The new edition of the *Curiosities* seems to swim. My father's memory has been kept alive and done justice to, which was the great, indeed sole object. *Bell's Messenger* says in the review: 'He is still more admired now that he is dead.' . . .

Grosvenor Gate, *Jan.* 22. — I have been obliged to come up suddenly for some public business. . . . Young Stanley's visit to Hughenden, though hurried, was very agreeable. He seemed charmed with the hill country, after

Lancashire, and with everything else. Having no horses, we took long walks together—one day to Hampden, which pleased him much; another to the Abbey:[1] no one there, so we rambled all over the park; the view of Hughenden from the heights is quite marvellous. I had never seen it before, and this must be the view which Stafford was full of in the House of Commons last year, when he returned from staying at the Abbey. We walked to Denner Hill and its sylvan neighbourhood, and on Sunday, after church, we walked on the hills in view of Dashwood's park, till we got to West Wycombe Church. There is a regular journal for you!

The political horizon seems fair, and I never knew a session about to commence with better prospects. . . .[2]

[1] Wycombe Abbey. [2] *Letters*, pp. 236, 237.

CHAPTER X

On the Brink of Office

1851–1852

The session of 1851 in the main bore out Disraeli's anticipations of better fortunes for the Conservative party. The Opposition leaders,[1] who dined with Stanley just before the meeting of Parliament, and sat talking politics, as Malmesbury tells us, till one in the morning, must have been in good spirits. The Government were very vulnerable both on the question of the land and on their anti-Papal policy, and on both subjects Disraeli struck, in the debate on the Address,[2] the note of his subsequent criticism. Ministers had lamented agricultural distress in the Queen's Speech, but without any suggestion of action. They expressed 'confident hope' that the depression would pass away; that, said Disraeli, was 'the language of amiable despair.' He gave notice that he should move in the matter on the earliest possible day. On the question of Ecclesiastical Titles he anticipated the paltriness of Ministerial intentions.

Russell lost no time in bringing in his Bill, which merely forbade the assumption by Roman Catholics of territorial titles within the United Kingdom under penalty of a fine, and rendered void all bequests or donations made to persons under such titles. The mountain had brought forth a mouse, as one of the Irish members said. It was a 'little paltry, miserable measure,' declared Bright. The Irish, the Radicals, and the Peelites, opposed it outright. Disraeli, in Stanley's words, gave it 'a contemptuous support.' He would vote for it in order that people might

[1] Besides Disraeli, Herries, Malmesbury, Redesdale (Chairman of Committees in the House of Lords, 1851-86), and Beresford, there was also present Edward Stanley. 'He is very discreet,' wrote his father in explanation.

[2] Feb. 4.

see what was the result of that remarkable agitation which had been fostered by the Government. The weapon they had forged was not equal to the office for which it was intended. Was this all? Was a piece of petty persecution the only weapon they could devise on a solemn political exigency? It was a purely technical remedy. No principle was asserted or vindicated, and no substantial evil would be remedied. Russell, said Disraeli, called the Pope's letter a 'blunder on the sudden.' But the Pope's action had been deliberate. He had no doubt been encouraged by Russell's opinion, given in Parliament in 1845, that there were no grounds for continuing the restriction which prevented a Roman Catholic Bishop in Ireland assuming a title held by a Bishop of the Established Church. Besides, the Government had received notice of the Pope's intentions through a communication made to Minto, but disregarded by him. Parliament might have legislated in reference to the recognition, on terms, of a Roman Catholic hierarchy; but the Government had shirked this difficult problem. Their Bill would effect nothing. Disraeli's position, in fact, was that the Government, if they were not prepared for comprehensive legislation, should have left the question alone altogether. This was, in his opinion, merely an electioneering Bill, his support was of an equally tactical character, to prevent the Whigs from extracting all the profit from the extravagantly Protestant humour of the nation. After a debate which raged for four nights, leave was given to bring in the Bill by an enormous majority consisting of the regular supporters of both front benches.

Before the vote was taken, Disraeli had brought forward, and almost carried, his motion on agricultural distress. It took the simple form of laying down that it was the duty of Ministers to introduce without delay effectual measures for the relief of a distress which they acknowledged to exist. He based his case on that concurrence of general prosperity and agricultural depression which he had written about in the recess. In that concurrence there must be something wrong which Ministers should remedy. The arguments he used in his long and elaborate, but studiously moderate, speech were necessarily familiar, as he had pleaded the cause again and again. He asked that the Minister, whose tone implied that he recognised in his heart the injustice suffered by the land, should act.

I am altogether innocent of mixing up this question with the passions of party politics. The speeches I have made in this House are not speeches which are adapted to please thoughtless societies out of doors or meetings which are often held in the country, at which my name is mentioned as one who does not do sufficient justice to the sufferings of those who complain. Sir, I pardon all these innuendoes; I can make allowance for the strong feelings of worthy men placed in the trying circumstances in which the farmers of England are now labouring. But, right or wrong, of this I am convinced, that the course I have taken with respect to their interests has been the result of long thought and careful observation, and that I have asked for nothing for them which justice does not authorise and policy recommend. . . . I now appeal to the House of Commons. . . . They may step in and do that which the Minister shrinks from doing — terminate the bitter controversy of years. They may bring back that which my Lord Clarendon called 'the old good-nature of the people of England.' They may terminate the unhappy quarrel between town and country. They may build up again the fortunes of the land of England — that land to which we owe so much of our power and of our freedom; that land which has achieved the union of those two qualities for combining which a Roman Emperor was deified, *Imperium et Libertas.* And all this, too, not by favour, not by privilege, not by sectarian arrangements, not by class legislation, but by asserting the principles of political justice and obeying the dictates of social equity.

It is difficult, after reading this eloquent and obviously sincere passage, to understand Russell's description of the speech, in his letter to the Queen, as 'not that of a man who was persuaded he was undertaking a good cause.' Ministers, and Graham and Cobden, who came to their rescue, had nothing to answer except that general prosperity must eventually benefit agriculture, and that the motion was in reality a demand for a return to Protection. This, which had been Peel's favourite argument on previous agricultural motions, carried less conviction when it no longer came from his lips. Moreover, Disraeli had in his original speech emphatically repudiated any interpretation of the kind. He would not, he said, in that Parliament make any attempt to restore an abrogated system. He could not consent that the laws regulating the industry of a great nation should be made the shuttlecock of party strife. Were it possible to bring Protection back by a chance majority, he would shrink from doing so. 'That must be done out of this House; and it must be done by no chance majority, but by, if not a unanimous, a very preponderating expression of public opinion.' Surely that was a sufficiently definite pronouncement, and he repeated it in his reply at the close of the second night's debate. It was on this occasion that Croker said to Disraeli, 'The speech was the speech of a statesman, and the reply was the reply of a wit;'[1] and Stanley characterised both speech and reply as masterly. The division[2] gave the Government a majority of only 14—281 against 267—on what amounted in effect to a vote of want of confidence. Disraeli's efforts for the reorganisation of his party had been crowned with success; but we must not forget that, as Stanley wrote to Malmesbury, 'our division . . . was not as good as it looked, for we had several with us on whose general support we certainly could not count.' The serious impression produced upon Ministers may be gathered from the fact that in the Budget, introduced four days later, they conceded, though in a minute fashion, the principle against which they had so obstinately contended, by proposing a grant-in-aid of £150,000 to be handed over to local authorities for the maintenance of pauper lunatics.

'Notwithstanding the efforts of all persons and parties to keep them in,' wrote Disraeli to Londonderry on February 19, 'I doubt whether the Government can

[1] See Vol. II., p. 227. [2] Feb. 13.

stand. The Budget is universally derided, and adds to their difficulties, when they have received a body-blow.' The very next day they suffered a defeat which drove them to resignation. A band of Liberals and Radicals had long been discontented with the Reform Act of 1832, and wished to widen the electorate; but they had been foiled by the apathy of the Whigs and of the public in general, and by Russell's unwillingness to reopen a question in the settlement of which he had borne so honourable a share. Locke King, the member for East Surrey, had taken in charge a cause of which Hume was the most prominent Parliamentary champion; and he repeated, on February 20, a motion which he had made unsuccessfully in the last days of the previous session, for leave to introduce a Bill to equalise the county and borough franchise. Russell resisted the motion on both occasions, but on the second occasion promised a Bill for the following session. Disraeli, in July, 1850, supported Russell in his resistance, and spoke on the same general lines as when he opposed Hume in 1848. The franchise, in his view, should be 'the privilege of civic virtues,' and not treated as a universal right. It was better to adhere to the 'mitigated monarchy of England, with power in the Crown, order in one estate of the realm, and liberty in the other.' But he had no dread of the people. If they had universal suffrage to-morrow, the artisans would not support the Radicals. They would be for Monarchy and the Empire, and would give a national verdict against any scheme of national degradation. Even with the support of Disraeli and the Conservatives, the Government had some difficulty in defeating Locke King in July. The numbers were 159 to 100. Now, in February, the Conservatives, while retaining their hostility to the motion, left Ministers to fight by themselves the battle with their unruly followers. Disraeli and his friends 'moved off,' says Hobhouse, 'almost in a body,' with the result that the Government were beaten by 100 to 54; and of the 54, 17 were Protectionists and 27 were officials, so that all the support they received from their own party amounted to ten votes! The Opposition believed that Ministers, embarrassed by the difficulties of their anti-Papal policy and the unpopularity of their Budget, were not honestly exercising their influence to defeat the Bill; and the facts certainly support this theory.

Whether they were riding for a fall or not, the Government resolved not to put up with treatment so ignominious, and resigned at once, Russell stating to the Queen that the smallness of the majority against Disraeli's motion, and the defeat on the franchise, showed that they did not possess the confidence of the House of Commons. Both the Queen and the retiring Minister were agreed that the proper course was to appeal to Stanley, whose first step was to consult his lieutenant in the Commons before his audience. 'Come down to me,' he wrote on February 22, 'as soon as you possibly can. I have received a summons to be at the Palace at 3 o'clock.' The Queen asked Stanley to form a Government; but he demurred, owing to his lack of available statesmen. 'There was one, certainly, of great ability and talent, Mr. Disraeli, but who had never held office before; and perhaps Mr. Herries.' He advised that an attempt should first be made to obtain a Coalition Ministry of Whigs and Peelites, and that he himself should not be called in except as a *dernier ressort*.[1] It was excellent advice, and it was followed. The Queen sent for Aberdeen, Graham, and Russell; and but for the Papal claims, on which Russell was deeply committed to legislate, while the Peelite statesmen would not hear of legislation, that Coalition, which was patched up somewhat factiously in December, 1852, in order to oust a Ministry which had abandoned Protection, would have come about naturally as the official recognition of what, in order to prevent a return to Protection, had been the working arrangement of the 1847 Parliament. A Coalition being found to be impracticable, the Queen turned to Aberdeen, but in vain.

[1] *Queen Victoria's Letters*, Memorandum by Prince Albert, Feb. 22, 1851.

The *dernier ressort* had been reached, and Stanley was summoned once more.

Disraeli, who felt from the outset that Protection would be the difficulty, endeavoured, between Stanley's first and second summons, to bring his chief's mind to contemplate a tariff, as we should now say, for revenue only, and merely incidentally protective.

To Lord Stanley.

Private. Sunday, Feb. 23, 1851.—Pardon the liberty I take of venturing to impress on you the importance, at this moment, of viewing the question of a countervailing duty on foreign grain in its pure and scientific character. It is a financial arrangement only, and in no degree an industrial one: in the same category as drawbacks. The highest authorities so view it. If it have also the effect of preventing an illimitable depreciation of the home market, that is a consequence that would make a countervailing duty *politic* as well as *just*—but this feature need not be dwelt on. Duties on foreign grain and foreign sugar may be completely vindicated without impugning any of the principles of the new commercial system.

Stanley had already, in his first audience, spoken to the Queen on the subject in a dubious sense, saying that he should propose to place a duty on corn, for revenue only; but the duty must be six shillings at least, to bring the price of corn to forty-five shillings, 'which Sir R. Peel had stated to the House of Commons was in his opinion the lowest price wheat would fall to after the abolition of the Corn Laws.' This moved the Prince Consort, very naturally, to call attention to Disraeli's recent tactics, which had certainly pointed to the abandonment of Protection.

I told him (the Prince wrote) the Queen and certainly myself had been under a delusion, and that I was sure the country was equally so, as to his intention to return to Protection. Sometimes it was stated that Protection would be adhered to, sometimes that it was given up, and that it was *compensation* to the landed interest which the Protectionists looked to. His last speeches and the motion of Mr. Disraeli led to that belief, but that it was of the highest importance that the country should know exactly what was intended.

Both the Court and Disraeli had realised the fundamental difficulty of the Conservatives, and the need for dealing with it in a drastic fashion.

Disraeli has left among his papers a most interesting memorandum, apparently drawn up during the long years of opposition in the early sixties, with reference to this abortive attempt to form a Conservative Government in 1851. Oddly enough, he makes no reference to Stanley's advice to the Queen, in his first audience, that Her Majesty should begin by trying to obtain a Coalition Ministry. Accordingly, it is not quite clear whether the conference of the two leaders described in the early paragraphs of the memorandum took place before Stanley's first summons to the Palace on Saturday, the 22nd of February, or before his second on Tuesday, the 25th. The word 'immediate' in the first sentence suggests the former date. The reference, later on, to the summons to Buckingham Palace 'early on the following morning' implies the latter date. The matter is of very slight importance.

This *coup d'état*, as Bankes called it, rendered an immediate conference between Lord Derby [then Lord Stanley] and myself necessary. There could be no doubt that the Queen would send for him: in fact, there was no other person. There had been long a House of Commons rumor that the Protectionists must try their hand. My agricultural divisions had brought it to this pass. Again the eternal question, How was a Government to be formed? Lord Derby thought he could manage sufficiently in the House of Lords, but at all times, when a party was rich in patrician statesmen, it was unwise to rest too much on the House of Lords for the materials of a Ministry: said he thought that 'Malmesbury would make a good Colonial Secretary.' Reducing it to a minimum, to be excused only by the extraordinary circumstances of the case, it was impossible to meet Parliament with less than six Cabinet Ministers on the front bench of the House of Commons; it ought to be eight. It did not appear that from our own resources we could furnish more than three men — Herries, Lord Granby, and myself — and of these three only one had any official experience, and though an able man was worn out, and the intended Leader of the House not only never having been in office, but with very little Parliamentary experience. Mr. Disraeli[1] had been ten years in Parliament — from 1837 to 1847 — and never been placed on any Committee; and it was only during the four subsequent years that he had had any opportunity of making himself in any degree acquainted with the multifarious duties of a leading member of the House of Commons.

It was evident that Lord Derby was sanguine of a fusion with the Peelites, and of the revival of the old connection. They sate (even Graham) on the Opposition benches; they were a staff without an army; it seemed a necessary and a natural solution. Graham had paid me a marked tribute in debate: Gladstone had supported my motion and voted with me. Mr. Disraeli was very much in favor of such an arrangement, and always encouraged it. But he was not sanguine as to the result. The difficulty was the Leadership of the Commons. It was impossible that the colleagues of Sir R. Peel, veteran and even illustrious statesmen, could be led by one who had stepped out of the ranks, had destroyed their famous leader, and covered them with confusion. For this reason, from the first, Mr. D. not only expressed his readiness to waive his claims, but impressed upon Lord Derby the necessity of such conduct on his part. Lord D., perhaps from delicacy or consideration for Mr. D.'s feelings, never reciprocated this feeling. Indeed, he once said that he had no idea that the man who had brought things to this point should not reap the great reward. But the truth is, the difficulty was one which could not be removed by individual sacrifice. The Protectionist party, though they were prepared (though not very willingly) to accept the services of the Peelites in a subaltern position, made it a condition *sine qua non* that the Ministry should be led in both Houses by their own chiefs. Irrespective of the Protectionist quarrel, the Peelites were very unpopular at this moment in the country on account of the line they had taken respecting the Papacy.

Lord Derby, evidently indisposed towards Graham, and neither desirous nor sanguine of any arrangement with him, was still more than hopeful that he should obtain Gladstone, and that G. by his influence and management would obtain sufficient aid from his friends to give us, in the present state of parties, a working majority. Still, it was necessary, with the royal audience impending, to contemplate the possibility of having to form a Government from our own resources, and ultimately I proposed to Lord Derby three names, in addition to the preceding ones, who I thought might be reputably introduced to Parliament as advisers of the Crown. These

[1] In the opening paragraphs of this memorandum Disraeli writes sometimes in the first person and sometimes in the third.

names were Sir Robert Inglis, whom I proposed for the India Board; Mr. Henley, who, I observed, had obtained a certain position in the House; and Mr. Henry Corry, who had been Secretary of the Admiralty under Sir Robert Peel, had the reputation of a good administrator, and always addressed the House on the duties of his department with fluency, clearness, and a knowledge of his subject.

Lord Derby shrugged his shoulders, but made no difficulties, which was not his way.

We parted, and I think that it was in the evening that I received a note from Lord Derby informing me that he had been summoned by Her Majesty to Buckingham Palace early on the following morning, and should call on me immediately after his audience.

The remainder of the memorandum describes what happened between noon on Tuesday, the 25th of February, when Stanley had accepted the Queen's commission, and four o'clock on Thursday afternoon, the 27th, when he notified her Majesty of his failure. Disraeli has compressed the events of the three days into two; the meeting at Stanley's house, which he so humorously describes, took place, not on the Wednesday, as the narrative suggests, but on the Thursday:

Accordingly, he [Stanley] called at Grosvenor Gate early — I should think by noon — and came upstairs to me in the blue room. His face was radiant, his eye merry, as he entered, and he said, raising, as was his custom, his mocking eyebrows, 'Well, we are launched!' And then he became serious. 'I have not kissed hands,' he said, 'but I have promised the Queen that I would try to form a Government.'

To effect this object, he informed H.M., that he would appeal for assistance to the followers of the late Sir Robert Peel, and that with that view [he] was willing that the question of Protection should be an open one until the country by a dissolution should have had the opportunity of giving its opinion upon it. He told me that Her Majesty had inquired of him to whom he proposed to entrust the Leadership of the House of Commons, and he had mentioned my name.

The Queen said: 'I always felt that, if there were a Protectionist Government, Mr. D. must be the Leader of the House of Commons: but I do not approve of Mr. D. I do not approve of his conduct to Sir Robert Peel.'

Lord Derby said: 'Madam, Mr. D. has had to make his position, and men who make their positions will say and do

THE MINISTERIAL CRISIS.

Mr. Disraeli, on hearing of the Ministerial crisis, immediately waited upon Fortune, but was not favoured with an interview.

On hearing that Lord Stanley had gone a second time to the Palace, Mr. Disraeli took his seat—and the oaths—as 'gentleman in waiting,' before the fire.

Such was the confusion of the ministerial movements and political promenades, that everybody went to call upon everybody. The hall porters were never known to have had such a time of it, but though knocking and ringing at doors continued throughout the whole day, nothing seemed to answer.

During the whole of the day, Mr. Disraeli was understood to be so particularly engaged, that, with the exception of Lord Stanley, he could see nobody. So important were Mr. Disraeli's interviews with himself during the Ministerial crisis, that it appears to have had the effect of shutting him up in the most extraordinary manner.

Reproduced by kind permission of the Proprietors, from 'Punch,' March 8, 1851.

things which are not necessary to be said or done by those for whom positions are provided.'

'That is true,' said the Queen. 'And all I can now hope is that, having attained this great position, he will be temperate. I accept Mr. Disraeli on your guarantee.'[1]

'And now,' said Lord Derby, 'I am going to write to Gladstone to call on me. Be with me late in the afternoon to know the result and consult.'

The interview[2] between Lord D. and G. was entirely unsuccessful. No question arose as to the materials of the Government, or as to Leadership of the House. Gladstone would not listen to Protection being an open question: he required an absolute renunciation of that policy; a specific declaration that the new Government completely accepted it —*un fait accompli*. Lord Derby was in good spirits. He told me that he had written to Sir Stratford Canning at Constantinople to offer him the Sec. for F.O., of which I greatly approved, and to the D. of Northumberland the Admiralty, than which nothing could be better. In fact, Lord Derby was full of resource, which was not his characteristic. 'I have written,' he said, 'to Ellenboro', and Lord Lonsdale, President of the Council, to Sir Robert Inglis, Henley, and Henry Corry, as you advise, to call on me to-morrow; and of course Herries and Granby. You will be with me early after breakfast.'

When I called the next morning, accordingly, he was in high spirits. He said: 'An answer from the Duke of N. accepting; Inglis has been with me and accepted. Ellenboro' is to be here in half an hour. No other answers.' Malmesbury was to be Secretary for the Col., Canning for the F.O., and myself Leader of the H. of C. and Home; Herries C. of Exchequer, Henley Board of Trade, Inglis India, and the Duke

[1] This conversation between the Queen and Stanley is given in the following form in Prince Albert's memorandum, dated Feb. 25, 1851, in *Queen Victoria's Letters*: 'Lord Stanley said he should have to propose Mr. Disraeli as one of the Secretaries of State. The Queen interrupted him by saying that she had not a very good opinion of Mr. Disraeli on account of his conduct to poor Sir R. Peel, and what had just happened did not tend to diminish that feeling; but that she felt so much Lord Stanley's difficulties, that she would not aggravate them by passing a sentence of exclusion on him. She must, however, make Lord Stanley responsible for his conduct, and should she have cause to be displeased with him when in office, she would remind Lord Stanley of what now passed. Lord Stanley promised to be responsible, and excused his friend for his former bitterness by his desire to establish his reputation for cleverness and sharpness; nobody had gained so much by Parliamentary schooling, and he had of late quite changed his tone.'

[2] This interview took place on Wednesday, Feb. 26, the very day of Gladstone's arrival from that Italian tour which resulted in his famous letters to Lord Aberdeen about Neapolitan misgovernment.

of Northumberland — a great card — Admiralty; Lord Lonsdale President. Things did not look very bad. They were showy, but, after all, the great thing was the House of Commons, and that was not settled.

While we were talking — in the library at his first house in St. James's Square (now Tollemache's) — Lord Ellenboro' was announced. He was, I think, to have been Privy Seal, but it never came to mentioning office to him. I would have retired, but Lord Derby told me to go into his dressing-room, that was adjoining, on the same floor, a spacious apartment, and conceal myself. In about half an hour I heard a merry shout: 'Come out from your dungeon!'

He was so gay that I was hopeful: but no! the mighty Earl had refused — on the same grounds, almost the same words, as Gladstone.[1]

'Never mind,' said Lord Derby. 'It's the House of Commons we must look after.' And almost as he was speaking, the Groom of the Chambers announced Mr. H. Corry in attendance. I returned to my dungeon, but was not kept there very long.

Henry Corry had not absolutely fainted, but had turned very pale when the proposition was made to him of becoming a leading member of a Protectionist Government, and had declined what, as Lord Derby said, under no conceivable circumstances, a year ago, could ever have been offered to him, and which never can be offered again.[2] Lord Derby was a little more serious, but still up to the mark. 'With Canning,' he said, 'we have still six Cabinet Ministers in the Commons.'

At two o'clock, which was now approaching, there was to be a general meeting: Lord Lonsdale, Lord Malmesbury, Lord Granby, Beresford (Chief Whip), Sir Edward Sugden, who had accepted the Chancellorship, and some others. Herries and Henley, who were also to have attended, but who were to have called previously, had never arrived. Just as the servant had informed Lord Derby that these personages were assembled, a letter arrived from Sir Robert Inglis withdrawing his assent. Lord Derby's countenance fell.

However, he came in and addressed his friends with cheerfulness and dignity (Henley had arrived). He told them that

[1] Stanley told the Queen that 'at one time Lord Ellenborough had accepted, but, having been sent on a mission to Mr. Goulburn in order to see whether he could convert him, he came home himself converted, and withdrew his acceptance again' (*Queen Victoria's Letters,* memorandum by Prince Albert, Feb. 27, 1851).

[2] An unfortunate prophecy. Henry Corry, father of Montagu Corry, Lord Rowton, was taken by Lord Derby into the Cabinet as First Lord of the Admiralty in 1867, on the resignation of Lord Cranborne, Lord Carnarvon, and General Peel.

the Queen, as they were aware, had sent for him; that he had undertaken to try to form a Government; that he had applied to Mr. Gladstone and his friends, but they refused, unless Protection was unequivocally relinquished; that we were therefore thrown on our own resources; that he had written to Sir Stratford Canning to accept the F.O., and that Lord Lonsdale, who had consented to be President of the Council, had kindly agreed to transact the duties of F.O. until Canning arrived; that the Duke of Northumberland had consented to be F.L. of Admiralty; that Lord Malmesbury was to be Secretary of State for Colonies; that what he wanted was official support in the House of Commons; that he felt confident that I would completely discharge the duties of Leader of that House; that he was sure the country would be satisfied if finance were entrusted to the experienced hands of Mr. Herries, whose unexpected absence he regretted; that Lord Granby would take a place in the Cabinet; that he hoped their friend Mr. Henley would consent to become President of the Board of Trade; that he had counted on the assistance of one or two more in the House of Commons, but had been disappointed, and now should like to hear their general views on the matter. Lord Lonsdale followed like a man of the world; said it was not a time to make difficulties; the Whigs were prostrate; we must support Lord D.; he would be provisional Secretary of State.

All this time, Henley, whom I believe Lord Derby did not personally know, or scarcely, sate on a chair against the dining-room wall, leaning with both his hands on an ashen staff, and with the countenance of an ill-conditioned Poor Law Guardian censured for some act of harshness. His black eyebrows, which met, deeply knit; his crabbed countenance doubly morose; but no thought in the face, only ill-temper, perplexity, and perhaps astonishment. In the midst of this Herries was ushered, or rather tumbled, into the room, exclaiming, 'What's all this?' Then there were explanations how and why he had not received a letter, and had not been there at 12 o'clock in the morning, to know that he was to be Chancellor of the Exchequer.

If Henry were mute and grim, without a word, suggestion, or resource, Herries, who had considerable experience of official life, to my great surprise was as unsatisfactory in a different manner. He was garrulous, and foresaw only difficulties. He seemed to be full of fear of Goulburn, who was to do this, and to prevent that, and in short render the administration of the finances by a follower of Lord Derby an impossibility. We none of us then knew much about finance, but the impression that Herries, who was deemed a great judge in such matters, contrived to convey was that our monetary affairs were in a critical state, and that Goulburn would eat us up alive if we presumed to touch them. It turned out afterwards that no difficulties of moment existed, but by postponing our Government we insured—as, for instance, in the matter of the Income Tax.

When Henley spoke at last, he flatly refused to take the Board of Trade: and, being a very suspicious man, it came out afterwards, as Herries told me, that he thought there was some sort of conspiracy to throw all the difficulties of the Government on himself and Herries, who would have had to fight the battle of the revised Tariff, which these profound statesmen were to introduce to counteract the free trade measures.[1]

Lord D. and myself exchanged looks, and I pretty well understood what was passing in his mind. Lord Malmesbury suggested some other place to Henley, murmured something about the India Board; Lord Lonsdale tried to soften him into an approach to the manners of civilised society. There was something like the general chatter of a club-room, when Lord Derby made a sign to me, and we withdrew to the end of the room.

'This will never do!' he said.

'I am not sanguine: but don't be in a hurry.'

After a few remarks on the extraordinary scene he returned to the table. There was silence, and he gave it as his opinion that it was his duty to decline the formation of a Government, and particularly from his inability to find members of the House of Commons who were prepared to co-operate with him.

Sir Edward Sugden, though he lost a peerage, agreed with Lord Derby; Lord Lonsdale seemed disappointed, Malmesbury distressed; Herries and Henley said nothing. Beresford frantically rushed forward and took Lord Derby aside, and said there were several men he knew waiting at the Carlton expecting to be sent for, and implored Lord Derby to reconsider his course. Lord Derby inquired impatiently, 'Who was at the Carlton?' Beresford said, 'Deedes.'[2]

'Pshaw!' exclaimed Lord D. 'These are not names I can put before the Queen. Well, my lords and gentlemen, I am obliged to you for your kind attendance here to-day: but the thing is finished. Excuse my leaving you, but I must write to the Queen at once.'

We dispersed: lingering in the hall, Lord Lonsdale said,

[1] Malmesbury, describing this meeting in his diary under date Feb. 28, 1851, says that 'Disraeli did not conceal his anger at [Henley's] want of courage and interest in the matter.'

[2] M.P. for East Kent.

'Never was such an opportunity lost. They were prostrate. We ought to have dissolved Parliament to-morrow.'

'The best thing the Country party can do,' said Malmesbury, 'is to go into the country. There is not a woman in London who will not laugh at us.'

Herries, who seemed annoyed that all was over, kept mumbling about not having received his summons till three o'clock: and that he remembered Governments which were weeks forming. Henley continued silent and grim. Beresford looked like a man who had lost his all at roulette, and kept declaring that he believed Deedes was a first-rate man of business.[1]

Disraeli was always in these earlier years for the bold course, and Stanley, who knew his feelings, tried to convince him that their failure was inevitable.

From Lord Stanley.

ST. JAMES'S SQUARE, *Feb.* 28, 1851.—. . . I am afraid you are not satisfied with the result of our deliberations yesterday. The more I reflect on the state of the case, the more I am satisfied it was inevitable, however mortifying to us as a party; and I think giving the explanation in the sense you suggested will save the *amour propre* of our friends, as far as it can be saved. I have only seen Hardwicke this morning. He is convinced we did right. I am sure we had got to the point at which boldness would have degenerated into rashness.

Disraeli concludes his narrative of the crisis thus:

As the Government had resigned, and Lord Derby had declined, it was necessary to extricate the Court, and everybody else, from an embarrassing and almost absurd position; so the Queen—after sounding Lord Aberdeen[2] (I believe), who shrank from the proffer—to act in a strictly constitutional manner, sent for the Duke of Wellington, who, of course, advised Her Majesty to request her late Ministers to continue in office. After all was arranged, His Grace called on Lord Derby and talked over affairs. He evidently thought them very satisfactory for Lord Derby, and generally for his old

[1] Stanley's statement in the House of Lords on Feb. 28 adds the information that he offered the Foreign Office unsuccessfully to Lord Aberdeen and to Lord Canning in succession. Also, one member who was prevented joining his Ministry 'by the pressure of extensive private affairs' must be Thomas Baring.

[2] The application to Aberdeen was before, not after, the second summons to Stanley.

political friends, with whom His Grace always sympathised. Thus he summed up the position: 'Well! they are in the mud, and now you can look about you.'

The Duke of Wellington contemplated the reunion of the Conservative party under Lord Derby when the next and inevitable crash took place. I did not take that view. The extraordinary circumstances of 1851 brought their moral to me, but it was different from the D. of W. The Whigs might be in the mud, but it was clear to me that another party was not in a more clean predicament.

One thing was established — that every public man of experience and influence, however slight, had declined to act under Lord Derby unless the principle of Protection were unequivocally renounced.[1]

Disraeli was seriously depressed at the timidity and mismanagement which had dashed the cup of office from his lips. And he must have shared the annoyance of the party generally at the terms in which Stanley, in his statement in the House of Lords, contrasted the inexperience of his own friends in the House of Commons with the experience and talents of the Peelites. He sympathised with the disgust of that stout old Protectionist Christopher, who wrote to him that, as official experience could not be learnt in opposition, the party must apparently wait till the Greek Kalends to acquire it. In his letters in the next couple of months to his sister he talks of the 'impenetrable clouds' in which public affairs are involved, costing him 'great trouble, and harass, and anxiety.' He intends 'to make another great rally of the party; but I fear it is too late.' Whatever his private reflections may have been, he did not slacken, but rather increase, his efforts to extricate his party from the 'mud' of Protection, so that they might be more prepared for office on the next occasion; and to plunge the Ministerialists deeper in their own 'mud,' the futile Ecclesiastical Titles Bill. When they returned to office, the

[1] During the crisis, Disraeli in the House of Commons gave a somewhat blunt contradiction to a statement made by Russell, correct as far as it went, but incomplete and therefore misleading, as to the outcome of Derby's first audience of the Queen. It was a trivial matter, but there was immense fuss at the time; and not only Russell, but the Court, were rather seriously offended. See *Queen Victoria's Letters*, under date Feb. 24 and 25, 1851.

Government reduced their unlucky measure to a simple prohibition, under penalty, of the assumption of the new titles. Still, the debate on the second reading extended over seven days. Disraeli made a short, scoffing speech on the last night. 'What a mockery,' he said, alluding to the practice in Ireland, 'when Her Majesty's Ministers themselves be-grace and be-lord these individuals, that they should now propose penal enactments because they are treated by the rest of Her Majesty's subjects with respect and with honour!' The Bill legislated against phrases, and not against facts. It asserted no principle, and was a mere spiteful enactment. But he could not agree with the line taken by the Peelites. In the speech of Gladstone, who preceded him, he discerned a reluctance to accept the royal supremacy over the Church of England. Graham had threatened the House with civil war in Ireland, and this gave Disraeli the opportunity for a remarkable deliverance on Irish policy:

> It is utterly impossible that Ireland can be again governed, openly or covertly, directly or indirectly, on the principle of Protestant ascendancy; but equally certain it is that no Government can exist which is not faithful and devoted to the Protestant Constitution of this country. In its maintenance are involved greater interests than the existence of a Government, the fate of a Crown, and the destinies of an Empire; and, trust me, among all the blessings which it insures to us, not the least important and not the least precious are the civil and religious liberties of the Catholics themselves.

The Bill passed through its various stages by enormous majorities, Disraeli constantly taunting the Government on their high-sounding words and trumpery proposals. *Punch*, in a famous cartoon, depicted Russell as a little boy who chalked up 'No Popery' on Cardinal Wiseman's door, and then ran away. Disraeli's criticism throughout was on these lines. They were meeting by 'petty religious persecution,' 'petty penal legislation,' what Russell had declared to be part of a conspiracy against the civil and political liberties of

Europe. Almost all the session was wasted over this measure; but, as was generally predicted, alike by Peelite opponents and by Conservative supporters, the Act was never put into operation, was gradually forgotten, and then twenty years afterwards was quietly repealed. But the Government had undoubtedly been rolled in the 'mud.'

Disraeli's other task, to extricate his friends from their own mire, was not so easy. His memorandum of the sixties, the beginning of which we have already quoted,[1] relates the development of the difference between himself and Stanley on Protection, and the action which he took after the failure of February, 1851.

In 1850 the relations between Lord D. [then Lord Stanley] and myself had become more cordial.[2] I had become the sole and recognised leader of the Tory party in the House of Commons, and had begun to shake the Ministry by my motions on Agricultural Relief. The possibility of 'a Protectionist Government' began to be talked about. I attempted on several occasions to bring Lord Derby to bear on the subject of Protection, but I soon found that his prejudices on the subject, and his distrust of me with regard to it, were not to be easily removed.

The ludicrous catastrophe of 1851 determined me no longer to trifle with the question, and I laid before him my views, that he ought to seize the opportunity afforded by his not being able to serve his sovereign, in consequence of inability to form an administration on the Protective principle, publicly to relinquish that ground, so that he might be free to act with other statesmen, and thus, Sir Robert Peel being no more, place himself at the head of the reconstructed Conservative party. I also in a full and unequivocal manner impressed him with my conviction, and the grounds for that conviction, that he misapprehended the feeling of the country on the subject, and even of his own friends; and I assured him, with no mean opportunities of observation on the matter, that the agricultural classes in the main looked upon a recurrence to Protection as an impossibility, and looked upon its advocacy as an obstacle to practically remedial measures. I intimated that every year, from the necessity

[1] Ch. 8.

[2] In May, 1850, Stanley changed the formal 'My dear sir' of his letters to his chief lieutenant, to 'Dear Disraeli.'

of things, a recurrence to an abrogated policy becomes more difficult, and I impressed upon him that I already saw changes in the state of affairs which indicated that the pressure on the land was diminishing.

Disraeli was unsuccessful in his attempts to persuade Stanley publicly to relinquish the protective principle; but he must have made a considerable impression by his representations, as the position which Stanley took up in his statement in the House of Lords after the crisis was of a moderate character. It was, first, that the income tax should not be allowed to degenerate into a permanent tax; second, that there should be a moderate countervailing duty on corn; and, finally, that the question of Protection must be settled, once and for ever, at the next General Election. If the country proved to be against it, Stanley would bow respectfully to its decision. He had no desire to reverse, but only to modify, Peel's commercial system. Disraeli was quite disposed to accept Stanley's view about the income tax. But he was opposed to insistence upon a countervailing duty on corn, because, though he held it to be right in principle, it was no longer possible of attainment. He cordially agreed that the question of Protection must be finally decided at the next General Election, but with the important proviso that the Conservative party should not go to the country identified, as a party, with Protection. He was confident that the country would maintain the new commercial system; and he was determined to make it clear that there was an important section of the party, headed by himself, who only asked for a verdict in favour of compensation to agriculturists, and not of Protection in any shape. With this view, though without any open breach with his chief, he pressed on several occasions during the remainder of the session the policy he had advocated in his motion on agricultural distress in February. He first fell upon Wood's amended Budget, which, while abolishing the window tax and establishing an inhabited house duty, withdrew the small grant-in-aid to local authorities. The orthodox Free Traders had frightened the Chancellor of the Exchequer from this act of justice, which, petty as it was, was the admission of a principle — a principle, it may be added, which, though Disraeli's own efforts were unsuccessful, has long since been accepted by both political parties in this country. Disraeli proceeded to make one more effort to get Parliament to accept the view that in any readjustment of taxation regard should be had to agricultural distress. He earnestly disclaimed any desire to set country against town, and so he made no objection to the repeal of the window tax. But he once more appealed to the House, not, indeed, to revert to an 'abrogated' policy — the constant repetition of the epithet is a feature of his speeches at this period — but to adopt some plan of compensation to the land by the relief of either rates or taxes. He hoped that 'the spirit of the great departed' would not be evoked to stand between an abundant Treasury and suffering farmers. Stanley's pronouncement in favour of a countervailing duty on corn lost Disraeli the support he had received in the previous year from Gladstone, who averred that he could no longer believe that the Protectionists were ready to acquiesce in the new commercial system. Bright, however, said he gathered from Disraeli's speeches that he was convinced that any project of returning to Protection was a delusion. No doubt Bright's perception of Disraeli's meaning was quickened by expressions used to him in private. But the whole drift of Disraeli's recent language could hardly be mistaken by an unprejudiced observer. The division,[1] 263 against 250, was better, by one, than that in February; but even the fact of getting within 13 of the Government forces failed to restore Disraeli's spirits.

To Sarah Disraeli.

Sunday, April 13, 1851. — I rose so late on Saturday, not having got to bed the previous night till past four o'clock, that I could not write you a line, and give you tidings of the

[1] April 11.

division, which has very much inspirited our friends; though the truth is, it now turns out, that we ought to have won, or at least reduced the majority to an almost infinitesimal quantity. However, our blood is up again, though I fear we shall never regain the occasion so sadly lost. In February the Whigs were prostrate, and even if beaten now, of which I have little or no hope, they will be formidable and well-organised foes. I spoke to my satisfaction, which is rarely the case. We shall go to Hughenden on Tuesday, thus closing a campaign seldom equalled for its events, its excitement, its chagrin and wasted energies. I am sorry, very, that I could not come down to see you before I went away, but, independently of the painful absorption of my pursuits, I have had little heart for the expedition. May, perhaps, may bring brighter skies and fortunes, though we cannot complain of fortune, only of our inveterate imbecility, which could not avail itself of her abundant favours. . . .[1]

To Lady Londonderry.

Hughenden, *April* 20, 1851. — . . . With respect to politics, the situation is this: The Whigs having become again elate, and talking of a working majority of fifty, I took advantage of a clear error of the Chancellor of the Exchequer in the reconstruction of the Budget — viz., the omission of the once proffered relief of the landed interest, and forced them once more to a trial of strength. I did it entirely on my own responsibility. Some of our friends — I might say many — faint-hearted after all that had occurred, were prophetic of overwhelming defeat, and believed the braggadocio of the Government, that they would have a majority of 80! Their majority was only a bare one — 13, one less than on my previous struggle at the beginning of the year. But the annoying thing is that, disheartened and misled by the enemy, enough of our good men were absent to have gained the victory! Among them, I am sorry to say, were the two sons of your great house. I did not much count on Castlereagh, but I am, for many reasons, annoyed about Seaham. However, we must forget it. Four men who voted for my first motion voted against me this time, making alone a difference of 8! In fact, the enemy was in our power, had not some of our friends mistaken their wooden guns for well-proved ordnance. The effect of this division, however, has shown that the Whigs are as weak as before, our troops have gone in great spirits into the country, and the after-Easter campaign will be a very active one. We shall certainly try

[1] *Letters*, pp. 238, 239.

to knock up the Government again, if only for the fun of the thing. But, seriously, Stanley has obtained some adherents whom he did not reckon on, and is prepared to take the helm, and I think will display a *personnel* for which the world does not give his Cabinet credit.

The struggle after Easter will, I anticipate, be rather of a religious than a fiscal or agricultural character. The Papal Bill comes on in Committee on the 5th. No doubt the Protestant party will move resolutions to make it more efficient, and no one, however learned in the House of Commons, can anticipate the consequences. There is no lull in the anti-Catholic feeling in this country; on the contrary, the middle classes are more alarmed than ever. The recent conversions sustain the excitement. James Hope, the glory and boast of Scotland, and who was to have been Sir Robert Peel's next Lord Advocate, the bosom friend of Gladstone, joined the true faith about a fortnight ago. Archdeacon Manning, the spiritual adviser of Sidney Herbert, about the same time, and, horrible to say, was received not merely by the Oratorians as Father Newman was — the Oratorians being a sort of Papistical Wesleyans — but by the Jesuits, whom he has joined. He was received in Farm Street Chapel, or rather Jesuit Church. The whole of the clergy of one of the principal churches in Leeds have gone over in a body, and part of their congregation. The people of this country are really very agitated, and it is difficult to calculate the extent of the consequences, were a man of very great station and abilities to put himself at the head of the Protestant movement. Some think that Gladstone has already joined Rome; S. Herbert is looked upon with a very suspicious eye; but the most remarkable rumour is a local one, told me by Lord Henry Bentinck — viz., that the Duke of Newcastle[1] is about to bow to the Vatican! But I confess, notwithstanding my safe authority, I am very incredulous as to this last. . . .

To Sarah Disraeli.

GROSVENOR GATE, *May* 24. — Yesterday our chief won the Oaks, a compensation for his other loss, or, as some think (not I), an omen of recovering it. The day before we met him at the Hardwickes' — a sort of Cabinet dinner (Cabinet of St. Germains), the Malmesburys, Redesdale, Herries, etc. On Wednesday we went to the Great Exhibition. You must contrive to go, if only for once, as I did. Any day you like to come up Mary Anne will go with you, who by that time will know all the points, for one wants a guide. . . .

[1] Lincoln, the Peelite, had succeeded his father as 5th Duke of Newcastle on Jan. 12, 1851.

I met at Stanley's the other day the new Irish M.P., Mr. Whiteside,[1] who promises, which is much more than our political prospects do. I am not in much spirits for writing, but send this line to keep up the chain, and show that you are not forgotten. . . .[2]

The Great Exhibition in Hyde Park, which was opened by the Queen on May 1, was a godsend for the Government, by diverting public attention from their blunders. It was a temple of Free Trade, and therefore not popular with the extreme Protectionists, who regarded it as facilitating the entry of foreign wares to compete with home products. Colonel Sibthorp described it as an 'unwieldy, ill-devised, unwholesome castle of glass,' but his leader, with more propriety, if in his most courtier-like manner, as 'that enchanted pile which the sagacious taste and the prescient philanthropy of an accomplished and enlightened Prince have raised for the glory of England, and the delight and instruction of two hemispheres.' This discrepancy of feeling was not the only sign of the gap which Disraeli's educative policy on the hopelessness of Protection was opening between him and his more reactionary supporters.

A motion by Hume on May 2 to limit the grant of the income tax to one year, instead of the three proposed by the Chancellor of the Exchequer, afforded Disraeli the opportunity of defeating the Government once more, and at the same time of making his own position clearer. Hume explained that his object was to obtain the revision, not the removal, of a tax which in its present form was unequal and unjust. But he was seconded by Alderman Thompson, a Protectionist, who expressed the view that a portion of the revenue should be raised by a duty on foreign corn; and supported by Granby, who declared himself against direct taxation. Cobden, though he was in favour of a revision of the tax, would do nothing to endanger the principles for the establishment of which it

[1] Afterwards Solicitor-General and Attorney-General for Ireland in the Derby-Disraeli Administrations, and ultimately Chief Justice of Ireland.

[2] *Letters*, p. 240.

was imposed; and Wood protested against placing £5,000,000 of annual revenue in jeopardy. Disraeli attempted, not very successfully, to show that Granby and others were not advocating a duty on foreign corn; but retorted, with more success, on Cobden, who now spoke of the income tax as the foundation of the new commercial system, his denunciations of it in 1845. Then Cobden said it was 'a fungus growing from the tree of monopoly'; 'one great monopoly, the Corn Law, alone renders that tax necessary.' This was the way public opinion was 'doctored and drilled.' It was intolerable that men who had made speeches of that sort should charge those who objected to income tax with putting forward that objection as a mask under which to attempt to get back abrogated laws. That was a 'stale old *ruse*.' Russell, in his reply, showed that he perfectly understood both Disraeli's policy and his difficulty. They never had, he said, a question brought forward in that House with regard to local taxation, or the malt tax, or any matter affecting the landed interest or the general taxation of the country, but some of Disraeli's supporters got up and made the avowal, 'After all, our real object is the restoration of Protection.' Then Disraeli had always to rise after them and say, 'Don't take them at their word; whatever you may have heard, I did not hear it.' Indeed, Disraeli always seemed to be in such a situation that he did not hear a word of Protection. He would get tired, if his friends were not more prudent. If they would always march forward when he wished them to keep back, he would, Russell thought, at last say, 'Upon my word, you are too bad; I will not march through Coventry with you any more.' Government were beaten by a majority of fourteen, but the differences among the Opposition could not be concealed. There was great disinclination, the Whip reported, to support Disraeli on June 30, when he followed up the victory over the income tax with a motion that, as that tax could no longer certainly be depended upon, and the surplus was therefore problematical, it would be wrong to make any material sacrifice of public income in effecting changes of taxation. The result was a minority of 113, in spite of the votes of Gladstone and Sidney Herbert.

The speech delivered on that occasion has a special interest as the considered utterance on the general principles of financial policy of one who was shortly to assume the mantle of the Chancellor of the Exchequer. He laid down in the course of it several principles, many of which are eminently sound. 'If you have to raise in a country like England a revenue of the amount which we at present do raise, it would be quite impossible to obtain such results by adhering strictly to any particular mode of taxation. I feel convinced that the greater the number, the more various the means of supply, the greater will be the facility for raising the revenue.' 'Direct taxation should be as general as indirect taxation,' is another of his maxims. That was the fault of the income tax, imposed by Peel for a temporary object; it was on too narrow a basis. 'If you maintain that the essence of direct taxation is that it should be limited to a class, that it should be founded on large exemptions, it is not so much a direct tax as a forced contribution. It is a tax upon capital. It is a constant invasion of the fund which is employing labour.' As to other kinds of direct taxation, 'a house duty is a duty as just in principle as can well be conceived.' A surplus should not be frittered away. 'It is much wiser, if you have a surplus, to do something that is efficient — to discover what interest is most suffering, what tax most oppressive, the remission of what duty would give the most elasticity to trade, or add most to the comfort and the happiness of the community, than to hold as a matter of course that the commercial class, the agricultural class, the inhabitant of the town, and the shipbuilder, should each have his share.' On what principle should taxes be chosen for remission? 'I am not one of those who think that there is any abstract excellence in a Customs duty — I am not one of those who think that, as a rigid rule, or even as a general rule, you should remit an Excise duty in preference to a Customs duty.' 'I think, if there be a particular interest in the country which is subject to great difficulty, is experiencing great distress, and incurring a long and continual depression, that it is the duty of the Chancellor of the Exchequer . . . to see whether the remission of any tax would tend to relieve it.' It was most important to do nothing to shake public credit. How was it that this little island produced a revenue greater than so many vast dominions? What was the magic spell? 'It is that in this country we have associated our material interests with the inspiration of a great moral principle, and that we have built up public wealth on the foundation of public credit. That is the choicest production of the British Isles, more precious than all the harvests of tropic climes, than all the gems of Golconda, or the auriferous deposits of the sierras of the Pacific.'

The repudiation of the theory that Customs duties are to be specially encouraged is a marked feature of the speech. Another feature was what his sister called the 'burning caustic' applied to an independent Conservative member who had criticised his agricultural motions.

The hon. member for Berkshire (Philip Pusey[1]) has lately made some comments upon my parliamentary career, which would have been less inconvenient, and certainly not less ingenuous, if they had been made here, and in my presence. The hon. gentleman is of opinion that the motions which I have brought forward were futile motions; and, secondly, that in bringing them forward the mover of them was insincere. These are very harsh opinions. It is possible that the motions which I have brought forward with the twofold object I have mentioned may have been futile, but at any rate motions that have been supported by a large party in the House of Com-

[1] An eminent agriculturist, who had become a Free Trader; 'by his lineage, his estate, his rare accomplishments and fine abilities, one of the most distinguished country gentlemen who ever sat in the House of Commons,' to quote Disraeli's posthumous praise of Pusey in 1875. At the General Election in 1852, after holding the seat for seventeen years, he 'was obliged,' in Greville's words, 'to retire from Berks'; and a regular supporter of Disraeli was elected in his place.

mons have upon their surface *prima facie* symptoms of not being considered altogether inefficient. It is possible that a member who brings forward a motion may be insincere, but it is difficult to penetrate the bosom of any man. We should rather give him credit for motives more natural, more obvious, and more charitable. I may have been mistaken, and not insincere; my reason may have been misled, vanity may have misguided me; I may have been a foolish man or a vain man; it is better to think that than that I should be an insincere man. At any rate, my motives under the circumstances may remain a question of controversy. But what are we to say of a member of Parliament who, when motions are brought forward which he believes to be futile, by a gentleman who he is convinced is insincere, omits no opportunity of following him into the same lobby, and supporting him by his suffrage?

The leadership to which Disraeli had attained was indeed no bed of roses; and, in spite of the apparent imminence of a Conservative administration, at least twice in the year between the failure of February, 1851, and the success of February, 1852, he seems to have been more than half inclined to give up the thankless task which in the winter of 1848–49 he had been so eager to undertake. On June 5 Thomas Baring proposed a motion to prevent the adulteration of coffee by mixing chicory with it; and Edward Stanley made an admirable speech on the same side. The Government resisted the motion, and were supported by several Protectionists, like Trollope and Tyrell, on the ground that chicory was a home product, and therefore to blend it with foreign coffee should not be treated as adulteration. But for this help, Ministers, who only had a majority of five votes, would have suffered another defeat; and Disraeli, discouraged by the ill-success of his efforts, and impressed by the mover's talents, appears to have tried to get Baring to come forward as leader in his place. Baring was disposed to regard the suggestion as *persiflage*, but, if it was to be treated seriously, said that he was incapacitated for a prominent position by want of ability, education, and energy, and that he preferred his occupations and his independence to political responsibility.

To Thomas Baring.

[*June* 6, 1851.] — . . . The more I reflect upon what passed between us, the more I am convinced that the suggestion I made, after long deliberation, was a right one for all persons and interests concerned. But I feel that it was crudely made. It required for success the opportunities of habitual intimacy. I was so sensible of the imperfect manner in which I had laid the matter open to you that I had intended in the country to have drawn up a memorandum for your private eye, in which I would have endeavored to place the subject in a complete light, to calculate the contingencies of the political world, and to indicate the means by which the too limited base of the party might be expanded into a broader and really conservative foundation. But I feel that the effort would be useless.

I can assure you that I am in no mood for *persiflage.* Totally irrespective of all personal considerations, which I trust I never intrude, I am naturally grievously distressed at leaving in so forlorn a condition a body of gentlemen who have conducted themselves towards me with great indulgence and cordiality, and for many of whom I entertain a sincere affection.

Nothing came of this overture to Baring, and Disraeli's despondency about the position continued.

Lord Malmesbury to Lord Derby.

ACHNACARRY, *Aug.* 19, 1851. — . . . I saw Disraeli the day before I left town. He seemed to me to be very much *down*, and full of fancies, one of which was that Graham wished to serve under you as *leader* of the H. of Commons. Whether he feared this as pushing him (D.) from his stool, or wished it as giving you a better chance of forming a Government, I could not make out, but one thing is certain — viz., that he *wants* to throw over 'Protection.' . . . Dizzy means to be perfectly quiet during the recess. . . .

The thirteenth Earl of Derby, who was an eminent naturalist, but who had never taken a prominent part in public life, died on June 30 of this year, and Disraeli's chief succeeded to the title which he was three times to inscribe on the roll of Queen Victoria's Prime Ministers; while Disraeli's friend and political pupil, Edward Stanley, became in turn by courtesy Lord Stanley. In the struggle which was now proceeding within the party over the abandonment of Protection, the two Stanleys, as we have seen, took opposite sides. The father, who had incurred the reproach of lukewarmness for the cause in 1846–1848, was now untimely resolute and Disraeli's principal obstacle; while the son, who had not entered the House of Commons till after Bentinck's death, had been almost a Free Trader from the beginning, and was Disraeli's warmest supporter in opposing policies of exclusion and restriction. Disraeli took the opportunity of two agricultural meetings in Bucks—one at Aylesbury on September 17, and the other at Salt Hill on October 7—to force the issue in a more unequivocal fashion than he had yet used. The harvest had been excellent; and the farmers, being more prosperous, were more likely to listen to his advice.

To Sarah Disraeli.

HUGHENDEN, *Sept.* 19, 1851.—I was at Aylesbury on Wednesday, where I dined with the old Society, Lowndes of Chesham in the chair. I made a good speech in a difficult position and on a difficult subject, and the meeting seemed in heart. I saw to-day in *The Times* two columns of incoherent and contradictory nonsense which made me blush, though I ought to be hardened by this time on such subjects. I am only afraid the world will think it all Delphic and diplomatic, and that the wordy obscurity was intentional, whereas I flattered myself I was as terse and simple as suited a farmers' table. . . .

HUGHENDEN, *Oct.* 4 [? 9], 1851.—On Tuesday I went to Salt Hill, expecting to find Labouchere in the chair, but he had not returned from Spain, and we had a regular political meeting, though against the rules. It went off well. . . .[1]

In both speeches Disraeli claimed always to have spoken on the question with the utmost frankness, and to be merely repeating and enforcing what he had been saying for three years in the House of Commons. When the protective system was attacked, he did his best to uphold it. 'No one fought more ardently, no one, I hope, fought more sincerely, than I did. My sabre was notched from top to bottom before I ceased to struggle.' 'But

[1] *Letters*, pp. 241, 242.

to uphold a system that exists, and to bring back a system that has been abrogated, are two different things, and I am convinced myself that . . . the protective system can never be brought back unless it is the interest of all classes — at least, of all classes of importance — that that should be the principle which should regulate the national industry, and unless the nation speaks out upon the question in an unmistakable manner.' The farmers could not obtain it by themselves. There must be 'an almost universal feeling in the country.' 'Protection to a particular class, irrespective of all other classes, is out of the question;' and 'all other classes almost are announcing to us that they are profiting' by Free Trade. He did not advise them to give up the principle of Protection for British Industry, but to remember that it was a system which no longer existed, and could not be got back in a hurry. Therefore they should not ask Ministers for a fixed duty or a sliding scale, to cure their suffering; but for political justice and financial equity; for the reduction of burdens, and the removal of restrictions, on the agricultural class. It is not to be wondered at that a leading farmer, at the close of the Aylesbury dinner, wanted to know if 'Protection' was a word which should be blotted out of our language.

Derby this time made no direct protest, but two or three weeks later, in a letter mainly occupied with other subjects, said that he thought Disraeli's line 'a judicious one, though of course it did not satisfy the more eager Protectionists, and though I myself am far from thinking that what you suggest will fully meet the justice of the case, nor should I be prepared to acquiesce in it as a final settlement of accounts.' But the extreme party felt that Disraeli had definitely made his choice, and would no longer fight for Protection. Lord Stanhope described the speeches as 'most indiscreet'; and even the faithful Sarah Disraeli, who was moving in very Protectionist circles in Herefordshire, doubted their policy. 'One thing everybody is certain of,' she wrote, 'and that is that whoever puts himself at this moment courageously at the head of the Protectionists must be Prime Minister two years hence. You are throwing it away.' What was of more consequence, immediately on reading the second speech, Granby, the recognised leader of the old guard, determined to resign his place on what he called 'the tripartite committee of management.' This defection was a blow to Disraeli, who was determined to carry the party with him. A visit of Granby to Hughenden did not bring the two men together. 'Granby's visit was very short,' Disraeli wrote to his sister on November 17. 'He stayed long enough, however, to ask Redrup,' the village butcher, 'to whom he paid a visit with me, "whether there was any land that had gone out of cultivation in this neighbourhood." The astonishment of Redrup, who has just sold his barley for 30s. per quarter, may be conceived.' Beresford, who saw Disraeli about the same time in the autumn, reported to Derby on November 26: 'I was with Disraeli on Monday for an hour and a half alone, and I own I heard from him certain opinions which struck me as anything but in conformity with the principles by which the party has been conducted and animated for the last five years, and he enunciated sentiments which appeared to me as antagonistic to the policy which you have hitherto held, and by which your administration was to have been guided, unless I very much mistake your views.'

Disraeli was quick to see what Granby did not see, and what most of the farmers refused as yet to recognise, that agriculture was beginning to revive, and therefore the restoration of Protection was rapidly ceasing to be a question of practical politics. As he told Derby this year, the pressure on land was diminishing.

To Sarah Disraeli.

HUGHENDEN, *Oct.* 17, 1851. — I think you err in what you say as to the price of wheat — 3s. per bushel, which would be 24s. per quarter. It is still much nearer to 40s. per quarter than 24s. At this moment, with the exception of wheat, all agricultural produce is as high as the average of the last twenty years — barley, oats, beans, horses and cart colts, cows, sheep, pigs, wool, and hay.[1] It is a question yet difficult to solve, whether wheat is to partake of their elevation, or they to sink to its depreciated level, as former experience has shown these disturbances of the general equilibrium to be but temporary. But circumstances are changed, and former experience may not be any longer a guide in this respect. It is possible that agriculture may flourish without a high price of wheat, and without producing any. There certainly seems to me no reason for its appearance in the Chilterns, unless it fetches a high price. I believe all the farmers in this district who have decent capital are much more than making both ends meet.[2]

Granby brought matters to a head by a very frank letter to Derby, written either in the end of December or on one of the first days of January.

Lord Granby to Lord Derby.

[*Dec.*, 1851, *or Jan.*, 1852.] — . . . From various causes, principally from my own want of energy and ability, the position I held was a mere nominal one, which I should not have minded if I had not also felt it was a false one, for I was held responsible, and supposed to be conversant with, counsels and tactics of which I knew nothing. Even this I might have borne if I had felt convinced it was for the advantage of the party, but it seemed to me, on the contrary, that it was rather a disadvantage than otherwise, inasmuch as it cast ridicule upon us, and laid us open to the sneers and taunts of our opponents.

What, for instance, could be more absurd than our position as a great party on the debate on the Income Tax?[3] Having to the best of my power stated what I believed to be the views of the party on that subject, Disraeli rose almost immediately afterwards and took an entirely different view. And when Charles Wood came and asked me what were the real views of the party, and whether Disraeli and Granby and Herries had not consulted together previously as to the line to be taken, I felt that the tripartite arrangement was an absurdity, and the sooner it was dissolved the better for the party. When first the Committee was arranged, I proposed

[1] Sarah Disraeli acknowledged her mistake as to the price of wheat, but added: 'No one will allow here [in Herefordshire] that wheat is the only depressed article; beans are as bad, and cattle worse — and everything else too.'

[2] *Letters*, pp. 242, 243.

[3] See above, pp. 303–4.

to Disraeli that we should meet once a week to talk matters over, and if that had been agreed to, this could not have happened. But such being the actual state of things, and the position of the party, it appeared to me that it was very desirable to free ourselves from this ridicule. And since Disraeli's talents and power of speech had become everywhere known and acknowledged I felt my name was no longer required, and by withdrawing I should not only follow my own selfish inclinations, but at the same time (by consolidating the leadership in the Commons) add weight and strength and unity to the Protection party. . . .

Granby added that he hoped he did not undervalue the relief that Disraeli proposed to afford by a reduction of burdens, a shifting of weight, and a revision of taxation; but as a national policy these were inadequate. There were two systems before the world, and England must choose. He was himself in favour of a protective policy for all classes. In view of Granby's attitude, Disraeli had taken steps to ascertain whether the party wished him to continue, and whether they would give him their confidence and cordial co-operation.

To Lord John Manners.

HUGHENDEN MANOR, *Jan.* 13, 1852.—. . . When I came down here before Christmas, I received two letters written 'by persons of quality,' not addressed to myself, but evidently written with the intention of being confidentially submitted to me: in one of which it was frankly stated that 'Mr. D. had ruined the agricultural party'; and in the other that 'steps should be taken to prevent Mr. D. giving that prominence to the subject of local taxation in the House of Commons which he hitherto has done,' quite forgetting that that prominence had given us last year the Government of the country.

This being the case, and having received a very friendly letter from Miles about the 'Political Biography,'[1] ending by wishing to know our plans for the ensuing session, I thought it best to communicate the contents of these two letters to him; to detail to him the appeal of Granby; to call his attention to the agricultural manifesto of November *Blackwood*, in which my policy was denounced as 'a policy of finesse,' an expression in conversation approvingly adopted by Granby; and finally stating that I considered the address of the National Protection Society, and the alleged causes of its extraordinary meeting in December, as an open vote of censure

[1] *Lord George Bentinck.*

on myself; and that under these circumstances I wished him, as a leading country gentleman and one who had busied himself in bringing me forward in the Protectionist party, to put himself in communication. . . .

The correspondence with Miles was calculated greatly to reassure the desponding leader. If Disraeli and Derby were agreed on vital points, Miles thought there would be no difficulty in placing Disraeli more firmly 'in that position which, with unwearied assiduity, talent, and energy, you have occupied for the last three sessions, to the advantage, as I believe, of the country, and to the admiration of those friends — and they are *more* than your too sensitive nature leads you to imagine — who, lacking ability in debate, and unused to contemplate and act upon a wide political field, were solely removed from contempt by the universality of your genius and powers of debate.' As to Protection, although profits and wages were less, trade was never in a sounder state, and the poorer classes were never better off. 'It would be a suicidal act . . . to endeavour to uphold early next session the obsolete question of Protection.' By January 19 Miles had collected, for Disraeli's information, the views of most of the leading members of the party in the House of Commons. With the exception of Henley, who complained that the party had no well-defined principle, and Stafford, who was offended — as was Henley too — by the famous chapter about the Jews in *Lord George Bentinck*, then just published, there was a chorus of approval both of Disraeli's leadership and of his policy in declining to call for Protection. Herries earnestly deprecated any personal changes, and thought a spontaneous Protectionist attack would be a most inexpedient course. Similar sentiments were expressed, generally in more cordial language, by Baring, Bankes, Trollope, H. Baillie; March, for his father the Duke of Richmond and himself; Worcester, for his father the Duke of Beaufort and himself; Roundell Palmer, an independent member; Jolliffe, who held that Protection for wheat would never be obtained by any direct act of legislation; and Christopher, who thought that, 'like all men of genius,' Disraeli was too sensitive. Buller considered this sensitiveness, in the circumstances, very natural.

Sir John Yarde Buller to William Miles.

DILHORNE HALL, *Jan.* 21, 1852.—. . . I am not surprised at his sensitiveness, for the way in which he is spoken of by Protectionists at the Carlton must have reached his ears; add to which *I* do think that we in the House of Commons have not placed him in the position he ought *now* to fill—namely, that of our *one* acknowledged leader—and I am ready to assist in placing him in that position. I have used the word 'now' because, when first Mr. Disraeli was mentioned as the successor of Lord George, I thought I saw the difficulties that were about him, and I ventured to say to some of our friends that I thought it would be better not to constitute him our leader then, but to wait till by his talent and by his management of our cause he had won the place. I think that he has done so, and I am ready to place my confidence in him. . . .

From William Miles.

LEIGH COURT, [*Jan.* 20, 1852].—I have received your kind invitation to dinner on Monday the 30th, to talk over the Queen's Speech; and I shall have much pleasure in attending upon you on that day. This is as it ought to be, Ld. Derby receiving the Lords, and yourself the Commons; and I do hope that, through Jolliffe's exertions, asperities may have been so smoothed down that we may be enabled to have at your house the meetings of the Commons this session, as I want you to be thoroughly recognised as our leader, mouthpiece, and adviser. It will be still Lord Derby's party; but the very fact of heretofore having always met at Lord Derby's for necessary discussion has led to the surmise that a want of confidence existed in the party towards yourself.

Now, as Lord Derby and yourself have, as I believe, always agreed, I think it would frequently be for his lordship's convenience that you should occasionally meet the Commons, and yourself explain what should be the united tactics of the party. You would thus become much better, more generally, known to individuals, and would, I feel confident, by degrees acquire that confidence which may now be wanting to make our party complete. . . .

This correspondence was most gratifying to Disraeli; but its underlying condition, as Miles constantly pointed out, was that Disraeli and Derby should be in agreement. The misfortune was that they were not.

From Lord Derby.

Confidential. KNOWSLEY, *Jan.* 18, 1852.—As I am sure that our communications ought to be without reserve, I have no hesitation in writing to you on the subject of a correspondence which I have seen between Mr. Knox of the *Morning Herald,* and Mr. S. Phillips, in consequence of the former having refused to insert a leading article sent by the former (*sic*), urging the necessity of the abandonment of Protection; to which Mr. Phillips replies that 'he knows exactly the wishes and views of Lord Derby,' and urges the necessity of preparing the way, by a series of articles, for my abandoning, as soon as I take office, the very question which placed in my hands the lead of the party. It is no very high compliment to my honesty that I should be supposed capable of meditating such a proceeding, even were I more anxious than I am to undertake the labour and responsibility of office; and I should have looked upon this assertion as only an unwarrantable piece of presumption on the part of Mr. Phillips had he not, while refusing to *name* the person from whom he derived his information, made use of terms which would lead to the inference that he spoke in consequence of communications which he had had with you.

Now, I know that you do not entertain any very strong idea that the result of the approaching election will be such as to render possible the reimposition of even a moderate duty on foreign corn; and I am ready to say again, as I have said already, that if that should prove to be the case, I was not prepared indefinitely to maintain a hopeless struggle; but until the country shall so have pronounced its opinion, I shall maintain my opinion, that on the grounds both of finance and of national interests a reimposition of duties on imports, including corn, is desirable, and shall seek to enforce and uphold a policy founded on that opinion; nor should I think it fair or becoming secretly to instruct our agents in the Press to throw cold water on the prospect of attaining that which our friends are desirous of attaining, and which has formed one of the chief bonds of our union. If, therefore, Mr. Phillips has referred to you, I am quite sure that he must wholly have mistaken any expressions of yours which have led him to form the inferences he apparently has done; and as I believe that you are in frequent communication with him, you will oblige me by correcting the misapprehension under which he apparently labours as to my 'views and wishes,' and also by hinting to him that he has no authority to be the exponent of my opinions, which, when necessary, I prefer explaining for myself. The time is very critical—the game is, I believe, in our hands; but in order to be played with ultimate success, it must be played honestly and manfully, and to take office with the purpose of throwing over, voluntarily, the main object of those who have raised us to it is to follow too closely an *exemplar vitiis imitabile*, to which I never can submit. . . .

As we meet on Thursday at Burghley, we shall have full opportunity to discuss our course of proceeding.

Disraeli describes this letter as 'written apparently with some irritation, for which there was no cause, as I had no communication whatever with the scribe to whose labours it relates.' In the end of 1848 and during 1849 Disraeli had been frequently in communication with Phillips;[1] but the correspondence had ceased for some time, and was not resumed till July 24, 1852, when Phillips wrote, 'In times past I had the good fortune to render you some service,' and suggested that he might be of some service again. So it was not difficult to pacify Derby on the personal question; but it was evident that the 'wishes and views' referred to, if not Derby's, were certainly Disraeli's. Strong, however, in the support of the other most important members of the party in the Commons, Disraeli held his own in the Burghley conferences, though he did not convert all his colleagues.

To Lord John Manners.

GROSVENOR GATE, *Jan.* 26, 1852.—Granby has given you an account of what took place at Burghley. The affair is skinned over, and we must all hope the best. I cannot but feel that there is some degree of estrangement between Granby and myself, and I deplore it. I take the blame entirely to myself. He has misapprehended some expressions and misconceived some actions. But explanations are seldom felicitous, and on the eve of the momentous and critical events with which I have now to deal, and for the result of which, right or wrong, I must be greatly responsible, I must dismiss the subject, tho' with regret, from my mind. . . .

To Sarah Disraeli.

GROSVENOR GATE, *Jan.* 26, 1852.— . . . We came from Burghley on Saturday night, having there a large party—Derbys, Salisburys, Granby, Herries, Malmesburys, etc. Lord

[1] See Ch. 5 and Ch. 8.

Derby is, fortunately, very well, much thinner for his illness, but looking, perhaps in consequence, ten years younger. He is in good heart and sanguine, but I see tremendous troubles ahead; if not breakers, waves mountains high. . . .[1]

Meanwhile Disraeli had published a book, in which he had sung the swan-song of Protection.

To Lord Henry Bentinck.

[*August*, 1850.] — . . . I have always been actively desirous of erecting some monument, I will not say more lasting than marble, to the memory of your brother. I am not myself an admirer of those biographies which start up at the death of an eminent man — *précis* of the moment, crudely accomplished. They generally bear the marks of their hurried parentage, and are usually deficient in discrimination and depth, and rarely take any hold on the public mind. From this reason I should under any circumstances have been silent in 1848, and last year, though often revolving the theme, my time was so taken up in endeavouring to control the provincial movement that I wanted the repose necessary to its proper treatment.

This year, however, I am resolved to be tranquil, and the death of Peel facilitates the historic treatment of our subject. I shall aim rather at a delineation of political character than at a formal biography, and I shall confine myself to the three years during which our lost friend took a leading part — three years which I find distinguished by three great subjects with which he identified himself. In 1846 Protection, 1847 the application of the credit of the State to the development of Irish resources, 1848 the relief of the sugar-growing Colonies by the Legislature, in which, notwithstanding he was a mere Member of Parliament, he succeeded. When a complete review is thus taken of his public character and achievements, I think the country will understand how much might have been expected from the man whom they have lost.

Why I particularly write to you now, tho' I should under any circumstances have written to you, is to consult you on the point of the introduction of his correspondence.

As I wish to make a popular book that all classes may read, and may come home to their business and bosoms, I should avoid the formal publication of letters; but I think it desirable to introduce into the narrative passages from his correspondence that may throw light upon his character, and interest the readers by the evidence they offer of his personal qualities.

For example, I purchased his correspondence with his Manchester agent. I may not extract twenty passages from these

[1] *Letters*, p. 246.

fifty letters, but still these passages may give a lively impression of his indefatigable industry and thirst for information. My own letters from him are numerous, and in many respects interesting; but they do not refer to his life in the House of Commons, from the natural reason that there we were always together. With whom was he in active correspondence during the Session of Parliament? With anyone? The Duke, for example? and if so, should I see these letters? Can I? Think of all these points, and let me know what you feel about them or any others connected with the subject.

We go to Knebworth to-morrow, Sir E. Lytton's, for a week, and then to Bucks, where I shall find complete solitude, and propose to dedicate my time to your brother's memory. I shrink from further delay from a feeling that, as far as I am concerned, if it be not done now it may be never done. . . .

To Lord John Manners.

HUGHENDEN, *Sept.* 13, 1850.

MY DEAR JOHN,—We only arrived at Hughenden yesterday, and your letter reached me this morning. We left town about a month ago for Knebworth, where we intended to stay a few days, and remained a fortnight! Bulwer has restored the seat of his ancestors in a manner which a 'large-acred' poet could alone imagine and accomplish. It is one of the best things in England: a rich Tudor edifice in an ancient deer-park, with towers, cupolas, gittering vanes, and embayed windows; within and without faultless. I find him a moderate Protectionist, and I think ready to act with us. The Lovelaces were there at the beginning of our visit, but latterly we were almost always alone, and nothing could be more agreeable. Our host is charming under such circumstances. We took long rides every day, and went to Hatfield, the Hoo, Brocket, etc., etc. After this we went to Downham, Norfolk, and stayed a pleasant week with the William Powletts: a good many people there, among them Seymour and Francis Baring and Hotham.

I have had holiday enough, and am at work at a political biography of Lord George Bentinck. It ought to have been done before, but I never have time. The Duke of Portland has sent me two chests full of papers. Lord Henry says that G. B. had an active correspondence with Mr. Chapman, whom he liked. I do not intend to publish any correspondence, but rather to insert passages in the narrative which may illustrate his character and doings. I think you know Chapman very well: perhaps you would communicate with him at your convenience, and see whether he would like me to look over this correspondence. . . .

I wish also, at your leisure, you would throw on paper some of your general impressions of G. B.'s character and career to guide me. I shall not publish it, so don't be nervous. Charles Villiers has been very kind in doing this. He was on the W. I. Committee, and has given me his impressions thereanent in a couple of sheets.

I hope you are well. Give my love to G[eorge] S[mythe], if you see him. Write to me whenever you can; as often and as long as you choose. You are the best correspondent in the world. Adieu, my dearest comrade.—D.

The work did not make the progress that autumn which the author hoped for. He wrote to Manners in October: 'I get on very slowly with the biography, for the subject expands under my pen, since it includes, in truth, every topic of present interest in the political world'; and in December: 'G. B.'s life expands into a rather great work. It . . . touches on such vast themes that the pen often pauses to think.' Accordingly, one autumn was not sufficient, and the work occupied the recess of 1851 as well as that of 1850, 'the last line of the last chapter,' as he told his sister, being finished on December 6. It was 'a mournful office,' he wrote to Londonderry, 'like commemorating the exploits of the Grand Army at St. Helena.'

Lord George Bentinck: A Political Biography, was published in December, 1851, though, in accordance with the then common practice, it bore the date 1852 upon the title-page. It was dedicated to Lord Henry Bentinck. Disraeli told Delane that the book was 'the Parliamentary history, and perhaps something more, of three eventful years.' As the Parliamentary history of the years 1846–1848, with Bentinck as the central figure, it has been necessarily the foundation of the last chapter of the previous volume, and some of the early chapters of the present volume, of this biography; and this aspect of it has been sufficiently illustrated by reference and quotation, though its graphic character can only be properly appreciated by those who read it through. But it is also 'something more.' There are various digressions in which Disraeli puts forward his own political views, most of them woven more or less closely into the general narrative, but some — and one especially, the twenty-fourth chapter on the Jewish question — rather in the nature of excrescences; and, of course, the book abounds in detatched expressions and sentences of Disraelian philosophy. In these respects it holds a unique position as an interpreter of his opinions; it is the one book of his political maturity which is not cast in the form of fiction; and therefore the views expressed in it may perhaps be taken literally with comparative immunity from misconstruction. With those expressed on the Jewish question, on the all-importance of race, on the mode of government of Europe, and on the influence of secret societies, we have already dealt. There are others which claim our attention.

The position of the Crown is only once touched on, but in an important passage it is strongly maintained that the royal veto on Bills passed by both Houses has not lapsed by disuse, but may yet in conceivable circumstances be employed with advantage to the State.

> As a branch of the legislature whose decision is final, and therefore last solicited, the opinion of the Sovereign remains unshackled and uncompromised until the assent of both Houses has been received. Nor is this veto of the English Monarch an empty form. It is not difficult to conceive the occasion when, supported by the sympathies of a loyal people, its exercise might defeat an unconstitutional Ministry and a corrupt Parliament.[1]

The Crown is therefore a reserved force in the constitution of the country. The actual holders of power should be the aristocracy, whose first duty it is 'to lead, to guide, and to enlighten; to soften vulgar prejudices and to dare to encounter popular passion.' 'England is the only important community that is still governed by traditionary influences, and amid the shameless wreck of nations she alone has maintained her honour, her liberty, her order, her authority, and her wealth.' Disraeli deplored the Radical tendency to 'yearn for the trans-

[1] Ch. 4.

atlantic type.' In America there was a virgin soil, no tradition, and no surplus population. 'There may be sympathy of feeling between Great Britain and the United States, but there is no analogy in their political conditions.' The governing aristocracy must be broadly conceived and widely recruited. 'The aristocracy of England absorbs all other aristocracies, and receives every man in every order and every class who defers to the principle of our society, which is to aspire and to excel.'[1] There is, in fact, a *carrière ouverte aux talents* in this country, by which Disraeli himself had profited. In this connection there is a well-known passage, written of Peel as an historical fact, but, we can hardly doubt, of the author himself as an aspiration — an aspiration by no means wholly fulfilled in 1851:

An aristocracy hesitates before it yields its confidence, but it never does so grudgingly. In political connections under such circumstances the social feeling mingles, and the principle of honour which governs gentlemen. Such a following is usually cordial and faithful. An aristocracy is rather apt to exaggerate the qualities and magnify the importance of a plebeian leader. They are prompted to do this both by a natural feeling of self-love and by a sentiment of generosity.[2]

The instrument by which government must be carried on is party — an instrument which Peel never fully appreciated. 'The first duty of an English Minister is to be faithful to his party. . . . Good and honourable government in this country is not only consistent with that tie, but in reality mainly dependent upon its sacred observance.'[3] This does not mean, of course, that statesmen are to prefer party to principle, but that a Minister should not use power conferred upon him by his party for one purpose to promote measures of an opposite character. Again in this connection we have a personal touch, based partly on experience and partly on aspiration:

The favour of courts and the applause of senates may have their moments of excitement and delight, but the incident of deepest and most enduring gratification in public life is to possess the cordial confidence of a high-spirited party, for it touches the heart as well as the intellect, and combines all

[1] Ch. 27. [2] Ch. 17. [3] Ch. 20.

the softer feelings of private life with the ennobling consciousness of public duty.[1]

The party which Disraeli led had been formed to maintain Protection, and the book is the history of its heroic but ineffectual fight for that policy under Bentinck. What bearing had the book on the issues of the moment in December, 1851, and what course did it recommend the party to pursue? Here Disraeli showed considerable reserve. But the farmers are told that they lost their opportunity by their apathy at the General Election of 1847, and have no right to be dissatisfied with 'the temperate course which is now recommended to them by those who have the extremely difficult office of upholding their interests in the House of Commons.' The Corn Law struggle is, moreover, treated as only one phase of 'the great contention between the patriotic and the cosmopolitan principle which has hardly begun, and on the issue of which the fate of this island as a community depends.' The suggestion clearly is that the ground should be shifted, so that the national and patriotic party might fight to more advantage. On only one aspect of the discarded system is stress laid in such a way as to imply an appeal for early reconsideration. Disraeli clings to the principle of reciprocity, and makes out an excellent case on its behalf. It appears, he says, 'to rest on scientific grounds, and it is probable that the experience may teach us that it has been recklessly disregarded by our legislators.'

With Irish policy, which occupies a considerable number of pages, we have dealt in part already, and shall return to it again. In regard to one or two isolated questions, the book throws an interesting light on Disraeli's opinions. Of the Anti-slavery legislation his view was very much that of Gladstone in his early days. 'The movement of the middle classes for the abolition of slavery was virtuous, but it was not wise.' The history of that movement and its consequences would be 'a narrative of ignorance, injustice, blundering, waste, and havoc, not easily paral-

[1] Ch. 8.

leled in the history of the world." These may seem hard sayings, but they would find even now many supporters in the West Indies and in South Africa. Disraeli criticises the county court system, just established, as impairing, if not destroying, 'that mighty fabric of centralised jurisprudence which was the most enduring element and perhaps proudest achievement of the Norman Conquest.' Was that progress, or reaction to Saxon ideas?

To revert to the main theme of the book, Lord George Bentinck and his three Parliamentary campaigns, it is impossible not to admire the manner in which the dignity of history is thrown round the narrative of what was almost contemporary politics. Though the pages are enlivened with wit and humour, there is a sense of seriousness and responsibility and balance throughout. 'Truth after all,' writes Disraeli in the opening chapter, 'is the sovereign passion of mankind'; and he claims to have combined 'the accuracy of the present with the impartiality of the future.' The claim has been generally conceded. In one respect he was conspicuously impartial—in his estimate of the qualities of his principal adversaries. We have already quoted his character of Peel.[2] Bright wrote of it at the time: 'I think it a very fair and a masterly picture of a great man. Disraeli never denies any merit his opponents may possess.'[3] Greville thought much the same, though his Peelite friends[4] naturally disagreed. Russell is always treated in the book with great respect. We read of his 'dignity,' of 'the lustre of his reputation'; he is called the 'somewhat rash but still unrivalled leader' of the Whigs. The Prime Minister reciprocated the courtesy shown him.

From Lord John Russell.

CHESHAM PLACE, *Jan.* 22, 1852.

MY DEAR SIR,—I wrote to thank you for your political life of Lord G. Bentinck before I had read it.

Having read it, you must permit me to express to you how

[1] Ch. 18. [2] Vol. II., pp. 305–8. [3] Trevelyan's *Bright*, p. 158.

[4] Graham told Greville that the character of Peel was 'a great and malignant outrage.'

much I have been interested and gratified The great struggle of 1846 is described in a masterly manner. Altho' the summary of Sir R. Peel's speeches is hardly fair, yet the character of the statesman and member of Parliament is drawn with great power and truth.

For my own part in these great affairs, altho' in some particulars you are mistaken, you have done me more than justice in the main. It was a disadvantage in a biography to have a hero whose forte was in statistics and arithmetical details, but with such a hero you have made your work very entertaining, while Mr. Canning, a wit and an orator, is reduced to commonplace by an ill-assorted fate of having a dull biographer.—I remain, yours truly, J. RUSSELL.

Of the last speech of the great Irish leader, O'Connell, with whom Disraeli had had angry differences in the past, he gives a sympathetic account. O'Connell spoke from the front Opposition bench. 'His appearance was of great debility, and the tones of his voice were very still.'

'It was a strange and touching spectacle to those who remembered the form of colossal energy, and the clear and thrilling tones that had once startled, disturbed, and controlled senates.' 'To the House generally it was a performance of dumb-show, a feeble old man muttering before a table; but respect for the great Parliamentary personage kept all as orderly as if the fortunes of a party hung upon his rhetoric.' Other distinguished men meet with similar appreciation. We hear of Graham's 'lucid arrangement of details' and 'comprehensive management of his subject'; of Molesworth's speeches as 'highly finished and full of thought and information'; of the 'multifarious information and the vast experience of Mr. Hume, who towers' among the English Radicals 'without a rival'; of the 'persuasive ingenuity of Mr. Cobden,' and elsewhere of 'that clear and saucy style which he knows how to manage'; of the 'terse eloquence and vivid perception of Charles Villiers'; of Charles Buller's 'vivacity and clear argument'; of 'the practised eye' of 'Bear' Ellice; of 'an orator no less accomplished than Mr. Shiel'; while Palmerston, Sir George Grey, Sir Charles Wood, and Lord Lincoln, are spoken of in complimentary language.

The merits of his own friends in the House of Commons are, as we have already seen,[1] naturally warmly acknowledged, and the character of the hero skilfully brought out. But there is one very curious feature, which was noticed at the time, and has frequently been matter for comment since: namely, the very slight mention—throughout what is mainly the story of the Protectionist party, its victories and its defeats—of the leader under whom Bentinck and the rest of the party fought. The references to Lord Stanley, who when the book appeared had just become Lord Derby, are indeed courteous. His conduct in quitting Peel receives its due meed of approbation; he was the 'one distinguished exception' in an unduly compliant Ministry. Disapproval is indeed hinted of his refusal to attempt to form a Government when that Ministry broke up in 1845, Peel's 'protesting colleagues' being criticised for having shrunk, when the opportunity offered, from 'the responsibility of officially vindicating their opinions.' Stanley, though acknowledged to have been Bentinck's 'political leader' in the Peel Ministry, appears in the book mainly as Bentinck's old friend; we hear of his 'warm personal and political sympathies' with him; of their joint secession from the Whigs; and of a couple of occasions in three years on which, in the House of Lords, the peer defended and vindicated the commoner. But that is all. In general his action is ignored, and his leadership of the Protectionist party is only referred to in a hypothetical way. It was believed in the early part of the session of 1846, we are told, that 'Lord Stanley might eventually think fit to guide [the party] by his counsels, and become, if necessary, personally responsible for its policy'; but we are never told that he actually assumed the position. The whole direction of the policy pursued by the party is ascribed to Bentinck, aided occasionally by that discreet 'friend' the author; though we know from other sources, as in the case of Disraeli's famous speech at the close of the session of 1848,[2] that the impulse came in many

[1] Ch. 5.

[2] See Ch. 4.

cases from Stanley, quite as much as from Bentinck or Disraeli.

Some of the reasons for this reticence are not difficult to see. Disraeli was a literary artist, and, as such, would naturally concentrate attention on his hero. The arena of the great fight for Protection was the House of Commons. It was there that Bentinck wielded his weapons; but there Stanley had no longer a place, and therefore he could not take so prominent a part in the battle as Bentinck. Bentinck, however, felt, as his frequent outbursts of dissatisfaction showed — and Disraeli probably shared the feeling — that, even so, Stanley had not done all he might. He allowed himself to be prevented, by the objections of the Duke of Wellington at the beginning of the session of 1846, from explaining and vindicating his position to Parliament and the country until the Corn Bill reached the Lords in May. During all these months Bentinck stood, in the popular eye, as the leader of the revolt against Peel, and was so regarded in many quarters at the election of 1847. Stanley, in fact, was only active in the cause by fits and starts. Still, reasons of this kind hardly cover the ground. Disraeli's artistic sense did not prevent him from digressions from his main theme on subjects of which his mind was full. Moreover, though Stanley's action was fitful, and he was of course unable to share in the attack on Peel in the Commons, he declared the fact of his opposition to Peel's policy quite early in the session of 1846; he was chosen Protectionist leader in March; he led the resistance to the Corn Bill in the Lords, and made fine speeches against it there; he was recognised by Bentinck as his chief at the Protectionist banquet in July; he was in frequent collaboration with Bentinck about the policy of the party; and it was to him that Bentinck wrote a formal notification of resignation. So it seems to be necessary to seek for more convincing reasons for Disraeli's unwillingness to place Stanley in a prominent light, and we may find them, perhaps, in the delicate relations of the two men. They were the leaders of the same party in their respective

Houses, and in frequent consultation; but there was at that time, as Disraeli has told us, 'no confidential intimacy' between them. It was difficult, it might be held to be in doubtful taste, either to praise or to criticise. The fact that Disraeli's main political preoccupation for two years had been to endeavour to persuade Stanley to abandon Protection might also suggest that it was inopportune to emphasise Stanley's share in the struggle to maintain it. Bentinck was dead; the limelight could be turned on to him without compromising present politics.

William Beresford to Lord Derby.

London, *Tuesday.*—. . . I have read over Disraeli's book again more carefully, and have taken notes for the purpose of looking to certain statements and facts which strike me as incorrect.

I am still of opinion that the work, brilliant as it is in the diction, acute and vigorous in its fine critical review of the debates, is disappointing as a biography. To you I freely say that it is untrue and unjust. The great hero of the book, either openly or by insinuation, is the author. In future times, a reader taking it up would consider that Lord Stanley was a secondary personage in the party and the legislature.

In regard to the treatment of Stanley, Beresford's criticism was justified. What about his further charge, that the real hero of the book is Disraeli himself? Some countenance to this view has been given in later times by Lord Rosebery, who, in his monograph on Lord Randolph Churchill, says that Disraeli had to justify in *Lord George Bentinck* the part that he himself had taken by Bentinck's side 'in violent polemics,' without mentioning his own name and without affectation, and that he succeeded. Further, that, as Bentinck was from the political point of view 'a difficult figure to drape with picturesque effect,' Disraeli made his book a political treatise in which Bentinck plays a minor part. That Disraeli wished to justify the course which he and Bentinck had taken together is evident, and also that he has woven into the narrative much of his political philosophy; but that, in so doing, he reduced Bentinck to a minor part is surely a strange misreading of the book. Rather is Mr. Whibley's[1] the

[1] Introduction to edition published in 1905.

truer appreciation: that the biography is a drama, with two chief actors, Bentinck and Peel, 'brilliantly disengaged from the dingy background of the House of Commons'; and that Disraeli modesty underrates the importance of his own part. He is a 'friend' who is always in intimate association and correspondence with the hero, and who makes him suggestions from time to time. But of his famous philippics which really overthrew Peel there is little trace, and an uninstructed reader would suppose that the decisive factors in the struggle were the tactical manœuvres and ponderous oratory of Bentinck. The digressions express, no doubt, Disraeli's rather than Bentinck's views; but, with the exception of the purple patch about the Jews, they can hardly be said to divert attention from the hero to the author. The book really fulfils the aim which Disraeli set before himself, as stated in his letter to Henry Bentinck, of depicting in high relief his friend's political action in regard to three great subjects in three successive years — Protection in 1846, the development of Irish resources by the credit of the State in 1847, and the relief of the sugar-growing Colonies in 1848.

To Lord Henry Lennox.

HUGHENDEN, *Aug.* 8, 1852.— . . . Tell Julian [Fane], with my kind regards, that his friend is quite at liberty to translate the 24th chapter [of *Lord George Bentinck*]; and would I were at liberty to think and write of no other subjects! I have never seen the book since it was written, and have no copy here to turn to: but a clergyman writes me that I have made the Crucifixion in the time of Aug. Cæsar — which, however, I did not do. What I wrote in my MS. was T. Aug. Cæs.: and my editor, tho' otherwise very accurate, not knowing that Tiberius was also Augustus, had it printed Aug. Cæsar. This should be changed in the translation to 'Tiberius Augustus Cæsar.'

I don't know of any other errors, for the passages denounced as heterodox by English clergymen, who are more ignorant of theology than any body of men in the world (the natural consequence of being tied down to 39 articles, and stopped from all research into the literature which they are endowed to illustrate), are only reproductions from St. Augustin and Tertullian.

Froude states that Disraeli 'received a large sum from a private hand' for *Lord George Bentinck;* but there is no trace of any such transaction in the Beaconsfield papers and Froude does not give his authority. The book only appealed to a political public, and therefore had not the sale of the more popular of the novels; but it went through four editions (2,750 copies) in half a year. The reviews, as was perhaps natural, ran rather on party lines; and, as the Press was overwhelmingly Free Trade in sentiment, they were generally somewhat unfavourable. Disraeli, like other authors before and since, and with equal want of success, endeavoured to select his own reviewer in *The Times*. He asked Greville, whose connection with Delane was known in political circles, to write the notice, but was told it was out of the question. The review which actually appeared in the great journal, though of very complimentary length — 'at least a great advertisement,' wrote Disraeli — was rather critical than appreciative. Bentinck's family expressed their gratitude, and Disraeli received the congratulations of his friends, though some of them echoed Manners's criticism that the insertion of the famous twenty-fourth chapter was unjustifiable. Greville, on the other hand, admired the Jewish episode for its courage. Sarah Disraeli was enthusiastic over the last book of her brother's that she was to read. 'Such a piece of English history must remain a classic so long as human nature endures. . . . It will be to the civilised Polynesians what Sallust is to us. . . . Surely a memorial so exalting never was raised by the hand of Friendship.' Lord Ponsonby called the book a 'triumph.' It showed doubters, he thought, that Disraeli was 'possessed of the qualifications necessary to a great stateman. The book, in all those parts of it where you treat general subjects of policy, is a convincing proof that you ought to be the directing mind in this country, as it shows that you have the wisdom to pardon as well as the generosity to praise many whom you might justly have censured.' Disraeli was in a few weeks to have his first opportunity of showing what he could effect, if not as the directing mind in the country, at least as the directing mind of a Ministry in the House of Commons.

CHAPTER XI

Chancellor of the Exchequer

1851–1852

'Affairs are very stirring,' wrote Disraeli to his sister on December 7, 1851, 'but how they are to turn out the most prescient can hardly see. There ought, I think, to be a Conservative Government.' He was quite right in his expectation; in less than three months there was a Conservative Government; and the stirring event which indirectly brought it about was Louis Napoleon's notorious *coup d'état* on December 2. That introduced a new factor into politics.

Till then, the English political situation had been dominated during the recess by the prospect of a Ministerial Reform Bill in 1852. The defeat on Locke King's motion had forced the Ministry into action. Disraeli had said in Parliament that, so long as the Reformers upheld their own Act of 1832, it would have been unwise to disturb it. Now that the very statesman who framed, modelled, and ushered that measure into the House gave up his own handiwork, Disraeli considered himself free. Naturally, his autumn correspondence with Derby dealt mainly with the prospects of Reform, and has a special interest as their first formal interchange of views on a subject so bound up with their political reputation.

From Lord Derby.

Knowsley, *Oct.* 26, 1851.—. . . Subject to what I may hear from you, and to the opinion which you can form far better than I can of the probable temper of the House of Commons, my idea is that we should abstain from pledging ourselves to resist any and every measure which may be brought forward, at the same time that we deprecate the introduction of any extensive alteration as uncalled for by any necessity or any strong public feeling, and as prompted in the present instance by a desire to save a tottering Administration by diverting public attention from its misgovernment to a subject of popular discussion and agitation. I should, nevertheless, express myself ready to hear their proposal, with the grounds on which they, and especially John Russell, justify its introduction; but I should declare that I would strenuously resist any measure which should have for its object to disturb the existing balance between different interests, to give additional power to the congregation of large masses, and to swamp the county representatives (which is the object of the Radical party) by assimilating the town and county franchise, as they have done in Ireland, and bringing the unrepresented towns to overbear by the household or a more extended franchise the county constituencies, which now rest in the main on landed property.

Pray tell me whether you concur generally in the policy of this game, and how far you think its announcement, if we decide on it, either publicly or privately, should precede the introduction of the Government plan. . . .

To Lord Derby.

HUGHENDEN, *Oct.* 30, 1851. — I was grieved to hear of your long sufferings; but as reaction is the law of life, I will indulge in the belief that you have now entered on a renewed lease of health.

Your theme is indeed a dreary one, but you mitigate its annoyance by your frankness and cordiality.

My impressions as to our conduct at this moment coincide, I think, in the main with those which you have expressed. As regards the impending Reform Bill, it would be dangerous for us to make the first move. I agree with you that there are some points on which we may at once decide. I think we should alike refrain from being anti-, or constructive, reformers. A vehement declaration in the first vein will gain us no strength, as the Finality School must go with us, and any concerted scheme of enfranchisement on our part must end only in distraction and discomfiture. The circumstances of the hour alone can bring a golden opportunity like the Chandos clause, and if it offer we can seize it. There is evidently a deadly silence on the subject at present, which we ought not to disturb; and were we to do so, we should be playing the game of the Whigs, who are watching for indications. I think all we ought to pledge ourselves to at present is professing our disposition to give a fair hearing to the

Government, to resist any scheme the main object of which is merely to consolidate the Whig party, or to check the constitutional influence of the land. These conditions would justify any degree of ultimate opposition. But reserve is our game. . . .

A few weeks later, Disraeli revived and elaborated a far-reaching suggestion which he had previously thrown out.

To Lord Derby.

Confidential. HATFIELD, *Dec.* 9, 1851.—. . . Is it impossible to make a great push, founded much on the alarming state of Europe and the consequently unstable character of our foreign trade, to reconstruct our Colonial system, or rather Empire, by freeing the Colonies from all duties, or some other mode, and conceding to them as represented in the Imperial Parliament the vacancy occasioned by the disfranchised boroughs, so bringing a third element formally into the House, and healing that too obvious division and rivalry between town and country? If feasible, it would allow us to prevent, perhaps, the increase of the town or democratic power, without the odium of directly resisting its demands.

This crude idea, more crudely expressed, might perplex some, but you will see at a glance what I mean, and have not pretended to convey, and will be able to decide better than any other person in the country whether the move is practicable.

Lord L[yndhurst] thinks we ought to be prepared for every hypothesis of change. The expediency of considering the question in the light intimated in this letter occurred to me in the train. It might blend many sympathies, commercial, political, and imperial, at this moment. . . .

Derby, in a long and carefully reasoned reply, pointed out the enormous difficulties in the way. How were the Colonial members to be elected? By the inhabitants or by their legislatures? What about Crown Colonies? How can Colonial representation be made to fit in with the Free Trade system? He had considered these questions carefully at the time of the great Reform Bill, and found no solution. Disraeli was not convinced.

To Lord Derby.

GROSVENOR GATE, *Dec.* 18, 1851.—. . . I have deeply considered your last letter in all its points, but have not yet relinquished the views I previously suggested to you. We should clear the course very much by confining ourselves now entirely to the political part of the subject, and on a future occasion, if Colonial members are sitting in the House, and we have an opportunity to revise and reconstruct our financial system, we may find them convenient allies. In the general management of the question I am much guided by the example of the United States towards their Colonies.[1] Altho' the American system is not one I should willingly appeal to for our domestic or foreign affairs, there is, I think, nearly a complete analogy between the two countries as regards their Colonies. The Senators at Congress are elected by the two Houses of each independent State, and this, I think, would do, if we could always find two chambers in our Colonial Constitutions. But in the last Australian Constitutions that was not the case. But these are very unpopular, and if we combined, with Imperial representation, an attempt to settle, on an intelligible principle, the construction of their municipal governments, the Australians would willingly surrender their one-chambered Constitutions, which are very unpopular with them, and we might appropriate all that section of what are called Colonial reformers, who hitherto have only been busying themselves with the municipal principle, and dissolving the Empire by mistaking it for what they call local government.

I can't help thinking that, if this move were matured and well managed, it might give a new phase to politics, appropriate a great section of support irrespective of our friends, tranquillise the Colonies, revive their affection to the Metropolis, and widen the basis and sympathies of our party. But the question is one so very much of detail that it is very difficult to write upon it. At present I would only impress two points: the expediency of postponing the commercial part of the question, and of finding in the American system some solution of the difficulties as to the constituent body of the projected Colonial members. . . .

I saw Lord Lyndhurst on Tuesday. He has had the gout, for the first time, and has been in bed for three days. He was on the sofa when I saw him, and otherwise extremely well. He had no information. I spoke to him, in complete confidence, on our Colonial idea, but rather to elicit his views than to develop our own. He was very favourable to the project at the first blush, as the only means of diverting an increase of the power of the towns, and as a method of consolidating Imperial strength. The Colonies are interested in

[1] Disraeli uses the term 'Colonies' of new States admitted to the Union. Florida, Texas, Iowa, Wisconsin, and California had all been admitted in the previous half-dozen years.

all questions of peace and war, and if they had, as it were their Ambassadors sitting in our Senate, their hearts would be with us in a struggle. It must be an organic principle of the arrangement that they are not to be liable for any portion of the public debt. I wrote to Stanley[1] on the 8th to Calcutta. If the views in this letter at all develop, I shall sadly miss him. Indeed, these are not times for him to be so long away.

Disraeli did himself an injustice in speaking of his idea as 'crude,' and representing it as having only occurred to him in the train. The possibility of combining the advocacy of Colonial representation with the Conservative attitude towards the Government Reform Bill may have only just suggested itself to him; but his mind had been dwelling on Colonial representation for some time, and he had even mentioned it in writing to his chief on December 28, 1849.[2] As he had then told Derby, he had been studying the whole Colonial question, and he discussed this particular point often with Edward Stanley. 'The Colonies still appear to me to be our safest card,' wrote Stanley to him on October 19, 1850; 'and I am firm in faith as to the ultimate popularity of Colonial representation; besides, popular or not, the thing ought to be done.' Disraeli was never content with the *laisser-aller* policy of many of the Whigs and most of the Radicals of the day — merely to give the Colonies representative institutions, and entirely disregard the use to which they might put them. He constantly sought methods by which, without impairing their local independence, he might bind them with a living interest to the Mother-Country and the Empire. Colonial representation was open, no doubt, to the detailed objections which Derby urged; but if the principle had been adopted sixty years ago, it is possible that we might by this time see our way

[1] Edward Stanley, in his early years of public life, was wont to spend much of the Parliamentary recess in foreign travel for purposes of political observation. Immediately after his grandfather's death he had started for the Far East. 'May our next campaign,' he wrote prophetically in a farewell note to Disraeli in July, 'instal you as leader of the House of Commons!'

[2] See above, p. 237.

to that representative organisation of the Empire which is the necessary alternative to ultimate disruption.

Disraeli communicated his idea to his Hatfield host, the second Marquis of Salisbury, father of the Prime Minister, who was much struck by it, and thought it might be 'most useful in reconciling our alienated Colonies and quickly nullifying the Free Trade policy,' and who also encouraged him to deal with franchise extension in a bold way. As finality had been given up, Salisbury wrote on January 17, 1852, it was all a question of expediency. 'It is difficult to give a reason why an £8 occupier in Ireland should be entrusted with a franchise which you would only allow to a £10 occupier in England. It is difficult to argue that a £6 occupier is not as fit to be entrusted with it as one who is rated at £8.' 'The popularity obtained by this extension of franchise would enable our party to make such regulations for the prevention of mischief as they never can hope to do under other circumstances. I believe that, if the present county franchise is to be materially altered, the lower you go the more influence you will give to property.' He was sensible that the Minister who carried out these suggestions must be a bold man, but it was a choice of difficulties. Comments of this kind from an unimpeachably orthodox Tory would confirm Disraeli in the belief that the party would follow him in a wide measure of Reform whenever he considered the moment favourable.

To Sarah Disraeli.

HATFIELD, *Dec.* 10 [1851].—. . . This is a splendid place, in the highest state of renovation. There was a ball last night in the great gallery, 500 persons. In the house are the Hardwickes (Lord Royston), Robert Grosvenor (one girl), Rokebys (three girls), and Henry Bulwer, and a multitude of dancing men; also the county member and his wife (Halsey), and the candidate for the county, Sir Lytton.

Lady Salisbury[1] is an admirable hostess and a very pleasing woman; great simplicity, quite a Sackville, with four most

[1] Afterwards wife of Edward Stanley, the 15th Earl of Derby.

beautiful young children — a boy just like a young Cantelupe. . . .[1]

Bulwer Lytton, at this time still Sir Lytton Bulwer, was a promising recruit whom the leadership of his friend Disraeli had attracted to the Conservative party. He had sat in the House of Commons as a Liberal, and even a Radical, from 1831 to 1841, but had failed to obtain a seat in either of the Parliaments which brought the free trade system into operation. Though a Liberal, he had always been a Protectionist, so the action of his party in combining with the Peelites to introduce the new system alienated his support. Like Disraeli, he was romantic rather than utilitarian, national rather than cosmopolitan in his politics; and very naturally, when his old party connection was severed, he rallied to his friend's standard. They had, apparently, not seen much of each other of late years, until Disraeli and his wife, in the early autumn of 1850, accepted an invitation to Knebworth. Bulwer had written: 'I don't think the wondermongers will find much to cavil at in our conjunction. After all, I am a Protectionist, and authorship is neutral ground.' The visit, which proved so agreeable to both host and guests that it was prolonged from a few days to a fortnight, seems to have finally determined Bulwer's course; and he had now become, with Disraeli's assistance, Conservative candidate for Herts. He brought a popular name and great oratorical gifts to a party which needed both; but, till he got back into Parliament, his assistance was necessarily of an imperfect character.

Russell's Reform Bill, which was introduced at the beginning of the session, proved to be by no means of the sweeping character which Disraeli expected. It merely proposed to lower the county franchise from £50 to £20, and the borough franchise from £10 to £5. Disraeli therefore did not treat it very seriously. He chaffed the Reformers about the short commons they had received, and expressed the opinion that the Bill did not necessarily

[1] *Letters*, p. 244.

call for opposition. He had always been an advocate of industrial suffrage. But the Bill discomposed Derby, and seemed likely to make a coolness between him and Disraeli. Malmesbury wrote on February 13, 1852: —

> Lord Derby seems quite knocked down by this Reform Bill, for which, strange to say, he seems to have been unprepared. I found him to-day without his usual energy. I am very anxious he should meet it by a counter Bill or resolution, but he will not hear of it, and treated Disraeli coldly when he proposed it. A mutual dislike between them might have serious consequences, but the two men are so different in character that it can hardly be otherwise; yet they cannot do without one another at present. I have great confidence in Disraeli's good-temper and ambition to see that such is the case.

The subsequent history of the Reform question shows that Malmesbury's confidence was justified. But this particular Reform Bill was never properly alive. Before the beginning of the session the quarrel between Russell and Palmerston had come to a head: Palmerston had been dismissed,[1] and the Russell Ministry, with its Reform Bill, was doomed. Palmerston's independent and masterful methods of conducting foreign affairs had brought him throughout the duration of the Ministry into frequent collision both with the Crown and with the Cabinet. The offence given in the autumn by his too sympathetic treatment of the exiled Kossuth was aggravated in December by his spontaneous and unauthorised declaration to the French Ambassador that he entirely approved of the *coup d'état* by which Louis Napoleon had forcibly made himself master of France. The Cabinet were anxious to express no opinion, and public feeling in England was strongly stirred against the President, no epithets being too bad for him in the Press. On hearing of the dismissal, Disraeli wrote to Lord Henry Lennox: 'I fancy the *coup d'état* of the 22nd December portends a Peelite reconstruction. The real question therefore is: what effect would a Peelite reconstruction have upon the

[1] Dec. 22, 1851.

prospects of our party? If you have any Christmas games going on, this will be a very good question to ask your friends.'

To Lady Londonderry.

HUGHENDEN, HIGH WYCOMBE, *Dec.* 28, 1851.—. . . The success of Napoleon seems to have given Johnny a taste for *coup d'états*. . . . They talk of a Peelite reconstruction; but if in embryo, it certainly is not hatched, and if born, will not live long.

The fact is the stroke of Napoleon has changed the whole complexion of politics, and for an English Minister to bring in a Reform Bill, in deference to the clamour of a very weak movement party, at the present moment is preposterous. Yet, if Lord John proposes anything temperate, the movement party will spring at him like hounds. In short, he ought to resign. . . .

Overtures were made by Russell first to Newcastle, and afterwards, as on several previous occasions, to Graham, but without result. The Government were evidently 'very sick,' as Disraeli wrote to Derby, in a long letter in which he told the story of Palmerston's dismissal as he heard it, obviously from Palmerstonian sources. 'I was not turned out; I was kicked out,' he reported to be Palmerston's own phrase. 'Lord P. was sacrificed to the mislikings of "the elder statesmen of Europe," and to a hoped-for *rapprochement* between Whigs and Peelites, impracticable while he was a Minister.' Disraeli told Derby that he heard confidentially that there was great alarm in the Cabinet lest the Conservatives were going to coalesce with Palmerston. 'I ridiculed the rumour and reprobated the factiousness of such a sudden alliance, adding we hoped we were strong enough to carry on affairs without taking in the discarded partner of an insolvent firm, and thought that with fair play we should not be driven to such a course. This morning I have a line from the same correspondent reminding me that six weeks ago he had informed me that Palmerston was doomed (which was true: it was about Kossuth), and now adding that another person (meaning Johnny) was in "as bad a plight."'

When Parliament met, it was found that it was not Russell, but Palmerston, who had a bad case. The Prime Minister had no difficulty in proving the disregard shown by Palmerston both for the Crown and for the Cabinet; and he revealed a memorandum of August, 1850, in which the Queen had laid down the duty of a Foreign Minister towards the Crown, which Palmerston had promised, but failed, to observe. Palmerston's reply was not successful. Russell was fully justified in reporting to the Queen that Palmerston 'made no case, and was not supported by any considerable party in the House. His approbation of the President's conduct seemed to confound the Liberal party.' Disraeli told Lord Normanby that he had watched Palmerston during Russell's speech, and doubted whether the hanging of his head were not merely acting; 'but before he had spoken two sentences he saw he was a beaten fox.' To Henry Bulwer also Disraeli exclaimed: 'There *was* a Palmerston.' Whatever he may have jestingly said, he was too shrewd to think anything of the kind. At any rate, in his speech — mindful, no doubt, of the probability that Palmerston, after his breach with Russell, would soon be acting with the Tories, in opposition if not in office — Disraeli treated the reasons assigned for the dismissal as unsatisfactory, and pointed out, with perfect justice, that down to this last escapade Ministers had adopted Palmerston's policy, and were responsible as a body for his blunders. If the policy were to be the same, he would prefer that the same Minister, who was an able man, should carry it out.[1]

To justify Palmerston's removal was easy; to carry on an already tottering Administration without one of the only two men who gave it distinction in the eyes of the world was impossible; and Palmerston had his 'tit for tat with John Russell' in little more than a fortnight from the

[1] A passage in this speech shows that Disraeli had begun to appreciate the middle classes. Their power and prosperity, he said, were 'inseparable from the greatness of England.' He owed his own seat to them, for 'the farmers of the United Kingdom are the most numerous and the most important portion of the middle class.'

opening of the session. The conditions of the Continent, and particularly of France, had directed attention, as often before and since, to our deficiencies in home defence; and Russell proposed to establish a militia force, not the old regular militia, but a local militia. Palmerston expressed strong approval of the general policy of strengthening our home defences, but moved, before the Bill was introduced, that the new force should follow the old plan of regular militia. Russell was indignant at a Government measure being treated in this cavalier fashion; but Disraeli supported Palmerston, and the Government were beaten by 135 to 126 votes.[1] The Whig Ministry, so feeble and so tenacious, so often threatened and so long-lived, had fallen at last. The opportunity of the Conservatives had come; but they were still hampered by the Protection policy, which all Disraeli's arguments had not persuaded his chief to discard.

How the crisis developed and the first Derby-Disraeli Ministry was formed is told in the memorandum of the sixties from which we have already quoted the introductory portions:—

In the autumn of this year [1851] the expulsion of Lord Palmerston from the Cabinet had taken place, and the Government was consequently more in the 'mud' than before. All indicated a crisis on the meeting of Parliament.

Lord Derby took the opportunity on the first night[2] (I think) of its meeting in 1852 to make a declaration on the subject of Protection. I really believe that, in taking this course, he was influenced by my representations, and wished to make a declaration that on the whole would reconcile all parties. His scheme seemed to be the adoption of the American tariff. It appeared to me to be Protection in its most odious form, and I was without hope.

Lord Palmerston lost not a moment in moving an amendment to the first Government measure, which insured their defeat (Militia Bill). An eager friend,[3] anticipating that

[1] Friday, Feb. 20.

[2] Disraeli seems to be confusing Derby's speech on the Address on Feb. 3 with his speech on taking office on Feb. 27. It was in this latter speech that he expressed approval of the American system as the most defensible in principle and the least burdensome in practice.

[3] Sir Benjamin Hall, M.P. for Marylebone.

Lord P. would be sent for by the Queen, would not allow Lord John Russell an opportunity of escape, but forced him to pledge himself that night to consider his Ministry finished.

But the Court, though it disliked the Protectionists, disliked Lord Palmerston, whom they had absolutely dismissed in the autumn, more, and Lord Derby, to the great astonishment of Lord Palmerston's friends, was again sent for.[1]

Lord Derby was not in town: he was at the Duke of Beaufort's, at Badminton, a shooting-party. I wrote to him from the House of Commons counselling him to seize the opportunity of forming a strong Government: to offer the leadership of the House of Commons to Lord Palmerston, and places in the Cabinet to such friends as he desired, and to assure Lord P. from me that he would find in me a loyal lieutenant. I sent off Mackenzie, the Junior Whip, at once to Badminton, who arrived there the following morning, before the news of the resignation was known.

To Lord Derby.

Confidential. Friday night.—Mackenzie will tell you the great event. Palmerston has defeated them by the militia, when the regular troops failed. As you will have a good opportunity to think over your many difficulties in your journey up, I write this to beg that I may not add to them. Don't let me be in your way. It is everything for your Government that P. should be a member of it. His prestige in the House is very great; in the country considerable. He will not give you trouble about principles, but he may about *position.* He would not like to serve under me, who he looks upon as a whippersnapper. I am sufficiently repaid in having gained your confidence and not altogether disappointed our friends, and I beg therefore you will understand this.

Here is Lord Derby's answer, just arrived in St. James's Square:—

From Lord Derby.

Confidential. St. James's Square, ½ past 9 [*Feb.* 21, 1852].—Whatever may be the issue of the present crisis, or the details of the arrangement consequent upon it, I shall never forget the generous self-sacrifice offered by the note which I received by Mackenzie at Badminton this morning. While I am sure that every instance of the kind tends to raise the character of public men generally, I am equally convinced

[1] Russell told the Queen that Palmerston had no party, and that he supposed Derby was prepared to form a Government.

that each case, even if the offer be accepted, must ultimately redound to the credit and advantage of the man who makes it from public motives. I have already had other intimations that P. is not unwilling to join us — but I shall studiously *not* see him till after I have had my audience of the Queen, which is appointed for ½ past 2 to-morrow. I am equally anxious that I *should* see *you*. Will you therefore have the goodness to call here at one o'clock to-morrow?[1]

On the previous evening I had met Lord Palmerston at Lady Foley's. He said to me inquiringly: 'Well, how long will Derby's Government last? He may have it for five years.'

'I think Lord Derby's Government might last more than five years if it be properly formed,' I replied. I was greatly tempted to open the subject to him at once, but from a feeling of delicacy towards Lord Derby refrained.

I saw Lord Derby before the audience.[2] He went resolved to form a Ministry and to kiss hands.

When Lord Derby informed the Queen of his intention of applying to Lord Palmerston to combine in forming a Government, and of offering him the leadership of the House of Commons, H.M. seemed distressed. 'If you do it,' she said, 'he will never rest till he is your master.'[3]

After leaving the Queen, Lord Derby had his interview with Lord Palmerston. Lord Derby had kissed hands, which Lord P. knew. What was Lord P.'s real view at that moment must remain a mystery. I am inclined to believe that he might have been induced to join Lord Derby. His political position was very desolate. He had no party. Not a single man of mark had followed him when he was ignominiously ejected from office. Indeed, only two individuals, and those obscure, had expressed their determination to blend their public fate with his. Lord Derby impressed upon him that the offer was made entirely with my sanction, and that he would find me an able, loyal lieutenant. Lord P. said he was quite satisfied on that head — he had no doubt of our getting on well together. With regard to friends for the Cabinet, he had none to suggest except on public grounds, equally open to Lord Derby as himself; with respect to any followers or private friends in regard to subordinate office, he had no wishes; there was nobody that he cared to provide for. This seemed promising enough; but then came the main principles

[1] These letters have been inserted in their proper places in the memorandum which refers to them.

[2] Sunday, Feb. 22.

[3] Derby told the Queen he was not afraid of Palmerston; he felt sure he could control him.

on which the Cabinet should be formed. Lord Palmerston did not think that Protection should be left an open question; that it could be left in an ambiguous position. He had no prejudices on the subject. He had always been in favour of a moderate fixed duty on foreign corn. He had advocated it in 1846 to the very last. But it was too late to think of such things in 1851. He would be party to no Ministry which contemplated the possibility of any change or modification in the Free Trade measures.

This ended the affair, and Lord Derby came to me from Piccadilly Terrace (Beaumont's house, where the Palmerstons then lived) at Grosvenor Gate. He would make no further overtures: in that he was wise, as it could only have been a waste of time. He recurred to my being Chancellor of the Exchequer, which he had opened to me before. I had then demurred, as a branch of which I had no knowledge. He replied: 'You know as much as Mr. Canning did. They give you the figures.' He said then definitely that Lord Malmesbury was to be Secretary for Foreign Affairs, but nothing of his position as regarded Sir Stratford Canning. Herries, he said, must be Colonial Secretary; Henley should go to the Board of Trade; Walpole, a recruit of last year, was to be Home Secretary; John Manners to be in the Cabinet, *vice* Granby. He must now go home at once: he had to write to the Queen, and to all these persons and many others, and begged me to be with him early on the morrow.

When I called on the morrow,[1] I found his house already full of people: men in every room. His servant told me Mr. Herries was with his Lord, and that he had inquired several times for me, and that my name was to be taken in immediately. A very few minutes elapsed before I was in his presence. It was rather a face of consternation. 'I really think we shall break down,' he said. 'What am I to do for a Colonial Secretary?'

So then it turned out, that Herries, evidently disgusted at not being C. of E., had peremptorily refused the Secretaryship. I instantly counselled my giving up the Chancellorship, which I didn't want, but Lord D. would not hear of it. The recollection of the scene of last year evidently influenced him; besides, he thought that the Leader of the House of Commons should be under the same official roof as himself. What was to be done?

'I know the man,' I said; 'he will do very well.'

'Who?'

'Pakington!'

'I have just sent for him to be U.S. to Walpole. It should

[1] Monday, Feb. 23.

be a country gentleman. I thought it was a capital arrangement. He will be here in a few minutes.'

Sir John Pakington was announced. He remained in the waiting-room, while I was convincing Lord Derby that he would make a competent Secretary of State. It was, naturally, rather hard work. I don't know that Lord Derby had even a personal acquaintance with Pakington at that moment. The exigency at last conquered him; he said, with an almost merry face of perplexity: 'Will you be bail for him?'

'To any amount,' I said.

I had only a public acquaintance with Pakington, who, though obliged to vote with the Protectionists, always kept aloof, and fetched up with the Peelites, for which Peel made him a Baronet. But I had observed him, especially on Lord G. B.'s colonial committee.

Pakington was introduced, elated with the impending destiny of becoming an U.S. Lord Derby explained the situation in his happiest manner. Never shall I forget Pakington's countenance, as the exact state of affairs broke upon him: never did I witness such a remarkable mixture of astonishment and self-complacency.

The cabinet was finally composed as follows: —

First Lord of the Treasury . . .	Earl of Derby.
Lord Chancellor	Lord St. Leonards.
Lord President	Earl of Lonsdale.
Lord Privy Seal	Marquis of Salisbury.
Home Secretary	S. H. Walpole.
Foreign Secretary	Earl of Malmesbury.
Colonial Secretary	Sir John Pakington.
Chancellor of the Exchequer . . .	B. Disraeli.
First Lord of the Admiralty . . .	Duke of Northumberland.
President of the Board of Control .	J. C. Herries.
President of the Board of Trade .	J. W. Henley.
Postmaster-General	Earl of Hardwicke.
First Commissioner of Works . .	Lord John Manners.

Outside the Cabinet the Earl of Eglinton was Lord-Lieutenant of Ireland, and Lord Naas Chief Secretary; Christopher was Chancellor of the Duchy of Lancaster, and Beresford Secretary at War. Stanley, who was still on his travels when the Ministry was formed, was appointed Under-Secretary for Foreign Affairs, and on his return represented his office in the Commons. Thesiger was

Attorney-General, and Fitzroy Kelly Solicitor-General, Bankes Judge-Advocate-General, and Trollope Chief Poor Law Commissioner. Lyndhurst, who was in his eightieth year, had declined the Chancellorship. Granby and his following stood aloof.

Of the members of the Cabinet only three — Derby, Lonsdale, and Herries — had been Cabinet Ministers before, and none of the rest was even a Privy Councillor. It was a memorable scene when they went to Windsor to receive the seals, and has been characteristically described by Disraeli himself in *Endymion:*[1] —

> A dozen[2] men, without the slightest experience of official life, had to be sworn in as privy councillors, before even they could receive the seals and insignia of their intended offices. On their knees, according to the constitutional custom, a dozen men, all in the act of genuflexion at the same moment, and headed, too, by one of the most powerful peers in the country — the Lord of Alnwick Castle himself — humbled themselves before a female Sovereign, who looked serene and imperturbable before a spectacle never seen before, and which, in all probability, will never be seen again.

'One of this band,' Disraeli continues, 'a gentleman without any official experience whatever, was not only placed in the Cabinet, but was absolutely required to become the leader of the House of Commons, which had never occurred before, except in the instance of Mr. Pitt in 1782.' It was a proud occasion for him. No wonder that at the mere prospect of it he should have 'felt just like a young girl going to her first ball,' as he told Malmesbury. He had now, with his whole party, 'got a *status*'; and he was to show whether one who, in the opinion of a Liberal historian,[3] was 'perhaps the best Leader of Opposition that the House of Commons has ever seen,' could lead the House itself with equal distinction, and prove himself a statesman as well as a great Parliamentarian.

At the dinner of the Royal Literary Fund, in May, Thackeray, who had often laughed at and parodied him,

[1] Ch. 100.

[2] The exact number of new Privy Councillors sworn in on this occasion was seventeen; but several of them were outside the Cabinet.

[3] Mr. Herbert Paul, in *A Modern History of England.*

hailed the romantic success of a brother-novelist in a speech which was half banter, half appreciation.

Could a romance writer in after-years have a better or more wondrous hero than that of an individual who at twenty years of age wrote *Vivian Grey*, and a little while afterwards *The Wondrous Tale of Alroy;* who then explained to a breathless and listening world the great Asian mystery; who then went into politics, faced, fought, and conquered the great political giant of these days; and who subsequently led thanes and earls to battle, while he caused reluctant squires to carry his lance? What a hero would not that be for some future novelist, and what a magnificent climax for the third volume of his story, when he led him, in his gold coat of office, to kiss the Queen's hand as the Chancellor of the Exchequer![1]

Disraeli's father was no longer alive to enjoy his triumph; but he could still count on his sister's sympathy and applause.

Sarah Disraeli to Mrs. Disraeli.

[? *Feb.* 26, 1852.]—I have fallen from the excess of light into such profound darkness and repose that I am bewildered, and should think all the wonderful events of these last seven days were so many dreams, were I not roused every now and then, and convinced that all the world are believing in their actuality.

I had to grant perpetual audiences yesterday to people who want something. First came my little postman to ask me to put him on the town district; he did not ask me for my interest, but requested me at once to transfer him. I noticed he spoke with a very tremulous voice, which impressed me strongly with a sense of my extraordinary power. Then came a friend of mine who wants the Chancellor of the Exchequer to read a pamphlet he had written on the currency. Then a letter from a lady who wants a place for her husband. . . .

Tell dear Dis I left the Board of Inland Revenue in a state of great flutter; all speculating on their new master. Mr. Pressly, one of the mainsprings—Dis knows him—had heard that he had grown somewhat grand of late.

Congratulations came from Disraeli's first political mentor, and also from an old follower and friend, now a political opponent.

[1] *The Times*, May 13, 1852. 'Great Asian mystery' has been substituted conjecturally for 'mystery of the great Caucasian theory' which appears in the actual report.

From Lord Lyndhurst.

Feb. 25.—I congratulate you most sincerely and warmly upon the high position which you have so deservedly attained. It recalls to my recollection in a very lively manner the political conversations and scenes which passed between us so many years ago, and which the course of events has brought to so brilliant a conclusion.

You will, I am sure, evince to the world that addition and subtraction are not the only qualifications for a Chancellor of the Exchequer.

From the Hon. George Smythe.

[*Feb.* 24, 1852.]—Those who hailed the dawn have the best right to salute the meridian. Believe, therefore, dear Dis, in the sincere congratulations with which I kiss Mrs. Disraeli's hand, and am, your affectionate opponent, G. SYDNEY SMYTHE.

I can't help laughing at your having disinterred Sir Roger de Coverley to stick him in the Colonies. It is so like one of your old strokes—in fiction.

Smythe's gibe at Pakington[1] is characteristic of the kind of reception which this untried team received from the public, and especially from the newspapers which supported Free Trade. They were at once dubbed the 'Who? Who?' Ministry, because the Duke of Wellington, partly from deafness and partly from unacquaintance with the new men, kept exclaiming 'Who? Who?' as the Prime Minister in the House of Lords repeated to him, one by one, the names of his colleagues. Palmerston said that there were only two real men in the Government, oddly forgetful of the fact that there were only two men who counted with the public in the late Government—Russell and himself. The Queen did not realise at first that there was more than one man; there was, at any rate, only one whom the Court really knew. She wrote to King Leopold on March 23: 'In the present case our acquaintance is confined almost entirely to Lord Derby, but then *he is* the Government. They do *nothing* without him. He has all the Departments to look after, and on

[1] Greville, in July, writes: 'The appointment that created the greatest surprise and was the most criticised, that of Sir John Pakington, has turned out . . . one of the best.'

being asked by somebody if he was not much tired, he said: "I am quite well with my babies."'

Of all the appointments, few were more unfavourably criticised than Disraeli's. That he should lead the House was not so surprising, but why put him at the Exchequer? It was a *mauvaise plaisanterie*, said one journal; he will find it difficult to be both a wit and a Chancellor of the Exchequer, said another. People had forgotten, or had paid little attention to, the remarkable speech on finance at the end of the previous session, from which we have culled in the last chapter some admirable financial maxims. At the same time it may be admitted that there was no special suitability in the post, except its comparative freedom from departmental duties, and the proximity of the official residence attached to it to that of the First Lord of the Treasury. But hitherto, when the Prime Minister was in the Lords, the leadership of the House had usually been associated with a Secretaryship of State; and such was the position assigned to Disraeli in the abortive negotiations of 1851. It is possible that the prejudice of the Court against Disraeli may have determined Derby to instal his colleague in an office that does not necessitate much personal intercourse with the Sovereign. In 1847 the Queen had been shocked at the mere suggestion that Disraeli was destined to hold high office in the next Cabinet, and in 1851 she had only accepted his nomination on Derby's guarantee. On the other hand, Derby was in real difficulty for a Chancellor of the Exchequer. Palmerston had refused; there is good reason to believe that Thomas Baring had refused; and, after Herries' timidity in the previous year, Derby was resolved not to give him another chance of the post. In the awkward position in which the party found themselves, part anxious to restore Protection, part resolved to get quit of that policy, the management of finance was a very delicate matter, and was naturally entrusted to the most dexterous hand.

It has been suggested that Disraeli had cherished the idea of uniting, like Canning, the leadership of the House with the Foreign Office. The interest in foreign affairs which he constantly manifested from the beginning to the end of his political career makes such an ambition a natural one; and a note written during the formation of the Ministry shows that Lyndhurst, who, as an old colleague of Derby's and friend of Disraeli's, was likely to be well informed, believed that Disraeli was to be Foreign Secretary. 'I think,' Lyndhurst wrote, 'you have chosen rightly in selecting the Foreign Office, for which you are admirably suited. We shall not, in future, blush for our foreign despatches, or foreign diplomacy.' Sir William Fraser, too, says that that Disraeli, who had become the headstone of the corner in 1878, had been rejected as Foreign Secretary by 'the builders' in 1852. It may be taken for granted that neither the Queen nor Derby would have consented to his appointment at that date; but there is no evidence, in the Beaconsfield papers or elsewhere, that he put himself forward for it. In the various lists of possible Ministries which he drew up during these years, he places himself sometimes at the Exchequer, sometimes at the Home Office, and sometimes at the India Office, but never at the Foreign Office. On the other hand, he did not entirely share the satisfaction which Derby entertained for Malmesbury's conduct of that office, at any rate during the Ministry of 1858; and in 1859 he roundly declared that Malmesbury 'must go'— 'at least, from his present position.'

To Sarah Disraeli.

March 2, 1852.—Having recovered from the horrors of a torpid liver, which has overwhelmed me the last few days, I send you an official letter, to tell you we get on very well: the Court gracious, the Press amiable, and our friends in the country considerate.

To-morrow is a levee; Friday a Council; and Saturday our first Cabinet.

A fortnight in my office without the H. of C. to distract me is a great advantage at starting.

My election is fixed for the 12th, the day the House re-assembles: rather awkward.[1]

[1] *Letters*, p. 246.

Disraeli's optimism was natural in his first week of high office. But the difficulties before him and the Government were serious. It was true that they had come in because the Whig Government could no longer hold together; but they were in a decided minority in the House of Commons, and the Free Traders, of all sections, were likely to unite against them in Opposition. Their own attitude to Protection constituted their main difficulty. It had already prevented Palmerston from joining them; it had in the previous year put a stop to the negotiations with Aberdeen, Graham, and Gladstone; it had frightened off Lord Canning, Ellenborough, and Henry Corry. No doubt the question was treated as a more open one in the formation of the Government this year than it had been in 1851; and Lord Hardinge, at any rate, accepted the post of Master-General of the Ordnance as an avowed Free Trader. But Derby, in his first declaration of policy on behalf of the Government in the House of Lords, on February 27, having, as he wrote to Disraeli, 'ticklish ground to go over,' held up the American tariff to admiration as compared with the Free Trade system, and restated his individual opinion that corn should be no exception to a general system of imposing duties on foreign imports; while declaring that no general financial scheme of the kind could be introduced except by a Government strong in the confidence both of Parliament and of the country. To Disraeli this seemed to be 'Protection in its most odious form,' qualified by postponement of action till after the General Election. His own first intimations of policy were much more cautious. He had, of course, to submit himself for re-election on taking office. In his address he told the electors of Bucks that the first duty of the new Government would be 'to provide for the ordinary and current exigencies of the public service; but, at no distant period, we hope, with the concurrence of the country, to establish a policy in conformity with the principles which in opposition we have felt it our duty to maintain. We shall endeavour to terminate that strife of classes which, of late years, has exercised so pernicious an influence over the welfare of this kingdom; to accomplish those remedial measures which great productive interests, suffering from unequal taxation, have a right to demand from a just Government.' They were 'favourable to progressive improvement in every department of the State.' In other words, his programme was not Protection, but justice to the agricultural interest by a readjustment of public burdens, coupled with administrative reform. On the hustings he went into more detail. Three great interests, he said — the agricultural, colonial, and shipping interests — had been injured by the legislation of 1846–1849; justice should be done to them, to the British producer as well as to the British consumer. The landed interest, especially, suffered under heavy burdens that must be redressed; the people of England, as things were then, were eating a farmer every night for their supper. A countervailing duty was recommended by eminent economists, and was probably the best method; but if the people of the country were — as he seemed to assume they were — opposed to it, then some other method would be found. The Government did not shrink from appealing to the people, but there was necessary business to get through before dissolution was possible, and defence and Chancery reform were ripe for treatment. Hobhouse found this speech as mysterious as those of Disraeli's colleagues; and no doubt Derby's indiscretion made it difficult for Disraeli to be plain.

This speech was delivered on March 12, the day Parliament met again after adjournment, and on the following Monday, the 15th, the attack on the Government began in both Houses. The Free Traders were, or professed to be, alarmed. The Anti-Corn Law League was revived in Manchester, and meetings of protest arranged in many big towns. The Liberals met at Russell's house, and under his inspiration determined that no close time should be accorded to the new-comers; Lord Grey, on March 6, told Malmesbury the Government would not last three weeks. In the Lords, Derby was asked whether it was the intention of the Government, in a new Parliament, to recommend an alteration in the present policy with regard to the importation of corn ; and he declined to say more than that the question could only be solved at the General Election, and that no duty should be imposed on corn by a bare majority, but only after a very general concurrence of opinion. The debate in the Commons was described by Disraeli in his first letter, as leader of the House, to the Queen. Disraeli's letters were a new experience to Her Majesty, differing greatly as they did from the somewhat stereotyped official form to which previous leaders of the House had accustomed her. She told her uncle on March 30 : 'Mr. Disraeli (*alias* Dizzy) writes very curious reports to me of the House of Commons proceedings — much in the style of his books.'[1]

To Queen Victoria.

House of Commons, *March* 15, 1852, *Monday night.* — The Chancellor of the Exchequer, with his humble duty to your Majesty, informs your Majesty of what occurred in the House of Commons this evening.

Mr. Villiers opened the proceedings, terse and elaborate, but not in his happiest style. He called upon the House to contrast the state of the country at the beginning of the year and at the present moment. But he could not induce the House to believe that 'all now was distrust and alarm.'

The Chancellor of the Exchequer, in reply, declined to bring forward in the present Parliament any proposition to change our commercial system, and would not pledge himself to propose in a future Parliament any duty on corn. He said a duty on corn was a measure, not a principle, and that if preferable measures for the redress of agricultural grievances than the five-shilling duty on corn (mentioned by Mr. Villiers) could be devised, he should adopt them — a declaration received with universal favour on the Government side.

Lord John Russell replied to the Chancellor of the Exchequer in consequence of some notice by the former[2] of the strange construction of a new Opposition to force a Dissolution

[1] Disraeli himself was often dissatisfied with the literary form of his reports. On Nov. 14 he apologized to the Queen for 'a somewhat crude note.' 'He humbly begs your Majesty will deign to remember that these bulletins are often written in tumult, and sometimes in perplexity ; and that he is under the impression that your Majesty would prefer a genuine report of the feeling of the moment, however miniature, to a more artificial and prepared statement' (*Queen Victoria's Letters*).

[2] Apparently a slip for 'latter.'

of Parliament by a Minister who, three weeks ago, had declared such Dissolution inexpedient. It was not a successful speech.

The great speech on the Opposition side was that of Sir James Graham: elaborate, malignant, mischievous. His position was this: that Lord Derby, as a man of honour, was bound to propose taxes on food, and that, if he did so, revolution was inevitable.

Mr. Walpole followed with great taste and moderation, confining himself to the constitutional question, and avoiding the statistics which Sir James introduced.

Mr. Gladstone and Lord Palmerston both spoke in the same vein: the necessity of immediate Dissolution after the passing of the 'necessary' measures; but the question soon arose, What is 'necessary'?

Lord Palmerston thought the Militia Bill 'necessary,' upon which the League[1] immediately rose and denied the conclusion.

There seemed in the House a great reluctance to avoid[2] a violent course, but a very general wish, on the Opposition side, for as speedy a Dissolution as public necessity would permit.

The evening, however, was not disadvantageous to the Government. All which is most humbly submitted to your Majesty, by your Majesty's most dutiful subject and servant, B. DISRAELI.[3]

Derby was naturally nervous about the performances of his 'team of young horses' in the Commons in their first trial, and was anxious before he went to bed to have a report from his lieutenant.

From Lord Derby.

ST. JAMES'S SQUARE, ½ *past* 10 [*March* 15].—I hear from many quarters that you made a *magnificent* speech, and after our conversation this morning I have no fear that there should appear any divergence of opinion which could by possibility be laid hold of between us. . . .

But if you have time for a line written on your knee, as you have no reply, and consequently nothing pressing upon you, I wish you would relieve my anxiety by letting me know what was John Russell's line, and its success; that our men have not marred the effect of your speech, and that the favourable commencement of the night has been sustained. Shall you get your vote of men and money? Remember *nothing* can be done till the Mutiny Bills are secure, and the defence of

[1] The Anti-Corn Law League.

[2] Disraeli seems to have meant 'reluctance to take' or 'desire to avoid.'

[3] *Queen Victoria's Letters.* The paragraph about Walpole's speech is omitted in the book.

the country must be the first step. I should not deprecate a little *factious* delay to our necessary measures, which should *unavoidably* carry on Parliament till June or July.

Disraeli's reply, written from his place in the House of Commons, was couched in much the same terms as his letter to the Queen, though he went into more detail about Russell's speech, which he declared to be 'a complete failure. He made a feeble reply to my attack, which forced him up, and then took refuge in a prepared glorification of his Government — speech of statistics, which, from the dulness and the dinner-hour combined, broke up the House.' Disraeli announced in his speech the measures which the Government hoped to pass: first, the Bill for the disfranchisement of St. Albans together with the Ministerial proposals for distributing the forfeited seats; secondly, Chancery reform; and, thirdly, a Militia Bill.

To Sarah Disraeli.

D[owning] S[treet], *March* 17, 1852.—I think we have turned the corner. The public seems with us, and our raw recruits have not made a single mistake. . . .

Ralph and M. A. keep you, I believe, somewhat *au fait* at what happens. For myself, I am very well, but I literally have not time to take my meals.

The Lord President,[1] however, gives to-day his first Cabinet dinner: so business and food may be combined. In the evening Lady Derby gives her first reception, which I shall attend, though otherwise I do not attempt to go anywhere. M. Anne, however, is very gay and ubiquitous.

On Monday night Lord Derby did wonders, and I, in the other House, did not disgrace our friends.

From Lord Derby.

Private. St. James's Square, *Thursday* [*March* 18]. — I hope you did not think that I urged too strongly last night at Lonsdale's my view of the course to be taken in the House of which you are the Leader. If I did, you must attribute it to my strong sense of what was essential for securing and strengthening our position.

[1] Lonsdale. It was the practice of this Government to hold Cabinet dinners on Wednesdays during the session.

I have this moment Lord Hardinge with me. He says, from Gladstone, that with an understanding that we are to have a dissolution in the summer, and a meeting in November, the body of the Peelites will support us through the session, resist an attempt to cut short our supplies, and not press for a second Parliamentary session of 1852. I have declined entering into any *engagement*, as Gladstone has no reciprocity to offer; but I have authorised Hardinge to tell him privately that such are my views, and that I agree that it is desirable that the country should have an intimation of our commercial policy, as early as is consistent with the object of making the *next* meeting of Parliament that for the session of 1852–53, and not a second session of 1852. If the Peelites act on their personal intentions, and we are firm, but temperate in tone, our game is won.

This expectation of support from the Peelites was fulfilled, save in one conspicuous instance; and consequently, as Derby wrote, down to the General Election the Government were secure. Derby and Disraeli were pleased with the outcome of their first debates, but they could not expect the Whig and Radical Opposition to be; and there is justice in the Queen's comment, in writing to King Leopold, that these debates were 'not satisfactory, because both Lord Derby and Mr. Disraeli refuse to give a straightforward answer as to their policy, the uncertainty as to which will do serious harm.' On Friday, March 19, Disraeli was again interrogated by Russell as to whether Ministers would advise a dissolution of Parliament with the least possible delay; and he gave the Queen this summary of his reply: —

He held it was not constitutional and most impolitic for any Ministers to pledge themselves to recommend their Sovereign to dissolve Parliament at any stated and specific time, as circumstances might occur which would render the fulfilment of the pledge injurious or impracticable; that it was the intention of the Ministers to recommend your Majesty to dissolve the present Parliament the moment that such measures were carried which were necessary for your Majesty's service, and for the security *and good government* of your Majesty's realm; and that it was their wish and intention that the new Parliament should meet to decide upon the question of confidence in the Administration, and on the measures which they could then bring forward in the course of the present year.[1]

Upon this answer an attempt was made by Bernal Osborne, who talked of a 'thimblerig Government,' to stop supplies on the ground of want of confidence in Ministers. The motion, though supported by Russell, Cobden, and Bright, was not carried to a division; and it was repelled with spirit by Disraeli, who characterised Russell's behaviour in first throwing up the Government, and then endeavouring immediately to force the new Minister to resign, as factious. It was a false move of Russell's; and, as Disraeli told the Queen, 'the discomfiture of the Opposition was complete.' The first week had certainly gone well for the Government, and Derby so reported to the Queen. Her Majesty's account of his conversation shows that Disraeli's arguments, or the manifest trend of public opinion, had already had an effect on his views; for he told her that, though he anticipated a Conservative majority at the General Election, it would not be a majority for the reimposition of a duty on corn, 'certainly not a majority large enough to justify him in proposing such a measure.' But his 'honour and credit' prevented him from abandoning Protection till the country had pronounced against it. The Queen interpreted this ambiguous statement, in the light of her strong common-sense, to mean that 'Lord Derby is quite prepared to drop Protection.' She told King Leopold that the Government would get through the session, dissolve in June or July, and meet Parliament again in November; 'and then Protection will be done away with.' That was what Disraeli foresaw and desired to be prepared for; what Derby was coming to expect, but would not provide against.

The Government lost no time in bringing in their Militia Bill. They proposed to create an additional permanent force of 80,000 men for national defence, to be raised by bounties of £3 or £4; the period of training and drilling to be twenty-one days, the Crown having

[1] *Queen Victoria's Letters.*

power, in case of necessity, to extend it to fifty-six days. The cost would be about £1,200,000. The Bill was introduced[1] by Walpole and generally welcomed; its only opponents were the Manchester School, whose arguments, said Disraeli, really meant that in the present state of the world no country need defend itself. An easy passage was expected for it; but on the second reading, to the general surprise, Russell supported a motion for its rejection, on the ground that it followed the plan of the old militia which his Government had condemned.

To Queen Victoria.

HOUSE OF COMMONS, *April* 19, 1852 (*Monday night, half-past twelve*).—The Chancellor of the Exchequer, with his humble duty to your Majesty, reports to your Majesty that, after a dull debate, significant only by two of the subordinate members of the late Administration declaring their hostility to the Militia Bill, Lord John Russell rose at eleven o'clock and announced his intention to oppose the second reading of it. His speech was one of the ablest—statesmanlike, argumentative, terse, and playful—and the effect he produced was considerable.

Your Majesty's Government, about to reply to it, gave way to Lord Palmerston, who changed the feeling of the House, and, indeed, entirely carried it away, in a speech of extraordinary vigour and high-spirited tone.

The Ministers were willing to have taken the division on his lordship sitting down, but, as the late Government wished to reply, the Chancellor of the Exchequer would not oppose the adjournment of the debate.

The elements of calculation as to the division are very complicated, but the Chancellor of the Exchequer is still inclined to believe that the second reading of the Bill will be carried.[2]

Russell had a second time since the formation of the Government made a false move, and Palmerston's protest against mixing up party feeling with the defence of the realm carried the House with it. On the morning of the division Disraeli wrote to his sister: 'Lord John, after much deliberation, has chosen his own field of battle, and if he get beat to-night, which I think he will, he will have

[1] March 25. [2] *Queen Victoria's Letters.*

proved himself a very unfortunate, not to say a very unskilful, general.' Many Whigs, as well as most of the Peelites, voted with the Government, who carried[1] their Bill by nearly two to one in a full House — 315 against 165. It was a notable triumph, and, though due to an extraordinary blunder in tactics of the leader of Opposition, none the less calculated to increase the hold of Ministers on Parliament and the country. The Bill passed through its remaining stages with little trouble, and, being blessed by the Duke of Wellington in the House of Lords, became law in almost exactly the shape in which it was introduced.

Russell did not propose to proceed in opposition with the Reform Bill which he had introduced on behalf of his Government; and the new Ministry naturally decided to leave the question alone. But Hume and Locke King were irrepressible, and Disraeli had to resist, and, with Russell's aid, defeat two familiar motions by these Reformers. In his speeches he said that neither he nor his party was opposed to Parliamentary reform, though they did not consider an extension of the franchise to be synonymous with the extension of democratic power. They were opposed to crude and unnecessary proposals, based on erroneous calculations, which would merely give further representation to property. It would be a different matter if a well-matured measure were brought forward, not for party purposes, but with the sincere desire of giving the deserving artisan the exercise of the suffrage in a manner consistent with the maintenance of the institutions of the country. Besides these Reform motions, Disraeli had to meet financial resolutions, brought forward in advance of the Budget, and calculated to deprive the Exchequer in one case of the income derived from the hop duty, and in the other of that arising from the paper duty and the newspaper stamp and advertisement duties. With both proposals, as we know, he had considerable sympathy; but, as a Chancellor of the Exchequer de-

[1] April 26.

fending the Treasury, he naturally opposed both. The Government could not pledge themselves, and he appealed, and appealed successfully, to be allowed to make his financial statement without being hampered by preliminary votes of the House.

These debates, and the multifarious duties devolving on a leader of the House with very insufficient support on his own bench, together with official work at which he was a novice, left the Chancellor of the Exchequer little opportunity to consider his Budget. 'I have neither time to feed nor sleep, though pretty well,' he tells his sister on the Monday before it was due ; 'great debates every night, and the Budget on Friday, for which I have literally not time to prepare.' The Queen, 'alarmed by vague rumours that it was the intention of the Government to propose great changes in the present financial system,' made inquiries about the Budget at the beginning of the week.

From Lord Derby.

Confidential. ST. JAMES'S SQUARE, *Sunday night* [*April* 25]. —The enclosed note from H.M. will show you that she means to know *everything* that is going on. I have sent her in answer one of our confidential printed papers of the Budget, and told her that, though at present we had come to no positive and formal decision, I apprehended we should have a 'provisional' Budget with one year's income-tax; I have told her the deductions to be made from any apparent surplus, and the necessity of keeping something in hand to go upon, *if, as appeared probable,* we could derive no income from foreign corn. . . .

As Derby now no longer concealed from the Queen or his colleagues that he was beginning, however reluctantly, to recognise the hopelessness of Protection, Disraeli determined to treat the Budget as a great opportunity for counteracting the ill effect of his chief's opening declaration on financial policy. Not that in his actual financial proposals there was any scope for showing the tendency of his mind. The Budget was necessarily provisional; and it was provisional, not merely because the Government were a Government without a majority and pledged not to modify the new commercial system till after the General

Election, but also because the income tax had only been voted, in 1851, for one year, and a Committee was sitting to take the whole question of that tax and its incidence into consideration. But it was obvious that the Chancellor of the Exchequer could not review the financial situation without giving a fairly clear indication of the principles on which he held that the taxation of the country must be based. This expectation, the piquancy of Disraeli's position, the fascination of his career, and the absurd *canards* circulated by the Free Traders as to the probability of reactionary proposals, produced more than the usual excitement and curiosity about the Chancellor's statement; and when he rose on April 30 the House was fuller than it had been since the great Pacifico debate.

From the beginning he struck the note of complete impartiality and detachment which he maintained throughout. He asked members to dismiss from their minds all prejudgments and prejudices, and join with him in an attempt clearly to comprehend the exact financial position of the country. Owing to Hume's motion in 1851, limiting the income-tax to one year, an important branch of the revenue had lapsed; what was the soundest means of supplying the deficiency? The revenue of the country was raised in three modes: first, by duties on articles of foreign import; secondly, by duties on articles of domestic manufacture; thirdly, by direct taxation. To which of these should he revert in his need? By the method of customs already a large revenue was raised; and since 1842 there had been a systematic and continuous reduction of these duties, amounting to £9,000,000 in all; so that, in the light of history, it would be presumptuous in him to recur to fresh customs duties to supply his deficiency. Were excise duties more encouraging? There were two parties in their financial controversies: one, the more prevalent, which was always in favour of reducing customs; but another, important though not triumphant, which desired to relieve native industry by reducing excise—a party to which his 'ever-lamented friend' Bentinck belonged. If one side of the House wished to reduce customs, and the other excise, what was a poor Chancellor with a deficiency to do? Besides, even those who considered customs duties the greatest of financial grievances had shown repugnance to raising revenue by excise; and, since 1842, excise duties had been relieved to the extent of £1,500,000. Only a week before a proposal had been made to repeal duties on paper and newspapers which would have meant a further loss of £1,400,000. It was, therefore, an extremely hopeless enterprise to supply his deficiency by increasing excise duties.

Some Liberals talked as if to raise money by direct taxation was a preferable method. The principal direct tax, the income tax, was introduced by one of the most eminent of modern statesmen in 1842 in order to effect reductions in duties; but it was introduced as an emergency measure, and the House and country could not be got to adopt it without its being framed on a large basis of exemption. Moreover, it was only renewed with difficulty, and had at last become so odious and unpopular that in 1851 it had only been continued for one year, on condition that it should be investigated by a Select Committee. That Committee, of which he himself was a member, was still sitting. One of the gravest objections to this tax was that there was no difference in the rate of assessment upon incomes of a temporary and of a permanent character. There were difficulties in adopting any scheme for remedying this defect. 'In questions of finance, the feelings of the people must be considered as well as the principles of science.' The Committee were unanimous that, if measures of direct taxation were to form a permanent feature of our finance, they could not rest upon a system of exemptions. Direct taxation, in Disraeli's opinion, should be nearly as universal in its application as indirect. Otherwise 'it is confiscation. It is making war upon the capital which ultimately must employ that very industry which you wish to relieve.' The instance of the income tax therefore hardly encouraged the Chancellor to turn to direct taxation. Besides, the principal feature of

ELECTRO-BIOLOGY.—AN AMUSING EXPERIMENT UPON MR. BULL IN A PERFECTLY WAKEFUL STATE.

Professor.—'THERE, SIR! THAT'S A LUMP OF SUGAR—YOU CAN'T MOVE IT, SIR; I DEFY YOU TO GET RID OF IT.'

the Budget of 1851 was the repeal of one of the most considerable sources of direct taxation — the window tax — at a loss of nearly £2,000,000. It was repealed on the 'plausible plea, but miserable pretext,' of sanitary consideration; and a house tax was substituted. But this new tax followed 'the vicious principle which pervaded all our direct taxation,' and only applied to 400,000 out of 3,500,000 houses. The policy of the last ten years had brought us to this result, that 'the House of Commons disapproves of all three methods of taxation.'

Disraeli now passed to the portion of his speech which provoked most comment — his description of the results attained under Wood's Free Trade Budget of the previous year. There was an excess in the receipts over the late Chancellor's estimates of £330,000; but even that statement did not do justice to his merits, as there had been vast remissions of taxation. There had been reductions on coffee, timber, and sugar, and Wood had therefore estimated for losses of £176,000, £286,000, and £335,000 respectively; but the losses had only been, in the three items, £112,000, £126,000, and £309, owing to the enormous increase in consumption. Hence the customs had exceeded the estimate by £270,000. There was the same tendency to rapid expansion shown in excise, stamps, taxes, and Post Office, though in the last case much must be attributed to the Great Exhibition. All this part of the speech was vociferously welcomed by the Opposition.

For the coming year, 'after the marvellous results which I have communicated to the House as the consequènce of the last reduction in the sugar duties, one is naturally sanguine' about the revenue. Assuming the income tax to cease, the amount to be collected under that head in the year would be only £2,600,000, and the total estimated receipts on the basis of present taxation £49,000,000, leaving a deficit of £2,125,000 for 1852–53, and of £4,250,000 for 1853–54. If the income tax was retained it would bring in £5,187,000, and give a surplus of £460,000. To retain the tax for a limited period was the only prudent course. That was what the Government recommended, and they proposed no change of taxation whatever.

Disraeli added a weighty passage on the importance of laying down clearly and decidedly the principles on which the public revenue should be raised. Had the Government been longer in office they would not have shrunk from this laborious task; and they would not be content again, if they had the opportunity, to make provisional propositions.

They look with great apprehension to the opinions prevalent in this House, which seem opposed to all the great sources of raising the revenue of this country. They consider that nothing would be more injurious than rashly and rapidly to reduce the sources of indirect taxation while you have come to no general conclusion as to the principles upon which direct taxation shall be levied. They are of opinion that if we continue in this mood of mind—admirable as is the industry, vast as is the capital, of this country, great as are the advantages which are received from our political institutions, which have secured it order, wealth, and liberty—it will be impossible to maintain the revenue of this country in that manner which the public credit and the wants of our national establishments require. Sir, we have a profound conviction upon that head. We deem it our duty to impress upon the Committee and upon the country the dangerous course in which they have embarked—to impress upon them the absolute necessity, now or in another Parliament, of arriving at some definite understanding on what principle the revenue of this country ought to be raised. They deem it their duty to denounce as most pernicious to all classes of this country the systematic reduction of indirect taxation, while at the same time you levy your direct taxes from a very limited class.

The speech was markedly successful, and showed, as Thomas Baring said, that the Chancellor of the Exchequer had a mind which could grapple with anything. It brought Disraeli what he greatly valued, his first letter from the Sovereign who had hesitated to accept his services, but who was eventually to set him above all her other Ministers in her esteem and regard.

From Queen Victoria.

BUCKINGHAM PALACE, *May* 1, 1852.—The Queen has read with great interest the clear and able financial statement which the Chancellor of the Exchequer made in the House of Commons last night, and was glad to hear from him that it was well received.

Admiration was, indeed, expressed on all sides for the speech itself, and there was general concurrence in the proposal to renew the income tax for a limited period. The Free Traders naturally exulted in the evidence given, in the speech, of the general prosperity. Wood regarded it as strong testimony to the complete success of the financial and commercial policy of the last ten years, and Gladstone was quite prepared to rest the whole case on it. Compliments came also from Bright and Labouchere. A few Liberal members, indeed — Hume, Reynolds, and Wakley — mingled with their approbation taunting references to Disraeli's conduct to Peel, whose principles they contended he was now vindicating; but the usual note of the Opposition was one of generous appreciation. The Conservative speakers — Thomas Baring, Tyrell, Alderman Thompson, and Hudson, the Railway King — were equally complimentary, but pointed out that it did not follow that, because the financial position of the country was good, there were not important interests suffering from distress; and also that the Chancellor had not attributed the prosperity of the country to Free Trade. These declarations show that Palmerston's and Greville's statements that the speech was received in 'sullen silence,' 'in silence and discontent,' by the supporters of the Government, are somewhat exaggerated; but those two shrewd observers were not far wrong in concluding that, after the speech, Protection, in the shape of a duty on corn, could no longer be attempted. One very important listener shared their sentiments. If Disraeli had been dissatisfied with Derby's declaration, Derby was no less disturbed by Disraeli's. His anxiety prompted him to write the same evening a long letter of remonstrance. Greatly as he admired the clearness and lucidity of the statement, 'I think the silence of our own friends, and the rapturous and triumphant cheers with which the opposite side of the House greeted each successive illustration of the financial result of the remission of taxes, and the advantage gained to the consumers, must have shown you, as you went on, that you were making out a triumphant case for the Free Trade policy which is the mainstay of our opponents.' What about the interest of the producer? 'It is impossible that you should have overlooked the fact that, with regard to two at least of the items you enumerated—coffee and sugar—and partially also as to timber, the increase of consumption has chiefly fallen on the foreign produce, while the diminution of price has mainly affected the home or the colonial producer.'

On the whole, I cannot but say that I should have listened with far more pleasure to your statement had I been able to shut my eyes, and to persuade myself that I was listening to Charles Wood congratulating the country on the eminent success of his financial policy, and encouraging the country to persevere in and extend it, exaggerating its advantages, and passing lightly over its injurious consequences, than I did when I remembered, able as it was, that it was the statement of the organ of a Government by whom that commercial policy had been, certainly not condemned in the abstract, but censured as having been carried to a reckless extent.

Derby anticipated—and with good reason—a 'yell of triumph' from the Free Trade paper; as he left the House he heard the remark, 'It was the eulogy of Peel by Disraeli.' He had seen no one, and might be mistaken as to the feelings of their own party; but 'I foresee great discontent among our friends, and great embarrassment when we come to the serious consideration of that financial system, on which, if we adopt without reserve the policy of our predecessors, we shall be justly stigmatised as impostors who have obtained office under false pretences; and if we depart from it, we shall be met with rather weighty arguments, drawn from your speech of this evening.'

It was, of course, Disraeli's object to force the note, in order that there might be no mistake about his resolve to extricate his party from a Protectionist policy. He was quite willing himself to make certain reserves, as he showed in the next few days. Derby, however, in spite of his growing conviction that Disraeli's course was the right one, did not content himself with a private grumble by letter, but took advantage of a City banquet to Ministers a few days later to utter some ambiguous words which once more suggested that Protection might be revived. Undoubtedly there had been annoyance at the Budget among extreme Protectionists; and the farmers, who, as Malmesbury tells us, 'though reconciled to Protection, expected some relief in other ways,' were disappointed at no hint having been given of a measure for their advantage, beyond the promise to examine the whole financial system after the election. Derby at the Mansion House was profuse in compliments to his lieutenant, whose speech had refuted the unworthy notion 'that a man possessing high ability, a vivid imagination, and great eloquence cannot master the driest commercial and financial topics.' But he said that, though Disraeli properly did not allude to the subject, no Government ought to lose sight of the interests of those large classes, unconnected with commerce, who were mainly producers. Government must reconcile apparently conflicting interests, and 'by mutual concessions and by mutual compromises' blend them in one harmonious whole.

'Mutual concessions and mutual compromises' might mean anything, and probably in Derby's mind meant no more than Disraeli's policy of compensation to the landed interest. But the phrase immediately aroused suspicions temporarily allayed by Disraeli's Budget speech. *Punch* asked, in a famous cartoon, which horse Derby declared to win with, Protection or Free Trade? The Peelites, who had hitherto supported Ministers, took alarm, and immediately inflicted on them the one serious rebuff of the session. One of the measures which Disraeli had declared to be 'necessary' in March was a Bill for assigning the four seats forfeited by the disfranchisement of St. Albans and Sudbury. On May 10 he moved for leave to introduce the Bill, and made the very reasonable proposal, which was subsequently carried out with slight variation by Palmerston's Government in 1861, to allot two seats to the West Riding of Yorkshire, and two to the south of Lancashire, both of them districts of great and growing population. In an interesting speech he discussed with sympathy, and only dismissed owing to practical difficulties, the suggestion of introducing new elements into the constituency by allotting these seats to learned societies, such as the Royal Society, the Inns of Court, or the unrepresented Universities. Gladstone got up immediately Disraeli sat down, and moved to disregard the motion and proceed to the orders of the day. It was not necessary or wise, he said, to deal with such a measure in a moribund Parliament. But his real reason for objecting was that the Government were at issue with Parliament on a cardinal point of policy. It was a solemn duty to bring the question to a formal and final issue, which could only be done by dissolution. That process should be expedited and the controversy ended. Government were beaten by eighty-six, and Palmerston as well as Gladstone voted against them. It was characteristic of Derby to write to Disraeli next day: 'I do not think there is much harm done, if any, by our defeat of last night'—a defeat due mainly to his own Mansion House declaration.

To Sarah Disraeli.

House of Commons, *May* 14.—A hurried line to tell you that, after many vicissitudes, affairs seem pretty well and smooth again, except this morning—Lord Derby has the gout! They say it is light; but he is in bed, and how things are to go on without him baffles my imagination.

Yesterday[1] I feasted my followers in a manner worthy of the cause, and as few Chancellors of the Exchequer have of late years. There was an enormous Drawing-room, the banquet and drum at Lady Derby's, not less, I should think, than a thousand. I never got upstairs. The Privy Seal, the Lord President, the Postmaster, all gave gratuitous feasts. The Duke of Northumberland, too—in fact, never was a faction so feasted! . . .[2]

By May 24 Derby had advanced so far in the way Disraeli desired the Government to go that he said openly

[1] Celebration of the Queen's birthday. [2] *Letters*, pp. 247, 248.

in the House of Lords, as he had already told the Queen and Disraeli, that he did not think it probable that so large a majority would be returned at the General Election in favour of an import duty on corn as would render it desirable to reimpose such a duty; and he repeated that without a decided and unequivocal majority the attempt ought not to be made. But even this was very negative and unsatisfactory as a programme for the elections, and Disraeli occupied the Whitsuntide recess in drawing up his address to his constituents, which should make it quite plain that the Government did not, as a Government, whatever subordinate individuals might do, go into battle under the flag of Protection. That there might be no doubt that this document was the authorised manifesto of the Government, he submitted it to Derby for revision, and adopted all the suggestions which he made.

From Lord Derby.

ST. JAMES'S SQUARE, *June* 3, 1852.—I have looked over your address, and have ventured on two or three suggestions of no great moment, but which I would recommend for your adoption. I think one sentence about 'recurrence to the abrogated laws' would appear to condemn in principle, as well as to admit to be impossible, the imposition of any duty—and it is well to let down the agricultural body as easily as we can. I do not like your last sentence. I think my 'auspices' had better be omitted, and the expression of 'making' the country, etc., implies too much as requiring to be done. You will easily amend it. . . .

The important paragraphs in the address, which was dated Hughenden Manor, June 2, and was issued two or three days later, were these:—

The time has gone by when the injuries which the great producing interests endure can be alleviated or removed by a recurrence to the laws which, previously to 1846, protected them from such calamities. The spirit of the age tends to free intercourse, and no statesman can disregard with impunity the genius of the epoch in which he lives. But every principle of abstract justice, and every consideration of high policy, counsel that the producer should be treated as fairly as the consumer, and intimate that, when the native producer is thrown into unrestricted competition with external rivals, it is the duty of the legislature in every way to diminish, certainly not to increase, the cost of production.

It is the intention of Her Majesty's Ministers to recommend to Parliament, as soon as it is in their power, measures which may effect this end.

One of the soundest means, among others, by which this result may be accomplished is a revision of our taxation. The times are favourable to such an undertaking; juster notions of taxation are more prevalent than heretofore; powerful agencies are stirring, which have introduced new phenomena into finance, and altered the complexion of the fiscal world; and the possibility of greatly relieving the burdens of the community, both by adjustment and reduction, seems to loom in the future.

What the exact remedy for the agriculturists 'looming in the future' might be was perhaps misty and doubtful. But that there was to be no recurrence to the old Corn Laws, but on the contrary, 'free intercourse' and 'unrestricted competition,' was made perfectly clear; and this policy received Derby's *imprimatur*. Disraeli summed up the issues before the country in the following words:

The country will have to decide whether it will maintain a Ministry formed on the principles of Conservative progress; whether it will terminate for ever, by just and conciliatory measures, the misconceptions which have too long prevailed between producer and consumer, and extinguish the fatal jealousy that rankles between town and country; whether our colonial empire shall be maintained and confirmed; whether the material development of Ireland shall at length be secured; whether such alterations as time and circumstance may appear to justify and require in the construction of the House of Commons shall be made in that spirit of revolution which has arrested the civilisation of Europe, or in the spirit of our popular, though not democratic, institutions; whether the Church of England shall still remain a national Church; whether the Crown of England shall still be a Protestant Crown.

It will be noticed that Disraeli vindicates the progressive nature of the Conservatism which he advocates, and especially its right to deal with the question of Reform; that he recurs to the material development of Ireland; and that he sounds the note of Imperialism.

To Sarah Disraeli.

June 8, 1852. — . . . The business is very hard and anxious; up to three o'clock every morning, and in my place in the House again at noon. It cannot, I suppose, last very long — at least, if it do, I shall not. However, on the whole, I keep my health. . . . M. A., I suppose, keeps you *au fait* to our, or rather to her, life. Mine you know by the newspapers; I go nowhere. Yesterday I was *not* at the Trinity House, and shall not be at a long series of civic feasts which are coming — E. I. Company, Skinners', M. Taylors' — being all, and perhaps fortunately, on House or Commons days.

I gave Graham a good dressing,[1] and he could not rally.

I am very glad young Stanley has come back.

On Sunday I was two hours with the Prince — a very gracious and interesting audience. He has great abilities and wonderful knowledge — I think the best-educated man I ever met; most completely trained, and not over-educated for his intellect, which is energetic and lively. — Adieu.[2]

It was not to be expected that Disraeli's address would prevent the Opposition from harping on the uncertain attitude of the Government towards Protection. The fear of Protection was by far their best electioneering card, and, before the session ended, it was again played for all it was worth by Russell. This was in a debate[3] which sprang up about the wrongs of a British subject, Mr. Mather, who was cut down in the streets of Florence by an Austrian officer. Malmesbury, as Foreign Secretary, had endeavoured to get compensation for him from Tuscany, and the Opposition contended that he should have applied to Austria. But Russell passed from this topic to a general review of the proceedings of the Government. He accused them of concealing their policy, and not telling the country clearly whether the new commercial system was to be tampered with or not. He contrasted the Budget speech and the address to the electors of Bucks with Derby's declarations, and wanted to know which the House was to believe. The country would never give its confidence to a Government which had no opinions and no principles. It was, of course, only a

[1] On June 7 Disraeli successfully vindicated, in reply to Graham, the management of public business by the Government.

[2] Part of this appears in *Letters*, p. 248.

[3] June 14.

re-hash of an attack that Russell had made more than once before during the session. 'The very first night I took my seat,' said Disraeli, 'the noble lord rose and opened his batteries. He has since returned to the attack; but his drums were muffled, and the fire slackened. Now we have a last effort, but it is a forlorn hope that will not take the citadel.' With regard to the charge of a change of opinions since 1846, he roundly denied it. He and his friends opposed the abandonment of the Corn Laws and the alteration of the sugar duties; but he denied that either he or the bulk of those with whom he acted had ever advocated a recurrence to the same laws that existed before 1846. 'You cannot recall a single speech to that effect; I defy anybody to quote any speech I ever made, or any sentence that I ever uttered, that recommended such a course as desirable or possible.' That statement has been denounced by Disraeli's traducers as audaciously false. The reader of this volume will recognise its substantial truth. Lord Derby, Disraeli admitted, had recommended a fixed duty on corn, though he had now intimated his belief that the country would not support such a policy. But a fixed duty was not a recurrence to the laws which existed before 1846. A fixed duty, as he had often pointed out, was recommended by McCulloch and other economic authorities. But it was not a principle, but a measure; and, as it was invested with popular odium, and repudiated by the popular will, he was not going to pin his political career to it, or make it the basis of his policy. The object of the Government was to do justice to the classes wronged in 1846, but 'without disturbing the system which is now established.' There could be no doubt now about Disraeli's meaning.

To Queen Victoria.

HOUSE OF COMMONS, *Monday,* ½ past 12 *o'clock* (*a.m.*) [*June* 15, 1852].—The Chancellor of the Exchequer, with his humble duty to your Majesty, reports to your Majesty that Lord John Russell made his 'observations on the present state of public affairs' this evening: appended to the Mather case.

This latter he treated very cleverly, and had the House with him; but his postscript, which was very general, marred all, and dissipated the attention of the House.

Lord Granby got into high Protection: Lord Palmerston attacked both Governments, but the present gently. The House seemed ill-disposed, and affairs looked black; but the Chancellor of the Exchequer was more fortunate than he expected or deserved. He is just down, and writes this humbly to say that your Majesty's Ministers have outlived a threatening night.

While there was great doubt in the popular mind at home, fomented by the Opposition for party purposes, as to the position of the Government, it is noteworthy that a shrewd and interested foreign observer had already, before the issue of the Bucks address and the debate on June 14, recognised that not only Disraeli, but Derby, had finally abandoned Protection. Metternich wrote to Disraeli from Vienna on May 24 : 'Vous avez du vous convaincre que je ne me suis point trompé sur les exigences de la situation dans laquelle se sont trouvés les chefs du parti réellement conservateur des intêrets de votre grand pays, sous le poids d'une qualification qui n'a trait qu'à une fraction de ses intérêts — sous un poids dont vous et votre noble ami ont déjà su se débarrasser au profit de la cause dont vous êtes les défenseurs.'

The anti-Catholic and anti-Ritualist feeling excited by the Pope's action about ecclesiastical titles in 1850, and by the proceedings of the Tractarians, was still strong in the country, and was reflected in motions in the House of Commons. On June 12 Disraeli wrote to the Queen : 'The feeling of the House of Commons, on both sides, is so determined against Tractarian principles, that the majority will support motions, of which they otherwise disapprove, if they think such votes may incidentally check the aggressions of the sacerdotal party.' In another letter to the Queen, describing a debate on education on June 21, Disraeli wrote : 'The feeling of the House of Commons, probably in this representing faithfully that of the country, is against both the violent parties in the Church, and in favour of a firm, though temperate, course on the part of the Crown, which may conciliate a vast majority, and tend to terminate dissension.[1]

In the latter part of the session, Spooner, a strong Protestant Tory, moved to inquire into the Roman Catholic College of Maynooth, which received a Government grant. The debate stretched over several days, and all parties except the Irish professed a willingness to have an inquiry, Walpole for the Government, Gladstone for the Peelites, and Russell for the Opposition. Though much strong language was used, nothing was eventually done, as the debate was not concluded till the session was nearly over, and it would have been ridiculous to appoint a Committee when Parliament was about to be dissolved. It was not a creditable spectacle; but all parties were playing for position at the General Election. Disraeli only took part to state that the Government would not abrogate the grant to Maynooth, and would not advise the appointment of a Royal Commission. Otherwise he let the debate take its course in the electioneering spirit which actuated Derby in writing to him, on one of the days when the subject came up: 'I think you must at all events let your men go as far as you can. Votes will be given to-night in reference to impending elections, and we must not be hard upon men, even in office, who may vote for Spooner, even if we propose, and he refuses, to limit the inquiry.'

To Sarah Disraeli.

DOWNING STREET, *June* 16.—Our unprecedented efforts have nearly steered the ship into port. The Speaker says he never remembers so much and such hard work. I think we shall carry every one of our Bills of the slightest importance; even the Crime and Outrage Bill, of which I once despaired. . . . Things look favourably. The Court is very gracious; I was with the Prince Consort two hours again on Sunday last. . . . The fish dinner is fixed for the 30th. I hope Parliament will be prorogued the next day, and the Queen will do so in person.[2]

Disraeli was perfectly justified in his complacency about the legislative results of the session, which compared

[1] *Queen Victoria's Letters.* [2] *Letters*, p. 248.

favourably with the recent muddles of the Whigs. The part of the session under the control of the new Ministers was but three months and a half, and in that time they had passed the Militia Act; an Act giving New Zealand a Constitution; various measures of legal reform, including Acts to diminish the technicalities of special pleading, to amend Common Law procedure, to reform the Court of Chancery, and to extend the jurisdiction of County Courts; and important sanitary measures, for improving the water-supply of London, and restricting intramural interments. Undoubtedly they had found many of these measures left by their predecessors in an advanced state of preparation; but to have passed them all, in the face of a captious Opposition who began by denying the right of the Government to do anything but dissolve forthwith, was a considerable achievement. No wonder that Lyndhurst took the opportunity of congratulating the Government at the close of the session, and that Derby pointed out in reply that it was to the firmness of the Government in resisting premature dissolution that this considerable harvest was due. It was due also to the tactful and judicious manner in which the new leader of the House of Commons had managed its business. Even Greville, who began, on second-hand reports, by abusing his leadership during the first fortnight, admitted his success at the close of the session. Though condemning him as 'a perfect will-o'-the-wisp' as regards his opinions, he added: 'He has given undoubted proofs of his great ability, and showed how neatly he could handle such a subject as finance, with which he never can have been at all familiar.' He exhibited conspicuously, among other things, one admirable quality which marked his leadership during each of his terms of office — a readiness to leave his colleagues to deal with their own departmental work in the House, and not to intervene himself *nisi dignus vindice nodus*.

His manner of speaking during this his first session as leader of the Government in the Commons is preserved for us in a lively, if somewhat unsympathetic, sketch of a visit to the House which appeared in the *Leader* on September 25 of this year. The visitor has been told that 'Mr. Disraeli is up,' has heard cheers as he approached, and is eagerly looking forward to a feast of oratory.

The House of Commons is before you, and your sensations undergo an instantaneous collapse. Your eye takes in the scene; a full House, listening, too, but lazily and loungingly, the cheer you heard having been made up of an aggregate half-laugh, half-sneer. You see the orator, there at the top. His body is half thrown across the table, one hand resting behind him, flirting with a laced cambric, the other white hand tapping gently a red box. And he is making a great speech? He is talking to Lord John, whose arms are crossed carelessly, whose thin lips are parted with an easy smile, and who seems to think the eloquence rather amusing. Mr. Disraeli has a most exquisite voice, and he is using only its gentlest modulations. He is quite colloquial, and his tone is friendly and familiar—especially when he comes to a bitter innuendo, when he turns his head to the country gentlemen, that they may hear it and laugh—a low, simmering chuckle, that just agitates the surface for a moment only, Lord John and the Whigs and the Radicals smiling, too, as though the sarcasm were a good-natured joke. Mr. Disraeli is getting near the end of his speech, and is now recapitulating and fastening all the points (not mathematical ones) together, as is his wont; and this is his argumentative style. He approaches the peroration—his forte; and here he raises his head, he throws back his collar, he puts by his cambric, he turns from Lord John, and faces the House. He speaks slower; he ceases his affected stammer; he is more serious and more solemn, but still quiet and unpretending. Talking now to the many, and not to one or two, he becomes more oratorical, and he fixes attention. What he is now saying is the manifesto of a party; not a syllable is lost. He is nearing a meaning, and his articulation is elaborate; and there is a dead silence. But he is still unexcited; dexterously and quietly he eludes the meaning—soars above it, in one or two involuted closing sentences, delivered with a louder voice and with more vehement gestures; and, having got the cheer at the right spot, this great orator, concluding, sinks into his seat, as nonchalant as though he had been answering a question about Fahrenheit, and immediately (Mackenzie having told him how the division will be) turns to ask Lord Henry Lennox whether Grisi was in good voice that night!

CHAPTER XII

The December Budget

1852

Parliament was prorogued on July 1, and dissolved the same day. Derby told the Queen on the last day of the session that he thought he would gain forty seats, which would give him an absolute majority of the House of Commons — of course, not for the imposition of a duty on corn. Such a duty, he added, might now be considered 'as abandoned under any shape whatever, whether for Protection or revenue.'

That was the policy with which Derby entered upon the General Election. But in those days peers did not issue manifestoes, still less make speeches, to influence the return of members to the House of Commons. Consequently the electors were never told by the Prime Minister what he had said to his Sovereign and his colleagues; and they might still legitimately doubt whether he had become completely converted to the views of the leader of the House of Commons. Disraeli's speeches in the election were as unmistakable as his address. At Newport Pagnell, on July 14, he said that, while Protection was sound in principle, 'if the country has chosen to abrogate that system, and if the majority of the people of this country are of opinion that it would be unwise to recur to it, I say we must seek by other means, and in another direction, to place the cultivators of the soil in a fair and just position.' The burdens of local taxation must be readjusted, and there must be such a revision of the system of national taxation as to reduce the cost of production. Granted that the bread of the people must be cheap, care must be taken that the producer of that bread should be able to produce it as cheaply as possible. On the hustings at Aylesbury two days later he said that he had been taunted with the usual question, 'Are you a Free Trader?' and that he was almost surprised that the big and little loaf had not appeared in the Liberal procession. But 'the time has gone by when these exploded politics could interest the people of this country. No one supposes that the present administration have any intention, or ever had any intention, to bring back the laws that were repealed in 1846.' The old members for the county, Du Pré, Disraeli, and the Whig Cavendish, were duly returned, the somewhat farcical opposition of a local Liberal, Dr. Lee, being easily disposed of.[1]

The official policy of the party involved the abandonment of Protection. But Derby had been brought into line too late to insure discipline among the rank and file, or even among Ministers themselves. Stanley, indeed, who was important, not only from his own abilities, but as the Prime Minister's son and heir, said at King's Lynn that Protection had been set at rest, and he was glad of it. But Herries and Manners, if not Walpole, Disraeli's Cabinet colleagues, Christopher, the Chancellor of the Duchy, and Fitzroy Kelly, the Solicitor-General, hinted that Protection might be again restored. Whig criticism suggested that Free Trade or Protectionist opinions were assumed by Conservative candidates solely in accordance with the proclivities of their constituencies; that in the counties they were Protectionists, and in the towns Free Traders. The contention of the Opposition was that by this profligate trifling with a great question the Government gained seats; but Disraeli, more reasonably, believed that, on the contrary, seats were lost owing to the uncertainty. He was convinced that, if his urgent advice had been taken earlier and Protection unquestionably abandoned by the whole party, the innate Conservatism of the country would have asserted itself, and the Government would have been accorded a fair trial. He, like Derby,

[1] The result of the poll was — Du Pré, 1,999; Disraeli, 1,968; Cavendish, 1,403; Lee, 665.

had been sanguine of a majority, not, of course, for Protection, but for a Conservative policy, which should give Ministers power to erect that barrier against revolution which Derby regarded as his mission. They were disappointed. The party had indeed some remarkable successes. None of their leading men were defeated, and their numbers were increased; but, all told, they did not exceed about 310 in a House of over 650. The numbers of the other parties may be put roughly at about 270 Whigs and Liberals, 35 or 40 Peelites, and 35 or 40 Irish Roman Catholic brigade. As a large but uncertain portion of the Conservatives had definitely abandoned Protection, there was a majority of nearly, if not quite, three to one in favour of Free Trade; but the Peelites, though their old leader's policy prevailed, were much weaker in the new Parliament than in the old. After the election of 1847 they were reckoned at nearly 100; but Disraeli's policy of readjustment of local and imperial burdens had rallied many of the rank and file to Derby's banner before the close of the Parliament, and after 1852 they were never counted as more than 40. They were weakened, too, by the defeat of Cardwell at Liverpool, Sir George Clerk at Dover, and Lord Mahon, the historian, at Hertford. George Smythe, too, lost his seat, but, Protection being abandoned, returned to his political allegiance to Disraeli. Important Liberals like Sir George Grey, Cornewall Lewis and Horsman, were also beaten; but Macaulay came back, after some years' absence, triumphantly for Edinburgh, and Lowe entered the House as member for Kidderminster. Lytton reappeared in Parliament as a Conservative, and the Tory party had a still more powerful reinforcement in the new member for Belfast, Hugh MacCalmont Cairns, afterwards Disraeli's Lord Chancellor. Another new member, who did not sit long in the 1852 Parliament, as his election was declared void for bribery, and whose subsequent appearances at Westminster were fitful, was Sir William Fraser,[1] a great hero-worshipper

[1] 1826–1898. M.P., Barnstaple, 1852–1853 and 1857–1859; Ludlow, 1863–1865; and Kidderminster, 1874–1880 — about ten years out of twenty-eight.

and collector of *ana*, chiefly about Wellington and Napoleon III. and Disraeli, the author of *Disraeli and his Day*, which enshrines, if it sometimes mangles, many of the best stories about its hero.

The successes of the Government had been sufficient to give them a fair chance of remaining in office, if only they could attract a little outside support. Palmerston, the most conspicuous personage in the House of Commons, with the possible exceptions of Russell and Disraeli, stood in rather an isolated position. He had quarrelled with the official Whigs, and had resolved, after the events of the last winter, never to serve under Russell again. He had rested his refusal to join Derby in February solely on the ground that Protection could not be left an open question, and had treated the Government throughout the session in a benevolent manner. Now that Protection had been definitely repudiated, it was to Palmerston that the thoughts of Ministers, anxious, as were Disraeli and Stanley, to broaden the basis of the Government, naturally turned. 'I quite agree,' wrote Stanley on July 19, 'that the ship requires fine steering; but she requires something else as well: an accession to the strength of the crew. There is an old helmsman who would be very useful in taking an occasional spell at the wheel.' He added: 'Lady P. has been going about remarking to everybody that no pledge had been given at Tiverton, and that he was free to act as he pleased.' Derby was ready for a negotiation of the kind, but, wrote Stanley, 'did not express himself very warmly about it.' It was, of course, out of the question to suggest giving Palmerston the Foreign Office, to which he himself had, indeed, no wish to return. He was supposed to prefer the Home Office, and Walpole was ready, he said, 'to do anything to promote the success of the affair.' It was suggested that the Speaker might be willing to retire and take his peerage, and that Walpole might fill his chair. On Palmerston's side there was, apparently, a disposition at least to listen.

From Samuel Phillips.

July 24, 1852.—. . . To-day I passed an hour with [Lord Palmerston]. . . . Your name, amongst others, was mentioned, and it was gratifying to note the respect with which Lord Palmerston adverted to his acquaintance with you. He told me how frequently he had been charged with not dealing with you as an inveterate foe . . . and how much he had been gratified with your conduct when you waited upon him in the matter of ——. I told Lord Palmerston that Mr. Macaulay had informed me not a week ago that he believed Mr. Disraeli would be delighted to act with the Foreign Secretary whom Lord John had discarded, and Lord Palmerston did not in any way indicate that he would be otherwise than delighted to act with Mr. Disraeli. . . .

Nothing, however, happened. No direct overtures were made at this moment; and to indirect overtures Palmerston only answered that he was content with his position. There was much to be said for waiting till the reassembling of Parliament, when the disposition of the various parties would be more defined.

To Lord Derby.

Private. HUGHENDEN, *Sept.* 5, 1852.—. . . Stanley, who is here still, harps upon reconstruction.

I look upon Parliamentary reconstruction as out of the question; but you have great external cards at your command—greater than any Minister ever yet had. Would Newcastle take India, and Canning Canada? You have also other things, if required. The Governor-Generalship of Australia—now a great post; Van Diemen's Land and Trinidad, both due or vacant.

After his letters to Talbot, the D. of Buccleugh would be the natural mediator, and his interference would not be displeasing to those with whom you are negotiating. It would save you the annoyance of a personal application and its possible mortifying results.

If successful, you would have a working majority of fifty; if it fail, provided the communication be carried on by the machinery I indicate, it would do us [no] harm.

If you act on this suggestion, I humbly advise that you should see the D. of Buccleugh yourself, and not write.

Mem. also that, irrespective of consolidating the Government, we are really terribly deficient in eminent administrators, and our party would be alike cheapened by continuing the present men or providing them with inefficient successors.

I hope you will be able to collect these hurried, but not hasty, hints.

The understanding on which the Peelites had supported the Government during the session, and on which the Liberals had eventually consented to allow necessary legislation to pass, was that the new Parliament should be called together before the end of the year; and that the Government should then produce at once their fiscal proposals, which were held in abeyance over the General Election. Disraeli, accordingly, as soon as his electoral campaign was finished, busied himself with preparations for his forthcoming Budget, during such time as could be spared from the general affairs of the Ministry. His autumn correspondence gives us evidences of his activity and of the trend of his thoughts. The most interesting, in many ways, of these letters were written to Lord Henry Lennox, a younger son of the Duke of Richmond, who had become member for Chichester in 1846, and continued to represent it for forty years. He was a bright and intelligent, but not highly educated, young man of fashion, who took a keen interest in politics. Disraeli was obviously much attracted by him, as he was wont to be attracted by a combination of youth, birth, smartness, and intelligence, and had put him in his own office as a Lord of the Treasury. It is clear from the correspondence that he imparted to him many confidences both as to his own political aspirations and as to the policy of the Government, and encouraged him to gird at Tory mediocrities whom he himself never suffered gladly. Henry Lennox, who had some of the Puckish qualities of George Smythe, talks, in his letters to his chief, of 'Walpole! the dear, the gentle Spencer!', of 'Pachy' as a 'cautious prig,' of Granby's 'incredible folly,' 'dogged obstinacy,' and 'pertinacious dunderheadism'; and even, in reference to a negotiation pending with the Vatican, of 'that dirty Pope.' This exuberance, which may have recalled memories of the *Letters of Runnymede*, far from shocking Disraeli, amused him, and he replied with great affection, and with little or no reproof.

To Lord Henry Lennox.

HUGHENDEN, *July* 18, 1852.

MY DEAR HENRY, — Assuming, which I think I may venture to do, that the poll to-morrow will be all right, I shall come up to town in the evening. The Cabinet, which I told the Captain to call on Tuesday, will be a sufficient excuse for not being present on the second day, and missing also the declaration, chairing, etc.

The Times sent down their best reporters on Friday, and conveyed my ideas, and almost my very expressions, to the world, instead of that incoherent rhodomontade which their provincial ally perpetrated at Newport.

Did you mark the leader in *The Times* yesterday on my Aylesbury speech? I thought it very significant. I have myself little doubt that, if I had been permitted to take the bold lead at once, and not have been forced back from the Budget position, *The Times* would never have deserted us, would have written us up, and that our returns would have been several seats better.

We framed an Opposition on Protection and Protestantism. When you commence your studies, and read *Coningsby*, which I will give you in a single volume, you will see how I have treated those exclusive and limited principles, clearly unfitted for a great and expanding country, of various elements, like this of ours. G. Bentinck would not stand Protestantism, and was cashiered in consequence, I believe, entirely by the influence of that master-mind, your friend, the Secretary at War. Notwithstanding all I said and did, they stuck to Protection till the country positively spat upon it. I tore away this millstone, but yielded reluctantly to the belief that the brother burthen, by a fortunate combination of circumstances, was to turn up trumps for us. It seems to me to have done us more harm than the South Sea house-bubble, for that was too absurd to achieve anything real — even mischief.

Utterly disregard what B[eresford] says about your Gladstone vote.[1] I am very glad you gave it. He is the only one of the Peelites between whom and myself there was some inkling of sympathy.[2] As for the rest, they may thank the *Morning Chronicle*, in a great measure, for their discomfiture,

[1] Lord Henry Lennox must have voted for Gladstone in his contest at Oxford University, when he was opposed by Dr. Bullock Marsham, the Warden of Merton.

[2] Gladstone, in his private correspondence about this time, was writing very differently of Disraeli. To Aberdeen, on Aug. 5, he was severe upon the 'unscrupulousness and second motives of Mr. Disraeli, at once the necessity of Lord Derby and his curse' (Morley's *Gladstone*, Bk. III., ch. 8).

which was, I believe, not under his influence, but rather under the judicious inspiration of Newcastle and Herbert. . . .

The nomination was a success. It was not in the Court, which you remember, but in the County Hall, three times at least the size, and seemed full of a turbulent and hostile audience: but I got them as still as the H. of C., and finally obtained almost an universal show of hands.

I am glad you are dull in my absence. I also feel lonely. . . .

Lennox reported from London, on August 6, a rumour, originating in the Peelite camp, that 'you intend to be so liberal as to break up the Conservative Government, and be received yourself into the bosom of the Progressive party.'

To Lord Henry Lennox.

HUGHENDEN, *Aug.* 7, 1852. — It was very kind of you to write to me, and most delightful to me to hear from you. Continual waterspouts have almost prevented me from leaving the house for five minutes, so I have worked very hard: indeed, have almost devoured all the papers I brought down for the autumnal gorge, and have greatly advanced many things. Work absorbs, or should absorb, one; nevertheless, I think very often of my young companion, and miss him sadly, for his presence to me is always a charm, and often a consolation.

The Speaker gives us a working majority of twenty, which will be increased, he adds, if there be anything approaching faction. As for what the Peelites intend to do, we must find out who the Peelites are: and as for what any men will do, three or four or six months hence, he is a bold one who, in this rapid age, will prophesy.

Many may be dead, who are now stumbling-blocks. By the bye, Dolly Vane ought to manage Durham, *vice* Granger, without much difficulty.[1]

As for myself, I consider that I am already 'in the bosom of the Progressive party.'

What you have done about the Press is very good. On this subject, always go directly to Stanley, who is master of it, and also knows every turn of my mind anent. You, my beloved, are a little fresh in supposing that your Phœnix[2] could

[1] T. C. Granger (Liberal), who had been elected at the head of the poll for Durham in July, died suddenly immediately afterwards, and Lord Adolphus Vane (Conservative) was returned at a by-election in December, but unseated on petition.

[2] Lennox had written: 'I have found a very clever fellow, who writes very well.'

choose his journal, and that the *Daily News*, incontinently, would permit him to uphold the great captain, and your graceless correspondent. . . .

To Lord Malmesbury.

HUGHENDEN, *Aug.* 13, 1852. — I return you Lord Cowley's confidential despatch. I am not disposed to reduce our duties on French brandies to obtain a reduction of their duties on our coals. We had better leave our mutual tariffs as they stand, unless the French are willing to treat these matters on a much more extensive scale. If they would reduce their duties on linen yarn, cottons, or iron, I should recommend our meeting them with reductions on their brandies and silks. The latter would be a great card for France. We ought now to be for as complete Free Trade as we can obtain, and let the English farmer, and the English landlord, too, buy the best and the cheapest silks for their wives and daughters.

In case anything is to be done in this respect, it should be done with as little knowledge of the Board of Trade as practicable. That office is filled with our enemies. Lord Cowley, therefore, should conduct the business entirely; or we should send some confidential and circumspect agent of our own.

It is useless now to vex ourselves about the Protectionist rock ahead. If this section exist, it can do nothing until the financial statement is made. Every expression of opinion on their side will be suspended until they have heard our financial measures. I confess I have no great fear of them, and I think they and their constituents will be satisfied.

This Fisheries affair is a bad business. Pakington's circular is not written with a thorough knowledge of the circumstances. He is out of his depth, more than three marine miles from shore.

These wretched Colonies will all be independent, too, in a few years, and are a millstone round our necks. If I were you, I would *push matters* with Fillmore, who has no interest to pander to the populace like Webster, and make an honourable and speedy settlement.[1]

The Fisheries dispute related to the encroachments of American fishermen upon Canadian and Newfoundland fishing-grounds — a question which has often disturbed Anglo-American relations. Pakington, by writing, shortly before a Presidential election, a perfectly justi-

[1] *Memoirs of an Ex-Minister*, under date.

fiable but imprudent despatch, had provoked Daniel Webster, the American Secretary of State, to the use of inflammatory language, and for a while the situation was critical. But Webster died in October, and Disraeli's advice to come to an arrangement with Fillmore, the outgoing President, was adopted with success. The petulant outburst about the 'wretched Colonies,' obviously inspired by the irritation of the moment, and scribbled in confidence to a Cabinet colleague, has sometimes been taken as an indication of Disraeli's real sentiments about the Empire. This superficial view is sufficiently disproved by the correspondence with Derby in the previous autumn, in which Disraeli urged the advisability of Colonial representation in the British Parliament, as well as by all his speeches on Colonial affairs. He did, indeed, fear for a moment, as he confessed in 1872, that the Radical policy of encouraging the Colonies to set up for themselves might be successful; but his own efforts were throughout directed to strengthening the bonds of Empire.

To Lord Derby.

Private. HUGHENDEN, *Aug.* 13, 1852.—. . . The Duke of Bedford, I hear, has had 'satisfactory communications' with D. of Newcastle, and says that Graham has agreed to serve under Lord John. This I expected. The Duke says also, I am told, that the only one he can make nothing of is Gladstone. . . .

My Budget greatly expands, and, I hope, matures, and, if we only had a majority to carry it, should give you the Government of this country as long as you liked. . . .

I have been reading my commissariat despatches from the Cape. The prospect is very gloomy. I have no confidence in our new General,[1] because, I observe, he has already changed his system and recurred to the already unsuccessful method of Sir H. Smith. This war is a terrible running sore in our finances. All these Generals of ours are too old. . . .

The Junior Lord of the Treasury, kept in London in the middle of August to transact official business, grew dispirited under these troubles about public affairs in

[1] Sir George Cathcart, who succeeded Sir Harry Smith, brought the Kaffir War to a successful conclusion in March, 1853.

America and Africa, aggravated by the prospect of a very wet harvest. What about his chief's expected Budget? 'Do not suppose that my faith in you and in the great scheme is wavering! No such thing! I am only considering the numerous difficulties you will overcome.' He proceeds to report a rumour that the party whom he calls 'the real Peelites' are going to acknowledge one whom he calls, in his irresponsible way, 'that pompous, becoroneted fool, Newcastle.'

To Lord Henry Lennox.

[? *Aug.* 17, 1852.]—Excuse my frankness, but I do not wish, too hastily, to look upon our friendship as the last of my illusions.

I shall be in D[owning] S[treet] to-morrow by two o'clock. I apprehend that my morning will be very much engaged, but I hope we may dine together, alone, at the Coventry.

Politics when we meet: I will only say now that, having vanquished a Sir Robert Peel, I am not going to be upset by a D. of Newcastle.

Lennox got his leave towards the end of the month, and went to Scotland, taking *Coningsby* to read on the way. From the train he wrote an ecstatic letter: 'How true! how painfully true! a picture of human nature! and what language!' and added: 'It strikes me . . . that our position as a party is, or has been for the last six months, nearly identical with the Conservative party in 1834, as described in the fifth chapter of the second book.'[1]

To Lord Henry Lennox.

HUGHENDEN, *Sept.* 1, 1852.—I cannot let another day close without thanking you for your letter, but I am so tired that I can only tell you that I love you.

I have had a great pressure of business this last week, and especially these last three or four days, and have sometimes had to work nine hours a day, till my hand and brain seemed both exhausted.

Write to me very often, and tell me how you are. I am amused about *Coningsby*, and am rather surprised that you never read it before.

[1] The chapter about the Tamworth manifesto of 1834; see Vol. II., pp. 289, 290.

Sir Robert Peel was so taken with it that he shut himself up a whole day in his dressing-room, and locked up the book when he went out, lest his family should get it. His son, the present Sir Robert Peel, told my wife this at the time. He wrote a letter to his sister, Mrs. Dawson, about it, which she showed me, and there he said what charmed him most were the descriptions.

Lord John Russell read *Coningsby* every evening to his wife, as she confessed to Madame Lionel de Rothschild, my informant. Madame R. asked what parts he liked best, expecting, of course, the political disquisitions, or Tadpole and Taper, at the least. Lady John said, 'The love scenes.' Johnny was often moved to tears, she added, while reading them.

Don't mention all this, told me by a woman in strict confidence; but I think it rather amusing: the two great politicians reading a political novel, and only reading it because it was a political novel — and we, domestically and familiarly, learning that one admired most the descriptions, and the other the passages of tenderness and passion.

If you ever have inclination or power to read another book — for reading, I suspect, is not your forte — you must manage to read *Sybil*,[1] and especially *Tancred*. I suppose there is a circulating library even at Johnny Groats, and if there be one, you are sure to find both or one of these books there.

I am very troubled about the Chairmanship. W[ilson] Patten will not take it — for private reasons — tho' he will vote for our man. But what man? Some say Newdegate. I don't think he would take it, but I am sure the House would not take him. They would think it as bad as voting for a five-shilling fixed duty.

I have encouraging reports from Rome.

My letter has swollen.

The appointment of Chairman of Committees in the new Parliament greatly exercised Derby and Disraeli. About the Speakership there was no question, when once the idea of putting Walpole in the Chair, to make room for Palmerston, had been abandoned. Shaw-Lefevre had been Speaker in three Parliaments, and by his dignity, courtesy, and tact, had endeared himself to the House. He was, of course, a Whig, and, if he were adopted by the

[1] When Lennox read *Sybil*, he wrote (Oct. 26) to Disraeli: 'I do hope we shall carry out the delightfully liberal, unrestricted views advocated so ably in its pages.'

Conservatives, was sure of re-election without opposition. For the Chairmanship, as the Government were still in a minority, it was important to nominate a man who would be acceptable to opponents as well as to friends. Derby was very anxious to secure for the post an old friend, who had been his colleague for years in the representation of North Lancashire, who had acted rather with the Peelites than with the Protectionists, and who was equally respected in the County Palatine and in the House of Commons, John Wilson Patten, afterwards created, on Disraeli's advice, Lord Winmarleigh. For long Patten refused, to the despair of the leaders, who could not think of any other suitable candidate. 'It would be a terrible thing,' wrote Disraeli, 'to start with being in a minority in almost the first week of a new Parliament; it would be like a paralytic stroke in youth.' Finally Patten yielded to Derby's importunities.

To Lord John Russell.

Confidential. *Aug.* 31, 1852.

MY DEAR LORD,—A new Parliament and an inexperienced leader offer rather perilous prospects, and you will therefore not be surprised that I have done my best to mitigate these difficulties by requesting Mr. Lefevre to allow himself again to be put in nomination for the Chair.

I think it very desirable, under existing circumstances, that the political party with which Mr. Lefevre is in connection should be represented in the proceedings, and, while he is proposed by some gentleman of standing on the Ministerial side, the seconder of the motion should be a follower of your lordship.

This course may be unusual, but it is not, I believe, irregular; and I think it would add to the authority with which Mr. Lefevre would resume the duties he has fulfilled so well.

I think the seconder should be a member of moderate opinions—that is to say, of Whig opinions. This is due to Mr. Lefevre himself, and I hope, also, that you will agree with me that it is expedient in the conduct of the House generally that we should encourage as much as possible the ancient connections and names.

I hope you will not think me arrogant in making these suggestions, for I make them in unaffected deference to your judgment, to which I am always inclined to bow, and which on several occasions has assisted me by its kind experience. Indeed, my powerful reason for thus troubling you is to beg you, if you do not disapprove of these views, to favor me by turning in your mind and fixing upon the person best qualified, in your opinion, to fulfil the office of seconder of the Speaker, and whom I would then address, mentioning that I did so with your approbation.

I hope Lady John is well, and all your hearth, and I beg you to believe me, with very sincere respect, your lordship's obliged and faithful servant, B. DISRAELI.

P.S. — Mr. Lefevre mentioned to me in confidence that Mr. Cayley had written to him offering to propose him, but Mr. Lefevre replied that the matter rested with the Government.

From Lord John Russell.

Private. THE GART, *Sept.* 3, 1852.

MY DEAR SIR, — I have received your letter of the 31st, and hasten to answer it.

I agree with you that it is desirable to have the mover and seconder of the Speaker of different political parties, and I acted on this opinion long ago, when I proposed to Lord Castlereagh to second the nomination of Mr. Manners Sutton.

The persons who occur to me as the most fit for seconders are Lord R. Grosvenor and Mr. Pendarves. Of these two I should prefer Lord Robert, as I believe Mr. Pendarves moved or seconded once before. But you may have reasons against both of which I am ignorant. In that case I will think of some others.

When you can make public your intentions respecting a successor to Mr. Bernal,[1] I shall be glad to know them. But I do not ask to be informed before you are in a condition to let your view be generally known.

Many thanks for your inquiries for Lady John. She is much the better for the Highland air, and all my family thrive upon it. I beg my compliments to Mrs. Disraeli, and remain, yours faithfully, J. RUSSELL.

To Lord John Russell.

DOWNING STREET, *Oct.* 9, 1852.

MY DEAR LORD, — I have written to Lord Robert Grosvenor, as I thought the selection most happy, so much so, indeed, that I have somewhat reconstructed my own arrangements to secure his co-operation. I had originally intended to have asked Lord Hotham to have proposed Mr. Lefevre, but it

[1] Chairman of Committees in the last Parliament.

occurred to me that two lords might be held a little too fine, and I have therefore modified the scheme by infusing a little democracy into the proceedings (to please you), but in the Conservative shape of Sir John Yarde-Buller.[1]

We shall recommend Mr. Wilson Patten for the Chairmanship. I should be happy if this proposition were to pass off as tranquilly as that of Mr. Lefevre. Unless the circumstances are very urgent, the choice of one to preside over our discussions is hardly, I think, the happiest conjuncture for a party struggle.

We shall have plenty of opportunities for crossing our swords without seeking our battle of Edge Hill in the Chairmanship of Ways and Means. But I feel it is presumption in me to say as much as this.

I beg my compliments to Lady John, and I remain, yours very faithfully, B. DISRAELI.

From Lord John Russell.

DOUGLAS'S HOTEL, EDINBURGH, *Oct.* 12, 1852.

MY DEAR SIR, — I think you are fortunate in having obtained the consent of Mr. Wilson Patten to serve in the Chair of the Ways and Means Committee. I cannot say there will be no contest, but I shall do nothing to encourage it, and shall be disposed to wait patiently till your real colours are hoisted. If it is the broad banner of Free Trade, I shall rejoice to see your standard. — I remain, yours faithfully, J. RUSSELL.

That broad banner it was certainly Disraeli's intention to hoist. The mere prospect of his financial measures, on a Free Trade basis, excited his young aristocratic disciple to quite a lyrical outburst : —

From Lord Henry Lennox.

GORDON CASTLE, *Saturday, Sept.* 11. — . . . I wonder if I am wrong, but I really feel as if your Budget would create a *furore.* Your career will be like William Pitt's; you will conciliate the Court, you will become the first Englishman of your time, and will make England the first country in the world. You will efface party distinctions by the introduction of a colossal measure of financial reform, as he did by the victories of our troops; and you will, like him, cajole the old Tory squires and make them give a hearty assent to all that they have passed their life in opposing. At least, such is my hope and *belief.* . . .

[1] It was Robert Palmer, M.P. for Berks, who eventually proposed Shaw-Lefevre; Lord Robert Grosvenor, as arranged, was the seconder.

To Lord Henry Lennox.

HUGHENDEN, *Sept.* 16, 1852. — Your letter was most agreeable, interesting, and, I need not add, most welcome.

I think your life a very wise one.

Although I have never slaughtered the antlered monarchs, I have endeavoured to describe them in some verses which I wrote for Mr. Scrope,[1] and which he printed in his *Deer-Stalking* — a capital work, and the happiest effusion of the gentleman littérateur which we have had this century.

The author was the most accomplished gentleman I ever knew, quite conscious that his fathers lived in the days of the Plantagenets, yet easy and polished. He was as great with the salmon as with the stag, having written, like a master, on both sports. He had a very happy pen, was a poet, a very fine scholar and linguist, and, as an amateur artist, superior, I think, to his friend and rival, Sir George Beaumont. He had also that rarest of talents — he could talk well. Add to this a very handsome person and ten thousand a year — so I think he drew a prize in the great lottery of life.

I am in mourning for him now, and wear my weeds sincerely, notwithstanding he left my wife, his kinswoman, a legacy, and me a picture, which I shall hang up in my dining-room at D.S., where I hope it may long remain.

The greater death, which all are talking and thinking of, has brought us a shoal of patronage; but I question whether its tendency, otherwise, is to strengthen the Government. The Duke was very warmly with us of late, and still exercised a beneficial influence for those he wished to serve.

Stanley is staying here, off and on. I have not seen him since the death, but now expect him.

Adieu, my dear Henry, and write to me whenever you can and like: even a line is pleasant from those we love.

The greater death, that of the Duke of Wellington, took place at Walmer Castle on September 14. Serious as the loss was to the party of order, Disraeli, as Chancellor of the Exchequer, took comfort — as it turned out, prematurely — in one reflection. He wrote to his Parliamentary Secretary of the Treasury: 'The death of the Duke ought to be the removal of an obstacle to military economy. Keep your eye awake to all this. Lord Hardinge [the Duke's successor as Commander-in-Chief], I fear, is very prone to expenditure. He must be met sternly.'

[1] See Vol. II., p. 56.

Two months later[1] it fell to Disraeli's lot to deliver a panegyric on the Duke in the House of Commons. The task had rather weighed upon him. He had written to his wife that he was 'a little disturbed by the Duke of Wellington, all the world expecting a great speech from me, and I at least resolved that I will make one without the word "duty" appearing.' The speech was very 'eloquent,' as Russell, who followed him and said he did not want to add a single word, called it; but it was rather laboured, and it has become notorious as containing perhaps the most striking of the many acts of plagiarism charged against Disraeli. It is often referred to as if the whole speech was borrowed; in actual fact, the passage in question is less than a quarter of the whole. He was describing the qualtities necessary to a great general, and he did so with ideas, and to a large extent in words, taken from an old article by Thiers on Marshal Gouvion de St. Cyr in a French review. The article was published in 1829, and reproduced in the *Morning Chronicle* in 1848. The discovery of the plagiarism was made by the *Globe*, Palmerston's organ, which printed speech and article in parallel columns. Thereupon, to quote *The Times* of a few days later, 'a shout of "Stop thief!" was raised, and a whole pack of jealous *littérateurs* were immediately on the scent of their offending, and perhaps too successful, brother.' Not all of his brethren of the pen took this ungenerous attitude. George Smythe, who had written the article in the *Morning Chronicle*, explained that Disraeli had himself called his attention to the passage from Thiers many years before, so that, instead of Disraeli being indebted to the *Morning Chronicle*, the *Morning Chronicle* was indebted to Disraeli. Monckton Milnes offered his services in a friendly way to put the matter straight:—

From Richard Monckton Milnes.

16, UPPER BROOK STREET, *Saturday* [*Nov.* 20, 1852].—Though politically opposed, we are literary *collaborateurs*. If

[1] Nov. 15.

you think it worth while to let me know anything of the circumstances of the passages from Thiers that made part of your speech on the Duke, which you would like me to state, authoritatively or unauthoritatively, in the society in which I live, I shall be glad to do so, as a plain matter of justice.

To Richard Monckton Milnes.

At Dinner. GROSVENOR GATE, *Nov.* 20, 1852. — Your note is like yourself; I really think you have the best disposition in the world.

The facts are these: A good many years ago — perhaps (I shudder to say it) a quarter of a century — I read the passage in question (*not passages*) in a defunct French journal, a sort of Gallic *Quarterly Review* — *Revue Trimestre*, I think — set up, I fancy, by the Broglie clique.

The way I knew it was that it had contained a review (and a review in French!) of *Vivian Grey*, which, of course, I thought was the finest thing in the world. It began: 'La carrière du roman politique est ouverte en Angleterre,' etc. I could repeat it now, after five-and-twenty years.

I never had heard then of M. Thiers, nor had anyone else. We were both of us then equally obscure.

The passage in question seized upon me, as passages in Mr. Burke, for example, which I have not read for a long time. It was engraven on my memory, though, of late years, I don't particularly remember to have recalled either its sentiments or its language.

Association of ideas brought it back when musing for a moment, amid the hurry and strife of affairs, over a late solemn occasion, and I summoned it from the cavern of my mind. Unfortunately, the spirit was too faithful.

Conceive my astonishment — I ought to say my horror — when I read the article in the *Globe*. Instead of cribbing it from the *Morning Chronicle*, the very fact of my having seen it in that journal would, of course, have prevented my using it.

Literary men may comprehend these psychological curiosities: the world never can. I appreciate your friendship, but I must submit to my fate. I am a Plagiary, but I must bear the mortification with temper, and not, at least, be Sir Fretful.

Milnes, or Disraeli himself, must have communicated this explanation to Delane, as *The Times* embodied it in a leading article on the following Monday, and treated the whole matter as trivial, save only as illustrating the absurd jealousy of literary men. 'Why are authors to drag down every one of their fraternity who may happen to become a Minister of State? . . . Authors will never have their proper consideration, in the face of dukes, millionaires, squires, and prize cattle, till they are loyal to their own body.' One of the most popular authors of the day, Bulwer Lytton, rallied promptly to his friend, and even sketched out a speech by which Disraeli should defend himself if he were challenged in the House of Commons! A 'dull friend in such cases,' he wrote in a hurried note, 'is often more suggestive than one's own bothered personalities.' No such direct reference was made in the House as compelled Disraeli to defend himself; but the curious will find in the Appendix[1] the passage from the speech, the passage from the French review, and Lytton's ingenious explanation. Most people will be content with Disraeli's own confession and avoidance in his letter to Milnes, and will think that, like greater literary men who have been hardened plagiarists, he improved what he borrowed. His reputation, however, suffered at the time, and the innumerable jokes in *Punch* and elsewhere did him and his colleagues no good.

As appeared from the letter to Malmesbury on August 13, Disraeli cherished the hope of signalising his Budget by a comprehensive commercial treaty with France. Such a scheme would carry out his leading ideas both in foreign policy and in finance. British foreign policy, he maintained, should be founded on a thorough understanding with France; foreign trade should rest on commercial treaties concluded on a reciprocal basis. Thanks to Louis Napoleon's friendship for Malmesbury and Malmesbury's tactful management, good relations were now established with France, in spite of the unmeasured licence which the British Press permitted itself to use about the author of the *coup d'état*, and in spite of the alarm felt in many quarters in England owing to the impending revival of the Napoleonic Empire. Those relations would be strengthened and rendered

[1] Appendix C.

permanent, and the trade of both countries would materially benefit, if the tariffs of the two countries were, by agreement, revised in each other's favour; but Disraeli insisted that the revision must be general, and not limited to one article, such as coal.

To Lord Derby.

D. S., *Oct.* 6, 1852.—I have just received a despatch from Lord Cowley, dated yesterday (5th Oct.), in reply to mine of a few days back, written at the request of Lord Malmesbury, in which Lord Cowley strongly expresses the willingness of the French Government to enter into a treaty of commerce on the broader basis, which I had indicated.

M. D[rouyn] de Lhuys was to leave Paris the 4th to join the President, and will not be back before the 12th; but he means to talk the whole question over with the President, who, he assures Ld. Cowley, is most anxious to improve the commercial relations of France with Gt. Britain. Ld. C. is to see him directly on his return, and will then write to me again.

The French Minister wishes that we should have a list prepared of the articles on which we are anxious to see the duties reduced.

Ld. Cowley adds that he gave him at once to understand, as I had desired, that the linen yarns of Ireland and other manufactures of that country would be an indispensable point with H.M. Government.

If we can manage all this, it will be a dainty dish for the meeting of Parliament. I could easily modify my scheme to catch this breeze. . . .

For awhile the negotiations proceeded favourably, and Disraeli arranged to send Sir Thomas Fremantle,[1] the Chairman of the Board of Customs, to Paris to advise Cowley. But the Board of Trade pointed out early in November that any reduction of duty conceded to France could be immediately claimed by Portugal, Spain, and Sicily; while any concession to any one of the three last could be claimed by either of the other two, but not by France. This and other difficulties it was not found possible to adjust in the short time available before the Budget, which could not be postponed beyond the be-

[1] Afterwards 1st Lord Cottesloe.

ginning of December. Disraeli had the political imagination to conceive, but not the time to mature, or the political forces to carry into effect, a great scheme of the kind. It was left to Cobden and Gladstone, eight years later, to win the credit of negotiating and conducting through Parliament a commercial treaty with France.

Besides French commercial negotiations, the Kaffir war, and the Fisheries dispute, other imperial and foreign questions which occupied Disraeli's mind during the autumn were the Burmese War and our relations with the Vatican. The Burmese War had been undertaken by Lord Dalhousie after a long series of grave complaints against the treatment meted out by the King of Ava to British subjects. Rangoon had been taken after obstinate resistance, and the question arose as to the extent to which hostilities should be carried and territory annexed.

To Lord Derby.

[*Aug.* 31, 1852.]—I write you hurriedly, but on a subject on which I have long and deeply reflected. Although I attach no authority to the statement, I see by the mail just arrived that we are to march to Ava. I cannot forget that Herries wrote to me that the mail of the 8th Sept. ought to carry out definite instructions on this subject. I hope, therefore, that you will not think these lines intrusive, for, irrespective of its being my duty humbly to offer you any suggestions which may occur on subjects of general policy, I cannot help feeling that the question at issue is one which particularly concerns my department.

I know there are authorities who maintain that Oriental States will never observe treaties by which they have lost territory, and that if the work be not done thoroughly it will have to be done again. There may be, and is, much truth in this general principle, and yet it may be a dangerous one to act upon.

Russia does not act upon this principle with regard to Persia; there in all her wars she is successful, yet she conquers in detail. She has pursued the same policy in other instances.

Remember Afghanistan; these general principles were very rife at the beginning of that war. I remember Sir James Hogg, a mere Calcutta lawyer, whose knowledge of Indian politics (now not inconsiderable) has been subsequently gained [in Leadenhall Street], boastfully exclaimed at the time that the Hindoocoosh was the natural boundary of our Empire. Yet what a rash and ignorant dogma! And what disasters followed its adoption!

I am not satisfied that, if we try to do it 'thoroughly' we shall succeed. We may take Ava as we took Caubul, and yet not retain it.

The mere appropriation of Pegu consolidates our territory, and enables us to pursue subsequent enterprises if necessary — and they may not be necessary for a quarter of a century — with comparative economy and ease. Admitting even that we shall hereafter have to commence a third Burmese war, I maintain that it is a preferable risk to the prosecution of the present one on a scale of general conquest.

But the ground on which I object to this project of complete conquest is a ground of finance.

The state of Indian finance already occasions me great disquietude. The Indian revenue has already a deficit of one million and a half sterling. A prolonged war must increase it. We cannot distinguish Indian from English finance ultimately: we cannot permit the Indian Government to be bankrupt. I need not point out the inevitable consequences on our Exchequer. . . .

The D. of W. is for complete conquest, but His Grace is not sufficiently impressed with the great fact that finance is now the most important element of our Indian Empire.

Disraeli's letter did not reach Derby till after the Prime Minister had sanctioned the despatch prepared by Herries, the President of the Board of Control, and by the Secret Committee, authorising further offensive operations. These, however, were not carried out on the scale which Disraeli deprecated, and no attempt was made to march to Ava, as Dalhousie, the Governor-General, in spite of exhortations to a forward policy from home, contented himself with capturing and holding Prome and Pegu, and annexing to the British Empire merely the Lower Province. Thus Disraeli's policy was in effect adopted, and his prediction that subsequent operations might not be found necessary for a quarter of a century was more than fulfilled. The next Burmese war, which resulted in the conquest of Upper Burma, did not break out till 1885.

Lennox, in one of his autumn letters, told Disraeli that there was a report in the Carlton that Sir Henry Bulwer was at Rome 'to try and make terms with the Pope about Bulls and about Ireland.' Rumour was not far out in this case. In spite of his jeers at Minto's mission in 1847, Disraeli found, in office, that good relations with the Vatican were desirable, especially for the Government of Ireland. The Conservative party had beaten the Protestant drum in the elections even louder than Russell and the Whigs, and were regarded in Rome as the uncompromising enemies of the Roman Catholics. Disraeli had never been easy in this situation, and, with Malmesbury's assent, asked Sir Henry Bulwer, then Minister at Florence, to go to Rome, and see what he could effect with the Pope. Bulwer, who, besides being an old friend, was very grateful to Disraeli for defending him when he was Minister in Madrid in 1848, threw himself willingly into the scheme. He did not, perhaps, achieve much; but at least he succeeded in altering the disposition of the Roman Government towards Disraeli and his colleagues from hostile suspicion to friendliness. Further, he received assurances that the Pope and Cardinal Antonelli, his Minister, strongly disapproved of violent language and political agitation in the Irish clergy, and would willingly restrain the extreme party in Ireland, were they not afraid of turning its violence against themselves. Under a Government like that of England, 'which permits everything to be said, and almost everything to be done,' they could expect little support in any efforts they might make beyond the strictest line of prudence.

To Sir Henry Bulwer.

[*Latter half of September*, 1852.]—Affairs in general are proceeding here favorably: the Government is daily strengthening, and the dangers to it which are spoken of are only on the surface, and are, in fact, already dissipated, though the common mind, as usual, does not recognise accomplished results.

I wish I could speak as easily of the embarrassments in embryo, and which relate to the country in which you now reside.

It is impossible to conceal from myself that the religious feeling of England is in a state which may lead to vast and fatal consequences — at least, in the estimation of those who desired a mild and enlightened administration of affairs.

The extreme indiscretions of the High Church party in England and the violence of the Roman Catholic priesthood in Ireland have combined to operate a strange and, even five years ago, inconceivable revolution in the public mind here, and it is just as well that you should be aware of this fact.

As regards our Roman Catholic fellow-subjects, this is not the England which you knew when you were in the House of Commons, nor is it the England, even, of the last years of Sir Robert Peel's Government.

Everything is really different from what it appears on the surface. Instead of the continuance of Lord Derby's Government being a circumstance hostile to the rights and privileges of our Roman Catholic population, the existence of that Government is at this moment the only cause which prevents an eruption of feeling against Roman Catholicism, such as this century at least has not witnessed.

You know what have ever been my views on this subject. They are such as every wise statesman would wish to be permitted to cherish.

When our Government was formed, I myself insisted on the nomination of Lord Naas, who, though a Protestant nobleman, was the representative of a Roman Catholic constituency — the county of Kildare — and who is a supporter of the endowment of Maynooth, to the office of Irish Secretary instead of a gentleman otherwise highly qualified for it, but of extreme Protestant opinions. I carried this appointment of Lord Naas with great difficulty, and as a necessary foundation for the system which I intended to pursue. I am informed it was very agreeable to the Roman Catholic leaders in the House of Commons, especially Mr. Keogh and Mr. Moore. Yet the moment it was made and Lord Naas vacated his seat on his acceptance of office in March last, the Roman Catholic priesthood rose against him in mass and expelled him from the county. The consequence of this has been that the policy I upheld in the Cabinet naturally received a blow from which it has never recovered. Hence all the hesitation and unsatisfactory discussions about Maynooth which took place in the last months of the Parliament, and many other disagreeable circumstances too obvious to require notice.

All our arguments in favor of a mild and friendly system,

which had made a due impression in the quarters to which they were addressed, were answered in a manner which seemed to prove their utter fallaciousness, and I now more than fear that, if some favourable change does not occur, no Cabinet will be permitted to govern England for any length of time which does not adopt repression of the Roman Catholic system as the basis of its policy.

It will be strange if for the mild wisdom of a Conservative Cabinet is substituted in this country a *soi-disant* Protestant Government sympathising with the Republicans of Rome; yet, believe me, stranger things have happened.

Even your friendly visit to the Eternal City is looked upon with a very evil eye, and the accounts of your proceedings which appear in the journals, though often exaggerated, and sometimes incorrect, have done no inconsiderable mischief.

The death of the Duke will probably occasion Parliament to be called together a week earlier than was contemplated.

Disraeli did not permit the ingratitude with which his efforts to introduce a conciliatory policy for Ireland were met to divert his course. We know from *Lord George Bentinck* and other sources how deeply he was impressed by the Report of the Devon Commission. He was anxious to carry out its recommendations, and he encouraged the Irish Law Officers, Napier and Whiteside, to prepare Bills which should constitute a complete code for Irish land. When Parliament met, the Queen's Speech announced 'a liberal and generous policy,' and Napier introduced four Bills: to give limited owners power to make improvements and charge them upon the inheritance; to extend the leasing powers of Irish proprietors; to permit limited owners to enter into contracts with tenants; and to give compensation to tenants for improvements, and retrospective compensation. It was not easy to secure the consent of Irish proprietors or of a Conservative Cabinet to these measures; but the principal opposition came from Sharman Crawford's new Tenant-Right party, who considered they did not go far enough, and introduced a Bill of their own. Disraeli hoped he had pacified them by arranging, at the cost of some internal friction in the Government, to send the Tenant Right Bill, along with Napier's Bills, to a Select Committee. The Tenant Right party, however, irritated perhaps by Derby's strong opposition to the principle of their measure, and also by the proposal to extend the Income Tax to Ireland, assisted in ejecting the Government from office; but they did not thereby avoid the Income Tax, nor did they receive from the succeeding Government even that compensation for improvements which Napier's code provided for. Disraeli maintained in the debates of 1870, that, had the Bills of 1852 been accepted and passed into law, there would have been no need for Gladstone's heroic legislation.

Disraeli, as became a man of letters, was very sensible of the duties of Government to literature, science, and the arts, and in his brief first term of office he took a keen interest in the Prince Consort's scheme for a great scientific and artistic institution at South Kensington. Derby wrote on May 31: 'I have been to-day for above an hour with the Prince, who wants us to take off his hands . . . about 21 acres of land which he has bought with the surplus money of the Commission [for the Exhibition of 1851], and which if we will purchase for a National Gallery, he will be able to buy largely in addition to complete a great scheme for collecting together various scientific establishments.' He sent Disraeli a draft plan of the South Kensington Buildings then suggested by the Prince.

To Lord Derby.

HOUSE OF COMMONS, *Friday morning* [*June* 4]. — I return you the draft report. The plan is worthy of Caliph Vathek. All we want is an architect, or architects, worthy of the vast occasion.

Were the case well put forward, I should not despair of kindling some enthusiasm in the House of Commons and carrying a good vote. The prestige of the Prince's taste and success would greatly aid us; the only difficulty is the prevalent feeling that no public edifice can be raised in this country which is not a failure, or a job, or both. Let us hope, however, that we have arrived at the end of such mortifications, and that the contemplated creation will redeem and sustain the taste and genius of the country. . . .

Disraeli wrote under the influence of the feelings provoked by the new Houses of Parliament recently opened. We are now accustomed to this pile, and dwell rather on its more admirable parts, such as the two fine towers; but the contemporary opinion was mainly one of condemnation, and Disraeli had even jestingly said, in a discussion in the House of Commons on Barry's building, that the low standard of architecture in this country was due to the fact that no architect had ever been shot, like Admiral Byng, *pour encourager les autres.* The Prince's plan was to establish the National Gallery on that part of the South Kensington site which faces Hyde Park, and, after several interviews with him, Disraeli consented to afford help from the Treasury. In December Disraeli moved and obtained a vote of the House of Commons of £150,000 towards the purchase of land at Kensington Gore; but the Ministry went out, and the Bill for removing the National Gallery to the new site was defeated on its introduction in 1856. Disraeli's action procured him an invitation, after the fall of the Ministry, to join the Commissioners of the Exhibition of 1851: —

From the Prince Albert.

WINDSOR CASTLE, *Jan.* 22, 1853.

MY DEAR MR. DISRAELI,—Considering the part which you took in obtaining from the House of Commons the grant founded upon the Report of the Commissioners for the Exhibition of 1851, the pledges which you gave to the House in your speech, and the warm interest with which you took up the plan for bringing arts and sciences more directly to bear upon our productive industry, I thought it of great importance that you should join our Commission as one of its members. The object of this letter is to ask you whether you would allow me to propose your name for election at our next meeting, on Tuesday next. I have ascertained the concurrence in my views of some of the most important members of our body, and cannot doubt, therefore, of its assent.

Should you be willing to accept my proposal and to trust so far to my preliminary assurance as to call at the Commission Room at the Palace of Westminster at ¼ before 12 on Tuesday, I feel sure that your presence would be very useful, as we are going to discuss the position of the Commission in relation to the Government and the late grant.—Ever yours truly, ALBERT.

The consideration of Disraeli's Irish policy and of his relation to the arts has diverted us from the main stream of politics. As the October Cabinets and the session approached, his frame of mind was hopeful. He wrote to his wife on October 8: 'I think things look well, though, to all appearances, the Waterloo will take place immediately on our meeting. The whole weight, therefore, must necessarily fall on me, as it will be finance. However, I am in good heart.' Serious difficulties, however, soon arose. On the one hand, it became evident that the French commercial treaty could not be obtained—at any rate in time; and, on the other, that more money would be required for the national defences. Both the Court and the public were alarmed about the projects of Louis Napoleon. Russia was busy on the Continent, arranging for a coalition against him, and did her best, but in vain, to induce England to join. She did not forget, we may be sure, that a good understanding with England would also contribute to her designs upon Turkey.

Shortly after the formation of the Government (wrote Disraeli many years afterwards), Baron Brunnow, the Russian Ambassador, proposed to Lord Derby an alliance between England and Russia, offensive and defensive. Lord Derby at once rejected the proposition. It was never brought before the Cabinet; but it was made. It should be remembered the position of France was then very menacing; the French Empire was nearly hatched. We had good information as to Louis Napoleon's (then President of the Republic for ten years) intentions on this head. A month before the imperial declaration, a drawing of Louis Napoleon in full imperial robes and paraphernalia was entrusted to a lithographic artist, with positive instructions to take off only one impression. One, however, was sent to me by a secret agent. I possess it now.

To the Continent a French Empire, with a Napoleon on the throne, seemed to foreshadow a repetition of the long years of war which were only terminated by Moscow and Leipzig and Waterloo. Russia, Austria, and Prussia came to an understanding as to common action in case the treaties of 1815 were threatened. King Leopold, whose kingdom had been, and, if war broke out, would probably again be, the cockpit of Europe, was naturally foremost in spreading the alarm and infecting his relatives at the English Court. One man in England, who knew the character and appreciated the position of the new Napoleon better than any other statesman, resolutely opposed the general view. Malmesbury told his Sovereign and his colleagues, and has recorded in his diary, that Louis Napoleon's object at that time was 'to gain and secure the alliance with England and consolidate his position with the Great Powers by a pacific policy.' He was perfectly right; but it is difficult to deny that the Queen also had reason on her side when she wrote to Derby on October 23: 'The Queen is no alarmist, but thinks that, the necessity of our attending to our defences once having been proved and admitted by Parliament and two successive Governments, we should not relax in our efforts until the plans then devised are thoroughly carried out.' Both the Admiralty and the War Office pressed for increases; and just before the session opened Disraeli received his first command to stay with his Sovereign at Windsor, where Her Majesty and the Prince urged on him the immense importance of complying with the demands of the military departments. The discussion with the Prince lasted for two hours and a half.

To Mrs. Disraeli.

WINDSOR CASTLE, *Nov.* 3, 1852.—A most successful and satisfactory visit. A very large dinner-party yesterday: the Duke and Duchess of Nemours, Duchess of Kent, etc.

Successful and satisfactory as the visit may have been in some respects, Disraeli came away in very low spirits. He 'ridiculed the panic,' Malmesbury tells us; and saw, in consequence of it, the balance of that Budget, on which the fortunes of the Ministry and the party depended, completely upset. He was always alive to the necessity of adequate national defences, but could not agree that a special effort was necessary at a moment when, as he rightly thought, no special danger threatened, and when nothing but a popular and successful Budget could keep the Government in power. However, the Prime Minister and the Cabinet supported the demands of the Court and of the services, and Disraeli, however dispirited, resolutely set himself to alter his arrangements to suit them.

The Court steadily kept up its pressure. On November 13 the Queen wrote strongly to Derby on 'the necessity of referring,' in the financial statement, 'to our defenceless state, and the necessity of a *large* outlay, to protect us from foreign attack.' Disraeli assured Her Majesty in reply, on November 14, that, in making the financial arrangements, he had left a very large margin for the coming year (April 1853–54), 'which will permit the fulfilment of all your Majesty's wishes with respect to the increased defence of the country, as he gathered them from your Majesty's gracious expressions, and also from the suggestions which afterwards, in greater detail, His Royal Highness the Prince deigned to make to him. The Chancellor of the Exchequer will deeply consider the intimation graciously made in your Majesty's letter to Lord Derby, as to the tone on this subject to be adopted in the House of Commons, and he will endeavour in this, and in all respects, to fulfil your Majesty's pleasure.' On the same day the Queen expressed her satisfaction in a letter to Disraeli, repeated that the need was '*very* urgent,' and said that Malmesbury, who had talked with the Prince on the subject, would communicate further with Derby and Disraeli on his return.[1]

Some ten days later Derby wrote that he wished to see Disraeli on the subject of '*immediate* naval preparation, about which the Queen is very urgent.' Could he see his way to providing for 5,000 extra seamen and 1,500 marines?

[1] *Queen Victoria's Letters.*

To Lord Derby.

GROSVENOR GATE, 11 *o'clock, Tuesday* [*Nov.* 23].— . . . What I have agreed to do with reference to defence was to carry into effect the complete wishes of Her Majesty and the Prince. I promised to do this, and, as far as I am concerned, I have done it. These arrangements include five thousand seamen and *two* thousand artillerymen. Hardinge only asked for one thousand, but, having told Her Majesty and the Prince that the plan submitted to me at Windsor should be completely carried into effect, I told Hardinge that I thought *two* thousand preferable. I have promised nothing about the Marines; the Prince never mentioned them or included them in his written memoranda. From what I have gathered, I have reason to believe that such augmentation is more than questionable. . . .

If the financial prospect was overclouded, in other ways the Ministerial outlook was not good. Certainly Ministers were not unpopular, and, as Greville noted, they had got 'the whole body of the agriculturists, all the Church, and a large proportion of the wealthy middle classes,' on their side; but their chief asset had been the disunion of the Opposition. Russell, who through his mistakes both as Minister and as leader of Opposition had lost ground with all sections of the Liberals, had hitherto persisted in maintaining his claim to the first place in the next Government. So long as he took this view, neither Palmerston nor the Peelites would join heartily in any attack on the existing Ministry. But, as the session approached, Russell modified his attitude, and announced that he was ready to waive his claims and serve under Lansdowne. Then a note of violent hostility to the Derby Government was struck by the Radicals. At a great meeting at Manchester of the Anti-Corn Law Leaguers held on November 2, Cobden, amid approving cheers, insisted that, if the Ministry were to remain in office, they must begin by a comprehensive recantation of the Protectionist heresy and a direct affirmation of Free Trade dogmas, with no nonsense about compensation to the landed interest.

The Speech from the Throne, read by the Queen in person on November 11, was not considered by the Free Traders sufficiently explicit or unambiguous on this point. The words were :—

> It gives me pleasure to be enabled, by the blessing of Providence, to congratulate you on the generally improved condition of the country, and especially of the industrious classes. If you should be of opinion that recent legislation, in contributing, with other causes, to this happy result, has at the same time inflicted unavoidable injury on certain important interests, I recommend you dispassionately to consider how far it may be practicable equitably to mitigate that injury, and to enable the industry of the country to meet sucessfully that unrestricted competition to which Parliament, in its wisdom, has decided that it should be subjected.

Derby, in the House of Lords, supplemented this passage by the announcement that he was prepared to bow to the decision of the country, and, while desirous, so far as possible, to mitigate the injury inflicted by the Free Trade policy, to adopt that policy and to carry it out frankly and loyally. He acknowledged that a great portion of the prosperity of all classes, and particularly of the labouring classes, was due to the Free Trade legislation which had given them cheap and abundant food. This sufficed for the Lords, and was characterised by Greville as a final and complete abandonment of Protection in the most clear and unequivocal terms. In the Commons the Opposition were very hostile, Gladstone and the Peelites, Malmesbury noted, being especially bitter. Villiers, the Parliamentary protagonist of Free Trade, or, as Disraeli called him, the 'stormy petrel of Protection,' rose immediately after the address had been moved and seconded, and described the speech as vague and deceptive. Protection was such an 'enormous mischief' that the new Parliament must solemnly renounce it. Without waiting for the explanations of the Government, he, acting in concert with Graham on behalf of the Peelites, gave notice of a Free Trade resolution for the earliest possible day. Russell also thought the language

THE POLITICAL TOPSY.

'I 'SPECTS NOBODY CAN'T DO NOTHIN' WITH ME?'—*Vide* '*Uncle Tom's Cabin.*'

Reproduced by kind permission of the Proprietors, from '*Punch,*' *October 23, 1852.*

of the speech evasive. The intentions of the Government ought to be announced in a clear and decided manner, and not enveloped in the mist in which Disraeli loved, like the goddesses of old, to enshroud himself. Gladstone wanted a full, final, and solemn settlement; Cobden insisted that the pure principle of Free Trade must be affirmed; even Palmerston thought a formal declaration of the House of Commons necessary in the public interest. Disraeli protested that there was no intention of disturbing the principle of unrestricted competition, or of producing artificial prices or granting compensation for losses; that what the Government proposed was to bring our financial system more into harmony with our commercial system. He suggested that the House should wait for a Free Trade discussion till he had explained the financial policy of the Government, which he would do at the earliest opportunity after the Duke of Wellington's funeral. But objection was taken to this delay, and, though no amendment to the Address was proposed, mainly owing to the fact that Parliament met under the shadow of the Duke's death, the Opposition determined to make Ministers swallow the leek.

This was not a very chivalrous proceeding, but some justification was found for it in the fact that a considerable section of the Ministerialists advocated a return to Protection at the elections, and that, while some of these were now ready to bow to the expressed will of the country, others, like Sibthorp, were not. During the discussions that followed there was an abundant outpouring of personal explanation as to the origin and drafting of the resolution as Villiers ultimately proposed it. 'The debate,' Disraeli wrote to the Queen on November 26, 'was very animated and amusing, from the rival narratives of the principal projectors of the demonstration, who, having quarrelled among themselves, entered into secret and — in a party sense — somewhat scandalous revelations, to the diversion and sometimes astonishment of the House.'[1]

[1] *Queen Victoria's Letters.*

In spite, or because, of all this wealth of explanation, there is still some obscurity as to what happened; but, in general terms, it appears that two groups were drafting resolutions simultaneously, Villiers and his friends on the one hand, and the Peelites, under Graham's inspiration, on the other. The Peelites took the language of the Speech about unrestricted competition, and the statements made by Derby in the Lords, as a basis, and endeavoured to omit any expressions which might be felt to be objectionable by Ministers and their friends. Their draft reached the hands of the Government; and, at a party meeting held in Downing Street on Monday, November 15, Derby advised his followers, if such a resolution were proposed, to accept it frankly. Meanwhile the situation had changed. Villiers, with Russell's assent, had drafted the following resolution: 'That it is the opinion of this House that the improved condition of the country, and particularly of the industrious classes, is mainly the result of recent commercial legislation, and especially of the Act of 1846, which established the free admission of foreign corn, and that that Act was a wise, just, and beneficial measure.' These 'three odious epithets,' as Disraeli called them, at once converted the motion into a party attack which Government was bound to resist. Russell, though he assented to Villiers's terms, apparently preferred the Peelite draft; but the scale was turned by the Manchester men, who insisted that the Free Trade party, *par excellence*, had a right to a deciding voice in a matter of this kind, and that the justice and wisdom of the Act of 1846 must be categorically affirmed. Villiers's resolution was therefore put upon the paper, and Disraeli gave notice of an amendment which acknowledged that the improvement of the condition of the working classes was mainly due to the cheapness of provisions produced by recent legislation, and that it was the duty of the Government unreservedly to adhere to unrestricted competition as the principle of our commercial system.

To Lord Derby.

Grosvenor Gate, *Nov.* 19, 1852. — I send a draft resolution for your sharpest criticism.

If, as I assume from all I observe, hear, and think, the object of the Villiers motion is not to break us up, but only to keep us in by a humiliating tenure, I think it not unlikely that a bold move may turn their flank.

It is pretty clear that they have neither a Government nor a policy ready, and they wish to keep us in till they have both. If this resolution of ours is carried and followed up by measures, we shall have not only a Government, but a policy; and, notwithstanding all our difficulties, I can't help fancying that the campaign is now in our hands.

In spite of Disraeli's optimism, his amendment, which was not specially to the taste of his own friends, did not at all satisfy the Peelites, and there seemed every prospect of an ordinary party fight, instead of a solemn pronouncement of national policy. The situation was saved by the action of one powerful personage, Palmerston, at that time very independent of party ties.

From Lord Palmerston.

Private and Confidential. Carlton Gardens, *Nov.* 22, 1852.

Dear Disraeli, — I dislike the condition in which the House of Commons is about to place itself in regard to Villiers's motion. I wished for a nearly unanimous affirmation of a great principle of domestic policy, and, instead of that, here we are going to be embarked in an ordinary party struggle. Is there no way of preventing this? and might not some third party propose some form of words which the great majority of the House might agree to? You have not stated your objections to Villiers's words, but I conclude your main objection is that many who are prepared to submit to an overruling necessity, and to acquiesce in the continuance of the Free Trade policy, are nevertheless unwilling to declare that they think the changes made in 1846 and following years were just. If that is your objection, might it not be removed by the substitution of a different form of words? Will you cast your eye over the accompanying draft, and let me know privately and confidentially, and, as the lawyers say, without prejudice, what your personal guess is as to the acceptation or rejection of such a resolution if I was to propose it as a middle term in the spirit of conciliation.

Your opinion shall be strictly kept to myself, whatever it may be, but it would serve to guide me in determining whether it would be worth my while to sound people on our side of the House in regard to such a proposal.—Yours sincerely, PALMERSTON.

The resolution which Palmerston enclosed was couched in very similar terms to the original Peelite draft; and this was natural, as he appears to have acted at the request of Gladstone and Sidney Herbert, who 'carried the amendment to him at his house.'[1] Disraeli encouraged Palmerston to proceed, and eventually withdrew the Government amendment in favour of his.

The debate in one form or another was carried on for three nights, November 23, 25, and 26. Villiers, in his opening speech, emphatically declared that he did not mean his resolution to be a motion of want of confidence in Ministers. But, repeating his expression on the Address, he maintained that 'enormous mischief' had been caused by Disraeli's attitude since 1846, and he asked him not to sit down 'without letting us at last know what he does really mean.' On this head Disraeli's answer was perfectly clear; Protection was abandoned. He said that there could be, and there was, no question in Ministers' minds as to the result of the elections. 'There was no doubt that there was not only not a preponderating majority in favour of a change in the laws passed in those years, but not even of modifying them in any degree; that there was a decisive opinion on the part of the country that that settlement should not be disturbed.' In a subsequent speech he repeated: 'The verdict of the country has been of an unmistakable character. We have bowed to that unequivocal declaration.' But he was careful to point out that the Government had not come in on Protection, and had not dissolved on Protection. 'If we had acceded to office in order to advocate a system of Protection—if we had dissolved on that question, and found that the country would not support

[1] Morley's *Gladstone*, Bk. III., ch. 8.

us, we should have felt it our duty immediately to relinquish the posts which we now occupy.'

When he got up to answer Villiers, Disraeli was suffering from illness. Just before the meeting of the House that afternoon, he wrote to Derby: 'I am terribly cut up with the influenza, but I am going down to the House, with no want of courage or confidence, as I think we have a triumphant case. . . . I will see you to-morrow, as I have no doubt a good speech, *sudor rhetoricus*, will cure my fever.' In spite of his illness he entered into an elaborate defence of the course pursued by himself and his friends since 1846, in order to disprove the charge that they had perpetrated 'enormous mischiefs.' Not a single attempt, he asserted, and, when met by cries of 'Oh!' emphatically repeated, had been made, with the sanction of any party, to abrogate the Act of 1846, or bring back the old system of Protection. In opposing the Act, he had acted mainly in the interests of labour; and it was because he found, after experience, that the labouring classes were not injured, though the farmers were, that he did not press for its abrogation. He reminded the House that in the 1847 election, owing to high prices, the farmers were apathetic, and that, when they did agitate for a return to Protection in 1850, the party advised them to look rather to relief of local burdens and revision of taxation. It was a motion of that sort which, being only rejected by a few votes, was the principal cause of the resignation of the Whig Ministry in 1851, and Derby's programme then, when he unsuccessfully tried to form a Ministry, did not involve a return to the Protection of 1846, but only a moderate countervailing duty. Derby also then announced that he would accept as final the verdict of the General Election. The Derby Government had come into power by no Protectionist intrigue, but because of the internal dissensions of their predecessors. They would not, however, be Ministers on sufferance. 'Whatever were the exigencies of the case in the old Parliament, we neither desire nor will we submit in the new to carry on the Government under any indulgence which is foreign to the spirit of the British Constitution.' He finished his speech with an appeal from the factious and vexatious conduct of the old Free Trade party to the new members in the new Parliament. 'I appeal to the generous and the young; and I ask them to pause, now they are at last arrived on the threshold of the Senate of their country, and not become the tools and the victims of exhausted factions and obsolete politics.'

To Queen Victoria.

HOUSE OF COMMONS, *Nov.* 23, 1852.—The Chancellor of the Exchequer, with his humble duty to your Majesty, reports to your Majesty that the first night on the debate of Mr. Villiers's motion has been very interesting.

After Mr. Villiers's speech, the Chancellor of the Exchequer endeavoured to make a vindicatory and conciliatory statement for the country, which was not unsuccessful.

Mr. Bright followed very violent; but late at night Lord Palmerston rose, and suggested a very temperate and middle course, which, by omitting the offensive epithets in Mr. Villiers's motion, would save the honour of the late Protectionist party, and yet would unequivocally affirm all that the House and the country could reasonably desire.

Judging from the feeling of the House, the Chancellor of the Exchequer thinks he shall be able to induce his friends to adopt the course suggested by Lord Palmerston, although it involves some admissions which without the previous discussion, they would certainly have not entertained. . . .

The Whigs, the Manchester men, and one, at any rate, of the Peelites, entirely declined to be appeased by Disraeli's speech, or to show the generosity which Palmerston counselled; but were very bitter and vindictive, though the admitted success of their policy might well have made them magnanimous. No doubt they had many old scores to pay off, and thought this was the opportune moment. Some of them roundly denied Disraeli's facts. Bright quoted some extreme sayings and doings of the high Protectionists, and asked if, in view of them, the Chancellor of the Exchequer seriously meant to say that his party were not attempting to repeal the Act of 1846. 'Why, everyone knows that your whole agitation for six years has been, the first part of the time calumniation of Sir Robert Peel, and during the latter part demands for the Protection you have lost, or for some compensation in place of it.' Cobden said that Disraeli had offered an insult to their reason, their common sense, and their moral feeling, in attempting to make it appear that he had not been leading or encouraging a party which had kept up this mischievous delusion out of doors. Bernal Osborne said that Protection was the only thing on which the Chancellor of the Exchequer had been consistent, and that it was most audacious that he should come down to the House, and, 'with a face which I never saw equalled in the theatre,' say that he had never attempted to reverse the policy of Free Trade. Bernal Osborne had ransacked Hansard for proof of his contradiction of Disraeli's claim, but could only produce a few doubtful sentences and votes, all of which have been quoted in previous chapters of this volume, and none of which proved his case. Granby, the leader of the high Protectionists, expressed his cordial agreement with Disraeli's statement. 'I fully admit that the right hon. gentleman never brought the question of Protection before the House of Commons.'

The taunts of Sidney Herbert and Russell were more damaging to Disraeli. 'I acquit the Chancellor of the Exchequer,' said Herbert, 'as far as his own convictions are concerned, of the charge of having ever been a Protectionist. I never for one moment thought he believed in the least degree in Protection. I do not accuse him of having forgotten what he said or what he believed in those years; I only accuse him of having forgotten now what he then wished it to appear that he believed.' And he recalled the attacks on Peel. 'I sat by him [Peel] night by night on that bench when he was attacked by the foulest language, and accused of the meanest crimes.' But Peel was of a generous nature, and would not have desired any man's humiliation. 'It is not words that humiliate, it is deeds. If a man wants to see humiliation — which, God knows, is always a painful sight — he need but look there,' pointing to the Treasury bench. Russell said that Disraeli had made out a technical case for himself, but not a pleasant one. 'Without thinking Protection could be restored, and being rather in favour of Free Trade, he has allowed this great party, the great party of the farmers of the country, to believe that he would restore Protection, when he never believed in or expected anything of the kind.' If the truth had been fairly told the farmers, the question would have been finally settled four years before. Disraeli, Russell maintained, had shown to the House that, while he was a Protectionist, he did not faithfully serve the cause of Protection; 'I say, therefore, now that he has espoused the cause of Free Trade, let us take care that he is not as faithless to the cause of Free Trade as he has been to that of Protection.'

What justification was there for these taunts, what truth in these charges? Was Disraeli a Free Trader at heart who pretended for awhile to be a Protectionist for his own selfish ends; or, on another theory, a Protectionist throughout who only rendered lip-service to Free Trade at the last to gain, or retain, office; or — a third discreditable alternative — an absolutely indifferent person who adopted either cause as his self-interest dictated? Was his conduct in 1852 comparable to that of Peel in 1845–46, and equally, or indeed much more, culpable? Did he betray either his principles or his party?

In the light shed by Disraeli's private papers on his public actions, no fair-minded person can adopt any of the crude theories for which party *animus* and Free Trade bigotry gained at one time widespread acceptance. It is evident that such ambiguities as appear in Disraeli's conduct during the six years between 1846 and 1852 are due to the struggle within the party between him and the high Protectionists, something of which was suspected but little definitely known before now. Disraeli took throughout his political life a middle course on the commercial question, and was never a fanatic for either Protection or Free Trade; but he definitely considered moderate Protection the better course for England, especially with a view to securing to the land what he regarded as its due influence in the Constitution. That opinion he never altered, though he did not think that the return to any form of Protection was practicable during his lifetime. Peel came into power pledged to moderate Protection, and used that power to overthrow it, thereby breaking his party into two fragments, of which only the smaller portion followed the Minister. Disraeli set himself, with Bentinck, to organise the larger party, but, recognising that a country could not be always chopping and changing its commercial policy, made no attempt, either at the General Election of 1847 or in Parliament, to upset the new system at once. Even at that time he saw that the sliding scale could not be revived, but that the choice lay between a fixed duty and some form of compensation. What he did at that period, and did effectively, was to show that Cobden's sanguine prophecies of peace and plenty had not been fulfilled in the first three years after the passing of the Act of 1846. But the whole of the commercial and industrial community accepted the new system, and considered that it had helped them to weather the bad times. When they were united, they outweighed the agricultural classes both in numbers and in wealth, and could have their will, even if those classes were agreed among themselves. But agriculturists were not agreed; even among the farmers there were many who thought that, by clinging to Protection, they lost the opportunity of getting help in other ways; and the labourers, who were at first suspicious of a policy promoted by the manufacturers and the middle class for their own ends, had become reconciled to a system under which they obtained cheap food. The well-being of the labourers especially appealed to the Disraeli of *Sybil*. He noted also the growing prosperity of the country, from 1849 or 1850 onwards, which was due, no doubt, largely to extension of railways and to gold discoveries, as well as to liberation from commercial shackles, but was attributed by the Free Traders entirely to their panacea. In these circumstances, from about the time of his recognition as leader, Disraeli became convinced that public opinion would not tolerate a reversion to the old commercial system. Thenceforward he steadily laboured to dissociate the party from Protection, as Russell and Bright themselves had pointed out in Parliament; and, so far from deluding the farmers, he set his face against G. F. Young's movement, and invited all those interested in the land to look elsewhere for their relief. It was a delicate business, in view of Derby's reluctance to face the facts and of the interests and prejudices of many of his followers; but it was done with consummate ability. He failed, indeed, to convert Derby till too late, but he succeeded in changing the general current of opinion in the party, and in keeping the party together, even after Free Trade was accepted.

Can anyone familiar with what is practicable in politics maintain that it was Disraeli's duty in opposition to proclaim upon the housetops in 1849 that Protection must be abandoned — not on principle, but because it could not be obtained — when the result must have been a further split in the party which he was so laboriously bringing together? For it is absurd to suppose that the rank and file of the party would have been content to follow the Peelite leaders, whom they stigmatised as traitors for their conduct in 1846, and whose Conservative principles they regarded as doubtful, owing to their constant association in political action with Whigs and Radicals. It must always be remembered that the Conservative party, as Walpole well pointed out in the debate, stood for much more than a mere commercial system, and that, in an age of unbounded faith in material progress, such a party was most necessary for the due balance of the State. No one can allege that Disraeli was remiss in doing his utmost to convert his party in private. It is difficult to see what other course in the circumstances he could have taken in public, than that of saying that, however right Protection might be in principle, however justifiable economically a countervailing duty on corn, the party and the agricultural interest must not expect to obtain any policy of the kind from Parliament, but must look to readjustment of local burdens and revision of taxation. It was his misfortune, and not his fault, that he had not wholly converted his colleagues when circumstances put them in office; but they did not obtain office on a Protective policy, and the programme on which, as a Government, they went into the elections was one of 'free intercourse' and 'unrestricted competition.' It may be that the process of conversion was hastened by office in the case of some of his colleagues, but Disraeli had urged the definite abandonment of Protection on Derby at least a year before.

In accepting and making the best of Free Trade after it had become a law, as soon as he was clear that the country was resolved not to go back upon its steps, Disraeli was only following the tradition of English politics — a tradition reinforced by the recent precedents of Roman Catholic emancipation and Reform. It was said that, for the party and the leader who had attacked and overthrown Peel on the question of Free Trade, to acquiesce in it themselves was a humiliation. Wherein did the humiliation consist? Not for a moment did the party thereby condone the use which Peel made of power conferred on him for exactly opposite purposes. It did not even abandon its theoretic belief in the system then discarded. What it did was to recognise the benefits conferred on all classes by cheap and abundant food, and to bow to accomplished facts, accepting the least unpalatable of the unpalatable motions presented to it. It set itself right with public opinion over a matter which public opinion had, with insufficient warrant, erected into a tenet of religion; it recited, in the fashion of the day, the shibboleth which public opinion exacted of all politicians as a condition of employment by the State.[1]

There were a few of the triumphant Free Traders who showed, in the debate on Villiers's motion, a due appreciation of the position of Disraeli and his party, and consideration for their feelings. One was Gladstone, who, however, somewhat marred the grace of his speech by a definite approval of Russell's criticisms. Gladstone pleaded that the House should imitate the magnanimity of Peel, who did indeed look for revenge, but not in stinging speeches or motions carrying a sense of pain or degradation to honourable men. Peel, he said, looked for the acceptance of his principles first by the country, and then by the world. The cause of the aristocracy should be redeemed from association with that 'obnoxious policy,' whose 'obsequies' they were celebrating in that debate. They should put away the desire to trample on those who had fought manfully, and merely rejoice in the great public good that had been achieved. It was Palmerston, however, who struck the note to which the House responded. 'Sir, we are here an assembly of gentlemen; and we who are gentlemen on this side of the House should remember that we are dealing with gentlemen on the other side; and I, for one, cannot at all reconcile it to my feelings to call upon a set of English gentlemen unnecessarily, for any purpose that I have in view, to express opinions

[1] Compare the letter of Manilius in the *Press* of May 14, 1853 : 'The first act of Lord Derby's Government, on the assembling of the new Parliament, was precisely that anticipated by every man of ordinary sense. It was the recognition of that principle which divides the rulers of a despotism from the Ministers of a Constitutional Monarchy — viz., the submission of men made responsible to the Sovereign for the security of the realm, to the power of public opinion when unequivocally expressed by a legitimate appeal to its verdict. Here all taunts as to the inconsistency of politicians who, in opposition, had opposed a law which in office they ratified, were absurd on the lips of those who had studied our history and comprehended our Constitution. To oppose a law, to represent the hardships it may inflict, to argue on the consequences it may entail, to advise, when it be passed, either congenial modifications or supplementary amendments — all this belongs to the first province of debate. But that law confirmed in all its integrity by fresh proofs of popular assent, and the modifications or amendments advised rendered as impracticable as the repeal — nothing remains for those who have passed from the freedom of opposition to the grave responsibilities of office but to accept the law, and seek, by means analogous to its spirit, remedies for whatever particular grievance it may inflict. See p. 496.

they do not entertain, or to recant opinions that may be still lingering in their minds.' He refused to join in taunting and reproaching those who yielded their early impressions to the inevitable force of events. All the country wanted was to be assured that Free Trade was the principle upon which their legislation was to be founded.

Villiers's motion was defeated by 336 to 256, Palmerston and the Peelites, including Graham, voting with the Government; and then Palmerston's amendment, being supported by the Government, the Liberals, and the Peelites, was carried by 468 to 53, about seventy of the rank and file of the Ministerialists declining to vote in the second division. The text of the resolution which marked the close of the great Free Trade controversy ran thus:

> That it is the opinion of this House that the improved condition of the country, and especially of the industrious classes, is mainly the result of recent legislation, which has established the principle of unrestricted competition, has abolished taxes imposed for the purposes of Protection, and has thereby diminished the cost and increased the abundance of the principal articles of the food of the people.
>
> That it is the opinion of this House that this policy, firmly maintained and prudently extended, will, without inflicting injury on any important interest, best enable the industry of the country to bear its burthens, and will thereby most surely promote the welfare and contentment of the people.
>
> That this House will be ready to take into consideration any measures, consistent with these principles, which, in pursuance of Her Majesty's gracious Speech and recommendation, may be laid before it.

It was hardly pretended that even this resolution was literally accepted by many of those who voted for it. Disraeli, in announcing his acceptance of it, said that it contained expressions to which he might demur, and which he should regret to see placed on the journals of the House with his individual authority or sanction; but that was a mere fighting about words, not about facts. As one of the Ministerial rank and file put it, the real question was the passing of a formal resolution that Free Trade was to be adopted. That was done, and, thanks to

Disraeli's management, done with little or no resentment even from the high Protectionists — such as Booker, who sat for Herefordshire; Ball, the farmers' friend; Isaac Butt; and even Granby — none of whom reproached the Government in the debate, but all promised cordial co-operation. The whole, with hardly an exception, of the 53 who voted in the minority, supported the Government in the critical division on the Budget. There were some angry expressions. Lennox reported, in the recess, his father, the Duke of Richmond, as saying of the Government: 'I can see they are, damn them! at the old game of throwing over their principles'; and Sibthorp, in the debate on the Address, talked of their 'duplicity.' But the party as a whole recognised that Disraeli's policy had been right and, indeed, inevitable. There was no cave formed and no serious discontent felt.

The question of reconstruction, which had only been toyed with in the autumn, naturally arose again on the evidence afforded by these debates that Palmerston and the Peelites were ready, in certain circumstances, to come to the aid of the Government against Whig factiousness. Palmerston, who at the moment was being roundly abused by the Whigs and Radicals, held the key of the situation. He always wrote and talked as if he had never seriously contemplated joining Derby's Government, but he certainly left the impression both on Ministers themselves and on shrewd outside observers, like Greville, that it was rather a question of terms. The only possible terms were, however, vetoed by the Crown. Derby was not permitted by the Queen to offer Palmerston the lead of the House of Commons; nor, indeed, did he himself desire, owing, apparently, to unwillingness to seem to slight Disraeli, to repeat his proposal of February. A private interview which Disraeli had with Palmerston on November 24 produced no result. According to Disraeli's report to Derby, Palmerston's language was perfectly friendly towards the Government; but 'he concluded by declaring that though he sat by Mr.

Sidney Herbert in the House of Commons, and was an old personal friend, he did not act in concert with him or with Mr. Gladstone; and that he did not see, on their part, any disposition to join the Government. After this declaration, Mr. Disraeli felt that it would be useless and unwise to sound him further as to his own ulterior views, and the conversation led to nothing.'[1] It does not appear whether Palmerston had heard of the royal veto; but the reports which reached Derby suggested that the Peelites would not join him unless Palmerston led the Commons, Gladstone refusing to serve under Disraeli. In these circumstances Derby reported to the Queen that he had taken no steps towards exercising the discretion she had entrusted to him.

Prince Albert to Lord Derby.

Private and Confidential. WINDSOR CASTLE, *Nov.* 26, 1852.

MY DEAR LORD DERBY,—The contents of the letter which you wrote to the Queen yesterday afternoon, and which she received this morning only, has caused us less surprise than it appears to have done to yourself. You will remember that we expressed some doubts as to the 'common accord' between the Peelites and Lord Palmerston.

My conviction is now further confirmed that Lord Palmerston is aiming at the leadership of the House of Commons, in order to possess himself of *absolute power*, and that he is taking his position in a way to obtain this, whether the debate may end in a junction of the Peelites with your Government or with Lord John Russell, whom he would in that case wish to see removed to the House of Lords.

Such a calamity for the interests of the country the Queen will feel it her duty to prevent by a firm opposition on her part. If you mean to negotiate further on a further change of Parliamentary prospects, your own and the Queen's safety will mainly depend on the instruments which you mean to employ for your negotiations. If left to be settled between Mr. Disraeli and Lord Palmerston, and the result only to be *reported* to you, I should feel very uneasy, considering the *laxity of the political consciences* which both these gentlemen have hitherto exhibited. You would in that case find it very difficult not to accept any arrangement which they may have preconcerted.

[1] *Queen Victoria's Letters.*

Should Mr. Disraeli have to relinquish the lead, Mr. Gladstone would be a much fitter successor than Lord Palmerston, for, whatever his peculiar crotchets may be, he is a man of the strictest feelings of honour and the purest mind.—Ever yours truly, ALBERT.

A memorandum of November 28 by the prince, printed in *Queen Victoria's Letters*, shows how Derby stood up for his colleague against this disparaging criticism. He declared that Gladstone was quite unfit to lead the House, and that he himself 'could not in honour sacrifice Mr. Disraeli, who had acted very straightforwardly to him as long as they had had anything to do with each other, and who possessed the confidence of his followers. Mr. Disraeli had no idea of giving up the lead.' In reply to a question from the Prince, Derby added that 'he did not think Mr. Disraeli had ever had a strong feeling, one way or the other, about Protection or Free Trade, and that he would make a very good Free Trade Minister.'

There is no reason to believe that Disraeli would have hesitated now any more than in the previous February, or in 1855, to make way for Palmerston, if that had been in question. To make way for a Peelite was another matter. Even if he had been willing, his followers certainly would not have permitted such an arrangement. Gladstone at this time, Lord Morley writes, was 'inspired by the strong hope of Conservative reunion'; but, in a friendly conversation with Derby, he spoke oracularly of 'many difficulties of a personal nature' in any conceivable Ministerial combination, and said that the attitude of the Peelites to the Government depended on the Budget. It was the misfortune of the Peelites, and of Gladstone in particular, and goes far to account for the little affection with which they were regarded, that they never seemed so friendly and so disposed to approximate to their old party as when they were on the eve of taking some definite step to widen the gulf and unite themselves more closely to the other side. Gladstone's friendly disposition now was the immediate precursor of a fatal blow dealt at the Budget; and again, in 1859, he actually voted with the Derby Government in the division which ejected them from office, and then, without hesitation, joined the Liberal Government which supplanted them.

All hope of reconstruction being abandoned, the Government had to face, without any new blood, the problem of the Budget. There is little in the Beaconsfield papers to show how the financial scheme developed in the Chancellor's mind, but some of the expressions in the Lennox correspondence suggest that Gladstone was not mistaken in his comment after the Budget speech: 'It is plain enough that, when its author announced something looming in the distance, he did not mean this plan, but something more extensive.' We know, of course, that Disraeli had hoped for a commercial treaty with France, which would have necessarily involved important changes in customs dues. That he desired to abolish the Law of Poor Law Settlement, and give the management of county rates to a more popular board, appears from Malmesbury's notes of Cabinet meetings. Above all, we know that the demands of the services, supported by the Crown, necessitated extra expenditure at the last moment, after all his calculations had been made, and curtailed the remissions of taxation which he hoped to announce. These demands were renewed at the eleventh hour.

To Lord Derby.

Private. D.S., *Nov.* 30, 1852.—I fear we are in a great scrape, and I hardly see how the Budget can live in so stormy a sea.

We have had no explanation from Stafford[1] as to his letter of this day to Hamilton[2] that the navy Estimates for 1853–54 will be increased nearly one million. I trust that the Admiralty have not got into debt, and are attempting to shuffle off this scot on future estimates. This will never do, for, if permitted, we shall never be safe.

We are pledged to the Queen, as far as the seamen and Marines are concerned, and we must not seem to waver; but I think you must exert your utmost authority that there shall be retrenchment, no matter at what inconvenience, in all in which her honour and safety are not concerned. I think Hardinge also ought to give up his extra 1,000 men.

But, turn the matter as I may, I see no way out of it, and

[1] Secretary of the Admiralty. [2] Secretary of the Treasury.

must deeply regret that we should have become involved in such a difficulty at such a moment; and that on the very eve of battle I should be suddenly called upon to change all my dispositions.

Derby replied that he had told Stafford to cut down all Admiralty expenses except those for the additional seamen and Marines; discussed which of the two great remissions contemplated by Disraeli had better be pared in consequence of the new demands; and continued, 'Put a good face upon it, and we shall pull through. *L'audace — l'audace — toujours l'audace.*'

Courage never failed Disraeli; but courage was certainly wanted when he rose on Friday, December 3, in a House (Greville says) 'crowded to suffocation,' to introduce the Budget which was to make or mar the Government. He had had but nine months' official or financial training; he had, indeed, delivered one Budget speech, but had then proposed no change of taxation. He faced adversaries who almost monopolised the official and financial experience of the day, and he faced them practically unsupported. There were opposite him three ex-Chancellors of the Exchequer — Wood, his immediate predecessor; Goulburn, who assisted Peel; and Sir Francis Baring, whose service at the Treasury was, however, of a remote date — and there was Gladstone, already a power in economic debate, and destined to be the most famous Chancellor of the Victorian era. There was Disraeli's old antagonist, Graham; Cobden, eager to detect Protectionist heresy; and the veteran Whig chief, Russell. From none of these men could he expect a favourable, or even impartial, hearing. The Whigs and Radicals were sore at the defeat of Villiers's motion; the Peelites cherished a personal resentment against the man who overthrew their chief. Wood, the most unlucky of Chancellors, had suffered severely under Disraeli's criticism for six years; and Gladstone, though he may have persuaded himself that he came to hear the Budget with an open mind, had really condemned it in advance. He wrote to Aberdeen on July 30 that the Government were chained to the Budget, and that he, for one, was not prepared to except Disraeli as a financial organ, or to be responsible for his financial measures; and he found Disraeli's Bucks speeches on revision of taxation each 'more quackish in its flavour than its predecessor.' On the morning of December 3 he wrote to Mrs. Gladstone that startling and dangerous, and perhaps outrageous, proposals were to be expected. Finally there was a feeling common to the Free Traders of all kinds, whether Peelites, Whigs, or Radicals, that it was a monstrous and unnatural thing that one who had been a Protectionist, and was still, though he accepted facts, unconverted in principle, should venture to stand up in the House of Commons and produce a Free Trade Budget.

Before opponents of this calibre and in this frame of mind, Disraeli had to lay no mere ordinary financial statement. It was no question of small increases or remissions of taxation, according as there was a deficit to supply or a surplus to spend. It was no provisional Budget, like that which he had introduced in the spring, which left taxes as they were, and only demanded lucid exposition in its author. This time he had announced his intention of bringing our financial system into harmony with our commercial system. It was his hope to allay the bitter feelings between country and town, to do justice to the interests which had lost Protection, and to equalise taxation while obviating existing anomalies. He had to satisfy the country gentlemen behind him within the limits of the new commercial system, and without rousing the anger of the towns. He had to do this, too, with no assured majority at his back, ready by sheer weight and solidity to push far-reaching proposals through Parliament; and at an awkward moment, long before the conclusion of the financial year, when estimates both of revenue and of expenditure must be largely guesswork. Moreover, it was impossible that a Chancellor of the Exchequer who was also leader of the House of Commons, and in many ways the animating spirit of the Government, should have been able to devote the personal attention and care he could wish to the details of his financial arrangements. Happily he had in Sir Charles Trevelyan, the permanent head of the Treasury, expert aid of the first quality, and it was believed that the Budget owed much to Sir Charles's experience and assiduity.

At the outset of his speech Disraeli asked the House to consider his proposals as a whole, a request to which, though it was refused by many of his opponents at the time, history is bound to attend. The principal boons offered by the Budget to the taxpayer were the remission of half the malt tax and half the hop duty; the gradual remission of half the tea duty; the assessment of income tax on one-third of the farmer's rental instead of one-half; the reduction of the rate of the tax on precarious incomes to three-fourths of the rate on realised incomes; the reduction of lighthouse dues and removal of the Admiralty grievances of shipowners; and permission to the sugar interest to refine in bond for home consumption. In order to make good the deficiency caused by these reductions and remissions, Disraeli proposed to extend the area and increase the amount of direct taxation. The income tax was to be extended to incomes of £100 a year of precarious income, and to £50 a year of permanent income, and was to apply to Ireland as well as to Great Britain. The house tax was to be extended to houses of £10 a year rateable value, and to be doubled in amount.

Thus the Budget was essentially based on Free Trade principles. 'The doctrine of unrestricted competition,' said Disraeli, 'is not consistent with restricted industry.' After the solemn verdict of the country, and the formal and definite establishment of the new system, the Government had to consider how they could best enable the community to encounter that universal competition which it must now be prepared to meet. That was to be done 'by cheapening as much as possible that which sustains their lives. We look, therefore, to articles of prime necessity.' 'It is the boast of hon. gentlemen opposite that they had given cheap bread to the community; but the principles upon which you have given cheap bread to the community are principles which ought to make you cheapen the sustenance of the community in every form.' He proposed, therefore, to reduce the malt tax and the tea duty, and give the community cheap drink as well as cheap food. The reduction of the malt tax was in the interest of the consumer, but it would also benefit agriculturists. As for tea, 'I hardly know anything more diverting than to open Pepys's Diary, where we see it stated, "Took a cup of the new China drink — very pleasant," and to remember that not two centuries have passed, and the exotic novelty that pleased one evening that fantastic gentleman is now the principal solace of every cottage in the kingdom.' He hoped to enable the people to have a supply at a very reasonable rate of a very favourite beverage, and at the same time to give a great stimulus to commerce, shipping, and manufactures. It was said that the consuming power of the people was diminishing, but he saw no evidence of it. There was no doubt considerable emigration; but 'every emigrant from England generally becomes an English colonist, and an English colonist becomes an English customer, and our markets are stimulated, our people are employed, and their wages are improved, by the very circumstances which some regard as tending to our decay and dissolution.'

But, though the Budget was based on Free Trade principles, relief was given to each of the interests — shipping, sugar, and agriculture — which had suffered through the change. Disraeli desired to remove well-founded causes of discontent, and enlist the sympathies of all classes in favour of the new system of taxation. The shipping interests were to be relieved in respect of lighthouses, and anchorage, salvage, and enlistment. In regard to these latter questions, he considered that the Admiralty had pressed hardly on the merchant service, but the Admiralty were prepared to yield their claims. In this connection, Disraeli entirely exonerated the Royal Navy from reprehensible conduct, and added: 'I have no doubt that in the navy, as well as in all departments of life, much more humanising tendencies are exerting their influence than there did twenty-five, or forty, or fifty years ago.' A harmless remark, one would have thought, especially with the qualification 'as well as in all departments of life'; but Croker regarded the passage as a personal attack upon himself, who had been Secretary to the Admiralty from 1809 to 1830, and he wrote an article for the forthcoming *Quarterly Review* criticising the Budget almost entirely in reference to this purely incidental point.

With regard to the sugar industry, which had undoubtedly been treated in a wanton and indefensible manner, Disraeli granted it the boon of refining in bond, but was unable to go farther, in view of the prosperous state of the trade at the time. In 1852, as compared with 1851, there was an increase in British sugar entered for consumption of 1,250,000 hundredweights, and a decrease in foreign sugar of 600,000 hundredweights.

> I may be called traitor, I may be called renegade; but I want to know whether there is any gentleman in this House, wherever he may sit, who would recommend a differential duty to prop up a prostrate industry which is actually commanding the metropolitan market, under the circumstances which I have placed before Parliament? It is unnecessary to enter into any argument on the point. No person could think of proposing an increase of differential duties except for the attainment of a definite object. If that object be to give the command of the home market to our colonies, it is already attained.

In dealing with the agricultural interest, Disraeli first considered the question of local taxation. This took three forms — the highway rate, the county rate, and the poor rate. A Bill would be introduced for the better administration of the highway rate. As the country rate was slight in amount, he did not propose to recommend any change — an announcement which was received with sensation in the House, causing Disraeli to remind members of his request that his proposals should be considered as a whole. Then he came to the poor rate, where the complaint of the landed interest was exceedingly well founded. The maintenance of the poor should undoubtedly be the subject of general taxation, and not fall on real property alone; but, since he first brought the question forward, the burden had diminished 25 per cent. In 1848 the expenditure amounted to £6,180,000, but in 1851 only to £4,962,000. At this there were, naturally, loud cheers from the opposition. 'I am afraid,' said Disraeli, 'that is really not a cheer on account of the diminution of pauperism. I am afraid it is a cheer for recent legislation.' He did not want to disturb recent legislation, but it had been shown that diminished poor rates might coexist with high prices of corn.

> But there are greater subjects for us to consider than the triumph of obsolete opinions. (Great laughter from the Opposition.) Yes, I look upon one-sided Free Trade as an obsolete opinion, just as you look upon Protection: obsolete, because they are lost in the great principle of the day—that of unrestricted competition.

As the burden was now less, Disraeli did not propose to relieve the agricultural classes by the way of local taxation, but he proposed to benefit them by the reduction of the malt tax and hop duty, and by the less onerous mode of assessing the income tax on farmers' profits.

A most important feature of the Budget was the manner of dealing with the income tax. It was clear that it could not be dispensed with at present, but Disraeli determined to deal with its anomalies in the spirit of his April Budget speech. He had then laid it down that direct taxation should be as general, so far as can be expediently managed, as indirect, and that a distinction should be drawn between precarious and permanent incomes; so he included Ireland, hitherto exempt, extended the tax downwards, and fixed the rate on the schedules dealing with trade earnings, professional incomes, and farmers' profits, at three-fourths of that charged on realised property. With extension of the franchise accepted in principle by leading politicians on all sides, it was a statesmanlike policy to provide, as far as possible, that no class should be exempt from taxation required for the benefit of all.

As the remissions provided in the Budget, together with increased expenditure (£600,000) for defence, would cost the revenue £2,100,000 in 1853–54, and more in subsequent years, it was necessary to find some addition to the resources of the country, and Disraeli looked boldly to direct taxation. That was an inevitable result of 'the principle of unrestricted competition, that all indirect taxes should be moderate in amount.' Gladstone and Harcourt and subsequent Chancellors of the Exchequer have found themselves compelled to follow the path pointed out by Disraeli, and to make use of the mighty engine of direct taxation in an increasingly oppressive manner. Disraeli selected the house tax, both for extension in accordance with his principle of avoiding exemptions as far as possible, and for increase. However economically sound, it was a bold decision, as in 1834 an agitation of the newly-enfranchised London householders caused the abandonment of the then existing house tax; and, when such a tax was reimposed in 1851, all houses below £20 value were exempted. Disraeli lowered the exemption limit to £10, and doubled the tax. He justified the increase by reference to the remissions of taxation since 1834, and to the boons conferred by the rest of his Budget, all of which would benefit the inhabitant householder.

The speech contained an eloquent passage on the national defences. Though the tendency of the age, said Disraeli, and the predominant feeling of the day, was peace, it was of primary importance that our shores should be protected. It would have been more convenient for the Government to defer action, but it was their paramount duty to bring the matter forward at once. 'The plans we have matured, and which, if the House will support our proposition, will be carried into complete effect, will be plans which will settle this question of national defences for ever'—a bold assertion, which events speedily falsified. 'You will have all your arsenals and strong points in the kingdom defended, and you will have a real Channel fleet, which can assemble from its different rendezvous at the moment necessary, and which is the proper garrison and protection of the country.' At the same time he promised a thorough overhauling of the administration in all departments, with a view to that efficiency, which, rather than retrenchment, was the true parent of economy. In conclusion he recommended the proposals of the Government as essentially practical measures. They proposed nothing on which they were not prepared immediately to act. That was the reason why they had not dealt with the succession duties. 'We think we have proposed enough to-night, and we think that what we proposed is of a character that, if acted upon, we can judiciously advance a step farther.'

This great effort lasted five hours, and Disraeli's wife and friends, remembering that he was only just recovering from an attack of influenza, were anxious about his health. The Parliamentary Secretary of the Treasury sent a couple of notes from the House to relieve Mrs. Disraeli's anxiety.

George A. Hamilton to Mrs. Disraeli.

Nine o'clock [*Friday, Dec.* 3, 1852]. — You will be anxious to know how matters go on. The Chancellor has made a most wonderful effort. He has been speaking nearly four hours, with unrelaxed energy and spirit. The speech has been on the whole very well received by a very critically disposed Opposition, and I am full of confidence.

10 *o'clock.* — The Chancellor has just finished; a more surprising effort has never been made, and he has been greatly cheered. I have no fear for the result. He is greatly fatigued. We must get him to go home as soon as possible.

As Hamilton wrote, the Opposition were very critically disposed, and some of the more important of them permitted themselves to misbehave during the delivery of the speech. Sir William Fraser, who was sitting in the side-gallery, noticed conduct which could not be seen by the majority of the House. 'Sir George Grey and Sir Charles Wood, nearly related,[1] facing Disraeli, the latter having been Chancellor of the Exchequer, kept interchanging signs, and nudging one another, laughing occasionally, while Disraeli was speaking ; in fact, turning him

[1] Wood had married Grey's niece.

into ridicule, in a manner which was not only unfair, but ungentlemanlike, considering their social position compared to Disraeli's, their life-long experience of the House, and his extreme difficulties — difficulties which he had encountered in a manly and well-bred manner.' Macaulay was more generous, and his comment in his diary is characteristic:

It was well done, both as to manner and language. The statement was lucid, though much too long. I could have said the whole as clearly, or more clearly, in two hours; and Disraeli was up five. The plan was nothing but taking the money out of the pockets of the people in towns and putting it into the pockets of growers of malt. I greatly doubt whether he will be able to carry it; but he has raised his reputation for practical ability.[1]

From Queen Victoria.

OSBORNE, *Dec.* 5, 1852. — The Queen thanks Mr. Disraeli for his note received yesterday, and must congratulate him on the very successful way in which he brought forward the Budget, and hopes that he has not suffered from the great exertion which it must have been to him.

From Lord Derby.

ST. JAMES'S SQUARE, *Saturday* [*Dec.* 4]. — I cannot resist congratulating you in writing, as I have already done verbally (at least, I hope Mackenzie delivered my message), on your masterly performance of last night. I had the satisfaction of hearing the whole of it, except the first half-hour; and I can truly say that I listened to the whole exposition with entire satisfaction, and admiration of the clearness and breadth with which you stated your views, and the skill with which you introduced the various topics and trod over very difficult ground. One ought not to be too sanguine, or to trust too much to first impressions; but I think you have weathered the really dangerous point, and that the ship is now in comparatively smooth waters. I am glad to find from H. Lennox that you are not bodily the worse, and mentally you must be much better. . . .

Lord Lyndhurst to Mrs. Disraeli.

Dec. 4, 1852. — . . . I cannot refuse myself the pleasure of congratulating you on Disraeli's great success, and on the skilful and brilliant manner in which he turned the weapons of the Free Traders and Radicals against themselves, pounding

[1] Trevelyan's *Macaulay*, p. 579.

them in their own mortar. The playful and easy manner in which he treated the subjects and his opponents was, as Derby, who sat next me, observed, quite charming.

The reception of the Budget, at first, was eminently favourable. *The Times* wrote next day that Disraeli had succeeded in showing that the country had new resources and new capabilities; and Greville, three days later, that he thought the Budget would 'go down, and make the Government safe.' On the Wednesday following, Derby and Disraeli had an enthusiastic reception in the City at the Lord Mayor's banquet, postponed from November 9, owing to the Duke's death and funeral. Disraeli, on rising to return thanks for the House of Commons, was received with protracted cheering. He expressed the hope that the new House would take a large view of national circumstances, forget party feeling, legislate not for classes, but for the community, in an impartial and patriotic spirit, and 'resolve, if the measures of Her Majesty's Government are entitled to public confidence and respect, that, they shall not be defeated by the manœuvres of faction.

The manœuvres of faction were already at work. The lead was taken by the Peelites, under the general superintendence of Aberdeen, but with Gladstone as the moving spirit. As early as Monday, December 6, Gladstone rose and strongly protested against any interference with the frame of the income tax, and, in concert with Goulburn, took up solemnly the extraordinary position that to differentiate between precarious and realised incomes was a breach of faith with the public creditor, inasmuch as thereby income derived from the funds was taxed more highly than income earned. The obvious answer was that income derived from the funds would be taxed at exactly the same rate as income from any other investment, and therefore the public creditor was treated exactly the same as every other creditor. Though these pedantic objections to the treatment of the income tax might produce little effect, there were other arguments against the Budget of a more popular character. To repeal half the malt tax and half the tea duty, especially when the latter was done by degrees, was of little value, it was said, to either consumers or producers and importers. There was something in the objection, and Disraeli could not bring forward in public the fact that, but for the increased expenditure on defences into which he was forced, he would have been able to deal more decisively with one, if not both, of these taxes. Again, in spite of Disraeli's expressed desire to reconcile town and country, an agitation was got up in the towns—on the basis of Macaulay's crude appraisement of the Budget as taking money from townspeople to put it into the pockets of malt-growers—to protest against the extension and increase of the house tax. The Irish naturally objected to the extension of the income tax to their island. There were also purists who said that it was monstrous, when you had a surplus, to impose fresh taxation, and not content yourself with distributing boons among the taxpayers. Disraeli was justifiably indignant at being taunted, in the exceptional conditions of his position, with not following 'the miserable routine of commonplace circumstances.'

The debate began on December 10, a week after the statement, and ended on December 16. Disraeli's difficulty in dealing with it was that all his opponents wanted his blood, but wanted it for different reasons. Wood, indeed, condemned the Budget generally as 'most visionary and most rash,' and said that no one in his senses would attempt in one year to deal with tea duties and malt tax, or to increase income tax and house duty. 'Take back your Budget,' he said. Reduce the tea duties, but leave malt tax alone, and give up the house tax. Disraeli need not be ashamed of doing what Pitt was compelled to do. 'I want you to reconstruct your own Budget. . . . Either you know nothing about it, or you have recklessly abused the knowledge which you possess.' Cobden would be glad to do away with the malt tax, if there were a surplus, but would not vote for any new tax in its place. Lowe thought the system of gradual reduction practised in regard to the tea duties was drawing bills on popularity and discounting them at once; and he also exhibited curious learning (not admitted by the head of the firm of Bass) on brewing. Goulburn harped once more on the injury to public credit. Graham protested against extending the area of direct taxation. It was the great resource in time of war; it should not be pressed unduly in time of peace. Much of the criticism of the Opposition was directed to a quite incidental proposal of Disraeli's, to put an end to the Public Works Loan Fund, which he maintained was of no present utility, and the repayments of advances under which he proposed to carry to revenue — £400,000 in all.

'The Budget,' says Sir Stafford Northcote,[1] 'presented too many assailable points to have much chance of being adopted.' That is true; but also, apart from its creator, it had a lamentable want of support in debate. The only speech of importance in its favour among the unofficial members was a spirited oration by Bulwer Lytton. Manners was overtasked in being put up to reply to Wood and Cobden, and Pakington was hardly a match for Goulburn and Graham. Walpole was the most successful Ministerial speaker. He vindicated Disraeli against the 'extraordinary attacks' upon him by the Opposition orators. Why was he assailed at every point? Were they jealous of his success?

> Is it because he has laboured hard and long, contending with genius against rank and power and the ablest statesmen, until he has attained the highest eminence which an honourable ambition may ever aspire to — the leadership and guidance of the Commons of England? Is it because he has verified in himself the dignified description of a great philosophical poet of antiquity, portraying equally his past career and his present position? —
>
> 'Certare ingenio; contendere nobilitate;
> Noctes atque dies niti præstante labore
> Ad summas emergere opes, rerumque potiri.'

Palmerston, who sincerely wished the Government well, and might perhaps have averted its fall by some such friendly action as he had taken on Villiers's motion, was

[1] *Twenty Years of Financial Policy*, p. 180.

laid up and prevented from going to the House during the debate. The only kindness he could show was to abstain from the division. His sentiments were conveyed to Mrs. Disraeli by Lady Bulwer: 'I have been to Lady P[almerston]'s — alas! without success. It seems he disapproves of the house tax, and would naturally have voted against it, but abstains from good-will towards the Government. . . . They wish you to stay in, and would do all they could for it. . . . She spoke of joining you, and wishes there were people to follow Lord P., but that the difficulty was for him to go alone.'

Disraeli had staked the existence of the Ministry on securing a general verdict in favour of the Budget. Being strongly possessed of the fighting instinct, and determined not to succumb until he had exhausted every resource, he endeavoured, as the discussion proceeded, to get the question on which the fateful division was to be taken put in such a manner as to give the Government the best chance of surviving. On this point there were many wrangles. The resolution referred to the house tax, and, in presence of the manifest repugnance of the representatives of towns to consent to its being doubled, Disraeli showed a disposition to accept the vote as only determining the principle of extension of area without pledging the Committee to an increase. This was warmly resented by the Opposition, who maintained with reason that without the doubling of the house tax the promised boons could not be given. Disraeli felt himself being driven into a corner, and, the night before the division, as a last resource, tried to obtain some support in a quarter where he had for long found considerable personal sympathy, even though coupled with strong political antagonism. It was a Wednesday, at that time an 'off' Parliamentary night, and he asked Bright to come and see him in Grosvenor Gate between ten and eleven. Bright had taken no part in the debate, save to say shortly that he did not see that any new tax was necessary; but that, if the necessity was proved to him, he would prefer to vote for a tax upon successions applying generally to all property.

He accepted Disraeli's invitation, and has left in his diary a full account of what his biographer calls a 'strange colloquy.'[1] Disraeli, who was found 'near the top of the house, in his morning gown, surrounded by books, pictures, mirrors, etc.,' unburdened his soul about that 'infernal question,' Protection, and those 'damned defences,' which had between them made such havoc of his Budget. He declared that he would not have touched the malt tax if he could have dealt with tea without doing so, and dwelt on the administrative economies the Government were effecting. All he wanted was a general vote for his Budget, and then he would give up malt tax and house duty, and remodel his scheme. His party had 'stood so much already,' that he did not see why he might not get rid of the 'old stagers' and 'red tapists,' and form a Government, not perhaps all at once, with Cobden and Bright. Disraeli's face, says Bright, was serious; but Bright laughed, and we may laugh with him at the mixture of earnestness and irony in his host's conversation. If Disraeli could get Bright and his friends to be neutral, it was all that he probably hoped for, and he trusted to his own dexterity for a fresh combination after the vote was obtained. But this was only one mood; and, when he found Bright quite irresponsive, he ended his talk in a deeper vein. 'No man knew what he had struggled against and overcome; he had been a Minister, and was now about to be beaten. He had always felt the insecurity of their position, and had not removed to Downing Street[2] on that account. He would not keep office or try to cling to it if they could not have *power*, and it was clear they had not the numbers with them to enable them to go on, and it was doubtful if they could live to Easter if they now escaped.'

This last mood corresponded to that of Disraeli's chief, who no doubt had a shrewd idea of what was passing in his mind, and who was writing to him at the very time

[1] Trevelyan's *Bright*, Journal, Dec. 15, 1852.

[2] Though Disraeli had not gone to live in Downing Street, he had decorated the reception-rooms. He wrote to his wife in September of this year from the official residence: 'The rooms look admirable. I think the saloon the most effective in London: the dining-room all right and very good.'

that this curious scene was being enacted in Grosvenor Gate.

From Lord Derby.

Private and Confidential. ST. JAMES'S SQUARE, *Wednesday night* [*Dec.* 15]. — The more I reflect upon the position of our affairs which you presented to me this evening, the less I am satisfied with the position which we shall occupy, if by any concession we obtain a respite from an adverse vote to-morrow night. The case may be different if we can obtain a respite without concession; but even then we shall not stand satisfactory to ourselves, nor, I am afraid, to the country. We may buy off a hostile vote before Christmas; but how shall we stand afterwards? We have abandoned the principle of Protection in deference to the voice of the country; we always said that we would do so. We prepared our Budget, of which one main element was the reduction of the malt tax as the *only* relief granted to the land, and that granted because it was only incidentally a relief to them, accompanying advantages, in the spirit of Free Trade policy, to the consumers. You say, and I believe truly, that in any case we cannot carry our reduction of the malt tax; but, if we cannot, can we carry any other reduction of taxation avowedly for the relief of the land? I think you will at once answer, No: and I am afraid it is so.

Now, if it be so, shall we not be justly exposed to a double attack, from our friends and our opponents, from the one that we are conferring no boon on them, but, on the contrary, subjecting real property to new imposts; and from the other, that we are needlessly involving ourselves in an extension of direct taxation, most unpopular in itself, and uncalled for by any public necessity? We have staked our existence on our Budget as a *whole* — we have asked for a decision of Parliament, which is to say whether as a whole they will accept it, and us to administer it; can we, with credit, accept a departure from it which, as a whole, doing impartial justice to all the various classes interested, will disturb the general balance, and force upon us, in point of fact, a complete reconstruction? And when we come to reconstruct, what shall we have to say to our agricultural supporters, who will find themselves without a vestige of relief, and even with an increased weight of taxation? We bound ourselves, before the dissolution, to abide by the decision of the country as to the maintenance of the system of Free Trade; but we bound ourselves no less strongly to relieve the land, to some extent, from the consequences of that Free Trade. How can we declare, by concession on the house tax, that we will deprive ourselves of the means of doing *anything* for that interest to which, after all, we owe our position?

If indeed you are of opinion that, by postponing the absolute decision on the amount of house tax, you will be enabled, abandoning the malt tax, to give such other relief to the land as may save our honour; or that you see your way to such a conclusion from a definitive abandonment of the double duty, and the adoption of a lower scale, I am ready to concur with you, though reluctantly, in deferring the crisis of our fate till after Christmas; but I own that if you are only to escape defeat to-morrow by a virtual surrender of your Budget — at least, of so much of it as promises *any* relief to our own friends, and without the prospect of the slightest step in their favour in our subsequent arrangements — I think the temporary respite will be dearly bought; and that you had better be defeated honestly in a fairly-fought field than escape under a cloud, to encounter aggravated defeat with alienated friends and sneering opponents. Perhaps I do not read the House of Commons aright, nor exactly know what are their feelings; but if we are to be a Government, we must be so by our own friends, and in spite of all combinations, and not by purchasing a short-lived existence upon the forbearance of the Radical party.

My deliberate opinion is, that the utmost amount of concession which you ought to make is to accept the principle of extension and increase of the house tax, without binding yourself or the House to the amount of the latter, reserving that for the calm consideration of the Government during the recess; but refusing to pledge yourself *against* the amount as originally proposed, or to any figure which may make the rest of your Budget *impossible*. If the House have not so much confidence in us as to place us in a majority on these conditions, it is high time that the country should satisfy itself whether any other possible combination possesses *more* of its confidence. If such a combination can be found, the business of the country may be carried on, and we shall be, though defeated, not discredited. If no such combination can be formed, we must very shortly return to power, with increased means from the failure of our divided oponents. This is my deliberate opinion, unbiassed, I hope, by any personal considerations; but if you have any doubt as to the course to be pursued, you had better call a Cabinet for to-morrow. I will see none of our colleagues, and my opinion shall be reserved until every member shall have expressed his own.

To Lord Derby.

Confidential. Grosvenor Gate, *Dec.* 16, 1852. — I do not think there is any necessity to call a Cabinet, for, I am sure, everyone must agree with you on the subject.

Your letter has removed the only dark spot in my political

career, which was the fear, from something you once said to me, that retirement from office would be the term of your public life. Personally, I should then feel isolated; but, as it is, I would prefer being your colleague in opposition to being the colleague of any other man as a Minister.

In accordance with the agreement manifested in these letters, Disraeli stated at the beginning of the final night's debate that the Government would regard the vote as involving an increase as well as an extension of the house tax; and thereupon issue was joined. It was shortly after ten when the Chancellor of the Exchequer rose to answer his assailants. 'During a whole week they had baited him; night after night they had derided and ridiculed him, taunted and twitted him, scoffed and scouted him,' writes a contemporary observer.[1] 'He scarcely seemed to hear, and not at all to feel;' his face wore 'that cold changeless look which, in natures such as his, covers depths of smouldering emotion. . . . So he sat, hour after hour, night after night, the full black eye gazing upon vacancy, his pale face veiled in apathy.' Now his hour had arrived. He was never so great as when at bay, and the welcoming cheers of his party showed at once their sympathy and their expectations. He began with studied calmness, and spoke throughout with such precise elocution that every word could be heard; and every word told. 'Superlative acting' it appeared to the moral sensitiveness of Gladstone; a more sympathetic and clear-sighted onlooker saw that 'feelings long restrained and painfully excited were struggling to escape and panting for expression.' Scorn, perhaps, was the prevailing feeling; irony and sarcasm the principal weapons.

Friends and foes alike admitted that the orator's powers had never been more brilliantly displayed. 'Sir,' he began, 'after four nights of criticism, conducted by some of the most considerable reputations in this House, on the financial propositions that I have laid on the table of the Committee, I now rise to vindicate those propositions.' He dealt first with the objections of detail, especially

[1] In *The Tablet and Telegraph*, Dec. 25, 1852.

those on his proposed dealings with the sum of £400,000, which were 'assailed in language and a tone somewhat unusual, certainly not very Parliamentary,' by Wood, who, instead of addressing the Chair, addressed Disraeli personally. Graham had talked of the benefits of this Public Works Loan Fund to country gentlemen. Why, it had been spent behind the back of the House on such profitless enterprises as a Thames tunnel and a park for Battersea, and the money had been lost. 'In stopping a system so iniquitous, I was only doing my duty as a guardian of the public purse.' He did not pay the sum into the balances of the Exchequer, as 'it would, in the present state of affairs, have been just the same as locking up that sum in an iron chest; it would have been immovable and unprofitable.' He apologised for troubling the House with these details of Treasury finance. 'My own knowledge on the subject is, of course, recent. I was not born and bred a Chancellor of the Exchequer; I am one of the Parliamentary rabble'—a mock depreciation of himself as compared with his opponents, which had an instant effect. Defending himself in regard to the drawback on malt to be payable in October, Disraeli held up to ridicule Lowe's ostentatious learning about brewing. 'Why fix the 10th of October?' Lowe had asked. 'Here is a plot; if we can only find out why the Government fix upon the 10th of October, we shall be able at once to penetrate these financial mystifications.' Disraeli was surprised that one who seemed so complete a master of the art of brewing, and had made so eloquent a defence of the system of credit to maltsters, should be unaware that the malting season was from October to May.

Passing to more serious subjects, Disraeli pointed out that, in contemplating a revision of the financial system, it was essential to discover how far the country would consent to direct taxation. For this, Graham, 'prompt in accusation at all times,' had accused him of pushing direct taxation to a rash extreme, and Wood had called him 'reckless.' This charge of recklessness was brought by one who seemed to forget that, when he, as Chancellor of the Exchequer, was in possession of both an income tax and a window tax, he came down to the House one day and proposed to a startled assembly to double the income tax. That might indeed have been called reckless — especially as on the first menace of opposition the same Minister withdrew his proposition.[1] The House was worked up to a high state of passion as Disraeli continued to pour scorn upon his hapless predecessor: —

> Talk of recklessness! Why, what in the history of finance is equal to the recklessness of the right honourable gentleman? And what was the ground on which he withdrew this enormous proposition — a proposition which only the safety of the State would have justified him in making? When he was beaten, baffled, humiliated, he came down to the House of Commons, and said he had sufficient revenue without resorting to that proposition! The future historian will not be believed when he states that a Minister came down with a proposition nearly to double the income tax, and, when that measure was rejected, the next day announced that the ways and means were ample without it. But then the right hon. gentleman tells me — in not very polished, and scarcely in Parliamentary language — that I do not know my business. He may have learned his business. The House of Commons is the best judge of that; I care not to be his critic. Yet, if he has learned his business, he has still to learn some other things — he has to learn that petulance is not sarcasm, and that insolence is not invective.

A storm of cheers and counter-cheers greeted this biting retort, and then Disraeli, in a lower key, dwelt for awhile on his proposals about income tax. The Government were determined to recognise a difference between precarious and realised incomes, but they were aware that 'to frame a complete measure on this subject would baffle the happiest genius in finance,' and therefore the details would be open to modification. Next he turned upon Graham, 'whom I will not say I greatly respect, but rather whom I greatly regard' — a phrase which roused Gladstone's subsequent indignation. There is, however,

[1] See above, pp. 105, 106. It was Russell, the Prime Minister, who actually brought the proposal to double the income tax before the House in 1848; but, of course, he was acting on behalf of the Chancellor of the Exchequer, Wood.

creased — has governed all recent financial schemes. The justice of taxing precarious — or, as the modern phrase is, 'earned' — incomes more lightly than realised incomes has been recognised. The malt tax has gone; the tea duties have been greatly reduced. One admirable principle which Disraeli laid down, that direct taxation should not be based on large exemptions, but should be, so far as practicable, as general as indirect, has indeed met with increasing neglect. But this result of democracy, which tends to exempt almost entirely from taxation the classes who hold political power, fills political philosophers with disquiet for the future.

Ministers resigned at once, and on the following Monday[1] Disraeli announced the fact in the House of Commons. After all the storms of the last few weeks, the parting scene was a peaceful one, to the astonishment of the Queen and the Prince, who had not expected to find the leading spirits of the Commons 'of a sudden all so well-bred.' Russell claimed the credit of having suggested to Disraeli the propriety of taking the initiative in frank apology. Disraeli did so, as Lord Morley says, 'with infinite polish and grace.' Fraser noted that he wore 'an exceptional air of gaiety,' and was particularly neat and spruce in dress and appearance.

I hope the House will not think it presumptuous on my part, if . . . I venture to offer them my grateful thanks for the indulgent, and I may even say the generous, manner in which on both sides I have been supported in attempting to conduct the business of this House. If, sir, in maintaining a too unequal struggle, any word has escaped my lips (which I hope has never been the case except in the way of retort) which has hurt the feelings of any gentleman in this House, I deeply regret it. And I hope that the impression on their part will be as transient as the sense of provocation was on my own. The kind opinion of the members of this House, whatever may be their political opinions, and wherever I may sit, will always be to me a most cherished possession, one which I shall always covet and highly appreciate.

To this overture Russell, Graham, and Wood responded suitably. Russell complimented Disraeli on the ability

[1] Dec. 20.

and gallantry with which he had carried on the struggle; Graham declared he had never failed to admire his talents; Wood was only too anxious to return to the old terms of reciprocal kindness with him. Perhaps the good feeling did not go very deep. The blunt Sibthorp, who definitely returned to his allegiance to Derby and Disraeli, said: 'I have heard that you may knock a man down, and then step forward with courtesy to give him a plaster. I neither quite subscribe to the knocking down, nor have I any faith in the sincerity of those who offer the plaster.' He regarded the Coalition as a 'phalanx of conspirators,' and meant to be on his guard against 'the man-traps and spring-guns of hon. gentlemen opposite.'

The grace of Disraeli's farewell was not confined to the House of Commons. To the Queen he wrote: 'Mr. Disraeli humbly begs permission to lay at your Majesty's feet his dutiful and grateful sense of the gracious and indulgent kindness which your Majesty has been pleased to bestow upon him;' and he assured the Prince that he would 'ever remember with interest and admiration the princely mind in the princely person,' and be at all times prepared to prove his devotion. To the Treasury, from which he had taken his private secretary, T. P. Courtenay,[1] and where he had made himself greatly liked, he did not stint his acknowledgments; and particularly to its permanent chief, whose reply is a valuable testimony, from one whose standard of public duty was notably high, to the spirit in which the retiring Chancellor of the Exchequer had performed the duties of his great office: —

From Sir Charles Trevelyan.

TREASURY, *Dec.* 29, 1852. — I sincerely thank you for your *parting kindness* in writing me a letter containing a great deal more than I deserve.

It is, nevertheless, a satisfaction to me to know that, having done *my best*, my exertions have been appreciated by you.

I feel grateful for the uniform cordiality and courtesy I have experienced from you, and I shall always recollect with pleasure and bear testimony to the direct and obvious regard you have had for public interests in all my intercourse with you.

[1] A member of the Devon family, who died prematurely in 1861.

I had been so long a public servant that perhaps this gives me more satisfaction than even personal kindness to myself. You have my best wishes for your health and happiness.

The Conservative Government had no reason to blush for the results of their ten months' term of office. They had been without a majority in the House of Commons, and the Court, though correct in its attitude, had been markedly unsympathetic. Nevertheless Derby could justly boast that, in spite of Malmesbury's inexperience, the foreign relations of the country were the better for his administration. The difficult question of the recognition of Louis Napoleon, and the still more difficult question of his title — the magic figure III., which had seemed to foreshadow a revival of Continental warfare — had been adjusted without conceding objectionable claims, and without imperilling the good understanding with France which was so valuable to this country. We had kept clear of the Russian combination against France, and shown the Emperor Nicholas that there were British statesmen who knew their own minds. Disraeli himself had been so occupied with the domestic battle that he had not played this time a leading part in the foreign discussions, though the results must have been thoroughly welcome to him. But he had helped, by the Militia Act and by his provision in the autumn, to strengthen the national defences. A Constitution had been given to New Zealand, and legal reform had been materially advanced. Government had been efficiently carried on in spite of the rawness of Ministers. Above all, the Ministry had relieved the country of the doubt about the permanence of the new commercial system which had paralysed so many energies. Free Trade was now established with the concurrence of the Conservatives. By his loyalty to his chief and to his colleagues Disraeli had exposed himself to virulent criticism, which circumstances prevented him from meeting conclusively. But he had, at any rate, shown the almost illimitable range of his political resources ; and his position as Leader had been confirmed by ten months of dexterous management. He had proved his capacity for the highest offices in the State.

CHAPTER XIII

Mrs. Brydges Willyams

1851—1863

About the time of Disraeli's first taste of office a new personality came into his life, and he formed an intimacy of a romantic character which was only broken by death. Though his friends were many, his intimates had been few; perhaps only three, indeed, down to this period — his father, his sister, and his wife. His father was dead; to his sister and his wife was now added — in the person of an elderly widow, Mrs. Brydges Willyams, of Mount Braddon, Torquay — a third woman friend, with whom his relations became only less intimate than with them, and with whom he maintained an affectionate correspondence for more than ten years. About the origin of this 'curious and delicate idyll,' as Froude happily terms it, many stories have been told, of varying degrees of inaccuracy. The true facts have been put on record, from personal knowledge, by Sir Philip Rose, in a detailed memorandum, dated May 1, 1882, which leaves little unexplained:

Prior to the year 1851 this lady appears to have occasionally written to Mr. Disraeli, either after one of his political speeches, or upon the publication of a new work, expressing her profound admiration for the author, and her sympathy with his noble vindication of the race of Israel; but, like most public men, accustomed to receive this sort of homage, especially from ladies, Mr. Disraeli had taken no notice of her letters, and had only ascertained, by a casual inquiry of a Devonshire friend, that a gentlewoman of that name resided at the address from which the letters were dated.

It subsequently transpired that Mrs. Brydges Willyams was *née* a Miss Mendez da Costa, of the race of Israel, though a professor of the Christian faith. Her mother was married a

From the photograph of a caricature in the possession of the Willyams family.

second time, to a Mr. Ford, and Miss Mendez da Costa married Colonel Brydges Willyams, who commanded the Devonshire[1] Militia, and who left her a widow without children.

She was a lady of advanced age, of moderate fortune, inherited from her own family, but of great intelligence and considerable intellectual powers, and had an enthusiastic pride in the race from which she sprung; this, in fact, was the tie that first attracted her to Mr. Disraeli, and secured her devoted attachment to him.

In the year 1851 Mr. Disraeli brought me a letter he had just received, which required an immediate answer. I remember his words: 'I have received an important letter, and I come to you, as my best friend, to ask your advice.' He then showed me a letter written in a large, bold hand, without the usual commencement or ending, but only the signature, 'S. Brydges Willyams.' Although all other letters seem to have been preserved, I have not, at present, lighted upon this one among Lord Beaconsfield's papers; but I have the clearest recollection of its contents, and even of the wording, which was original and peculiar, and, to the best of my recollection, as follows:

'I have often before addressed you in reference to your political speeches and your published works; but I now write to you upon a private subject. I am about to make my will, and I have to ask, as a great favour, that you will oblige me by being one of the executors.'

She then went on to mention some trifling matters in which she was interested, and concluded her letter thus:

'I think it right to add that whoever are my executors will also be my residuary legatees, and that the interest they will take under my will, although not a considerable one, will, at all events, be substantial.'

We consulted over this letter, and I gave my advice, which was in accord with Mr. Disraeli's own instinct, that he ought not to be hasty or eager in accepting the proposal; and, beyond a simple acknowledgment of the receipt of the letter, and stating that the subject required consideration, he allowed a month or six weeks to elapse before giving any definite answer; and then he wrote only a conditional acceptance, suggesting that, as he wished for more information, and his arrangements for the autumn recess included some visits in Devonshire, he would take the opportunity of calling upon her at Torquay and making her personal acquaintance.

Upon returning from his first visit to Torquay, Mr. Disraeli brought me a memorandum from Mrs. Brydges Willyams of

[1] It was the Cornish, and not the Devonshire, Militia, which Colonel Brydges Willyams commanded.

her wishes, and a request from her that I would act for her professionally, and prepare a will for carrying them out. As I saw by the memo that there was a pecuniary benefit intended for Mr. Disraeli, I told him that, looking to his interest alone, I thought I had better not act for Mrs. Brydges Willyams, but that he should suggest to her to apply to some local solicitor of high standing. . . . The advice was followed. . . .

As the acquaintance thus formed grew and ripened into a most intimate friendship, other wills were made from time to time, the latest being executed in 1857, by which the residue of her estate, subject to legacies of a considerable amount, was bequeathed to Mr. Disraeli absolutely, Mr. Disraeli and a Mr. Stephen Wilson being appointed executors. Mr. Wilson predeceased the testatrix, who died in 1863. Her estate was sworn under £40,000. The legacies bequeathed by the will would have reduced the residue to about £20,000; but as several of the principal legatees had also predeceased the testatrix, and consequently their legacies had lapsed, the amount of residue actually realised somewhat exceeded £30,000. . . .

Daniel Mendez da Costa, a well-known and prosperous member of the Da Costa family, was the grandfather of Sarah Brydges Willyams; and her father was apparently Abraham Mendez da Costa, of Bath, who died in 1782, while his children were quite young.[1] So Mrs. Willyams must have been at least seventy when Disraeli first corresponded with her in 1851. She was probably older. Her husband, James Brydges Willyams, of Carnanton, St. Columb, Cornwall, an eldest son, who predeceased his father, and so never came into the family property, died in 1820, at the age of forty-eight. It was believed in the Willyams family that his wife was older than himself. In that case she must have been eighty in 1851, and over ninety when she died in 1863.

It was in the spring of 1851 that the correspondence began; and the natural inference from Sir Philip Rose's memorandum is that it was in the autumn of that year that Disraeli first visited Torquay and made Mrs. Will-

[1] I am indebted for this information about the Da Costas to Mr. Lucien Wolf, whose authority on such matters is unquestionable. The ordinary books of reference appear to be wrong in giving Emanuel Mendez da Costa as Mrs. Willyams's father.

yams's personal acquaintance. It may very well have been so, but it was presumably only a flying call; for the earliest letters preserved make no reference to any visit before August, 1853, when, as on all subsequent occasions, Mrs. Disraeli accompanied her husband. It was not till after this period that the correspondence assumed its very affectionate and intimate character. It opened with mutual presents of books.

To Mrs. Brydges Willyams.

GROSVENOR GATE, *Aug.* 2, 1851.

MY DEAR MADAM, — I must offer many apologies for not previously acknowledging your obliging remembrance of me, but the death of the late Lord Derby and the illness of the present one have combined to overwhelm me with affairs. I leave town on Monday for Hughenden Manor, where I shall find an entire, and most welcome, repose.

Brown was a favourite writer of my father, who looked upon him as the most sensible and satisfactory of the metaphysicians; and his collected works were very welcome to me.

You will receive to-morrow, or Monday, *Tancred*, which, notwithstanding it is in the form of a novel, I hope you will read, and read even with attention, as it is a vindication, and, I hope, a complete one, of the race from which we alike spring. I have added to the packet the last, and classical, edition of the *Curiosities of Literature*, which you may place by the side of *Charles the First*. In a memoir of my father, prefixed to this edition, you will find the name of your family incidentally mentioned. Adieu! dear madam. — Yours sincerely, D.

From Mrs. Brydges Willyams.

MT. BRADDON, *Aug.* 4, 1851.

MY DEAR SIR, — I thank you gratefully for a fine logical speech, which I have circulated to enlighten some of my friends, and for two most admirable works, which I shall reserve to devote my time to when I return from London. I am going there to-morrow for a fortnight, to see the Great Exhibition, with one of my nieces who has seen it throughout, and has such an uncommonly fine memory that I could not have a better cicerone. I am extremely glad that you are enjoying 'an entire repose,' so essential to the mind and to existence. If, however, you should happen to come to town whilst I am there, and could appoint a time and place at the Crystal Palace, I should be delighted to meet you, and to pay my lawful debts; as to other debts, I must not soar to impossibilities. — Ever sincerely yours, S. B. W.

I have taken an apartment at 6, Bryanston Street, Portman Square.

Disraeli had left town when Mrs. Willyams arrived, and did not return to meet his correspondent at the Crystal Palace. Always courteous to ladies, and anxious to show special courtesy to a devoted admirer and benefactress, he reverted more than once, in subsequent letters, to his regret at missing her on this occasion. Two years afterwards he sent her his portrait as a kind of return visit; and eleven years afterwards, at the time of the next Exhibition, he again recalled her invitation and his default.

To Mrs. Brydges Willyams.

GROSVENOR GATE, *Feb.* 25, 1853. — I fear the portrait of an ex-Minister can hardly be a very acceptable offering to anyone, but I have, nevertheless, taken the liberty of directing Messrs. Colnaghi to send you one of myself, which they have published.

As I was prevented, by absence from town, having the pleasure of meeting you two years ago, you must kindly interpret the arrival of this silent guest as, in a manner, returning your visit to London, which I should be very glad to hear that you thought of repeating this season. — Ever yours, D.

HOUSE OF COMMONS, *May* 9, 1862. — . . . The Great Exhibition is not as fascinating a one as that you remember, when you made me an assignation by the crystal fountain, which I was ungallant enough not to keep, being far away when it arrived at Grosvenor Gate. But, tho' not so charming, it is even more wonderful. One was a woman; this is a man! . . .

These letters, and Sir Philip Rose's memorandum, seem entirely to dispose of Froude's account[1] of the origin of the friendship. Froude tells us that the lady asked for a meeting at the fountain in the Great Exhibition; that, after some hesitation, Disraeli went; that she told him an unintelligible story, and gave him a packet which proved to contain a case for submission to lawyers and a banknote for £1,000 to pay his election expenses.

[1] *Life of Beaconsfield*, ch. 12.

In reality the first meeting was at Torquay, and not in London, the only question being whether it took place in 1851 or 1853. Mrs. Willyams did not suggest an appointment at the Exhibition till after she and Disraeli were already in friendly correspondence, and that appointment he was unable to keep. The document that brought them together was her proposed will in his favour, and not a case for submission to lawyers; and if, as is quite possible, she ever gave him £1,000 for his election expenses, it was not after the mysterious fashion of this legend, for which Froude gives no authority.

To Mrs. Brydges Willyams.

GROSVENOR GATE, *Dec.* 21, 1851.

MY DEAR MADAM, — Passing thro' town, from Hatfield to Hughenden, I took the liberty, yesterday, of sending you a copy of a work which I have just published [*Lord George Bentinck*]. The strife of parties will not be very interesting to you, but, in the treatment of my theme, there may perhaps be some traits of character and some subjects touched upon, which may attract a thoughtful and instructed mind. — Believe me, sincerely yours, D.

Further progress with the friendship thus pleasantly begun was delayed by the formation of the first Derby-Disraeli Ministry. He had little time for letter-writing, and she would not encroach upon his scanty leisure. But a touching letter which she wrote, as the public funeral of the Duke of Wellington was approaching, shows how anxiously she was watching his career, and how quick she was to anticipate any risks to which his health might be exposed:

From Mrs. Brydges Willyams.

MT. BRADDON, *Sept.* 29, 1852.

MY DEAR SIR, — The assurance of your friendship, which will never be effaced from my remembrance, leads me to express my most earnest wish that you would get a substitute for yourself to attend the grand public funeral in contemplation. I would most gladly vote for medals and monuments that might be a beacon to seamen and a protection to our coast, but not for a fleeting, pompous, melancholy spectacle which involves a sacrifice of time, health, and life. — With best wishes, I am ever, truly yours, S. B. W.

When in Opposition, Disraeli wrote again, resuming the theme of race:

To Mrs. Brydges Willyams.

GROSVENOR GATE, *Feb.* 28, 1853. — . . . It is race, not religion, that interests me in the instance in question. All Europeans, and many others, profess the religion of the Hebrews.

I, like you, was not bred among my race, and was nurtured in great prejudice against them. Thought, and the mysterious sympathy of organisation, have led me to adopt the views with respect to them, which I have advocated, and which, I hope I may say, have affected in their favor public opinion. . . .

I beg to assure you that I am not at all 'unapproachable' to those who tenderly interest me, like yourself. If you come to town this season, I hope to see you, and very often. And if you do not come, it shall go hard if, before the year elapses, I do not visit your sunny hill on our western coast. — Ever yours, D.

Mrs. Willyams did not come to London, and accordingly the Disraelis went to her at Torquay after the close of the session in the middle of August.

To Mrs. Brydges Willyams.

TORQUAY, *Tuesday* [*Aug.* 16, 1853]. — Mrs. Disraeli is very anxious to have the pleasure of being presented to you, and we propose, if a word by the bearer does not tell you are engaged, to take your mountain fortress by assault this morning, and early — about noon. Ever yours, D.

The Disraelis stayed a week in Torquay, and returned charmed with the kindness and sympathy of their new friend, who, on her part, was confirmed in her devotion to him and attracted by his wife. Till they came again she would, she told them, 'live on retrospection.' 'We passed a most agreeable week,' he wrote on August 25, 'and have done nothing but talk of you and yours ever since.'

To Mrs. Brydges Willyams.

HUGHENDEN MANOR, *Sept.* 29, 1853. — My life is so uneventful that you must take a letter from me as a morning call from some insipid country neighbour, who begins by talking about the weather. I won't do that, but I must talk about myself, which is still worse.

I thought your criticism on *Ixion* as brilliant as anything in its pages, and was very much gratified by it. I quite forgot to mention, in a little advertisement to the volume, that *Ixion* and the *Infernal Marriage* were written more than twenty years ago. Many of the allusions, now obsolete, require this. Jupiter, for example, was George IV., and Apollo, Lord Byron. So in the *Infernal Marriage* there is a great deal of the politics of the Duke of Wellington and Lord Grey's Government; and Tiresias was Talleyrand, and Mantho, his niece, the Duchess of Dino. I had sketched, some years ago, the conclusion of this masqueraderie, but it was stolen from my chambers, with some other MSS. and property, in my days of solitariness, and I never had heart to undertake it again.

I have scarcely left the grounds since our return; books and writing fill up the tranquil hours, occasionally disturbed by a letter from some statesman out of office, raising the spectre of unsatisfied ambition. If it were not for the point of honor, I would abjure politics, having had my dream, tho' not altogether a very brilliant one. Two living statesmen, however, appeared on Tuesday week last, and stayed till Saturday — Lord Henry Lennox, one of my aide-de-camps, and whom I had the pleasure of making a Lord of the Treasury for ten months; and Mr. Smythe, the eldest son of Lord Strangford, and who, both as to ability and acquirement, is perhaps the most brilliant man of the day, tho' more adapted to social and literary pursuits than the stern business of politics. It was his first visit to Hughenden, tho' not Lord Henry's. Their presence occasioned us a few days of unusual exertion, and I showed them the land around, as you showed me Ugbrook and Berry Pomeroy, and the wooded banks of the Dart. Our country is not so fair and soft, but it has some charms with sunbeams. My nearest neighbour has historic interest of a very peculiar kind. The estate is that famous Hampden where ship-money was refused. Mr. Hampden died 200 years ago fighting *against* Charles Stuart; his considerable estate, descending thro' the female line, is now the property of Cameron of Lochiel, the great Highland Chief, whose ancestor 100 years ago (1740) died fighting *for* Charles Stuart. Such is history, and such is life! Strange things both.

All this part of England is History. The great events of the Parliamentary struggle of 1640, in fact, were confined to the Metropolitan counties — Beds, Bucks, Huntingdonshire, etc.; and you may travel from this place to Kimbolton Castle in the latter county, and mark, the whole way, the seats and residences of the leaders of those days.

What you did me the honor of quaffing at Torquay was not seltzer, but old-fashioned *soda* water. When I called for the former, the landlord was exhausted, and, it being Sunday, he could not replenish his stores. I have myself no faith in soda water, tho' I think it must be free from vitriolic acid. The characteristic of Struve's seltzer is *carbonic acid gas*, which he obtains from marble. Lord Hardwicke told me that, when in 1848–49 he was serving on the Italian coasts, he found large blocks of Carrara marble perpetually shipping to Struve at Brighton, as the finest source of carbonic gas.

How often I wish that next summer may be green and golden, and that you may be under this roof, and a visitant to many places which I think would interest you! and how often I recall, with charm, and often with consolation, the kindness which you have shown to me, and the mysterious sympathy which now binds us together! — Ever yours, D.

HUGHENDEN, *Oct.* 21, 1853. — I fear my despatches will be almost as numerous as those of the Great Powers to the Porte, but, altho' I wrote yesterday on another and graver subject, I must send one line to say that the illustrious characters have arrived at Hughenden Manor, and made as great a sensation as any at the Congress, or Conference, of Vienna, being habited in scarcely less gorgeous costume.

How kind of you to send me so magnificent a gift — and what taste in its selection!

My library is my weak point. It is that of which, of all material possessions, I am most proud and fond. I inherited and I enriched it. I shall place your interesting and gorgeous tomes by some worthy brothers. May you some day see them!

The last present you gave me was a singular — but not a very tender — one. It was a thunderbolt! When you see it again, you will find it set in marble, and forming my principal paper-weight. The inscription on it is *From Ixion in Heaven*.

I will not defend Struve any more.

Galen tells us in an ancient passage, which has influenced me often in life, that we should 'thicken the blood before we slumber.' I remark you do not follow this archaic dogma of health. Something taken half an hour before repose, very nutritious but very light, might charm your eyelids, and make you dream only of your friends.

One scribbles to you now — very hastily — but he is obliged to send to-day a very grave despatch to Paris. — Adieu, D.

I have got the militia[1] quartered here, and am obliged to

[1] In another letter to Mrs. Willyams, Disraeli wrote: 'It is astonishing how quickly the ploughboys turn into martinets.'

give, what Lord Londonderry would call, 'great military banquets.' I want you on my arm to help me. You would be quite at home.

The beginnings of this romantic correspondence have been set forth at some length. For the subsequent ten years, till Mrs. Willyams's death, it is one of the first-hand authorities for Disraeli's life, and will be frequently quoted in this biography. Disraeli wrote whenever he had time, and Mrs. Disraeli took his place when he was too busy. A chronicle of Disraeli's doings, and a reflection of many of his thoughts, was regularly transmitted to Torquay. The correspondence began at a time when that between Disraeli and his sister was failing, and to a large extent fills its place, though it is less spontaneous and more mannered. Politics, literature and society, family affairs and country pleasures — each takes its turn in his letters; often, indeed, they are all blended in one characteristic epistle. The intercourse was almost wholly carried on by letter. There is no reason to suppose that Mrs. Willyams, though often asked, ever visited the Disraelis either at Grosvenor Gate or at Hughenden. After her venture to the Great Exhibition in August, 1851, she seems to have been either too infirm or too home-keeping to pay visits. Once a year, and no more, the Disraelis spent a week, or perhaps a fortnight, at Torquay. For the first four years, 1853-1856, this visit was paid in August or September; for the last six, in the winter. They did not stay with Mrs. Willyams in her villa, Mount Braddon, but they put up at an hotel, spending, however, most of their afternoons and evenings with their friend.

There was an unceasing exchange of presents between Hughenden and Torquay. Not only books, as we have seen, but flowers, were constantly passing to and fro. Roses came from Torquay, and violets from Hughenden. Torquay also sent, year after year, cuttings which were planted at Hughenden, and greatly added to its amenities. Mrs. Disraeli kept Mrs. Willyams supplied with newspapers

political triumphs and defeats, of her hero. Her sympathy was sought when James Disraeli's wife died in 1857—'a bride, a mother, and a corpse, in eight months'; and when Sarah Disraeli died in 1859, 'I do not like you to know anything from a newspaper,' wrote Mrs. Disraeli, 'which has made us so unhappy.' When Disraeli regained office in February, 1858, he caused a telegram, in days when telegrams were rare portents, to be sent her immediately. A year later he wrote from Downing Street: 'This is the anniversary of our entering office. I thought you would like to have a line upon such a day, though I write from the field of battle and with as many cares upon my shoulders as man can well bear.' And when he left office his final letter was for her:

To Mrs. Brydges Willyams.

DOWNING STREET, *June* 17, 1859.—I send you my last official letter, as I am now going down to the House of Commons to announce the formation of the New Government, and to-morrow morning I go down to Windsor, to resign my seals to her Majesty.

I thought you would like to have the last line I write from Downing Street.

In answer to the last line from Downing Street, Mrs. Willyams expressed a wish that, 'instead of wasting breath in the Lower House, you would take a step higher.' Mrs. Disraeli replied: 'He would not, my dear, go to the Upper House for the world, not for many, many years; he enjoys his fame too much in the Lower House. He could not take the red ribbon without being knighted, and that would be dreadful—to be called Sir B. Disraeli. The Queen is all kindness to Dis, and would give him anything.'

What manner of woman was Disraeli's 'benefactress,' as he was proud to call her? Her most striking characteristic was the abnormal development in her of the feminine capacity of devotion. She had worshipped Disraeli, and determined to make him her heir, before she knew him, and acquaintance only intensified her feelings.

She was absolutely wrapped up in her 'dear Dizzi,' and could never be grateful enough to him for giving her, as she quaintly phrased it, a place in his 'domain of peace and concord.' 'My happiest moments,' she told him, 'are when I think of your friendship.' His 'incomparable letters' were her greatest comfort. 'I wish I could give adequate acknowledgement for so much indulgence.' She was full of anxiety whenever she heard that he was indisposed. 'You sacrifice too much to fame. . . . What can be hoped from only three days at Hughenden?' Her confidence in his political genius was boundless. 'Your touch on politics is always harmonious. My idea is that the masses only wait for a rallying cry to rise here and there. My trust is in your prescience!' Devotion such as this appealed powerfully to his affectionate nature; and he paid her in return the compliment, not merely of that somewhat Oriental flattery which he always used with women, but of admitting her into his family circle and making her a sharer of his actions and his thoughts. 'Your constant kind and affectionate thoughts of him,' wrote Mrs. Disraeli to her, 'add much to the happiness of our lives. I never heard him appreciate so highly as yourself anyone, man or woman.'

Though she was a considerable reader, intellectually Mrs. Willyams was rather limited; and her letters hardly justify Sir Philip Rose's high praise of her mental powers. Of this limitation she was herself quite aware. Early in the acquaintance she wrote to Mrs. Disraeli: 'I am sorry to say that my head is my vulnerable point, and that in submission I deny myself of daily papers.' When the Disraelis had taken care that she was duly supplied with the London journals, she wrote: 'I indulge too much in lounging all the finest part of the day with the variety on my table. If ever I am to amend my ways, I must beg you will not be so profuse in treating me with the absorbing news of the day. . . . If I had memory, I might be a tolerable *superficial* politician, but, as it is, I am good for nothing except to join in a chorus of praise to the unrivalled genius of dear Dizzi.'

Though Mrs. Willyams's mental powers were limited, they were keen enough within their own range. Eccentric she may have been, and was; but she was a shrewd observer of people and things. She had, besides, many interests in common with her friends, especially delight in Nature, in country sights and sounds, and in gardening. Above all, the bond between her and Disraeli was the bond of race. In her will she gave as her reason for leaving him her fortune that it was done 'in testimony of my affection and of my approbation and admiration of his efforts to vindicate the race of Israel, with my views respecting which he is acquainted, and which I have no doubt he will endeavour to accomplish.' She was a Mendez da Costa; he believed himself to be a kinsman of the Laras; both Da Costas and Laras being aristocratic families of Peninsular Jews.[1] So when she wanted to get her coat-of-arms investigated and regularised by the Heralds' College, he entered eagerly into her project, and gave himself an infinity of trouble, during a space of nearly three years, to settle, satisfactorily to her, a business over which she showed herself rather captious and tiresome. The question was opened when he was in office in 1859, and was not finally closed till March, 1862. Incidentally in the course of the correspondence he explained and justified his own crest and quarterings. A few of his many letters on this somewhat esoteric subject will probably be enough.

To Mrs. Brydges Willyams.

HUGHENDEN MANOR, *June* 16, 1859.—... The last thing I did in office was to receive a communication from the Spanish and the Portuguese Ambassadors here, respecting the arms of the families of Mendez da Costa and Lara, respecting which they had for some time been making inquiries and researches for me....

[1] This was the belief both of Disraeli and of Mrs. Willyams; but Mr. Lucien Wolf claims to have shown that the Portuguese Jewish Laras, with whom the Disraelis were connected, had no connection with the Spanish noble family of Lara.

Grosvenor Gate, *July* 20, 1859.—I have forwarded to you to-day, by railroad, the emblazonment of the arms of Mendez da Costa. . . . The drawing was taken (from which the shield was emblazoned) from a tomb more than three hundred years old.

The quarterings are singular: the Lion of Leon, and a winged arm, holding a sword in the hand. Was it the arm of an archangel?

People put blocks of ice in their rooms, which produce a refreshing temperature. Try some thirty pounds of rough ice in this fashion. It will revive you—in heat which even the Mendez da Costas in their most fervent days, amid the sierras and skies of Andalusia, could not exceed!

I also (the Laras) quarter the Lion of Leon *rouge*.

Grosvenor Gate, *July* 23, 1859.—The Spanish families never had supporters, crests, or mottoes. The tower (Castle) of *Castille*, which I use as a crest, and which was taken from one of the quarters of my shield, was adopted by a Lara in the sixteenth century in Italy, where crests were the custom—at least, in the North of Italy—copied from the German heraldry. This also applies to my motto. . . .

Carlton Club, *July* 12, 1861.—The Heralds give me a great deal of trouble, but they are very positive people, and it will not do to make any mistake in their craft. They have promised this morning to give me a correct drawing of your shield on Tuesday next. They say that all your previous quarterings have been wrong—that is to say, that the arms of Legh ought never to have been introduced into your shield, your mother not having been an heiress—but that your own arms of Mendez da Costa ought to have been emblazoned. . . . They were anxious to know how you had obtained them, as nothing is more difficult than correct emblazonments of ancient Spanish arms. I told them that they had been copied from the Queen of Spain's own golden book, which was kept under her own key, which seemed to make their mouths water. I am sorry for these delays, but it will be a satisfaction to you that you will now have everything quite correct—the arms of Brydges Willyams and Mendez da Costa in a lozenge. They have the arms of Brydges Willyams registered, with a Cornish motto; but, as ladies do not use mottoes or crests, this does not concern us. . . .

So keen was Mrs. Willyams's pride in her family, and so convinced was she that Disraeli shared it to the full, that in her will she expressed a wish that he should use and adopt the names and arms of the families of Lara and Mendez da Costa in addition, or precedent, to that of Disraeli. In this, however, he disappointed her, being no doubt sensible of the ridicule to which the assumption of these sonorous names by a statesman of sixty would expose him.

Though Mrs. Willyams never saw Hughenden, her memory is closely bound up with it. The correspondence between her and the Disraelis is full of Hughenden. It was there, during the Parliamentary vacations, that he wrote her his longest and most frequent letters. He told her of all his doings there, of the visitors who came, the changes that were made, the growth of the trees, the beauty of the gardens. It was with the object of embellishing the rooms and the flower-beds of Hughenden that she made many of her presents; and she never wearied of hearing the smallest details of its growth and progress. From his letters to her we can largely reconstruct his life in the country, and complete the picture outlined in Chapter VI.

To Mrs. Brydges Willyams.

HUGHENDEN MANOR, *Wednesday* [*Dec.* 26, 1855]. — Yesterday there was a ball and a supper at Hughenden Manor, but Mrs. Disraeli and myself were not invited. Our household and their guests were dancing till past five o'clock this morning; you must have heard the fiddle, I think, at Torquay. But this is the reason that my despatch did not go by yesterday's post. They were all too busy, and all the people have gone to their work this morning, without ever having retired to rest. What rural rakes!

Aug. 28, 1858. — . . . I will give you some account of the present condition of some of the many offerings which you have been so kind as to make to this place.

In the first place, the small-leaved rose, trailed over a wire frame, lotus-shaped, has become a considerable bush, and was this season, at one time, the bearer of more than sixty flowers. Its surprising beauty was, I am told, greatly admired, but, alas! not by us, for, while it was flourishing and diffusing sweets, I was laboring to purify the Thames at Westminster. The gardener, however, has succeeded in grafting several very fine specimens from the parent stem, and these are all now alive and brilliant, to greet us with their presence.

HUGHENDEN MANOR, 1848.

From a water-colour drawing.

The two splendid jars are installed in the chief saloon, each on the top of a cabinet, and have a very excellent effect. The cabinets have long required a crowning decoration of this character.

In the library, on a stand built for the occasion, a number of Gould's *Birds* is always open, and they are really so life-like that, when one enters the room, one is almost tempted to walk on tiptoe, lest one might frighten them away.

The chief business of Mrs. Disraeli, during this residence, has been to adorn her terrace in the Italian style with a beautiful series of vases, which came from Florence, and which sparkle in the sun, their white and graceful forms well contrasting with the tall geraniums and blue Agapantha lilies which they hold. I think you would admire this terrace very much. It has only one fault — that you never walk on it. . . .

With regard to Mrs. Kneller's request,[1] I beg leave to say, that if it would please you that I should endeavour to assist her son, I will make the attempt with sincere gratification; but it will be to please you, and no one else, for I do not care one rush for Lord Bolingbroke, dead or living.

I shall try to send you some violets by this post, if I find any as sweet as some that charmed me a few days back.

Oct. 20, 1858. —. . . We were absent nearly a fortnight, and I find a great difference in the color of the trees — the limes all golden, the beeches ruddy brown, while the oaks and elms and pines are still dark and green, and contrast well with the brighter tints. But not a leaf has fallen; they want the first whisper of the frost, and then they will go out like lamps when the dawn breaks on a long festival. . . .

Aug. 31, 1859. —. . . Here our life is so monotonous that our only incident almost has been a rural fête, which Mrs. Disraeli gave to her schools — a hundred strong, and a hundred neighbours to meet them. They feasted and danced in the park, with my election banners, no longer lawful, to inspire them, and a most capital band. It really was a sight worthy of Watteau, and I preferred it infinitely to the fête given by H.R.H. the Duchess d'Aumale at Orleans House, which we had the honour to attend a few days before we left town, and which was in beautiful gardens, with gondolas on the river, and Princes and Princesses trifling and gliding thro' the berceaus. We had, among many other pastimes, a lottery, in which there were no blanks, there; but such games of chance are only for the heirs of the inheritance of Condé!

[1] Disraeli wrote to Mrs. Willyams from Windsor Castle, Nov. 15: 'I have sent, to-day, a nomination to a clerkship, in the national debt office, to the son of Mrs. Kneller.'

Baron Rothschild and all his family came and stayed two days with us. He brought me a dessert from Paris—of the most wonderful pines, peaches, and melons. I gave a dinner to the neighbourhood the second day, that he might meet the notables, and his dessert, *à la Russe*, was grouped round the little lemon-tree which you gave us two or three years ago, and which this year has *eight* fine golden fruit upon it. So, I flatter myself, I beat even the dessert of Paris.

Sept. 4, 1861.—A clear case of sympathy; for while, yesterday morning, you were sending us some of our most favorite delicacy, which are so difficult to get good, and which were in this instance delicious, we were trying to catch you a trout in our stream. The morning, however, was so bright that, after hours, we were unsuccessful; nevertheless, the sport in the bright park, and by the side of rippling waters, was delightful, tho' fruitless. After the arrival of your case, we determined to try again, a little before sunset, and in the first twilight landed a gentleman 4¼ pounds in weight!—pretty well for our little stream, that was dry for three years. I packed him up in the flags among which he was caught last evening, and sent him off instantly from the river-side. You ought to have had him *early* this morning, so he is as fresh as day; and I told them to put a brace of grouse in the basket. . . .

Aug. 21, 1862.—Here I have been 10 days, and meant to have written to you the very first. And yet I have done nothing; but have remained in a state of complete languor and apathy. It is always so. The sudden change and contrast from a life of unceasing excitement acts most strangely on the nervous system, and it takes me some time to acclimatise.

Not that it is *ennui*. For here is a great deal to do. No one could have been absent eight months from his Estate, and find *ennui* on his arrival—but I am incapable of performing what awaits me, and which, in its sort and manner, is also urgent, as much as affairs of State.

I begin, however, to thaw. It is so long since I was here, that even my ancient trees seem to have grown, and the modern conifers have wondrously shot up. . . . As for flowers, all Hughenden sparkles with the Microfolia rose, the numerous and brilliant offspring of the colony you sent from Mt. Braddon. Thus you see how races are propagated and how empires are formed!

But our public buildings are still more striking: a new school nearly finished, and a monument to my father, raised, in my absence, by my wife, and which, both for design, execution, and even material, is one of the most beautiful things not only in the County of Buckingham, but in England. . . .

Private. Sept. 1, 1862.—I am quite myself again, and, as I have been drinking your magic beverage for a week, and intend to pursue it, you may fairly claim all the glory of my recovery—as a fairy cures a knight after a tournament or a battle. I have a great weakness for mutton broth, especially with that magical sprinkle, which you did not forget. I shall call you in future after an old legend and a modern poem, 'The Lady of Shalott'!

I think the water of which it was made would have satisfied *even you.* For it was taken, every day, from our stream which rises among the chalk hills, glitters in the sun over a very pretty cascade, and then spreads and sparkles into a little lake, in which is a natural island. Since I wrote to you last, we have launched in this lake two most beautiful cygnets, to whom we have given the names of Hero and Leander. They are a source to us of unceasing interest and amusement. They are very handsome and very large, tho' as yet dove-colored.

I can no longer write to you of Cabinet Councils or Parliamentary struggles: here I see nothing but trees and books, so you must not despise this news of my swans!

Oct. 14, 1862.—. . . Last night I returned from Quarter Sessions, always a busy scene in our provincial life. It is, in fact, the old assembling of the Estates of a Province, with the Governor, or Lord-Lieutenant, in the chair, and all the notables around him: great debates about little things. In this county there is a regular magistrates' mess, so we don't dine together at an hotel or a pot-house, as in many other counties, but under our own roof, sitting on our own furniture, and drinking our own wines out of our own cellar—all which makes us a little pompous, especially the Wine Committee, who, you would think, were a Council of State.

On Thursday next we open our new school. It is built by the same architect who restored the crypt, designed the two sarcophagus', and also my father's monument, which latter erection is much admired by all the world. It is fifty feet high, and of the Italian style of the Renaissance period, which is, at the same time, rich and graceful. . . .

We are to walk to the school, which is in the village, one mile and a half away—a sort of procession—but, alas! what weather! 'Tis the middle of the equinoctial gales, which are a fortnight after their time. Think of us on Thursday—and pity me—addressing the infant generation under the new roof, probably wet to the skin!

Sept. 20, 1863.—. . . Here we are full of harvest-homes! a novel feature, as now practised, of our English country life. In old days, or, rather, two or three years ago, every farmer, after the harvest, gave a supper to his hinds, where they guzzled and got tipsy, and resumed their work in the morning with aching heads, after a rural debauch.

Now, instead of an isolated nocturnal revel in a farmhouse kitchen, all the farmers of the parish unite together and give to their collected laborers a festival in a tent, which will hold hundreds, with banners and a band. A day is set apart: all go in procession to the church, which is adorned with flowers and sheaves, the children sing chorales, and everyone has a favor, and a stalk of corn in his buttonhole.

The clergy are at the bottom of this movement: it connects the harvest with religion and the Church. Even a *dissenting* farmer can scarcely refuse to walk in the procession on such an occasion.

Unconsciously, all are reviving pagan rites, and restoring the Dionysian festivals!

Sept. 28, 1863.—You live in the world to what I do, who never see anything but books and trees. When we left Hughenden last year we sent in an architect and suite, and tho' ten months have elapsed, some workmen still linger about. We have realised a romance we had been many years meditating: we have restored the house to what it was before the Civil Wars, and we have made a garden of terraces, in which cavaliers might roam, and saunter, with their ladye-loves! The only thing wanting is that you should see it; but I am going to have in due time a competent artist down, who will photograph the house, gardens, terraces, monument, etc., etc., in every aspect, and these shall be sent, or, I hope, *brought*, to you, for the time is approaching when we must turn our thoughts to the western ocean, the classic waves of gigantic soles and colossal prawns!

All these alterations have prevented our receiving our friends this year, so I have been like a man in a desert island—beautiful, tho' lonely, and free from the despair of a Robinson Crusoe or an Alexander Selkirk, for I have a future—at Mount Braddon!

In making the alterations here, a great number of owls have been disturbed among the yew-trees; but they have been religiously cared for, as if I were the priest of Minerva, and now they have resumed their haunts. Their hooting at night is wilder and louder than the south-west wind, which, indeed, is only the accompaniment to their weirdish arias. And they tap at the windows with their fell beaks!

Not only was Mrs. Willyams keenly interested in Hughenden during her life, but by her own desire she was buried there. She died somewhat suddenly on November 11, 1863. Disraeli's last letter to her was written only on November 5. He was, clearly, quite unaware that she was ill, and was looking forward to his winter visit to Torquay. 'Adieu! we shall soon meet,' he concluded. He hurried to Torquay, but arrived too late. 'I have lost a kind and faithful friend,' he wrote to Derby, 'but I have lost her in the fulness of years, and she has made me the heir to her not inconsiderable fortune.' It was her wish to lie in the family vault in Hughenden Church, where her friend and his wife expected in their turn to be buried; but, to Disraeli's disgust, the vault was found to be closed.

To Philip Rose.

Dec. 1, 1863. — What are my rights as to vault in Hughenden Church? My benefactress was to have been buried in my vault there. Mr. Clubbe[1] wrote to me that Interment Act prevented burials in a church, and that the vault in the chancel (which I called, and believed to be, *my* vault) was closed accordingly.

I told him that Burials Act, in my belief, did not apply to country churches, and that the vault ought not to have been closed. It was impossible, however, at such a moment to have a controversy, and I was obliged, by great exertions, to have a vault made in the churchyard, contrary to the express wishes of the deceased, and where neither my wife nor myself will be buried, preferring even Kensal Green to anything so unprotected. . . .

It was found impossible to reopen the family vault, and both Disraeli and his wife subsequently overcame their objection to the site of Mrs. Willyams's grave. All three, benefactress and beneficiaries, now lie together just outside the east end of the church, and one monument, on the outer wall of the De Montfort Chapel, records the names and legends of them all.

[1] Vicar of Hughenden.

CHAPTER XIV

THE COALITION AND THE 'PRESS'

1852–1854

The Coalition which Disraeli anticipated and denounced was formed in December, 1852, with Aberdeen as Prime Minister, but not without many difficulties and searchings of heart. Disraeli wrote to Londonderry on December 21: 'I apprehend that the difficulties of the *personnel* — sixteen Secretaries of State — are minor obstacles compared with the daily, or rather hourly, increasing *émeute* of Brooks's and the Reform; especially the latter, the mainstay of a Liberal Government, and now finding the cake is to be cut up without their having a slice.' It took a week to compose the difficulties, and the Cabinet, as finally settled, contained six Whigs, six Peelites, and one Radical. As the party support consisted, according to Derby's estimate, of 120 Whigs, 30 Peelites, 150 Radicals, and 50 Irish Brigade, there was an obvious want of proportion in the division of the spoils which must lead to future trouble. For the present, however, all seemed well. The Court, which had worked for some time for this result; the public, who desired a fusion of moderate men; the Press, which saw with satisfaction such an array of administrative talent in office, congratulated themselves on having at last secured a strong and durable Government; and accepted as satisfactory Aberdeen's assurances that the Ministerial measures would be both Conservative and Liberal, and that the country was sick of distinctions which had no real meaning, and which only prevented from acting together men who were able to perform good public service. Russell went to the Foreign Office[1] with the lead of the House of Commons, Gladstone to the Exchequer, Palmerston to the Home Office, and Graham to the Admiralty. The Cabinet contained also Lansdowne, Argyll, Granville, Newcastle, Cranworth, Wood, Sidney Herbert, and Molesworth; while Villiers, Cardwell, Lowe, Bernal Osborne, Cockburn, and Bethell, filled important offices outside. Well might Palmerston say that the administration combined 'almost all the men of talent and experience in the House of Commons, except Disraeli.'

To the ejected Conservatives the situation presented a very different appearance. Aberdeen and Gladstone had been protesting during great part of the year that nothing separated them from their old party but Protection. Protection had been abandoned, but Aberdeen, Gladstone, and the rest, at once coalesced with the Liberals. Aberdeen and Palmerston stood for opposite principles in foreign policy, and had been violently opposed within a year. Yet they went now into the same Cabinet. No wonder that Derby in the Lords denounced the arrangement as unprincipled, and held even stronger language in private. It was difficult, he thought, to account for it save by personal hatred of Disraeli. Disraeli took much the same view.

Lord Derby to Lord Londonderry.

Dec. 21, 1852.—. . . How it is possible that Lord Aberdeen can carry it on, unless he throws himself into the hands of the extremist parties, I am unable to conjecture. I earnestly regret the course which he has pursued, which is wholly inconsistent with his repeated declarations to me that there was only one subject of difference between us; that, that once removed, nothing would give him greater pleasure than again to act with me; and that, happen what might, no consideration should ever induce him to join the Whigs! I am afraid that personal feeling has had much to do with this step, and that the course pursued is mainly to be attributed to the

[1] In a few weeks he gave up the Foreign Office to Clarendon, retaining the lead of the House of Commons without any portfolio.

jealousy and hatred (the word is not too strong) felt by the Peelite party in the House of Commons towards Disraeli. The breach is now, I fear, wider than ever.

To Lord Londonderry.

Private. GROSVENOR GATE, *Dec.* 31, 1852.—. . . Clarendon is not a deep man, and always writes and talks of public affairs as if he were a third-rate partisan.

The existence of the Coalition will be brief, and its end ignominious.[1] It will be followed by the strong Government which it absurdly professes to be. . . .

With respect to public affairs, I keep myself quite aloof; but everybody writes to me, and from all sections. My opinion is that there is coalition, but no fusion; widespread discontent and hourly increasing spirit of vengeance. It is a place-hunting cabal, and they were so rapacious after their prey that they forgot, in their chase after *office,* to settle their *policy.* We had the details of the whole combination long ago, but, to mature their arrangements, it was necessary that we should remain in until after Christmas. This determined our course. . . .

The situation produced somewhat strained relations between Disraeli and Gladstone; and a correspondence which before its close became unfriendly passed between them on the question of the furniture in Downing Street, which was taken over by the incoming from the outgoing Chancellor of the Exchequer.

From William Ewart Gladstone.

DOWNING STREET,
Jan. 21, 1853.

MY DEAR SIR,—I owe you many apologies for having made no communication to you at an earlier date on the subject of the furniture belonging to you, and remaining in this house. The cause has been this, that it has been under consideration whether, after the change made by the late Government, it might not be the most convenient arrangement that *all* the furniture in the house should belong to the Crown, with provisions for charging the wear and tear of all except the official rooms upon the Chancellor of the Exchequer. Until this was

[1] Speaking in the House of Commons on July 13, 1854, Disraeli said: 'When the Coalition Government was formed, I was asked how long it would last, and I ventured to reply, "Until every member of it is, as a public character, irretrievably injured."'

settled, I did not know whether your furniture would be taken over on my behalf or on that of the Office of Works. It has now been settled that it shall be done by the latter, and Sir W. Molesworth has put the matter in train for being despatched forthwith.

There is, I believe, a robe which passed down under some law of exchange from one Chancellor of the Exchequer to another, and I shall be very happy to receive it from you on the ordinary footing, whatever that may be. — I remain, my dear Sir, faithfully yours, W. E. GLADSTONE.

To William Ewart Gladstone.

GROSVENOR GATE,
Feb. 26, 1853.

DEAR SIR, — As I understand you have been for some time residing in Downing Street, I think it would be convenient that our arrangements with respect to the furniture of the official residence should no longer remain unsettled.

On my accession to office I paid to Sir Charles Wood immediately, at his request, for furniture alone the sum of £787 12s. 6d., taking many things which I did not require, but complying with what was represented to me by him as the invariable rule of the office.

This rule having occasioned considerable dissatisfaction among some of my colleagues, the system attracted the attention of the First Ld of the Treasury, who greatly modified it, directing that all furniture in rooms of public reception should be taken by the Crown. In consequence of this arrangement, I received in the autumn a drawback of £479 16s. from the Office of Works, which left a balance in my favor of £307 16s. 6d.

Assuming that you would, under any circumstances, be content with the valuation which was so recently made by Messrs. Overen on the part of Sir C. Wood, and Messrs. Banting on mine, and that you certainly would not contemplate a repetition of so expensive a ceremony for so comparatively trifling an amount as you will have to pay, I would suggest that your cheque for £307 16s. 6d. would, as between us, properly conclude the business.

With reference to your letter of the 21st ult., stating as the cause of delay that the Board of Works had resolved to take the remaining furniture of the official residence, and that you had not then received the consequent payment, I would venture to observe that such payment is a matter of business between you and the Bd of Works, and that it should not interfere with the arrangement between us any more than

abstains from them only because he perceives that they are unwelcome.

It is quite clear that Disraeli was right in the main subject of dispute, though the two months' delay and the display of red tape provoked him to unwonted and hardly courteous acerbity. Gladstone ought to have settled with his predecessor for the furniture on the basis of the system in force when the transfer of office took place. Subsequent arrangements made by the new Government with the Office of Works could only properly apply to the next transfer. But it is amusing to note that, under cover of indignation at Gladstone's conduct about the furniture, Disraeli evades altogether the question of the robe, where he was apparently withholding what in the ordinary course would have been transferred for payment to his successor. The robe descended, or was believed by Disraeli to descend, from Pitt; Disraeli was very proud of the association, and could not bring himself to give Gladstone the option of purchasing what he himself had bought from Wood. He wore it again during his two subsequent tenures of the Chancellorship of the Exchequer, and it remains as an heirloom at Hughenden Manor.

Disraeli did not think the Coalition could long hold together; and he began at once to prepare for the future. There was much in his favour. His party was far the largest single party in the House of Commons, three hundred or more in all, though no doubt many of them would be content with the Aberdeen Ministry so long as it exhibited its Conservative side. In spite of the trials of the last few months, the Conservatives were in fair spirits, and there was not so much recrimination as usually follows defeat. Croker was the natural recipient of some grumbles. Lonsdale wrote to him, bewailing Disraeli's excessive confidence in his powers of speech. 'He thinks always . . . he will carry the whole House with him. He has been deceived so often that he ought to be wiser. As a party leader he will be encouraged, but I doubt if there is a single man that would be his follower. He is our best man, but we have great difficulty in keeping our troops in discipline.'[1] Criticism of this kind was not very serious. It was obvious, too, that the Conservatives might easily find reinforcements. Of the four parties supporting the Aberdeen Ministry, only one, the Peelite group, was really satisfied. The Coalition had rewarded the Irish Tenant Leaguers for their assistance in the crucial division, not by accepting their policy, but by giving office to two of their least respected members, Sadleir and Keogh, and thus disgusting the rest. Gavan Duffy wrote to a subordinate member of the late Government on January 10: 'I hope your friends do not despair in Opposition. Three-and-thirty of the Irish party will sit there along with them, making a majority of the whole House if Mr. Disraeli can keep his own party together.' Irish support, however, as Disraeli had already learnt by experience, was of a very untrustworthy character; as Stanley wrote, the Brigade 'oppose for opposition's sake, and because it is their habitual policy,' not for love of any English party. Again, the Whigs grudged bitterly the excessive toll of places exacted by the Peelites; and one very influential group, the Greys, conspicuous in Russell's Administration, were entirely omitted. They might be disposed in certain circumstances to rally to a national party; and Disraeli, as we shall see, made during the session a serious bid for a Whig alliance. Then there were the Radicals, who had only one representative in the Ministry, and to whom, in his interview with Bright in December, Disraeli had already made tentative overtures. There is no doubt that throughout this session his mind played a good deal round the possibility, if the Whigs proved obdurate, of approximating to the Manchester School. The Ministry were the Mandarins of both parties, the official class who had hitherto monopolised office, whichever party was in power. With the exception of ten months of 1852, there had been no period in the last twenty years when either Russell,

[1] Croker, iii. 257.

Lansdowne, Palmerston, and Wood, or Aberdeen, Graham, Herbert, Newcastle, and Gladstone, had not been holding high administrative posts. Disraeli still retained his youthful preference for intellect and originality over experience and official gravity. He discerned in Bright and his friends a kindred dislike for 'old stagers' and 'red-tapists.'

The question of organisation was pressed on him by Malmesbury, who wrote of the absolute necessity of reforming the *personnel* of the party. 'Had you twice the talent and eloquence you possess, you could do nothing with the incapacity which prevents our details from being properly managed. It is better to fail in orators to back you by words than in men to back you by votes. We lost the election by bad management.' He thought that, if Disraeli did not attend to this, nobody would or could. Disraeli, we know, agreed with Malmesbury in condemning the party management, and there was an opportunity this year for a complete change. Beresford, who had been principally responsible for the management of the General Election, was rather under a cloud owing to the censure passed on him by a Committee of the House, who found a reckless indifference to consequences in his relation to systematic bribery at Derby at the last election. Forbes Mackenzie, the Whip, was unseated for bribery at Liverpool. Disraeli got Sir William Jolliffe, afterwards Lord Hylton, an energetic and popular member, to look after Conservative interests in the House of Commons, and he relied upon his friend and confidential agent, Rose, who had been working under Beresford since 1851, for the chief management of the party outside. But his mind was mainly given to policy. Now he was in opposition again, he was determined to move more decidedly in the direction foreshadowed in *Coningsby* and *Sybil*, and to attract public support and Parliamentary co-operation for his party by discarding, at the risk of some dissension and confusion at first, whatever was exclusive and restrictive in its programme. In this he was warmly seconded by Stanley, and to some extent by Malmesbury, though all of them felt that Derby's sympathy would be imperfect. Stanley wrote on January 20: 'The Captain does not care for office, but wishes to keep things as they are, and impede "Progress." . . . Don't let us plunge into a reactionary course of opposition and suffer political martyrdom for a cause in which we neither of us believe. Your influence is more powerful than that of anyone, as it ought to be. Use it.' The three colleagues exchanged ideas about Reform, and Stanley wrote on January 27: 'You cannot go ahead too fast or too far for *one* of your followers, nor for the official members of our party, generally speaking. But it will be very difficult, and require all your diplomacy, to persuade the squires to consent to any plan of Reform.' Malmesbury wrote on February 3: 'I agree entirely with you that our party is repugnant to the urban taste, and that we should try something to recover the towns' interest, but no operation can be compared in difficulty to it. . . . I trust to your genius to give us a standard and war-cry.'

From Lord Derby.

Private. KNOWSLEY, *Jan.* 30, 1853.— . . . We shall have a difficult game to play. We must to a certain extent keep up the spirits of our party; but we must exercise, and get them to exercise, great patience and forbearance, if we do not wish, by an active and bitter opposition on our part, to consolidate the present combination between those who have no real bond of union, and who must, I think, fall to pieces before long, if left to themselves. You must not build upon any possible union between me and the ultra-Whigs, such as Lord Grey, or the Manchester School. Such an union is simply impossible, and I name it only because I infer from Edward's language that such an idea had passed through your mind. I hardly think it could long dwell there.

It was not domestic policy or the tactics of the Opposition that was to overthrow the Coalition, but foreign policy, and the vacillation resulting from the co-existence in the same Cabinet of incompatible aims in foreign affairs.

When the Derby Government resigned, good relations had been established with France, in spite of the internal convulsions through which she had passed; and the international position of England was clear. If any Power contemplated a policy of adventure in Europe, it would have to reckon with the two western Powers; and any disposition to adventure which Louis Napoleon himself might feel was held in check by the necessity of carrying public opinion in England along with him. The change of Government at once threw doubt on England's attitude. Palmerston was the French Emperor's only friend in the new Cabinet, and he was relegated to the Home Office. Aberdeen had worked cordially with the France of Louis Philippe, but preferred Russia to the France of Louis Napoleon, and was believed to be favourably disposed to the extreme pacificism preached by the Manchester School. It was by no mere coincidence that, within a fortnight of Aberdeen's accession to office, the Emperor Nicholas opened to the British Ambassador at St. Petersburg his designs upon the Sick Man, and his hopes of securing the co-operation of Great Britain. Disraeli was guided by a sure instinct when he based his first arraignment of the Coalition on their apparent indifference to the maintenance of a cordial understanding with France. Ever since the *coup d'état* Louis Napoleon had been assailed with unbounded licence in the English Press, and therefore it particularly behoved statesmen who valued the understanding to be careful to give no countenance to this campaign of abuse. Yet Ministers of the importance of Graham and Wood had demeaned themselves to tickle the ears of the groundlings by joining in it themselves. The First Lord of the Admiralty told his constituents that the French Emperor was 'a despot who had trampled on the liberties of forty millions of men.' The President of the Board of Control said to his constituents: 'Take our nearest neighbours. Such a despotism never prevailed in France, even in the time of Napoleon I. The Press gagged; liberty suppressed; no man allowed to speak his opinion.' The ruler of whom responsible Ministers thus spoke had just been twice acclaimed by an overwhelming vote of the French people.

These imprudent speeches immediately worked mischief abroad. Malmesbury, from his knowledge of the foreign situation, was very indignant. He wrote to Disraeli to encourage him to notice them in the House, reminding him that the Derby Government had successfully separated France from the three despotic Powers of the Continent, and that 'when we recognised the Empire there was no one thing she would not have done *for* us and *with* us.' Accordingly Disraeli, in spite of some doubts by Derby, delivered an important speech on Foreign Policy and the Coalition on first going into Committee of Supply.[1] He earnestly impressed on the House the immense importance of a cordial understanding with France, ridiculing the notion of hereditary hostility. He recognised that prejudice had naturally been excited against the Emperor for having terminated a Parliamentary constitution and curtailed the liberty of the Press. 'It is unnecessary for me to say that it is not probable I shall ever say or do anything which would tend to depreciate the influence or to diminish the power of Parliament or the Press. My greatest honour is to be a member of this House, in which all my thoughts and feelings are concentred; and as for the Press, I am myself a "gentleman of the Press," and bear no other escutcheon.' But suppose there was a disputed succession in England; a young Charles Stuart at Breda, or a young Oliver Cromwell at Bordeaux, publishing manifestoes and issuing missives to powerful parties in this country. Or suppose a great revolution here, the monarchy subverted, a centralised republic established by a minority, and then the army called in by the people against that minority. Would liberty of the Press be then enjoyed even here? He respected Napoleon III., but he had sympathised with Louis

[1] Feb. 18.

Philippe. After a long reign of unbroken prosperity, Louis Philippe 'was rudely expelled from his capital, and was denounced as a poltroon by all the journals of England, because he did not command his troops to fire upon the people. Well, other powers and other princes have since occupied his seat, who have asserted their authority in a very different way, and are denounced in the same organs as tyrants, because they did order their troops to fire upon the people.' What was the moral? 'That it is extremely difficult to form an opinion upon French politics; and that so long as the French people are exact in their commercial transactions, and friendly in their political relations, it is just as well that we should not interfere with their management of their domestic concerns.'

This sentiment was loudly cheered on both sides of the House, and Disraeli proceeded to show that both Russell and Lord Grey a year before had expressed similar views about Napoleon and about the attacks on him in the Press, which they had deprecated. But what was the attitude of Aberdeen's Government? Did Graham express it? Did the Cabinet regard the Emperor as a despot or the French as slaves?

If I had to form an opinion of the policy of the Cabinet from the first declaration made by so eminent a member of it as the First Lord of the Admiralty, I should certainly be induced to suppose that some great change was about to occur. How are we to account for such a declaration? I will not be so impertinent as to suppose it was an indiscretion. An indiscretion from 'All the Talents'—impossible! Can it, then, be design? . . . The present Government tell us that they have no principles—at least, not at present. Some people are uncharitable enough to suppose that they have not got a policy; but, in Heaven's name, why are they Ministers if they have not got discretion? That is the great quality on which I had thought this Cabinet was established. Vast experience, administrative adroitness, safe men who never would blunder—men who might not only take the Government without a principle and without a party, but to whom the country ought to be grateful for taking it under such circumstances. Yet at the very outset we find one of the most experienced of these eminent statesmen . . . holding up to public scorn and indignation the ruler and the people, a good and cordial understanding with whom is the cardinal point of sound statesmanship.

Wood's punishment followed Graham's on the same lines. Incidentally Disraeli touched on the Eastern Question — a problem which had always been treated by English statesmen through a cordial understanding with France. As long as France and England thoroughly understood each other on that great question, the peace of the world and the interests of civilisation and humanity were not in peril. Aberdeen had told the House of Lords that there was no need to dilate on the foreign policy of the Coalition, as the same system had been pursued for thirty years. And yet, a year or two ago, Aberdeen had called Palmerston's policy 'abominable,' and Russell, by indicating Palmerston as the Minister, not of Russia or Austria or France, but of England, had implied that Aberdeen was acting in foreign interests. Disraeli added that not only was foreign policy uncertain, but it was uncertain who was Foreign Minister. Inspired paragraphs said that Russell was going to cease to be Foreign Secretary, but retain a room in the Foreign Office. 'Sir, I confess I must protest against this system of shutting up great men in small rooms, and of binding to the triumphal chariot wheels of administrative ability all the fame and genius of the Whig party. I think I have a right to ask the noble lord frankly: "Are you Secretary of State or are you not?"' It was only a few days later that Russell gave way to Clarendon as Foreign Secretary.

Disraeli finished up this damaging attack upon the Coalition — an attack which recalled the philippics of seven years before against Peel — with the following peroration: —

We have at the present moment a Conservative Ministry and a Conservative Opposition. Where the great Liberal party is I pretend not to know. Where are the Whigs, with their great traditions — two centuries of Parliamentary lustre and deeds of noble patriotism? There is no one to answer. Where are the youthful energies of Radicalism, its buoyant expectations, its sanguine hopes? Awakened, I fear, from the first dream of that ardent inexperience which finds itself at the same moment used and discarded—used without compunction, and not discarded with too much decency. Where are the Radicals? Is there a man in the House who declares himself to be a Radical? (A voice, 'Yes!') Oh, no! you would be afraid of being caught and changed into a Conservative Minister. . . . We have now got a Ministry of Progress, and everyone stands still. We never hear the word 'reform' now; it is no longer a Ministry of Reform; it is a Ministry of Progress, every member of which agrees to do nothing. All difficult questions are suspended. All questions which cannot be agreed upon are open questions. Now, I do not want to be unreasonable, but I think there ought to be some limit to this system of open questions. . . . Let Parliamentary reform, let the ballot, be open questions, if you please, let every institution in Church and State be open questions; but at least let your answer to me to-night prove that among your open questions you are not going to make an open question of the peace of Europe.

'An open question' was exactly what the Coalition did make of the peace of Europe, and in consequence drifted into war. The speech was a word in season, and not easy to answer. Malmesbury wrote: 'I have been revelling in your speech. . . . Is C. Wood alive?' and Stanley: 'You have put new life into the party, and I don't think there is any harm done among the waverers.' It was naturally treated by Russell in the House as factious,[1] and by Greville in his Journal as 'a speech of devilish malignity, quite reckless and shamelessly profligate.' A newspaper which shared the prevailing Gallophobia called Disraeli 'Louis Napoleon's Attorney-General, *vice* Malmesbury, invalided.' Russell assured the House of Commons that the Government were, and meant to remain, on terms of amity with France, in spite of the 'incautious' expressions of his colleagues. To the charge of want of principle in the Coalition he replied

[1] Some Conservatives, notably Thomas Baring, took the same view, fearing that the speech might increase the mischief already done by the indiscretions of Ministers.

that it consisted of men who had fought side by side for years on behalf of Free Trade against Protection. In other words, it was founded on agreement in the past about a question which was now settled. This was not an answer, but an admission.

To R. Pemberton Milnes.[1]

East Indian Committee,
March 4, 1853.

My dear Squire, — I have little to say, and write from the Black Hole of Calcutta, where I have been shut the whole morning.

Everything is very flat, though our friends keep together beyond my hopes. The other day I sounded the bugle, and exercised them a little, and to-night[2] we are to have a regular encounter. India and the Income Tax are the features of the future, and may disturb, though I should hardly think dislodge, the Government. . . .

Vernon Smith came to me yesterday to beg me to choose a day to dine with him, as Ld. Fitzwilliam was so disappointed that he had not met me at Fryston or Burghley (which latter place we quitted the day he arrived) that he had devised these means for our meeting.

Is he to convert me, or the reverse? Or is he, an old Whig, as disgusted as V. S. himself? However, on Tuesday next we are to dine together. Adieu, my dearest Squire. — D.

I have made Annabel's[3] acquaintance, and found her all you prepared me for — most pleasing, and very clever and intelligent.

It was not merely in Parliament that Disraeli meant to carry on the fight against the Coalition. 'A gentleman of the Press' himself, he was not likely to be indifferent to the influence of effective journalism on party prospects. The Conservative party, since the breach with Peel, had received very poor support in the newspapers. *The Times*, which enjoyed a far larger circu-

[1] In the *Life of Lord Houghton*, this letter is wrongly treated as if addressed to Monckton Milnes, the son, instead of to Pemberton Milnes, the father.

[2] On the Clergy Reserves (Canada) Bill.

[3] The Hon. Annabel Crewe, wife of R. Monckton Milnes, and mother of the Marquis of Crewe.

lation than any other journal, and had an authority corresponding to its circulation, was against them, though it generally treated Disraeli with respect; the *Morning Chronicle* was the organ of the Peelites and the *Globe* of Palmerston; the *Daily Telegraph* and the *Daily News* both supported the Liberals. Against these the Conservatives could only set the *Morning Post* and *Standard*, both at that time of small circulation and importance, and of doubtful loyalty to the leaders of the party; and the *Morning Herald*, which was the original organ of the Protectionists, but which was constantly annoying their leaders, from Bentinck onwards, by its extreme narrowness and bigotry. The only weekly journals of political consequence, the *Examiner* and *Spectator*, were Liberal; *John Bull*, their Conservative rival, had not maintained the position which Theodore Hook, its founder, had secured for it. Consequently, in the correspondence of Disraeli and his friends, we find frequent complaints of the party Press. In November, 1849, Malmesbury wrote indignantly to Disraeli about the conduct of the *Morning Post*, and elicited from him the comprehensive condemnation: 'The state of our Press is deplorable.' In the following year Disraeli began to take steps to supply the want. He was vigorously seconded by the younger Stanley, who shared his liberal sentiments, and was anxious to permeate the party with them. From Stanley's letters we find that there were negotiations in 1850 for purchasing *John Bull*. But the plan that commended itself to both, though it took long to carry into effect, was to start a new journal. 'What have you effected touching the new journal?' wrote Stanley in October, 1850. In January, 1851, the idea had made progress.

From the Hon. Edward Stanley.

KNOWSLEY, *Jan.* 8, 1851.—. . . What you say about the paper is satisfactory. . . . A good start is everything, new ideas and new men. I have said nothing to our chief, but I know that his opinion of the value of the Press has undergone a great change, and I expect to find him favourable. The *Herald* is worse than no paper at all; its dulness reflects on us, while its Exeter Hall articles disgust our High Church supporters. . . . For my own part, I am willing to give all the time and trouble that can be spared from the House. . . .

Nothing, however, seems to have been done in 1851, and it needed the bitter experience of the first Derby-Disraeli Ministry, which was the target of newspaper abuse, and was very inadequately defended in the Press, to compel Disraeli and his friends into action. During the autumn of their year of office, as we have seen from Disraeli's correspondence with Lennox, he was in close consultation on the subject with Stanley, who wrote in September: 'I think we have found a journalist.' This appears, from another letter of Stanley's, to have been D. O. Maddyn, a competent writer who had served on the *Morning Chronicle*, and who became a regular contributor to the new journal, though he proved not to be of sufficient calibre for the editorship. The circumstances in which the Ministry were defeated gave Disraeli the final stimulus. An unprincipled Coalition, whose only common bond was a desire to be revenged on himself, and who yet were covered with laudation by the Press, must by the Press be exposed and defeated. For that purpose, as well as to raise the level of Conservative journalism, and to propagate his own Tory Democratic ideas, it was necessary to have a definite organ; and he began at once to make serious preparations for the new venture. In the first months of the New Year he applied to his rich friends for support. To Henry Hope, to whom he had dedicated *Coningsby*, he wrote: 'I am thinking of starting almost immediately a weekly journal of a somewhat peculiar character. . . . As the paper, though Tory, is of a very progressive and enlightened design, I can neither ask nor desire general aid from the party, and am forced therefore to appeal to private sympathy.' Other friends, with whom he was less intimate, Disraeli approached by circular:—

Circular about the Press.

[? *March*, 1853.]—The state of the Press as regards our party has become so intolerable that we think of making a great effort to terminate a condition of affairs which exercises a very bad influence on our prospects. It seems that the whole ability of the country is arrayed against us, and the rising generation is half ashamed of a cause which would seem to have neither wit nor reason to sustain and adorn it.

Experience has shown that propping up obsolete organs is a mere waste of energy and capital. We require something which will produce as striking and as rapid an effect on opinion as the *Anti-Jacobin* when it was started by Mr. Canning, or the *Edinburgh Review* when it first rose.

A plan has been matured which, if carried into effect, might, we believe, produce this result, and bring an amount and variety of brilliant talent to bear on opinion which has rarely been equalled; but it demands not only funds, but considerable funds, for the launch and the maintenance of the organ for the first year.

My friends have requested me confidentially to ascertain whether the necessary support can be secured.

It is desirable to obtain the amount from as small an area as is consistent with not unduly pressing on any individual. It is recommended that there should be no shares, no annual subscription, and no project of refunding.

Some members of the late Cabinet have largely contributed, and I have taken the liberty, after reflection, to lay the circumstances before your lordship for your best consideration.

The new journal was to be issued weekly, and to be called the *Press*. Sufficient support was obtained to make a beginning. Samuel Lucas, a distinguished Oxford man, who had quitted the Bar for literature and journalism, and was for many years a well-known writer on *The Times*, was appointed editor, and early in March was engaged in collecting his staff, mainly under Disraeli's inspiration. Disraeli proposed to write regularly himself, and so did Stanley; Disraeli's brilliant friends, Bulwer Lytton and George Smythe, were immediately enlisted. The writers mostly belonged to the forward school, or left wing, of Conservatism. Among the contributors to the early numbers were Shirley Brooks and Tom Taylor, successively editors of *Punch;* Henry Longue-ville Mansel, the metaphysician, afterwards appointed, on Disraeli's recommendation, Dean of St. Paul's; Sir James Emerson Tennent, traveller and author, who had held subordinate office in the 1852 Ministry; Lord Maidstone, who was something of a poet as well as a politician, and (wrote Disraeli) 'full of humour,' afterwards eleventh Earl of Winchilsea; Augustus Stafford, recently secretary of the Admiralty, who had been one of the 'Young England' party;[1] Isaac Butt, the Conservative Home Ruler; and a versatile barrister and *littérateur*, who in later life became notorious as counsel for the Tichborne claimant, Edward Vaughan Kenealy. Disraeli, who had a high opinion of Kenealy's abilities, was anxious for his co-operation, and explained his ideas to him in a personal interview on April 13. Kenealy wrote an account of what passed while it was fresh in his memory. He found Disraeli greatly changed since he had last seen him in 1846, and thought him old and thin, restless, and with a House of Commons mannerism.

We plunged at once *in medias res.* He said, from his knowledge of my great learning, classical tastes, and peculiar genius, he was led to mention me as one of the confraternity of supporters who were to bring out the new weekly paper; that it was intended to be highly classical in its style, and quite the opposite of the barbaresque style of composition which at present prevails, making the daily newspapers absolutely unreadable; that the master-minds of the eighteenth century were to be the models, and that a combination of sound political philosophy with Aristophanic pleasantry was what was most desired; . . . that Lord Stanley, of whom he spoke highly as a young man of solidity and great skill, and pointed him out as probably a future Prime Minister, and Smythe, late of Canterbury, were others of the brotherhood on whom he depended.

The *Anti-Jacobin* was to be, to a certain extent, the model; and those who, like myself, had political tendencies, would find this one of the best modes of advancing them. The Coalition was to be attacked, and the true principles of the Tory party were to be put forward. The Tories were at present a great mass, but destitute of ideas, and the *Press* was to furnish them with these. . . .

[1] See Vol. II., p. 195.

The political leaders in the new paper are to be first-rate, like *The Times*, and Canning and Frere would be the models for those of lighter nature.[1]

Kenealy's connection with the paper, in spite of Disraeli's obvious anxiety to secure and retain him, was very short. He wrote several squibs for the first few numbers, but then withdrew, as he could not brook any sort of editorial control.

The *Press*, which was published every Saturday morning, price sixpence, was both a newspaper and a review. It contained a shortened report of the Parliamentary proceedings of the week, and many of the familiar news features of a daily paper—law and police reports, obituary, naval and military information, ecclesiastical and University news, Court and fashion intelligence, and the latest despatches from foreign capitals—as well as leading articles on home and foreign politics, and critical estimates of literature and the arts. In size and shape, it resembled the weekly reviews of to-day, such as the *Spectator;* but it was slightly broader, and had three columns instead of two to a page, except on the two central pages of the normal twenty-four, where some letter or poem or burlesque, to which special importance was attached, was displayed in double column, followed by the curious facetiæ and squibs which were in fashion at the time. The serious political articles occupied the front and early pages.

The first number, which appeared on May 7, opened with a leading article on 'Coalition,' which was written by Disraeli himself and described the standpoint of the new journal. 'The state of political parties in England at the present moment,' it began, 'is very peculiar, and, with a prosperous and tranquil surface, not without considerable danger. The administration of our affairs is carried on by a Coalition of individuals who have avowedly no opinions in common, except upon a subject which is no longer a matter of public controversy, the principles

[1] E. V. Kenealy's *Memoirs*, ch. 7.

of our commercial system.' The Coalition was carried on, it was pointed out, not even by a compromise, but by 'a mere suspension of principle.' The Government 'administer affairs, but they represent no opinion. The excellence of representative government, however, is that it should represent opinion.' This was done through party, or political connection. But parties were now dissolved. 'It is conveniently maintained that, in consequence of the abrogation of the protective principle in commerce, the distinctive characters of the two great parties in the country no longer exist.' This absurd tenet was turned into ridicule, and the article concluded in the right Disraelian spirit: —

Why has the constitutional habit of the realm been disturbed and discontinued? Why is the country governed neither by the Liberal nor by the Conservative party? From personal and petty causes only. The Chancellor of the Exchequer, professing high Conservative opinions, will not, from a personal feeling, combine with the leader of the Conservative party in the House of Commons. The morbid vanity of Woburn Abbey must be represented without an interval in the royal councils. The Whigs may perish, but the Duke of Bedford must be satisfied. To accomplish these noble ends, to gratify a prejudice, and to pander to an oligarch, an austere intriguer, without any following in the country, and without any lustre of career, is installed in the high place. Around him are clustered a motley crew of statesmen, who, magnanimously forgetting careers of recrimination, and veiling their mutual aversion with sinister frankness and affected cordiality, devote their heterogeneous energies to the service of a perplexed Sovereign and an amazed country.

The most striking feature of the early numbers of the new journal was a lively series of 'Letters to the Whigs,' signed 'Manilius,' reproaching the leaders of that historic party with coalescing with Peelites, Radicals, and the Irish Brigade, instead of those who were more nearly allied to them in political opinion, the Conservative Opposition. These letters, owing both to their style and to their sentiments, have been unhesitatingly attributed to Disraeli himself by two competent critics; by Mr.

Walter Sichel, in his suggestive *Disraeli, a Study in Personality and Ideas*, and by Mr. William Hutcheon, in his interesting volume of Disraelian by-products, *Whigs and Whiggism*. Undoubtedly there is internal evidence to support this attribution; but it so happens that we have first-hand testimony to the contrary. In the bound copy of Volume I. of the Press, preserved at Knowsley, Stanley, who, after the editor and Disraeli, was in the best position to know, has entered in his unmistakable handwriting the names of the contributors at the end of all the principal articles in the first eleven numbers; and the 'Letters to the Whigs' are ascribed in each case to Bulwer Lytton. This brilliant piece of journalism is therefore a feather in Lytton's cap and not in Disraeli's; and 'Manilius' was not putting the curious off the scent, but correctly indicating his own political position, when he described himself as one standing 'somewhat distinct from the ordinary relations of party, and altogether remote from the interests of official ambition.' But, as the two men were at the time in very close political agreement, as similar sentiments to those of 'Manilius' were expressed in Disraeli's speeches during this session, as the letters were given the most prominent place in the centre of the paper, and as the copy apparently reached the Editor through Disraeli's hands, we may confidently assume that the ideas were Disraeli's as well as Lytton's, and that Disraeli was specially anxious to impress them upon the political world.

The main theme was that the nation was divided between two great parties, the supporters of Cobden and Bright and the supporters of Derby and Disraeli, and that the Whigs must make their choice. They must realise that their day of power was past, and that they could only continue to enjoy that office, which they regarded as their appanage, either by merging themselves in the Radicals or by allying themselves with the Tories. The argument indicated a change of attitude towards Disraeli's old opponents, the Venetian oligarchy. But the change had been gradual, and was foreshadowed in a letter to Manners nearly seven years before, when Disraeli intimated that there must 'ultimately be a fusion between the real Whigs and us.'[1]

'Manilius,' speaking for Disraeli as well as for Lytton, wished now for a 'manly alliance' of Whigs and Tories 'upon the broad understanding that reforms are to cement the foundation of monarchy, and not attempt the anomalous paradox of uniting democratic institutions to a defenceless throne.' This would give the Whigs 'electoral numbers,' and strengthen 'the liberal disposition of Lord Derby's partisans' by giving them what they wanted — 'colleagues experienced in office and eloquent in debate.'[2] Lytton and Disraeli had penetrated, with real insight, into the heart of the political situation; and the Whigs would have been driven at that time either to merge themselves in the Radicals, or to ally themselves openly with the Tories, but for the influence of one dominating personality. Palmerston, who rose to the first place during the Crimean War, and retained power, with one brief interval, till his death, succeeded, by pursuing a Conservative policy at home and a Liberal policy abroad, in combining under his banner Whigs and Radicals without any fusion, and in disarming Conservative opposition. When Gladstone took the place of Palmerston, the disintegration began, but its progress was delayed owing to party and personal antagonism to Disraeli. After Disraeli's death it proceeded apace, till it culminated in the Liberal-Unionist secession of 1886. Consequently the Whig houses of Cavendish, Grosvenor, Fortescue, Elliot, Dalrymple, Fox, Wood, and many more, have formed that 'manly alliance' with the Tories which Disraeli desired. The Russells, the Leveson-Gowers, the Petty-Fitzmaurices, and the Greys, are divided, but in each case the elder branch has left the Liberal party; only a few, such as the Spencers, the Harcourts, and the Caringtons, remain in their old party connection,

[1] See above, p. 10. [2] *Press*, June 11.

and these have ceased to exercise any perceptible Whig influence on policy.

From Lord Stanley.

Private. ST. LEONARDS, *May* 17, 1853.—I hear [the *Press*] everywhere well spoken of in general, but everywhere with one qualification. They say we are too much of an essay, and too little of a newspaper; that we do not give a sufficient quantity of news, and are rather too exclusively political. I have mentioned this to Lucas, but, as you are in fact the manager of the machine, I report it to you. . . .

Disraeli contributed to all the early issues. Out of the eleven numbers where we have Stanley's authority to guide us, Disraeli wrote the first leading article in ten, Stanley taking his place in the issue of July 2. He sometimes wrote also a subsidiary article, and contributed occasionally skits making game of his political adversaries in the shape of 'Imaginary Conversations of Eminent Men,' or 'Imaginary Bribery Commissions,' with Ministers giving evidence.[1] He exercised, moreover, a continual supervision over the whole production; but he was very careful to keep his newspaper activities a secret. Even to Kenealy, one of his contributors, he wrote shortly before the issue of the first number; in which the leading article was from his own pen: 'I am so very much engaged

[1] The following is a complete list of the articles attributed to Disraeli by Stanley in the first eleven numbers of the *Press*.

No. 1. Leading article, 'Coalition.'
No. 2. Leading article; article, 'The Budget as a Whole.'
No. 3. Leading article.
No. 4. Leading article; 'Meeting of the Special Commission under the new Act to inquire into the practices by which Her Majesty's Ministers obtained their present seats.'
No. 5. Leading article; article, 'Ministerial Finance'; 'Adjourned Meeting of the Special Commission,' etc.
No. 6. Leading article.
No. 7. Leading article; 'Adjourned Meeting of the Special Commission,' etc.
No. 8. Leading article; 'Imaginary Conversations of Eminent Men.'
No. 9. Special news about the Eastern Question.
No. 10. Leading article; Special news about the Eastern Question; 'Alarming Rumour of the Resignation of Lord Aberdeen.'
No. 11. Leading article; Memorandum on the Relations between the Governments of England and France during the administration of the Earl of Derby.

at the present moment that I can only give Mr. Lucas and his enterprise my good wishes'; and in the second number he criticised his own Budget speech of December as, 'in our opinion, much too long, and savouring somewhat of the Yankee school of Rhetoric.' Lucas wrote to Disraeli in March: 'No one will be able to say through me, "I know the originators and inspirers of this organ to be so-and-so," for I shall stand firmly and impenetrably between you and the public'; and in October: 'I invariably *myself* destroy *your* copy.' Stanley also was writing constantly for the paper lengthy reviews of serious books, as well as political articles, and at the beginning of the recess, on August 20, asked: 'Does Lucas want regular assistance? or has he filled up our places with other contributors?'

The attack on the Coalition, begun with vigour on the first page of the first number, was continued persistently, not only in serious articles, but in squibs, burlesques, and pasquinades. Disraeli conducted the attack in the main himself. His serious writing in his journal was, as ever, vigorous and effective, if somewhat highly coloured for modern taste; but it must be confessed that the savour has almost entirely departed from his lighter pieces. The following quotations are taken from his leading articles: 'Those whom an intrigue has placed in present power represent nothing, and have made up their minds to nothing'—a charge with much truth in it; Aberdeen was 'qualified to be the Minister of a second-rate German State.'[1] 'We live in an age of great events and little men. The star of England pales. . . . Something ignominious is impending.'[2] In the fifth number there is a specially pungent article, in which Aberdeen is treated in the most merciless fashion:—

His mind, his education, his prejudices, are all of the Kremlin school. Now that he is placed in a prominent position, and forced to lead English gentlemen, instead of glozing and intriguing with foreign diplomatists, not a night

[1] *Press*, May 21. [2] *Press*, July 9.

passes that his language or his demeanour does not shock and jar upon the frank and genial spirit of our British Parliament. His manner, arrogant and yet timid—his words, insolent and yet obscure—offend even his political supporters. His hesitating speech, his contracted sympathies, his sneer, icy as Siberia, his sarcasms, drear and barren as the Steppes,[1] are all characteristic of the bureau and the chancery, and not of popular and aristocratic assemblies animated by the spirit of honour and the pride of gentlemen.

If war break out—*and the present prospect is that war will break out*—this dread calamity must be placed to the account of this man, and of this man alone.[2]

The *Press* was started, as this extract reminds us, at the moment when the Eastern Question was beginning to assume a menacing aspect; and the subject, treated under Disraeli's direction with special knowledge and acumen, soon took the leading place in its columns.[3]

The principal domestic question of the day, Parliamentary Reform, was discussed in a liberal spirit. In the third number it was laid down, by Disraeli himself, that, in regard to Reform, 'there are two men in England who occupy intelligible positions, and only two. They are both Liberals, both Reformers, and both Lancashire men; and these are Lord Derby and Mr. Bright.' Derby's prominent share in the passage of the Great Reform Act was recalled. Derby was a disciple of progress as much as Bright; but Derby's was English progress, in the spirit of the English Constitution and the national character, while Bright's was American progress, in the spirit of the American Constitution and the American character. Derby would effect change by a wise management of traditionary influences; Bright by means of a tyrant majority. 'Between these two intelligible systems the people of this country must, sooner or later, choose.'[4] The subject was developed in a more conservative sense in July. 'The principal depository of power should be the land—the only basis of a free and

[1] Disraeli wrote to Lucas on June 3: 'Alter, in the leader, "sarcasms meagre and barren as the Steppes" to "sarcasms drear and barren," etc.'

[2] *Press*, June 4. [3] See below, ch. 15. [4] *Press*, May 21.

genuine aristocracy.'[1] 'The possession of land has at all times brought with it as much of duty as enjoyment, and it is the only property in which all men take an interest. They willingly accord power, and even privilege, to that which, in the very necessity of things, must be held for the common good.'[2] These are very Disraelian sentiments, which constantly recur in his speeches and writings. Later in the year Reform was taken up again in a somewhat different spirit, the writer this time being Stanley. The idea of 'representatives of education' having been discussed and rejected, 'we are,' it was said, 'thrown back upon the stern, simple elements of property and population.' The conclusion finally arrived at was certainly a sweeping one.

> It is the duty of statesmen . . . to bring within the pale of the Constitution everyone whose admission cannot be proved dangerous. Is this policy, at once conciliatory and conservative, practicable? Can the franchise be placed on such a basis as, while giving to intellectual and social superiority their due weight, to admit all, save the actually houseless and pauper, to some participation in its privileges? We do not positively answer 'Yes'; yet the possibility merits inquiry; the object all must acknowledge to be good; the means may fairly be discussed hereafter.[3]

This article, which Disraeli did not see till after publication, somewhat fluttered orthodox dovecotes. It was called by so whole-hearted a supporter of Disraeli's as Mandeville 'a regular Radical article.' Mandeville probably made a shrewd guess at the author. 'If our party,' he wrote, 'objected to Stanley's pamphlet on Church rates, as you know, they will object, and with much more reason, to this article on the Franchise.' Disraeli no doubt felt his young colleague had gone too far, for in the next week's issue it was suggested that the Conservative party should for the present hold aloof, and wait to see the Government proposal.[4]

[1] *Press*, July 23.
[2] *Press*, July 30.
[3] *Press*, Nov. 5.
[4] *Press*, Nov. 12.

The great difficulty of the *Press* was, as always with a new publication, the financial one. In October it was losing £90 a week; but Disraeli was ready himself, with his wonted disregard of pecuniary considerations, to spend from his own very moderate means to keep the journal afloat.

From Lord Stanley.

KNOWSLEY, *Aug.* 24, 1853.—. . . It is all we could expect—2,000 and upwards in less than three months. If we go on to 3,000 in the next three months we ought to be landed.

Next session will decide the fate of the party and that of the paper.

Circulation — Total Sales: May 7, 807; July 30, 2,039.

Advertisements: May 7, £53 17s.; July 30, £10.

KNOWSLEY, *Monday, Oct.* 10, 1853.—. . . This, then, is our position: Present deficiency; probable but not certain solvency at the end of a few months, so far as paying our way, but no prospect of getting back from the profits of the paper any portion of the original outlay; funds exhausted; resources from subscriptions nearly at an end; and yourself, as I understand, responsible for the deficit. . . .

You and I at least, and probably some others, are known to all London as having been concerned in the affair: and our own failure, besides the general injury to the party, will tend to throw us back again into the hands of the ultras from whom we have separated, and who will never receive us except with suspicion, even if we could join them with satisfaction to ourselves. In other words, if the *Press* breaks down it will be inferred, and reasonably, that the opinions of the Conservative party are those of the *Herald.* This must not be, if it can be helped. . . .

My father . . . I have no hope of his helping us in any way. . . .

Anything is better than that you should injure your private fortune in pushing party interests. Parties, like nations, have no gratitude. . . .

To Philip Rose.

HUGHENDEN, *Oct.* 30, 1853.—I have completely examined the accounts of the *Press*, which make the matter entirely clear to me.

Considering all things, and provided energy and judgment are now exercised, I think the result may be satisfactory.

The weekly expenditure must be cut down to £100, which in round numbers will be a weekly loss of £50—*i.e.*, £200 per month.

If the whole number printed (say 3,000) be absorbed by a real sale, and the advertisements be doubled, the paper would then pay; and I think, if an effort be made at the meeting of Parliament, we may count on these results when it has completed about its twelfth month (May, 1854).

Our resources must be devoted to the inner page and the staff. Amateur correspondents may be encouraged, but not paid, and all little features, which occasion expenditure, terminated.

The success of the paper will now depend upon its authentic intelligence, the spirit of its inner page, and the vigor of its leading article. Hitherto it has fought its way, without any great policy to advocate; but that will come, and if such a time arrives, and finds a journal of this description with a prepared sale of 2,000 or 3,000, it may mount to considerable position.

I beg your earnest attention to the enclosed. I send also a cheque for £1,000 for the *Press.*

The sale of the paper slowly increased, and at the end of 1853 was 2,250. It was, however, still run at a loss, though Disraeli felt justified, after a year's experience, in giving a favourable report to the friends who had assisted him. The following letter, which is printed from a draft among the Beaconsfield papers, was probably circulated to all who gave financial support :

To Lord Bath.

GROSVENOR GATE,
March 30, 1854.

MY DEAR LORD,—As you were one of the earliest supporters of the *Press*, I think it may not be uninteresting to you to see the result of the effort.

Its success has justified our best expectations. Launched at a moment when the party was disorganised and depressed, and not sufficiently encouraged at its commencement, it has greatly contributed to the subsequent rally, very much affected opinion, has been referred to in both Houses of Parliament, given a tone and cue to the country's journals, and in ten months secured a genuine sale exceeding that of the *Spectator* and *Examiner,* which have been established for twice as many years.

Nevertheless, there is, and must be for some time, a loss

upon its production. We must remember that in this undertaking, as commercial profit is not contemplated, the most expensive article is given at the cheapest rate, and that it would require another year before that force of advertisements could be obtained which may prevent loss.

It is possible to curtail the expenditure, but that would be at the cost of progressive influence, and of destroying the school of writers which we have with difficulty and by a wise liberality created.

Very little dependence can be placed on amateur writing; and although one or two of our friends have done more than was ever contemplated, it is as an habitual exertion found incompatible with their other duties.

At the same time it seems to be of great importance to the party, that this organ should be maintained and pushed until it is self-supporting, which at its present ratio of increase may be counted on in the course of another year!

Either because of the lack of financial success, or because a better man was available, Disraeli and his friends changed their editor at the close of the first year. On May 11, 1854, Rose wrote to Disraeli: 'Lucas has resigned very peaceably'; and it was arranged that he should continue to write for the paper. The new editor, David Trevena Coulton, had some years previously founded and conducted a paper, the *Britannia*, with much the same aims and objects as inspired the *Press*—to extend and popularise the principles of Conservatism; but he had retired for seven years from active journalism to a farm in Kent, and his only writing was done for the *Quarterly Review*. He was a delicate man, and yielded reluctantly to the importunities of Disraeli and others; but having yielded, he threw himself into the work with great vigour and energy, and three years later (May, 1857) died at his post. Disraeli conceived, and retained, a very high opinion of him. Eight years after his death, he wrote of him to Rose: 'Coulton was a powerful political writer, a true man of letters, and of signal integrity. He was not a hireling, but wrote from conviction, and was always animated by a high sense of duty. He died in harness, writing the best articles in the *Press* newspaper, which, had he lived, would, I think, have been established as a powerful organ.'

While Lucas was editor, Disraeli seems himself, as a rule, to have written the principal leading article. Coulton took this labour off Disraeli's shoulders, without any loss of inspiration for the paper. He used to go, Mr. T. E. Kebbel tells us, to the House of Commons on Friday nights, to be primed by Disraeli with the latest information and the freshest arguments, and then return to the office to reduce his notes into the form of leading articles. Besides the writers already mentioned, Coulton could rely, then or subsequently, upon Richard Holt Hutton, editor of the *Economist*, afterwards editor of the *Spectator;* John Robert Seeley, author of *Ecce Homo* and of *The Expansion of England;* F. W. Haydon, Benjamin Haydon's son, who acted as subeditor, and apparently at a later date as editor; and Mr. Kebbel,[1] the sole survivor of a noteworthy group. At a still later period the paper enjoyed the services of Mortimer Collins, the novelist, and Edward Pember, the Parliamentary counsel. In its best days it seems to have had a circulation of from 3,000 to 3,500 — quite a considerable figure for a weekly journal at that period, and one which compared favourably with that reached by most of its rivals.

Down to February, 1856, the communications between Disraeli and the editor were constant, and the paper evidently closely reflected his views. Subsequently his interest slackened, and he rather left its management, along with other party and personal matters, to Rose, who wrote on October 5, 1857, that the finances of the journal were, on the whole, satisfactory. 'The ship is therefore afloat. My chief difficulty now arises from occasional insubordination among the crew, which has too much Irish material in its composition.' A few months afterwards, on acceding to office in 1858, Disraeli sold the paper; and eight years later, in 1866, its brief,

[1] All students of Disraeli are under obligations to Mr. Kebbel for the light he has thrown in many published works on Disraeli's career, and especially for the admirable collection of *Selected Speeches.*

but at first brilliant, career came to an end. It could, however, at least boast that it had long survived that Coalition which it was its original mission to expose and destroy.

The Coalition, in spite of their popularity with the country, fared in the early months of 1853 rather indifferently in the House of Commons, where they were defeated on minor points three times in one week. But their credit was restored by Gladstone's Budget, one of the financial landmarks of the century. Like Disraeli, he based himself upon direct taxation, but in a different fashion. He proposed to renew the income tax for seven years, gradually diminishing the rate during that period, with a view to the extinction of the tax at its close; and, like Disraeli, he proposed to extend it to Ireland, and to incomes of £100 a year. But he constructed an elaborate argument to show that it was impossible to correct its anomalies and injustices, and his authority sufficed for more than fifty years to prevent an obviously just distinction being drawn between earned and unearned incomes. For further direct taxation he proposed a succession duty on land, in addition to the existing legacy duty on personalty; he also proposed to increase the Scottish and Irish spirit duties. By these means, in addition to the large surplus which his predecessor had bequeathed him, Gladstone calculated that he would have on the current year over £2,000,000 available for remissions of taxation. He took over Disraeli's proposal for the gradual remission of the tea duty; he repealed the soap duty; lowered the advertisement and newspaper duties; reduced the assessed taxes; and reduced or repealed a long list of customs duties. By the boldness of his scheme, the ingenuity of his argument, and the loftiness of his tone, the Chancellor of the Exchequer produced a great effect on the House and on the country.

'We cannot cling to the rags and tatters of a protective system' had been a protestation of Disraeli's earlier in the session. Accordingly, he rather congratulated the

Chancellor than condemned his Budget; indeed, he was able to boast,[1] with considerable justification, that not only was there similarity in several details, but that many of the principles of Gladstone's Budget were identical with those of his own two Budgets of the previous year.[2] Financial policy had been assimilated with the new commercial system; new taxes had been imposed to supply the deficiency created by remissions; provision had been made for dealing with the finances of more than one year. These were all principles which Disraeli had recommended, but which the combination which overthrew him scoffed at and protested against. But he maintained that there were two great blots in the Budget — the renewal of the income tax for seven years without any mitigation of the inequalities of assessment, and the injustice shown to the land.

With regard to the income tax, Disraeli shrewdly declined to believe in its abolition at the end of seven years or at all. Those who kept their eyes open and marked the signs of the times must recognise that the income tax would take a perpetual place in the revenue; but, if it was to be a permanent item in our finance, it ought not to be extended to new classes and countries without an attempt to mitigate its injustices and inequalities. With regard to the land, he pointed out that it was proposed to leave the malt tax unmodified while the tea duty was reduced, and at the same time to increase the burdens on land by a succession duty. The Budget thus aggravated the pressure of indirect taxation upon the British producer, while it imposed a fresh direct tax on the possessor of the soil; yet when those interested in the land complained, they were met with taunts and jeers — told they must take this measure or they would get worse.

Disraeli hoped the old feud between town and country was over; there was no longer any difference of material interests between them. The greatness of the country consisted in its national character created by its institu-

[1] May 2.

[2] 'The Budget as a whole is a caricature and exaggeration of Mr. Disraeli's financial projects and speeches' (*Press*, May 14).

tions, which had their root in the soil. The owners of the soil were no exclusive class; why, then, this hostility to the land? Should the representatives of the towns remain still alienated from the agricultural interest, and 'proceed in their illusory progress, they may perhaps arrive at the goal which they contemplate, they may perhaps achieve the object they have set before them; but I believe they will be greatly disappointed in the result, and they will find they have changed a first-rate kingdom for a second-rate republic.' This was a phrase that Disraeli had used before, and expressed his strong conviction of the tendency of the Manchester School. So long as Palmerston and Russell were the leading figures in Liberal politics, this tendency was checked; but under Gladstone it had for some years free scope, and the influence of Great Britain in the councils of the world suffered a steady and lamentable decline, till it was restored by Disraeli himself in his great Government.

The principal features of the Budget were carried by majorities of seventy, and it went through with comparatively little change. One change Disraeli was largely concerned in effecting. Before the Budget was introduced, Milner Gibson had proposed, and with Disraeli's aid carried against the Government, a resolution for the repeal of the advertisement duty. Gladstone only proposed to reduce it; but he was forced in Committee to accept the decision of the House against it. Disraeli had before protested against taxes on knowledge, and he told the House that the repeal of the advertisement duty had been decided on in principle by the Derby Government, and only abandoned owing to the increase in expenditure. The Budget of 1853 was one of many evidences of the incurable optimism which permitted the Coalition to drift into war. It postulated continuity of financial policy, neither fresh remissions of taxation nor fresh additions to expenditure, and, above all, peace. With the coming of war the gradual diminution and final extinction of the income tax went by the board, and there was no opportunity for financial schemes on a large scale till Gladstone returned to the Exchequer in 1859.

Distinctions which he valued came to Disraeli this year. He presided in May over the anniversary of the Royal Literary Fund, and was warmly welcomed by his brother craftsmen. He told them that literature and politics were like night and morning ; each had its alluring charm and dazzling attributes, and he declined to give a decision in favour of either. The appreciation of generous youth was even dearer to him than that of men of letters, and he had it in full measure from the Oxford undergraduates in June. Derby had succeeded the Duke of Wellington as Chancellor of the University, and he included Disraeli in the list of his recommendations of distinguished men for honorary degrees at his installation. 'We shall have to run the gauntlet of the public opinion of the undergraduates,' Derby wrote to him, adding, 'I do not think, however, that we have much to apprehend on that score.'

In spite of Derby's assurance, there is ground for thinking that Disraeli was nervous about his reception ; but he found himself, as *The Times* said, 'the lion of the solemnity,' even though persons so considerable as Derby himself, Macaulay, Gladstone, Bishop Wilberforce, Grote, Bulwer Lytton, Aytoun, Samuel Warren, and Judge Haliburton, were present. Never before, except perhaps when the Duke of Wellington was installed, was there such an enthusiastic welcome in the Sheldonian Theatre as on his appearance. Pale, stoical, and impassive, save that his lips slightly quivered, he walked up to the Chancellor, while the theatre was ringing with plaudits; and, in answer to the formal question, *Placet-ne vobis, Domini?* the undergraduates in the gallery shouted, *Maxime placet! Immense placet!* Fraser noted that after, 'with a considerable lighting up of his face,' he had moved to his seat, he looked with his eyeglass along the ladies' gallery, caught sight of his wife, and kissed his hand to her. Further evidence of his popularity was given after a

Christ Church banquet to Derby which he attended. The undergraduates assembled in Tom quadrangle, in spite of the rain, to cheer 'Dizzy' as he left the hall, and escorted him to the gate with what is described as a 'spontaneous shout of enthusiasm.' 'Gentlemen,' he said, 'within these classic walls I dare not presume to attempt to thank you! but, believe this, never will I forget your generous kindness.'

At this period Disraeli wanted all the sympathy of his admirers, for the India Bill, now the principal measure before Parliament, brought out into the open the dissatisfaction of many of his followers. The Government of India at that period rested with three powers: the Governor-General in India; and at home the Court of Directors of the British East India Company on the one hand, and on the other the Board of Control, a department of the British Administration with a Cabinet Minister, the President, at its head. It was a compromise between Company Government and Cabinet Government, in which the Cabinet had the last word, and, in its present form, dated from 1833. The Act in operation expired in 1854, and had to be either renewed for a term or altered. Disraeli's experience, on a Committee of the House of Commons which had investigated the system of Indian Government, had convinced him that this complicated arrangement ought not to continue, and that the time had come for more direct assumption of authority by the Crown and Parliament. Ministers proposed, however, substantially to prolong the present arrangement with modifications in the Court of Directors, introducing, indeed, at the same time the important principle of unlimited competition for Indian appointments, and thus obtaining the warm commendation of Macaulay. The Bill did not at all satisfy Bright, who was the principal advocate of radical change in the Indian Government, and who desired to have Indian affairs continuously subject to the interference of Parliament. Disraeli, while not prepared to go so far as the Manchester

School, was opposed to passing in a hurry, at the end of a session, a Bill which perpetuated most of the anomalies of the existing system;[1] and under his influence Stanley put down an amendment to the second reading, recommending delay and reconsideration with a view to the attainment of a final and permanent settlement.

From Lord Derby.

St. James's Square, *June* 20, 1853.—I am sorry to say that I find among our own friends a great division of opinion on the subject of Stanley's motion on Thursday, and an amount of discontent which requires very careful handling to prevent its breaking out into open mutiny in the camp. Tom Baring's[2] opinion we knew before. Henley has to-day been with me, and reports, as his own view as well as that of Herries, that it is not desirable to interfere to prevent legislation in the present Session; and I have received a message from Lonsdale that the members on whom he exercises some influence have a strong feeling on the subject, as I was aware that he had himself. I have begged that all will attend the meeting to-morrow; but to me it is abundantly clear that we have no chance of carrying with us anything like the united strength of our party, and that I must be very guarded in the language which I hold.

I should not do my duty by you and by the party if I did not frankly express to you my opinion that a considerable portion of the dissatisfaction which has shown itself is attributable to an uneasy feeling among our Conservative friends as to a supposed understanding, and to a certain extent combination, between yourself and the Manchester School; and to an apprehension that under the cover of delay there may be sought to be introduced changes very agreeable to that sort of gentlemen, but not reconcilable with the safe administration of our Empire in India; and they are unwilling, apparently, to unite with men of whose intentions they entertain no favourable view, for the purpose of overthrowing the Government. I confess that I share this latter

[1] An article in the *Press*, July 9, on 'The Crown or the Company,' expressed Disraeli's view; it was written by Stanley. 'A feeble despotism is a political impossibility. . . . The question is not between bureaucracy and representative government; it is between bureaucracy ably conducted, openly acknowledged, answerable for its acts to Parliament; and bureaucracy which excludes ability, disavows responsibility, works in the dark, and, receiving no ostensible pay, pays itself (with permission of the authorities) in the corrupt use of patronage. Which of these two is the preferable alternative? or, rather, which of these two is the lesser evil?

[2] Baring had been the chairman of the Indian Committee.

feeling, and should be sorry to see the Administration displaced by a vote produced by a junction of the most conflicting elements, when the means of forming a new Government are not very obvious, and when the country is involved in very serious external difficulties.

I ought to add, speaking with entire unreserve, that the impression which I have mentioned of your understanding with Bright and Co. has been heightened, and the discontent of our supporters in the House of Commons aggravated, by the friendly terms in which you spoke of Keogh the other night, and by your abstaining from throwing a shield over Naas, who was placed in direct collision with him.[1] I have also heard strong comments on the fact of your having left the House the other night just before the division on the ballot, and upon your absence from any of the divisions or discussions which have taken place on the succession duty.

In short, I cannot conceal it from you that there is reported to me to be a growing fear, and the Government Press does its utmost to keep up the opinion, that you are gradually withdrawing yourself more and more from the Conservative portion of our supporters, and seeking alliances in quarters with which neither they nor I can recognise any bond of union. And I think it is to this feeling more than anything else that is to be attributed the division which at present prevails, and which I am confident will manifest itself to-morrow. If it does, as I expect it will, my language must be that of stating my own views, but not urging them strongly in a party sense. I see no other mode of escaping a signal defeat, in the most mortifying way, by the defection of our own followers—the result of which would be not only the present strengthening of a Cabinet which has no elements of strength in itself, but the permanent disruption of our party in the House of Commons. Personally, I should look on this result with great indifference; but I think it would be unfortunate for the country, and therefore I have not shrunk from pointing out to you the nature and the causes of the danger which I see; and I trust that, in opening to you my whole mind, I have not done it in a way to cause you personal pain, though I know that I must have given you some annoyance. Can you call here at eleven to-morrow to talk it over?

Disraeli was not to be moved from his course either by Derby's representations or by the grumbles of his party. His imagination, like Burke's, had been powerfully affected by India, and he was resolved to do his best

[1] Disraeli, as leader of Opposition, had endeavoured to smooth over and compose a bitter personal dispute, instead of being content to espouse his late colleague's side.

to make his countrymen realize their responsibilities towards their Eastern Empire. He told the House frankly that he had the misfortune to differ on this question from many of his political friends for whom he entertained, not only great respect, but personal regard; but he could not approve a measure continuing a system of Government for India which was cumbrous, divided, tardy, and deficient in clear and complete responsibility. The Constitution established in 1833 had failed, because there were the same complaints in 1853 as there had been in 1833 — 'constant wars; constant deficits; no education; few public works; maladministration of justice.' The small alterations which the Bill made he ridiculed. The existing Court of Directors, numbering thirty, was to choose fifteen of its own number to be the future directors. The proposal reminded Disraeli of a subject in which the Indian Government had greatly distinguished itself — the putting down of Thuggee.

The House, I am sure, knows what a Thug is. A Thug is a person of very gentlemanlike, even fascinating manners. He courts your acquaintance, he dines with you, he drinks with you, he smokes with you; he not only shares your pleasures, but even your pursuits. Whatever you wish done, he is always ready to perform it. He is the companion of your life, and probably a member of the direction of the same joint-stock company; but at the very moment when he has gained your entire confidence, at the very moment when you are, as it were, reposing on the bosom of his friendship, the mission of the Thug is fulfilled, and you cease to exist. I confess I shall be curious to see who are the fifteen Thugs. I want to know who will be the first innocent victim to be selected.

The speech, of which Lady Waldegrave (*née* Braham), who was in the Ladies' Gallery, said that it made her proud of her race, contained other characteristic passages. He said that no one had defended the Bill (though many were not going to vote for the amendment) who was not in office; there was Macaulay, to be sure, but he ought to have been in office. Macaulay's speech was 'one of those bursts of conversation which would have charmed the breakfast or cheered the dinner table.' With regard to the proposal to have an Indian Budget in the House of Commons, Disraeli uttered a prophecy which has been amply fulfilled :

> Is anything more dreary than a financial statement? What is it that at all excites attention, but the desire to know how much we are going to receive, how much we are going to pay? But we are to have an Indian Budget when we can receive nothing, and cannot control the expenditure. The powers of the Government to maintain a House are remarkable, but I think that their House-collecting, or House-containing, powers will be taxed to the utmost on the night when the Indian Budget . . . is coming on.

The Government had invited attention to the state of the Near and Far East as a reason for haste. It was said 'that Austria was in a state of uncontrolled fanaticism — that the position of the Turkish Empire was most perilous and critical. . . . I was very sorry to hear that the Coalition had brought things to such a pass in the Levant. But I have heard it laid down as a rule of law that no man has a right to take advantage of his own wrong, and it is no argument for misgoverning India that you have misgoverned your foreign affairs.' He thought the Government might have very well suggested delay themselves; they had only been in office a few months, and had had much else to do. But Disraeli's arguments had no effect on Ministers, who merely made game of the divisions of the Opposition. He was supported by only 140 votes in the lobby, against 322, and the Bill was carried. The form of Government thus established lasted only five years. The Indian Mutiny came in 1857, to show that Disraeli's pessimism was better justified than the official optimism; and in 1858 Disraeli, as Leader of the House, presided over the transference of India from the Company to the Crown, thus effecting himself that complete change which he had pronounced in opposition to be necessary.

Disraeli was educating his party, but the momentary effect was to throw their affairs into more confusion than ever. The success of Gladstone's Budget had placed the

Government in a much stronger position, and the blunders of coalition diplomacy in the Eastern Question were as yet either not known or not realised to be blunders. Accordingly the session ended favourably for the Government, and badly for their opponents. Parties in opposition have a tendency to fall foul of their leaders. One section of the Conservatives appealed to Lonsdale to help to depose Disraeli, laying great stress on the Liberal votes that had been given by his friend Stanley. Pakington, who had apparently not been admitted to Disraeli's councils in opposition, was suggested as a possible successor. Many Conservatives looked to Palmerston, who was supposed to be uncomfortable under Aberdeen, as their future leader. There were others who held, as Rose wrote to Disraeli, that nothing could be done while Derby remained leader, and that many of the Whigs, who would never join Derby, would be content to follow Disraeli. Malmesbury wrote to Derby, September 8: 'I believe nothing can rally us but the greatest personal exertions on your part in seeing and talking over individuals who possess influence over sections of the House of Commons; in coming to a clear understanding with Disraeli respecting his language and conduct, and insisting on his riding to orders; and, lastly, in laying before the party (as far as it can be done) a programme of our plan for the Session.' Malmesbury apparently had rallied to Derby's views, and deserted Disraeli and Stanley, with whom he was working in the spring, and whom he had helped to found the *Press*.

From Lord Malmesbury.

ACHNACARRY, FORT WILLIAM, *Sept.* 18, 1853. — . . . When Protection went by the board we were lighter by a heavy spar, but that spar was our mainmast. We brought a new army into the field, one-half of which were recruits, or fine-weather soldiers, and the army was defeated in our first pitched battle. We, the leaders, then ran away, and in our flight and subsequent retreats and skirmishes we have only found the old guard firm — namely, those men who had fought with us for five years. Put them at 150, and you have got all you can trust to. . . .

Disraeli was not seriously dispirited. He wrote to Ferrand at the beginning of the vacation: 'Politics are quite dead, and the chicken-hearted are all despairing; but I am an orthodox believer in the resurrection of the factions, and am too old a stager ever to give up the game.'

With the end of the session came the retirement of an old colleague, Herries, and the election to Parliament for Stamford in his place of one who was to be the severest of Disraeli's Tory critics and the intimate ally and successor of Beaconsfield. In making the announcement, Herries wrote: 'I understand that Lord Robert Cecil will be a valuable accession to the Conservative party in the House of Commons.'

To John Charles Herries.

Aug. 11, 1853 —I received your letter of the 8th inst., and read it not without emotion. The close of a public career so honorable and distinguished and of such duration as your own is an incident which must interest all your friends, and must touch more nearly those who have had, however adverse the circumstances, the honor of being your colleagues.

I confess I am not surprised at your determination. Nothing can be more unsatisfactory than the condition of the Tory party. It is, perhaps, the necessary result of a false position; but whatever the cause, the consequence is certain, and your successor may well be a young man, if he aspires to witness the triumph of his confederation.

Lord Derby had not prepared me for your communication. Goodwood and the gout have prevented my seeing him of late. . . . I trust that repose and the resources of the beautiful scene to which you have retired will renovate your health and insure you many years of enjoyment and honor.

The new member for Stamford made his maiden speech against the Oxford University Bill in the next session. It was praised by Gladstone in the House of Commons, and by Disraeli in a letter to his late colleague, Lord Robert Cecil's father. 'I have no hesitation,' Disraeli wrote, 'in saying that if he will work — and he has a working look — I will soon make a man of him.' 'It is a very great satisfaction to me,' Salisbury replied, 'that Robert's first attempt has met with your approbation. I am afraid that your praise may be a little increased by the friendship which I hope you entertain for his father.'

CHAPTER XV

'A COALITION WAR'

1853–1855

Disraeli had no responsibility whatever for the Crimean War. He was in office neither during the diplomatic negotiations which led up to it, nor during any part of its actual progress; and he always maintained that the war was the disastrous result of a Coalition in which two opposed principles of foreign policy were struggling for ascendancy, and that it would never have happened but for the defeat of the Derby Ministry. 'We are as a people fond of facts,' wrote the *Press* under his inspiration on September 24, 1853, 'and this one fact is too significant to be passed by unnoticed. The formation of the Aberdeen Ministry was the signal for the Cabinet of St. Petersburg to commence its attack on the independence of the Porte.' Nearly twenty years afterwards, in a speech at Manchester,[1] he repeated his view in the most categorical terms:

> The Crimean War need never have occurred. . . . There was not the slightest chance of a Crimean War when we retired from office; but the Emperor of Russia, believing that the successor of Lord Derby was no enemy to Russian aggression in the East, commenced those proceedings with the result of which you are familiar. I speak of what I know — not of what I believe, but of what I have evidence in my possession to prove — that the Crimean War would never have happened if Lord Derby had remained in office.

We may accept Disraeli's hypothesis, without being able to understand what evidence could have absolutely proved it. It is at least certain that the Derby Ministry spoke with one voice in foreign policy, and the Aberdeen

[1] April 3, 1872.

Ministry with two; and that by the change of Government the close understanding with France, which was then the necessary preliminary to a firm policy in the Near East, was placed in jeopardy, only to be restored after serious delay. Clarendon, Aberdeen's Foreign Minister after Russell's retirement from the post, told Greville over and over again, in the spring and summer of 1853, of the great difficulties of his task in the Cabinet, 'standing between and mediating between Aberdeen and Palmerston, whose ancient and habitual ideas of foreign policy are brought by this business into antagonism. . . . He is therefore obliged,' was Greville's comment, 'to take a great deal upon himself, in order to prevent any collision between Palmerston and Aberdeen.'[2] As Aberdeen was Prime Minister, and Palmerston had been relegated to the Home Department, what wonder that the Emperor Nicholas should have supposed that Aberdeen would guide English policy, and should have pushed forward with confidence, only to find that, after all, the resolve of the English people was expressed by Palmerston, and not by Aberdeen?

As Disraeli had no responsibility, his biographer is spared the task of repeating, save in the briefest outline, a familiar story. There was a secular quarrel between Latin and Greek monks about the guardianship of the Holy Sepulchre and the other Sacred Places in Palestine. One Church relied on France, the other on Russia, while Turkey was the Sovereign of the country. France meant Louis Napoleon, who was on his probation; Russia meant the Emperor Nicholas, who thought the 'Sick Man' was near to dissolution. Louis Napoleon, anxious to gain a reputation both for Catholic zeal and for power, obtained from Turkey by pressure certain privileges for the Latin Church in the way of keys to the Holy Places. This was bitterly resented by Nicholas, who despised Napoleon III. as an upstart, and who took very seriously

[1] 'England and France are the two policemen of Europe, and they can always keep the peace.' — Disraeli in the *Press*, May 28.

[2] Greville, under date June 22, 1853.

his own headship of the Greek Church. He sent Prince Menschikoff in the spring to Constantinople, ostensibly to demand a satisfactory settlement in regard to the Holy Places, but in fact to extort from the Porte an engagement to give Russia the definite protectorate of the Christians in Turkey, and thus to bring Turkey under Russian control. He would not believe that Aberdeen could possibly push resistance to such a policy to the point of war; and Aberdeen and Clarendon, on their part, accepted the Emperor's assurances, through his Ambassador, Brunnow, that he had no hostile or sinister intentions, and that Menschikoff's mission was of a very limited scope. Lord Stratford de Redcliffe, British Ambassador at Constantinople, understood Nicholas better. His authority with the Porte was exceptional, and under his influence the question of the Holy Places was isolated and a settlement readily arranged, but the Russian demand for a protectorate was rejected. Menschikoff left Constantinople towards the end of May; and Nicholas sent his troops across the Pruth, and occupied the principalities of Moldavia and Wallachia [1] early in July, declaring that this was not an act of war, but merely in order to obtain security for the Sultan's compliance with his views. Clarendon's confidence in the Emperor was now shaken, and he inclined to Palmerston rather than to Aberdeen. The English and French fleets came up to Besika Bay, just outside the Straits, to support the Sultan, France being more forward in aggressive movement than England.

Public feeling, however, was rising in England. British policy had been for some time, on the one hand, to support the integrity and independence of the Turkish Empire, as a necessary make-weight in Eastern Europe; but, on the other hand, to press for internal reforms and better treatment of the subject Christian races. The two aspects of British policy, the first represented at this time by Palmerston, and the second by Aberdeen, have

[1] Now united into independent Rumania; then under the suzerainty of the Sultan.

not always been easily reconcilable. But in this case there was a justifiable doubt whether any benefit whatever would accrue to the Christian inhabitants of the Balkan provinces by exchanging the yoke of a Mohammedan Sultan for that of the Christian ruler of an empire itself only slowly emerging from primitive conditions, and with its society still on a servile basis. The policy, which has since proved fruitful and successful, of encouraging on the Danube and in the Balkans the creation of Christian States independent both of Russia and of Turkey, was quite impracticable till after Russian ambitions had been curbed. The fundamental principle of British foreign policy seemed to be challenged by Nicholas's aggressive tendencies and his commanding influence in the councils of the German Powers, coupled with Russia's apparently inexhaustible resources — the principle, namely, that England could not, with due regard to her own safety, permit any single Power absolutely to dominate the Continent of Europe. In bringing, or appearing to bring, diplomatic pressure to bear on Russia, Austria and Prussia were ready to unite with France and England; and, with a view to peace, the four Powers drafted at Vienna a note to be addressed by Turkey to Russia, which might placate the latter without endangering the interests of the former. Maladroitly, they only secured the assent of Russia, and not that of Turkey, to the note; and it was discovered that Russia meant to construe it in such a way as to give her that protectorate over Christians in Turkey which she demanded. Turkey sent an ultimatum requiring the evacuation of the principalities, and on its rejection by Russia war broke out between these two Powers. The English and French fleets came through the Dardanelles to Constantinople, and on November 30 the Russian fleet attacked and destroyed the Turkish in Sinope Harbour. After the indignation caused in England by this achievement, there was little hope of keeping out of the war.

Throughout the session Ministers deprecated debate, and put off questioners by reassuring replies, minimising

Menschikoff's mission and the ominous proceedings of Russia. Disraeli contented himself with asking questions, though he viewed the diplomacy of Ministers with ever-increasing distrust, and exposed, through the *Press*, their hesitations and inconsistencies. The gravity of the situation was insisted upon from the third number[1] onwards, and the Ministers responsible for the failures of our diplomacy were mercilessly scourged. The violence of Disraeli's attacks on Aberdeen in the *Press* may surprise those who have learnt, owing to the publication of contemporary memoirs and correspondence, how many high qualities Aberdeen concealed under a repellent exterior, and how greatly he was esteemed by those admitted to his confidence. But he had not the qualities necessary for the Prime Minister of a Coalition in a troubled time. He had, indeed, the patience to suffer discordant colleagues even to an extreme degree, but not the vigour to dominate them; and he was so self-sacrificing as to remain in office to carry out a policy which he abhorred and had unsuccessfully resisted. Moreover, owing to a bad Parliamentary manner, he had no personal hold on Parliament—a strange position for a Prime Minister under a Parliamentary Constitution.

> Lord Aberdeen seems paralysed with the responsibility of action, and Lord Clarendon only whimpers and wrings his hands. . . . The curse of 'antiquated imbecility' has fallen, in all its fulness, on Lord Aberdeen. His temper, naturally morose, has become licentiously peevish. Crossed in his Cabinet, he insults the House of Lords, and plagues the most eminent of his colleagues with the crabbed malice of a maundering witch![2]

In the seventh number Disraeli gave a timely warning:

> We are on the eve of great events; and it is just as well that the people of this country should be prepared for their occurrence. . . . A single blunder in the conduct of our foreign affairs may cost us as much as a series of bad harvests. . . .
>
> The designs of Russia are to be resisted by a vigilant and skilful diplomacy, resting on an assured basis of material power; nor is there, in general, any fear of Russia attempting

[1] *Press*, May 21.

[2] *Press*, June 11.

to advance those projects which British policy deems so dangerous, except at periods when she finds our diplomacy napping, and the administration of our affairs in the hands of incompetent persons.[1]

After the event the Foreign Secretary himself realised how well-founded was this line of criticism. Clarendon wrote to Aberdeen on November 4 that the point of danger then reached might have been avoided by firm language and decided action at the outset.[2] When the Russians crossed the Pruth, Disraeli in the *Press* summed up the futile proceedings of four months thus:

We have had . . . stout declarations by Ministers in both Houses of Parliament; bold notices of motions given and withdrawn by docile members of the same; we have had both the English and the French Cabinets nearly broken up, and the Turkish Cabinet quite changed; we have had endless despatches, protests, ultimatums, proclamations; notes, parting, explanatory, and circular; orders for admirals to act and to be inert; combined fleets and contradictory allies;—and what have we done? Why, we have recommended the Sultan not to consider the invasion of his dominions by a foreign army as a *casus belli.* A *casus belli?* Why, it is no longer a question whether it is a case for war; *it is war*, and war the most triumphant and successful.[3]

Disraeli, it is not surprising, thought the time for debate had now arrived, and on July 13 he pressed on Russell to give a day for a motion which Layard had had for some time on the paper. In this reasonable request, Greville, whose pages teem with Clarendon's confessions, nevertheless could see nothing but wanton mischief-making. Russell pleaded successfully the Vienna negotiations as a reason for further postponement; and no regular discussion took place in the House of Commons until the eve of prorogation in the middle of August, nor did Disraeli himself speak even then. But his feelings and judgment throughout were with the Palmerston section of the Cabinet. He and the Opposition leaders generally realised the meaning of the Menschikoff mission, to which

[1] *Press*, June 18. [2] Maxwell's *Clarendon*, vol. ii., p. 8.
[3] *Press*, July 16.

Clarendon and Aberdeen were blind. 'A palsied hand,' wrote the *Press* on September 3, 'was fumbling with the reins of empire.' Malmesbury's policy was expressed laconically on September 18: 'To stop the modern Attila is a great and sound game.' Disraeli agreed that Nicholas must be stopped, but he did not regard him as a Hun. In 1849 he had described him in Parliament as 'a man of intellectual power who had upon the whole exercised his influence with a due regard to his duties, and was in advance of the people he governed'; and he always held similar language, in the *Press* as well as in the House of Commons.

To Lord Londonderry.

Confidential. HUGHENDEN MANOR, *Sept.* 26, 1853.— Altho' we may differ on Russian politics, we do not differ as to the abilities of the Czar. What is occurring is what I foresaw and mentioned, tho' it is occurring under aggravated circumstances of British incapacity. Such conduct as that of the English Government cannot, however, be accounted for by mere want of ability. It is one of the inevitable consequences of a coalition between statesmen of totally different systems.

I do not agree with you about Napoleon. Altho' personally, from the first, he was disinclined to war, he has behaved towards us most honorably. True it is, that Drouyn de Lhuys and Walewski were both of them warlike, but he would soon have thrown them over, had he wished to have left us in the lurch. Against his own feelings and immediate interests he was prepared to act, for the sake of the English alliance; but the conduct of our Government to him has been so inconsistent, and often so mistrustful, that we have absolutely encouraged him to leave us in the lurch.

As far as I hear, whether it be at St. Petersburg or at Paris, it ends by all agreeing that Aberdeen is not up to the mark. What will come of it, I pretend not to predict, but that there are dissensions in our Cabinet is, I think, evident.

Your 'strong Derbyite friend' must have been indulging in a little romance.[1] Statesmen do not much meddle with politics in September, and my despatches from Knowsley have only taken the shape of haunches of venison; but I don't think the present aspect of affairs is exactly one to induce a

[1] Londonderry's Derbyite friend had told him that the 'Chief [Derby] has thrown up his cards, and the troops turned to the right about, all to peg on to the Thane [Aberdeen] if they can, or to Palmerston.'

Minister out of office to 'throw up the cards.' With a fall of ten per cent. in consols since we retired, an European war at hand, mainly, if not entirely, occasioned by the vacillation and mutual jealousy of our opponents, much commercial and financial difficulty impending, precipitated and aggravated by the singular imprudence of the Chancellor of the Exchequer, I don't think Ld. Derby would feel it consistent either with his duty or his inclination to retire from the scene: tho' a mere reproduction of the late Government is impossible, nor was it ever contemplated. . . .

Writing to Mrs. Willyams on October 10, Disraeli says: 'I have sent Lord Henry Lennox on a secret mission to Paris, and his despatches are very curious and exciting.' Here is one of them:

From Lord Henry Lennox.

PARIS, *Oct.* 6 [1853].—. . . I went to see the Pss. Lieven. I found her seated on a low sofa, surrounded by a screen which was amply provided with *abat-jours* to conceal the ravages of time and anxiety. She was extremely depressed, and frequently burst out during our interview with, 'Mais c'est embêtant, ça; c'est détestable, et tout pour a few Grik Prists!!' She told me her news was of the worst, and that she had now *almost* given up the last ray of hope. She considers the thing has been mismanaged by all, and in some degree even by the Russians. 'La diplomatie à Vienne n'a pas brillé,' she said. The next observation was, 'They tell me the Derby party are willing to support Palmerston and a war Ministry; I cannot believe it, but as you are *très lié* with Mr. Disraeli you can tell me your *avis*.' I replied that I really knew not—that such a contingency had not been talked of while I was in England, and added, by way of drawing her out, 'Fancy Aberdeen *after all* finding himself at the head of a Ministry which declares war against Russia and his old ally Brunnow!' She did not hear me to the end, but in the most excited manner protested against the possibility of it. 'Mais moi, je vous dis que ça n'arrivera pas; *je sais* qu'Aberdeen ne consentira jamais à déclarer la guerre contre la Russie.' I then tried her again by saying, 'How annoying it would be to Ld. Aberdeen to go out *alone*, and at such a crisis!' She rose again and firmly protested that certainly S. Herbert and Newcastle would never leave him. . . .

A woman, a friend of mine, saw Pr. Jérôme yesterday; he said that the French Emperor had *quite made up his mind*, and that he only waited for us to do so, that he might declare war against Russia and carry it out, added Jérôme, *corps et âme.* This is authentic. . . .

Lennox's mission in Paris was to act as a kind of Special Correspondent of the *Press*, which kept up during the autumn a sustained attack on the Government, and in particular on the Prime Minister. 'The truth is that, amidst professions of peace, we are sacrificing its reality to its shadow';[1] 'the time has come when grave pomposity can no longer pass for wisdom, or moroseness for courage';[2] 'Lord Aberdeen has precipitated the convulsion, and is, at the same time, alike unfit and unprepared to control the storm';[3] 'he will betray the honour and the interests of our country — it is the law of his nature and the destiny of his life.'[4] Certainly most, and probably all, of these sentences were written by Disraeli himself. It is hardly surprising that Aberdeen should have turned on his tormentor in the House of Lords in the following spring and denounced 'a publication which is supposed to enjoy great authority; at all events, from its malignity and misrepresentations, the origin of it is not perhaps very difficult to discover.'[5] Disraeli retorted in the *Press* that 'malignant misrepresentation' was 'a splenetic misnomer for "inconvenient truths."'[6]

Mrs. Disraeli was seriously ill in the autumn of 1853. She was 'greatly suffering,' her husband told Londonderry, 'from a state of nervous debility.' 'As she is the soul of my house, managing all my domestic affairs, it is, irrespective of all other considerations, a complete revolution in my life. Everything seems to me to be anarchy.' It was not until the middle of November that her health sufficiently improved to allow the Disraelis to leave Hughenden for a little visiting. They went to Merstham in Surrey to stay with the Jolliffes, to Wimpole to stay with the Hardwickes, and to Heron Court to stay with the Malmesburys; and between these last two visits Disraeli went, for

[1] *Press*, October 1.
[2] *Press*, October 15.
[3] *Press*, November 26.
[4] *Press*, December 16.
[5] March 31, 1854.
[6] *Press*, April 8, 1854.

the first time, as a guest to his chief's house at Knowsley. The two leaders had corresponded but little during the autumn. The course which Disraeli had thought it best to take in the House of Commons had not commended itself to Derby, and both probably felt that the less said the better. Besides, the gout was particularly persistent in its attacks on Derby this autumn. Disraeli was the first to break silence.

To Lord Derby.

Confidential, HUGHENDEN, *Oct.* 28, 1853.—I have not troubled you all this time, notwithstanding events, because I thought you must be sick of us all, and would like, for a while, to forget party and politicians; but a rather restless letter from Malmesbury a few days ago makes me feel that you might misinterpret my silence, and suppose it to arise from indifference to our fortunes, for which I should be sorry.

I need not say I should like very much to know your general opinion as to affairs, and I give my own rough impressions in sincere deference to them.

I collected from Fremantle at Q. Sess. that the Government flatter themselves that they shall still weather the storm and meet Parliament with peace. This does not accord with what reaches me from the Continent, either from Paris or from my mysterious correspondent, Prince Frederic,[1] who is now in Germany. Madame de Lieven said some ten days ago that there were two things 'certain.' First, that the Emperor would not quit the Principalities. Secondly, that Lord Aberdeen would never declare war against Russia.

So much for war. As to Finance, I doubt whether the *malaise* be so profound as it appears. . . .

The third point of importance is the Reform Bill. I have pursued my researches and calculations which I made in 1851 on that question, adapting them to the new Census, and testing them by it. The result is a triumphant case for the territorial constitution. . . .

The state of the party is the fourth point which I would notice. I cannot help believing that there is more anarchy, in that respect, in the Houses of Parliament than in the country. Jolliffe, who, I hope, will be here in a few days, seems to have found a very general, and on the whole satisfactory, response to his circular respecting the registration, and is immersed in a very extensive correspondence. I have no doubt his sedulousness, tact, and courtesy, have worked well at the juncture, and that the new organisation we estab-

[1] Of Holstein.

lished is quietly but efficiently operating. I don't care so much for the personal feelings of Parliament if the people out of doors are true. A single motion, often a single speech, at the right moment, in either House, will clear the skies.

The result of all this is that I have felt, generally speaking, we could not be too quiet. . . .

Derby was too ill to reply until November 14, when he somewhat deprecated Disraeli's optimism about the state of the party. The effect of 'a single motion,' or 'a single speech at the right moment,' was, he thought, only temporary. 'The clouds will gather again, unless there is in the party a strong foundation of personal confidence, which must be maintained by constant attention, and even by some indulgence to the prejudices of those whom we lead.'

Before Disraeli reached Knowsley, rumours of Cabinet dissensions and of Palmerston's dissatisfaction with his colleagues became more rife than ever, and worried the Conservative leaders. Stanley sent Disraeli, on November 28, a sketch of his own and his father's preoccupations: 'Supposing resignations, Palmerston becomes master of the situation; will he be content to play a secondary part? Will he lead the Commons under my father? And in that event, you co-operating with him as joint leader, what becomes of Gladstone? G. and his follower, S. Herbert, are to all appearance very strongly bound by personal ties to Palmerston. Can that connection be broken? Or, supposing P. to take the command in person, what will be our position? It is evident to me that few of our friends would oppose *him*, consequently that our *rôle* as an Opposition will speedily become absurd.' Disraeli refused[1] to believe in any such 'mortifying decomposition of our friends.' And he asked Derby not to be offended 'if I take the liberty of saying what I once said to George Bentinck in his darkest hour, that "come what will, we will stand or fall together."'

Disraeli's visit to Knowsley lasted three days, from December 9 to 12; and, according to Malmesbury, who

[1] December 2.

was a fellow-guest, his arrival 'bored' Derby, as it obliged him to turn from translating Homer to talking politics, and to hold at least one 'Cabinet Council' of the ex-Ministers staying in the house — Disraeli, Malmesbury, and Hardwicke. Disraeli's own impression of Derby's humour was that he was anxious to obtain office again and 'full of fight.'

To Mrs. Disraeli.

KNOWSLEY, *Dec.* 12, 1853. — This place is remarkable: a wretched house, yet very vast: an irregular pile of many ages: half of it like St. James' Palace, low, red, with turrets: the other like the Dutch façade of Hampton Court. It appears to me that, like many other old great places, it has been built originally on the road side, with the park behind; so that now all the lands, through which you approach the residence, have a bare and comparatively modern look, as made up, which was doubtless the case, of fields, while behind the house is a park almost as large as Windsor, and with great beauty. I think it is a circumference of more than ten or twelve miles, with red deer, as well as fallow deer, oak forests, a splendid lake, great undulation, and in the moorland, or, as it is called in Lancashire, moss, the landscape is all rhododendron on a large scale.

Our party, the Ossulstons, who have come over from Chillingham with Lady Malmesbury to meet my lord, Lord Hardwicke, Anson, and some other men.

Lord Derby looks very thin and pale, but I think improved: he looks so very young.

Palmerston's resignation, about which there had been so much speculation and so much prophecy, was announced on December 16, and remained effective for just ten days, when it was withdrawn and everything went on as before. Dissatisfied as he was with much of the Aberdeen and Clarendon diplomacy, it was not on the Eastern Question, but on Russell's Reform proposals, which he found too Radical,[1] that he actually resigned; but as he returned on the entreaty of his colleagues and the assurance that the details of the Reform Bill were open to discussion, and as public opinion had treated his

[1] Disraeli told Lady Malmesbury that the Bill was a 'slashing' one; 'every town in which there was a statue of Peel was to have a member.'

presence in the Cabinet as indispensable, his influence was rather increased than diminished by the episode. The hopes and fears of the Conservative party were naturally much excited. Disraeli, writing on December 18, told Pemberton Milnes that Palmerston was 'furious that his resignation should be solely, or even mainly, placed upon Parliamentary Reform. He resigned on the broad grounds of "Antiquated Imbecility."'[1] Stanley drew the proper moral from what had happened, and rescued for us a prediction of Disraeli's which was abundantly justified, when he wrote to him on December 29: 'It really looks as if your prophecy were coming true: "a war and no Reform."'

To Lord Derby.

Grosvenor Gate, *Dec.* 19, 1853.—. . . The Government have no root in the country. Their plan of reform is an attack on the aristocracy, while at the same time it disgusts the working classes, while from their Puseyism the Cabinet cannot excite any enthusiasm among the middle classes. A clique of Doctrinaires, existing as a Government by Court favor, cannot last in troubled times like these—irrespective of the unpopularity which the management of their foreign affairs has brought to them.

What gladdens my heart is that the tactics we followed in resigning last year, and in which our friends had lost all faith, if they ever had any, have proved to have been founded on a deeper knowledge of men and things than our critics gave us credit for.

I apprehend you will not be much troubled any longer with grumblers in our party. I fancy, from some letters I have received and from some receptions which have greeted me, that 'confidence' is wonderfully restored. . . .

But the most funny thing of all, and the most delightful, is that Palmerston has contrived to land the Peelites with the Movement party. Remember Gladstone's Conservative peroration this time last year. I have no doubt myself, looking to the character of the man, his extreme caution as to acting alone, etc., that he did not make the *coup* until he had felt

[1] 'It is true that the policy of Lord Palmerston has, in the main, been followed, but it has been always followed too late' (*Press*, Dec. 17). 'Antiquated Imbecility' was a phrase which Palmerston had used of Aberdeen's principles when he and Aberdeen were opposed.

his way with, or probably been egged on by, most of the principal Whig houses; and although Lord Lansdowne has withdrawn his withdrawal, the moral effect of the first step remains. . . .

To Mrs. Brydges Willyams.

HERON COURT, CHRISTCHURCH, *Dec.* 30, 1853.

MY VERY DEAR FRIEND, — We are here on a visit to Lord and Lady Malmesbury, in a very wild scene; a land of four rivers, a true Punjaub, abounding in every species of wild-fowl, and the finest sport. I have sent you some of mine for your New Year's dinner. . . . The Government seem to have had a paralytic stroke, but they have administered cordials to the patient, and it will linger on awhile. Its alternative is Reform or War. This is a pleasant choice. . . .

Writing to Lennox on January 13, Disraeli said: 'I am disgusted with the silly *Herald* and the stupid *Standard* mixing themselves up in the mud. There were plenty of scavengers among the *canaglia.*' The mud in which the *Herald* and *Standard* were dabbling was a violent and unjustifiable attack begun by the Radical Press, but continued by these Conservative journals, against the Prince Consort, charging him with improper and unconstitutional interference in public affairs, and in particular with influencing British foreign policy in the interests of Germany and Russia. The Conservative leaders exerted themselves to stop, so far as they could, these libels in papers professing Conservatism, but did not entirely succeed in their object or in avoiding the unfounded suspicion of encouraging them. When Parliament met, the spokesmen of both parties severely reprobated the campaign of falsehood.

To Lord Ponsonby.

Jan., 1854.— I received your letter last night, and read it with astonishment and some sorrow. That 'very many people' should 'suppose' that I should in any way sanction, or not earnestly prevent, had I the power, attacks upon the Prince Consort, justifies on my part both feelings.

Having had the honor to serve Her Majesty, and having experienced from the Court always candor and courtesy, such conduct on my part would not be merely disloyal or dishonorable — it would be infamy. Irrespective, however, of these considerations, the opportunity which office afforded me of becoming acquainted with the Prince filled me with a sentiment towards him which I may describe without exaggeration as one of devotion. Nothing will induce me to believe that the Prince, with his knowledge of character and power of calculating conduct, has ever given credence to the insinuation you mention, or to recognise it as anything else but a malignant manœuvre of party.

But this accusation is not merely false; it happens to be absurd. Far from having 'much influence' over the papers you mention, I not only have none, but they are my secret or my avowed foes, and have several times attacked me with acrimony. Notwithstanding the unceasing assaults which in every form are levied against me from the Peel school,[1] you will never observe any formal defence of me in any of these journals. It is right, however, that I should state that other leading members of the party, whom one would think were more advantageously placed with respect to these journals, have made the most earnest representations of the injustice and folly of the course which they are pursuing with respect to the Prince, and entirely without effect.

The truth is, great errors exist as to the influence of party leaders over what are esteemed party journals. Where a party is the proprietor of a newspaper or assists it with a subvention, as, in the instance of the *M[orning] C[hronicle]*, no doubt they can do what they like; but that is not the case with the journals you mention. Holding them by no proprietary tie, and indebted to us for no pecuniary aid, they look only to their circulation, and will follow up any cry which they believe tends to increase their sale.

With regard to the second point of your letter — namely, the elevation of Palmerston or his union with myself, which are assumed to be the secret objects of these attacks — I need not, happily, trouble you at any length. I have never seen Palmerston or heard from him directly or indirectly during all these events. Indeed, I very much doubt whether I have spoken to him since he joined the administration of Lord Aberdeen. What may be his objects I pretend not to decide, but I doubt whether they be as towering as his enemies fear or his friends hope. He does not appear to me to be a man capable of availing himself of a great occasion.

My letter has spread to such a length that I will say nothing

[1] These attacks culminated this month in the publication, by a publisher of repute, of an anonymous volume entitled 'The Rt Honble Benjamin Disraeli MP. A Literary and Political Biography addressed to the new generation.' It was an elaborate arraignment, running to over 600 octavo pages, of the whole of his career, and it solemnly found him guilty of high political crimes, such as unscrupulousness, immorality and infidelity.

about politics in general. You know I am of a sanguine temperament, but I admit to you now that the state of affairs in this country is serious. We are instantly menaced with war and domestic revolution; and neither of these calamities has arisen from the necessities of things, but has been produced by the incompetence or the short-sighted ambition of second-rate men.

To Lord Henry Lennox.

GROSVENOR GATE, *Jan.* 23, 1854.—The Captain kept me so late at work in St. James' Sqr. on Saturday that I missed the post, so that I could not thank you for your magnificent present,[1] which will come very apropos to a Parliamentary dinner, which he insists on my giving on the 30th.

I am not at all 'depressed,' tho' I have got the prevalent catarrh, which is eno' to crush anybody. I think the Government is in great straits, and I am not at all afraid of Portal's[2] men in buckram, tho' I am sorry to lose such a nice young fellow as himself. Adhesions come in from all quarters, and so far as numbers are concerned, it will be the most powerful Opposition that ever met Parliament.

Parliament was to assemble on January 31, and more elaborate preparations were made by the party than usual, dinners being arranged both at Derby's and at Disraeli's for the eve, and a great meeting at Derby's for the actual morning. To the meeting, on Disraeli's suggestion, all Conservatives, and not merely Derbyites, were invited, so as to attract Peelites who disliked the Coalition into which their leaders had entered,[3] and Disraeli had other plans, detailed in a well-known letter to Malmesbury, for heartening his followers in the Commons.

To Lord Malmesbury.

GROSVENOR GATE, *Jan.* 24, 1854.—It is said that everything depends on a great muster at the Captain's on the morning of the 31st. A great muster will be better for us at this moment than a great division.

[1] Of truffles.

[2] M.P. for Hampshire. Lennox had reported him as saying that there were fifty men he knew of in the party who would vote to keep Gladstone in rather than that Disraeli should return.

[3] The most eminent anti-Coalition Peelite was Sir Stafford Northcote, who had been Gladstone's private secretary, but who was not to enter Parliament for another year. He has left it on record that he 'always abhorred' 'that miserable Coalition.'

To insure this, all his men ought to be asked to dine with him. He has offered only three dinners; the cards are out, they will only include ninety of his followers. There wanted nine dinners. The cards should all be out; if the dinners took place a month hence it would not matter. What they want is to be asked to their leader's, and to have their cards meeting them on their arrival in town.

You must remember this is a new Parliament, full of *new men who have never entered his house*, for last year *he gave no dinners at all*, from domestic circumstances.

Those who understand these things have all been to me to say how critical this is; every man who is not asked is offended. I cannot mention these matters to him; you are the only person who can.

Lord Salisbury also should be asked to invite the men. His dinners last year did great good, when our fortunes were darkest.

I have given the *Press* another £500, which will keep them till the end of March; during the interval we must consult as to the course we ought to pursue. The sale increases greatly, and its influence: but the expenses do not much diminish. You had better keep the subscriptions you have received till we meet and consult on this.

The enclosed will show you that the *actual sale* has increased six hundred per week since I left Hughenden in November.[1]

To Lord Londonderry.

GROSVENOR GATE, *Monday, Jan.* 30, 1854.—I never heard of your illness[2] for a long time, living in the country, and, like Mr. Roebuck, 'reading only *The Times*.'

I first saw the paragraph reproduced in a weekly journal in town one day, but I learnt, at the same time, on the authority of one of your most intimate acquaintance, that there was no truth in it, and that you were, happily, quite well. I am most grieved to hear that all this was inaccurate.

As for the D[israeli]s, tho' not utterly defunct, they have been nearly so. We stopped in town, at the end of the year, coming from Heron Court, for my wife to consult Dr. Ferguson, and on a debilitated frame she caught the London Influenza in its most aggravated form. We got down to the country as soon as we could, but she has been reduced to the

[1] In *Memoirs of an Ex-Minister* this letter is wrongly dated 1853. The reference to the *Press*, which was only started in May, 1853, and to the meeting of Parliament on Jan. 31, show that it was written in January, 1854.

[2] Londonderry died on March 6. This was apparently Disraeli's last letter to him.

last extremity, and tho' she has wonderfully rallied, at one moment the physicians hardly gave me a hope.

To complete my troubles, tho' myself extremely well, about ten days ago or so, I caught the disorder from her, for it is an epidemic; and tho' my attack has been comparatively light, it has nevertheless been very depressing, and rendered me almost incapable of business.

In such a state, and with such gloomy, uninteresting materials, I could not venture to attempt to write to Lady Londonderry; she deserves a happier subject and a brighter pen.

I am most annoyed and vexed, that you do not dine with Ld. D. I have to receive the Commons to-day for the first time at his especial desire; but I am in poor cue for a host.

I know very little about politics, except that the Cabinet are all at loggerheads.

Her Majesty was very gracious indeed to Ld. D.

I fancy to-morrow will be quiet; when much is expected, nothing occurs. It is impossible to ask the opinion of Parliament on affairs, with papers unread.

As for the Prince, I should think it will all blow over. . . .

Parliament did open quietly. The grave words of the Speech from the Throne about the necessity of supporting British representations by augmented naval and military preparations were presently emphasised by a declaration made by Clarendon, that the country was 'drifting towards war,' though Aberdeen continued to ingeminate peace. In spite of the threatening aspect of foreign affairs, Ministers proposed a full programme of important legislation, including a Reform Bill. Disraeli protested on the first night. He could not conceive, he said, that a body of statesmen who believed they were about to embark in a great European struggle would have asked Parliament to reform the Civil Service, the Ecclesiastical Courts, the Poor Law, and the House of Commons. 'I thought we were going to make war upon the Emperor of Russia. I find we are only going to make war upon ourselves.' Because the Government had been formed on the principle of the necessity of Parliamentary Reform, they were going to do what in existing circumstances was little short of madness. In spite of protests, Russell brought forward the Reform Bill in the early days of the session. It is unnecessary to consider here the details of a measure which should never have been introduced, and the consideration of which was first postponed, and then, after the declaration of war, abandoned. These strange proceedings gave Disraeli abundant opportunity for sarcastic comment. On the motion for postponement,[1] he asked whether it was for the public advantage that a Minister should always be laying siege to the Constitution? That the most eminent man in the House of Commons should announce that he disapproved of its character, and thought it should be materially changed, and yet, though unable to pass any measure of the kind, should remain Minister? The whole difficulty arose from the Coalition; 'a large measure of Parliamentary reform,' in Graham's words, was the talisman that brought Ministers together. When the Bill was withdrawn,[2] Disraeli, with some compliments to Russell, whose character and career were, he said, precious possessions of the House, reinforced his previous arguments. A Reform Bill, he pointed out, was a measure to change the principal depositary of power in the State. If it was produced by a Minister, and not proceeded with, disaffection was created in the minds of those who would have obtained political power under it, and dislike among those whose power it would have taken away; the constituted authorities and established institutions of the country were weakened and enfeebled. There had been far too much levity, for party purposes, in dealing with questions of organic change in the Constitution. Russell and the Government had embarrassed themselves by pledges, and he hoped they would learn the lesson. Reform could only be carried by a great preponderance of public opinion.

To Lady Londonderry.

COVENTRY, *Feb.* 11, 1854. — . . . Public opinion — that, if Russian aggression must be resisted, it has been occasioned by English infirmity; as for Reform, if Lord John proceeds,

[1] March 3. [2] April 11.

all agree the Cabinet will break up, and the general conviction is that he will proceed.

Thus, you see, affairs are so critical and capricious that, unless you come to town, it will be impossible to convey an accurate idea of them to you.

Lord Derby is well and sanguine—our party in good heart—a large number of the Whigs disaffected. . . .

To Lord Henry Lennox.

HOUSE OF COMMONS, *Feb.* 27, 1854.—. . . Affairs here are smouldering: much in the same way as you left them: threatening spontaneous combustion to such a degree that, some days, I consider it inevitable. One hardly knows what a day may bring forth![1]

Let us hope the best. I am all right with the Prince again, and am working with him. . . .

March 14, 1854.—. . . 'The Hounds' are damaged daily: but I don't see the turning of the lane yet. If Johnny can be kept to Reform, it is all up with them: but that seems a poor chance. . . .

A motion by Layard gave Disraeli early opportunity of defining the attitude of the Opposition towards Ministerial diplomacy and the approaching war. He devoted the greater part of a long speech[2] to a minute examination of the voluminous Blue Books which had been presented to Parliament. This was received with some impatience by the majority, who were in the humour expressed by Graham when he deprecated 'pottering over Blue Books.' Disraeli maintained that the vacillating course which British diplomacy had pursued must have been due either to credulity or to connivance. If to credulity in believing Russia's assurances, there might be a long and severe war, but one carried on for great objects, which might end in great public benefit. 'You may have a war which may restore Bessarabia to the Porte, may convert the Crimea into an independent country destined to flourish under the guarantee of the Great Powers, a war that may make the Danube a free river, and the Euxine

[1] To Malmesbury Disraeli wrote on Feb. 28: 'My conclusion is that the Cabinet is in convulsions; whether it may be soothed by any Daffy's Elixir remains to be proved, but, at the best, it's a poisonous remedy.'

[2] Feb. 20.

a free sea.' But if the vacillations of our diplomacy were due to connivance with the policy of bringing the independence and integrity of Turkey to an end, it would be a timid and vacillating war, ending with some transaction similar to Menschikoff's note or to the arrangements of the Vienna Conference. The first result would be welcome, the latter entirely unsatisfactory, to the British people. Look at the vacillating orders given to the fleets, first sent into the Black Sea and then brought back. 'When I heard of the return of our squadron to Constantinople, I could not help recalling the words of a great orator when he was addressing an assembly not less illustrious than this, when he said: "O Athenians, the men who administer your affairs are men who know not how to make peace or to make war."' So much for the diplomacy which had brought the country to the brink of war; but at this crisis the Opposition would not hamper the Government.

Whatever might be our opinion of the conduct of the Government in the management of those transactions which have led to this terrible conclusion, I cannot suppose that on these benches there could be any difference of opinion as to the duty which we have to fulfil—to support our Sovereign and to maintain the honour of our country. I can assure the noble lord that, so long as the Opposition benches are filled by those who now occupy them, he will at least encounter men who will not despair under any circumstances of the resources and of the fortunes of their country. . . . I cannot but believe that the noble lord must have drawn his opinion of those who sit opposite him from his recollection of other and preceding Oppositions. I do not know whether on the part of the noble lord it was an impulse of memory or of remorse. But this I can say, I can answer for myself and for my friends, that no future Wellesley, on the banks of the Danube, will have to make a bitter record of the exertions of an English Opposition to depreciate his efforts and to ridicule his talents. We shall remember what we believe to be our duty to our country; and however protracted may be the war, however unfortunate may be your counsels, at least we shall never despair of the Republic.

Patriotic support for the war combined with a persistent exposure of the vacillation of the Ministry was the note of Disraeli's speeches through the session. In a speech[1] on the Budget, he put very clearly his view of the responsibility of the Coalition for an unnecessary war:—

The war has been brought about by two opposite opinions in the Cabinet. These conflicting opinions have led to all the vacillation, all the perplexity, all the fitfulness, all the timidity, and all the occasional violence, to which this question has given rise; and I must say that if the noble lord the leader of this house [Russell]—I speak my solemn conviction—had remained Prime Minister of this country, or if the noble lord the Secretary of State [Palmerston] had been Minister of this country, or if Lord Derby had continued Minister of this country, nay, if Lord Aberdeen—I wish to state the case fairly—had been Minister of this country, with a sympathising Cabinet, there would have been no war. It is a coalition war. Rival opinions, contrary politics, and discordant systems, have produced that vacillation and perplexity, that at last you are going to war with an opponent who does not want to fight, and whom you are unwilling to encounter. What a mess for a great country! And all brought about by such distinguished administrative ability! . . .

And then they say, if we criticise their policy, we are bound immediately to come forward and propose a vote of no confidence in them. I tell them again I will not propose a vote of no confidence in men who prove to me every hour that they have no confidence in each other.

When war was actually declared, Disraeli, in supporting an address to the Crown,[2] fixed the responsibility for what had happened more particularly on the Prime Minister, Aberdeen, who was hampered by the understanding which he, as Foreign Secretary, had come to with the Emperor Nicholas in 1844, that the future of Turkey should be decided by Great Britain and Russia, the interests of France being ignored. Nicholas had presumed on Aberdeen's acquiescence, and the Cabinet had not frankly warned him, at the time of the Menschikoff mission, that they would act with France, and would not permit the partition of Turkey. Had they met him in that way, the Emperor, 'a Prince of great sagacity, shrewdness, and ability,' would have drawn back. But

[1] March 21. [2] March 31.

British opposition to Russian policy in Turkey was thoroughly justifiable. 'We oppose the policy of Russia,' Disraeli said, 'because, if she succeeds in getting possession of Constantinople, we believe she will exercise such a preponderating influence in European politics as would be fatal to the civilization of Europe, and injurious to the best interest of England.'

Disraeli did not consider that support of what he tersely described as 'a just but unnecessary war' bound the Opposition to support without question the financial expedients which Ministers resorted to in order to raise money to carry it on. Gladstone's first Budget, introduced on March 6, before the actual declaration of war, provided for an increase in income tax to pay for the expenses of the expedition to the East. To this Disraeli made no opposition, though he did protest against the doctrine that all coming emergencies should be met by enhancements of direct taxation. Gladstone had laid it down that war expenditure ought to be met out of income, and that recourse should not be had to loans save in the last extremity. Even when proposing in his second Budget, on May 15 — in addition to a further increase of the income tax and to increased taxes on spirits and malt — to issue Exchequer bonds, 'that is to say,' as Northcote puts it, 'loans in advance of taxes,' the Chancellor expatiated on Pitt's 'miserable policy' of 'loan, loan, loan.' Disraeli's rebuke was well merited. He advised Gladstone to 'give over these unworthy sneers levelled at the reputation of a great Minister,' one 'still dear to the people of England,' and confine himself in future to self-glorification. 'Let him remember that Mr. Pitt, whatever may have been his failings, held with a steady hand the helm when every country but Great Britain was submerged in the storm; and when he taunts Mr. Pitt with courting bankers and moneylenders, he might also remember that that Minister owed to a grateful country an eleemosynary tomb.'

Disraeli opposed the increase of the malt tax on the

ground that, as it had been to the patriotism of the territorial class that Ministers had particularly appealed for war service, this should not be the class specially singled out for increased taxation. Throughout the session there were constant attacks upon Gladstone's finance, in which Disraeli took a prominent part.[1] The glamour with which the Chancellor of the Exchequer's success of the previous year had invested him had largely disappeared. Several of his minor proposals had failed; and the reproach of having proposed a great peace Budget in 1853, on the eve of war, tarnished his reputation in spite of several fine fighting speeches which he made in his defence. But, whatever members may have thought of the merits of his new financial measures, a House of Commons determined, and rightly determined, to prosecute the war to a successful issue, voted them all by considerable majorities.

The war, in fact, was this session the salvation of Ministers; and Malmesbury records that Disraeli was 'furious' with it for this reason. On all other matters they suffered constant defeats and humiliations, and, but for the war, could not possibly have survived. They had to withdraw their Reform Bill, and to modify in several most important particulars their Oxford University Bill; and they were even defeated on their Parliamentary Oaths Bill, though in other sessions Russell had never any difficulty in carrying in the Commons his Jewish relief measures. Failure also attended Ministerial attempts to legislate on the Law of Settlement, Scottish Education, Civil Service Reform, and Bribery Prevention. When the Attorney-General announced the withdrawal of his Bribery Bills on May 29, Disraeli took occasion to review the blunders of the Government and to point the moral. They enjoyed, he said, the inesti-

[1] Incisive and elaborate criticism of the proposals and the Parliamentary behaviour of the Chancellor of the Exchequer was a marked feature of the *Press* during this year. He was charged with a want of public morality, want of strict accuracy, and want of temper. He was described as 'unable, from the ambidextrous constitution of his mind, to make a candid statement'—a phrase that reads like Disraeli's own.

mable happiness of having affairs conducted by men of remarkable ability who had made enormous sacrifices for their country — and for themselves. No man had made greater sacrifices than Russell. He had thrown overboard all his old friends and colleagues, who were banished to invisible corners of the House, and he sat surrounded by a coterie of public men who had spent their lives in depreciating his abilities and decrying his career. What compensation had been received by the House for the breaking up of parties and departing from the spirit of the Parliamentary constitution? They had been told that, though the Government had no principles, it had all the talents; and yet they had never had those well-digested and statesmanlike measures they had been led to anticipate. These sarcasms brought Russell to his feet. Other Ministers, he said, had been disappointed about their Bills. Disraeli himself had brought forward a financial measure which he failed to carry. It was true that Disraeli resigned, and the present Government did not. But, then, Disraeli had never ventured to propose, in regard to the war, a vote of want of confidence in the Government, and its supplies had been granted by majorities of one hundred. There was little in this part of the speech which needed an answer. But at the close Russell unwisely and ungenerously permitted himself to taunt Disraeli with insincerity in his support of the Jewish cause because of his recent vote against the Oaths Bill.

This taunt, undeserved as we have already shown[1] it to have been, stung Disraeli to a warmth of reply unusual with him. An eyewitness described him as trembling with passion when he rose to speak, and as discarding his wonted *persiflage* and irony for the most fiery eloquence. He towered, we are told, above the whole House in the fulness of his superb indignation. He was not surprised, he said, at Russell's not resigning. He knew he would govern on sufferance. He had seen him submit to the most humiliating and disgraceful defeats with a

[1] Ch. 3.

patriotism or pertinacity most admirable. He amended his charge against the Government, that in their Eastern diplomacy they had been actuated by either credulity or connivance, into a charge that their conduct could only be accounted for by both credulity and connivance. Then he attacked Russell for his factious conduct to the Derby Government, instancing his opposition to the Militia Bill and the Bill for Chancery Reform. Another measure which the Derby Government brought forward, for disposing of the vacant seats, was opposed by Gladstone's 'sanctimonious rhetoric,' on the plea that a Government on sufferance could not be permitted to deal with Parliamentary Reform. 'I suppose the vision of a perfect Reform Government passed before the prescient and prophetic glance of the right hon. gentleman. Yet what have you got in the way of Parliamentary Reform from the Government of All the Talents ?' When the financial measures of the Derby Government failed, they resigned. 'Whatever others may consent to do, I will never be a Minister on sufferance.' Russell had broken up his party and parted from his friends in order to carry great measures dealing with reform, education, and religious liberty. All these measures had failed, yet he still retained his post. And what a post it was for the most eminent statesman of this country to hold — a subordinate office under his ancient and inveterate political opponent, whom only four years ago he denounced as a conniver with foreign conspirators ! 'And now the noble lord comes down and tells me that this vote the other night, which he admits was an overwhelming defeat, was caused by my being false to the principles which I profess in this House !'

Disraeli easily vindicated his sincerity on the Jewish Question. Russell did not dispute the vindication, and justified his own acceptance of office in the Coalition by reference to Lansdowne's and Macaulay's opinion, that acceptance was his plain duty. For Disraeli the whole evening was a triumph. Bright enforced his argument about the powerlessness of the Government, and the lack of confidence generally felt in them. Walpole and Pakington defended their leader with cordiality and success, and an attempt by Bernal Osborne to support the charge of insincerity broke down completely.

The one measure of importance which the Government succeeded in passing, in however mutilated a shape, was the Oxford University Reform Bill. The freedom of local government, as opposed to a centralised bureaucracy, was always Disraeli's ideal. Accordingly, though he did not directly oppose the second reading, in one of the debates he expressed his dislike of a policy which, in his opinion, struck a fatal blow at the self-government and independence of the University. Moreover, the Bill outraged the principle of prescription, on which English institutions depended, for the sake of removing a few anomalies and imperfections. England was ruled, as he had written in *Lord George Bentinck*, by traditionary influences, the Universities being not the least considerable of them. He would accord authority to the Universities, if they wished it, to increase their power and enlarge their sphere of action; but he objected to placing them under the control of the State. Happily, the reform of Oxford and Cambridge has, so far, respected to a large extent the principle laid down by Disraeli; but some modern educationists do not conceal their impatience of an independence which mars bureaucratic symmetry. Disraeli could report in July to Mrs. Brydges Willyams that it had been 'on the whole a satisfactory campaign. The Opposition has become consolidated and powerful; the Government, though still a Government, is broken and infirm. The two bodies have changed their relative positions since last year.'

Disraeli was much struck, during the session of 1854, with the strong Protestant feeling of the House of Commons.' The spirit roused by the Papal Aggression in 1850 was still powerful, and showed itself in resistance to any modification of the Parliamentary oath, in motions for inspection of Roman Catholic monasteries and nunneries, and in attacks on the Maynooth grant. In the closing days of the session, in a debate raised by Spooner on Maynooth, Disraeli appealed to the Government to settle all questions of the kind in a comprehensive manner, taking up much the same line as he had taken on the Ecclesiastical Titles Bill. He asked:

Have we or have we not a Protestant Constitution? If we have a Protestant Constitution, what does it mean? Let Government come forward; let it declare by legislation what are the functions, what the attributes, what the influence, and what is the bearing, of that Protestant Constitution. Let every man, whether he be a Protestant or a Roman Catholic, clearly understand what are the rights and privileges which he enjoys under that Constitution, what he may do and what he may not do.

Russell, he thought, was in the most happy position for effecting a settlement; he was the champion of civil and religious liberty, and himself both a supporter of Roman Catholic emancipation and the promoter of the Ecclesiastical Titles Bill. No one could better vindicate the Protestant Constitution. Russell, however, declined the delicate task; and, indeed, it is easier to see that the request was very embarrassing to a Government which depended equally on the writer of the Durham letter and on Peelites inclined to Puseyism, than it is to conceive what kind of legislation could possibly satisfy the conditions. The speech made Disraeli for a time the Protestant hero, and letters and addresses poured in upon him. He was a little uneasy in the part, and so were some of his friends. Stanley wrote in the autumn: 'In the summer of 1852 you repeatedly told me that our chance at the elections had been ruined by our taking up high Protestant politics. I agreed with you then, as I do now. Shall we gain in 1854 by repeating the mistake of 1852?' And again: 'I fear you will burn your fingers with that infernal "Protestantism."' Walpole also wrote very sensibly: 'It would hardly do for us to *originate* a motion or measure of that kind in time of war, as they would accuse us (unjustly !) of making differences or disunion among the people, when there ought to be nothing but concord and harmony.' But it may be doubted whether Disraeli ever contemplated action on the part of the Opposition. In an answer which he wrote to a Protestant Association in Lancashire which promised him support 'to their utmost power in the maintenance of a sound Protestant policy,' there is more evidence of a desire to make the Coalition ridiculous, and secure a little party capital, than of any intention seriously to take in hand and settle the relations between emancipated Roman Catholics and a Protestant Constitution. It was, indeed, an 'admirably ironical epistle,' calculated 'to outdo the famous Durham letter.'[1]

To the Rev. Christopher Robinson.

HUGHENDEN MANOR, *Sept.* 16, 1854.—. . . I beg you to offer the Association my thanks for this mark of their approbation, which I value. Public men in this country depend upon public confidence. Without that they are nothing.

Far from wishing to make the settlement of this all-important question a means of obtaining power, I would observe that I mentioned, at the same time, in my place, the various and eminent qualifications which, I thought, Lord John Russell possessed for the office, and my hope that he would feel it his duty to undertake it.

In that case I should extend to him the same support which I did at the time of the Papal Aggression, when he attempted to grapple with a great evil, though he was defeated in his purpose by the intrigues of the Jesuit party, whose policy was on that occasion upheld in Parliament with eminent ability and unhappy success by Lord Aberdeen, Sir James Graham, and Mr. Gladstone.

I still retain the hope that Lord John Russell will seize the opportunity which he unfortunately lost in 1851, and deal with the relations in all their bearings of our Roman Catholic fellow-subjects to our Protestant Constitution. But, however this may be, there can be no doubt that, sooner or later, the work must be done; with gravity, I trust, and with as little heat as is possible in so great a controversy, but with firmness and without equivocation; for the continuance of the present state of affairs must lead inevitably to civil discord, and perhaps to national disaster.

[1] Madden's *Lady Blessington*, Vol. III., ch. 4.

To Lady Londonderry.[1]

CARLTON CLUB, *July* 19, 1854. — . . . The Government in a dreadful state, but will, I suppose, hold on a little longer. On Monday they received official intimation that Austria would not enter the Principalities or otherwise act against Russia, and recommending revival of Vienna Conference: Clarendon in despair, and said that nothing could be worse.

They have been trying it on very strongly with the Château,[2] as to your friend,[3] and H.M. much harassed.

At Duchess of Gloucester's infantile assembly it came out; the Prince of Wales said, *Papa is going to France.* Upon which there was a hush, and Rev. Gibbs put his finger to his lip, and somebody else her hand on his R.H.'s mouth; but the murder was out. Lady Jersey and Co. caught the flying words. It seems the Prince is to go in September, but I believe alone.[4] This will hardly satisfy your friend, who naturally wants someone else. . . .

It began to be realised in the summer of 1854 that the allied armies of France and England, so long as they remained in the Balkan Peninsula, could deal no decisive blow at the enemy who had evacuated the Principalities; and the two Governments, impelled by public opinion, resolved on further aggressive action.

To Frances Anne, Lady Londonderry.

Strictly confidential. HOUSE OF COMMONS, *Aug.* 7, 1854. — . . . The Government have staked their future on an autumn campaign in the Crimea, with the hope of re-establishing their position. The prospects are not good, and the chances are that we shall make a fiasco.

I am not myself very anxious to precipitate affairs. I have received from the highest quarter an intimation that, if things take their due course, the next and, I hope, very lasting Tory Government may be under a head which I never contemplated. I hardly know whether I should consider the intimation a gratifying one. I already feel, in the position I now occupy, the want of sufficient fortune. There are a thousand things which ought to be done which are elements of power, and which I am obliged to decline doing or to do at great sacrifice. Whether it be influence with the Press, or organisation throughout the country, everyone comes to me, and everything is expected from me. Tho'

[1] Now a widow. [2] Windsor Castle. [3] Napoleon III.

[4] Prince Albert paid a visit to the Emperor at Boulogne, Sept. 4–8.

Frances Anne, Marchioness of Londonderry,
with her Son, afterwards fifth Marquis.
from the portrait by Sir Thomas Lawrence, P.R.A.
in the possession of Lord Londonderry.

Printed in England.

so many notables and magnificoes belong to the party, there never was an aggregation of human beings who exercised less social influence. They seem to disregard or to despise all the modes and means of managing mankind.

As for our chief, we never see him. His house is always closed; he subscribes to nothing, though his fortune is very large, and expects, nevertheless, everything to be done. I have never yet been fairly backed in life. All the great personages I have known, even when what is called 'ambitious' by courtesy, have been quite unequal to a grand game. This has been my fate, and I never felt it more keenly than at the present moment, with a confederate always at Newmarket and Doncaster, when Europe — nay, the world — is in the throes of immense changes, and all the elements of power at home in a state of dissolution. If ever there were a time when a political chief should concentrate his mind and resources on the situation, 'tis the present. There cannot be too much vigilance, too much thought, and too much daring. All seem wanting. — Alas! and adieu! always your attached D.

This is an extraordinarily interesting letter. The statement that Disraeli had received an intimation 'from the highest quarter' that he, rather than Derby, would be asked to form the next Tory Government, seems almost incredible when we consider not only the point which he mentions himself, the insufficiency of his personal position, but the great ascendancy which Derby's talents, character, experience, and station had given him in the party, and also the disposition of the Court towards the two men. It is probable, indeed, that increased knowledge of Disraeli may have already modified in some degree the original distrust of him felt by the Court; and the Prince Consort, absorbed as he was himself in his delicate constitutional duties, would probably discover in the long run that he had more in common with the persistent watchfulness of Disraeli than with the intermittent brilliance of Derby. But there had as yet been no sufficient time, and no sufficient opportunities of association, to effect a change. Moreover, when an attempt was made to form a Tory Government in the following year, there was no manifestation of any such disposition on the part of the Court as Disraeli's language implies. The only explanation which occurs to the bewildered student, other than the assumption of a complete misapprehension on Disraeli's part, is that the Court may have believed that the constantly recurrent and increasingly severe attacks of gout to which Derby was now subject had rendered him incapable of serving the Crown again as First Minister. If so, the mistake was comparable to that of Derby and Disraeli themselves, six months later, in treating Palmerston, on the threshold of his ten years' domination of English politics, as a worn-out Pantaloon.

Apart from this point, the letter throws a flood of light on Disraeli's relations to the 'magnificoes' of the party, and to his chief. It is a repetition, in a much more accentuated form, of the criticism hinted in his letter to Malmesbury at the beginning of the session, when his immediate object was to get Derby to give a comprehensive series of Parliamentary dinners.[1] The notables were glad enough to make use of Disraeli's services, but were disinclined to put their own shoulders to the wheel, or even to turn to due account on behalf of the party those social influences which they wielded so easily, but which meant so much to others. Of Derby himself, Disraeli's complaint is much the same as Bentinck's was. Whereas men like Peel, Russell, Palmerston, Aberdeen, Bentinck during his last three years, Gladstone, and Disraeli, whatever other interests they might have, treated politics as their serious profession, Derby in politics was always the brilliant but incalculable amateur. Strenuous and keen as he could be for a period, Derby was only too apt to lose sight of the whole political struggle for weeks together while he devoted himself entirely to other pursuits, it might be racing or shooting, Homer or local interests. It was especially difficult to secure his attention for politics when he was in opposition and when office did not appear to be imminent. Such being his disposition, it testifies all the more to his amazing aptitude for that sphere

[1] See above, p. 532, 533.

of action which he treated so lightly, that he should have been regarded during the Reform Ministry as the inevitable heir to Whig leadership; and then for the rest of his life, after he had quitted the Whigs and joined the Tories, as the indispensable leader of his new party.

To Frances Anne, Lady Londonderry.

HUGHENDEN, *Aug.* 21, 1854.—I have been here ten days, and should have earlier advised you of my removal, had not that happened to me which has happened every year for the last quarter of a century, and which, every year, always takes me by surprise—namely, that, tho' I left town quite well, I had not been eight and forty hours before I found myself in a complete state of nervous prostration, and quite unable to write the shortest letter on the most ordinary business. I suppose it is the sudden cessation of excitement, too complete and abrupt for our mortal frames; but, whatever the cause, the result is undoubted and most distressing. However, I will not dwell upon such egotistical twaddle. I am a little better, and this is my first attempt at a recurrence to the interest of existence—that is, to write to you. . . .

HUGHENDEN, *Sept.* 3, 1854.—. . . The elements seem always to save the Russians. A correspondent of mine, who had seen Madame Lieven, about a month ago wrote to me that she was *au desespoir*, and that he had got out of her that the Emperor had only 30,000 men in the Crimea, and ought to have had at least 100,000. Indeed, he never expected war, and had made no fitting preparations. The defense at Bomarsund seems hardly superior to that of the Chinese forts, and it is likely that Sebastopol would have fallen; affairs, however, may be very different next year, even if Austria does not wind up the business in the interval.

I have been reading here, with infinite delight, Ségur's Memoirs. He was French Ambassador at the Court of Catherine the Great, and accompanied her on her great expedition to the Crimea. Did you ever read them? I once did years ago. If you never came across them, I know no book more exactly in your way. It is all about what we are all thinking and talking of. Never was a Court painted in more lively colors, or more authentically; and the charming circle surrounding the Empress in her voyage, Potemkin, the gay Prince de Ligne, the high-bred, melancholy Fitz-Herbert, Ségur himself, the King of Poland, and Momonoff, live as the characters do in Boswell's Johnson.

The Disraelis paid in September and October a series of visits in the West of England, staying with Lady Rolle, the Palks, the Yarde Bullers, and others, and spending several days with Mrs. Willyams at Torquay. In his social occupations Disraeli seldom entirely forgot politics. 'We passed a delightful month in Devon and Cornwall,' he wrote to Lennox; 'and where, so far as political prospects are concerned, I was greatly satisfied. The Whigs throughout the West of England have entirely renounced the Coalition.'

To Lord Henry Lennox.

HUGHENDEN, *Dec.* 2, 1854.— . . . [Lord Derby] seems to be full of his ancient spirit, and which dealing with 'producers and consumers' appeared to have cowed.

The present men are in a great mess, and the country is beginning to hate them: but unless there be some mutual drinking of Brighton waters, or some similar beverage, I don't foresee change. Mere criticism will not upset even a Coalition Ministry, but their rapidly increasing unpopularity may stimulate new formations. In the meantime, 'Heaven is above all.' . . .

To Mrs. Brydges Willyams.

HUGHENDEN, *Dec.* 6, 1854.—We have had very absorbing and sad times since I last wrote to you. We have lived here quite alone, reading only the ensanguined newspapers, and learning, each day, of the loss of our dearest friends. What tragedies!

My Parliamentary staff has suffered more than that of any of the Generals of Division. I think I told you that the chief of my staff, Sir William Jolliffe, had lost his eldest son in the Guards, before Sebastopol, of cholera; and that his second, and prime hope, charged with Lord Cardigan at Balaclava, and after a fortnight's terrible existence under the telegraphic bulletin, that reported the whole of the light cavalry as destroyed, turned up as one of the three officers in his regiment of Dragoons who was unscathed; but the father looks ten years older than he did last session. Colonel Hunter Blair, of the Scotch Guards, one of my most active aide-de-camps, and really invaluable both as a partisan and a friend, [was] shot in the tenderest part and died in awful torments. This is a severe loss to me. My second aide-de-camp, Lord Mandeville, writes to me that he has had four cousins killed and one severely wounded.

In the midst of all this, Parliament is called suddenly together, and the pressure on me for the last week has been very great. We go up to town to-morrow, for, to complete our troubles, our house is full of workmen, and yet on the morning of the 12th I must contrive to receive two hundred members of Parliament! . . .

It was time that Parliament should meet. The invasion of the Crimea had turned out a larger and more difficult business than a sanguine people and an eager Press had foreseen. Disraeli had had his misgivings from the first. On September 4 he wrote to Mrs. Willyams: 'We seem to have fallen into another Walcheren Expedition, and in my opinion the Ministers ought to be impeached.' On October 25 Walpole wrote to Disraeli: 'I am as clear as you that the expedition to the Crimea was a great mistake. As long as we stood on the high moral grounds of right and justice, we were invincible; the moment we attempt either the humiliation or dismemberment of Russia, no one can conjecture to what extremities we might be driven.' What was the position at the beginning of December? The allied forces had won victories at the Alma and at Inkermann, and in these battles and at Balaclava the British soldier had shown all his old steadiness and heroism; but the losses had been very severe, Sebastopol had not fallen, and the armies were settling into winter-quarters for the siege. Meanwhile, in published narratives and private correspondence, there came terrible revelations of mismanagement and incompetence, of cholera and scurvy, of troops without food and clothing, with food and clothing rotting hard by on the beach. Letters to Disraeli from Lady Londonderry, whose son, Lord Adolphus Vane, had gone to the front, show what the mothers of our soldiers were feeling.

From Frances Anne, Lady Londonderry.

Nov. 26, 1854. — Surely there must be an hour of reckoning for this hateful Government who go to war without providing an army. It is actual murder to let this little heroic wreck of an army fight those hordes and masses of barbarians who reinforce by tens of thousands while we hardly do so with hundreds. And that wintering in the Crimea, without comforts, habitations, hardly provisions, etc.—it is all heartbreaking. . . . I think of nothing else even in my sleep, and if I were younger I am sure I should seize on the idea of *The Times*, and get a yacht and go there. It seems so dreadful to sit at home and do nothing.

Dec. 20.—I have deplorable accounts—floating encampments on mud, no fresh meat even for the officers, pork and biscuit, horses dying all round, and none to be got even to bring up the supplies taken out. There seems neither care nor thought, and a total indifference as to what becomes of the wreck of this fine army, and the brave spirits who seem tasked beyond human endurance.

The ***Press***, on November 25, added its voice to the chorus of indignation in the newspapers:

This is no time to mince words, or to seek for emasculated paraphrase, in place of honest English. The nation knows that the army has been abominably treated, and that its condition at this moment is one of peril and suffering. Public indignation demands that every exertion be instantly made for the succour and solace of the troops now sentenced to a Crimean winter. Hands, hearts, purses, are all open if the Government will do its duty. There is nothing which the nation will refuse to the Administration—except confidence.

The line of the Opposition in the forthcoming debates was discussed in a letter from Derby to Disraeli on November 28. 'Of course,' he wrote, the Government 'will introduce no debatable matter into the Address; of course we must have no amendment; of course we must support them in the vigorous (?) prosecution of the war; and equally of course we must give them the benefit of our unreserved opinion of the way in which they have mismanaged and starved it. This last topic may lead to divisions, as well as debates, in your House, if Gladstone adheres to his absurd crotchet of paying for the war within the year. . . . As to the past, I think our chief topic should be want of foresight, every step being a "leap in the dark," and every measure adopted too late.' But Derby did not seem to contemplate that the revelations of mismanagement might upset the Government. Disraeli was more clear-sighted, and, with a view to the formation of an Administration capable of extricating the country from its enormous difficulties, tried, but without success, to strengthen the Opposition by overtures through the Duke of Richmond to Lord Fitzwilliam and the old Whigs. His growing influence with his own party was shown by his holding, for the first time, a meeting of the Conservative members of Parliament in his own house at Grosvenor Gate on the morning of the opening of the session. Hitherto party meetings had been held at Derby's house, for Commoners as well as Peers. Derby congratulated him: 'I rejoice in the necessity in which you find yourself, of thus taking the lead of the Commons at the commencement of the session.'

The Queen's Speech announced that Parliament had been called together at an unusual period in order to take measures for prosecuting the war with the utmost vigour and effect; and the feeling of Parliament, with the exception of the small minority represented by Bright, was entirely in harmony with the spirit of the Speech. But there was a strong conviction, which Newcastle and Sidney Herbert, the Ministers principally responsible, did not succeed in dispelling, that the Government had so far shown little prudence or vigour. Of this conviction Disraeli made himself the exponent. When Ministers declared war, he pointed out, they did so in most favourable circumstances. They had had a unanimous Parliament and people, unlimited supplies, an overflowing Exchequer, and the most powerful ally in the world; and yet what had they accomplished? 'I now ask the House,' he said, 'for a moment to turn round and consider, not whether there were sufficient nurses or surgeons at Scutari, not what was the number of pots of marmalade which should be sent out to the support of our starving troops, but I ask the House to consider what have been the results which this Ministry with these enormous advantages have obtained.' The great armada which had been despatched to the Baltic with Graham's benison and under the command of a 'true Reformer,' Sir Charles

Napier, had done nothing but destroy the fortifications of Bomarsund. In the Black Sea, an army of 20,000 or 30,000 men had been sent against a fortress as strong as Gibraltar; it was sent at the wrong time, and no provision was made for its maintenance or reinforcement. Why was not the militia embodied when the war began? Ministers had managed to bring the country into a state of war with the greatest empire of the world, because they were a Coalition, each with an *arrière pensée*, no two of them ever of one mind. They expected that their negotiations would end in peace, and that they would never be called upon to act: from the first they flattered themselves with the belief that the circumstances they had now to encounter would never happen during their lives. They had done everything unexpectedly and everything too late. Now they were relying on an alliance with Austria. What assistance did she propose to give? France had acted. Would Austria act? Or merely watch the game and profit by it in the end? Disraeli's scepticism as to the value of the Austrian alliance was justified, as Russell had to admit that the treaty which had just been signed only bound Austria to act in certain eventualities in the future.

It was an unpleasant surprise for Parliament and the country to find that the principal measure introduced by Ministers, in this December sitting, for the more vigorous prosecution of the war, was a Bill to enable the Government to enlist 10,000 foreigners in the British army, to be drilled in this country. This Foreign Enlistment Bill was felt to be very wounding to the national pride; and here, again, the Opposition, led by Derby and Ellenborough in the Lords, and by Disraeli in the Commons, undoubtedly represented popular opinion in their protest. The Bill was only carried by majorities of 13 in the Lords, and of 39 and of 38 in the Commons. Disraeli said that he had no objection to our countrymen fighting by the side of foreigners who were our allies, but he did object to their fighting by the side of mercenaries — the *condottieri* of modern Europe. Wellington's correspondence showed that no dependence could be placed on the fidelity of foreign mercenaries whose political sympathies were not engaged. The measure would therefore prove ineffectual; but it was also impolitic, as the world outside would draw the inference that our recruiting capacity was exhausted, and at home the power of the Government would be paralysed and the spirit of the country depressed. Why had not the necessary preparations for a great war been made in time? Even now they should have confidence in themselves and their own resources, and should not, in this situation of danger, doubt, and anxiety, 'bring in a Bill in order to enlist foreign mercenaries to vindicate the fortunes of England.' The only answer of Ministers, and perhaps the sufficient answer, was that they must obtain the command of numbers at once, and by all available means.

Parliament, which met on December 12, adjourned on December 23 for the Christmas holidays. 'I hear from all quarters that the ten days' campaign had set us up greatly in public opinion,' wrote Stanley on January 1. That was Disraeli's own view; 'the Ministers were much shaken, and their prestige is destroyed,' he told Mrs. Willyams. To Lennox, on January 11, he wrote of the Ministry: 'I hear that the cement consists entirely of a postponement of decision on all points, whether political or financial, at present; they are to meet Parliament, trusting that some event may occur which will give a preponderance to either of the rival systems. If war on a great scale is in the ascendant, then Aberdeen and Co. will retire, and there is to be an attempt at a Whig Government, which I should not be sorry to see.' The news of the Crimean winter that came from the front intensified public feeling against Ministers, and there was a growing movement in the Tory party that formal expression should be given to this feeling directly Parliament reassembled. Derby demurred. He feared that a vote of censure might be defeated, that it would only consolidate the Government, and prevent the Opposition from obtaining reinforcements. When the House of Commons met,[1] the matter was at once taken out of Conservative hands by a Radical, Roebuck, on the mere notice of whose motion for a Committee of Inquiry into the war Russell resigned. He had never been content with his secondary position in the Coalition Government, and had frequently threatened the desertion which he now carried out. The cement had given way, and it was with difficulty that after this blow the Cabinet were brought to consent even to meet the debate in office. 'Appearances are,' wrote Disraeli to Lady Londonderry on January 23, even before Russell's resignation was known, 'that the Government will not survive the next ten days or so.' At the same time Derby was writing in quite an opposite strain to Disraeli—that he concluded that Roebuck's motion must be supported; 'but whether meant in earnest or not, I think it will do the Government good, and regret it accordingly.' But it soon became evident that Disraeli was right. Russell's resignation rather than face inquiry, and his condemnation of Newcastle's administration of the war, appeared to be conclusive arguments in favour of Roebuck's motion. When Lytton said in the debate, 'Dismiss your Government and save your army,' it was felt he was rightly interpreting public opinion. Even Derby was driven at last to admit that the Opposition must take the responsibility of a direct attack on the Government. At 9.40 p.m. on the final day of the debate (January 29) he wrote to Disraeli: 'The case has now grown to such importance that I think *you must* speak—but not till the last moment; if after Palmerston, so much the better.' Gladstone, not Palmerston, was the Government mouthpiece, and Disraeli followed him. His predictions of Coalition incompetence had been verified; the world now recognised what he had pointed out two years before. There was no valid answer to his peroration.

[1] Jan. 23, 1855.

There is no stain upon the character or honour of public men, or inconvenience to the public service, in statesmen, however they may have at one time differed, if they feel themselves justified in so doing, acting together in public life. All that the country requires of public men when they do so act together is, that they should *idem sentire de republicâ*—that upon all great questions they should entertain the same views, that in subjects of policy, whether foreign or domestic, they should be animated by the same convictions and the same sympathies. But with regard to the existing Government—all have seen that, during their career, it does not appear that upon any great question, whether domestic or external, they have been animated by the same spirit and sympathies. It is to that circumstance that we must attribute the fact that they have been so unsuccessful in carrying their measures or prosecuting their policy. . . .

Sir, I have no confidence whatever in the existing Government. I told them a year ago, when taunted for not asking the House of Commons to ratify that opinion of mine, that, as they had no confidence in each other, a vote of want of confidence from this side of the House was surplusage. I ask the House of Commons to decide if twelve months have not proved that I was right in that assumption, although its accuracy was then questioned. What confidence has the noble lord, the late President of the Council, in the Minister for War? What confidence have this variety of Ministers in each other's counsels? They stand before us confessedly as men who have not that union of feelings and of sympathy necessary to enable them successfully to conduct public affairs.

Conservatives, Russellite Whigs, and Radicals went together into the Opposition lobby; and Roebuck's motion was carried by 305 to 148 votes, a crushing majority of 157 against Ministers. They immediately resigned; and thus fell unregretted, after little more than two troubled years, that Coalition from which the Court and the public had hoped so much. 'The country was governed for two years,' writes Disraeli in *Endymion*,[1] 'by all its ablest men, who by the end of that term had succeeded, by their coalesced genius, in reducing that country to a state of desolation and despair. "I did not think it would have lasted even so long," said Lady Mont-

[1] Ch. 100.

fort; "but, then, I was acquainted with their mutual hatreds and their characteristic weaknesses. What is to happen now? Somebody must be found of commanding private character and position, and with as little damaged a public one as in this wreck of reputations is possible."'

Two men stood out prominently before their countrymen at the moment as fulfilling in the main Lady Montfort's conditions — Derby and Palmerston. Aberdeen, the head of the fallen Administration, and Russell, the previous Whig Prime Minister, were both discredited — the first as responsible for the failures in foreign policy and war, the second by his desertion of his colleagues at a critical moment. From the general condemnation of the Coalition Ministers, Palmerston was exempted. He had filled an office, that of Secretary of State for Home Affairs, which gave him no direct influence on foreign policy or military administration; and the public believed that if he had been at the Foreign Office our diplomacy would have been more resolute, and if he had been at the War Office the breakdown in our military arrangements would have been impossible. Derby was in a still better position. Many believed, with Cobden and Bright, that, if his Ministry had remained in office, the Crimean War would have been honourably avoided. At any rate, he had no responsibility for the half-hearted policy and feeble administration which had brought the country into such peril, and, while criticising Ministerial blunders, he had been careful to maintain a patriotic attitude towards the war. He had a lieutenant in the Commons, Disraeli, whose position was equally favourable. The names of Derby and Palmerston were thus in everybody's mouth; that one of them, and if possible both — one leading the Lords, and the other the Commons — should take office was the general desire. 'The great necessity of the country at this hour,' wrote the *Press* on January 27, 'is a War Cabinet, constituted with the single purpose of prosecuting hostilities with energy, of repairing past errors, of saving the remnant of our army, of sustaining the reputation of our arms, and of grappling with our foe till he confesses himself vanquished and sues for peace.' 'Ask any intelligent politician of the Continent,' it maintained three weeks later, 'what Administration would prove most formidable to Russia, and he would reply: "Lord Derby, Lord Ellenborough, Lord Palmerston, and Mr Disraeli."'

Derby was sent for by the Queen, as his party 'was numerically the strongest, and had carried the motion.' Disraeli at once facilitated his task by showing the same abnegation as in 1852—an abnegation all the more praiseworthy as his leadership was now a matter of considerable duration and notable success. He would gladly act under Palmerston's direction, and hoped that his surrender would promote the accession of Palmerston's friends, who might not be willing to act under himself. 'There was only one feeling in the Conservative party,' as was explained in the *Press* on February 3—'namely, to resign all individual claims for the sake of giving the country the advantage at this critical period of a strong Government.' Disraeli has, unfortunately, left no memorandum describing this crisis and his own share in it. But we know that in his judgment it was an occasion which should have been boldly seized; and he must have cordially agreed with Ellenborough's appeal to Derby not to leave Her Majesty's room without kissing hands. The bold course was not taken. The Queen offered Derby the Government,[1] but his acceptance was of a conditional character, recalling very much his attitude at his first audience in 1851. The Queen's memorandum[2] of January 31, 1855, shows what his views were:—

He owned that his party was the most compact—mustering about two hundred and eighty men—but he had no men capable of governing the House of Commons, and he should not be able to present an Administration that would be accepted by the country unless it was strengthened by other combinations; he knew that the whole country cried out for Lord Palmerston as the only man fit for carrying on the war

[1] Jan. 31.

[2] *Queen Victoria's Letters.*

with success, and he owned the necessity of having him in the Government, were it even only to satisfy the French Government, the confidence of which was at this moment of the greatest importance; but he must say, speaking without reserve, that, whatever the ignorant public might think, Lord Palmerston was totally unfit for the task. He had become very deaf as well as very blind, was seventy-one years old, and . . . in fact, though he still kept up his sprightly manners of youth, it was evident that his day had gone by. . . . Lord Derby thought, however, he might have the lead of the House of Commons, which Mr. Disraeli was ready to give up to him.

For the War Office, Derby considered there were only two men — Lord Grey, with whom, however, he disagreed in general politics; and Lord Ellenborough, whom the Court thought almost mad. 'To be able to meet the House of Commons,' he wanted men like Gladstone and Sidney Herbert; for Foreign Affairs he would return to Malmesbury, who had done well before. But 'should he not be able to obtain strength from the Peelites, he could not be able to form a creditable Government; he must give up the task.' Only after the Queen had tried every other quarter would he 'be ready to come forward to the rescue of the country with such materials as he had, but it would be "a desperate attempt."'

Derby thus in advance, at his first audience, pronounced himself incompetent to form a creditable Government out of the resources of his own party, and refused even to make the attempt until all other combinations had been tried. Malmesbury suggests that Derby believed that neither Russell nor Palmerston could succeed in forming a Government; that he would then come in on his own terms, and be 'a most powerful Minister.' A note among Disraeli's papers makes the same suggestion:

After the break-up of Lord Aberdeen's Government, Lord John Russell and Lord Derby both made great mistakes in the course they took — the latter almost a ruinous one; both said and acted on the belief that 'Lord Palmerston could not form a Government.' Yet Lord Russell and Lord Derby were two of the most experienced men in our public life then existing.

But Derby's language to the Queen is hardly compatible with the belief that a final resort to himself was inevitable; nor, indeed, is the speech in the House of Lords in which he explained his action and disparaged his party. The theory reads rather like an excuse put forward after the event, when Derby came to realise that he had made an irreparable mistake.

To endeavour to secure Palmerston, the only undamaged reputation in the Coalition, was obviously Derby's right course in the circumstances, whatever may be thought of overtures to the Peelites. Directly he left the Queen, Derby went to Palmerston, to whom he offered the presidency of the Council with the lead of the House of Commons. Palmerston was asked to sound Gladstone and Sidney Herbert, and promised to do so; but he said the new Government must be a Coalition, and not only the taking in of one or two persons, and suggested that Derby should endeavour to retain Clarendon's services at the Foreign Office — a suggestion which Derby naturally found unpalatable, but which he afterwards told Malmesbury he would have adopted if thereby he secured Palmerston.

In spite of these observations, Derby's impression from his interview was that Palmerston was inclined to join, provided that Gladstone and Herbert would accompany him; and so he told the Queen and his principal colleagues. Disraeli wrote to Lady Londonderry on that afternoon that Derby had 'accepted the mission to form an Administration, and Lord Palmerston has agreed to act under him on certain conditions as regards his colleagues — difficult to comply with, but I think not insuperable.' Ellenborough accepted the Ministry of War, and Malmesbury the Foreign Office. To the latter Derby 'appeared in high spirits and confident of success; and when I told him I should like to go to Heron Court for forty-eight hours to settle my private affairs, he consented, saying: "Make haste back; you will find everything settled by that time."' So confident was Malmesbury that a Derby Government was in process of formation that he wrote from Heron Court to Disraeli making suggestions for many appointments, some quite minor ones. 'I write to say I hear Sir E. Dering would take office with us. If Canning held what he has got, and came in with us, it would be a stone out of the Peelite wall and bring us four or five peers. I find Hardwicke was much liked at the Post Office. . . . Would Bentinck do as Secretary of Admiralty? . . . Have you thought of Blandford? What Naval Lords of A. have you?' That Palmerston seriously thought of a combination with Derby at one period of this eventful January 31 seems clear; but it may be doubted whether he did not contemplate throughout being himself, rather than Derby, First Minister. He knew that he would have the effective backing of Napoleon III., our ally, with whom it was essential that the British Government should act harmoniously.

From George A. Hamilton.

20, CHESTER SQUARE, *Wednesday*, 4 *o'clock* [*Jan.* 31]. — A friend of mine whose *veracity* may be relied upon, and who is an intimate friend of the Palmerstons, saw Lady P. this morning on some family matter. She told him Lord Derby had been sent for, questioned him a good deal about the feeling of the Conservatives towards Lord P., intimated that, if Lord P. should be sent for, 'it would be delightful if Lord Derby should have the management in the Lords.' She said no one party was strong enough to carry on the affairs of the country, that she saw no reason why Lord D. and Lord P. should not act together, and she left the impression on my friend's mind that Lord P. would serve *under* Lord D.

My friend is known to be a strong adherent of our party, and this conversation must have been intended to be made known.

By the time that Palmerston saw Gladstone, which was about four o'clock, it is clear that he had realised that, if Derby failed, his own opportunity would come. He told Gladstone that he felt disinclined to accept, 'but that if he refused it would be attributed to his contemplating another result, which other result, he considered, would be agreeable to the country.' Gladstone, on the other hand, represents himself as having been disposed to join,[1] if he could obtain Aberdeen's approval, rather than that Derby should give up the commission. But neither Gladstone nor Herbert would join without Palmerston; and Palmerston, after consulting Clarendon, who was resolutely opposed to the arrangement, definitely made up his mind to refuse. He wrote that, on reflection, he had come to the conclusion that he would not, by joining the new Government, give to it that stability which Derby anticipated; but he promised support to any Government which would carry on the war and maintain our alliances. Derby, who had been waiting hopefully all the afternoon, received the note at dinner-time.

From Lord Stanley.

Private. Jan. 31, 11.30 *p.m.*—Bad news needs no messengers. You will have heard that P. declines. His note arrived about 9.30.

My father thereon wrote to the Queen. . . .

I don't give up the game yet: if it is lost, *vendetta* must be our consolation—and of that we shall have enough.

From Lord Derby.

Thursday, 8.50 *a.m.* [*Feb.* 1, 1853].—I have received the combined letters—civil, but distinct refusals on the part of all three. I sent Palmerston's down to the Queen late last night, and shall go down with the others myself this morning. I will call on you on my way soon after ten.

Gladstone added to his refusal some encouraging words: 'Any Government owing its origin to the late vote of the House of Commons and honestly endeavouring to do its duty, must have peculiar claims to support in connection with the great national interests involved in the questions of War and Peace. On public grounds I am dis-

[1] Lennox, however, reported to Disraeli on Feb. 4 that he heard on good authority that 'the Derby Coalition hung fire on account of G. and S. H. being determined not to sit in the Cabinet with the "Peel-smasher."'

posed to believe that the formation of a Government from among your own political connections would offer many facilities at this moment, which other alternatives within view would not present: and unless where my opinions might not leave me a choice, it would be my sincere desire to offer to an Administration so constructed under you an independent Parliamentary support.' Herbert gave similar assurances. He was convinced, he wrote, 'that any Government now to be formed is entitled to that liberal construction of its acts which is necessary to a fair though independent Parliamentary support.' These two letters — Gladstone's particularly — were rather markedly cordial in their tender of support to a Derby Administration; and we can well believe that Disraeli pointed this out and urged Derby to proceed, notwithstanding the impossibility of obtaining extraneous aid. But Derby was resolved to abandon the task. 'As to the independent support' proffered by the Peelite leaders, he told the Queen 'it reminded him of the definition of an independent member of Parliament — viz., one that could not be depended upon.'[1]

Even the most loyal of his colleagues doubted the wisdom of his course. Almost alone, Stanley was clear that his father was right, and that the ball must come again to his feet before long. Pakington wrote to Disraeli: 'I think Lord D. was, on the whole, right in his late difficult decision; but I feel the force of what you said about the probable effects upon our own party; and if we go on treating Ministers like ninepins — only bowling them down to set them up again — we shall be bowled down ourselves.' Ellenborough's opinion has already been quoted. Malmesbury, who was woke up next morning at Heron Court at four o'clock by George Cavendish Bentinck to hear of the collapse, has recorded his judgment in his diary that Derby showed a want of nerve and courage, and missed a great opportunity. To Derby himself he made the best of the situation.

[1] *Queen Victoria's Letters.*

Lord Malmesbury to Lord Derby.

Heron Court, *Friday* [*Feb.* 2, 1855].—I was just getting into my carriage to come up by the earliest train this morning, when I got a note from Stanley informing me of the state of things, so I shall put off my journey till Monday. I think your conduct must stand before the country in a very favourable contrast with that of the public men who oppose us, and if it has not its effect on the nation, I for one don't deem it worth governing.

I believe that we could have gone on with the *old lot* by attaching to them Ellenboro', Lytton, etc., for a time, but that your present game is the best.

As to Gladstone, much is to be said. This is the third time he shies at us, and I am certain that he is so hated by some of our best friends that he would lose us several votes. He is looked upon as a Tartuffe, and we have already one man whose eloquence is his only respectable quality. I cannot say, therefore, that I regret him.

Malmesbury's strange outburst against Disraeli, with whom he was then on very friendly terms, suggests that the critical situation had got on the nerves of more than one of the leaders. Disraeli's own feelings were undoubtedly bitter. Lennox wrote to him: 'S[tanley] asked me whether "our friend" were not much annoyed, to which I replied that, knowing what you had sacrificed of time, labour, and talents, I concluded you must be utterly disgusted.' As Lord Morley says, Disraeli 'beheld a golden chance of bringing a consolidated party into the possession of real power flung away.' Malmesbury, in his diary, writes of him, after Derby's explanation in the House of Lords, as being 'in a state of disgust beyond all control; he told me he had spoken his mind to Lord Derby, and told him some very disagreeable truths.' It seemed to him a failure in political courage—a quality which had once particularly distinguished Derby before he had become such a martyr to gout, and which was one of Disraeli's own characteristic virtues. It so happened that an old friend of his, the Ambassador Lord Ponsonby, who was now near his end, had just been exhorting him to show this quality, and in his last letter pointed to the present conjuncture as the right moment for its display.

From Lord Ponsonby.

Jan. 14, 1855. — You, I am certain, will know that, when I give you an opinion, I am moved by my desire to be of use to you towards the acquisition by you of a commanding position in this country. . . . I hope that you may now be disposed to take the bull by the horns, to be yourself the Antagonistes. You must command, not solicit, power; you have the abilities that are needful, if you have the courage to exert them. I have no such opinion of those who are with you as coadjutors. The world may not be as favourable to you, from inclination for you, as you might like it to be, but it is ready to submit to your pre-eminence if you will assume that position and bid your will avouch the deed. All animals follow the most daring individual of their race. Man is not a whit better than the ass or the goose, and the mass will obey you if you assert your *natural* right to authority. Look around you and observe what a crowd it is of poor talking creatures they are who have authority enough to play the miserable part they fill! You had best speak out and act audaciously: our people will follow you if that be your game. Our people are looking for a leader. They are tired of rhetorical humbuggers in speaking and writing, such as those for the most part are who occupy our Senate with palaver and our Sovereign with twaddle. . . .

Believe me to be one who likes you very much as well as has the highest opinion of your intellectual powers, and is merely very much *inclined* to believe in your political courage.

Feb. 1, 1855. — Seeing your courage successful will make me quite well. The game *is yours*, if you *resolve* to win it.[1]

'Resolve' as he might, if he could not stir Derby into action, Disraeli was for the time helpless. Derby could not, indeed, manage the party in the Commons without Disraeli, but without the prestige of Derby's name and fame Disraeli could not at this time have collected a sufficient following for any purposes of government. He could only pour out his heart to his close friends.

To Frances Anne, Lady Londonderry.

Confidential. CARLTON CLUB, S.W., *Feb.* 2, 1855. — I was so annoyed and worn out yesterday that I could not send you two lines to say that our chief has again bolted!

[1] His last letter to Disraeli. He died February 21. See below, p. 572.

This is the third time that, in the course of six years during which I have had the lead of the Opposition in the House of Commons, I have stormed the Treasury Benches: twice fruitlessly, and the third time with a tin kettle to my tail, which rendered the race almost hopeless. You cannot, therefore, be surprised that I am a little wearied of these barren victories, which, like Alma, Inkermann, and Balaclava, may be glorious, but are certainly nothing more.

What is most annoying is that, this time, we had actually the Court with us, for the two Court favorites, Aberdeen (of the Queen) was extinct, and Newcastle (of the Prince) in a hopeless condition; and our rivals were Johnny in disgrace and Palmerston ever detested. The last, however, seems now the inevitable man; and though he is really an impostor, utterly exhausted, and at the best only ginger-beer, and not champagne, and now an old painted pantaloon, very deaf, very blind, and with false teeth, which would fall out of his mouth when speaking, if he did not hesitate and halt so in his talk, here is a man which the country resolves to associate with energy, wisdom, and eloquence, and will until he has tried and failed.

What then? John Russell, they say, has lost his character, but he is one of the few men who can do without that necessity, having the D. of Bedford always to go bail for him.

The Queen is in town, the flag flying at the Palace; but I know nothing authentic. . . .

The party generally were profoundly disappointed. Their only consolation was that the Peelite leaders, whom they completely distrusted, had not returned to the fold. 'The Carlton is frenzied with rage,' wrote Lennox; 'all at D[erby]'s final decision, and part at his attempted Coalition. . . . Hoping for better days ! Worse cannot be !' The party held that Derby had acted a timid part; and many were disposed to give in their allegiance, as one of them wrote, 'to Lord Palmerston, who has the courage to face difficulties before which Lord Derby succumbs.' For Palmerston's anticipations proved correct. Russell endeavoured to form a Ministry, but found his friends generally unwilling, after his recent escapades, to enlist under his banner; and Palmerston became Prime Minister, and even succeeded for a few weeks in retaining the services of all the leading Peelites except Aberdeen and Newcastle. Then Graham, Gladstone and Herbert resigned because the House of Commons persisted in prosecuting Roebuck's inquiry. Not altogether unfairly, the public were inclined to take the view which Sarah Disraeli expressed to her brother on February 11: 'As to the wretched Peelites, miserable as administrators, they are now shown to be selfish intriguers.'

Derby had plenty of the courage that faces and mollifies angry followers; and he justified himself successfully to a party meeting.

To Mrs. Disraeli.

Feb. 20, 1855—The meeting was very large, and on the whole very successful: more than 230 persons, including however, fifty peers. I never heard a finer speech than Derby's: the ablest he ever made. It met everything except the chief point—namely, that we did not accept office because we were afraid and incompetent. However, all were satisfied, and even enthusiastic, and we must hope the best, though we deserve little.

Derby 'met everything except the chief point.' It was difficult to meet that successfully, and both Derby's biographers, Mr. Kebbel and Mr. Saintsbury, have given up the attempt. Gladstone, too, held that 'Lord Derby's error in not forming an Administration was palpable, and even gross. . . . Had Lord Derby gone on, he would have been supported by the country, then absorbed in the consideration of the war. None of the three occasions when he took office offered him so fine an opportunity as this; but he missed it.'[1] It was clear that the Minister who brought the war to a successful end would win the gratitude of the people. It was equally clear that, though the Conservatives were in a minority in Parliament, the constituencies would not have tolerated intrigues by a discredited Coalition against a Ministry honestly endeavouring to extricate the country from its difficulties. Palmerston, who was nearly as conservative

[1] Morley's *Gladstone*, Bk. 4, ch. 6, where there is an interesting examination in detail of this whole political crisis.

as Derby in home politics, seized the occasion, and was, with a brief interval, Minister for the rest of his life. In 1855 the Opposition leaders were stronger in *personnel* than in 1852. In the first place, the majority of them now had enjoyed and profited by official experience, and Disraeli himself, Malmesbury, Pakington, St. Leonards, and others, had shown official aptitudes; and, next, they had some promising recruits — Ellenborough, of great abilities, but more doubtful judgment, in the Lords; and Bulwer Lytton, a versatile and accomplished politician, in the Commons. Moreover, Stanley, who was too young to be more than an Under-Secretary in 1852, was now qualified for high office, as he showed in 1858. And, if Derby had been quick to appreciate rising talent, he would have seen in Lord Robert Cecil, who now sat for Stamford in Herries's place, a notable acquisition for the front bench. The only one of Derby's pleas, in his defence of his *gran rifiuto* in the House of Lords, that carries much weight is his statement that the country was demanding the leadership of Palmerston. There was undoubtedly a movement of the kind, but there was also one in favour of Derby; 'it is difficult to make it understood,' writes Fraser, 'how vehement was the feeling in his favour at the time.' Confirmation of this statement is found in the Beaconsfield papers. A friend reports to Disraeli that men of all parties were saying during this winter: 'Lord Derby is a man of resolution, energy, and spirit; with him there would have been no divided counsels and no want of promptitude.' Had Derby succeeded in doing what Palmerston did, he might well have rallied most of the Peelites naturally to his banner, and at the next General Election won that Conservative victory which was delayed till 1874, after his death.

Disraeli at least had nothing to reproach himself with. He had brought the Coalition into hopeless discredit. He had led his troops to victory in the House of Commons. He had once again shown his disinterestedness by waiving his claims in favour of Palmerston. He had done his best to put heart and audacity into his chief. He had loyally upheld Derby's course in the *Press*, allowing no sign of his own disapproval to appear. Now that the matter was over, he was prepared to regard it in a philosophic spirit, and look out for fresh occasions which a Ministry, apparently with a very insecure tenure of office, could hardly fail to afford. In the *Press*, on February 10, he recommended the Conservative party to be patient but vigilant. Office was not their object, nor yet a personal triumph. They might control, if they did not direct, the course of public affairs. 'Your time will not be long delayed; justice will be done you by the people.'

To Mrs. Brydges Willyams.

Grosvenor Gate, *Feb.* 25, 1855.—Since I last wrote to you, events have made weeks as long as months. The political volcano has not been content with a single eruption. It has groaned, and heaved, and vomited forth streams, which are not yet cool, and are even still glowing. The surrounding earth is covered with corpses and fragments and ruins. Every day there are fresh victims or new portents. Nor is it probable that even the present form of affairs will long continue.[1]

Whether Lord Derby was justified in declining the task imposed on him, time can alone satisfactorily prove. Our acceptance would certainly have prevented some political scandals, but, on the other hand, a strong and permanent Government must, in the present, or rather late, unnatural state of parties, be preceded by a period of Parliamentary anarchy and spasmodic weakness.

Let us try to think of more agreeable matters. You have presented us with an aviary, without any of the inconveniences of that receptacle of the feathered race, and with almost all its beauties. Never was there so interesting and so magnificent a present. It never palls, for it is full of nature: faithful, picturesque, strange, and animated. I often

[1] In the first edition of *Haworth Churchyard*, dated April, 1855, Matthew Arnold scathingly described the political eruption of this spring as

> This ignominious spectacle,
> Power dropping from the hand
> Of paralytic factions, and no soul
> To snatch and wield it.

Palmerston did snatch and wield it, and Arnold expunged the lines.

delight myself in turning over its pages when I have a quiet evening, and thank you very heartily for companions who seem always to bring me messages of friendship and affection from Torquay. . . .

The great hero of London at present is Lord Cardigan, who relates with sufficient modesty, but with ample details, the particulars of his fiery charge at Balaclava, to willing audiences — as often as they like.

Amid all the strange events of this marvellous period, the most singular appears to be the now accredited incident of the departure of the Emperor Napoleon for the Crimea.[1] He is to take Sebastopol. His absence agitates the funds and disquiets statesmen.

To Frances Anne, Lady Londonderry.

Grosvenor Gate, *Feb.* 25, 1855.—I have been wishing to write to you every day, but have fallen into one of those fits of prostration which follow excitement, and which are sometimes both the consequence and the refuge from a surfeit of pusillanimity and incompetence.

The political volcano still heaves and vomits forth its lava. In a month's time Aberdeen, Newcastle, John Russell, and now the whole of the Peelites, have been overthrown, and the well-accredited rumour of yesterday was that the Special Envoy[2] was telegraphed back again, and, climax of all degradation, had agreed to take office under Palmerston, and sit as his subordinate, in his presence, in the House of Commons, as Secretary of State for the department which S. Herbert has just vacated, before the returning officer's signature was dry.

Others believe that Palmerston will go to the Upper House, which it is supposed may best suit his years, though still First Minister; while friends of both parties opine that if this be the case John Russell will trip him up by Easter.

The Cabinet, they say, is formed, but its elements are doubtful. Whether a man of the people, in the shape of Baines as Chancellor of the Exchequer, is to be included, for popularity, or whether it is to be exclusively Whig and family-party, by the promotion to that post of Cornewall Lewis, Clarendon's brother-in-law, is doubtful.[3] In this latter case, Layard, Lowe, Laing, Horsman and Co. are to have all the highest of the subordinate posts by way of hedge. If Layard, whose exclusion from office the Peelites made a condition of their precipitate adhesion to Palmerston, on account of his

[1] The Emperor was, fortunately, dissuaded by Clarendon from this resolve.

[2] Russell had accepted a special mission to Vienna.

[3] Cornewall Lewis was made Chancellor of the Exchequer.

attacks on Aberdeen, be placed, and highly placed, and John Russell return to the Treasury Bench, it will not be long before the seceding members are at open war with their late colleagues.

There is a strong belief in the best quarters that peace is impending — some think will even be immediate.

Poor Lord Ponsonby has gone, and I follow his remains on Wednesday. His death was at last very sudden. He was only seriously indisposed for a day, and his intellect clear until the last hour, when the ruling passion was strong, and his last words were: 'Write instantly to the Queen, and tell her that if she trusts Palmerston she is ruined. . . .'

It was mainly due to Disraeli that the House of Commons determined, in spite of Aberdeen's fall, to appoint the Committee which it had voted on Roebuck's motion. Palmerston asked the House to let the Government be its Committee; but Disraeli insisted that, after Russell's resignation and admissions of maladministration, the House would stultify itself if it did not proceed with the inquiry into the mysterious disappearance of one of England's finest armies. Palmerston gave way; the Peelites resigned; and their places were taken by Whigs, Russell consenting to hold the Colonial Office under his old subordinate. The Committee's report, which was presented in June, justified Disraeli's criticisms, though it must be admitted that the most decisive sentences were only adopted by the casting vote of Roebuck, the Chairman: —

Your Committee report that the sufferings of the army mainly resulted from the circumstances under which the expedition to the Crimea were undertaken and executed. The Administration which ordered that expedition had no adequate information as to the amount of the forces in the Crimea. They were not acquainted with the strength of the fortresses to be attacked, or with the resources of the country to be invaded. They hoped and expected the expedition to be immediately successful, and, as they did not foresee the probability of a protracted struggle, they made no preparation for a winter campaign. . . . Your Committee will now close their report with a hope that every British army may in future display the valour which this noble army has displayed, and that none may hereafter be exposed to such sufferings as have been recorded in these pages.

APPENDIX A

BENTINCK'S LAST LETTER TO DISRAELI

(Page 113)

In the final chapter of *Lord George Bentinck,* Disraeli gives the following description of Bentinck's occupations on the last morning of his life, before he started on the afternoon walk to Thoresby which proved fatal: —

On the 21st of September, after breakfasting with his family, he retired to his dressing-room, where he employed himself with some papers, and then wrote three letters — one to Lord Enfield, another to the Duke of Richmond, and the third to the writer of these pages. That letter is now at hand; it is of considerable length, consisting of seven sheets of notepaper, full of interesting details of men and things, and written not only in a cheerful, but even a merry mood.

In December, 1849, the Duke of Richmond stated at a public meeting that the main purport of Bentinck's letter to him was an expression of the regard which the writer entertained for Disraeli, and of the great obligations which the whole party were under to him, for the display of unrivalled talent, undaunted courage, and firmness of purpose. Here is Bentinck's letter to Disraeli: —

From Lord George Bentinck.

Welbeck, near Worksop, Notts, *Sept.* 21, 1848.

My dear D., — I got your interesting letter from Wynyard yesterday. Peel takes a different view from Graham in respect to the payment of the Irish Roman Catholic Priesthood. My brother-in-law Evelyn Denison[1] met Peel at Nuneham in July. The party consisted of Sir Robert and Lady Peel, Gladstone and his wife, Norreys and Lady Norreys, E. Denison and my sister, and Shiel. . . .

Peel talked frankly about Ireland, and especially to *Shiel*, observing that *now* was the time to settle the question of the Irish Church; that the time was come when it was no longer possible to leave the Irish Roman Catholic Priesthood in their present position; that the present moment was, in his opinion,

[1] Afterwards Speaker of the House of Commons, and eventually Viscount Ossington.

peculiarly favourable; that the extreme poverty, the absolute state of starvation, of the Irish Priesthood would be favourable to their assent to some arrangement; that a deep religious feeling, on the other hand, was spreading over the public mind, and was working a desire to see some religious education and provision made for the Irish People, and therefore he thought the opportunity on every account favourable for some settlement of the question.

Shiel upon this observed: 'Well, Sir Robert, you have settled two great questions: why should you not be the man to come in and settle this great question?'

Peel smiled and smirked, and freely replied: 'I am too old to do it, but it must be done. I don't say but that any Government that attempted to settle the matter might be overthrown in the attempt; but, whatever might be the Government that succeeded to them, that Government would find the impossibility of refusing to settle the question.'

Upon this Evelyn Denison put in his word, observing that the People of this country would not suffer the Roman Catholic Priesthood to be paid out of the consolidated fund, and asking Sir Robert Peel whether he had not been a little struck by the presentation by Law of a Petition signed by 3,000 Protestant Clergymen against any payment of the Romish Priesthood.

Peel answered: 'I was very much surprised. Still, when the time comes for the payment of the Roman Catholic Priesthood, *means will be found for that purpose*.'

My conviction is that the Whigs will not attempt the settlement of this question, but Peel will; he will find the means, and will find himself not too old.

When all is said, the Irish Poor Rate in but a single Union equals 5s. 11½d. in the £1, and averages somewhere about 2s. (Connaught, 2s. 0¾d.; Munster, 2s. 8¾d.; Leinster, 1s. 7¼d.; Ulster, 1s. 7¾d.). This produces £1,300,000 a year. One shilling additional in the £1 would make a very handsome provision for the Irish Roman Catholic Clergy; it would give £240 a year to 2,500 Priests, and leave £50,000 a year to be distributed among her Bishops.

Then there would be Churches and Glebe Houses to be built; 2,500 of these at £5,000 a piece would be £1,250,000—at 4 per cent. would be £50,000 a year more to be provided for; that would be about ¾d. in the £1 more.

John Bull would rather enjoy seeing the Irish Landlords fleeced a little; but I have no doubt but that, when once a Priesthood were arrayed on the side of order and industry, Irish Estates would be increased in value far more than 1s. 0¾d. in the £1.

Graham humbugged your wife about his obligations to me; I am not conscious that I ever obliged him in any way further than sticking to him and Stanley when they seceded from the Whigs.

Will Graham join in the assault upon the Household Troops? Does the Court care about them? It is rather a difficult case to defend.

The British Army would 'make soup' or 'cook bullocks' if those duties were required of them. I dare say the army is ill provided with marching and fighting equipment just now, but these would soon be forthcoming. As regards railways, the defending army must derive a mighty advantage from them, and would easily prevent their being broken up.—Ever yours most sincerely, G. BENTINCK.

E. Denison thinks the Government, and Ld. John specially, very weak, and that Peel's party look confidently to a new Government of which *Peel's party is to be the* PIVOT. . . .

Sir William Symonds (late Surveyor of the Navy) is here, and declares that the greatest benefit that could be conferred on the Navy would be *to disfranchise* the Dockyard men. There are 13,000 of them, and he declares half the number would perform the same duties; but, being almost all of them voters, every idle, inefficient, worthless fellow is kept on, for fear of his vote being turned against the Government candidate.

APPENDIX B

METTERNICH ON CONSERVATIVE LEADERSHIP

(PAGE 134)

From Prince Metternich.

BRIGHTON, *ce* 25 *Janvier*, 1849.

MON CHER DISRAELI,—J'ai reçu votre lettre du 13 de ce mois! Je vous rends, par les mots de satisfaction et de frayeur, l'impression que votre lettre, et la prière que vous avez bien voulu y joindre, ont produit sur moi. Le premier de ces sentiments tire sa source de la justice que vous rendez à la pureté de mes intentions; le second est la conséquence de la gravité du sujet sur lequel porte votre expédition et de la distance qui existe entre mon individualité et les éléments dont se compose la situation. Tout homme qui est appelé à donner un conseil, doit, pour pouvoir répondre à l'objet, chercher son point de départ dans la conscience, d'être maître de la matière qui forme l'objet de la consultation. L'étoffe me manquant à cet égard et désirant, d'un autre côté, vous prouver combien je suis sensible à la preuve de confiance que vous me donnez, je m'attacherai à l'élément qui toujours est à la disposition des hommes doués d'un esprit droit—à l'examen de la situation.

Celle dont il s'agit se présente à ma vue sous l'aspect suivant:

Dépouillée de tout fard et réduite à sa véritable valeur, la question est celle de soutien de la raison dans la lutte qui généralement est engagée aujourd'hui entre les partis conservatif et destructeur. Il est dans la nature de ces partis, que celui conservatif a, pour avoir de la force, besoin d'être discipliné, tandis que celui destructeur peut avec plus d'impunité se passer de cet élément de salut. *Tout* n'est point propre à la conservation ni à la construction, pendant que *tout* peut être employé à l'œuvre de la déstruction. Aussi l'embarras qui fait le sujet de notre entretien réside-t-il sur ce champ. Le Leader du parti protectioniste est mort, et ce parti est dès-lors à la recherche d'un conducteur nouveau.

J'arrive ici à une question, qui ayant déjà été effleurée par moi dans notre dernière rencontre ne vous surprendra pas. De quel parti s'agit-il; est-ce de celui *conservatif*, ou de celui *protectioniste?* Il s'agit du sécond et ce fait même renferme une faiblesse et un embarras. L'une et l'autre sont davantage propres aux questions *spéciales* qu'à celles *générales* qui s'élévent à la hauteur d'une cause, dans la nature desquelles se trouve l'avantage de ne point pouvoir mourir. Ce ne sont en effet que les questions de détail, qui dans leur réunion acquièrent la valeur d'une cause impérissable, qui peuvent, selon les temps et les circonstances, perdre de leur importance relative. Tel, si tout ne me trompe, est le cas du parti *protectioniste*, et celà non parceque le sujet dont ce parti porte le nom se serait effacé, mais parcequ'il ne renferme plus la matière réquise pour justifier sa dénomination. Le sujet s'est fondu dans la cause générale, dont la protection due aux intérêts agricoles forme sans contredit l'un des éléments les moins périssables. Je vous ai déjà dit que je croyais que le parti protectioniste ferait bien de renoncer à son titre. Une conséquence naturelle du fait serait celle de placer le parti de Manchestre en face *de la cause* conservative toute entière et de changer ainsi la lutte, qui entre ce parti et celui protectioniste porte le caractère *d'un combat singulier*, en une *opération de guerre* contre les principes de conservation. Tout *parti* perd de sa force par un changement de position pareil.

Il y a, à mon avis, un autre avantage attaché à ce qui à mes yeux aurait la valeur d'une utile fusion *d'un parti dans un grand tout*, et cet avantage serait celui, d'élargir le champ pour les combattants pour une même cause. Il est dans la nature des dénominations particulières, de restreindre ce champ par l'appel qu'elles font aux rivalités particulières entre ceux qui, en dernière analyse, veulent la même chose.

Ces remarques, mon cher Disraeli, peuvent être taxées d'être entachées d'une polémique qui ne conduit pas à une solution de la question posée. Je dois convenir que la remarque ne manque pas de fondement; n'en cherchez pas la raison en moi mais dans la nature de l'objet et dans la condition dans laquelle je me trouve placé à son égard, dans la pire des conditions dans laquelle puisse se trouver placé l'homme consulté, dans celle d'un manque de connaissances réquises pour répondre consciencieusement à la demande qu'un ami lui adresse. Lord Stanley a des scrupules que d'autres de vos amis ne partagent pas; ce en quoi toutes les opinions se rencontrent, c'est dans la justice qu'ils rendent à vos grands capacités. Vous de votre côté êtes également dans le vrai en tenant compte de ce que des conditions, contre lesquelles *nul ne peut*, peuvent amener à leur suite. Dans une situation de choses pareille ce n'est que vous-même qui devez vous placer à l'aiguille de la balance et pondérer le pour et le contre de la situation et arriver au prononcé de la chance qui a le succès en sa faveur. Ce qu'en tout état de cause vous ne pourriez mettre en doute, c'est la sincérité des vœux que je forme en faveur des bonne chances. Je suis né et j'ai vécu défenseur de la cause conservative, et je mourrai dans les rangs des soutiens de cette cause. La base pratique que vous devrez soumettre à la pondération des chances, c'est la somme du secours dont vous aurez à vous regarder comme assuré et cela en évaluant à la fois la force qui réside en vous-même.

Restez en tout cas fidèle à la cause, qui déjà vous a valu des succès incontestés et dont vous êtes dans mon intime conviction un défenseur aussi habile que déjà puissant. Vous savez que mon opinion à cet égard date de longue main; je ne sais pas en former à la légère.

Mille sincères et affectueux hommages. — METTERNICH.

APPENDIX C

THE PLAGIARISM FROM THIERS

(PAGE 395)

From Disraeli's Speech, November 15, 1852.

It is not enough to say that [a great general] must be an engineer, a geographer, learned in human nature, adroit in managing mankind—that he must be able to fulfil the highest duty of a Minister of State, and then to descend to the humblest office of a commissary and a clerk; but he has to display all this knowledge and to exercise all those duties at the same time, and under extraordinary circumstances. At every moment he has to think of the eve and the morrow—of his flank and of his rear—he has to calculate at the same time the state of the weather and the moral qualities of men; and all those elements that are perpetually changing he has to combine, sometimes under overwhelming heat, sometimes under overpowering cold—oftentimes in famine, and frequently amidst the roar of artillery. Behind all these circumstances there is ever present the image of his country, and the dreadful alternative whether that country is to welcome him with laurel or with cypress. Yet those images he must dismiss from his mind, for the general must not only think, but think with the rapidity of lightning; for on a moment more or less depends the fate of a most beautiful combination—and a moment more or less is a question of glory or shame. Unquestionably, Sir, all this may be done in an ordinary manner, by an ordinary man, as every day of our lives we see that ordinary men may be successful Ministers of State, successful authors, and successful speakers; but to do all this with genius is sublime.

To be able to think with vigour, with depth, and with clearness, in the recesses of the cabinet, is a great intellectual demonstration; but to think with equal vigour, clearness, and depth, amidst the noise of bullets, appears to me the loftiest exercise and the most complete triumph of human faculties.

From 'La Revue Trimestre' of 1829.

(*Quoted by the Hon. George Smythe in the Morning Chronicle, July*, 1848.)

An engineer, a geographer, a man of the world, metaphysician, knowing men, knowing how to govern them, an administrator in great things, a clerk in small—all these things it is necessary to be, but these are as yet nothing. All this vast knowledge must be exercised on the instant, in the midst of extraordinary circumstances. At every moment you must think of the yesterday and the morrow; of your flank and of your rear—calculate at the same time on the atmosphere and on the temper of your men; and all these elements, and so various and diverse, which are ceaselessly changing and renewed, you must combine in the midst of cold, heat, hunger, bullets. . . . Farther off, and behind them, is the spectacle of your country, with laurel or with cypress. But all these images and ideas must be banished and set aside, for you must think, and think quickly: one minute too much, and the fairest combination has lost its opportunity, and instead of glory it is shame that awaits you. All this, undoubtedly, is compatible with mediocrity, like every other profession; one can also be a middling poet, a middling orator, a middling author; but this done with genius is sublime. . . .

To think in the quiet of one's cabinet, clearly, strongly, nobly, this undoubtedly is great; but to think as clearly, as strongly, as nobly, in the midst of carnage and fire is the most perfect exercise of the human faculties.

From Sir Edward Bulwer Lytton.

1, Park Lane, *Sunday* [*Nov.* 21, 1852].

My dear Dis, — From what I accidentally pick up in the gossip of clubs, etc., I think it possible some such direct reference may be made to the Wellington speech as may oblige you to speak. I have well thought over the matter, and it occurs to me that you can easily get out of it. If you are at home, shall I step up to you with my ideas? If not, shall I send them to you in writing?

[*Later on, the same day.*]

I send you a rough sketch of my idea. Spoken well and boldly, I think it would bring you out with credit. Of course you will dress up the general idea in your own way. . . . — Yours ever, E. B. L.

[Enclosure.]

Begin anyhow.

Certainly I did not plagiarise from any extracts from the *M. Chronicle* in 1846. But it did so happen that, when I was very young, in 1829, I read an article in a French review in which there was a summary of the intellectual capacities necessary for a great general, that struck me forcibly and retained a strong hold on my memory. Subsequently, in the course of my reading, I found that this summary comprised or resembled passages in some of the most celebrated classical authors, who have treated of the Art of War. It was, in fact, a résumé of brilliant sayings by great authorities, amassed by scholarship and vivified by genius. And what if afterwards I discovered that the writer of this article (then unknown to me) was M. Thiers? What more natural than that, when I, a Civilian, was called upon by the post which I had the honour to hold in this House to pass a deserved eulogium upon our greatest military Chief — what, I say, more natural than that I should make the very historian of the times and the wars in which that Chief had attained his renown become, out of his own lips, the witness of the events to which in his history M. Thiers never appeared to me to have rendered sufficient justice? True that M. Thiers had concentrated all his eloquence and learning on a third-rate French general, of whom, perhaps, some of us never heard. St. Cyr has passed out of date, but the manner in which the contemporaries and countrymen of the Duke of Wellington received that summary of the requisite capacities of a general really great showed that every sentence, enriched by that learning and adorned by that genius, illustrated the actual character and imperishable services of him we mourned.

It was not to be expected that I could quote from a writer so eminent as M. Thiers upon an occasion of interest so universal as that of the funeral obsequies of the D. of Wellington — but what I must be aware that the charge of plagiarism now made would be brought against me. And I was prepared for it. If the natural and decorous spirit of national pride forbade the French people to send to the Funeral rites of the Conqueror of Waterloo their military delegates, at least we had present one of their greatest statesmen, their most popular historians, their most eloquent writers, himself unconsciously to bear witness to that rare combination of qualities which the world may not acknowledge in St. Cyr, but which all England recognised in Wellington.

The House, Sir, may thus divine my motive. Whatever my faults and deficiencies, I humbly presume that I should be scarcely deemed wanting in the ordinary invention of a man of letters, or the ordinary fluency of a Parliamentary debater. Easier for me to say something of my own than to quote or to plagiarise from another. But I was not thinking of myself. I was thinking how best to honour the illustrious subject of our grief and our eulogies; and thus I left half of his funeral oration to be uttered, through my feebler lips, by the historian of the Consulate and Empire.

If I have erred in this, it was not through design nor through negligence; it is one of those matters of criticism and taste which we can scarcely discuss in this House, and which I must be contented to leave to the acquittal of those who may well conceive that I would desire to enforce any panegyric of my own, by all which classical erudition and the practised analysis of military achievements could supply to the Historian who has immortalised those noble armies, which it was the destiny of our Wellington to encounter and subdue.

INDEX